Economics of Pessimism and Optimism

Kiyohiko G. Nishimura · Hiroyuki Ozaki

Economics of Pessimism and Optimism

Theory of Knightian Uncertainty and Its Applications

Springer

Kiyohiko G. Nishimura
National Graduate Institute for Policy Studies (GRIPS)
Minato-ku, Tokyo
Japan

Hiroyuki Ozaki
Faculty of Economics
Keio University
Minato-ku, Tokyo
Japan

ISBN 978-4-431-56725-7 ISBN 978-4-431-55903-0 (eBook)
DOI 10.1007/978-4-431-55903-0

Softcover reprint of the hardcover 1st edition 2017

Printed on acid-free paper

This Springer imprint is published by Springer Nature
The registered company is Springer Japan KK
The registered company address is: Chiyoda First Bldg. East, 3-8-1 Nishi-Kanda, Chiyoda-ku, Tokyo 101-0065, Japan

Preface

Real life is full of surprises. Not only do ordinary people in the street face unexpected events, but experts in financial districts and policy-makers in capitals around the globe are often also caught off guard by "once-in-a-century" unanticipated events. One such surprise event was the sudden collapse of European interbank markets on August 9, 2007, which then sparked the global financial crisis. The ramifications of this massive event, largely unexpected, shaped the financial landscape for the entire tenure of one of the coauthors (Nishimura) as Deputy Governor of the Bank of Japan.

Faced with the real possibility of surprise events, human emotions often swing between optimism and pessimism. Just before the global financial crisis, financial markets around the world showed great optimism that "this time" was different and we would see sustained prosperity. Immediately after the crisis was perceived as being real, the same financial markets displayed extreme pessimism leading to failures of financial institutions and even closure of some markets.

As economists, we face two challenges: first, to explain the behavior of people including experts and policy-makers facing such unexpected events according to the first principles of economics; and second, to predict these people's behaviors when another unexpected event occurs so as to better cope with such an event. The purpose of writing this book is to present the groundwork from which these challenges can be addressed.

A theoretical precursor of our work concerns the so-called Knightian uncertainty. Knight (1921) deliberately distinguished between "measurable uncertainty" or "risk" on one hand, and "unmeasurable uncertainty" that cannot be represented by numerical probabilities on the other, which is now known as "Knightian uncertainty." Knight also claimed that people face "Knightian uncertainty" in most situations that prevail throughout their lives.

The problem posed by Knight, however, was considered to be at least tentatively resolved by the celebrated theorem of Savage (1954): if the decision-maker's behavior complies with some axioms that appear plausible, she behaves *as if* she possesses a unique probability with which she computes the expected utility and then chooses an act that maximizes it. If one accepts this concept, "Knightian uncertainty" is reduced to mere risk. What is important here is that the decision-maker herself need *not* have a clear concept of probability, but rather that we as analysts (not the decision-maker) *can* assume the existence of the probability the decision-maker employs for psychic computations when we construct an analytic framework.

Ellsberg (1961) challenged Savage's subjective probability theory and argued that the concept of uncertainty advocated by Knight (i.e., "Knightian uncertainty") still prevails. He presented a famous experiment, known as "Ellsberg's paradox," in which the choice patterns of participants can never be explained if they use a probability to evaluate various acts. In particular, he showed that one of the axioms imposed by Savage, known as the "sure-thing principle," is always violated by the participants' behavior. Ellsberg's argument was fairly convincing, and it *is* still convincing today. Nevertheless, Ellsberg's paradox was regarded as a special case and for a time it was essentially "ignored" in the disciplines of economic science and decision science. This is because Savage's subjective expected utility (SEU) theory is extremely practical and it makes model building in economics easy in both microeconomics and macroeconomics.

The situation changed in the 1980s. A series of papers by David Schmeidler and Itzhak Gilboa (1982, 1986, 1989) developed operational forms of "Knightian uncertainty," known as the "Choquet expected utility (CEU)" theory and the "maxmin[1] expected utility (MEU)" theory, with sound axiomatic foundations. The CEU theory assumes that the decision-maker uses a *nonadditive* probability, while the MEU theory assumes that the decision-maker uses a set of probabilities instead of a single probability. Furthermore, both theories do not assume the sure-thing principle and they *can* explain Ellsberg's paradox.

Since the breakthrough made by Schmeidler and Gilboa, the utility of their theories motivated economists to apply the CEU and MEU theories to model the economic phenomena that we face. As a result, a large literature has been generated in various areas in economics.

Until the global financial crisis, however, these applications of Knightian uncertainty were relatively limited in scope, and were motivated more by theoretical curiosity and the desire to amend the apparent limitations of existing theory in explaining anomalies often found in peripheral phenomena. The situation has changed drastically since the global financial crisis, and there has been a vast expansion of the Knightian uncertainty literature that has been impossible to monitor fully. At the same time, the literature has become methodologically diverse, and in some ways it may be difficult to have a coherent view about Knightian uncertainty.

That said, this book anticipates two types of readers: researchers who have a technical orientation and nontechnical general readers who are interested in the implications of Knightian uncertainty and its relationship with optimism and pessimism.

---

[1]The terms maxmin and maximin are both used in the literature.

For researchers with technical orientation, the objective of this book is to equip the reader with the mathematical and economic methods necessary to understand the contents of this book and to conduct their own research along the lines developed in this book. To this end, the book provides a thorough discussion of mathematics and decision theory in a self-contained manner.

For nontechnical general readers, the book may seem overly formalized or mathematical to understand the real essence of Knightian uncertainty and the characterization of optimism and pessimism. However, the ideas behind the results reported in this book are very intuitive, even though they are (unfortunately) buried in rigorous mathematical detail. To assist nontechnical readers in comprehending the underlying principles, each chapter in the main body of this book provides a detailed "Introduction and Summary" section, in which the essence of the argument developed in the chapter is presented. In some chapters, an "Examples" section is also provided.

Our joint research dates as far back as the very beginning of the twenty-first century, when Ozaki presented a paper at the University of Tokyo. The paper, coauthored with Peter A. Streufert, covered the optimal growth model where the representative agent exhibited uncertainty aversion. Ozaki thought (and still thinks) that the paper was interesting because all the dynamic programming techniques could be invoked even though the agent aggregated uncertainty in a "nonlinear" manner. Furthermore, the paper germinated the ideas of an "ordered set of functions" and the "stochastic nondecrease" when the probability is not additive in the framework of a finite state space. The readers will see that these ideas are thoroughly exploited in both finite and infinite state spaces in this book.

Nishimura, then at the University of Tokyo before joining the Bank of Japan, did not share Ozaki's enthusiasm. Nishimura thought (and still thinks) that the introduction of a new concept, like a nonadditive probability, must generate new implications that could not be derived from a traditional framework that employed traditional concepts. Then, what might or could be changed by explicitly thinking of a probability that was not necessarily additive? Nishimura's insight was that an increase in risk represented by an additive probability and an increase in "uncertainty" represented by a nonadditive probability should have opposite effects on the value of waiting for the representative agent. This needed to be proven by solving the agent's dynamic optimization problem, and this was exactly what Ozaki liked to do by invoking dynamic programming techniques!

Our first joint paper was thus completed in a true collaboration and was published in the *Journal of Economic Theory* in 2004 (Chap. 9 of this book comprises its outgrowth). Since then, the collaboration has continued to this day, often enhanced by the synergy of Nishimura whose interests concern the application of theories to explain real economic phenomena from the policy perspective (especially since the global financial crisis), and that of Ozaki whose interests focus on the beauty of the theory and elaboration of it. These activities culminated in joint articles and discussion papers, and then the concept of this book emerged after Nishimura's term as Deputy Governor ended and he returned to academia. The actual publication plan started in 2014 with help of Ms. Juno Kawakami (Springer, Japan). We are thankful to Ms. Kawakami on this matter.

It is typical that writing a book owes much to many people. This case is no exception, but we can only name a handful here. We are particularly grateful to Itzhak Gilboa, who, with David Schmeidler, was the intellectual source of our scientific endeavor, and gave us warm encouragement in various stages of our study. Ozaki thanks Peter A. Streufert, who was and has been his only teacher during his career as a professional economist. He learned from Peter that we economists must be extremely prudent and precise in applying mathematics to economics (math is not that superficial tool we can handle easily!) and he also learned from Peter everything about dynamic programming in a verbatim meaning. We hope that Chap. 7 reflects what Ozaki learned from Peter correctly. Chapter 6 is based on a collaborative work of one of us (Ozaki) with Eisei Ohtaki, and we express our deepest thanks to him for allowing us to include it in the book.

Preliminary drafts of the book were used in many graduate classes including those of Hitotsubashi University, the University of Tokyo, and Keio University. We are grateful to the audiences of these lectures. In particular, Daiki Kishishita and Satoshi Nakada proofread the book with great care, which significantly improved the book. Austin Schultz copyedited the draft and helped with both English usage and academic writing. Nevertheless, the book, which is so lengthy, may contain some typographical errors for which we are solely responsible.

Finally, we close the preface with a slight variation of a quote from a French movie[2]: We hope readers enjoy reading the book as much as we enjoyed writing it!

Tokyo, Japan

Kiyohiko G. Nishimura
Hiroyuki Ozaki

References

Knight, F. 1921. *Risk, Uncertainty and Profit*, Boston: Houghton Mifflin.

Savage, L.J. 1954. *The Foundations of Statistics*, New York: John wiley (2nd ed., 1972, Dover, New York).

Ellsberg, D. 1961. Risk, ambiguity, and the Savage axioms. *Quarterly Journal of Economics* 75: 643–669.

Schmeidler, D. 1982. Subjective probability without additivity (Temporary Title). Working Paper, The Foerder Institute for Economic Research, Tel Aviv University.

Schmeidler, D. 1986. Integral representation without additivity. *Proceedings of the American Mathematical Society* 97: 255–261.

Schmeidler, D. 1989. Subjective probability and expected utility without additivity. *Econometrica* 57: 571–587. (Its working paper is first published in 1982)

Gilboa, I. and Schmeidler, D.1989. Maxmin expected utility with non-unique prior. *Journal of Mathematical Economics* 18: 141–153.

[2]*La Nuit américaine* (1973). English title: *Day for Night.*

Contents

About the Authors

Kiyohiko G. Nishimura is emeritus professor of economics and distinguished project research fellow at The University of Tokyo and a professor in the National Graduate Institute for Policy Studies (GRIPS). Before returning to academia, he was deputy governor of the Bank of Japan for 5 years until March 19, 2013, one of the most turbulent periods in the history of the world economy and central banking. He has been particularly influential in the debates over macro-prudential policies, especially in pointing out the critical importance of demographic factors on property bubbles and financial crisis. His work and speeches on demography and economic policy have been cited widely and policy makers around the world have increasingly been recognizing the urgency of the problem.

He received his B.A. (1975) and M.A. (1977) from The University of Tokyo and his Ph.D. (1982) from Yale University. He was an Arthur M. Okun Research Fellow (1981–1982) at the Brookings Institution in Washington, D.C., before joining the Faculty of Economics at The University of Tokyo in 1993, where he was associate professor (1983–1994) and professor (1994–2005). He was appointed as an executive research fellow of the Economic and Social Research Institute of the Cabinet Office of the Government of Japan between 2003 and 2005, before joining the Bank of Japan as a Member of its Policy Board (2005–2008), and then as deputy governor (2008–2013). After returning to academia, he was dean of the Graduate School of Economics and chairman of the Faculty of Economics at The University of Tokyo (2013–2015). He was jointly appointed by The

University of Tokyo and the National Graduate Institute for Policy Studies (2015–2017) until his retirement from The University of Tokyo. Since February 2014, he has been chairman of the Statistics Commission of the Government of Japan, which oversees the official statistics of Japan, and he is leading a sweeping reform of economic statistics in Japan. He has been a member of the Board of Trustees of Japan Women's University since April 2016.

Dr. Nishimura's academic research focuses on a wide span from economic theory such as mathematical economics and the microeconomic foundation of macroeconomics, to economic policy, and to management studies about areas including property markets and the e-business of automobile distribution. He received the Nikkei Prize in 1993 for his book *Imperfect Competition, Differential Information, and Microeconomic Foundations of Macroeconomics* (Oxford University Press, 1992), the Japan Economist Prize in 1997 for his book *Macroeconomics of "Price Revolution"* (Nihon Keizai Shinbun, 1996), the Japan Association of Real Estate Sciences Prize in 2005 for his book *Economic Analysis of Property Markets* (Nihon Keizai Shinbun, 2002), and the TELECOM Social Science Award in 2006 for his book *Advancement of Information and Communication Technology and Its Impacts on the Japanese Economy* (Yuhikaku Publishing, 2004). He was also the winner of the Japanese Economic Association Nakahara Prize in 1998 for his outstanding international contribution to mathematical economics and economic theory. He was awarded Emperor's Medal of Honor with Purple Ribbon in 2015 for his outstanding contribution to theoretical economics.

Dr. Nishimura is now a senior advisor of the Asian Economic Panel and a member of the editorial board of several international academic journals in economics and management sciences. He also held business positions before joining the Bank of Japan: he sat on the Advisory Board of the Fujitsu Research Institute (Japan) and he was an academic advisor of Recruit Ltd. (Japan) and the Investment Property Databank (U.K.). From July 2014 until March 2017, he was an independent director of Cookpad Inc., a global IT company managing the world's largest recipe-exchange site on the smartphone platform. Since December 2014, he has been a member of the MNI Connect Advisory Board of Market News International, a leading provider of news and intelligence for the global foreign exchange and fixed income markets. Beginning in October 2015 he has also been an advisor to the Zymax Real Estate Research Institute for property market research and to Nowcast Inc. since February 2015, for using big data in macroeconomic research. Since June 2017, He has been an advisor to O-uccino Inc., a real estate agent and internet service provider managing the largest list of previously owned properties for sale in Japan.

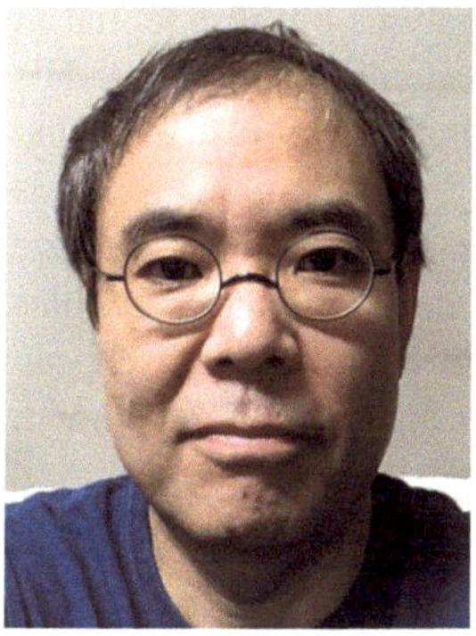

Hiroyuki Ozaki is professor of economics at Keio University. He has been particularly active in developing the theory of dynamic decision making, where non-additive probability measures are used that are substantially more general than additive probability measures, with applications to general equilibrium models and to elucidation of macroeconomic phenomena that are hard to explain in the traditional additive probability framework.

He received his B.A. (1986) from Keio University and his Ph.D. (1992) from The University of Wisconsin at Madison, where he majored in economics and minored in mathematics. He was assistant professor at The University of Western Ontario (1993–1996) and associate professor at Tohoku University (1996–2005) before joining the Faculty of Economics at Keio University in 2005. He has been professor at Keio University since then. He also has been serving as vice director of the Institute of Economic Studies of Keio University since April of 2015.

Dr. Ozaki's academic research focuses on mathematical economics and the decision-theoretic foundation of economic agents' behavior, which is often observed in the real economy and is at odds with rational behavior assuming additive probability measures. Among his numerous contributions to this field, most notable are: "Dynamic programming for non-additive stochastic objectives," *Journal of Mathematical Economics* 25 (1996), 391–442 (with Peter A. Streufert), which developed powerful tool kits for dynamic analyses that can be available in a very general economic environment; "Search and Knightian uncertainty," *Journal of Economic Theory* 119 (2004), 299–333 (with Kiyohiko G. Nishimura), which applied these tools to the everyday phenomenon generating from people's searching behaviors; and "Conditional implicit mean and the law of iterated integrals," *Journal of Mathematical Economics* 45 (2009), 1–15, which succeeded in explaining the often-found persistent behavioral biases in decision making in a rational way.

From a very early stage of his career as an economist, Dr. Ozaki has believed that mathematics is not a mere tool for economics analyses but is essential in modeling reality such as economic phenomena. His research activity is largely enhanced by his belief that economics must be "correct" in the sense that it is subject to the grammar of mathematics once we have chosen it as a method of constructing economics models, and by his belief that mathematics itself can shed light on how to model complex reality in a much better way.

Chapter 1
Overall Introduction

This book is about "uncertainty" in decision science and economic science and its application to everyday problems we face. A concept that is closely related to "uncertainty" and more commonly used is "probability." While we use the word "probability" very casually in everyday life, its true meaning is not so straightforward. We begin our exploration with some reflections on this concept, and then continue on to "risk and uncertainty" in this context.

1.1 What Is Probability?

1.1.1 Knowledge and States of the World

What is probability? Before answering this question, we need to define the particular event for which the probability is being considered.

To answer the latter question, we start by thinking about our view of the way the world ought to be. An abstraction we always make is that the world, or the universe, is a collection of "states." More formally, a *state of the world* is a thorough and complete description of the nature of the entire world during a relevant time period. For example, each state of the world is the list of the dates of both births and deaths of all people in some region on the earth during some time period, the temperature and humidity in that region every day during that time period, the constellation configuration every night seen from that region during that time period and so on.

There must exist one and only one state that describes the world *correctly*. We name it the *true* state of the world. Thus, any state of the world except for the true one describes the world somewhat incorrectly. Importantly, each state of the world needs to describe the entire world with crystal clarity and fully enough for us to be able to judge whether the given state of the world is true *if* indeed we know the

K.G. Nishimura and H. Ozaki, *Economics of Pessimism and Optimism*,
DOI 10.1007/978-4-431-55903-0_1

true shape of the world. Knowing that some state of the world is actually the truth is one thing, but knowing whether it is either the truth or not is another. In the latter sense, a state of the world is a *proposition*.[1] Thus defined, the states of the world are mutually exclusive and exhaustive descriptions of the world, one of which must be true. Any other must be false in principle regardless of whether we know which is the true state.

The set of all states of the world is called the *state space*. The state space is typically denoted by S in this book.[2]

It is reasonable to consider that the state space varies over time. This might happen if our knowledge of the whole world increases, or decreases because of memory loss. For example, suppose that a new atom is unexpectedly has been discovered. The atom may be very unstable and may not exist for a long time. However, the discovery of the new atom *does* alter S because each state of the world may now include a description of the percentage of the content of this atom in the whole atmosphere at some instant in time, and thus, the number of the elements of S will increase (S will dilate). A similar example is that of "Schrödinger's cat." The cat must have drastically changed the state space (or the whole universe itself!).

In this way, the state space may change according to a change in the amount or the depth of our knowledge at some point in time. Thus, the state space can be thought to embody all the *knowledge* we possess at that time.

Asking how our knowledge about the world is acquired and asking how a formation of the state space itself should be made in the first place are fundamental questions worth pursuing in themselves. Nevertheless, this book focuses on a world in which recognition via the state space has already been accomplished. Alternatively, we assume that the level of our knowledge about the world does not change at least over the time span we are considering. In any event, this book assumes that the state space S does not change over time and is fixed throughout.

1.1.2 Information and Events

We have defined what the "states of the world" mean in the preceding subsection. Note that the only a single state represents the truth of the world.[3]

The next important ingredient to a mathematical model of uncertainty is "information." If we know what the truth is, or equivalently, if we know exactly which

---

[1] In mathematics, a *proposition* is a statement that is either *always true* or *always false*. For example, the statement that a Martian lives on Mars is a proposition, and the statement that living on Mars is not comfortable is not.

[2] When we take "time" into consideration explicitly, we use S to denote a state space for one period and then use its "self-product" to denote the state space over the entire time span; that is, the "true" state space according to the context of the main text. Another common symbol for the state space is Ω.

[3] Mathematically, a single state, often denoted by s, is an *element* of the state space S. With the symbols, we write $s \in S$.

single state represents the truth, the story would be quite simple. Unfortunately, this is not typically the case.

To clarify the precise meaning of "information," consider the following simplified state space. Suppose that the only matter we are concerned about is tomorrow's weather. Also, assume that as a matter of possibilities, it will be sunny, rainy, or snowy tomorrow. Because it is assumed that exactly one of these weather conditions is realized tomorrow, this will constitute a complete list of the states of the world. Therefore, the state space S is given by $S =$ {"sunny", "rainy", "snowy"}.

A possible interpretation is that the truth (tomorrow's actual weather) will be determined tomorrow, and, until then, the truth is still indeterminate. Another interpretation is that the truth is already determined (while we don't know it yet), and it may be *revealed* tomorrow. We (and possibly many other researchers) adopt the latter interpretation.

Then the *information*, or, more precisely, the *information structure*, is any family of subsets of S satisfying some mathematical conditions that have very natural interpretations.[4] Assume that the information structure is now given by {"sunny"} and {"rainy", "snowy"}.[5] This list of subsets of S turns out to satisfy the above mentioned conditions, and thus, is certainly an example of the information structure.

Any element of the information structure is called an *event*.[6] An event has *occurred* by definition if the true state of the world is an element of that event. In the above information structure, the event {"rainy", "snowy"} occurred if "rainy" were the true state of the world.

We understand that an event is a set of states of the world about whose occurrence we can definitely know only with the given information structure. It is certainly the case that depending on a situation into which we are placed, we could know that the true state of the world is included by some event even if we didn't know exactly which state of the world is the truth. Thus, we may conclude that defining "information" possessed by an agent by using a family of events is a reasonable mathematical definition.

According to this interpretation, the information structure presented in the earlier paragraphs represents the situation where we will know tomorrow that "sunny" has occurred or not, but we will *never* know whether "rainy" or "snowy" has occurred. That is, we can't distinguish between a rainy day and a snowy day even if one of these occurs. The reason why we can't do so is not that important. What is really

---

[4] A family of subsets satisfying these conditions is named the *algebra* or the *σ-algebra*. See Chap. 2.

[5] If we state it with more mathematical precision, it is given by $\{\phi$, {"sunny"}, {"rainy", "snowy"}, $S\}$ because the empty set and the whole state space are always included by any information structure. This is because some whether *must* take place tomorrow, leading to our always knowing that S has occurred and that ϕ has never occurred. See the next paragraph for discussion of "occurred".

[6] The mathematical requirements for a subset of S to be qualified as an event have natural interpretations. They are important not only mathematically, but also in terms of economics. See Chap. 2 for the precise statement of these requirements and see Sect. 3.12 for further discussions on this "eventness".

important here is that the information structure may impose strong restrictions on our ability to conceive the true state of the world.[7]

We are now ready to answer the question raised in the first paragraph of Sect. 1.1.1. Basically, we can speak of "probabilities" *only of events*.[8] When we say "probability," it always refers to the occurrence of an event. This convention seems to be both natural and intuitive to some extent because it is difficult to consider the "probability" of something whose occurrence can never be observed nor verified.

In the following sections, we turn to the fundamental question of this section: What does the "probability of an event" exactly mean?

1.1.3 Frequentist Approach

The assignment of a probability to each event is a central issue throughout this book. Needless to say, then, the term of "probability" must convey its *precise* meaning whenever it is used. Unfortunately, this is not an easy task. For example, think about the next question: "What is the *probability* that an earthquake with a magnitude greater than 8 will strike Japan in the next 10 years?"[9] It is not immediately obvious how to really answer this question.

There are many different approaches that can be used to define what the "probability" is here. We consider three typical approaches in turn by using an extremely simple "coin-toss" example.

The first is the so-called *frequentist* or *classical* approach. Pick up one coin and consider tossing this coin many times (say, n times). In what follows, H means that the Head appears and T means that the Tail appears. According to the frequentist approach, *the* probability of the event that the head appears for this *specific* coin would be

$$\lim_{n\to\infty} \frac{\#H}{n}$$

where $\#H$ denotes the total number of heads occurring up to the n-th toss. Here, the symbol "lim" means some definite number, called the *limit*, which the ratio $\#H/n$ approaches more closely as we toss the coin more and more times up to infinity.[10]

---

[7]By "learning," we may become more informed about the true state of the world. As such, the information structure may change over time. As a result of some "learning," say, by a new possibility of observing the stock price of a firm that produces snow tires, the information structure may become "finer" and it may become represented by *singleton* events: {"sunny"}, {"rainy"}, and {"snowy"}. We consider this sort of "learning" process in Chaps. 13 and 15.

[8]For the reason why we say "basically," see the above footnote and Sect. 3.12.

[9]Note that the event given by the question is defined well enough in light of the preceding two subsections.

[10]With the full rigor of mathematics, the limit might not exist. To avoid such an issue, we may replace "lim" with, say, "lim sup".

We are quite sure that the probability of H thus defined would never be equal to a half *precisely*, although some may accept a half as a "plausible" number representing the probability of H. We are sure about this because the coin may not be a "perfect" coin; that is, because each coin has its own peculiarity and two distinct coins can never be the same, even if tossing may be made ideally randomized. For example, one coin may be worn down more than the other. Hence, the limit defined above for a specific coin cannot be exactly equal to a half even if it might be very close to it.

Furthermore, such coin-tossing trials cannot be repeated up to infinity for every coin. Thus, when so conceived, the probability according to the frequentist approach is difficult to incorporate into tractable models of decision-making.[11]

Another disadvantage of the frequentist approach is that we cannot calculate the probability of an event that rarely occurs. Recalling the earlier question about the probability of a high-magnitude earthquake, the frequentist approach fails in this instance for this reason. This urges us to move on to a second approach that differs substantially from the frequentist approach, namely, the subjectivist approach.

1.1.4 Subjectivist Approach

The so-called *subjectivist* approach is quite easy! If people or a single person *believes* that H occurs with $\alpha\%$ chance when tossing a coin, *the* probability of H is simply $\alpha\%$.

Here, we do not ask why that person believes that the event will occur precisely with that percentage. For example, if the person believes that H absolutely happens with 100% certainty and that T will never happen (say, because of a supernatural power that she believes she has), then the probability of H is 1 to her.

Note that the number of "1" used here does not convey any special meaning. We are just calling the probability that corresponds to 100% certainty as unity. It could be 2 or any other peculiar number. On the other side of the coin, the probability of T may be called "zero" or "nullity" in this case. Once again, any number can be used as long as it is different from 1 (and preferably less than 1).[12]

This approach is considered to be the other extreme of the frequentist approach. Assigning the probability to an event according to the subjectivist approach does not require any precedent for that event. In some cases, this can be regarded as an advantage of the method.

In fact, the question about the probability of a large earthquake may be answered simply by asking somebody: "What do you think?"

---

[11] Some attempts have been made toward incorporating the frequentist approach into a framework of decision-making. For example, see Gilboa and Schmeidler (2001). Their theory is known as *case-based decision theory*. It develops a concept of the *similarity function* that gauges the frequency of an events.

[12] Note that 0 is special because it is the unique number satisfying $0 + 0 = 0$. The "additivity" we mention in the next subsection forces the probability of an event that never happens to be 0.

On the other hand, this is also a weakness of the method. Almost anything can qualify as the probability of an event according to the subjectivist approach. This approach does not impose any restriction on probabilities, which means it lacks sufficient content to serve as a foundation for a decision-making theory.

1.1.5 Axiomatic Approach

There are long-standing disputes between the frequentist and subjectivist approaches, mainly in terms of frequentist and Bayesian statistics. We do not discuss the relative merits of these two approaches other than noting that both approaches have some deficiencies as mentioned in the preceding sections.

A clever way to avoid these disputes is to formulate some axioms at the outset. Here, the *axiom* is a "rule" whose legitimacy and infallibility are not supposed to be discussed.[13]

As the minimum requirements, the axioms that are assumed together, sometimes called an *axiomatic system*, must be both mutually independent and not contradicting each other. The *mutual independence* is warranted whenever one axiom is not implied by the other axioms, and the *noncontradiction* is valid as long as two distinct axioms can hold logically true simultaneously. Any axiomatic system considered in this book always satisfies these two requirements.

We may frame a set of axioms that conveys substantial contents and we may *define* any object that satisfies these axioms as *the* probability. This method of defining the "probability," called the *axiomatic approach*, was initiated early in the 20th century by a Russian mathematician, A.H. Kolmogorov.

The axioms known as *Kolmogorov's axioms* appear quite reasonable for treatment of "probability." Apart from seemingly innocuous normalization by "0" and "1" (see Sect. 1.1.4 above), it requires that the probability of the "union" of "mutually disjoint" events be equal to the sum of probabilities of each single event, where the "union" of events occurs if any event constituting that union occurs, and the two events are "mutually independent" if they never occur at the same time.[14] We call this axiom the "additivity."

Anything that satisfies Kolmogorov's axioms is *defined* as *the* probability. In this way, we can dispense with (sometimes metaphysical) discussions about what the word "probability" should mean. We sometimes refer to this probability as an *additive* probability to emphasize that it satisfies the "additivity" axiom.[15]

---

[13]An extremely famous example of an axiom is Euclid's fifth axiom in geometry: "Two parallel lines never intersect." While there is no argument about the axiom's legitimacy and infallibility, we may deny this axiom to use non-Euclidean geometry, e.g., Riemannian geometry.

[14]The precise definitions of these mathematical terms are given in Chap. 2.

[15]This suggests that there might exist a probability that is *not* additive, which turns out to be true later.

Despite its simple appearance, the additivity axiom is a strong rule that the "probability" should obey. For example, according to the axiomatic approach with additivity, the probability of H not occurring (i.e., T occurring) *must* be $(1 - \alpha)\%$ whenever the probability of H occurring is $\alpha\%$.[16] This is indeed *everything* we can deduce about the probability from the axioms, and it appears that the "probability" does not convey much information.

This impression, however, is wrong. In fact, the additivity is so strong that the implications of this axiom are far sharper than one might think at first glance. We will see many such implications later in this book and that some of them are, in not a few cases, in direct opposition to phenomena observed in the real world.

1.1.6 Objective Probability and Randomizing Device

In this book, we call the probability that is defined in view of the frequentist approach the *objective* probability.

Note that when talking about the objective probability, we assume that it satisfies Kolmogorov's axioms implicitly (and sometimes, explicitly).[17]

To be consistent with the frequentist method according to which the probability is defined, we assume the existence of an "ideal" and "perfect" coin. For this coin, the ratio of a head occurring out of n-time tosses $(\#H/n)$ goes to precisely 0.5 as the number of coin tosses approaches infinity. In terms of the limit that we defined in Sect. 1.1.3, this is equivalent to saying that the limit of that ratio is exactly equal to 0.5 when n goes to infinity. We refer to such a coin as being *fair*.

Similarly, we assume that there exists a dice, a roulette wheel, and so on, that can generate any number precisely as the limit of frequencies. This routine is summarized by referring to a *fair* dice, a *fair* roulette wheel, and so on.

When talking about an objective probability, we always assume the existence of such a machine behind the scene, referred to as a *randomizing device*, that can generate that probability according to the frequentists' view. The concept of the randomizing device is very convenient because we can produce any number as the objective probability by using it.

Of course, the existence of randomizing devices is hypothetical, and, in light of Sect. 1.1.3, their existence in reality is very hard to assume. Nonetheless, we keep using this convention. This is because such virtuality allows us to greatly simplify matters in any theory of decision-making (e.g., see Anscombe and Aumann's theory in Sect. 3.8 on this subject).[18]

---

[16]This fact follows from the additivity axiom because the probabilities of H and T need to add up to unity.

[17]The additivity of the probability defined as the "limit" of ratios *needs* to be proven. This could be a big issue although it has never been discussed to our knowledge. We do not address this issue in this book.

[18]The existence of randomizing devices is essential in some areas of economics. For example, in defining the so-called "mixed strategy" in game theory, a randomizing device plays a central role.

1.1.7 Subjective Probability and Ir/rationality

In this book, we call the probability that is defined in view of the subjectivist approach the *subjective* probability.

Recall that almost anything can be a probability if we follow the subjectivist approach. We now discuss the relationship between the subjective probability and the axiomatic approach argued in Sect. 1.1.5.

We may relate the former with the latter so that a subjective probability that satisfies Kolmogorov's axioms is *rational* and one that does not is *ir*rational. Here, the word "rationality" may be used interchangeably with "plausibility as a way of thinking." Then, the plausibility of Kolmogorov's axioms becomes a central issue in terms of rationality. For example, we may ask ourselves if the additivity axiom is plausible as a natural way for people to form beliefs about an event occurring, possibly by resorting to introspection.

Is this, however, an appropriate treatment? In other words, should the eventual justification of the rationality be sought solely in these axioms? Is this a correct way to judge the rationality of a subjective probability?

An alternative way of answering the question of rationality is to compare predictions of human behaviors based on the subjective probability obeying Kolmogorov's axioms and the actual observations made about them. If there exist significant and persistent discrepancies between them, we may say that both Kolmogorov's axioms and the probability based on it are not necessarily "rational" in the sense of plausibility. The alternative is to make a self-contradicting statement that a person's actual behavior is not plausible.

Many examples are presented later in this book where the predictions are clearly denied by the actuality. Thus, we may conclude that the subjective probability that always satisfies Kolmogorov's axioms is *not* necessarily rational according to the criterion offered in the previous paragraph.

Rather, examples of this kind suggest that considering an "irrational" subjective probability, that is "irrational" in the sense of violating Kolmogorov's axioms, may lead to improved predictions of human behaviors and economic phenomena caused by the behaviors.

The literature has proposed alternative axioms to those of Kolmogorov and some authors have called something that satisfies these alternative axioms "probability." These "probabilities" could be labeled as "rational" in the sense of plausibility; that is, they show good performance both in explaining the ongoing economic phenomena and in predicting economic phenomena in the future.

That said, it is true that the concept of rationality is still elusive and there is no consensus. Concerning the rationality of the subjective probability, we take the standpoint that its capability of explaining the reality is the most important criterion for judging its rationality. This book discusses some of the important alternative axioms and aims to show that the "probability" satisfying these alternatives does much better in explaining the reality than the traditional probability satisfying Kolmogorov's axioms.

1.2 Risk and Uncertainty

1.2.1 Frank Knight and Leonard Savage

According to the treatment of Frank H. Knight,[19] risk and uncertainty are deliberately distinguished from each other.

Suppose that the states of the world and the information structure are given. Then, a human being faces *risk* if either (1) she believes that the *objective* probability is known to her, or (2) a *single* subjective probability of her that satisfies Kolmogorov's axioms is given. Otherwise, she faces *uncertainty*. The true uncertainty in this sense is named *Knightian uncertainty* after Knight, an economist who emphasized the importance of distinguishing between risk and uncertainty.

Thus defined, Knightian uncertainty means a truly uncertain situation where the agent is unsure about the possibility of the occurrence of an event and the uncertainty cannot be summarized by a single additive probability whether it is objective or subjective.

Suppose that an agent faces uncertainty. Also consider some set of "behavioral" axioms (that are defined precisely and mathematically later in this book) that are stated as the axioms imposed on the pattern of her behaviors, although they may or may not be satisfied by that pattern.

Leonard J. Savage proved[20] that if her behavioral pattern completely complies with this set of behavioral axioms, she acts in such an uncertain situation as if she faces risk in the sense of (2) above.[21] Thus, we may practically assume that she knows *the* probability if we admit these behavioral axioms as totally plausible.

According to Savage's theory, known as *subjective expected utility* (SEU) theory, uncertainty is reducible to risk. This means that there would be no positive reason why uncertainty and risk should be distinguished.

Therefore, whether we should make this distinction between risk and uncertainty hinges upon the plausibility of thinking that people's behaviors satisfy all of Savage's axioms. Unfortunately, however, there exists at least one axiom among them whose plausibility has been controversial for a long time. This axiom is known as Savage's *sure-thing principle* and it, for example, requires that the agent's decision be independent of her actions that would not have been conducted in fact. (In retrospection, is this reasonable enough to postulate?) Furthermore, there is a lot of imaginary and/or

---

[19]Knight (1921).

[20]Savage (1954).

[21]Savage proved much more than this. According to Savage's theorem, if her behavioral pattern complies with the axioms, she behaves as if she calculates the mathematical expectation of her prospects of random utility by using *the* subjective probability. If she chooses a specific action, she should maximize her expected utility thus calculated. In the main text, we focus on the existence of the single probability that is included among the claims of his theorem. Furthermore, if we only care about the existence of the single additive subjective probability, Savage's axioms can be weakened. See Machina and Schmeidler (1992) and Sect. 3.6 of this book.

actual experiments in which people exhibit behavioral patterns that expressly violate the sure-thing principle.

The most famous experiment of this type was that submitted by Ellsberg (1961). In his experiment, the subjects show the robust patterns of choices that clearly violate Savage's sure-thing principle. Furthermore, this pattern of choices cannot be explained as far as we simply assume that each subject has a single additive subjective probability. (See, however, Sect. 1.3.4 below.) Because Ellsberg's experiment, known as *Ellsberg's paradox*, is of fundamental importance, we will carefully discuss this topic later in this book (Sect. 3.7).

If we do not consider Savage's axioms to be sufficiently reasonable to be imposed on the patterns of human behaviors as encouraged by the above-mentioned paradoxes, then we must allow a situation where people face (Knightian) uncertainty that is *ir*reducible to risk.

1.2.2 Maxmin Expected Utility (MEU) and Choquet Expected Utility (CEU)

Knightian uncertainty describes a situation where the uncertainty a human being is faced with is so deep that it cannot be summarized by a *single* probability. The alternative is a *set* of probabilities rather than a single probability. The situation where information is too imprecise to be summarized by a single probability but precise enough to be summarized by a set of probabilities is called *ambiguous*. Thus, ambiguity is a special case of Knightian uncertainty.

Gilboa and Schmeidler (1989) proposed a set of behavioral axioms that require much less than those of Savage. In particular, they drop Savage's sure-thing principle. Then, they prove that if a decision-maker's behavior complies with all of their behavioral axioms, we may assume that she makes decisions based upon some *set* of additive subjective probabilities, instead of a single additive subjective probability.

In addition, one of their axioms, known as *uncertainty-aversion*, implies that she always picks up the "worst" probability in evaluating each uncertain prospect. This "worst" probability may vary depending upon the situation she faces. That she always weighs heavily on the "worst" probability may be considered to represent her *pessimistic* attitude toward Knightian uncertainty.

The theoretical framework described in the previous paragraph is called *maxmin expected utility* (MEU) theory; it has drawn much attention as a remarkable theory of Knightian uncertainty.[22] Since this theory appeared, it has been extensively applied to concrete economic models in almost all areas of economics and this book itself may be placed along this line of research.

[22]"Knightian uncertainty" means the situation where a probability does not yet exist; "ambiguity" means that the decision-maker is endowed with a set of probabilities; "maxmin" behavior is a decision-maker's specific attitude toward ambiguity.

An alternative set of behavioral axioms, which also requires much less than that of Savage, was proposed by Schmeidler (1989).[23] Among his set of axioms, Schmeidler weakens Savage's sure-thing principle to a large extent, and proves that if a decision-maker's behavior complies with all of his behavioral axioms, we may assume that she makes decisions based upon "something" that looks like a subjective probability, but is *not* exactly a subjective probability because it does not necessarily satisfy the additivity axiom among Kolmogorov's axioms.

We may call it "probability" in accordance with the philosophy expressed in Sect. 1.1.7 and we actually do so in this book.[24] However, care must be taken in this matter in economic and mathematical senses. We call the probability that appears in Schmeidler's theorem a probability *capacity* and we call the probability satisfying all of Kolmogorov's axioms a probability *charge* or a probability *measure*.[25] The probability charge and the probability measure satisfy the additivity axiom of Kolmogorov, but the probability capacity may not. That is, a capacity may be *non*additive in the sense that it does not satisfy the additivity stated in Sect. 1.1.5. The capacity satisfies only the weak requirement that the capacity of a "large" event should be larger than that of a "small" event that is completely contained by the "large" event. In other words, people know that any event is more likely to occur than its "portion" if they are equipped only with the capacity.

According to Schmeidler (1982, 1989), Knightian uncertainty is so deep that it can be summarized only "imprecisely" by a probability capacity. This is called *Choquet expected utility* (CEU) theory after Gustave Choquet, a French mathematician who developed the concept of a capacity and an integral theory with respect to a capacity in the first place.

In addition to this imprecision, if a CEU maximizer is "uncertainty-averse" in some sense, which will be stated formally and mathematically in Chap. 3, the CEU theory turns out to be a very special case of MEU theory.[26] That is, when people are "uncertainty-averse," the capacity characterizing their view on uncertainty is still nonadditive, but it obeys some strong law or pattern about the way of its being nonadditive, called *convexity*.[27]

Furthermore, the behavior of a CEU-maximizer with a convex capacity can be described as an MEU-maximizer equipped with a very special set of probability

[23]His work first appeared in 1982 as a working paper. Hereafter, we refer to his work as Schmeidler (1982, 1989).

[24]We use the word "probability" to mean that it obeys the "0–1" normalization. See Sects. 1.1.4 and 1.1.5.

[25]The distinction between a charge and a measure is truly mathematical. The details are shown in Chap. 2.

[26]Chronologically, the axiom of *uncertainty aversion* appeared first in Schmeidler (1982, 1989), and then in Gilboa and Schmeidler (1989). The two versions of uncertainty aversion are similar, but remain slightly different. See Chap. 3.

[27]Roughly speaking, a capacity is *convex* if the capacity of the union of the mutually disjoint events is *larger* than or equal to the sum of the capacities of each single event. For the precise definition, see Chap. 2.

charges known as the *core* of the convex capacity. Henceforth, we refer to the CEU employing a convex capacity as the *convex* CEU.

One important novelty of MEU theory and convex CEU theory is that the agent who maximizes the MEU or the convex CEU *does* precisely exhibit the choice pattern observed in Ellsberg's experiment mentioned in Sect. 1.2.1, which can never be explained by SEU theory.

In this book, we mainly apply the "intersection" of MEU theory and CEU theory; that is, *convex CEU theory*. This is basically because of its mathematical tractability[28] (Chaps. 6 and 14 are exceptions).[29]

1.2.3 Pessimism and Optimism

The assumed behaviors of people in both MEU theory and convex CEU theory as its special case convey people's "pessimistic" views of the world when they are faced with truly uncertain prospects. Such behaviors can be characterized by both the multiplicity of probability charges representing uncertainty and people's inclination of choosing the "worst" probability charge representing the "worst-case" scenario in each opportunity of decision-making.

In a symmetric manner, people's "optimistic" views on the world when faced with uncertain prospects can be modeled by the "maximax" theory, where uncertainty is represented by a set of probability charges and people use the "best" probability charge at each opportunity for decision-making. CEU theory with a "concave" capacity is a special case of the maximax theory.

People's "pessimistic" and "optimistic" attitudes toward uncertainty are important to understand real-life economic phenomena. The sudden market collapse triggered by the bankruptcy of Lehman Brothers, the so-called "Lehman shock," and the unpredictable stock price volatility that is observed everyday, among many others, are two good examples of economic phenomena where people's pessimistic and/or optimistic views about the market play central roles.

The theory of Knightian uncertainty presented in this book focuses on MEU theory and convex CEU theory representing people's pessimistic views. Conversely, it also represents their counterparts with optimistic views, and thereby provides a theoretical framework that is not only interesting but also powerful in analyzing real-life economic phenomena.

---

[28]Mathematical expression is helpful when we analyze dynamic economic models with Knightian uncertainty. See, for example, Sect. 2.5.

[29]We can consider a "hybrid" of MEU theory and CEU theory. We may assume that the agent is endowed with a set of probability capacities that are not necessarily additive. Although interesting, we do not pursue this line of research in this book.

1.3 What Is This Book Going to Achieve?

Given all mentioned so far, the objective and the goal of this book is multi-fold. We see this in turn in what follows.

1.3.1 Indeterminacy of Equilibrium Prices

In this book, we assume that people face Knightian uncertainty that is too deep for it to be reduced to mere risk. This fundamental uncertainty urges us to replace the SEU-maximizers in traditional economic models with the MEU-maximizers (or their maximax counterparts) and/or CEU-maximizers with a convex capacity (or their counterparts with a concave capacity).

We examine if this replacement makes any difference in implications of traditional economic models; we will observe that it makes a "big" difference. We will then ask if the models with MEU- or CEU-maximizers can explain the economic phenomena observed in the real world better than the traditional models with SEU-maximizers. Again, the answer is "yes."

Roughly speaking, there are at least two directions of research that emphasize the difference between the implications of the MEU or CEU models and those of traditional models.

One is that the existence of uncertainty-averse agents can explain some sort of "multiplicity," or equivalently, "indeterminacy," of equilibria in an economy. The concept of generating this sort of "indeterminacy" by using MEU-maximizers or convex CEU-maximizers was first invented by Dow and Werlang (1992). This mechanism is so important that we devote a whole chapter (Chap. 4) to explain their model.

It has been long known in the stock market that in reality, there exists a range of prices where no trade occurs. Essentially, nobody buys or sells short an asset when the price falls within this range. This range of prices is called "bid-ask spread" and its effect on the market is well-known as "portfolio inertia."

However, the traditional model that uses a unique additive probability has failed to explain this phenomenon in the framework of a single agent's choice of optimal portfolio. This is because in such a model, the price under which the agent is indifferent between buying and selling short is determined *uniquely* (Arrow 1965). On the other hand, a pessimistic agent who is endowed with multiple beliefs has an indifference curve that is *kinked*. Thus, there are *multiple* prices that "support" the position that corresponds to this kink.

This simple mechanism of generating multiple supporting prices can be applied to a static equilibrium model with many heterogeneous agents equipped with multiple beliefs, leading to multiple equilibrium prices (e.g., Dana 2004). It can also be applied to a dynamic asset pricing model with a representative agent equipped with multiple beliefs, leading to a continuum of equilibrium prices (e.g., Epstein and Wang 1994).

One novelty of these models that can bring about equilibrium indeterminacy is that they can support "badly-behaved" prices as equilibrium prices. A model with a single equilibrium price is more powerful in its capability of prediction than these models. However, it fails to explain the price that is actually observed in the real world because the unique equilibrium price is usually "well-behaved" and the observed price is typically "badly-behaved".[30]

A huge mass of literature about the indeterminacy of equilibrium prices has since followed, but any model in the subsequent literature has been a variation of Dow and Werlang's model. We give an overview of these models and look at them in detail in later chapters (Chaps. 5, 6, and 8).

It is well-known that this sort of indeterminacy of equilibrium prices in the presence of uncertainty-averse agents is "rare" or not robust in a sense that is made precise later in this book (Rigotti and Shanon 2012). To generate "robust" indeterminacy, we need an additional factor beyond multiple priors held by the agents, which is a typical assumption in theories of Knightian uncertainty. One such factor is the incorporation of "money" into a model as in Ohtaki and Ozaki (2015); Chap. 6 explains in detail how this change enables us to have robust indeterminacy.[31]

1.3.2 Increase in Risk Versus Increase in Uncertainty

Another line of research that emphasizes the distinction between the implications of assuming risk and those of assuming uncertainty was initiated by Nishimura and Ozaki (2004, 2007).

Traditional economic theories do not clearly distinguish between risk and uncertainty; thus, the precise meaning of an *increase in uncertainty* has not been seriously discussed or clearly defined. On the other hand, an *increase in risk* has been discussed quite well when uncertainty is represented by a single additive probability, that is, in the case of risk. One important concept of increased risk is the mean-preserving spread.

One probability distribution is a *mean-preserving spread* of another by definition if the mean of both distributions is identical but the degree of "dispersion" of the former distribution is bigger than that of the latter.[32] One situation is *riskier* than another by definition if the former situation is represented by a single probability distribution that is a mean-preserving spread of another probability distribution that

---

[30]The unique equilibrium price in a dynamic economic model is quite often "well-behaved" in the sense that it is "stationary" and "Markovian." For example, it depends on the weather on that day rather than on the date or the weather of the past week. Hence, the booms and crashes of the *equilibrium* prices are difficult to explain by such a model. See Epstein and Wang (1995) in this regard.

[31]Chapter 6 is an expanded version of Ohtaki and Ozaki (2015).

[32]In the definition of the mean-preserving spread, the meaning of being "more disperse" is defined precisely via mathematics. Importantly, this sense of dispersion does not coincide with the mathematical "variance" in many cases.

represents the latter situation. Furthermore, this concept of increased risk has a sound preference-theoretic foundation. That is, *any* SEU-maximizer with an increasing and concave utility index exhibits aversion to an increase in risk (Rothschild and Stiglitz 1970, 1971).

It is well-known that the *option value of waiting* increases when the risk increases in the sense of the mean-preserving spread if the risk is concerned with the realization of outcomes. This is because the *upper* (i.e., "better") tail, which is upper when compared to some benchmark that is above the mean, of the distribution becomes thicker and because the probability of getting a higher outcome by waiting becomes larger according to this change in risk. An increase in the option value of waiting leads to an increase in the reservation wage in the context of a job search. Here, the *reservation wage* is defined as some wage level, if any, such that if the current wage offer is above this level, then the unemployed worker should take that job. Otherwise, she should stay unemployed rather that get hired to maximize her happiness measured in terms of her lifetime income.

When we say "uncertainty has increased," it is more likely that we really mean that the prospects about the future economic situations are more uncertain. Thus, if uncertainty has increased and *if people hate uncertainty*, people will act to resolve uncertainty as soon as possible. As a result, the reservation wage would be lowered, instead of being raised. The interpretation of increased uncertainty would be supported by actual data showing decreased rate of people leaving their jobs.

Our intuition stated in the last paragraph and the theoretical consequence of an increased risk stated in the paragraph before contradict each other. One reason for the contradiction is that the traditional approach defined "increased uncertainty" incorrectly (it defines "increased uncertainty" as "increased risk"). This observation leads to thinking of an alternative definition of "increased uncertainty" by Nishimura and Ozaki.

If we assume an MEU-maximizing agent or a CEU-maximizing agent with a convex capacity, instead of a SEU-maximizing agent, it means that she is endowed with a set of probabilities, instead of a single probability. It is then natural to define an increase of uncertainty by an *expansion* or a *dilation* of this set.

Nishimura and Ozaki (2004) showed that if uncertainty increases in this sense and if people exhibit aversion toward uncertainty in the form of MEU or CEU with a convex capacity, then the reservation wage *de*creases rather than increases. This is consistent with our intuition given above and with the decreasing rate of people leaving their job observed in actual data.

This book devotes three chapters (Chaps. 9, 10, and 11) to studies on this discrepancy between an increase in risk and that in uncertainty in different environments.[33] Chapter 9 is concerned with a job search in which the job is assumed to be permanent. Thus, risk and uncertainty both fade after accepting the job.

---

[33] Chapters 9 and 10 are based on a job search model by Nishimura and Ozaki (2004) and a continuous-time real option model by Nishimura and Ozaki (2007). The basic concept of Chap. 11 appears in Nishimura and Ozaki (2014).

In contrast, Chap. 10 considers a real option of whether to buy a patent of infinite life right now or to wait. The return from the patent is either risky (in the traditional framework) or uncertain (Knightian in our framework). Here a stark contrast is found in the value of this patent: in the traditional framework, an increase in risk increases the value of the patent for the same reason as in Chap. 9, while an increase in uncertainty decreases the value of the patent, because purchase of the patent exposes the investor to uncertainty.

Chapter 11 examines recurrent uncertainty. It adopts the cash-in-advance framework with periodic utility of Stokey and Lucas (1989), and examines the difference between a *permanent* increase in risk and that in uncertainty. We reinterpret this framework as a portfolio manager's problem of investing in illiquid assets, so that money holdings can be interpreted as speculative holdings kept only for investing later. The result shows again a stark contrast between the two. A permanent increase in the risk increases the value of waiting as in Chaps. 9 and 10, and thus increases the time average of speculative money holdings. In contrast, a permanent increase in the uncertainty makes the uncertainty-averse investor resolve uncertainty more often than before and thus reduces the time average of money holdings. That is, when the uncertainty increases, the fund-manager who hates uncertainty prefers to make the gross return determinate rather than indeterminate (in the form of money holdings) as a random variable depending on the future state's realization. These results also produce an interesting implication in the Stokey–Lucas framework of the cash-in-advance economy for consumption: a permanent increase in uncertainty in the future tends to increase current consumption.

It is important, however, to note that Chaps. 9, 10 and 11 assume that uncertainty is represented by a set of probabilities and that people show an aversion to this form of uncertainty. Thus, their comparative statics depend heavily *both* on an increase of uncertainty in the form of an expanding set of subjective beliefs and on people's pessimistic attitudes toward uncertainty where they always use the "worst" probability in each opportunity of decision-making. The axioms for the MEU and the CEU with a convex capacity inevitably characterize these two essentially distinct aspects of human behavior *simultaneously*.[34]

Some attempts have been made to axiomatically disentangle people's subjective uncertainty represented by a set of probabilities and their pessimistic attitude represented by the "worst" acting probability when they are faced with such uncertainty.[35] To study the economic consequences of a "pure" increase in uncertainty thus defined without assuming any specific form of pessimism or optimism seems to be interesting, but is, unfortunately, beyond the scope of this book.

---

[34]Note, however, that the behavior of a CEU-maximizer with a capacity that may be neither convex nor concave is not necessarily explained by either the "worst" or the "best" probability. Such a behavior is characterized by Schmeidler (1982, 1989) *without* the axiom of uncertainty-aversion.

[35]Among others, Klibanoff et al. (2005) is noteworthy. However, they assume that uncertainty can be parameterized and that the distribution of the parameter is known, rather than *un*known. In this book, uncertainty is so deep that even the *family* of distributions is unknown.

1.3.3 The ε-Contamination: Analytic Workhorse of Knightian Uncertainty

Besides these two main streams of research of Knightian uncertainty, this book contains several other topics.

The *ε-contamination* is a specific form of ambiguity. Here, the agent is "almost but not completely" sure about risk she faces. More precisely, she is sure about the "true" (additive) probability with a conviction of $(1 - \varepsilon) \times 100\%$. Otherwise, she has no idea about it and thinks that any probability, even wildly different from the true one, is possible.

Note that the ε-contamination is represented by a set of probability distributions, rather than a single probability distribution. That set consists of a $(1 - \varepsilon)$-to-ε combination of the unique probability (conceived as true by the agent) and any logically possible probability. Given the set of probabilities thus defined, the agent faces ambiguity, which is by definition characterized by a set of probabilities, rather than a single probability.

We call the MEU-maximizing behavior with the ε-contaminated set of probabilities the case of the ε-contamination of confidence, or simply ε-contamination (in the narrow sense). In the latter nomenclature, we follow the convention of the literature. Note that the ε-contamination (in the narrow sense) conveys people's pessimistic attitude or aversion toward uncertainty because they always pick up the "worst" probability in the ε-contaminated set in each situation where they must make a decision.

In reality, however, people are not always that pessimistic, and in some cases they are very optimistic. This situation can be captured by the following formulation. Consider a maxi*max*-expected-utility-maximizing behavior with an ε-contaminated set of probabilities, which can be called the *ε-exuberance*. Symmetric to ε-contamination (in the narrow sense), the ε-exuberance conveys people's optimistic attitude or affinity toward uncertainty because they always pick up the "best" probability in the ε-contaminated set in each of such situations.

The ε-contamination (in both senses) is an analytic "workhorse" throughout this book because of its analytical tractability. We make heavy use of it because it can provide very good illustrations in explaining the mechanics generating economic implications of the models with Knightian uncertainty of this book.

We also present an axiomatic foundation of ε-contamination. This includes a set of behavioral axioms that characterizes the agent's preference represented by the ε-contamination (in a narrow sense equipped with aversion toward uncertainty), and another set of axioms that characterizes the agent's preference represented by the ε-exuberance (Chap. 12).[36]

---

36 The first half of Chap. 12 relies on Nishimura and Ozaki (2006), but the chapter also contains many new results.

Note that the ε-contamination (in the narrow sense) is a further special case of the MEU and the convex CEU. Therefore, our axioms are naturally strengthening those of Gilboa and Schmeidler (1989) and Schmeidler (1982; 1989), where the way to cope with the irrelevance axiom is a crucial issue. The intuition behind our axioms for the ε-contamination is that the "worst" event with an $\varepsilon \times 100\%$-conviction is always "irrelevant," because such an event is always considered by the agent.

Since this result was first published in 2006 (Nishimura and Ozaki 2006), the research program for finding other types of axiomatic foundations for the ε-contamination (in the narrow sense) has become very active.[37]

1.3.4 Concept of "Expectation" Extended: Ellsberg Paradox and Persistent Bias

One strong rationale for the existence of Knightian uncertainty and people's aversion to it is Ellsberg's paradox. As we claimed above, the MEU and the CEU with a convex capacity are possible resolutions for the paradox and this fact justifies and even encourages the use of these preferences in economics.

They are, however, not the only option to resolve the paradox.[38] We propose a new theory that can explain Ellsberg's pattern of choices within a traditional environment of risk; that is, with a *single* and *additive* subjective probability of an agent (Chap. 13).[39] We can do so by introducing some information structure defined and discussed in Sect. 1.1.2 above into Ellsberg's experiment and by extending the concept of "expectation" to define a new scheme for updating an "expectation."

Given a single additive probability, the traditional concept of "expectation" (the *mathematical expectation* of a random variable) is a *certainty equivalent* (a constant) of that random variable, which is the "best" because it minimizes the *mean squared-error*.[40] It should be noted that the term of "best" refers to the error-minimization, where the error is the mean squared-error. This means that the agent thinks positive and negative surprise (error) symmetrically in a very particular way.[41]

---

[37] See, for instance, Kopylov (2009, 2016) and Alon (2015).

[38] See Epstein (1999) and Sect. 3.12 of this book about his critique of the CEU preference with a convex capacity with respect to Ellsberg's paradox.

[39] Although the essence of Chap. 13 relies on Ozaki (2009), the chapter contains many new results and economic applications.

[40] It should be noted that a constant is the only "measurable" function when no information is available, since a constant can be evaluated correctly without knowing any information about whichever event has occurred actually.

[41] The *conditional* mathematical expectation of a random variable is the "best" approximation of it by another random variable, i.e., by a "measurable" function, which is "measurable" with respect to some partial information that is coercer than the information with respect to which the original random variable is measurable. These simple mathematical facts are often overlooked. This may be because both the definition and the existence-proof of the conditional mathematical expectation are formally conducted through the Radon–Nikodym derivative in standard textbooks of mathematics.

There is, however, no a priori reason to assume so. Some people may like positive surprise more than negative surprise, while others may be inclined the opposite way. Thus, it is natural to explore implications of other error functions (people's attitude to surprise) in decision-making. This is what we are doing in this book. Ozaki (2009) introduced the concept of the *implicit mean* based on this idea. It should be noted that not all error functions work naturally in the information structure we consider. However, he was able to completely characterize a class of error functions and resulting certainty equivalents called implicit means, which work well in the sense that both the conditional implicit mean and the unconditional implicit mean are well-defined.[42]

In general, the implicit mean of the conditional implicit mean thus defined may *not* equal the (unconditional) implicit mean. That is, the *law of iterated integrals* does not hold for the implicit mean, while the law always holds concerning the mathematical expectation.

To exploit this "bias," we focus on some specific class of error functions that generates some specific form of the implicit mean. This class of error functions gauges approximation errors asymmetrically between overestimate and underestimate, and we call it the *asymmetric error function*.

Interestingly, the asymmetric error function raises the "bias" in a very systematic way that corresponds to people's "pessimism" and/or "optimism" when they face an opportunity of information acquisition in the future. Furthermore, the "pessimism" and/or "optimism" are "persistent" in the sense that will be clarified later in this book.

We apply this idea to Ellsberg's experiment and then show that the typical choice patterns in it can be well explained by the "pessimistic" and/or "optimistic" features built into the asymmetric error function *within the framework of a single additive probability*.

The theory described so far in this subsection is *not* that of Knightian uncertainty in the sense that people can still summarize the uncertainty by a unique additive probability. But it does provide one possible theoretical framework that explains people's aversion to uncertainty and their pessimistic behaviors (and symmetrically, their affinity to it and optimistic behaviors). As such, this approach deserves its own coverage in this book (Chap. 13).

---

[42]If we could find a function that gauges an error when approximating one random variable by another, which we call *error function*, and *if* the "best" approximate of the former random variable by a constant via this error function *were* the given certainty equivalent, we might use this error function to define a *conditional certainty equivalent* given some coercer information. If this conditional certainty equivalent, which itself is a *function* like a conditional mathematical expectation, were uniquely defined for any coercer information, we might define it as *the* conditional certainty equivalent.

Ozaki (2009) proves that the conditioning scheme proposed in the preceding paragraph actually works "nicely" for some class of certainty equivalents called the *implicit means*, leading to an invention of the *conditional* implicit mean.

1.3.5 Learning Under Knightian Uncertainty

In a situation where only risk is present, that is, the unique and additive subjective probability is known to the agent, her "learning" behavior can be described in quite a natural way.

Assume that the agent knows that the uncertainty is represented by the normal distribution, but that she does not know the "true" value of the mean of this normal distribution.[43] Then, she may assume some distribution (known as a prior distribution) *of* the mean of the normal distribution. After making some observations, she updates the prior distribution by Bayes' rule. The resultant distribution is known as the posterior distribution.

If both the prior and posterior distributions belong to the same parametric family of distributions, it is very convenient. Such a distribution, if any, is called the *conjugate family* of the given distribution. (In the current example, it is the normal distribution.) There exist thorough studies on the pairs of the given family of distributions, which is supposed to bring about the samples we actually observed, and its conjugate family. (In the current example, it is the normal distribution with an unknown mean and its conjugate family.)[44]

These studies show that the posterior distributions within the conjugate family tend to become more concentrated around a particular value (in the current example, it is the "true" value of the mean) as the agent makes more observations. Continued observations update the prior distributions into the posterior distributions arbitrarily many times, under certain conditions.[45]

Thus, the agent's conviction about the "true" distribution becomes strengthened *if she knows at least the family the distribution belongs to*. (In the current example, it is the family of normal distributions.)

However, what about the case where the agent has no idea about the "true" distributions describing the uncertainty she faces? What about the case of Knightian uncertainty where the uncertainty is so deep that the agent does not know the shape of the "true" distribution?

We consider the case of *ambiguity* where the uncertainty is represented by a set of probability distributions, and not by a single probability distribution. This set may contain some families of distributions that are distinct from one another.

We consider (and precisely define) the two most plausible ways for the agent to update ambiguous beliefs, and we show that the "degree" of uncertainty she faces *increases*, rather than decreases, if she "learns" according to these updating schemes. This is because the set of probability distributions describing her state of

[43]Recall that the normal distribution is completely characterized by its mean and variance.

[44]See, for example, DeGroot (1970). The conjugate family of the normal distribution with an unknown mean and an unknown variance turns out to be the bivariate distribution. The conditional distribution of the mean given a variance is a normal distribution, and the marginal distribution of the reciprocal of the variance is a Gamma distribution.

[45]For these conditions, see DeGroot (1970).

uncertainty may *dilate*, rather than shrink, when we characterize the ambiguity by the ε-contamination (our workhorse!) (Chap. 14).

Again, we arrive at a stark contrast between risk and uncertainty. When people face risk, the learning procedure works appropriately to strengthen their conviction. On the contrary, when they face true uncertainty, the learning procedure may not work at all because they lose their conviction about the "truth" over that process and their perceived uncertainty increases.

This occurs because learning may do harm if people learn that they have no clear picture of the relevant situation. In such cases, learning only makes the matter more complicated and even worse.[46]

1.4 Organization of This Book

The previous section outlines the economic content of this book. Although the main body of each chapter is based on mathematics, we provide a nontechnical introduction and summary section in each chapter to explain the main results, and a section of simple examples where appropriate. In the remainder of this chapter, we explain the organization of this book from a modeling viewpoint.

1.4.1 Mathematics: Chap. 2

Chapter 2 provides mathematical results that are essential to analyze economic models with Knightian uncertainty. Of note, the probability capacity, that is, a "nonadditive probability" is introduced and the integral with respect to it, known as the *Choquet integral*, is defined.

We devote Chap. 2 to mathematics partly because of the convenience of its expression; it is repeatedly referenced in later chapters.

However, Chap. 2 is not a mere collection of related mathematical results. There are many "new" results, some of which appeared first in the authors' own works. Among others, there are three versions of the ε-contamination (Sect. 2.3.3), the *orderedness* of measurable functions (Sect. 2.4.2), and *upper quasi-continuity*, *upper semi-continuity*, and *stochastic nondecrease* of the capacitary kernels (Sect. 2.5).

A version of the ε-contamination (*δ-approximation of ε-contamination*) first appeared in Nishimura and Ozaki (2004). This concept is extremely helpful in providing tractable examples of dynamic models of Knightian uncertainty.

The orderedness of measurable functions is a concept that plays a key role in explaining equilibrium in/determinacy of an economy in a unified manner. While a version of this concept appeared in Ozaki and Streufert (2001), its current version

[46] Basic ideas of this chapter were first developed in Nishimura and Ozaki (2002).

first appeared and was extensively exploited in an unpublished manuscript by Ozaki (2000). It will appear repeatedly in this book.

Roughly speaking, the *capacitary kernel* is a dynamic extension of a probability capacity and/or a set of additive probabilities.[47] The three concepts about it mentioned above are indispensable when we analyze dynamic models with Knightian uncertainty by invoking the dynamic programming techniques (see Sect. 1.4.4 below).

These mathematical treatments are sufficiently interesting to warrant presentation as Chap. 2, rather than just using them as convenient glossaries.

1.4.2 Decision Theory: Chap. 3

It is assumed that there exists fundamental uncertainty in the world that cannot be reduced to mere risk. This is largely based on evidence of the pessimistic and/or optimistic patterns in people's behaviors observed in the real world. *Decision Theory* is a branch of economics that studies human behaviors and uses a set of "behavioral" axioms to characterize behavior.[48]

When an individual holds a unique additive probability, it can be used to calculate the mathematical expectations of random outcomes resulting from their actions, and one of these actions can be chosen based on the maximized mathematical expectation. Such patterns of choice may or may not be treated with an *"if-and-only-if"-type statement*.[49]

This approach allows us to judge the plausibility of assuming a specific principle that rules human behavior because this judgment can be made based upon the patterns of choices that are *observable* in everyday life.

If an individual's known behavior contradicted any of the axioms, we may safely conclude that the behavioral principle characterized by these axioms *is* incorrect because of the nature of the "if-and-only-if"-type statement.

Chapter 3 offers the behavioral axioms that characterize the SEU-, MEU-, and CEU-maximizing behaviors introduced in Sects. 1.2.1 and 1.2.2.

---

[47] In other words, it is a "nonlinear" extension of a transition probability, or Markov chain with a finite state space.

[48] See Sect. 1.2.1 for the term "behavioral" axiom.

[49] To see an example of the "if-and-only-if"-type statement, consider ten objects of choice among which the agent must choose the best alternative. Two possible "behavioral" axioms may look like (1) she can name the best object, the second-best object and the worst object given any three objects in this set of ten objects, and (2) once she names one object better than another, then she always names so in any situation of choice. An "if-and-only-if"-type statement should be as follows: she satisfies these two axioms *if and only if* she makes a choice about these ten objects as if she puts a mutually distinct number to each of the ten objects and she always chooses the object that is labeled by a higher number in any situation of choice.

The decision theory presented in Chap. 3 motivates the overall economic perspective of the following chapters, so we discuss the behavioral axioms and the relation among them with considerable care. We provide the proofs of the characterization theorems in as much detail as possible although much of the detail is relegated to the Appendix.

1.4.3 Statics: Chaps. 4, 5, 6 and 12

The remaining chapters of the book are divided into two main parts according to the typical dichotomy employed by economics: *static* analyses in the first half and *dynamic* analyses in the later half (except for Chap. 12).

Three out of four chapters constituting the static analyses of the book concern the indeterminacy of equilibria described in detail in Sect. 1.3.1.

Chapter 4 presents the model by Dow and Werlang (1992) and clarifies the mechanism that generates the continuum range (the indeterminacy) of prices where no trade take place as a result of the agent's optimizing behavior in the presence of both Knightian uncertainty and people's aversion to it.

The single agent's framework can be naturally extended into a truly equilibrium framework. This was achieved by Dana (2004), among others, and the purpose of Chap. 5 is to identify the mechanism of generating the indeterminacy of equilibrium prices and allocations in her model, where many agents endowed with the CEU with the *common* convex capacity make trades in a pure-endowment economy.

The equilibrium indeterminacy in Dana's model rises by the same logic as Dow and Werlang's model. As stressed earlier, any model with multiple equilibrium prices equipped with Knightian uncertainty is more or less a variation of Dow and Werlang's model.

The multiplicity of equilibrium prices in those variants of Dow and Werlang's model is typically not "robust" and it will disappear if we "shake" the model slightly.[50,51] Thus, to generate "robust" indeterminacy, an additional mechanism other than "kinks in indifference curves" is required.

One such mechanism is the introduction of fiat money into the model and this is done in Chap. 6. To justify the introduction of money into the model, Chap. 6 considers a stochastic overlapping-generations economy where the young and the old coexist in each period. In this sense, the model is not purely static. However, we include this model into the first half of the book because the logic used in Chap. 6 is very closely related to that used in the static models.

---

[50]The precise meaning of the terms of "robust" and "shake" are given in Chap. 6.

[51]An important exception is Rinaldi (2009).

Chapter 12 is separated from the other chapters on static analyses, but it also treats a static theory. This treatment is described later because Chaps. 12, 13, and 14 each shed light on people's behaviors, focusing on their pessimistic and/or optimistic traits.

In a static framework, Chap. 12 presents an axiomatic foundation for the preference that is represented by the ε-contamination together with aversion to uncertainty and/or by the ε-contamination together with affinity to it (i.e., the ε-exuberance). This is an extremely intuitive way of showing people's pessimism and/or optimism via multiple beliefs in the form of a set of probabilities, or ambiguity. For more detail, see Sect. 1.3.3 above.

1.4.4 Dynamics: Chaps. 7, 8, 9, 10 and 11

The dynamics part of the book is further divided into two subgroups. The first subgroup, Chaps. 7, 8, 9, 10 and 11, exclusively studies *infinite-horizon* models.

When we discuss the infinite-horizon models, one of the central issues is the dynamic consistency of the agent's preference.[52] The agent's preference is *dynamically consistent*[53] if she never has a motivation to invert her original plan made in the very first period after some lapse of time. Intuitively, this means that her preference has a "nest" structure with respect to her own preferences she possesses in the future after some passage of time.

A major advantage of assuming a dynamic consistent preference in an infinite-horizon model is that we may invoke a very strong mathematical tool of *dynamic programming*. Its application to the model largely facilitates the analyses and provides clear results. We present mathematics of dynamic programming in Chap. 7, which is an adaptation of a general theory developed by Ozaki and Streufert (1996) in the current context of Knightian uncertainty. This approach is new in the literature of mathematics and economics, and we apply this to several specific economic models in Chaps. 8, 9, 10 and 11.[54]

Provision of a dynamically consistent preference over multiple periods with some sound axiomatic foundation is not an easy task in the presence of Knightian uncer-

[52]The issue of dynamic consistency arises even in the two-period model. It is of extreme importance when we consider an infinite horizon because such consistent structure of a preference is fully exploited when we analyze the models by some mathematical method named *dynamic programming*.

[53]We use the terms of "dynamical consistency" and "time consistency" interchangeably.

[54]Chapter 10 considers a continuous-time model and the claim that the contents of Chap. 7 concerning dynamic programming are used in that chapter stands only heuristically. Furthermore, searching a firm mathematical foundation for dynamic programming techniques for continuous-time optimization problems is still ongoing. The results currently available in the literature for continuous-time models are basically derived by the "variational method." The authors believe that the assumption necessary for solving the problems can be significantly weakened if we invoke dynamic programming techniques by assuming a dynamically consistent preference like the one in Chap. 10.

tainty. Two such achievements were made by Epstein and Schneider (2003), who extended the atemporal MEU preference to its dynamic version so as to make it satisfy the dynamic consistency, and by Wang (2003), who extended the atemporal CEU preference to its dynamic version. We assume the existence of such dynamic preferences and, in that sense, we presuppose their characterization results for those preferences by some axioms.

Nevertheless, we give a simple axiomatization result for a dynamic preference based on the CEU in Sect. 3.13 because the above representation theorems are still complicated and it is hard to see if their axioms are consistent with people's real behaviors.

It is still arguable whether we can safely assume that people behave in a dynamically consistent manner over time. There is much research where the economic agents' preferences are assumed to be dynamically *in*consistent.[55] In particular, it is known that the dynamic consistency and assuming the existence of the unique additive probability upon which people base their decisions are intimate in some axiomatic frameworks.[56]

Nevertheless, we assume that people's preferences are dynamically consistent and can be represented by an MEU-type or a CEU-type function that is *recursive*. This means that people can apply the atemporal MEU or atemporal CEU iteratively to eliminate uncertainty period by period. These preferences have an axiomatic foundation and simplify the mathematics drastically. This helps to justify the employment of these preferences in the models equipped with Knightian uncertainty.

Chapter 8 uses such a recursive utility function to show that equilibrium prices can be indeterminate in a truly dynamic framework following Epstein and Wang (1994) in the presence of Knightian uncertainty. The mechanism generating the indeterminacy is basically the same as that used by Dow and Werlang (1992) and Epstein and Wang's model is nothing than a variation of theirs.

Chapters 9, 10 and 11 are devoted to research about the reversal effects of an increase in risk and uncertainty, which was initiated by the authors own. These contrasting effects between risk and uncertainty are shown to be the cases in the search behaviors, the decision-making about real options and the optimal money-holding, in each of these three chapters.

We have described the mechanism of these reversal effects in some detail in Sect. 1.3.2 and we need not repeat it. However, we need to emphasize that the analyses are far simplified by the application of dynamic programming techniques that are possible thanks to the assumption of dynamic consistency we impose on the preferences. This assumption may not be essential to obtain these results on the reversal effects of risk and uncertainty.

---

[55]See, for example, the theory and its applications of *quasi-hyperbolic discounting*, which leads to dynamically inconsistent preferences (Laibson 1997).

[56]See Epstein and Le Breton (1993).

1.4.5 Two-Period Models: Chaps. 13 and 14 and Future Research: Chap. 15

The remainder of the book considers two-period models as a purification of finite-horizon economies. We consider the two-period models simply because the models are already complicated enough and the ideas in these chapters can be highlighted if we focus on the simplest two-period case. Nevertheless, the extension of these models into an infinite horizon would be interesting and worthwhile future research.

Chapter 13 explains people's pessimistic and/or optimistic behaviors within a framework of risk; that is, by still assuming that people base their decision upon a single additive probability. We explain the patterns of choices in Ellsberg's experiment without resorting to the MEU or the convex CEU. See Sect. 1.3.4 for more details.

Chapter 14 considers the updating rules for multiple probabilities to model learning behaviors in the presence of Knightian uncertainty. We make a use of the ε-contamination axiomatized in Chap. 12 to show that learning may increase perceived uncertainty when the uncertainty is too deep in the sense of Knight. See Sect. 1.3.5 for more details.

Finally, Chap. 15 explores a new approach that updates Knightian uncertainty. To determine the effects of learning under Knightian uncertainty, Chap. 14 considers two well-known updating rules for the set of probabilities and two corresponding updating rules for a convex capacity, but there we took them for granted. In the final chapter, we apply the error-function approach developed in Chap. 13 to the framework for updating, or equivalently, conditioning a convex capacity. We present a new result where the updating scheme thus generated for a convex capacity coincides with some existing method of updating a convex capacity.

We admit that the theory presented in the final chapter is rather speculative and the result is primitive. Nevertheless, we have included it in this book to motivate further research along this line. We believe that such research would be fruitful in terms of modeling people's behaviors about information acquisition in the presence of Knightian uncertainty.

In Chap. 15, we also suggest some directions of further research along the lines developed in this book, focusing on the "learning" behaviors of economic agents. We conclude by introducing some of the authors' research that is currently ongoing in close relationship with the studies outlined in this book.

The References in the final section of each chapter contain the full details of the books, articles, and other sources cited in this book. Note, however, that the list is not a thorough description of the literature on Knightian uncertainty and ambiguity, which is too vast to cover in this book. Rather, it focuses on the methods of thinking about uncertainty in a unified manner and provides the logic and tools to apply them to important economic problems.

References

Alon, S. 2015. Worst-case expected utility. *Journal of Mathematical Economics* 60: 43–48.

Arrow, K.J. 1965. The theory of risk aversion. In *Aspects of the theory of risk bearing*. Helsinki: Yrjo Jahnsonin Saatio.

Dana, R.-A. 2004. Ambiguity, uncertainty aversion and equilibrium welfare. *Economic Theory* 23: 569–587.

DeGroot, M.H. 1970. *Optimal statistical decisions*: McGraw-Hill.

Dow, J., and S.R.C. Werlang. 1992. Uncertainty aversion, risk aversion, and the optimal choice of portfolio. *Econometrica* 60: 197–204.

Ellsberg, D. 1961. Risk, ambiguity, and the Savage axioms. *Quarterly Journal of Economics* 75: 643–669.

Epstein, L.G. 1999. A definition of uncertainty aversion. *Review of Economic Studies* 66: 579–608.

Epstein, L.G., and M. Le Breton. 1993. Dynamically consistent beliefs must be Bayesian. *Journal of Economic Theory* 61: 1–22.

Epstein, L.G., and M. Schneider. 2003. Recursive multiple-priors. *Journal of Economic Theory* 113: 1–31.

Epstein, L.G., and T. Wang. 1994. Intertemporal asset pricing under Knightian uncertainty. *Econometrica* 62: 283–322.

Epstein, L.G., and T. Wang. 1995. Uncertainty, risk-neutral measures and security price booms and crashes. *Journal of Economic Theory* 67: 40–82.

Gilboa, I., and D. Schmeidler. 1989. Maxmin expected utility with non-unique prior. *Journal of Mathematical Economics* 18: 141–153.

Gilboa, I., and D. Schmeidler. 2001. *A Theory of Case-Based Decisions*. Cambridge University Press.

Klibanoff, P., M. Marinacci, and S. Mukerji. 2005. A smooth model of decision making under ambiguity. *Econometrica* 73: 1849–1892.

Knight, F. 1921. *Risk, uncertainty and profit*. Boston: Houghton Mifflin.

Kopylov, I. 2009. Choice deferral and ambiguity aversion. *Theoretical Economics* 4: 199–225.

Kopylov, I. 2016. Subjective probability, confidence, and Bayesian updating 62: 635–658.

Laibson, D. 1997. Golden eggs and hyperbolic discounting. *The Quarterly Journal of Economics* 112: 443–478.

Machina, M.J., and D. Schmeidler. 1992. A more robust definition of subjective probability. *Econometrica* 60: 745–780.

Nishimura, K.G., and H. Ozaki. 2002. Economics of self-feeding fear, Discussion Paper 2002-CF-175, University of Tokyo.

Nishimura, K.G., and H. Ozaki. 2004. Search and Knightian uncertainty. *Journal of Economic Theory* 119: 299–333.

Nishimura, K.G., and H. Ozaki. 2006. An axiomatic approach to ε-contamination. *Economic Theory* 27: 333–340.

Nishimura, K.G., and H. Ozaki. 2007. Irreversible investment and Knightian uncertainty. *Journal of Economic Theory* 136: 668–694.

Nishimura, K.G., and H. Ozaki. 2014. Liquidity preference and Knightian uncertainty, Discussion Paper Series CARF-F-337, The University of Tokyo. http://www.carf.e.u-tokyo.ac.jp/english/workingpaper/F337e.html.

Ohtaki, E., and H. Ozaki. 2015. Monetary equilibria and Knightian uncertainty. *Economic Theory* 59: 435–459.

Ozaki, H. 2000. Choquet capacity, Knightian uncertainty and indeterminacy of equilibrium prices, Tohoku University, mimeo.

Ozaki, H. 2009. Conditional implicit mean and the law of iterated integrals. *Journal of Mathematical Economics* 45: 1–15.

Ozaki, H., and P.A. Streufert. 1996. Dynamic programming for non-additive stochastic objectives. *Journal of Mathematical Economics* 25: 391–442.

Ozaki, H., and P.A. Streufert. 2001. Solutions for some dynamic problems with uncertainty aversion. *The Japanese Economic Review* 52: 251–283.

Rigotti, L., and C. Shannon. 2012. Sharing risk and ambiguity. *Journal of Economic Theory* 147: 2028–2039.

Rinaldi, F. 2009. Endogenous incompleteness of financial markets: The role of ambiguity and ambiguity aversion. *Journal of Mathematical Economics* 45: 880–901.

Rothschild, M., and J. Stiglitz. 1970. Increasing risk I: A definition. *Journal of Economic Theory* 2: 225–243.

Rothschild, M., and J. Stiglitz. 1971. Increasing risk II: Its economic consequences. *Journal of Economic Theory* 3: 66–84.

Savage, L.J. 1954. *The foundations of statistics*. New York: Wiley. (2nd ed., 1972, Dover, New York).

Schmeidler, D. 1982. Subjective probability without additivity (Temporary Title), Working Paper, The Foerder Institute for Economic Research, Tel Aviv University.

Schmeidler, D. 1989. Subjective probability and expected utility without additivity. Econometrica 57: 571–587. (Its working paper is first published in 1982).

Stokey, N.L., and R.E. Lucas Jr. 1989. *Recursive Methods in Economic Dynamics*: Harvard University Press.

Wang, T. 2003. Conditional preferences and updating. *Journal of Economic Theory* 108: 286–321.

Chapter 2
Mathematics for Reading Later Chapters

2.1 Introduction and Summary

This chapter covers a number of mathematical concepts that are used in the following chapters. The basic concepts that play important roles in this book are the *probability capacity*, which is a set function defined on the state space that is not necessarily additive over a disjoint family of subsets, the integral with respect to a probability capacity, called the *Choquet integral*, and an extension of a probability capacity to a Markovian stochastic environment, which we call the *capacitary kernel*. We define these concepts carefully and then present some of their important properties, which we repeatedly use in this book.

Some results are well known and their proofs are easily available in the literature unless otherwise stated. Regularly cited works include those of Dellacherie (1970), Shapley (1971), and Schmeidler (1986).

On the other hand, some results first appeared in the authors' own works. If such cases, we provide the proofs as fully as possible and the readers are referred to the Appendix.

2.2 Probability Charges and Probability Measures

2.2.1 *Algebra, σ-Algebra, and Measurable Spaces*

Let S be a set. We call a family of subsets $\mathcal{A}$ of a set S an *algebra* if it satisfies the three conditions: (1) $\phi \in \mathcal{A}$, (2)[1] $A \in \mathcal{A} \Rightarrow A^c \in \mathcal{A}$, and (3) $A, B \in \mathcal{A} \Rightarrow A \cup B \in \mathcal{A}$. Furthermore, consider the following condition that strengthens (3): (4) $A_1, A_2, \ldots \in \mathcal{A} \Rightarrow \cup_{i=1}^{\infty} A_i \in \mathcal{A}$. Condition (4) is clearly strengthening of (3), because we can simply set $A_3 = A_4 = \cdots = \phi$ in (4). We call a family of subsets $\mathcal{A}$ of a set S a

[1] Here, A^c denotes the complement of A in S.

K.G. Nishimura and H. Ozaki, *Economics of Pessimism and Optimism*,
DOI 10.1007/978-4-431-55903-0_2

σ-algebra if it satisfies (1), (2), and (4). An element of an algebra and a σ-algebra is called an *event*. A pair of a set and an algebra or a σ-algebra defined on that set, $(S, \mathcal{A})$, is a *measurable space*. While it is often the case that whether we are talking about an algebra or a σ-algebra is clear from the context, we will be as specific as possible. The family of subsets of a given set S consisting of all its subsets is called the *power set* and is denoted by 2^S. Clearly, 2^S is a σ-algebra and $(S, 2^S)$ is a measurable space.

2.2.2 Probability Charge and Finite Additivity

Given a measurable space $(S, \mathcal{A})$, a set function $p : \mathcal{A} \to [0, +\infty]$ that satisfies the following two conditions is called a *finitely additive measure* or a *charge*:

$$p(\phi) = 0 \text{ and} \tag{2.1}$$

$$(\forall A, B \in \mathcal{A}) \quad A \cap B = \phi \;\Rightarrow\; p(A \cup B) = p(A) + p(B)\,. \tag{2.2}$$

Condition (2.2) is called a *finite additivity*. It immediately follows that a charge p is *monotonic* in the sense that

$$(\forall A, B \in \mathcal{A}) \quad A \subseteq B \;\Rightarrow\; p(A) \leq p(B)\,. \tag{2.3}$$

To see this, note that for any A and B such that $A \subseteq B$, it holds that $B = A \cup (B \backslash A)$ and $A \cap (B \backslash A) = \phi$. This implies that $p(B) = p(A) + p(B \backslash A) \geq p(A)$, where the equality holds by the finite additivity of p and the inequality holds by the fact that p takes on only non-negative values.

A charge p that satisfies $p(S) < +\infty$ is a *finite charge* and a finite charge that satisfies $p(S) = 1$ is a *finitely additive probability measure* or a *probability charge*. We denote the set of all probability charges on a measurable space $(S, \mathcal{A})$ by $\mathcal{M}(S, \mathcal{A})$.

A probability charge p is *simple* if the set given by $\{\, s \in S \mid p(\{s\}) \neq 0 \,\}$ is a finite set. In particular, we write the simple probability charge such that $p(\{s\}) = 1$ for some $s \in S$ as δ_s. That is, δ_s is a point mass concentrated at s.

A probability charge p on a measurable space $(S, \mathcal{A})$ is said to be *convex-ranged* or *strongly nonatomic* if it satisfies the condition: $(\forall A \in \mathcal{A})(\forall r \in [0, p(A)])(\exists B \in \mathcal{A})\ B \subseteq A$ and $p(B) = r$. Roughly speaking, the convex-rangedness or strong nonatomicity requires that the measurable space together with the given charge should have a "rich" structure. A closely related concept is *nonatomicity*. A probability charge p on a measurable space $(S, \mathcal{A})$ is said to be *nonatomic* if it satisfies $(\forall A \in \mathcal{A})\,[\, p(A) > 0 \;\Rightarrow\; (\exists B \in \mathcal{A})\ B \subseteq A$ and $p(B) \in (0, p(A))\,]$. As the names suggest, if a probability charge is convex-ranged or strongly nonatomic, then it is nonatomic. However, the converse does not hold in general.[2]

[2]See, however, Proposition 2.2.1.

2.2.3 Dunford-Schwartz Integral with Respect to Charge

This subsection briefly explains the *Dunford-Schwartz integral* with respect to a probability charge. If a charge happens to be a measure, which will be defined in the next subsection, it coincides with the well known Lebesgue integral.

Let S be a set and let $\mathcal{A}$ be an algebra on it. We denote $B(S, \mathcal{A})$, or more simply B, as the set of all $\mathcal{A}$-measurable and bounded real-valued functions defined on a measurable space $(S, \mathcal{A})$. Here, a function $a : S \to \mathbb{R}$ is *$\mathcal{A}$-measurable* if for any Borel set E on $\mathbb{R}$, $a^{-1}(E) := \{ s \in S \mid a(s) \in E \} \in \mathcal{A}$. We denote by $B_0(S, \mathcal{A})$ or B_0 the subset of $B(S, \mathcal{A})$ consisting of functions, called *simple functions*, whose ranges are finite sets.

Given a probability charge on $(S, \mathcal{A})$ and $a \in B(S, \mathcal{A})$, the Dunford-Schwartz integral of a with respect to p is denoted by

$$\int_S a(s)\, dp(s)\,.$$

The Dunford-Schwartz integral is a functional defined on B or B_0. Instead of defining it formally, we choose to characterize it by some axioms. For its definition, see Dunford and Schwartz (1988) and Rao and Rao (1983).

To this end, we introduce some definitions about a functional. Let $I : B \to \mathbb{R}$ be a functional on a measurable space $B(S, \mathcal{A})$. It is *homogeneous* if for any $x \in \mathbb{R}$ and for any $a \in B$, $I(xa) = xI(a)$, and it is *additive* if $(\forall a, b \in B)\ I(a+b) = I(a) + I(b)$. A functional I is a *linear functional* if it is both homogeneous and additive. Also, a functional I is *monotonic* if $(\forall a, b \in B)\ a \geq b \;\Rightarrow\; I(a) \geq I(b)$. Finally, a functional I is *norm-continuous* if for any sequence $\langle a_n \rangle_{n=1}^{\infty} \subseteq B$ and for any element $a \in B$, $\|a - a_n\| \to 0 \;\Rightarrow\; |I(a) - I(a_n)| \to 0$, where $\|\cdot\|$ is the sup norm on B.

The Dunford-Schwartz integral is linear and norm-continuous. One of the most important results of the Dunford-Schwartz integral is that the converse holds.

Theorem 2.2.1 (Riesz Representation Theorem) *For any linear functional $I : B \to \mathbb{R}$ that is norm-continuous and satisfies $I(\chi_S) = 1$, it holds that*

$$(\forall a \in B) \quad I(a) = \int_S a(s)\, dp(s)\,. \tag{2.4}$$

Here, p is the probability charge on $(S, \mathcal{A})$ defined by $(\forall A \in \mathcal{A})\ p(A) = I(\chi_A)$.

In the theorem, χ denotes the *indicator function*. That is, for any $A \in \mathcal{A}$, χ_A is the measurable function on $(S, \mathcal{A})$ such that $\chi_A(s) = 1$ if $s \in A$ and $\chi_A(s) = 0$ if $s \notin A$. For the proof of the Riesz Representation Theorem, see Rao and Rao (1983, p.135, Theorem 4.7.4).

It is often not easy to verify the norm-continuity of a given functional. In that case, the next corollary is convenient. Let K be a convex set that satisfies $[-1, 1] \subseteq K \subseteq \mathbb{R}$ and denote the subset of B (resp. B_0) consisting of all the K-valued functions by $B(K)$ (resp. $B_0(K)$).

Corollary 2.2.1 *Let $I : B(K) \to \mathbb{R}$ be a functional. If I is additive, monotonic, and satisfying $I(\chi_S) = 1$, then (2.4) holds with B replaced by $B(K)$.*

2.2.4 *Probability Measure and σ-Additivity*

Let $\mathcal{A}$ be a σ-algebra and let p be a charge on $(S, \mathcal{A})$. A charge p that satisfies the following condition is called a *σ-additive measure* or simply a *measure*: $(\forall i, j$ such that $i \neq j)\ A_i \cap A_j = \phi$

$$\Rightarrow\ p(A_1 \cup A_2 \cup \ldots) = p(A_1) + p(A_2) + \cdots . \tag{2.5}$$

Note that $\mathcal{A}$ needs to be a σ-algebra. Otherwise, the second line of (2.5) is not well defined. The condition (2.5) is called *countable additivity* or *σ-additivity*. Clearly, σ-additivity implies finite additivity because we may set A_i to be ϕ except for finite i values and because $p(\phi) = 0$ by (2.1).

A measure p on a measurable space $(S, \mathcal{A})$ that satisfies $p(S) = 1$ is called a *probability measure*. In other words, if a set function $p : \mathcal{A} \to [0, +\infty]$ satisfies (2.1), (2.5) and $p(S) = 1$, then p is called a probability measure. These conditions constitute the so-called *Kolmogorov's Axioms*.

In a very similar manner, we may define the convex-rangedness (or equivalently, the strong nonatomicity) and the nonatomicity for probability measures. Unlike probability charges, however, these two concepts coincide as the next proposition states[3]:

Proposition 2.2.1 *A probability measure is convex-ranged if and only if it is nonatomic.*

Note that a probability measure p is *continuous from below* in the sense that $(\forall \langle A_i \rangle_i \subseteq \mathcal{A})\ A_1 \subseteq A_2 \subseteq A_3 \subseteq \cdots \Rightarrow p(\cup_i A_i) = \lim_{i\to\infty} p(A_i)$ and that it is *continuous from above* in the sense that $(\forall \langle A_i \rangle_i \subseteq \mathcal{A})\ A_1 \supseteq A_2 \supseteq A_3 \supseteq \cdots \Rightarrow p(\cap_i A_i) = \lim_{i\to\infty} p(A_i)$. Therefore, a probability measure p is *continuous* in the sense that it is continuous from below and above. Note that when $\mathcal{A}$ is a σ-algebra, if a probability charge defined on $(S, \mathcal{A})$ is continuous, then it turns out to be a probability measure (that is, it is σ-additive).

[3]For the proof, see Rao and Rao (1983).

2.3 Probability Capacity

2.3.1 Basic Definitions

Let $(S, \mathcal{A})$ be a measurable space, where $\mathcal{A}$ may only be an algebra (instead of a σ-algebra). A set function $\theta : \mathcal{A} \to [0, +\infty]$ is a *nonadditive measure* or a *capacity* by definition if it only satisfies both (2.1) and the monotonicity condition, (2.3). As we have already seen, a charge is monotonic. However, the monotonicity never implies finite additivity.

A capacity θ such that $\theta(S) < +\infty$ is called a *finite capacity* or a *game*. A finite capacity that satisfies $\theta(S) = 1$ is a *probability capacity* by definition.[4]

A probability capacity θ is said to be *convex* if it holds that

$$(\forall A, B \in \mathcal{A}) \quad \theta(A \cup B) + \theta(A \cap B) \geq \theta(A) + \theta(B). \tag{2.6}$$

If the converse inequality always holds in (2.6), θ is said to be *concave*. Note that if the inequality always holds with an equality, θ turns out to be a probability charge.

Given a probability capacity θ, we can define its *conjugate*, denoted by θ', by $(\forall A \in \mathcal{A})\ \ \theta'(A) := 1 - \theta(A^c)$. It can be easily verified that if a probability capacity is convex, then its conjugate is concave, and vice versa. Because the convexity implies that $1 = \theta(S) \geq \theta(A) + \theta(A^c)$, $\theta(A) \leq 1 - \theta(A^c) = \theta'(A)$ holds if θ is convex.

Similar to charges and measures, a probability capacity θ is said to be *convex-ranged* if the next condition holds: $(\forall A \in \mathcal{A})(\forall r \in [0, \theta(A)])(\exists B \in \mathcal{A})\ B \subseteq A$ and $\theta(B) = r$.

When $\mathcal{A}$ is a σ-algebra, a probability capacity θ is *continuous from below* if

$$(\forall \langle A_i \rangle_i \subseteq \mathcal{A}) \quad A_1 \subseteq A_2 \subseteq A_3 \subseteq \cdots \Rightarrow \theta(\cup_i A_i) = \lim_{i \to \infty} \theta(A_i) \tag{2.7}$$

and it is *continuous from above* if

$$(\forall \langle A_i \rangle_i \subseteq \mathcal{A}) \quad A_1 \supseteq A_2 \supseteq A_3 \supseteq \cdots \Rightarrow \theta(\cap_i A_i) = \lim_{i \to \infty} \theta(A_i). \tag{2.8}$$

A probability capacity θ is *continuous* if it is continuous both from below and above. Note that any finite *measure* is continuous, and that continuity and finite additivity together imply countable additivity.

Remark 2.3.1 Assume that S is a topological space. Then, let $\mathcal{A}$ be the Borel σ-algebra on S, that is, the smallest σ-algebra that contains all open sets on S. Sometimes, a set function $\theta : \mathcal{A} \to [0, +\infty]$ is *defined* as a capacity if it satisfies (2.1), (2.3) as well as (2.8) and if (2.7) also holds when A_i is restricted to be open

---

[4]In the definitions that follow, unity can be replaced by $\theta(S)$ for a finite capacity, while we exclusively consider probability capacities in this book.

(see, for example, Huber and Strassen, 1973). However, in this book, we stick to (2.1) and (2.3) as defining properties of the capacity.

2.3.2 Decomposability

Given a probability capacity θ on $(S, \mathcal{A})$ and a nondecreasing function $g : [0, 1] \to [0, 1]$ such that $g(0) = 0$ and $g(1) = 1$, we define a mapping $g \circ \theta : \mathcal{A} \to [0, 1]$ by $(\forall A \in \mathcal{A})$ $g \circ \theta(A) = g(\theta(A))$. Then $g \circ \theta$ is a probability capacity. Furthermore, $g \circ \theta$ is convex (resp. concave, continuous) when both g and θ are convex (resp. concave, continuous). (See A.1.2 in the Appendix.)

Given a probability charge p on $(S, \mathcal{A})$ and a nondecreasing function g on $[0, 1]$ that satisfies $g(0) = 0$ and $g(1) = 1$, we define a mapping $\theta = g \circ p : \mathcal{A} \to [0, 1]$ by

$$(\forall A \in \mathcal{A}) \quad \theta(A) = g \circ p(A) = g(p(A)). \tag{2.9}$$

Then, θ is clearly a probability capacity. However, it is not true that any probability capacity can be decomposed in this way as the next example by Chateauneuf (1991, Example 4, p.364)

Example 2.3.1 Let $S := \{1, 2, 3, 4\}$ and define a mapping $m : 2^S \to [0, 1]$ by $m(\{1\}) = m(\{3\}) = \frac{1}{5}$; $m(\{2\}) = m(\{4\}) = m(\{2, 4\}) = \frac{1}{6}$; $m(S) = \frac{1}{10}$ and for any other $A \subseteq S$, $m(A) = 0$. Furthermore, if we define a mapping $\theta : 2^S \to [0, 1]$ by: $(\forall A)$ $\theta(A) = \sum_{B \subseteq A} m(B)$, then it can be easily verified that θ thus defined is a convex probability capacity. Now suppose that (2.9) holds for some probability charge p and for some nondecreasing function g. Then, it holds that $\theta(\{1\}) = \theta(\{3\}) = \frac{1}{5} > \frac{1}{6} = \theta(\{2\}) = \theta(\{4\})$ and that $p(\{1\}) > p(\{2\})$ and $p(\{3\}) > p(\{4\})$ because g is nondecreasing, and hence, it follows that $p(\{1, 3\}) > p(\{2, 4\})$. However, because $\theta(\{1, 3\}) = \frac{2}{5} < \frac{1}{2} = \theta(\{2, 4\})$, we obtain a contradiction. ■

Some conditions for a probability capacity to be decomposable as in (2.9) are known. A probability capacity θ is *weakly additive* if it satisfies the next condition: $(\forall A, B, E, F \subseteq S)$ $[E \subseteq A \cap B, F \subseteq (A \cup B)^c, \theta((A \backslash E) \cup F) > \theta((B \backslash E) \cup F)$ $\Rightarrow \theta(A) > \theta(B)]$. Then the next theorem holds.

Theorem 2.3.1 (Scott) *Let $\mathcal{A}$ be 2^S. Then, for any convex-ranged probability capacity θ on $(S, \mathcal{A})$, it is weakly additive if and only if there exists a unique strictly increasing function $g : [0, 1] \to [0, 1]$ and a unique convex-ranged probability charge p such that $\theta = g \circ p$.*

Note that the function g in the theorem must be *strictly* increasing. Gilboa (1985) proved that it can be only nondecreasing if the weak additivity is replaced by "almost weak additivity" and "infinite decomposability." See Gilboa (1985) for these axioms and for more details.

2.3.3 The ε-Contamination

A very important example of a probability capacity is the *ε-contamination*, which is used repeatedly in this book. The ε-contamination is a sort of distortion of a given probability charge p obtained by "contaminating" p in the degree of ε. We present three versions of ε-contamination in this subsection.

Example 2.3.2 (**The ε-Contamination**) Let $p \in \mathcal{M}(S, \mathcal{A})$, let $\varepsilon \in [0, 1]$ and let θ be defined by

$$(\forall A \in \mathcal{A}) \quad \theta(A) = \begin{cases} (1-\varepsilon)p(A) & \text{if } A \neq S \\ 1 & \text{if } A = S\,. \end{cases}$$

The probability capacity thus defined is called the *ε-contamination of p*. It can be easily verified that θ is a convex probability capacity. Note that the ε-contamination is *not* in general[5] continuous from below even if the charge p is continuous. To see this, consider an increasing sequence of measurable sets such that each component is not equal to the whole state space and the limit (the union) is equal to it. ■

Example 2.3.3 (**The Naïve ε-Contamination**) Let $p \in \mathcal{M}(S, \mathcal{A})$, let $\varepsilon \in [0, 1]$ and let $\hat{\theta}$ be defined by

$$(\forall A \in \mathcal{A}) \quad \hat{\theta}(A) = \begin{cases} (1-\varepsilon)p(A) & \text{if } p(A) \neq 1 \\ 1 & \text{if } p(A) = 1\,. \end{cases}$$

The probability capacity thus defined is called the *naïve ε-contamination of p*. The naïve ε-contamination of p can be decomposed as $g \circ p$ where $g : [0, 1] \to [0, 1]$ is defined by $g(x) = (1-\varepsilon)x$ if $x < 1$ and $g(1) = 1$. By the observation made in the previous subsection, the naïve ε-contamination is convex because g is convex. However, the naïve ε-contamination is *not* in general continuous from below even if p is continuous because the mapping g defined above is not continuous. ■

While the difference between the naïve and ordinary ε-contamination is subtle, they *are* in fact different. To see this, let p be a probability charge on $(S, \mathcal{A})$. Note that the two concepts of the ε-contamination are distinct if there exists a set A such that $A \neq S$ and $p(A) = 1$ because $\hat{\theta}(A) = 1$ and $\theta(A) = 1 - \varepsilon$. However, such a situation is common. For instance, let $S = [0, 1]$, let $\mathcal{A}$ be the family of Lebesgue measurable subsets of $[0, 1]$, let p be the Lebesgue measure, and let $A = (0, 1)$.

Example 2.3.4 (**The δ-Approximation of the ε-Contamination**) Let $p \in \mathcal{M}(S, \mathcal{A})$, let $\varepsilon, \delta \in (0, 1]$ and let θ_δ be defined by

$$(\forall A \in \mathcal{A}) \quad \theta_\delta(A) = \begin{cases} (1-\varepsilon)p(A) & \text{if } p(A) \leq 1-\delta \\ (1-\varepsilon)p(A) + \varepsilon\left(\dfrac{p(A)-1}{\delta} + 1\right) & \text{if } p(A) > 1-\delta\,. \end{cases}$$

[5] We say "in general" because the correctness of this statement hinges upon the information structure as assumed.

The probability capacity thus defined is called the *δ-approximation of the ε-contamination of p*. It can be decomposed as $g \circ p$ where $g : [0, 1] \to [0, 1]$ is some convex function that can be easily figured out (see Sect. 9.3.2), and hence, it is a convex probability capacity. Importantly, the δ-approximation of the ε-contamination *is* continuous when p is continuous because the mapping g thus figured out *is* continuous. ■

The δ-approximation of the ε-contamination was introduced by Nishimura and Ozaki (2004). We discuss this probability capacity in more detail in Chap. 9.

2.3.4 The Core

We denote by core(θ) the *core* of a probability capacity θ and define it by

$$\mathrm{core}(\theta) := \{\, p \in \mathcal{M}(S, \mathcal{A}) \mid (\forall A \in \mathcal{A}) \;\; p(A) \geq \theta(A) \,\}\,.$$

The inequalities must hold for all events, and hence, writing $p(A) \geq \theta(A)$ is equivalent to writing $\theta'(A) \geq p(A) \geq \theta(A)$. If a probability capacity θ turns out to be a probability charge, core(θ) consists only of θ itself. Furthermore, it can be shown that if $\mathcal{A}$ is a σ-algebra and if θ is continuous, any element of core(θ) is countably additive; that is, a probability measure.

Any element of the core of θ can be thought of as an allocating scheme that cannot be blocked by any coalition in the cooperative game characterized by θ.[6] It is well known that the core of a "convex game" is nonempty. (See Shapley 1971.)

Proposition 2.3.1 *When θ is convex,* core (θ) is nonempty.

Conveniently, the core of some probability capacity can be calculated explicitly.

Example 2.3.5 (**The ε-Contamination**) Let $p \in \mathcal{M}(S, \mathcal{A})$, let $\varepsilon \in [0, 1]$, and let θ be the ε-contamination of p. Then, the core of θ is given by the following simple form:

$$\mathrm{core}\ (\theta) = \{\ (1-\varepsilon)p + \varepsilon q \mid q \in \mathcal{M}(S, \mathcal{A})\ \}\ . \tag{2.10}$$

The set itself of probability charges defined by the right-hand side of (2.10) is often called ε-contamination of p. We sometimes denote it simply by $\{p\}^{\varepsilon}$. See Chaps. 12 and 14. ■

Here, we remark that (2.10) is the core of the ε-contamination of p, *not* that of the *naïve* ε-contamination of p. Actually, in general, the former is a *proper* superset of the latter. To see this, let $S = \{1, 2\}$, let p be the probability charge such that $p(\{1\}) = 0$ and $p(\{2\}) = 1$, and let θ and $\hat{\theta}$ be the ordinary and naïve ε-contamination of p,

---

[6] In this context, the requirement that a capacity (and a charge) of the whole space be unity is a mere normalization. See the discussion in Sect. 1.1.4.

respectively. Then, $\text{core}(\theta) = \{(x, 1-x) \mid x \in [0, \varepsilon]\}$ and $\text{core}\,(\hat{\theta}) = \{(0, 1)\}$, the former of which equals (2.10).

For the core of the δ-approximation of the ε-contamination, see Chap. 10.

2.3.5 Updating Probability Capacity

To conclude this section, we introduce the concept of *updating*. Let θ be a probability capacity on $(S, \mathcal{A})$, and let $A, B \in \mathcal{A}$. By writing $\theta_B(A)$, we mean the probability capacity of A when we know that the event B has already occurred. We always require that given $B \in \mathcal{A}$, $\theta_B(\cdot) : \mathcal{A} \to [0, 1]$ should be a probability capacity. If this is the case, $\theta_B(A)$ is a *conditional probability capacity* given B or an *update* of θ given B.

We discuss three updating rules, all of which are identical and coincide with Bayes' rule for a probability charge p; i.e., $p(A \cap B)/p(B)$, if θ is a probability charge (that is, it is additive).

The most simple updating rule for a probability capacity is the *naïve Bayes' rule*, or equivalently, the *generalized Bayesian updating rule*, which is a natural extension of Bayes' rule for probability charges. Thus, it is defined by $(\forall A)\ \theta_B^{\boldsymbol{B}}(A) := \theta(A \cap B)/\theta(B)$ as far as $\theta(B) \neq 0$. It is easy to see that $\theta_B^{\boldsymbol{B}}$ is convex as far as it is well defined if θ is convex.

The next updating rule is what Denneberg (1994) calls the *general updating rule*. This is studied by Denneberg (1994) and the authors cited there. According to this rule, the conditional probability capacity of $A \in \mathcal{A}$ given $B \in \mathcal{A}$, denoted by $\theta_B^{\boldsymbol{G}}(A)$, is defined by

$$\theta_B^{\boldsymbol{G}}(A) := \frac{\theta(A \cap B)}{\theta(A \cap B) + \theta'(A^c \cap B)}.$$

This updating rule is well defined as far as $\theta(B) > 0$ if θ is convex because $\theta(A \cap B) + \theta'(A^c \cap B) = \theta(A \cap B) + \theta(S) - \theta(A \cup B^c) \geq \theta(A \cap B) + [\theta(A \cup B^c) + \theta(B) - \theta(A \cap B)] - \theta(A \cup B^c) = \theta(B) > 0$ where the weak inequality holds by the convexity of θ and the fact that $(A \cup B^c) \cap B = A \cap B$ and $(A \cup B^c) \cup B = S$. Therefore, the general updating rule $\theta_B^{\boldsymbol{G}}$ is well defined if θ is convex and if $\theta(B) > 0$. It can be also shown that $\theta_B^{\boldsymbol{G}}$ is convex as far as $\theta(B) > 0$ if θ is convex (Denneberg 1994, Proposition 2.3 (ii), (iv), and Proposition 2.5). Furthermore, if θ is convex, it follows that

$$(\forall A \in \mathcal{A}) \quad \theta_B^{\boldsymbol{G}}(A) = \min\{\, P(A \cap B)/P(B) \mid P \in \text{core}(\theta)\,\} \tag{2.11}$$

(Denneberg 1994, Theorem 2.4). That is, the general updating rule coincides with the minimum of the updates of the probability charges in the core of θ.

The final updating rule we introduce in this subsection is the *Dempster-Shafer updating rule*. According to this rule, the probability capacity of $A \in \mathcal{A}$ updated given $B \in \mathcal{A}$, denoted by $\theta_B^{\boldsymbol{DS}}(A)$, is defined by

$$\theta_B^{DS}(A) := \frac{\theta((A \cap B) \cup B^c) - \theta(B^c)}{\theta'(B)} .$$

This updating rule is well defined as far as $\theta(B) > 0$ if θ is convex because $\theta'(B) \geq \theta(B)$ when θ is convex. Also, it turns out that θ_B^{DS} is convex as far as $\theta(B) > 0$ if θ is convex.[7]

Gilboa and Schmeidler found another important expression of the Dempster-Shafer updating rule. They showed that the following holds true: $(\forall A)$

$$\theta_B^{DS}(A) = \min \left\{ \frac{P(A \cap B)}{P(B)} \,\middle|\, P \in \text{core}(\theta) \text{ and } P(B) = \theta'(B) \right\} \tag{2.12}$$

(Gilboa and Schmeidler 1993, Theorem 3.3, and Denneberg 1994, Theorem 3.4). Because $(\forall B)\ \theta'(B) = \max\{P(B) \mid P \in \text{ core } (\theta)\}$ by Corollary 2.4.1, (2.12) shows that the Dempster-Shafer updating rule is equal to the *maximum-likelihood updating rule*: it keeps the priors in the core of θ, which assign the maximum probability charge to the actually realized event and then minimizes the conditional probabilities of these remaining priors. It is obvious from (2.11) and (2.12) that $(\forall A)\ \theta_B^G(A) \leq \theta_B^{DS}(A)$, and hence, the general updating rule by Denneberg is more "cautious" than the Dempster-Shafer rule.[8]

We take up these updating rules again when we discuss conditional preferences and their representations by the updated probability capacities in Sect. 3.13, and when we develop an economic model where a learning process takes place under Knightian uncertainty in Chap. 14.

2.4 Choquet Integral

2.4.1 Definition

Recall from Sect. 2.2.3 that we denote by $B(S, \mathcal{A})$, or more simply B, the set of all $\mathcal{A}$-measurable and bounded real-valued functions defined on a measurable space $(S, \mathcal{A})$. We also denote by $B_0(S, \mathcal{A})$, or B_0, the subset of $B(S, \mathcal{A})$ consisting of simple functions.

[7]To see this, note that θ is convex $\Leftrightarrow$ θ' is concave $\Rightarrow$ $(\theta')^B$ is concave $\Leftrightarrow$ $\left((\theta')^B\right)'$ is convex $\Leftrightarrow$ $((\theta')')^{DS}$ is convex $\Leftrightarrow$ θ^{DS} is convex, where the second and fourth arrows are by Denneberg, 1994, Proposition 3.2 (vi) and (iv), respectively.

[8]Another important distinction between these two updating rules exists in the consequence of their iterated applications. Let $B, C \in \mathcal{A}$ be such that $\theta(B \cap C) > 0$. Then, $\left(\theta_B^{DS}\right)_C^{DS} = \theta_{B\cap C}^{DS}$ while $\left(\theta_B^G\right)_C^G \geq \theta_{B\cap C}^G$ (Gilboa and Schmeidler (1993), Theorem 3.3, and Denneberg (1994), Proposition 2.6 and Proposition 3.2 (viii)). The equality above for the Dempster-Shafer updating rule is referred to as the *commutativity* by Gilboa and Schmeidler (1993).

Given a probability capacity θ, we define a (nonlinear) functional $I : B \to \mathbb{R}$ by: $(\forall a \in B)$

$$
\begin{aligned}
I(a) &= \int a\, d\theta = \int_S a(s)\, d\theta(s) \\
&= \int_{-\infty}^{0} (\theta(a \geq y) - 1)\, dy + \int_0^{+\infty} \theta(a \geq y)\, dy \\
&= \int_{-\infty}^{0} (\theta(\{ s \mid a(s) \geq y \}) - 1)\, dy + \int_0^{+\infty} \theta(\{ s \mid a(s) \geq y \})\, dy\,.
\end{aligned}
\tag{2.13}
$$

Here, the two integrals in the third line are Riemann integrals in a broad sense. To see that these integrals are well defined, first note that the integrands are nonincreasing functions because of the monotonicity of θ. Because a nonincreasing function has at most countably many discontinuous points, it is Riemann integrable. Second, note that a is a bounded function. Therefore, a Riemann integral in a broad sense here is a finite number. The functional I defined by (2.13) is called a *Choquet integral*.

One of immediate consequences of the definition of the Choquet integral is the following fact: $(\forall a \in B)$

$$
\begin{aligned}
\int (-a)\, d\theta &= \int_{-\infty}^{0} (\theta(-a \geq y) - 1)\, dy + \int_0^{+\infty} \theta(-a \geq y)\, dy \\
&= \int_{-\infty}^{0} (\theta(a < -y) - 1)\, dy + \int_0^{+\infty} \theta(a < -y)\, dy \\
&= \int_{-\infty}^{0} (1 - \theta'(a \geq -y) - 1)\, dy + \int_0^{+\infty} (1 - \theta'(a \geq -y))\, dy \\
&= \int_0^{+\infty} (1 - \theta'(a \geq y) - 1)\, dy + \int_{-\infty}^{0} (1 - \theta'(a \geq y))\, dy \\
&= -\int_{-\infty}^{0} (\theta'(a \geq y) - 1)\, dy - \int_0^{+\infty} \theta'(a \geq y)\, dy \\
&= -\int a\, d\theta'\,,
\end{aligned}
$$

where the first and last equalities are definitional; the second equality is trivial; the third equality holds by the definition of the conjugate; the fourth equality holds by the change of variable $(-y \to y)$; and the fifth equality holds by exchanging the first and the second terms. The combined equalities thus imply the next proposition.

Proposition 2.4.1 (Choquet Integral by the Conjugate)

$$
(\forall a \in B) \quad \int_S a\, d\theta' = -\int_S (-a)\, d\theta
$$

where θ' is the conjugate of θ.

For a function $a \in B$, if we let $\underline{a} := \inf_s a(s)$, then $a - \underline{a} \geq 0$ and it holds that:

$$\int (a - \underline{a})\, d\theta = \int_0^{+\infty} \theta(a - \underline{a} \geq y)\, dy = \int a\, d\theta - \underline{a}\,. \tag{2.14}$$

By (2.14), we may apply only the definition of the Choquet integral for non-negative functions:

$$I(a) = \int_0^{+\infty} \theta(\{\, s \mid a(s) \geq y \,\})\, dy$$

when we calculate the Choquet integrals of bounded functions, which largely simplifies the story.

The expression of the Choquet integral is largely simplified when the integrand is a simple function. Given $a \in B_0$, we denote it by $a = \sum_{i=1}^{k} \alpha_i \chi_{E_i}$. Here, we let $\alpha_1 \geq \alpha_2 \geq \cdots \geq \alpha_k \geq 0$ and $\langle E_i \rangle_{i=1}^{k}$ is a partition of S such that $(\forall i)\ E_i = a^{-1}(\{\alpha_i\})$. Because a is $\mathcal{A}$-measurable, E_i is certainly an event for each i. (Such a partition is called an *$\mathcal{A}$-measurable partition*.) Then, the definition of a Choquet integral (2.13) implies

$$\begin{aligned} \int a\, d\theta = \int a(i)\, \theta(di) &= \sum_{i=1}^{k} (\alpha_i - \alpha_{i+1}) \theta \left(\cup_{j=1}^{i} E_j \right) \\ &= \alpha_1 \theta(E_1) + \sum_{i=2}^{k} \alpha_i \left(\theta \left(\cup_{j=1}^{i} E_j \right) - \theta \left(\cup_{j=1}^{i-1} E_j \right) \right) \end{aligned} \tag{2.15}$$

where $\alpha_{k+1} := 0$.

Finally, we define the Choquet integral of a function that is not necessarily bounded in a similar fashion. Let $L(S, \bar{\mathbb{R}})$ be the space of $\mathcal{A}$-measurable functions from S into $\bar{\mathbb{R}}$, where $\bar{\mathbb{R}}$ denotes the set of extended real numbers, $[-\infty, +\infty]$, and define the *Choquet integral* of $u \in L(S, \bar{\mathbb{R}})$ with respect to a capacity θ by (2.13) unless the expression is $(-\infty) + \infty$.

2.4.2 Properties of Choquet Integral

For the remainder of this chapter, θ is a probability capacity on $(S, \mathcal{A})$, where $\mathcal{A}$ is an algebra on S.

The following two results are immediate from the definition of the Choquet integral.

Proposition 2.4.2 (Monotonicity)

$$(\forall a, b \in B) \quad a \geq b \Rightarrow \int_S a\, d\theta \geq \int_S b\, d\theta\,.$$

Proposition 2.4.3 (Positive Homogeneity)

$$(\forall a \in B)(\forall \lambda \geq 0) \quad \int_S \lambda a \, d\theta = \lambda \int_S a \, d\theta \, .$$

The next result concerns the convexity and the concavity of a probability capacity.

Proposition 2.4.4 (Super- (Sub-)Additivity) *A probability capacity is convex (resp. concave) if and only if*

$$(\forall a, b \in B) \quad \int (a + b) \, d\theta \geq (\text{ resp. } \leq) \int a \, d\theta + \int b \, d\theta \, .$$

As this result indicates, the Choquet integral is not linear in general. However, there is an important case where it does become linear. For any pair of functions $a, b \in B$, they are said to be *co-monotonic* if it holds that $(\forall s, t \in S)$ $(a(s) - a(t))(b(s) - b(t)) \geq 0$. The co-monotonicity requires that two functions should move in the same direction when the state changes. Intuitively, one function does not work as a "hedge" of the other function.

The co-monotonicity has an important implication for the Choquet integral. It immediately follows that for any pair of functions $b, c \in B_0$, they are co-monotonic if and only if there exist a natural number k, an $\mathcal{A}$-measurable partition $\langle E_i \rangle_{i=1}^k$, and two k-dimensional vectors $(\beta_1, \beta_2, \ldots, \beta_k)$ and $(\gamma_1, \gamma_2, \ldots, \gamma_k)$ such that $\beta_1 \geq \beta_2 \geq \cdots \geq \beta_k$ and $\gamma_1 \geq \gamma_2 \geq \cdots \geq \gamma_k$ and such that $b = \sum_{i=1}^k \beta_i \chi_{E_i}$ and $c = \sum_{i=1}^k \gamma_i \chi_{E_i}$. It also can be shown that for any function $a \in B$, there exists a sequence of pairs of co-monotonic simple functions, (a_n, b_n), which satisfies that $(\forall n)$ $a_n \leq a_{n+1} \leq \cdots \leq a \leq \cdots \leq b_{n+1} \leq b_n$ and $\lim_{n \to \infty} I(a_n) = I(a) = \lim_{n \to \infty} I(b_n)$. These two facts are used to show the next proposition.

Proposition 2.4.5 (Co-monotonic Additivity) *For any pair of functions $a, b \in B$, if a and b are co-monotonic, then it holds that*

$$\int_S (a + b) \, d\theta = \int_S a \, d\theta + \int_S b \, d\theta \, .$$

The next result is extremely important in the interpretation of the Choquet integral in the framework of economics. Therefore, we name this result the *fundamental theorem of the Choquet integral*.

Theorem 2.4.1 (Fundamental Theorem of Choquet Integral) *A probability capacity θ is convex if and only if*

$$(\forall a \in B) \quad \int_S a \, d\theta = \min \left\{ \int_S a \, dp \, \middle| \, p \in \text{core}(\theta) \right\} .$$

The integral in the right-hand side is the Dunford-Schwartz integral (Sect. 2.2.3). Note that because a is bounded and measurable and the core is compact in the weak * topology, the minimum is actually attained.[9]

Let θ be a convex probability capacity and let $a \in B$. Because the fundamental theorem of the Choquet integral applies to $-a$, we have

$$\begin{aligned} -\int_S (-a)\, d\theta &= -\min \left\{ \int_S (-a)\, dp \,\middle|\, p \in \operatorname{core}(\theta) \right\} \\ &= \max \left\{ \int_S a\, dp \,\middle|\, p \in \operatorname{core}(\theta) \right\} . \end{aligned}$$

Because, however, the first term is equal to the Choquet integral of a with respect to the conjugate of θ by Proposition 2.4.1, we have established the next corollary.

Corollary 2.4.1 *A probability capacity θ is convex if and only if*

$$(\forall a \in B) \quad \int_S a\, d\theta' = \max \left\{ \int_S a\, dp \,\middle|\, p \in \operatorname{core}(\theta) \right\} ,$$

where θ' is the concave *conjugate probability capacity of θ.*

Given any convex probability capacity θ and any bounded measurable function a, we define a set of probability charges, $\mathcal{P}(\theta, a)$, by

$$\mathcal{P}(\theta, a) := \arg\min \left\{ \int_S a\, dp \,\middle|\, p \in \operatorname{core}(\theta) \right\} . \tag{2.16}$$

This is the set of probability charges on S that are "equivalent" to θ with respect to the Choquet integral of a given the fundamental theorem of the Choquet integral. The same theorem guarantees that $\mathcal{P}(\theta, a)$ is nonempty. Rather, in general, it is not a singleton set unless θ happens to be a probability charge.

---

[9]To be more precise, let $p : \mathcal{A} \to \mathbb{R}$ be a *bounded charge* on $(S, \mathcal{A})$. That is, p satisfies a finite additivity (2.2) and is such that $(\exists M > 0)(\forall A \in \mathcal{A})\ |p(A)| < M$. The set of all bounded charges on $(S, \mathcal{A})$ is denoted by $ba(S, \mathcal{A})$ and it turns out that $ba(S, \mathcal{A}) = B^*(S, \mathcal{A})$, where B^* denotes the *dual* space of B, *i.e.*, the space of linear functionals on B that are continuous with respect to the sup norm topology on B (Dunford and Schwartz, 1988). Note that the linearity does not imply the continuity automatically for infinite-dimensional spaces. Also note that any linear functional on B is specified by the Dunford-Schwartz integral by some bounded charge, which is a version of Riesz Representation Theorem (Theorem 2.2.1). Therefore, B^* can be identified as a set of bounded charges. Furthermore, the unit ball in B^* is *weak * compact* by Banach-Alaoglu's theorem (Dunford and Schwartz, 1988, p.424). Here, the weak * topology, or equivalently, $\sigma(ba, B)$-topology, refers to the *weakest* topology on B^* with respect to which any element of B should be continuous, in which we identify any element of B as a linear functional on B^* in a natural way. As is well known, B^{**}, the dual of $B^* = ba$, is a *proper* superset of B. Hence, the weak * topology is strictly coarser than the weak topology on B^*. Finally, because $\operatorname{core}(\theta)$ is the weak * closed subset of the unit ball in ba, and hence, it is weak * compact (Munkres, 1975, p.165, Theorem 5.2) and because a is assumed to be an element of B, Weierstrass' theorem (Munkres, 1975, p.167, Theorem 5.5) proves the claim in the main text.

Given a pair of bounded and measurable functions on $\mathcal{A}$, (u, v), v is *u-measurable* if v is measurable with respect to the smallest algebra on S that makes u measurable. A function v is *u-ordered* if u and v are co-monotonic and if v is u-measurable. As for the u-measurability and u-orderedness, the following result is of importance.

Theorem 2.4.2 *Let θ be a convex probability capacity on $(S, \mathcal{A})$, let u be a bounded and measurable function on it, and let $P, Q \in \mathcal{P}(\theta, u)$. If v is u-measurable, then*

$$\int_S v\,dP = \int_S v\,dQ\,,$$

and if v is u-ordered, then

$$\int_S v\,dP = \int_S v\,dQ = \int_S v\,d\theta\,.$$

The proof of this theorem can be found in Ozaki (2000).

The next result is easy to prove, but essential in solving dynamic economic models that appear later in this book. (See Sect. 7.1.)

Theorem 2.4.3 *Let θ be a convex capacity. Then,*

$$(\forall u \in B(S, \mathbb{R})) \quad \left|\int u\,d\theta - \int v\,d\theta\right| \leq \int |u - v|\,d\theta'\,.$$

We have already seen that the Choquet integral is monotonic and co-monotonically additive. Similar to the Riesz Representation Theorem, we now see that these properties are sufficient to characterize the Choquet integral. A functional I is *co-monotonically additive* if $(\forall a, b \in B)$ $I(a+b) = I(a) + I(b)$ whenever a and b are co-monotonic. If I is co-monotonically additive, it is homogeneous with respect to positive rational numbers. To see this, let $r = m/n$ $(m, n \in \mathbb{N})$. Then the co-monotonic additivity implies that $nI((m/n)a) = I(n(m/n)a) = I(ma) = mI(a)$. Also, in a similar manner to the proof of Corollary 2.2.1, if a functional $I : B \to \mathbb{R}$ is co-monotonically additive, monotonic, and satisfies $I(\chi_S) = 1$, then I satisfies the norm-continuity. Therefore, if I is co-monotonically additive, monotonic, and satisfies $I(\chi_S) = 1$, then it is homogeneous with respect to positive rational numbers and it is norm-continuous; hence, it follows that it is positively homogeneous.

The next theorem is a Choquet integral version of the Riesz Representation Theorem.

Theorem 2.4.4 (Schmeidler's Representation Theorem) *Suppose that $I : B \to \mathbb{R}$ is a functional satisfying $I(\chi_S) = 1$. Then I satisfies the co-monotonic additivity and monotonicity if and only if I can be represented by the Choquet integral with respect to the probability capacity θ defined by $(\forall A \in \mathcal{A})$ $\theta(A) = I(\chi_A)$.*

For proofs of this and the following theorems, see Schmeidler (1986). Note that there is a stark contrast between this theorem and Corollary 2.2.1. In this and the next theorems, B and $B(K)$ can be replaced by B_0 and $B_0(K)$, respectively.[10]

Theorem 2.4.5 (Schmeidler 1986) *Suppose that a functional* $I : B(K) \to \mathbb{R}$ *satisfies the following three conditions: (i)* $(\forall \lambda \in K)\ I(\lambda \chi_S) = \lambda$*; (ii) For any triplet of functions,* (a, b, c)*, any two of which are co-monotonic, if* $I(a) > I(b)$*, then it holds that* $(\forall \alpha \in (0, 1))\ I(\alpha a + (1 - \alpha)c) > I(\alpha b + (1 - \alpha)c)$*; and (iii)* $a \geq b \Rightarrow I(a) \geq I(b)$*. Then the function* I *can be represented by the Choquet integral with respect to the probability capacity* θ *defined by* $(\forall A \in \mathcal{A})\ \theta(A) = I(\chi_A)$.

The remaining results of this section assume that a probability capacity is continuous.

Theorem 2.4.6 (Monotone Convergence Theorem) *Let* $(S, \mathcal{A})$ *be a measurable space where* $\mathcal{A}$ *is a* σ*-algebra and let* θ *be a probability capacity on it. (a) Suppose that* θ *is continuous from below and let* $\langle u_n \rangle_{n=0}^{\infty}$ *be a sequence of* $\mathcal{A}$*-measurable functions such that* $u_0 \leq u_1 \leq u_2 \leq u_3 \leq \cdots$ *and* $\int u_0\, d\theta > -\infty$*. Then,*

$$\lim_{n\to\infty} \int u_n\, d\theta = \int \lim_{n\to\infty} u_n\, d\theta\,.$$

(b) Suppose that θ *is continuous from above and let* $\langle u_n \rangle_{n=0}^{\infty}$ *be a sequence of* $\mathcal{A}$*-measurable functions such that* $u_0 \geq u_1 \geq u_2 \geq u_3 \geq \cdots$ *and* $\int u_0\, d\theta < +\infty$*. Then,*

$$\lim_{n\to\infty} \int u_n\, d\theta = \int \lim_{n\to\infty} u_n\, d\theta\,.$$

Note that by the monotone convergence theorem, all of the above properties of the Choquet integrals hold true for any continuous capacity θ and for any function $u \in L(S, \bar{\mathbb{R}})$ whenever the integral is well defined.

Theorem 2.4.7 (Fatou's Lemma) *Let* θ *be a probability capacity that satisfies: for any decreasing sequence of* $\mathcal{A}$*-measurable subsets of* S*,* $\langle A_n \rangle_{n=1}^{\infty}$*,* $\lim_{n\to\infty} \theta(A_n) \leq \theta\left(\lim_{n\to\infty} A_n\right)$*. Also, let* $\langle u_n \rangle_{n=1}^{\infty}$ *be a sequence of non-negative* $\mathcal{A}$*-measurable functions such that* $(\exists M \in \mathbb{R})(\forall n)\ u_n \leq M$*. Then,*

$$\overline{\lim_{n\to\infty}} \int u_n(s)\, \theta(ds) \leq \int \overline{\lim_{n\to\infty}}\, u_n(s) \theta(ds)\,.$$

2.5 Capacitary Kernel

A mapping $\theta : S \times \mathcal{A} \to [0, 1]$ is a *capacitary kernel* (from S to S) if it satisfies $(\forall s \in S)$ θ_s is a probability capacity on $(S, \mathcal{A})$, and $(\forall B \in \mathcal{A})$ $\theta_{\cdot}(B)$ is $\mathcal{A}$-measurable.

[10]We only need to assume here that K is convex.

A capacitary kernel is *convex* (resp. *continuous*) if θ_s is convex (resp. continuous) for all s. In particular, if θ_s is a probability measure for all s, θ is called *stochastic kernel* (Stokey and Lucas, 1989, p.226).

As for a capacitary kernel, the next result is used repeatedly.

Theorem 2.5.1 (Fubini Property) *Let θ be a* continuous *capacitary kernel. Then for any $(\mathcal{A} \otimes \mathcal{A})$-measurable function u, the mapping*

$$s \mapsto \int u(s, s_+)\, \theta_s(ds_+) \tag{2.17}$$

is $\mathcal{A}$-measurable.

In this theorem, the continuity of θ cannot be dispensed with, as the following example shows.

Example 2.5.1 Let $(S, \mathcal{A})$ be a measurable space such that any singleton set is included in $\mathcal{A}$, and let a capacitary kernel θ be defined by

$$(\forall A \in \mathcal{A})(\forall s \in S) \quad \theta_s(A) = \begin{cases} 0 & \text{if } A \neq S \\ 1 & \text{if } A = S\,. \end{cases}$$

It is immediately apparent that θ thus defined is certainly a capacitary kernel that is convex. Furthermore, for any $(\mathcal{A} \otimes \mathcal{A})$-measurable function u, it turns out that

$$\int_S u(s, s_+)\, \theta_s(ds_+) = \inf_{s_+ \in S} u(s, s_+)\,. \tag{2.18}$$

To see this, fix $s \in S$. Then, there exists a sequence $\langle s_+^n \rangle_{n=1}^{\infty} \subseteq S$ such that $u(s, s_+^n) \to \inf_{s_+ \in S} u(s, s_+)$. For each n, we denote by δ^n the point mass concentrated at s_+^n. By the weak *-compactness of the core, there exists a subsequence, $\langle \delta^{n_j} \rangle_{j=1}^{\infty}$, of $\langle \delta^n \rangle_{n=0}^{\infty}$ that converges in the weak *-topology to some probability charge p^0 in the core of θ_s because each δ^n is obviously in the core. Thus, p^0 actually attains the infimum in the right-hand side of (2.18) because $u\left(s, s_+^{n_j}\right) \to \inf_{s_+ \in S} u(s, s_+)$ and

$$u\left(s, s_+^{n_j}\right) = \int_S u(s, s_+)\, \delta^{n_j}(ds_+) \to \int_S u(s, s_+)\, p^0(ds_+)$$

by the weak *-convergence of $\langle \delta^{n_j} \rangle$. (Note that p^0 may not be a point mass.)

Note that for any $a \in \mathbb{R}$, $\{s \mid \inf_{s_+ \in S} u(s, s_+) < a\} = \{s \mid (\exists s_+)\, u(s, s_+) < a\}$, the latter of which is the projection of the set $\{(s, s_+) \mid u(s, s_+) < a\}$ onto S. Unfortunately, the projection of a measurable set is not necessarily measurable (for instance, the projection of a Lebesgue measurable set in $\mathbb{R}^2$ onto $\mathbb{R}$ is not necessarily Lebesgue measurable). Therefore, the right-hand side of (2.18) is not necessarily $\mathcal{A}$-measurable as a function of s.

The set that is defined as the projection of the measurable set in the product measurable space is called *analytic* set. For the analytic set, see Dellacherie and Meyer (1988), Bertsekas and Shreve (1978), and Remark 2.5.1 right below. ■

The Fubini property is key for dynamic analyses conducted in the latter half of this book. An extension of the ε-contamination to a capacitary kernel inherits the same difficulty as Example 2.5.1. The δ-approximation of the ε-contamination (Example 2.3.4) is a mechanism to resolve this problem. See Chap. 9.

Remark 2.5.1 Note that the capacitary kernel in Example 2.5.1 *is* continuous from above but is *not* continuous from below. Furthermore, if we assume that S is a topological space and if we define the capacity by way of Remark 2.3.1, the "continuity from below" in the weak sense described there follows because the conjugate of θ_s is "continuous" with respect to a decreasing sequence of closed sets by the finite intersection property of compact sets. (Munkres 1975, p.170, Theorem 5.9) If we assume that θ_s is a capacity in the sense of Remark 2.3.1, the mapping defined by (2.17) is always $\mathcal{A}$-*analytic* instead of $\mathcal{A}$-measurable. (Dellacherie and Meyer 1988) The analyticity is a concept that is weaker than the measurability and Epstein and Wang (1995) use this concept to analyze asset pricing in the presence of Knightian uncertainty (see Chap. 8).

The rest of this chapter assumes that S is a nonempty Borel-measurable subset of a *Polish* space (*i.e.*, a Borel-measurable subset of a topological space that is a homeomorph of a *complete separable metric* space). Also, when S is a topological space, the algebra on it should be always understood to be the *Borel σ-algebra*, which is the smallest σ-algebra containing all open sets. We denote it by $\mathcal{B}_S$, and hence, $\mathcal{A} = \mathcal{B}_S$ in what follows.

A capacitary kernel θ is *strongly continuous* if $(\forall \langle s^n \rangle_{n=1}^{\infty} \to s^0)$ $\sup_{E \in \mathcal{B}_S} |\theta_{s^n}(E) - \theta_{s^0}(E)| \to 0$.

The concept of upper quasi-continuity was introduced by Ozaki and Streufert (1996) for a more general class of operators that includes as a special case the Choquet integral with respect to a capacitary kernel. A capacitary kernel θ is *upper quasi-continuous beneath* a function $\bar{u} \in L(S, \bar{\mathbb{R}})$ if $(\forall \langle s^n \rangle_{n=1}^{\infty} \to s^0 \in S)(\forall \langle u_n \rangle_{n=1}^{\infty} \leq \bar{u})$

$$\overline{\lim_{n\to\infty}} \int_S u_n(s)\theta_{s^n}(ds) \leq \int_S \overline{\lim_{n\to\infty}}\, u_n(s)\theta_{s^0}(ds)\,.$$

The concept of upper semi-continuity was introduced by Ozaki (2002) for a more general class of operators that includes as a special case the Choquet integral with respect to a capacitary kernel. Assume that X is another Polish space. A capacitary kernel θ is *upper semi-continuous on $S \times X$ beneath* a function $\bar{u} \in L(S, \bar{\mathbb{R}})$ if $(\forall \langle (s^n, x^n) \rangle_{n=1}^{\infty} \to (s^0, x^0) \in S \times X)(\forall u \in L(S \times X, \bar{\mathbb{R}}))$

$$u \text{ is upper semi-continuous and } (\forall n \geq 1)\ u(\cdot, x^n) \leq \bar{u}$$
$$\Rightarrow \overline{\lim_{n\to\infty}} \int_S u(s, x^n)\,\theta_{s^n}(ds) \leq \int_S u(s, x^0)\,\theta_{s^0}(ds)\,.$$

The next result is proved by Ozaki (2002), and it states that the upper quasi-continuity is a stronger assumption than the upper semi-continuity.

Theorem 2.5.2 *Suppose that a capacitary kernel θ is upper quasi-continuous beneath a function $\bar{u}$. Then for any Polish space X, θ is upper semi-continuous on $S \times X$ beneath $\bar{u}$.*

The next theorem provides a sufficient condition for θ to be upper semi-continuous.

Theorem 2.5.3 (Upper Semi-continuity) *Assume that a capacitary kernel θ is strongly continuous and that $(\forall s)\ \theta_s(\cdot)$ is continuous from above. Then, for any Polish space X, θ is upper semi-continuous on $S \times X$ beneath any constant function.*

For the remainder of this chapter, we exploit the orderedness of the state space by setting $S = Z := [\underline{z}, \bar{z}]$ for some $\underline{z}$ and $\bar{z}$ such that $0 \leq \underline{z} \leq \bar{z} < +\infty$. We let $\mathcal{A} := \mathcal{B}_Z$, the Borel σ-algebra on Z.

A capacitary kernel θ is *stochastically nondecreasing* if for each nondecreasing function $h : Z \to \mathbb{R}$, the mapping defined by

$$z \mapsto \int_Z h(z')\, \theta_z(dz') \tag{2.19}$$

is nondecreasing. The definition of the stochastic nondecrease here extends that of (Topkis 1998, p.159) for a probability measure to a probability capacity. The concept of the stochastic nondecrease for the capacitary kernel first appeared in Ozaki and Streufert (2001), where the state space is assumed to be a finite set.

Topkis uses (2.20) below for additive θ to define this concept, which turns out to be equivalent to the definition that uses (2.19). This equivalence also holds for nonadditive θ as the next theorem shows.

Theorem 2.5.4 (Stochastic Nondecrease) *A continuous capacitary kernel θ is stochastically nondecreasing if and only if a mapping defined by*

$$z \mapsto \theta_z(\{z' \in Z | z' \geq t\}) \tag{2.20}$$

is nondecreasing for each $t \geq 0$.

Similarly, a capacitary kernel θ is *stochastically convex* if for each nondecreasing function $h : Z \to \mathbb{R}$, the mapping defined by (2.19) is convex. For this concept, we have a counterpart of Theorem 2.5.4.

Theorem 2.5.5 (Stochastic Convexity) *A continuous capacitary kernel θ is stochastically convex if and only if a mapping defined by (2.20) is convex for each $t \geq 0$.*

Some of the assumptions on capacitary kernels introduced so far remain to be satisfied even after some distortion. The next theorem shows this fact.

Theorem 2.5.6 *Assume that* $f : [0, 1] \to [0, 1]$ *is a convex and continuous function satisfying* $f(0) = 0$ *and* $f(1) = 1$. *Also, assume that* θ *is a convex and continuous capacitary kernel that is stochastically nondecreasing (resp. stochastically convex, upper semi-continuous). Then, a mapping* $f \circ \theta : Z \times \mathcal{B}_Z \to [0, 1]$ *defined by* $(\forall z)(\forall A)\ (f \circ \theta)_z(A) = f(\theta_z(A))$ *is a convex and continuous capacitary kernel that is stochastically nondecreasing (resp. stochastically convex, upper semi-continuous).*

In general, a stochastic kernel need not be stochastically nondecreasing nor upper semi-continuous. The next example provides a stochastic kernel P that is strongly continuous, stochastically nondecreasing, and stochastically convex. Because a stochastic kernel is automatically continuous from above, P in the example is also upper semi-continuous by Theorem 2.5.3.

Example 2.5.2 Let $Z = [0, 1]$ and let P be a stochastic kernel defined by

$$(\forall z, t \in Z) \quad F_z(t) = P_z([0, t]) := \int_0^t (2 - z)\, d\mu\,,$$

where F is the associated (conditional) distribution function and μ is the Lebesgue measure. That is, $P_z(\cdot)$ is the uniform distribution on $[0, 1/(2 - z)]$. Then, P is strongly continuous, stochastically nondecreasing, and stochastically convex. (See A.1.12 in the Appendix.)

Suppose that P is a stochastic kernel that is upper semi-continuous, stochastically nondecreasing, and stochastically convex. The existence of such a stochastic kernel is guaranteed by Example 2.5.2. Also, suppose that $f : [0, 1] \to [0, 1]$ is a convex and continuous function satisfying $f(0) = 0$ and $f(1) = 1$. Then, by Theorem 2.5.6, $\theta := f \circ P$ is convex and a continuous capacitary kernel that is upper semi-continuous and stochastically nondecreasing, as well as stochastically convex, and hence it satisfies all the assumptions for some results appearing in Chap. 11.

2.6 Remarks: Upper Quasi/Semi-Continuity of a Stochastic Kernel

Easily verifiable conditions for the upper quasi-continuity and the upper semi-continuity are still unknown. We only have the following conjecture.

Conjecture 2.6.1 (Upper Quasi-continuity) *A capacitary kernel* θ *is upper quasi-continuous beneath* $\bar{u} \in L(S, \bar{\mathbb{R}})$ *if* $(\theta, \bar{u})$ *satisfies*

M1. $\left(\forall \langle s^n \rangle_{n=1}^{\infty} \to s^0\right) \quad \sup_{E \in \mathcal{B}_S} |\theta_{s^n}(E) - \theta_{s^0}(E)| \to 0$ *and*

M2. $\left(\forall \langle s^n \rangle_{n=1}^{\infty} \to s^0\right) \quad \lim_{b \to +\infty} \overline{\lim_{n \to +\infty}} \int_{\{s' \mid \bar{u}(s') \geq b\}} \bar{u}(s')\, \theta_{s^n}(ds') = 0\,.$

The conjecture holds true if θ is a *stochastic kernel* (see Ozaki and Streufert (1996), p.424, Lemma C.1).

For the upper semi-continuity capacitary kernel, we have

Conjecture 2.6.2 (Upper Semi-continuity) *Let X be a Polish space. Then a capacitary kernel θ is upper semi-continuous on $S \times X$ beneath $\bar{u} \in L(S, \bar{\mathbb{R}})$ if $(\theta, \bar{u})$ satisfies **M2** and*

M1$^-$. $\left(\forall \langle s^n \rangle_{n=1}^{\infty} \to s^0\right)$ *θ_{s^n} converges to θ_{s^0} "weakly" as $n \to +\infty$.*

We think that the strong continuity of a capacitary kernel assumed in Theorem 2.5.3 that gives sufficient conditions for the upper semi-continuity may be too strong. We think so because the above conjecture holds true if θ is a *stochastic kernel* (see Ozaki 2002, p.30, Theorem 1) where the sense in which θ weakly converges is clear. For a general capacitary kernel, there are several proposals about what a weak convergence is. See, for example, Narukawa et al. (2003).

References

Bertsekas, D.P., and S.E. Shreve. 1978. *Stochastic optimal control: the discrete time case*. Academic Press.

Chateauneuf, A. 1991. On the use of capacities in modeling uncertainty aversion and risk aversion. *Journal of Mathematical Economics* 20: 343–369.

Dellacherie, C. 1970. *Quelques commentaires sur les prolongements de capacités*, Seminaire Probabilités V, Strasbourg, Lecture Notes in Math., vol. 191, Springer-Verlag, Berlin and New York.

Dellacherie, C., and P.A. Meyer. 1988. *Probabilities and potential C*. New York: North-Holland.

Denneberg, D. 1994. Conditioning (updating) non-additive measures. *Annals of Operations Research* 52: 21–42.

Dunford, N., and J.T. Schwartz. 1988. *Linear operator part I: general theory*. Wiley Classics Library.

Epstein, L.G., and T. Wang. 1995. Uncertainty, risk-neutral measures and security price booms and crashes. *Journal of Economic Theory* 67: 40–82.

Gilboa, I. 1985. Subjective distortions of probabilities and non-additive probabilities, Working Paper, The Foerder Institute for Economic Research, Tel Aviv University.

Gilboa, I., and D. Schmeidler. 1993. Updating ambiguous beliefs. *Journal of Economic Theory* 59: 33–49.

Huber, P.J., and V. Strassen. 1973. Minimax tests and the Neyman-Pearson lemma for capacities. *The Annals of Statistics* 1: 251–263.

Munkres, J.R. 1975. *Topology: a first course*. New Jersey: Prentice-Hall.

Narukawa, Y., T. Murofushi, and M. Sugeno. 2003. Space of fuzzy measures and convergence. *Fussy Sets and Systems* 138: 497–506.

Nishimura, K.G., and H. Ozaki. 2004. Search and Knightian uncertainty. *Journal of Economic Theory* 119: 299–333.

Ozaki, H. 2000. Choquet capacity, Knightian uncertainty and indeterminacy of equilibrium prices, Tohoku University, Mimeo.

Ozaki, H. 2002. Dynamic programming with upper semi-continuous stochastic aggregator. *Advances in Mathematical Economics* 4: 25–39.

Ozaki, H., and P.A. Streufert. 1996. Dynamic programming for non-additive stochastic objectives. *Journal of Mathematical Economics* 25: 391–442.

Ozaki, H., and P.A. Streufert. 2001. Solutions for some dynamic problems with uncertainty aversion. *The Japanese Economic Review* 52: 251–283.
Rao, K.P.S.B., and M.B. Rao. 1983. *Theory of charges*. Academic Press.
Schmeidler, D. 1986. Integral representation without additivity. *Proceedings of the American Mathematical Society* 97: 255–261.
Shapley, L.S. 1971. Cores of convex games. *International Journal of Game Theory* 1: 11–26.
Stokey, N.L., and R.E. Lucas Jr. 1989. *Recursive methods in economic dynamics*. Cambridge: Harvard University Press.
Topkis, D.M. 1998. *Supermodularity and complementarity*. Princeton, New Jersey: Princeton University Press.

Chapter 3
Decision-Theoretic Foundations of Knightian Uncertainty

3.1 Introduction and Summary

This section surveys the decision-theoretic foundations of economic models with Knightian uncertainty. In later chapters, we often assume that the economic agents exhibit aversion to Knightian uncertainty in opportunities of decision-making. One of the main objectives of this chapter is to characterize the behaviors of such agents by some set of behavioral axioms that are imposed directly on their primitive preferences over "acts." Then these preferences turn out to be represented by means of mathematical objects such as a probability capacity and the Choquet integral as introduced in Chap. 2.

Our approach assumes that people's attitude toward Knightian uncertainty is described by their aversion to it, and this needs to be justified by the plausibility of these behavioral axioms. One of the most important rationales for these axioms is that they *are* consistent with the choice patterns in Ellsberg's (1961) experiment. It is well known that the traditional subjective expected utility (SEU) approach employing an additive probability is *in*consistent with these choice patterns, and that these choice patterns are now understood to be quite natural in the real world. Thus, one way to overcome this difficulty is to replace the axioms for the SEU representation with those used for the representation by the Choquet integral.

This research agenda was accomplished in the 1980s in a series of works by Gilboa and Schmeidler and is now known as the *maxmin expected utility (MEU) theory* and the *Choquet expected utility (CEU) theory*. Since then, their theory has been applied to economics as one of the most important theories of (aversion to) Knightian uncertainty. This chapter explains their theory along its development in some detail.

As we remarked in Chap. 1, risk and uncertainty are distinct concepts in economics. In a risky situation, the probability charge that describes the uncertain prospects are known. A preference over probability charges are first characterized as the mathematical expectation of some utility index with respect to each of these probability charges. The set of axioms for this characterization is known as the

K.G. Nishimura and H. Ozaki, *Economics of Pessimism and Optimism*,
DOI 10.1007/978-4-431-55903-0_3

von Neumann and Morgenstern (1947) axioms after the authors who first proved this remarkable result, while this theory is known as *expected utility theory*. Their theory is extended to a more general space called mixture space, an example of which is a set of probability charges, by Herstein and Milnor (1953). Remarkably, the proof of Herstein and Milnor is quite elegant and simple.

The representation theorem for an uncertain situation was first made by Savage (1954). Suppose that an agent has some preference over the set of state-contingent plans, which Savage calls *act*. He proved that if the agent's preference complies with some set of axioms, her preference is represented by the mathematical expectation of some utility index with respect to *some* probability charge. This celebrated theorem is referred to as the *subjective* expected utility (SEU) theory.

One fatal problem of SEU theory is that it *cannot* explain the robust preference ranking shown in Ellsberg's experiment. As far as assuming that the set function appearing in the representation is additive over a family of disjoint sets, this paradox remained unexplained. This problem was resolved in the 1980s by Schmeidler (1982, 1989), whose theory is named the *Choquet expected utility* (CEU) theory, and by Gilboa and Schmeidler (1989), whose theory is named the *maxmin expected utility* (MEU) theory. They use a *nonadditive* set function, which we call a probability capacity in this book, for the representation and they provided a set of axioms for this representation. In particular, they use Anscombe and Aumann's (1963) framework instead of Savage's framework. Anscombe and Aumann proved the subjective expected utility theorem with a mixture space developed by Herstein and Milnor and thanks to this, their proof is quite elegant and simple. In contrast, Savage's proof is quite lengthy and difficult because he directly applies von Neumann and Morgenstern's theorem.[1] Because Schmeidler and Gilboa use Anscombe and Aumann's framework, their proofs are relatively simple in this technical aspect.[2]

Finally, we include a discussion of dynamic preferences that can be represented by an *iterated* Choquet expected utility, which is based on Nishimura and Ozaki (2003). This sort of *dynamically consistent* preferences will be used repeatedly in the dynamic analyses in the latter half of this book.

For further details on the subject, the readers are referred to a monograph and a survey article by one of those who developed this research areas (Gilboa 2009; Gilboa and Marinacci 2013).

3.2 Preference Order

Let $\mathcal{X}$ be any set. We write generic elements of $\mathcal{X}$ as $x, y, z, \ldots$. Any subset $\succ$ of $\mathcal{X} \times \mathcal{X}$ is a *binary relation* and we write it as $x \succ y$ when $(x, y) \in \succ$.

[1]To be fair, Anscombe and Aumann need some randomizing device to generate an *objective* probability charge, and hence, it is difficult to call their theory a "truly" subjective expected utility theory.

[2]To this point, see also Sect. 3.14.

A binary relation $\succ$ is *asymmetric* by definition if $(\forall x, y \in \mathcal{X})\ x \succ y \Rightarrow y \not\succ x$, where $y \not\succ x$ means that $(y, x) \notin \succ$, and it is *negatively transitive* by definition if $(\forall x, y, z \in \mathcal{X})\ x \not\succ y$ and $y \not\succ z \Rightarrow x \not\succ z$. A binary relation $\succ$ is a *preference order* or a *preference relation* when it is both asymmetric and negatively transitive. Given a preference order $\succ$, the binary relation $\succeq$ is defined by

$$(\forall x, y \in \mathcal{X}) \quad x \succeq y \ \Leftrightarrow \ y \not\succ x \tag{3.1}$$

and the binary relation $\sim$ is defined by $(\forall x, y \in \mathcal{X})\ x \sim y \Leftrightarrow x \not\succ y$ and $y \not\succ x$. Then, $\succeq$ turns out to be transitive and complete, where $\succeq$ is *transitive* by definition if $(\forall x, y, z \in \mathcal{X})\ x \succeq y$ and $y \succeq z \Rightarrow x \succeq z$ and it is *complete* by definition if $(\forall x, y \in \mathcal{X})\ x \succeq y$ or $y \succeq x$ or both. A binary relation $\sim$ defined above is called an *indifference relation*.

A binary relation is a *weak order* if it is both transitive and complete. Alternatively, we may start with a weak order $\succeq$ and then define a binary relation $\succ$ by $(\forall x, y \in \mathcal{X})\ x \succ y \Leftrightarrow y \not\succeq x$. The binary relation $\succ$ thus defined *is* a preference order. Furthermore, if we *re*define $\succeq$ from this $\succ$ by (3.1), then $\succeq$ coincides with the weak order we started with.

Let $u : \mathcal{X} \to \mathbb{R}$ be a real-valued function defined on $\mathcal{X}$. A function u *represents* a preference order $\succ$ if it holds that $(\forall x, y \in \mathcal{X})\ x \succ y \Leftrightarrow u(x) > u(y)$.

3.3 Expected Utility Theory Under Risk à la von Neumann–Morgenstern

Let X be a set. We think of X as a set of rewards, prizes, or consequences and call X the *set of outcomes*. Let $\mathcal{A}$ be an algebra on X. We denote by $P(X)$ the set of all probability charges on the measurable space $(X, \mathcal{A})$ and write the generic elements of $P(X)$ (i.e, probability charges) as $p, q, r, \ldots$.

Let $\succ$ be a binary relation defined on $\mathcal{P}$, an arbitrary convex subset of $P(X)$. (That is, $\succ$ is any subset of the Cartesian product of $\mathcal{P}$ with itself.) A utility function u defined on $\mathcal{P}$ is an *affine function* if it holds that $(\forall p, q \in \mathcal{P})(\forall \lambda \in [0, 1])\ u(\lambda p + (1-\lambda)q) = \lambda u(p) + (1-\lambda)u(q)$.

Consider the following three axioms with respect to a binary relation $\succ$ on $\mathcal{P}$. Here, p, q, r are arbitrary elements of $\mathcal{P}$ and λ is an arbitrary real number such that $\lambda \in (0, 1)$.

A1(Ordering)	$\succ$ is a preference order
A2(Independence)	$p \succ q \ \Rightarrow \ \lambda p + (1-\lambda)r \succ \lambda q + (1-\lambda)r$
A3(Continuity)	$p \succ q$ and $q \succ r$ $\Rightarrow \ (\exists \alpha, \beta \in (0, 1))\ \ \alpha p + (1-\alpha)r \succ q$ and $q \succ \beta p + (1-\beta)r$

Then, the following theorem holds.

Theorem 3.3.1 (von Neumann and Morgenstern 1947) *Let $\succ$ be a binary relation defined on an arbitrary convex subset of $P(X)$, $\mathcal{P}$. Then, $\succ$ satisfies Axioms A1, A2, and A3 if and only if there exists an affine function u on $\mathcal{P}$ that represents $\succ$. Furthermore, if another function u' also represents $\succ$, then there exist real numbers $a > 0$ and b such that $u' = au + b$.*

We say that u is *unique up to* a positive affine transformation when it is unique in the sense stated in Theorem 3.3.1. A function u in the theorem is called von Neumann-Morgenstern's *utility index*, or more simply, a *utility index*. Let u be a utility index derived in the theorem and, with some notational abuse, define $u : X \to \mathbb{R}$ by $(\forall x \in X)\ u(x) := u(\delta_x)$, where δ_x is a point mass defined in Sect. 2.2.2. Then the affinity of u implies that for any simple probability charge p, it holds that

$$u(p) = \int_X u(x)\,dp(x) = \sum_{x \in X} u(x)p(x)\,.$$

3.4 Mixture Spaces and Representation Theorem à la Herstein–Milnor

A set Ψ is a *mixture space* if it is equipped with a function $h : [0, 1] \times \Psi \times \Psi \to \Psi$ that satisfies the following three axioms:

M1. $h_1(\psi, \rho) = \psi$
M2. $h_a(\psi, \rho) = h_{1-a}(\rho, \psi)$
M3. $h_a(h_b(\psi, \rho), \rho) = h_{ab}(\psi, \rho)$

Here, the first argument is expressed by a subscript. For instance, any convex set of probability charges considered in the previous section is a mixture space with $h_a : \mathcal{P} \times \mathcal{P} \to \mathcal{P}$ defined by $h_a(p, q) = ap + (1 - a)q$. Consider the following three axioms with respect to a binary relation $\succ$ defined on a mixture space:

B1(Ordering) $\succ$ is a preference order
B2(Independence) $\psi \succ \rho \Rightarrow (\forall a \in (0, 1])(\forall \mu)\ h_a(\psi, \mu) \succ h_a(\rho, \mu)$
B3(Continuity) $\psi \succ \rho$ and $\rho \succ \mu$
$\Rightarrow (\exists a, b \in (0, 1))\ h_a(\psi, \mu) \succ \rho$ and $\rho \succ h_b(\psi, \mu)$

Then, the following theorem holds.

Theorem 3.4.1 (Herstein and Milnor 1953) *A binary relation $\succ$ defined on a mixture space Ψ satisfies Axioms B1, B2, and B3 if and only if there exists a function $F : \Psi \to \mathbb{R}$ that satisfies*

Representation $\psi \succ \rho \Leftrightarrow F(\psi) > F(\rho)$ *and*
Affinity $(\forall a, \psi, \rho) \quad F(h_a(\psi, \rho)) = aF(\psi) + (1 - a)F(\rho).$

Furthermore, F is unique up to a positive affine transformation.

The proof of this theorem can be conducted exactly in the same way as the proof of von Neumann–Morgenstern's theorem (Theorem 3.3.1) provided in the Appendix because the latter proof only exploits the properties that are satisfied by any mixture space.

3.5 Subjective Expected Utility Theory Under Uncertainty à la Savage

3.5.1 Existence of Subjective Probability

Let S be a set. We think of each element of S as a description of a specific state of the world. Each of two distinct elements describes a state of the world that is different from that described by the other element. Also, the set S is exhaustive in the sense that it includes as its element each of all possible states of the world. The set S is called a *state space* or the set of *states of the world*.

Let $\mathcal{E}$ be an algebra consisting of subsets of S. An element of $\mathcal{E}$ is called an *event*. In this chapter, we set $\mathcal{E} = 2^S$. A binary relation $\succ_\ell$ on $\mathcal{E}$ is a *qualitative probability* by definition if it satisfies the following four axioms:

QP1 $\succ_\ell$ is a preference order
QP2 $(\forall E \in \mathcal{E}) \ E \succeq_\ell \phi$
QP3 $S \succ_\ell \phi$
QP4 $(\forall E, F, G \in \mathcal{E}) \ E \cap G = F \cap G = \phi \Rightarrow [E \succ_\ell F \Leftrightarrow E \cup G \succ_\ell F \cup G]$

Here, $\succeq_\ell$ is derived from $\succ_\ell$ by (3.1). If a binary relation $\succ_\ell$ is a qualitative probability, it follows that $(\forall A, B \in \mathcal{E}) \ A \subseteq B \Rightarrow B \succeq_\ell A$. Also, it is immediate that $\succ_\ell$ must be a qualitative probability if it can be represented by some probability charge p: $(\forall A, B \in \mathcal{E}) \ A \succeq_\ell B \Leftrightarrow p(A) \geq p(B)$. To show the converse, the next condition is necessary:

$$\textbf{QP5} \quad F \succ_\ell G \Rightarrow (\exists \langle E_i \rangle_{i=1}^n \subseteq \mathcal{E})(\forall k = 1, \ldots, n) \ F \succ_\ell G \cup E_k,$$

where $\langle E_i \rangle_{i=1}^n$ is a *finite partition* of S.[3] Savage (1954) proved the next theorem.

[3]A *finite partition* of the state space S is any family of subsets of S such that $E_i \cap E_j = \phi$ if $i \neq j$ and $\cup_{i=1}^n E_i = S$.

Theorem 3.5.1 (Subjective Probability Theorem) *A binary relation $\succ_\ell$ satisfies QP1-QP4 as well as QP5 if and only if there exists a unique convex-ranged probability charge on $(S, \mathcal{E})$, which represents $\succ_\ell$.*

3.5.2 Act

Let X be a set of outcomes. We do not assume topological, measurable, or any sort of structure on X. Also, denote by $P_0(X)$ the set of all simple probability charges on X. A function from S into X is called a *Savage act*, or more simply, an *act*. An act f is *simple* if the image of S by f, $f(S) := \{x \in X \mid (\exists s \in S)\ f(s) = x\}$, is a finite set. The set of all simple acts is denoted by F_0. In what follows, when we refer to an act, it always means a simple act unless otherwise stated.

Assume that an agent's preference between acts is given by a binary relation $\succ$ on F_0 and derive binary relations $\succeq$ and $\sim$ from $\succ$ in a way already mentioned. An event $E \in \mathcal{E}$ is said to be *null* with respect to $\succ$ if any pair of acts that differ only on E is always indifferent to each other. We induce a binary relation on X from a binary relation $\succ$ on F_0 and denote it by the same symbol $\succ$ as follows with some notational abuse: $(\forall x, y \in X)\ x \succ y \Leftrightarrow f \succ g$, where $(\forall s)\ f(s) = x$ and $g(s) = y$. The acts f and g used in this definition are referred to as *constant acts*. In what follows, we use a notation such as

$$f = \begin{bmatrix} x & \text{on} & A \\ g & \text{on} & A^c \end{bmatrix}$$

to denote an act f such that f always takes on $x \in X$ on an event A and coincides with an act g on A^c.

3.5.3 Savage's Axioms and Representation by Subjective Expected Utility

Consider the following axioms:

P1 (Ordering) $\succ$ is a preference order
P2 (Sure-Thing Principle) For any act f, f', g, g' and for any event A,

$$\begin{bmatrix} f & \text{on} & A \\ g & \text{on} & A^c \end{bmatrix} \succ \begin{bmatrix} f' & \text{on} & A \\ g & \text{on} & A^c \end{bmatrix} \Leftrightarrow \begin{bmatrix} f & \text{on} & A \\ g' & \text{on} & A^c \end{bmatrix} \succ \begin{bmatrix} f' & \text{on} & A \\ g' & \text{on} & A^c \end{bmatrix}$$

P3 (Eventwise Monotonicity) For any outcome x and y, for any non-null event E and for any act f,

$$\begin{bmatrix} x & \text{on} & E \\ f & \text{on} & E^c \end{bmatrix} \succ \begin{bmatrix} y & \text{on} & E \\ f & \text{on} & E^c \end{bmatrix} \Leftrightarrow x \succ y$$

P4 (Weak Comparative Probability) For any event A and B and for any outcome x, x', y, y' such that $x \succ x'$ and $y \succ y'$,

$$\begin{bmatrix} x & \text{on} & A \\ x' & \text{on} & A^c \end{bmatrix} \succ \begin{bmatrix} x & \text{on} & B \\ x' & \text{on} & B^c \end{bmatrix} \Leftrightarrow \begin{bmatrix} y & \text{on} & A \\ y' & \text{on} & A^c \end{bmatrix} \succ \begin{bmatrix} y & \text{on} & B \\ y' & \text{on} & B^c \end{bmatrix}$$

P5 (Nondegeneracy) There exists a pair of outcomes (x, x') such that $x \succ x'$

P6 (Small Event Continuity) For any outcome x and for any act f and g such that $f \succ g$, there exists a finite partition, $\langle E_i \rangle_{i-1}^n$, of S such that

$$(\forall i, j \in \{1, 2, \ldots, n\}) \quad f \succ \begin{bmatrix} x & \text{on} & E_i \\ g & \text{on} & E_i^c \end{bmatrix} \text{ and } \begin{bmatrix} x & \text{on} & E_j \\ f & \text{on} & E_j^c \end{bmatrix} \succ g$$

Then, the next theorem holds:

Theorem 3.5.2 (Savage 1954) *A binary relation $\succ$ on F_0 satisfies P1, P2, P3, P4, P5, and P6 if and only if there exist a unique convex-ranged probability charge μ on $(S, \mathcal{E})$ and a real-valued function u on X that is unique up to a positive affine transformation such that*

$$f \succ g \Leftrightarrow \int_S u(f(s))\, d\mu(s) > \int_S u(g(s))\, d\mu(s).$$

3.6 The Sure-Thing Principle and Probabilistic Sophistication

Savage's sure-thing principle is an axiom strong enough to force the preference to be represented separably over the state space. Furthermore, the sure-thing principle is quite often violated as we show by Ellsberg's paradox in Sect. 3.7. Machina and Schmeidler (1992) succeeded in dropping this axiom (with a cost of slightly strengthening Axiom P4) while still representing a preference in a convenient way. Such a preference is called *probabilistically sophisticated*.

Given an act f and a probability charge μ on $(S, \mathcal{E})$, we define some element of $P_0(X)$ by $(\forall x \in X)$ $\mu(f^{-1}(\{x\}))$ and denote it by $p_{f,\mu}$ or simply by p_f when μ is obviously understood. Let $\succ$ be a binary relation on F_0. For $p, q \in P_0(X)$, *p stochastically dominates q* if $(\forall x \in X)$ $\sum_{\{i \mid x_i \preceq x\}} p_i \leq \sum_{\{j \mid y_j \preceq x\}} q_j$. Here, we write as $p = (x_1, p_1; \ldots; x_m, p_m)$ and $q = (y_1, q_1; \ldots; y_n, q_n)$ and mean that an outcome x_1 occurs with a probability p_1 under p, for example. If a strict inequality holds for some outcome x, we say that p *strictly* stochastically dominates q.

Consider a binary relation $\succ_P$ defined on $P_0(X)$. If for any $p, q, r \in P_0(X)$, $\{\lambda \in [0,1] \mid \lambda p + (1-\lambda)q \succeq_P r\}$ and $\{\lambda \in [0,1] \mid \lambda p + (1-\lambda)q \preceq_P r\}$ are closed sets, then a binary relation $\succ_P$ is *mixture-continuous*. If a binary relation is mixture-continuous, it turns out to be continuous in the sense of Axiom A3 of von Neumann–Morgenstern's Theorem. (The converse does not hold. See Fishburn 1982, p.16.) Also, a binary relation $\succ_P$ on $P_0(X)$ is *monotonic* if $p \succeq_P q$ whenever p stochastically dominates q and if $p \succ_P q$ whenever p strictly stochastically dominates q.[4]

Similarly, consider a real-valued function $V : P_0(X) \to \mathbb{R}$ defined on $P_0(X)$. If for any $p, q, r \in P_0(X)$, $\{\lambda \in [0,1] \mid V(\lambda p + (1-\lambda)q) \geq V(r)\}$ and $\{\lambda \in [0,1] \mid V(\lambda p + (1-\lambda)q) \leq V(r)\}$ are closed sets, then a function V is *mixture-continuous*. Also, a function $V : P_0(X) \to \mathbb{R}$ is *monotonic* if $V(p) \geq (>)\, V(q)$ whenever p (strictly) stochastically dominates q.

Now, consider the following axiom on a binary relation $\succ$ on F_0:

P4* (Strong Comparative Probability) For any mutually disjoint event A and B, for any outcome x, x', y, y' such that $x \succ x'$ and $y \succ y'$, and for any act g and h,

$$\begin{bmatrix} x & \text{on} & A \\ x' & \text{on} & B \\ g & \text{on} & (A \cup B)^c \end{bmatrix} \succ \begin{bmatrix} x' & \text{on} & A \\ x & \text{on} & B \\ g & \text{on} & (A \cup B)^c \end{bmatrix}$$
$$\Leftrightarrow \begin{bmatrix} y & \text{on} & A \\ y' & \text{on} & B \\ h & \text{on} & (A \cup B)^c \end{bmatrix} \succ \begin{bmatrix} y' & \text{on} & A \\ y & \text{on} & B \\ h & \text{on} & (A \cup B)^c \end{bmatrix}$$

Axiom P4* implies Axiom P4. Axiom P4* and Axiom P2 are mutually independent but all the Savage axioms imply P4*. For any pair of mutually disjoint events A and B, we write as $A \succ_\ell B$ if there exist a pair of outcomes (x, x') with $x \succ x'$ and an act g such that

$$\begin{bmatrix} x & \text{on} & A \\ x' & \text{on} & B \\ g & \text{on} & (A \cup B)^c \end{bmatrix} \succ \begin{bmatrix} x' & \text{on} & A \\ x & \text{on} & B \\ g & \text{on} & (A \cup B)^c \end{bmatrix}. \tag{3.2}$$

Under the presence of Axiom P4*, $\succ_\ell$ does not depend on the choice of x, x', g. Furthermore, if we define $A \succ_\ell B \Leftrightarrow A \backslash B \succ_\ell B \backslash A$ for not necessarily disjoint events A and B, it follows from P4* that $\succ_\ell$ is a preference order on $(S, \mathcal{E})$. Then, the next theorem holds.

Theorem 3.6.1 (Machina and Schmeidler 1992) *A binary relation $\succ$ on F_0 satisfies P1, P3, P4*, P5, and P6 if and only if there exist a convex-ranged probability charge*

[4]We sometimes use the "abbreviated" expression for the two *if* conditions, that is, we sometimes write as "if $p \succeq_P (\succ_P)\, q$ whenever p (strictly) stochastically dominates q."

μ on $(S, \mathcal{E})$ that represents $\succ_\ell$ defined by (3.2) and a mixture-continuous monotonic function $V : P_0(X) \to \mathbb{R}$ such that $f \succ g \Leftrightarrow V(p_f) > V(p_g)$.

Note that in the theorem, the axioms inevitably force the preference to be monotonic. This monotonicity requirement cannot be overlooked as we see in the next subsection, while the requirement of mixture-continuity seems to be rather technical.

3.7 Ellsberg's Paradox

An essential critique to the subjective expected utility theory by Savage is given by *Ellsberg's Paradox*.

Example 3.7.1 (Ellsberg 1961) There are 90 colored balls in an urn. While 30 balls are known to be red (R), the remaining 60 balls are either black (B) or white (W) and their ratio is not known. Now consider the betting options when a ball is drawn from this urn and a reward is given depending on the color of that ball. In particular, suppose that there are four betting options described by the table below. For example, f_1 means betting such that a reward of \$1,000 is given if a red ball is drawn but nothing is given otherwise.

	R	B	W
f_1	\$1,000	\$0	\$0
f_2	\$0	\$1,000	\$0
f_3	\$1,000	\$0	\$1,000
f_4	\$0	\$1,000	\$1,000

Consider a preference order with respect to these betting (acts) such that $f_1 \succ f_2$ and $f_4 \succ f_3$. In fact, this seems to be a plausible preference order. However, with any utility index u and with any probability charge (i.e, a probability of R, B, and W in a usual sense), this preference order cannot be represented by the subjective expected utility. ■

To see why the expected utility fails to represent this preference order, suppose that $u(\$1{,}000) > u(\$0)$. By the affinity of the utility index, we can set $u(\$1{,}000) = 1$ and $u(\$0) = 0$ without loss of generality. If the decision-maker assigns x as a probability of B and she is a subjective expected-utility maximizer, she must assign $2/3 - x$ as the probability of W. Then, the ranking $f_1 \succ f_2$ implies that $x < 1/3$ and the ranking $f_4 \succ f_3$ implies that $x > 1/3$. Thus, the rankings in the paradox are not explained by the subjective expected-utility theory.

Furthermore, the situation is not improved even if the decision-maker is only probabilistically sophisticated. Such a decision-maker would assign some probability x to B and the probability $2/3 - x$ to W. Suppose that $x < 1/3$. Then, the distribution induced by f_1 strictly stochastically dominates the one by f_2, and the distribution induced by f_3 strictly stochastically dominates the one by f_4. The probabilistically sophisticated decision-maker must comply with the stochastic dominance relation and thus the rankings in the paradox are impossible.

The paradox denies the assumption that the decision-maker's preference may be described by a single probability charge.

3.8 An Alternative Framework à la Anscombe–Aumann

The cerebrated theorem by Savage (1954) states that if the decision-maker's behavior complies with some set of reasonable axioms, then her behavior can be described as if she tries to maximize the expected utility with respect to some subjective probability. The proof of Savage's theorem is quite lengthy (for example, see Fishburn 1970). In contrast, Anscombe and Aumann (1963) greatly simplified the story by introducing a randomizing device that generates an objective probability. For this simplicity, the CEU and MEU theories by Schmeidler and Gilboa that resolve Ellsberg's paradox use this framework.

It should be noted, however, that the original proof by Anscombe and Aumann assumes that the state space is finite (see also Kreps 1988). This section extends their result to a general state space that is not necessarily finite by using the Riesz representation theorem. The proof we provide in the Appendix is simple and quite easy to follow.

3.8.1 Lottery Act

In this section, we assume that a pair of a state space and a set of events is given by a measurable space $(S, \mathcal{A})$, where $\mathcal{A}$ is an arbitrary algebra on S, which is not necessarily equal to 2^S. Different from Savage's framework, a set of outcomes is now given by a mixture space Y. For example, let X be a set of prizes and let Y be the space of all simple probability charges on X. Then, Y thus constructed becomes a mixture space. In this framework, we require that the outcome space be "convex." This is a severe restriction on the current model because the outcome space can be any set in Savage's model. On the other hand, the set of events can be any algebra here while it is forced to be the power set in Savage's model.

A function from S into Y is called an *Anscombe–Aumann (A-A) act* or a *lottery act*. A lottery act whose range is a finite set and which is $\mathcal{A}$-measurable when its range is endowed with the discrete topology is called a *simple* lottery act. The set of all simple lottery acts is denoted by L_0. As before, we hereafter suppress "simple." The set of lottery acts whose range is a singleton (i.e., *constant lottery acts*) is denoted by L_c. Let $\succ$ be a binary relation defined on L_0. We use constant lottery acts to induce the binary relation on Y from $\succ$. That is, with some notational abuse, $(\forall y, y' \in Y)\ y \succ y' \ \Leftrightarrow\ f \succ g$ where $(\forall s)\ f(s) = y$ and $g(s) = y'$.

In this framework by Anscombe and Aumann (1963), we can construct a "mixture" of two lottery acts. To see this, let f and g be two lottery acts. Let h be a mixture function with which Y turns into a mixture space. Then, use h to define the mixture of f and g by $s \mapsto h_a(f(s), g(s))$. Then, it can be easily seen that the set L_0 becomes a mixture space by this operation. We write the mixture of f and g thus defined as $af + (1-a)g$.[5] This mixture of lottery acts is often referred to as a *compound lottery act*.

3.8.2 Anscombe–Aumann's Axioms and Representation by Subjective Expected Utility

Consider the following axioms that may be imposed on a binary relation $\succ$ on L_0. Here, f, g, h are any element of L_0 and λ is any real number such that $\lambda \in (0, 1]$.

AA1(**Ordering**)	$\succ$ is a preference order
AA2(**Independence**)	$f \succ g \Rightarrow \lambda f + (1-\lambda)h \succ \lambda g + (1-\lambda)h$
AA3(**Continuity**)	$f \succ g$ and $g \succ h$ $\Rightarrow (\exists \alpha, \beta \in (0,1))\ \alpha f + (1-\alpha)h \succ g$ and $g \succ \beta f + (1-\beta)h$
AA4(**Monotonicity**)	$(\forall s \in S)\ f(s) \succeq g(s) \Rightarrow f \succeq g$
AA5(**Nondegeneracy**)	$(\exists f, g \in L_0)\ f \succ g$

Independence Axiom (AA2) requires that a mixture of the third lottery act should not reverse the preference order between two lottery acts. It is a key axiom for a preference order to be represented by a probability charge as the form of expected utility that is additively separable on the state space.

In the next theorem, the affinity of u refers to that in Herstein–Milnor's Theorem.

Theorem 3.8.1 (Anscombe and Aumann 1963) *A binary relation $\succ$ on L_0 satisfies AA1, AA2, AA3, AA4, and AA5 if and only if there exist a unique probability charge μ on $(S, \mathcal{A})$ and an affine function u on Y that is unique up to a positive affine transformation such that*

$$f \succ g \Leftrightarrow \int_S u(f(s))\, d\mu(s) > \int_S u(g(s))\, d\mu(s)\,.$$

[5]Here, the expression "$af + (1-a)g$" appears to contain the scalar multiplication and the vector addition, but this is not necessarily so. We use this expression only for notational convenience.

3.9 Choquet Expected Utility Theory à la Schmeidler

3.9.1 Representation by Choquet Expected Utility

We proceed with the Anscombe–Aumann framework. Given two lottery acts f and g, they are *co-monotonic* if $(\forall s, t \in S)\ f(s) \succ f(t) \ \Rightarrow\ g(t) \not\succ g(s)$. Here, the binary relation should be understood to be the one between two constant lottery acts. Intuitively, the co-monotonicity means that each of the two lottery acts cannot serve as a *hedge* to the other. That is, if one lottery act gives a better outcome at some state, the other also must give an outcome at least as good at that state.

Consider the following axioms that may be imposed on a binary relation $\succ$ on L_0. Here, f, g, h are any element of L_0 and λ is any real number such that $\lambda \in (0, 1]$.

S1(**Ordering**)	$\succ$ is a preference order
S2(**Co-monotonic Independence**)	For any f, g, h such that any two of them are mutually co-monotonic, $f \succ g \ \Rightarrow\ \lambda f + (1-\lambda)h \succ \lambda g + (1-\lambda)h$
S3(**Continuity**)	$f \succ g$ and $g \succ h$ $\Rightarrow\ (\exists \alpha, \beta \in (0,1))\ \ \alpha f + (1-\alpha)h \succ g$ and $g \succ \beta f + (1-\beta)h$
S4(**Monotonicity**)	$(\forall s \in S)\ f(s) \succeq g(s) \ \Rightarrow\ f \succeq g$
S5(**Nondegeneracy**)	$(\exists f, g \in L_0)\ \ f \succ g$

The Co-monotonic Independence Axiom (S2) requires that a mixture of the third lottery act should not reverse the preference order between two lottery acts *only when* any of the three lottery acts does not serve as a hedge to the others. Hence, Co-monotonic Independence Axiom (S2) is much weaker than Independence Axiom (AA2). Because of this, the representation of a preference order may not necessarily be additively separable on the state space.

Schmeidler (1982, 1989) proved the representation theorem by *Choquet expected utility* (CEU) under these axioms.

Theorem 3.9.1 (Representation by CEU) *A binary relation $\succ$ on L_0 satisfies S1, S2, S3, S4, and S5 if and only if there exist a unique probability capacity θ on $(S, \mathcal{A})$ and an affine function u on Y that is unique up to a positive affine transformation such that*

$$f \succ g \ \Leftrightarrow\ \int_S u(f(s))\, d\theta(s) > \int_S u(g(s))\, d\theta(s)\,.$$

3.9.2 Rank-Dependent Subjective Expected Utility

A binary relation $\succ$ on L_0 is represented by the *rank-dependent subjective expected utility* if there exist a convex-ranged probability charge p on $(S, \mathcal{A})$, a real-valued function u on X that is unique up to a positive affine transformation, and a strictly increasing function $g : [0, 1] \to [0, 1]$ such that

$$f \succ g \Leftrightarrow \int_S u(f(s))\, d(g \circ p)(s) > \int_S u(g(s))\, d(g \circ p)(s)\,,$$

where the integrals are the Choquet integrals. To characterize the preference that can be represented in this way, we need to impose some axioms on the preference so that the probability capacity derived in Schmeidler's theorem satisfies the weak additivity in Scott's theorem (Theorem 2.3.1). Such an axiomatization is not yet known as far as we know.

It is important to note that while the rank-dependent subjective expected utility is one special case of Choquet expected utility, it *cannot* explain the Ellsberg paradox. This is because the rank-dependent expected utility is probabilistically sophisticated because the function g is *strictly* increasing. To explain the rankings in the paradox, g needs to be *nondecreasing* rather than strictly increasing. In this regard, the theorem of Gilboa (1985) is important (Sect. 2.3.2); it concerns the decomposition of a probability capacity by a probability charge and a nondecreasing function.

3.9.3 Uncertainty Aversion

A binary relation $\succ$ on L_0 exhibits an *uncertainty aversion* if it satisfies $(\forall f, g \in L_0)(\forall \alpha \in [0, 1])\ f \succeq g \Rightarrow \alpha f + (1 - \alpha)g \succeq g$. When $\succ$ is a preference order, this statement is equivalent to $(\forall f, g, h \in L_0)(\forall \alpha \in [0, 1])\ f \succeq h$ and $g \succeq h \Rightarrow \alpha f + (1 - \alpha)g \succeq h$. That is, the preference order is uncertainty-averse if it is quasi-concave. The concept of uncertainty aversion was first introduced by Schmeidler (1982, 1989).

Theorem 3.9.2 *Suppose that a binary relation $\succ$ satisfies Axioms S1, S2, S3, S4, and S5, and that θ is the unique probability capacity derived by Theorem 3.9.1. Then θ is convex if and only if $\succ$ is uncertainty-averse.*

3.9.4 Ellsberg's Paradox Reconsidered

Recall Ellsberg's paradox. Define a set function θ as follows: $\theta(\phi) = 0$, $\theta(\{R\}) = \frac{1}{3}$, $\theta(\{B\}) = \theta(\{W\}) = \frac{1}{9}$, $\theta(\{R, B\}) = \theta(\{R, W\}) = \frac{4}{9}$, $\theta(\{B, W\}) = \frac{2}{3}$, and $\theta(\{R, B, W\}) = 1$. The set function thus defined is clearly nonadditive. For example, $\theta(\{B, W\}) \neq \theta(\{B\}) + \theta(\{W\})$. In fact, it can be easily verified that θ is a *convex* probability capacity. Then, for any u such that $u(\$1{,}000) > u(\$0)$ (i.e, if the lottery act that certainly guarantees \$1,000 is strictly preferred to the one that always gives nothing), the preference order in Ellsberg's paradox can be represented by CEU with θ defined above.

3.10 Maxmin Expected Utility Theory à la Gilboa-Schmeidler

3.10.1 Representation with Multiple Priors

We proceed with the Anscombe–Aumann framework again. Consider the following axioms that may be imposed on a binary relation $\succ$ on L_0. Here, f, g, h are any element of L_0 and λ is any real number such that $\lambda \in (0, 1]$.

GS1(**Ordering**)	$\succ$ is a preference order
GS2(**C-Independence**)	For any constant lottery act $h \in L_c$,
	$f \succ g \Rightarrow \lambda f + (1-\lambda)h \succ \lambda g + (1-\lambda)h$
GS3(**Continuity**)	$f \succ g$ and $g \succ h$
	$\Rightarrow (\exists \alpha, \beta \in (0,1))\ \alpha f + (1-\alpha)h \succ g$ and
	$g \succ \beta f + (1-\beta)h$
GS4(**Monotonicity**)	$(\forall s \in S)\ f(s) \succeq g(s) \Rightarrow f \succeq g$
GS5(**Nondegeneracy**)	$(\exists f, g \in L_0)\ f \succ g$
GS6(**Uncertainty Aversion**)	$f \sim g \Rightarrow \alpha f + (1-\alpha)g \succeq f$

Gilboa and Schmeidler (1989) proved a representation theorem by *maxmin expected utility* (MEU) under these axioms. In this theorem, the closedness of the set C is with respect to the weak * topology defined on the set of all probability charges on $(S, \mathcal{A})$. Therefore, the existence of the minimum is guaranteed by Weierstrass's theorem.

Theorem 3.10.1 (Representation by MEU) *A binary relation $\succ$ on L_0 satisfies GS1, GS2, GS3, GS4, GS5, and GS6 if and only if there exist a unique nonempty closed convex subset C of probability charges on $(S, \mathcal{A})$ and an affine function u on Y that is unique up to a positive affine transformation such that*

$$f \succ g \Leftrightarrow$$
$$\min\left\{ \int_S u(f(s))\, dp(s) \,\middle|\, p \in C \right\} > \min\left\{ \int_S u(f(s))\, dp(s) \,\middle|\, p \in C \right\}.$$

3.10.2 Ellsberg's Paradox Re-Reconsidered

Recall Ellsberg's paradox again. Consider two (additive) probabilities, $\boldsymbol{p} = \left(\frac{1}{3}, \frac{1}{9}, \frac{5}{9}\right)$ and $\boldsymbol{q} = \left(\frac{1}{3}, \frac{5}{9}, \frac{1}{9}\right)$, for Red (R), Black (B), and White (W) in a casual sense and then denote by p and q the corresponding probability charges in a formal sense. Then, for any u such that $u(\$1{,}000) > u(\$0)$ (i.e., if the act that guarantees \$1,000 is strictly preferred to the one that always gives nothing), a preference order in Ellsberg's paradox can be represented by MEU with C defined by the convex hull of $\{p, q\}$.

3.11 A Relation Between CEU and MEU

If a probability capacity θ is convex, the fundamental theorem of the Choquet integral (Theorem 2.4.1) implies that

$$\int u(f(s))\,d\theta(s) = \min\left\{ \int u(f(s))\,dp(s) \;\middle|\; p \in \operatorname{core}(\theta) \right\}.$$

Therefore, *if θ is convex* (i.e., *if the preference order is uncertainty-averse*), CEU is a special case of MEU with $C = \operatorname{core}(\theta)$.

However, the converse is not necessarily true. To see this, suppose that C is an arbitrary closed convex set of probability charges on $(S, \mathcal{A})$. Then, if there exists a probability capacity θ such that $(\forall a \in B(S, \mathcal{A}))$

$$\int a(s)\,d\theta(s) = \min\left\{ \int a(s)\,dp(s) \;\middle|\; p \in C \right\},$$

it must hold that $(\forall A \in \mathcal{A})$

$$\theta(A) = \min\{\, p(A) \mid p \in C \,\} \tag{3.3}$$

(let $a := \chi_A$). However, as the following two examples by Huber and Strassen (1973) show, it is not guaranteed that the probability capacity θ defined by Eq. (3.3) from C is convex nor that $\operatorname{core}(\theta) = C$ even if it is convex by accident. In summary, for an arbitrarily given set C, there does not necessarily exist a convex probability capacity that generates C as its core.[6]

Example 3.11.1 Let $S = \{1, 2, 3, 4\}$ and let $\mathcal{A} = 2^S$. Let $\boldsymbol{p} = \left(\frac{5}{10}, \frac{2}{10}, \frac{2}{10}, \frac{1}{10}\right)$ and $\boldsymbol{q} = \left(\frac{6}{10}, \frac{1}{10}, \frac{1}{10}, \frac{2}{10}\right)$ be (additive) probabilities in a casual sense, let p and q be corresponding probability charges on $(S, \mathcal{A})$, and let C be the convex hull of a set $\{p, q\}$. Define sets A and B by $A = \{1, 2\}$ and $B = \{1, 3\}$. If we compute a probability capacity θ from C by Eq. (3.3), we obtain $\theta(A) = \theta(B) = \frac{7}{10}, \theta(A \cap B) = \frac{5}{10}, \theta(A \cup B) = \frac{8}{10}$. However, θ is *not* convex because $\theta(A \cup B) + \theta(A \cap B) = \frac{13}{10} < \frac{14}{10} = \theta(A) + \theta(B)$. ■

Example 3.11.2 Let $S = \{1, 2, 3\}$ and let $\mathcal{A} = 2^S$. Let $\boldsymbol{p} = \left(\frac{1}{2}, \frac{1}{2}, 0\right)$ and $\boldsymbol{q} = \left(\frac{2}{3}, \frac{1}{6}, \frac{1}{6}\right)$ be (additive) probabilities in a casual sense, let p and q be corresponding probability charges on $(S, \mathcal{A})$, and let C be the convex hull of a set $\{p, q\}$. If we compute a probability capacity θ from C by Eq. (3.3), we obtain $\theta(\phi) = 0$, $\theta(\{1\}) = \frac{1}{2}, \theta(\{2\}) = \frac{1}{6}, \theta(\{3\}) = 0, \theta(\{1, 2\}) = \frac{5}{6}, \theta(\{1, 3\}) = \frac{1}{2}, \theta(\{2, 3\}) = \frac{1}{3}$, and $\theta(S) = 1$. It can be easily verified that θ *is* a convex probability capacity. Furthermore, it can be seen that the core of θ is given by the set of probability

[6] In general, a probability capacity θ is *exact* if $\operatorname{core}(\theta)$ is nonempty and it holds that $(\forall A \in \mathcal{A})\ \theta(A) = \min\{\, p(A) \mid p \in \operatorname{core}(\theta) \,\}$. Clearly, the convexity implies the exactness. For more information, see Schmeidler (1972).

charges given by $\left\{\left(\frac{3+t}{6}, \frac{3-t-s}{6}, \frac{s}{6}\right) \mid s, t \in [0, 1]\right\}$. From this, it immediately follows that C is a *proper* subset of core(θ). For example, think of $\left(\frac{1}{2}, \frac{1}{3}, \frac{1}{6}\right)$. Therefore, core($\theta$) $\neq C$. ■

3.12 Epstein's Definition of Uncertainty Aversion

Epstein (1999) showed that assuming that a preference order is represented by CEU with a convex probability capacity is not necessary nor sufficient to explain the behaviors prominent in Ellsberg's paradox.

First, define a probability capacity θ by $\theta(\phi) = 0$, $\theta(\{R\}) = \frac{1}{3}$, $\theta(\{B\}) = \theta(\{W\}) = \frac{7}{24}$, $\theta(\{R, B\}) = \theta(\{R, W\}) = \frac{1}{2}$, $\theta(\{B, W\}) = \frac{13}{24}$, and $\theta(\{R, B, W\}) = 1$. Then, CEU with this θ can justify the preference order in the paradox, but θ is *not* convex. That is, the convexity of a probability capacity is not necessary to explain the paradox.

Next, consider another probability capacity θ defined by $\theta(\phi) = 0$, $\theta(\{R\}) = \frac{1}{12}$, $\theta(\{B\}) = \theta(\{W\}) = \frac{1}{6}$, $\theta(\{R, B\}) = \theta(\{R, W\}) = \frac{1}{2}$, $\theta(\{B, W\}) = \frac{1}{3}$, and $\theta(\{R, B, W\}) = 1$. The probability capacity θ thus defined *is* convex, but CEU with this θ cannot explain the paradox.

Epstein argues that if the behavior in Ellsberg's paradox embodies an aversion to "uncertainty" itself, CEU (and hence, MEU) representation fails to capture the attitude toward uncertainty.

Epstein proposes an alternative definition of uncertainty aversion. A family $\mathcal{A}$ of subsets of S is a *λ-system* if $S \in \mathcal{A}$, $A \in \mathcal{A} \Rightarrow A^c \in \mathcal{A}$ and it holds that $A_1, A_2 \in \mathcal{A}$ and $A_1 \cap A_2 = \phi \Rightarrow A_1 \cup A_2 \in \mathcal{A}$. Given a λ-system $\mathcal{A}$, we call any Savage act $f : S \to X$ *unambiguous* if it is $\mathcal{A}$-measurable in the sense that $f^{-1}(\{x\}) \in \mathcal{A}$ for any $x \in X$. A preference order $\succ^2$ on F_0 is *more uncertainty-averse* than $\succ^1$ if for any unambiguous act h and any act e, it holds that $h \succ^1 (\succeq^1)\ e \Rightarrow h \succ^2 (\succeq^2)\ e$. Finally, Epstein defines a preference order $\succ$ as *uncertainty-averse* if there exists a probabilistically sophisticated preference $\succ^{ps}$ such that $\succ$ is more uncertainty-averse than $\succ^{ps}$. Here, a preference is *probabilistically sophisticated* if it satisfies all the axioms in Machina and Schmeidler's Theorem (Theorem 3.6.1).

In this context, Epstein (1999) proves that the rankings in Ellsberg's paradox imply that the preference *is* uncertainty-averse in this sense. Furthermore, he also proves that if the preference is uncertainty-averse in this sense, then that preference *never* exhibits the rankings obtained by replacing "$\succ$" with "$\prec$" in Ellsberg's paradox.

3.13 Dynamic Preferences

This section adopts Nishimura and Ozaki (2003) and presents a dynamic preference and some axioms imposed on it so that the preference satisfying this set of axioms should be represented by an *iteration* of the Choquet integrals. For simplicity, we consider only two periods and a finite state space for each period. Although an extension to an infinite horizon and general state spaces should not be difficult, its exact exposition will be a subject for future research. Such a dynamic preference is dynamically consistent and is covered in later chapters in this book.

3.13.1 Unconditional and Conditional Preferences

Suppose that there are two periods. Let $m, n \in \mathbb{N}$ and let the state space of the first and second periods be given by $S := \{s_1, \ldots, s_m\}$ and $T := \{t_1, \ldots, t_n\}$, respectively. Therefore, the whole state space is given by $\Omega = S \times T$. A generic element of Ω is denoted by ω or (s, t). Let Y be an outcome space. We assume that Y is a mixture space. We call an element y of Y a *lottery* and we denote by $\lambda y + (1 - \lambda)y'$ the *compound lottery* given $y, y' \in Y$ and $\lambda \in [0, 1]$ as we did in Sect. 3.8.1.

We follow Anscombe and Aumman's (1963) framework and define a *simple lottery act* as a Y-valued function on Ω whose range is a finite subset of Y. The set of simple lottery acts is denoted by L_0. We henceforth refer to a simple lottery act as a lottery act by suppressing the adjective "simple." A lottery act whose range is a singleton set is referred to as a *constant act* and the set of constant acts is denoted by L_c, exactly as before. A lottery act f is *1st-period-measurable* if $(\forall s)(\forall t, t')\ f(s, t) = f(s, t')$. As its name suggests, the outcome of the 1st-period-measurable lottery act is completely determined only by the state realized in the first period. We sometimes write the outcome of a 1st-period-measurable lottery act f at (s, t) as $f(s)$ instead of $f(s, t)$.

In the world with two periods, the decision-maker's preference is given by a *class* of binary relations, $\{\succ_i\}_{i=0,1,\ldots,m}$, on L_0. We understand that $\succ_0$ is the decision-maker's *un*conditional preference before any event occurs and $\succ_i$ is her *conditional* preference after she knows that $s_i \in S$ has been realized in the first period. The two classes of binary relations, $\{\succsim_i\}_i$ and $\{\sim_i\}_i$, are derived from $\{\succ_i\}_i$ exactly by the same way as described in Sect. 3.2. For each $i \in \{0, 1, \ldots, m\}$, we define a binary relation on Y by restricting $\succ_i$ on L_c and denote it by the same symbol $\succ_i$. This is also the same convention we made before. A pair of acts, f and g, are *co-monotonic with respect to* $\succ_i$ if $(\forall \omega, \omega')\ f(\omega) \succ_i f(\omega') \Rightarrow g(\omega) \not\prec_i g(\omega')$. Note that the co-monotonicity is defined in terms of the preference induced on Y from $\succ_i$.

3.13.2 Axioms and Representation

We take as a primitive a class of binary relations, $\{\succ_i\}_{i=0,1,\ldots,m}$, of the decision-maker on L_0, and we consider the following axioms that may be imposed on that class of binary relations. In the axioms, f, g, and h denote arbitrary elements in L_0 and λ denotes an arbitrary real number such that $\lambda \in (0, 1]$.

A1 (Ordering) For each $i \in \{0, 1, \ldots, m\}$, the binary relation $\succ_i$ is a preference order.
A2(0) (Constrained Co-monotonic Independence) If f, g, h are 1st-period-measurable and pairwise co-monotonic with respect to $\succ_0$, then $f \succ_0 g \Rightarrow \lambda f + (1-\lambda)h \succ_0 \lambda g + (1-\lambda)h$.
A2(1) (Conditional Co-monotonic Independence) For each $i \in \{1, \ldots, m\}$, if f, g, h are pairwise co-monotonic with respect to $\succ_i$, then $f \succ_i g \Rightarrow \lambda f + (1-\lambda)h \succ_i \lambda g + (1-\lambda)h$.
A3 (Continuity) For each $i \in \{0, 1, \ldots, m\}$, if $f \succ_i g$ and $g \succ_i h$, then $(\exists \alpha, \beta \in (0,1))$ $\alpha f + (1-\alpha)h \succ_i g$ and $g \succ_i \beta f + (1-\beta)h$.
A4 (Monotonicity) For each $i \in \{0, 1, \ldots, m\}$, if $(\forall \omega \in \Omega)$ $f(\omega) \succeq_i g(\omega)$, then $f \succeq_i g$.
A5 (Nondegeneracy) $(\exists f, g \in L_0)$ $f \succ_0 g$.

A6 (Independence of Unrealized Events) $(\forall i \in \{1, \ldots, m\})$ $f(s_i, \cdot) = g(s_i, \cdot)$ $\Rightarrow f \sim_i g$.
A7 (Ordinal Preference Consistency) $(\forall i \in \{1, \ldots, m\})(\forall y, y' \in Y)$ $y \succ_0 y' \Leftrightarrow y \succ_i y'$.
A8 (Dynamical Consistency) $[(\forall i \in \{1, \ldots, m\})$ $f \succeq_i g] \Rightarrow f \succeq_0 g$.

The main result of this section is the following theorem. The theorem shows that under Axioms A1–A8, the unconditional preference $\succ_0$ is represented by an *iterated* Choquet expected utility with respect to some class of probability capacities (see (3.4) in Theorem 3.13.1) and each conditional preference $\succ_i$ is represented by its restriction over $\{s_i\} \times T$ (see (3.5) in Theorem 3.13.1). The proof of Theorem 3.13.1 is relegated to the Appendix.

Theorem 3.13.1 (Nishimura and Ozaki 2003) *A class of binary relations, $\{\succ_i\}_{i=0}^m$, satisfies A1-A8 if and only if there exist a unique probability capacity θ_0 on S, a unique class of probability capacities $\langle\theta_{s_i}\rangle_{i=1}^m$ on T, and a nonconstant affine function $u : Y \to \mathbb{R}$, which is unique up to a positive affine transformation, such that*

$$f \succ_0 g \Leftrightarrow \int_S \int_T u(f(s,t))\, \theta_s(dt)\, \theta_0(ds) > \int_S \int_T u(g(s,t))\, \theta_s(dt)\, \theta_0(ds) \tag{3.4}$$

and $(\forall i \in \{1, \ldots, m\})$

$$f \succ_i g \Leftrightarrow \int_T u(f(s_i,t))\, \theta_{s_i}(dt) > \int_T u(g(s_i,t))\, \theta_{s_i}(dt)\,. \tag{3.5}$$

3.13.3 Discussion of Each Axiom

This section discusses the axioms in Theorem 3.13.1 and their relations to axioms in the existing literature. The whole set of the axioms is divided into two subgroups; that is, Axioms A1 through A5 and Axioms A6 through A8.

Except for Axiom A2, each axiom in the first group, A1 and A3-A5, requires that all of the binary relations, $\{\succ_i\}_{i=0}^m$, should satisfy each of Schmeidler's (1982, 1989) axioms with the same name. Note that while Axiom A5 requires the nondegeneracy only for $\succ_0$, Axioms A4 and A5 applied to $\succ_0$ and Axiom A7 together imply that $\succ_i$ also satisfies the nondegeneracy for all i.

Axiom A2(1) (conditional co-monotonic independence) requires that all *conditional* preferences should satisfy Schmeidler's co-monotonic independence. See Sect. 3.9.1 for the motivation of the co-monotonic independence axiom.

In contrast, Axiom A2(0) (constrained co-monotonic independence) is new and it is concerned with the *un*conditional preference. *If* the full-spec version of the co-monotonic independence axiom were applied to the unconditional preference, it would require

A2(0)′ (Co-monotonic Independence) If f, g, h are pairwise co-monotonic with respect to $\succ_0$, then $f \succ_0 g \;\Rightarrow\; \lambda f + (1-\lambda)h \succ_0 \lambda g + (1-\lambda)h$.

On the other hand, Axiom A2(0) requires the co-monotonic independence to hold only among acts that are 1st-period-measurable; it does not say anything about a triplet of acts at least one of which is not 1st-period-measurable. Clearly, Axiom A2(0) is implied by Axiom A2(0)′. Actually, it is substantially weaker than A2(0)′. We come back to this point in the next subsection.

Among the second group of axioms, Axiom A6 (independence of unrealized events) applies only to the conditional preferences. It is also well known as the *consequentialism*[7] and it requires that if two acts behave exactly in the same way after the state s_i occurs, the conditional preference given s_i should evaluate these two acts indifferently. Axiom A6 forces the representation of $\succ_i$ to be independent of unrealized states, s_j for $j \neq i$ (see (3.5) in the theorem).

The last two axioms are concerned with the connection between the unconditional preference and the conditional preferences. The former, Axiom A7 (ordinal preference consistency), is also well known[8] and it requires that all the preferences should evaluate constant acts in the same way. This axiom implies that the von Neumann-Morgenstern's utility index, u, may be set to become common for all representations in Theorem 3.13.1 (see (3.4) and (3.5) in Theorem 3.13.1).

---

[7] See, for example, Axiom 7 of Ghirardato (2002), which, in the Savage-act framework, axiomatizes the class of unconditional and conditional preferences that can be represented by the expected utility with respect to some probability charge P and the conditional expected utilities with respect to the conditional probability charges that were updated from P by Bayes' rule.

[8] See, for example, Axiom 3 of Ghirardato (2002), cited in the previous footnote.

The latter, Axiom A8 (dynamical consistency), is a version of other well-known axioms of dynamical consistency.[9] To see an implication of this axiom, suppose that the axiom is now violated so that there exists a pair of acts, f and g, such that $(\forall i)\ f \succsim_i g$ and $g \succ_0 f$. Then, there are two possible cases: (a) $(\forall i)\ f \sim_i g$ and $g \succ_0 f$; and (b) $(\forall i)\ f \succsim_i g, (\exists i)\ f \succ_i g$ and $g \succ_0 f$, in the latter case of which there exists some state such that the decision-maker has a definite incentive to abandon her initial plan after observing that state. Axiom A8 requires that there should be no such pair of acts that either (a) or (b) is the case.

3.13.4 Dynamical Consistency and Its Implication

We now turn to a discussion of implications of the axioms as a whole. In particular, we argue that although the dynamical consistency (A8) seems to be a mild requirement, its implication is fairly strong in the presence of other axioms.

To see this, assume that all the axioms of the theorem are satisfied. Furthermore, assume that Axiom A2(0) is now strengthened to Axiom A2(0)$'$. Then, by Axioms A1, A2(0)$'$, and A3–A5, Schmeidler's (1982, 1989) theorem implies that there exists a unique probability capacity θ on Ω and an affine function $u : Y \to \mathbb{R}$ such that

$$f \succ_0 g \Leftrightarrow \int_\Omega u(f(\omega))\,\theta(d\omega) > \int_\Omega u(g(\omega))\,\theta(d\omega)\,, \tag{3.6}$$

where the utility index u may be assumed, without loss of generality, to be the same as the one in our theorem.[10] Furthermore, our theorem shows that (3.4) holds with some family of probability capacities, θ_0 and $\langle \theta_{s_i} \rangle_i$. Therefore, it follows that[11]

$$(\forall f \in L_0) \quad \int_\Omega u(f(\omega))\,\theta(d\omega) = \int_S \int_T u(f(s,t))\,\theta_s(dt)\,\theta_0(ds)\,. \tag{3.7}$$

Now we define a totally new and quite artificial probability capacity $\hat{\theta}$ on Ω from θ_0 and $\langle \theta_{s_i} \rangle_{i=0}^m$ as follows. Here, $\left(\theta_0, \langle \theta_{s_i} \rangle_{i=1}^m\right)$ is of course the family of probability

---

[9]Another version of the dynamical consistency, which is conceptually close to ours but adapted to a different framework, appears as Axiom 5 (Consistency) in Wang (2003). However, comparison with Wang's axiom is not easy because he employs a rather complicated hierarchical domain of preferences over information filtrations in the Savage-act framework.

[10]From (3.6), it follows that u is an affine function that represents $\succ_0$ on Y. The utility index in our theorem is also an affine function representing $\succ_0$ on Y. Therefore, one index is an affine transformation of the other, and hence, we can take u in (3.6) to be the same as u in our theorem.

[11]To see this, note that the both sides of Eq. (3.7) coincide when f is a constant act. We can prove that for any $f \in L_0$, there exists a constant act that is indifferent to f with respect to $\succ_0$ (see, for example, the first paragraph of A.2.5 in the Appendix). Therefore, both sides of Eq. (3.7) must coincide for *any* $f \in L_0$ because they both represent $\succ_0$.

capacities whose existence is guaranteed by our theorem. Given $A \in 2^{\Omega}$, define $\hat{\theta}(A)$ by

$$\hat{\theta}(A) := \int_S \int_T \chi_A(s,t)\, \theta_s(dt)\, \theta_0(ds)\,. \tag{3.8}$$

It is quite easy to verify that $\hat{\theta} : \Omega \to [0, 1]$ thus defined is in fact a probability capacity on Ω. By letting a lottery act $f^A \in L_0$ be such that $u(f^A(\cdot)) = \chi_A$ for each A,[12] the Eqs. (3.7) and (3.8) immediately imply that $(\forall A)\ \theta(A) = \hat{\theta}(A)$.

Furthermore, observe that $(\forall E \subseteq S)(\forall F \subseteq T)$

$$\hat{\theta}(E \times F) = \int_S \int_T \chi_{E\times F}(s,t)\, \theta_s(dt)\, \theta_0(ds) = \int_S \theta_s(F)\chi_E(s)\, \theta_0(ds)\,,$$

from which it follows that

$$(\forall E)\ \ \hat{\theta}(E \times T) = \int_S \theta_s(T)\chi_E(s)\, \theta_0(ds) = \theta_0(E)$$

$$\text{and}\ \ (\forall i)(\forall F)\ \ \hat{\theta}(\{s_i\} \times F) = \int_S \theta_s(F)\chi_{\{s_i\}}(s)\, \theta_0(ds) = \theta_0(\{s_i\})\theta_{s_i}(F)\,.$$

We therefore obtain $(\forall F)\ \theta_{s_i}(F) = \hat{\theta}(\{s_i\} \times F)/\theta_0(\{s_i\}) = \hat{\theta}(\{s_i\} \times F)/\hat{\theta}(\{s_i\} \times T)$ as far as the denominators are nonzero. Because $\theta = \hat{\theta}$ as we remarked above, we conclude that

$$\theta_0 = \hat{\theta}(\cdot \times T) = \theta(\cdot \times T) \text{ and } \theta_s = \frac{\hat{\theta}(\{s\} \times \cdot)}{\hat{\theta}(\{s\} \times T)} = \frac{\theta(\{s\} \times \cdot)}{\theta(\{s\} \times T)}\,. \tag{3.9}$$

It is well known that the probability capacity θ, which satisfies both (3.7) and (3.9), must be additive.[13] Therefore, a class of unconditional and conditional preferences that satisfy Axioms A1, A2(0)′, A2(1), and A3–A8 *must* be represented by the expected utility with respect to a unique probability *charge* and conditional expected utilities with respect to the conditional probability *charges* updated by Bayes' rule.

Epstein and Le Breton (1993) observed that in the Savage-act framework, if the unconditional preference is represented by using a unique probability charge P (but not necessarily in a form of expected utility), the axiom of dynamical consistency implies that each of the conditional preferences *must* be represented by using the conditional probability charge updated from P by Bayes' rule (again not necessarily

---

[12]Such a lottery act certainly exists. See the first paragraph of A.2.5 in the Appendix (let f^A be such that $f^A(\omega) = y^*$ if $\omega \in A$ and $f^A(\omega) = y_*$ if $\omega \notin A$).

[13]See, for example, Yoo (1991).

in a form of conditional expected utility).[14] The discussion in the previous paragraph shows that if both unconditional and conditional preferences are represented by the *non*-iterated Choquet expected utilities (under Axioms A1, A2(0)′, A2(1), and A3–A5), the axiom of dynamical consistency (as well as Axioms A6 and A7) implies that the representation of the preferences must be the unconditional and conditional expected utilities with respect to a probability charge and the conditional probability charges updated by Bayes' rule. This is a variant in our lottery-act framework of the observation made by Epstein and Le Breton.

Furthermore, in lottery-act framework such as ours, Gilboa and Schmeidler (1993) showed that if both unconditional and conditional preferences are represented by the *non*-iterated Choquet expected utilities, the dynamical consistency must be violated except for the trivial case where the probability capacity is additive (i.e., a probability charge).[15] In contrast, we require that the unconditional preference be represented only by an *iterated* Choquet expected utility by substantially weakening A2(0)′ to A2(0). By this, the class of unconditional and conditional preferences restores the dynamical consistency while still allowing the conditional preferences to be represented by the Choquet expected utility with respect to a probability capacity that is not necessarily forced to become a probability charge.

3.13.5 Two Updating Rules

As by-products of the previous subsection, we illustrate the two of updating rules we introduced in Sect. 2.3.5, i.e., the *naïve Bayes' rule* and the *Dempster–Shafer rule*, by showing that applying either of these two rules to a "product" probability capacity will regenerate the "conditional" probability capacities from which the "product" was made.

Let $\hat{\theta}_0$ be any probability capacity on S and let $\langle \hat{\theta}_{s_i} \rangle_{i=1}^m$ be any family of probability capacities on T. Then we define a probability capacity on $\Omega = S \times T$ by

$$(\forall A \in \Omega) \quad \hat{\theta}(A) = \int_S \int_T \chi_A(s,t)\, \hat{\theta}_s(dt)\, \hat{\theta}_0(ds)\,.$$

Thus defined, $\hat{\theta} : \Omega \to [0, 1]$ turns out to be a probability capacity.

First, observe that $(\forall E \subseteq S)(\forall F \subseteq T)$

$$\hat{\theta}(E \times F) = \int_S \int_T \chi_{E\times F}(s,t)\, \hat{\theta}_s(dt)\, \hat{\theta}_0(ds) = \int_S \hat{\theta}_s(F)\chi_E(s)\, \hat{\theta}_0(ds)\,,$$

[14] Their work is largely motivated by Machina and Schmeidler's (1992) theory of probabilistically sophisticated preferences discussed in Sect. 3.6.

[15] To be more precise, they show that both unconditional and conditional preferences are represented by the *non*-iterated Choquet expected utilities if and only if the class of unconditional and conditional preferences satisfy what they call an *f-Bayesian rule* with f being an act that takes on either the best or the worst outcome.

from which it follows that

$$(\forall E)\ \hat{\theta}(E \times T) = \int_S \hat{\theta}_s(T)\chi_E(s)\,\hat{\theta}_0(ds) = \hat{\theta}_0(E)$$

$$\text{and } (\forall i)(\forall F)\ \hat{\theta}(\{s_i\} \times F) = \int_S \hat{\theta}_s(F)\chi_{\{s_i\}}(s)\,\hat{\theta}_0(ds) = \hat{\theta}_0(\{s_i\})\hat{\theta}_{s_i}(F)\,.$$

We thus conclude that $\hat{\theta}_{s_i}(F) = \hat{\theta}(\{s_i\} \times F)/\hat{\theta}_0(\{s_i\}) = \hat{\theta}(\{s_i\} \times F)/\hat{\theta}(\{s_i\} \times T)$ as far as the denominators are nonzero. This is an updating rule that would be obtained if we simply applied Bayes' rule to $\hat{\theta}$ by thinking of $\hat{\theta}$ as if it is simply a probability charge. This updating rule is called the *naïve Bayes' rule*. (See Sect. 2.3.5.)

Second, observe that $(\forall i)(\forall F)$

$$\begin{aligned}
\hat{\theta}\left((\{s_i\} \times F) \cup (S\backslash\{s_i\} \times T)\right) &= \int_S \int_T \chi_{(\{s_i\}\times F)\cup(S\backslash\{s_i\}\times T)}(s,t)\,\hat{\theta}_s(dt)\,\hat{\theta}_0(ds) \\
&= \int_S \left(\hat{\theta}_{s_i}(F)\chi_{\{s_i\}}(s) + \chi_{S\backslash\{s_i\}}(s)\right)\hat{\theta}_0(ds) \\
&= (1 - \hat{\theta}_{s_i}(F))\hat{\theta}_0(S\backslash\{s_i\}) + \hat{\theta}_{s_i}(F) \\
&= (1 - \hat{\theta}_0(S\backslash\{s_i\}))\hat{\theta}_{s_i}(F) + \hat{\theta}_0(S\backslash\{s_i\})\,,
\end{aligned}$$

from which we conclude that

$$\begin{aligned}
\hat{\theta}_{s_i}(F) &= \frac{\hat{\theta}\left((\{s_i\} \times F) \cup (S\backslash\{s_i\} \times T)\right) - \hat{\theta}_0(S\backslash\{s_i\})}{1 - \hat{\theta}_0(S\backslash\{s_i\})} \\
&= \frac{\hat{\theta}\left((\{s_i\} \times F) \cup (S\backslash\{s_i\} \times T)\right) - \hat{\theta}(S\backslash\{s_i\} \times T)}{1 - \hat{\theta}(S\backslash\{s_i\} \times T)}
\end{aligned}$$

as far as the denominators are nonzero. This is an updating rule for probability capacities and is known as the *Dempster–Shafer rule* in the statistics literature. (See, for example, Dempster 1967, 1968; Shafer 1976. Also see Sect. 2.3.5 of this book.)

3.14 Remarks

Finally, we briefly mention some atemporal representation theorems that use Savage acts instead of lottery acts.

The CEU theorem with Savage acts was first proved by Gilboa (1987) and then his axioms were largely simplified by Sarin and Wakker (1992). In Savage's theorem, the state space S must be an uncountable set because the probability charge derived in the theorem needs to be convex-ranged as a direct consequence of Axiom P6. A representation theorem by subjective expected utility (SEU) with a probability charge when the state space is a finite set was proved by Gul (1992). A representation theorem by CEU for the finite state space was proved by Nakamura (1990).

On the other hand, a representation theorem by MEU with Savage acts was proved by Casadesus-Masanell et al. (2000). This theorem applies regardless of whether the state space is a finite set or an infinite set. Also see Alon and Schmeidler (2014) who does not assume an objective probability to generate lottery acts in the framework of MEU theory.

References

Alon, S., and D. Schmeidler. 2014. Purely subjective maxmin expected utility. *Journal of Economic Theory* 152: 382–412.

Anscombe, F.J., & Aumann, R.J. 1963. A definition of subjective probability. *Annals of Mathematical Statistics* 34: 199–205.

Casadesus-Masanell, R., P. Klibanoff, and E. Ozdenoren. 2000. Maxmin expected utility over savage acts with a set of priors. *Journal of Economic Theory* 92: 35–65.

Dempster, A.P. 1967. Upper and lower probabilities induced by a multivalued map. *Annals of Mathematical Statistics* 38: 325–339.

Dempster, A.P. 1968. A generalization of Bayesian inference. *Journal of Royal Statistics Society, Series B* 30: 205–247.

Ellsberg, D. 1961. Risk, ambiguity, and the Savage axioms. *Quarterly Journal of Economics* 75: 643–669.

Epstein, L.G. 1999. A definition of uncertainty aversion. *Review of Economic Studies* 66: 579–608.

Epstein, L.G., and M. Le Breton. 1993. Dynamically consistent beliefs must be Bayesian. *Journal of Economic Theory* 61: 1–22.

Fishburn, P.C. 1970. *Utility Thoery for Decision Making*. New York: Wiley.

Fishburn, P.C. 1982. *The Foundations of Expected Utility*. Dordrecht: Reidel.

Ghirardato, P. 2002. Revisiting Savage in a conditional world. *Economic Theory* 20: 83–92.

Gilboa, I. 1985. Subjective distortions of probabilities and non-additive probabilities, Working Paper, The Foerder Institute for Economic Research, Tel Aviv University.

Gilboa, I. 1987. Expected utility theory with purely subjective non-additive probabilities. *Journal of Mathematical Economics* 16: 141–153.

Gilboa, I. 2009. *Theory of Decision under Uncertain*. New York: Cambridge University Press.

Gilboa, I. and M. Marinacci. 2013. Ambiguity and the Bayesian paradigm. In *Advances in Economics and Econometrics*, ed. D. Acemoglu, M. Arellano, and E. Dekel, vol.1, 179–242. Cambridge: Tenth World Congress, Cambridge University.

Gilboa, I., and D. Schmeidler. 1989. Maxmin expected utility with non-unique prior. *Journal of Mathematical Economics* 18: 141–153.

Gilboa, I., and D. Schmeidler. 1993. Updating ambiguous beliefs. *Journal of Economic Theory* 59: 33–49.

Gul, F. 1992. Savage's theorem with a finite number of states. *Journal of Economic Theory* 57: 99–110.

Herstein, I.N., and J. Milnor. 1953. An axiomatic approach to measurable utility. *Econometrica* 21: 291–297.

Huber, P.J., and V. Strassen. 1973. Minimax tests and the Neyman-Pearson lemma for capacities. *The Annals of Statistics* 1: 251–263.

Kreps, D. 1988. *Notes on the Theory of Choice*. Boulder: Colorado, Westview Press.

Machina, M.J., and D. Schmeidler. 1992. A more robust definition of subjective probability. *Econometrica* 60: 745–780.

Nakamura, Y. 1990. Subjective expected utilityr with non-additive probabilities on finite state spaces. *Journal of Economic Theory* 51: 346–366.
Nishimura K.G. and H. Ozaki. 2003. A simple axiomatization of iterated Choquet objectives, unpublished manuscript.
Sarin, R., and P. Wakker. 1992. A simple axiomatization of nonadditive expected utility. *Econometrica* 60: 1255–1272.
Savage, L.J. 1954. *The Foundations of Statistics*, (2nd ed., New York: Dover). New York: Wiley.
Schmeidler, D. 1972. Cores of exact games I. *Journal of Mathematical Analysis and Applications* 40: 214–225.
Schmeidler, D. 1982. Subjective probability without additivity (Temporary Title), Working Paper, The Foerder Institute for Economic Research, Tel Aviv University.
Schmeidler, D. 1989. Subjective probability and expected utility without additivity. *Econometrica* 57: 571–587. (Its working paper is first published in 1982).
von Neumann, J., and O. Morgenstern. 1947. *Theory of Games and Economic Behavior*, 2nd ed. Princeton: Princeton University Press.
Shafer, G. 1976. *A Mathematical Theory of Evidence*. Princeton: Princeton University Press.
Wang, T. 2003. Conditional preferences and updating. *Journal of Economic Theory* 108: 286–321.
Yoo, K.-R. 1991. The iterative law of expectation and non-additive probability measure. *Economics Letters* 37: 145–149.

Chapter 4
Portfolio Inertia

4.1 Introduction and Summary

One of the most important implications of assuming an uncertainty-averse economic agent was presented by Dow and Werlang (1992). They considered an investor who does not hold any asset currently but who contemplates whether to take either a long or short position for some asset by anticipating any return from that asset in the future. Suppose that the investor is risk-averse in the sense that her utility index is concave and she is uncertainty-*neutral* in the sense that she evaluates uncertain prospects by a probability charge; that is, an *additive* set function. Arrow's (1965) result shows that in this situation, there exists some single price of the asset such that if the current price of the asset is lower than this price, she definitely should buy the asset, while if it exceeds this price, then she definitely should make a short sale. Importantly, such a benchmark price is determined *uniquely*.

In stark contrast, Dow and Werlang proved that if the agent is risk-averse as well as uncertainty-*averse* in the sense of Chap. 3, there exists a range of prices such that if the current price of the asset is lower than the greatest lower bound of this price range, she should buy the asset. However, if the price is higher than the least upper bound of this price range, she should make a short sale of this asset. This price range is known as the *bid-ask spread*. Where any trade of assets takes place, a situation called *portfolio inertia* is often observed, and the bid-ask spread is a clever explanation for it. This, together with a sound behavioral foundation, has allowed Dow and Werlang's model to become a cornerstone of applications of Choquet expected utility theory. This chapter explains their theory including the proof of their main theorem.

The reason that portfolio inertia takes place is quite simple. For simplicity, assume that there are only two states: a "good" state and a "bad" state. If we draw an uncertainty-averse agent's indifference curves in the coordinate of "good" state consumption and "bad" state consumption, then the indifference curves have kinks at the 45° line. At this point, "good" state consumption and "bad" state consumption are equated, or, in other words, full insurance is attained by keeping the curve convex toward the origin of the coordinate because of risk aversion and uncertainty

K.G. Nishimura and H. Ozaki, *Economics of Pessimism and Optimism*,
DOI 10.1007/978-4-431-55903-0_4

aversion. This takes place because the probability charge that is "active" in calculating the Choquet expected utility (i.e., the probability charge in $\mathcal{P}(\theta, u)$) suddenly changes across the 45° line, because the "active" probability charge is dependent on the rank of utility for each state in the Choquet integral. This "non-differentiability" of indifference curves immediately implies that there are multiple prices that support identical consumption profiles where the level of consumption does not change over state as utility-maximizing. In turn, this implies the multiplicity of prices under which no trade of assets takes place; that is, portfolio inertia.

Dow–Werlang's model considers only a single-agent optimization problem. However, the very same idea can be also applied to equilibrium models almost as it is. We will study the multiplicity of equilibria in a static general equilibrium model à la Arrow–Debreu (Chap. 5) and the multiplicity of equilibrium prices in a dynamic general equilibrium model with a representative agent à la Lucas (Chap. 8). We will see that these models generate the multiplicity of equilibrium prices by the same mechanism as Dow–Werlang model.

4.2 Non-differentiability of Choquet Integrals

Let θ be a convex probability capacity on $(S, \mathcal{A})$. We now consider (non-)differentiability of Choquet integrals in the following sense. Suppose that a function $x : S \times \mathbb{R} \to \mathbb{R}$ satisfies the following two conditions:

D1. $(\forall z \in \mathbb{R})\ x(\cdot, z)$ is measurable and
D2. $(\forall s \in S)\ x(s, \cdot)$ is a differentiable concave function.

Below, we denote by x_2 the derivative of x with respect to its second argument. Because the function $z \mapsto \int x(s, z)\theta(ds)$ is a concave function when θ is convex by the positive homogeneity and the sub-additivity of the Choquet integral (Propositions 2.4.3 and 2.4.4), there exist the left and right derivatives with respect to z. Actually, both coincide *if* θ is additive. To see this, assume that S is a finite set and that $\mathcal{A}$ is given by 2^S for simplicity. Then,

$$\begin{aligned}
\frac{d}{dz}\int x(s,z)\theta(ds) &= \lim_{\Delta z \to 0}\left[\int x(s, z+\Delta z)\,\theta(ds) - \int x(s,z)\,\theta(ds)\right] \Big/ \Delta z \\
&= \lim_{\Delta z \to 0}\int \frac{x(s, z+\Delta z) - x(s,z)}{\Delta z}\,\theta(ds) \\
&= \int \lim_{\Delta z \to 0}\frac{x(s, z+\Delta z) - x(s,z)}{\Delta z}\,\theta(ds) \\
&= \int x_2(s,z)\,\theta(ds),
\end{aligned}$$

where the first equality is definitional; the second equality holds by the additivity of θ; the third equality holds by the dominated convergence theorem and by the assumption that S is finite; and the last equality holds because x_2 exists by assumption.

However, in the general case of nonadditive θ, it is not guaranteed that the function defined above is differentiable, as the next example shows.

Example 4.2.1 Let $S := \{1, 2\}$ and let $\mathcal{A} := 2^S$. Define a probability capacity θ on $(S, \mathcal{A})$ by $\theta(\phi) = 0$, $\theta(\{1\}) = \theta(\{2\}) := 1/4$, and $\theta(S) = 1$. Also, define a function $x : S \times \mathbb{R}_+ \to \mathbb{R}$ by $x(s, z) := z^{s/2}$. Then, for each s, x is convex and differentiable with respect to z. Furthermore, it follows that

$$\begin{aligned}\frac{d}{dz}\int x(s,z)\theta(ds) &= \frac{d}{dz}\int z^{\frac{s}{2}}\theta(ds)\\ &= \frac{d}{dz}\begin{cases}(z^{\frac{1}{2}} - z)\frac{1}{4} + z & \text{if } z < 1\\ (z - z^{\frac{1}{2}})\frac{1}{4} + z^{\frac{1}{2}} & \text{if } z > 1\end{cases}\\ &= \begin{cases}\frac{1}{8}z^{-\frac{1}{2}} + \frac{3}{4} & \text{if } z < 1\\ \frac{3}{8}z^{-\frac{1}{4}} + \frac{1}{4} & \text{if } z > 1,\end{cases}\end{aligned}$$

and hence, it holds that

$$\frac{d}{dz_-}\int x(s,z)\theta(ds)\bigg|_{z=1} = \frac{7}{8} > \frac{5}{8} = \frac{d}{dz_+}\int x(s,z)\theta(ds)\bigg|_{z=1}.$$

■

To calculate the left and right derivatives directly, we may invoke Aubin's theorem (1979, p. 118, Proposition 6), which applies to general situations. (Also see Hiriart-Urruty and Lemaréchal 2001).

Theorem 4.2.1 (Aubin 1979) *Let Π be a nonempty subset of a metric space and let $\{f_\pi\}_{\pi\in\Pi}$ be a collection of functions from $\mathbb{R}$ to $\mathbb{R}$. For each $x \in \mathbb{R}$, define $g(x) := \inf_{\pi\in\Pi} f_\pi(x)$ and $\mathcal{M}(x) := \{\pi \in \Pi \mid g(x) = f_\pi(x)\}$. Suppose that* (a) *$\Pi$ is compact;* (b) *for each $x \in \mathbb{R}$, there exists a neighborhood X of x such that functions $\pi \mapsto f_\pi(y)$ are continuous (in the metric topology) for all $y \in X$; and* (c) *for all $\pi \in \Pi$, f_π is concave and differentiable. Then, g is differentiable at x both from the left and the right and it holds that*

$$\frac{d}{dx_-}g(x) = \max_{\pi\in\mathcal{M}(x)}\frac{d}{dx}f_\pi(x) \quad \textit{and} \quad \frac{d}{dx_+}g(x) = \min_{\pi\in\mathcal{M}(x)}\frac{d}{dx}f_\pi(x).$$

Recall from Sect. 2.4.2 that given a convex probability capacity θ and a bounded measurable real-valued function x, $\mathcal{P}(\theta, x)$, defined by (2.16), denotes the set of probability charges that are "equivalent" to θ with respect to a calculation of the Choquet integral of x because of the fundamental theorem of the Choquet integral

(Theorem 2.4.1). That theorem also shows that $\mathcal{P}(\theta, x)$ is nonempty while it is not necessarily a singleton.

Given these facts, we can obtain the following important result for the left and right derivatives as a direct consequence of Aubin's theorem.

Theorem 4.2.2 *Assume that a probability capacity θ is convex and that a function $x : S \times \mathbb{R} \to \mathbb{R}$ satisfies the conditions D1 and D2. Then, the following holds:*

$$(\forall z) \quad \frac{d}{dz_-} \int x(s, z)\theta(ds) = \max\left\{ \int x_2(s, z)P(ds) \middle| P \in \mathcal{P}(\theta, x(\cdot, z)) \right\}$$

$$(\forall z) \quad \frac{d}{dz_+} \int x(s, z)\theta(ds) = \min\left\{ \int x_2(s, z)P(ds) \middle| P \in \mathcal{P}(\theta, x(\cdot, z)) \right\},$$

where $\mathcal{P}(\theta, x(\cdot, z))$ is defined by (2.16).

Example 4.2.2 (*Continued*) We apply Theorem 4.2.2 to Example 4.2.1. In this example, because $\mathcal{P}(\theta, x(\cdot, 1)) = \text{core}(\theta)$,

$$\begin{aligned} \frac{d}{dz_-} \int x(s, z)\theta(ds)\bigg|_{z=1} &= \max\left\{ \int x_2(s, 1)P(ds) \middle| P \in \mathcal{P}(\theta, x(\cdot, 1)) \right\} \\ &= \max\left\{ \int \left(\frac{s}{2}\right) P(ds) \middle| P \in \text{core}(\theta) \right\} \\ &= \left(\frac{1}{2}\right)\left(\frac{1}{4}\right) + \left(\frac{2}{2}\right)\left(\frac{3}{4}\right) = \frac{7}{8} \end{aligned}$$

and

$$\begin{aligned} \frac{d}{dz_+} \int x(s, z)\theta(ds)\bigg|_{z=1} &= \max\left\{ \int x_2(s, 1)P(ds) \middle| P \in \mathcal{P}(\theta, x(\cdot, 1)) \right\} \\ &= \max\left\{ \int \left(\frac{s}{2}\right) P(ds) \middle| P \in \text{core}(\theta) \right\} \\ &= \left(\frac{1}{2}\right)\left(\frac{3}{4}\right) + \left(\frac{2}{2}\right)\left(\frac{1}{4}\right) = \frac{5}{8}, \end{aligned}$$

which verify the result obtained in Example 4.2.1. ■

4.3 Portfolio Choice Model à la Dow–Werlang

Consider an optimal investment problem of an investor who is uncertainty-averse. Let $W > 0$ be her initial wealth, let X be the stochastic present value of the dividend of an asset, let z be the volume of a purchase (or a sale) of the asset, and let q be the price of the asset. Assume that the preference relation of the investor is represented by CEU with a probability capacity θ, which is convex and that her utility index u satisfies $u' > 0$ and $u'' \leq 0$. That is, the investor is assumed to be averse with respect to uncertainty and averse or neutral with respect to risk. Dow and Werlang proved the next theorem.

Theorem 4.3.1 (Dow and Werlang 1992) *Suppose that*

$$\int X d\theta < q < \int X d\theta' .$$

Then, the investor does not change the current position: i.e., she does not purchase or sell the asset. Furthermore, if it holds that

$$q < \int X d\theta \quad \left(resp. \quad q > \int X d\theta' \right),$$

she purchases (resp. sells) the asset.

Proof We prove only the first half. The second half can be proved similarly. The objective function of the investor is

$$\int u\left(W - qz + zX\right) d\theta .$$

By Propositions 2.4.3 and 2.4.4, the convexity of θ, and the assumption that $u'' \leq 0$, it turns out that this objective function is concave in z. Hence, it is the best for the investor to keep the current position if the following holds:

$$\frac{d}{dz_+} \int u\left(W - qz + zX\right) d\theta \bigg|_{z=0} < 0 < \frac{d}{dz_-} \int u\left(W - qz + zX\right) d\theta \bigg|_{z=0} .$$

By applying Theorem 4.2.2 to the right and left derivatives, it turns out that these strict inequalities are equivalent to the following series of strict inequalities:

$$\begin{aligned}
&\min \left\{ \int u'(W)(-q + X) dP \,\middle|\, P \in \mathcal{P}(\theta, u(W)) \right\} \\
&< 0 < \max \left\{ \int u'(W)(-q + X) dP \,\middle|\, P \in \mathcal{P}(\theta, u(W)) \right\} \\
\Leftrightarrow &\min \left\{ \int u'(W)(-q + X) dP \,\middle|\, P \in \mathrm{core}(\theta) \right\} \\
&< 0 < \max \left\{ \int u'(W)(-q + X) dP \,\middle|\, P \in \mathrm{core}(\theta) \right\} \\
\Leftrightarrow &\min \left\{ \int X dP \,\middle|\, P \in \mathrm{core}(\theta) \right\} < q < \max \left\{ \int X dP \,\middle|\, P \in \mathrm{core}(\theta) \right\}
\end{aligned}$$

$$\Leftrightarrow \int X d\theta < q < \int X d\theta'$$

where the first equivalence holds because $\mathcal{P}(\theta, u(W)) = \text{core}(\theta)$ given that W is constant, the second equivalence holds because $u' > 0$ by assumption, and the third equivalence holds by the fundamental theorem of the Choquet integral (Theorem 2.4.1) and Corollary 2.4.1. ■

This theorem is quite interesting in showing the existence of portfolio inertia where no trade takes place when the investor is uncertainty-averse. When θ is additive, the bid-ask spread given by $\int X d\theta < \int X d\theta'$ disappears and the model is reduced to the classical one described by Arrow (1965).

References

Arrow, K.J. 1965. The theory of risk aversion. *Aspects of the theory of risk bearing*. Helsinki: Yrjo Jahnsonin Saatio.

Aubin, J.P. 1979. *Mathematical Methods of Game and Economic Theory*. Amsterdam, North-Holland.

Dow, J., and S.R.C. Werlang. 1992. Uncertainty aversion, risk aversion, and the optimal choice of portfolio. *Econometrica* 60: 197–204.

Hiriart-Urruty, J.-B., and C. Lemaréchal. 2001. *Fundamentals of Convex Analysis*. New York: Springer.

Chapter 5
Equilibrium Indeterminacy in Arrow–Debreu Economy with Knightian Uncertainty

5.1 Introduction and Summary

This chapter describes the Arrow–Debreu economy with Knightian uncertainty as developed by Dana (2004). We show that indeterminacy can arise in this economy, although it is very "rare" in the sense we make clear below.

Dana's model is an extension of that of Dow and Werlang (1992) to an equilibrium model in which each consumer is endowed with the Choquet expected utility in a pure-exchange, finite-state-space framework. In Dow–Werlang's model, the consumer's indifference curves have kinks, meaning there are multiple prices that can support a point at some kink as utility maximizing, with that point corresponding to the consumer's position to neither buy nor sell short. In Dana's model, there are more than one consumer whose indifference curves have kinks. For multiple prices to support an equilibrium allocation, that allocation must take place where the kink of a consumer's indifference curve touches another consumer's kink. If this is the case, there are many prices supporting this allocation as an *equilibrium* allocation. That is, the allocation and one of the supporting prices satisfy both each consumer's utility maximization under her or his budget constraint and market clearing in each market for state-contingent consumption goods. The kinks only occur at the "45° lines" and hence for the kinks to touch one another, the "45° line" must be common to some set of consumers. This commonality in turn requires that there is no aggregate shock, at least locally. In summary, for the indeterminacy to take place in Dana's economy, there must be at least two distinct states such that the total endowments at each of these states are the same in her framework of the pure-exchange economy.

Any pure-endowment Arrow–Debreu economy with a finite state space can be characterized by its initial endowment profile if we fix the consumer's preferences. Then the set of such economies that some line is shared as some consumers' 45° line has at most zero Lebesgue measure. In this sense, the indeterminacy of Dana's economy is a "rare" event. In other words, the indeterminacy is not "robust" because it disappears if we shake the economy even slightly. We return to this question of robustness in the next chapter.

K.G. Nishimura and H. Ozaki, *Economics of Pessimism and Optimism*,
DOI 10.1007/978-4-431-55903-0_5

All proofs are both easy and heuristic. In fact, they are a combination of the treatment by Mas–Collel, Whinston and Green (1995, Chap. 19) and the mathematical tools introduced in Chap. 2. Therefore, all the proofs are shown in the main text and are not relegated to the Appendix.

5.2 Arrow–Debreu–Dana Economy

5.2.1 *Initial Endowments*

The state space of the model is finite and we denote it by $S = \{1, 2, \dots, k\}$ with $k < +\infty$. We consider a pure-exchange economy with the initial endowments. There are a finite number of consumers ($i = 1, 2, \dots, n$) in the economy and the i-th consumer's initial endowment vector is given by $w_i = (w_i(1), w_i(2), \dots, w_i(k)) \in \mathbb{R}^k_{++}$. The total endowment vector of the economy is then denoted by $w = (w(1), w(2), \dots, w(k))$ where $(\forall j = 1, 2, \dots, k)$ $w(j) = \sum_{i=1}^n w_i(j)$. There exists *no* aggregate risk in the economy if $w(1) = w(2) = \cdots = w(k)$, there exists *complete* aggregate risk in the economy if $w(1) < w(2) < \cdots < w(k)$ without loss of generality (rename each state if necessary), and there exists *partial* aggregate risk in the economy otherwise.

5.2.2 *Consumption and Preferences*

The consumption of consumer i at state j is denoted by $C_i(j)$. Each consumer i is endowed with a von Neumann–Morgenstern utility index $U_i : \mathbb{R}_+ \to \mathbb{R}$. We assume that for each i, U_i is twicely differentiable with $U_i' > 0$ and $U_i'' < 0$. The preference of each consumer is represented by the Choquet expected utility with respect to the *common* convex probability capacity, θ. That is, the consumer i maximizes

$$\int_S U_i(C_i(j))\, d\theta(j)$$

which is henceforth denoted simply by $E_\theta[U_i(C_i)]$.

5.2.3 *Arrow–Debreu Equilibrium*

A pair of prices and the consumption profile, $(p^*, C^*) \in \mathbb{R}^k_+ \times \mathbb{R}^{kn}_+$, form an *Arrow–Debreu equilibrium* or simply an *equilibrium* if the following two conditions are met: $(\forall i)$ C_i^* maximizes $E_\theta[U_i(C_i)]$ subject to $\sum_{j=1}^k p^*(j)C_i(j) = \sum_{j=1}^k p^*(j)w_i(j)$, and $(\forall j)$ $\sum_{i=1}^n C_i^*(j) = \sum_{i=1}^n w_i(j)$. The first condition requires that each consumer should maximize her or his utility function under the budget constraint. The second condition requires that all the contingent-claim markets should clear.

Except that θ is not necessarily additive, the model is a standard Arrow–Debreu economy.

5.3 Indeterminacy of Equilibria

5.3.1 Preliminary Results

Let w be such that $w(1) = \cdots = w(\ell) < w(\ell + 1) < \cdots < w(k)$ for some $\ell \in [1, k-1]$, by renaming each state if necessary. This configuration loses the full generality of the initial endowment configuration among the consumers. For example, there might exist two mutually disjoint non-empty subsets of the state space, where the total endowments within each subset are the same but are different between the two subsets. This is clearly not covered by the configuration we posed in the first sentence. Nevertheless, we retain this convention because this is easy to handle while still preserving generality to a large extent. The essence of this chapter can be fully captured only by considering the configuration thus postulated.

Let $\pi \in \mathcal{P}(\theta, w)$. Then, we may set

$$\pi(\{\sigma(j)\}) = \theta(\{\sigma(j), \sigma(j+1), \ldots, \sigma(\ell), \ell+1, \ldots, k\}) - \theta(\{\sigma(j+1), \ldots, \sigma(\ell), \ell+1, \ldots, k\}) \text{ if } j \leq \ell \tag{5.1}$$

$$\pi(\{j\}) = \theta(\{j, j+1, \ldots, k\}) - \theta(\{j+1, \ldots, k\}) \text{ if } j > \ell \tag{5.2}$$

where σ is a permutation from $\{1, \ldots, \ell\}$ onto $\{1, \ldots, \ell\}$. For notational ease, we henceforth write as $\pi(\sigma(j))$, instead of $\pi(\{\sigma(j)\})$, for a singleton set. To see that we may set as (5.1) and (5.2), note that by (2.15) and (5.2), it holds that $E_\theta[w] = w(\ell)(1 - \theta(\{\ell+1, \ldots, k\})) + \sum_{j=\ell+1}^{k} w(j)(\theta(\{j, j+1, \ldots, k\}) - \theta(\{j+1, \ldots, k\})) = x(\ell)(1 - \theta(\{\ell+1, \ldots, k\})) + \sum_{j=\ell+1}^{k} w(j)\pi(j)$. Furthermore, it follows from (5.1) that $\sum_{j=1}^{\ell} \pi(\sigma(j)) = \theta(\{\sigma(1), \sigma(2), \ldots, \sigma(\ell), \ell+1, \ldots, k\}) - \theta(\{\ell+1, \ldots, k\}) = 1 - \theta(\{\ell+1, \ldots, k\})$. Given that $w(1) = \cdots = w(\ell)$, we have $E_\theta[w] = \sum_{j=1}^{\ell} w(j)\pi(\sigma(j)) + \sum_{j=\ell+1}^{k} w(j)\pi(j)$. Finally, $\pi(\sigma(j)) \geq \theta(\sigma(j))$ for $j \leq \ell$ and $\pi(j) \geq \theta(j)$ for $j > \ell$ by the convexity of θ. Therefore, we have verified that $\pi \in \mathcal{P}(\theta, w)$.

We now compute π for a simple example.

Example 5.3.1 Let $S := \{1, 2, 3\}$, let $w(1) = w(2) < w(3)$, let $p := \left(\frac{1}{5}, \frac{2}{5}, \frac{2}{5}\right)$, and let θ be the ε-contamination of p with $\varepsilon = \frac{3}{8}$. First, consider the permutation: $\sigma(1) = 1$ and $\sigma(2) = 2$. Then, $\pi(1) = \frac{1}{2} > \frac{1}{8} = \theta(1)$, $\pi(2) = \frac{1}{4} = \theta(2)$ and $\pi(3) = \frac{1}{4}$. Second, consider the permutation: $\sigma(1) = 2$ and $\sigma(2) = 1$. Then, $\pi(1) = \frac{1}{8} = \theta(1)$,

$\pi(2) = \frac{5}{8} > \frac{1}{4} = \theta(2)$ and $\pi(3) = \frac{1}{4}$. Note that two π values are the "rims" of admissible probability charges. ■

Let w be a total endowment vector and let π be a probability charge (*i.e.*, it is additive). The Arrow–Debreu equilibrium of the economy is renamed the π*-equilibrium* when θ is replaced by π.

Proposition 5.3.1 *Let a pair of prices and consumption profile, $(p^*, C^*) \in \mathbb{R}^k_{++} \times \mathbb{R}^{kn}_{++}$, be a π-equilibrium. Then, the following holds:*

$$(\forall i) \quad \frac{p^*(j+1)}{p^*(j)} = \frac{\pi(j+1)U_i'(C_i^*(j+1))}{\pi(j)U_i'(C_i^*(j))}, \tag{5.3}$$

$w(j) = w(j+1) \Rightarrow (\forall i)\ C_i^*(j) = C_i^*(j+1),$ *and* $w(j) < w(j+1) \Rightarrow (\forall i)\ C_i^*(j) < C_i^*(j+1).$

Proof The first statement simply says that for any consumer, the marginal rate of substitution between two contingent claims should be equal to their price ratio at any interior equilibrium; that holds true now because π is additive.

To show the second and third statements, note from (5.3) that

$$(\forall i) \quad \frac{U_i'(C_i^*(j+1))}{U_i'(C_i^*(j))} = \frac{p^*(j+1)\pi(j)}{p^*(j)\pi(j+1)},$$

the right-hand side of which is independent of i. Therefore, if it holds true that $C_i^*(j) < (=)\ C_i^*(j+1)$ for *some* i, then it holds true for *all* i because $U_i'' < 0$ for each i. The claims then follow from the market-clearing condition of the equilibrium. ■

Note that to obtain (5.3), we use the additivity of π. That is, the non-differentiability issue in Chap. 4 never arises. Also note that Proposition 5.3.1 states that for any i, C_i^* is w-ordered. (For the definition of "orderedness," see Sect. 2.4.2.)

5.3.2 Indeterminacy Theorem

The next theorem is a key result to show the indeterminacy of equilibria.

Theorem 5.3.1 *A pair (p^*, C^*) is an equilibrium if there exists $\pi \in \mathcal{P}(\theta, w)$ such that (p^*, C^*) is a π-equilibrium.*

Proof Let (p^*, C^*) be a π-equilibrium for some $\pi \in \mathcal{P}(\theta, w)$. Then, it follows immediately from the fact that $(\forall i)$ C_i^* is w-ordered (see the remark right after Proposition 5.3.1) and Theorem 2.4.2 that $(\forall i)\ \ E_\theta[U_i(C_i^*)] = E_\pi[U_i(C_i^*)]$.

Next, observe that for any i and for any consumption C_i', it holds true that

$$\sum_j p^*(j)C_i'(j) \leq \sum_j p^*(j)w_i(j) \Rightarrow E_\pi[U_i(C_i')] \leq E_\pi[U_i(C_i^*)] \tag{5.4}$$

because C^* is the π-equilibrium allocation. Because $E_\theta[U_i(C_i')] \leq E_\pi[U_i(C_i')]$ given that $\pi \in \text{core}(\theta)$, combining this with (5.4) and the first paragraph shows that for any i and for any consumption C_i', $\sum_j p^*(j)C_i'(j) \leq \sum_j p^*(j)w_i(j) \Rightarrow E_\theta[U_i(C_i')] \leq E_\theta[U_i(C_i^*)]$, that in turn shows that $(\forall i)$ C_i^* is maximizing her or his utility. Because C^* clears all markets, the proof is complete. ∎

We prepare one lemma before presenting the main theorem.

Lemma 5.3.1 *Assume that* $w(1) = \cdots = w(\ell) < w(\ell+1) < \cdots < w(k)$ *for some* $\ell \in [1, k-1]$ *and that* $\pi \in \mathcal{P}(\theta, w)$. *Then, the* π*-equilibrium allocation* C^* *satisfies the next equation:* $(\forall i)$

$$C_i^*(1)U_i'\left(C_i^*(1)\right)\left(\sum_{j=1}^{\ell}\pi(j)\right) + \sum_{j>\ell} C_i^*(j)U_i'\left(C_i^*(j)\right)\pi(j)$$
$$= \sum_{j=1}^{k} w_i(j)U_i'\left(C_i^*(j)\right)\pi(j). \tag{5.5}$$

Proof Because the equilibrium price, $(p^*(j))_{j=1}^k$, associated with the π-equilibrium is proportional to $\left(U_i'\left(C_i^*(j)\right)\pi(j)\right)_{j=1}^k$ because of (5.3), the consumer i's budget constraint implies that $\sum_{j=1}^k w_i(j)U_i'(C_i^*(j))\pi(j) = \sum_{j=1}^k C_i^*(j)U_i'(C_i^*(j))\pi(j) = \sum_{j=1}^{\ell} C_i^*(j)U_i'(C_i^*(j))\pi(j) + \sum_{j=\ell+1}^k C_i^*(j)U_i'(C_i^*(j))\pi(j) = \sum_{j=1}^{\ell} C_i^*(1)U_i'(C_i^*(1))\pi(j) + \sum_{j=\ell+1}^k C_i^*(j)U_i'(C_i^*(j))\pi(j)$, where the last equality holds because $C_i^*(1) = \cdots = C_i^*(\ell)$ by the w-orderedness of C_i^* (Proposition 5.3.1). ∎

Theorem 5.3.2 *Assume that* $w(1) = \cdots = w(\ell) < w(\ell+1) < \cdots < w(k)$ *for some* $\ell \in (1, k-1]$ *and that there exist* $\pi, \pi' \in \mathcal{P}(\theta, w)$ *such that for some* i, $E_\pi[w_i] \neq E_{\pi'}[w_i]$. *Then, the equilibrium is indeterminate.*

Proof Note that the π- and π'-equilibria for this economy certainly exist because then the model is nothing but the standard equilibrium model of Arrow–Debreu type. Assume that the equilibrium allocations associated with π and π' coincide. We then show that this leads to a contradiction. We denote this common allocation by $C^* = \left(C_i^*\right)_{i=1}^n$.

First, note that it follows from (5.2) that $\pi(j) = \pi'(j)$ for all $j > \ell$, and hence, that $\sum_{j=1}^{\ell}\pi(j) = \sum_{j=1}^{\ell}\pi'(j)$. Second, because C^* is the π'-equilibrium, Lemma 5.3.1 proves that $(\forall i)$

$$C_i^*(1)U_i'\left(C_i^*(1)\right)\left(\sum_{j=1}^{\ell}\pi'(j)\right)+\sum_{j>\ell}C_i^*(j)U_i'\left(C_i(j)\right)\pi'(j)$$

$$=\sum_{j=1}^{k}w_i(j)U_i'\left(C_i^*(j)\right)\pi'(j)\,. \tag{5.6}$$

Third, because the left-hand sides of (5.5) and (5.6) are the same, it holds that $(\forall i)\ \sum_{j=1}^{k} w_i(j)U_i'\left(C_i^*(j)\right)\pi(j)=\sum_{j=1}^{k} w_i(j)U_i'\left(C_i^*(j)\right)\pi'(j)$. By noting that $(\forall i)\ C_i^*(1)=\cdots=C_i^*(\ell)$ and that $\pi(j)=\pi'(j)$ for $j>\ell$, we have reached $(\forall i)\ U_i'\left(C_i^*(1)\right)\sum_{j=1}^{\ell} w_i(j)\left(\pi(j)-\pi'(j)\right)=0$, which implies that $E_\pi[w_i]=E_{\pi'}[w_i]$ for all i, leading to a desired contradiction.

We thus conclude that the equilibrium allocations associated with π and π' are distinct. By Theorem 5.3.1, both allocations are the equilibria, and hence, the equilibrium is indeterminate. ■

We now turn to the economy where there exists no aggregate risk.

Corollary 5.3.1 (No Aggregate Risk) *Assume that* $w(1)=w(2)=\cdots=w(k)$ *and that* $\pi\in$ *core*(θ). *Then, the* π*-equilibrium,* (p^*, C^*)*, is the equilibrium,* p^* *is proportional to* π*, and* C^* *is given by* $(\forall i)\ C_i^*(1)=C_i^*(2)=\cdots=C_i^*(k)=E_\pi[w_i]$.

Proof Let $\pi\in$ core(θ) and let (p^*, C^*) be the π-equilibrium. Then the second statement of Proposition 5.3.1 shows that $(\forall i)\ C_i^*(1)=\cdots=C_i^*(k)$, and (5.3) in turn shows that $(p^*(j))_{j=1}^k$ is proportional to $(\pi(j))_{j=1}^k$. Furthermore, (p^*, C^*) is the equilibrium by Theorem 5.3.1 because $\pi\in\mathcal{P}(\theta, w)$, which is in turn because $\mathcal{P}(\theta, w)=$ core(θ) by $w(1)=\cdots=w(k)$. Finally, the fact that $(\forall i)\ C_1^*(1)=E_\pi[w_i]$ follows from (5.5). ■

5.4 Two-Consumer Two-State Case: The Edgeworth Box

This section assumes that there are two consumers named 1 and 2 and that $S=\{1,2\}$. In this economy, we have either no aggregate risk or complete aggregate risk.

First, assume that $w(1)=w(2)$, that is, the case of *no* aggregate risk. Then, $p^*(1)\big/p^*(2)=\pi(1)\big/\pi(2)$, where $\pi\in$ core(θ), by Proposition 5.3.1. For this case, any relative price of good 1 to good 2, $p^*(1)\big/p^*(2)$, is possible as far as[1] $p^*(1)/p^*(2)\in[\theta(1)/(1-\theta(1)),\,(1-\theta(2))/\theta(2)]$. See Fig. 5.1, where consumer 1's indifference curves are drawn by the red curved lines and consumer 2's indifference curves are drawn by the blue curved lines. There, we assume that $w(1)=w(2)=5$. When $C_1(1)<C_1(2)$, then consumer 1 uses $\overline{\pi}(1)=1-\theta(2)$ and $\pi(2)=\theta(2)$ to calculate her Choquet expected utility, while otherwise she uses $\underline{\pi}(1)=\theta(1)$ and $\underline{\pi}(2)=$

[1] In fact, it holds that $\theta(1)/(1-\theta(1))<(1-\theta(2))/\theta(2)$ by the convexity of θ.

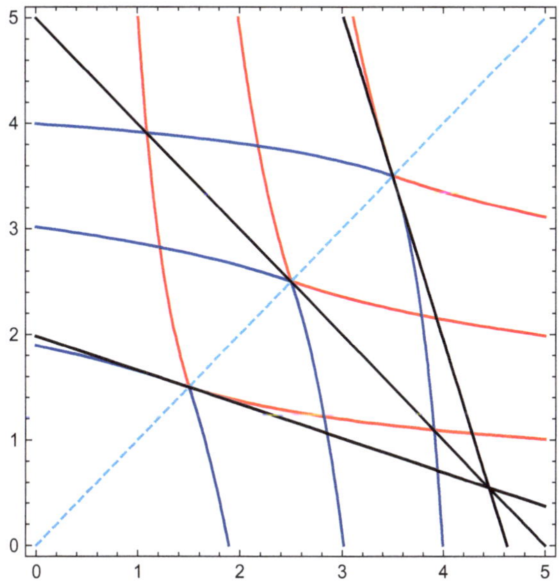

Fig. 5.1 Aggregate risk is not present

$1 - \theta(1)$ to calculate it. Therefore, her indifference curves have kinks on the 45° line. Similarly, the indifference curves of consumer 2 also have kinks on the 45° line. Furthermore, if $w_1(1) < w_1(2)$, consumer 1's "worst" equilibrium consumption is $C_1^*(1) = C_1^*(2) = E_{\underline{\pi}}[w_1]$ and her "best" equilibrium consumption is $C_1^*(1) = C_1^*(2) = E_{\bar{\pi}}[w_1]$. The (slopes of) black straight lines in Fig. 5.1 are all equilibrium prices corresponding to some given ω, one of which is the "worst" for consumer 1 and one of which is "best" for her. Note that there is a continuum of equilibria.

Second, assume that $w(1) > w(2)$ without loss of generality, that is, the case of *complete* aggregate risk. Again, the indifference curves of both consumers have kinks. However, the 45° line is not common to both consumers, and hence, the indifference curve of each consumer is *tangential* to the other. The equilibrium is thus unique and it coincides with the π-equilibrium where $\pi \in \mathcal{P}(\theta, w)$, which is now a singleton set.

See Fig. 5.2. There, we assume that $w(1) = 8$ and $w(2) = 5$. We can see that the 45° line (dotted line) is not common to both consumers and that the indifference curve of each consumer is tangential to the other. Each of tangent points is supported by only a unique equilibrium price.

5.5 Nonrobustness of Indeterminacy

From Sect. 5.4, we see that the equilibrium is indeterminate if and only if there exist j and j' such that $j \neq j'$ and $w(j) = w(j')$. If we keep θ fixed, each economy is characterized by the initial endowment profile $(w_i(j))_{i,j} \in \mathbb{R}^{kn}_{++}$. Then we know that

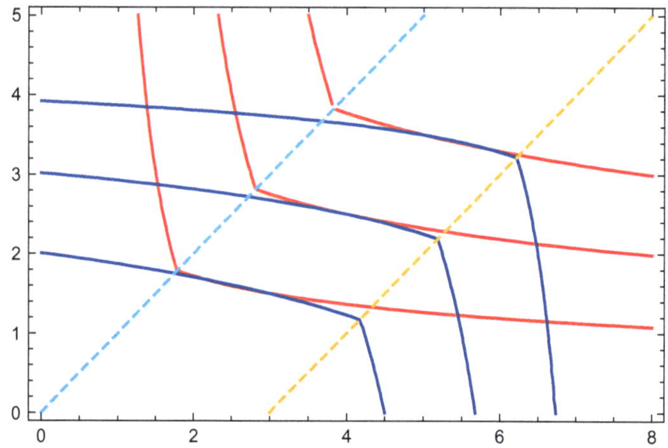

Fig. 5.2 Aggregate risk is present

the set of economies whose equilibria are indeterminate has the Lebesgue measure of zero. This means that any equilibrium indeterminacy disappears if an economy is perturbed slightly in the sense that the configuration of the initial endowment changes slightly.

To generate "robust" indeterminacy, we need a mechanism. This question is addressed in the next chapter.

References

Dana, R.-A. 2004. Ambiguity, uncertainty aversion and equilibrium welfare. *Economic Theory* 23: 569–587.

Dow, J., and S.R.C. Werlang. 1992. Uncertainty aversion, risk aversion, and the optimal choice of portfolio. *Econometrica* 60: 197–204.

Mas-Collel, A., M.D. Whinston, and J.R. Green. 1995. *Microeconomic Theory*. New York: Oxford University Press.

Chapter 6
Monetary Equilibria and Knightian Uncertainty

6.1 Introduction and Summary

In the past two decades, the implications of Knightian uncertainty have been explored in several general equilibrium settings. As shown by Dow and Werlang (1992), Tallon (1998), Chateauneuf et al. (2000), Dana (2004), one of the most important findings in the existing literature is that indeterminacy of equilibria can be generated in the static Arrow-Debreu economy under Knightian uncertainty when there is *no* aggregate uncertainty.[1] Here, no aggregate uncertainty means that the total endowment does not change over the state space.[2]

However, Rigotti and Shannon (2012) argued that such indeterminacy is not robust in the canonical Arrow-Debreu economy, meaning that the equilibrium is generically determinate. Roughly speaking, this means that indeterminacy would disappear if the economy was "shaken" only slightly. In fact, the set of Arrow-Debreu economies with no aggregate uncertainty has zero Lebesgue measure. Chapter 5 carefully discloses the intuition behind Rigotti and Shannon (2012) by means of Dana's (2004) model.

This suggests the importance of determining the mechanisms that can generate *robust* equilibrium indeterminacy under Knightian uncertainty by embedding it into the general equilibrium framework. The main subject of this chapter is to present

[1]See also Billot et al. (2000).

[2]Epstein and Wang (1994) use similar logic toward no aggregate uncertainty to show indeterminacy of equilibria in an intertemporal general equilibrium model with an infinitely lived representative agent. Note, however, that they only demonstrated *nominal* indeterminacy in this setting; i.e., they demonstrated the indeterminacy of the equilibrium asset prices but not of the equilibrium allocation. In their model, the single representative agent consumes the sum of the initial endowment and the dividend at each date along the equilibrium price path, and hence, real indeterminacy does not occur by the definition of the equilibrium. Also note that Epstein and Wang (1994) assume an uncertainty-averse representative agent in Lucas' (1978) model. Essentially, the former is different from the latter only in this respect although the former assumes that consumptions are *continuous* over the state space to avoid some mathematical difficulty which would arise when consumptions were only measurable. Epstein and Wang (1995) overcome this difficulty by using the concept of *analyticity*.

K.G. Nishimura and H. Ozaki, *Economics of Pessimism and Optimism*,
DOI 10.1007/978-4-431-55903-0_6

such a mechanism by embedding Knightian uncertainty into a stochastic overlapping generations (OLG) economy.

The OLG model is an intertemporal general equilibrium model that has a demographic structure with overlapping generations. Although the OLG model can be considered at various levels of generality, this chapter emphasizes the role of Knightian uncertainty by considering a simple but rather canonical stationary pure-endowment stochastic OLG model. Time is divided into discrete dates and runs from 1 to infinity. At each date, one of the finite states is realized. A history of states is called a "date-event." At each date-event, a single perishable commodity is available and a new agent that lives for two consecutive dates is born. Each agent has the opportunity to trade a single infinitely lived outside asset (money), which has a constant supply and yields no dividend. There exists neither storage technology nor production. Therefore, the ingredients of our model are almost the same as those found in a canonical stochastic OLG model. A remarkable departure of this chapter from the standard stochastic OLG model is that each agent is endowed with the MEU preference.

This chapter will make four main achievements. First, we show that a stationary monetary equilibrium is characterized by a system of inclusions, not by that of equations. As the second and central achievement, we show the *robust* indeterminacy of the stationary monetary equilibrium, which is a time-invariant equilibrium with circulating money. To make the meaning of robustness clear, let us call a pair of initial endowments in the first and second periods of the agent's life an *economy*. Then the second result is that there is a nonempty open set of economies, each element of which generates a continuum of stationary monetary equilibria. Furthermore, we argue that such economies exhibit aggregate uncertainty. Third, we conduct comparative statics of Knightian uncertainty. We show that an increase in Knightian uncertainty (in the sense that the set of priors dilates) increases the sizes of both the range of the stationary monetary equilibria and the set of economies generating a continuum of stationary monetary equilibria. Finally, we show that each of these stationary monetary equilibria is conditionally Pareto optimal. In other words, the equilibria are not Pareto comparable with each other.

The chapter is organized as follows. Section 6.2 presents some relevant results from the existing literature. Section 6.3 describes the details of our model. Section 6.4 provides two-state examples that illustrate the mechanism generating indeterminacy of equilibria. Section 6.5 demonstrates that stationary monetary equilibrium can be characterized by a system of inclusions, and then shows the existence and robust indeterminacy of stationary monetary equilibria. Section 6.6 conducts comparative statics that illustrate the effect of greater Knightian uncertainty on the equilibrium outcomes. Section 6.7 examines the optimality of stationary monetary equilibria. Proofs are relegated to the Appendix.

6.2 Related Literature

This chapter builds on a number of contributions. As mentioned in the Introduction and Summary, the static Arrow-Debreu model under Knightian uncertainty can generate indeterminacy of equilibria (for example, when there exists no aggregate uncertainty). However, such indeterminacy is not robust. To generate robust indeterminacy in a general equilibrium setting under Knightian uncertainty, "some other ingredient has to be inserted" as proposed by Mukerji and Tallon (2004a, p.285). The most recent studies found some situations that exhibit robust indeterminacy in a general equilibrium setting under Knightian uncertainty. Mukerji and Tallon (2001, Theorem) incorporated an idiosyncratic component of the asset returns[3] into the Arrow-Debreu model to argue the incompleteness of financial markets and indeterminacy of equilibria.[4] Furthermore, Mandler (2013, Proposition 1) recently developed a near Arrow-Debreu model by introducing a productive asset and sequential trades. He found robust indeterminacy of equilibria. In his model, the production was used to drive the economy to a point where agents face decision-making in a setting in which there exist no aggregate uncertainty. The observation made in this chapter contributes to this line of the literature by providing a new mechanism that generates robust indeterminacy of equilibria in a general equilibrium model under Knightian uncertainty. That is, we use the intuition obtained from the static Arrow-Debreu model and embed Knightian uncertainty into a stochastic OLG model with money. We can adjust the value of money in each state to make the environment similar to the one with no aggregate uncertainty. One may consider that this mecha-

---

[3]Here, an "idiosyncratic component of the asset returns" refers to the asset payoff difference across some states over which endowments remain identical. While "no trade" can occur over some price range when endowments are universally identical according to Dow and Werlang (1992); Epstein and Wang (1994) showed that it can still occur even with idiosyncratic shocks in this restricted sense. In their framework of a representative agent, the state of no trade is equivalent to an equilibrium and hence the presence of some price width with no trade implies indeterminacy of equilibria. Mukerji and Tallon (2001) incorporate Epstein and Wang's (1994) idea into a truly general equilibrium setting and showed a "no trade" result and indeterminacy. Mukerji and Tallon (2004b) use this idiosyncratic shock to solve a "puzzle" that the public want to denominate contracts in currency units. They extend Margil and Quinzii's (1997) general equilibrium model where both nominal and indexed bonds are available for trade by assuming uncertainty-averse agents and then derive conditions under which there is no trade in indexed bonds in any equilibrium. Furthermore, Ozsoylev and Werner (2011) use a similar idiosyncratic shock to show emergence of illiquid rational expectations equilibria by demonstrating that there exists a range of values of the signal and random asset supply over which the arbitrageurs, the suppliers of money, cease the trade in an asset pricing model with information transmission and with uncertainty-averse agents.

[4]See Rinaldi (2009) for additional information. Note, however, that because the MEU preference is a special case of the variational preference axiomatized by Maccheroni et al. (2006) and because any variational preference may be approximated arbitrarily well by another *smooth* variational preference, Rinaldi's (2009) result is not a confirmation that Mukerji and Tallon's (2001) result works for the whole class of variational preferences. In a similar fashion, the robust indeterminacy in this chapter is concerned with the robustness with respect to only the initial endowments and not the robustness with respect to *both* the initial endowments and the *preferences*. That is, the preferences are supposed to be fixed. Also see Guidolin and Rinaldi (2013).

nism is, in some sense, similar to Mandler's (2013). However, they are quite distinct from each other because, in our model, the *flexible* adjustment of the real price of money (not the production) makes the environment with which the agents are faced similar to the static one. In summary, by introducing a demographic structure with overlapping generations and an infinitely lived asset (money) in a constant supply to an intertemporal general equilibrium setting, we can generate robust indeterminacy of equilibria under Knightian uncertainty.

Our observations also contribute to studies on stochastic OLG models of the general equilibrium. The proposed model is simple but rather canonical and similar to those considered in the literature. For examples, see Magill and Quinzii (2003); and Labadie (2004); and Ohtaki (2011). However, the central subjects of these preceding works are different from ours.[5] We should note that Ohtaki and Ozaki (2015), on which this chapter is based, is the first that introduces the MEU preferences to the stochastic OLG model with money.[6]

Our model is canonical except for the preferences, but the density of the stationary monetary equilibria is quite different from the preceding studies. In representative agent models, Manuelli (1990, Proposition 1), Magill and Quinzii (2003, Proposition 1), and Ohtaki (2011, Proposition 1′) reported several sufficient conditions for the uniqueness of stationary monetary equilibrium.[7] Furthermore, Gottardi (1996, Theorem 1) showed that a stationary monetary equilibrium generically exists and is locally isolated in a more complicated stochastic OLG model with many one-period securities and many agents endowed with smooth preferences. With the MEU preferences that are known to be nonsmooth, in contrast, we show that the indeterminacy of stationary monetary equilibria can arise even when the sufficient conditions provided in the preceding works for the uniqueness of stationary monetary equilibrium are satisfied.

Finally, we mention our observation on the optimality of equilibria. The optimality of equilibrium allocations has been characterized by Manuelli (1990), Aiyagari and Peled (1991), Chattopadhyay and Gottardi (1999), Demange and Laroque (1999), and Ohtaki (2013) among others. These studies presumed that the preferences were smooth. However, the MEU preferences are nonsmooth as mentioned in the previous paragraph. Therefore, we cannot directly apply the characterization results developed in these preceding studies to the current model.[8] Instead of applying the established characterization results, we have more directly demonstrated the optimality of stationary monetary equilibria by tailoring Sakai's (1988) proof to our model.

---

[5] Labadie (2004) explored financial arrangements that could realize optimal allocations. Magill and Quinzii (2003) examined the asymptotic properties of monetary equilibrium processes.

[6] Fukuda (2008) introduced firms with convex Choquet expected utility preferences to Diamond's (1965) OLG model with a capital accumulation.

[7] Interested readers may also see Ohtaki (2015).

[8] Recently, Ohtaki and Ozaki (2013) extended the standard dominant root characterization of the optimal allocations to the economy under Knightian uncertainty.

6.3 The Model

We consider a stationary, pure-endowment, stochastic overlapping generations economy with money, where agents' beliefs about uncertain situations are represented by multiple priors, and not by a single prior.[9]

6.3.1 *Stochastic Environment*

Time is discrete and runs from $t = 1$ to infinity. Uncertainty is modeled by a date-event tree with a time-invariant finite state space S. For each $t \geq 1$, we denote the state realized in period t as s_t. This is called the *period t state*, where the (conceptually defined) period 0 state $s_0 \in S$ is treated as given. To be more precise, the date-event tree, denoted by Γ, is defined as follows: (i) the root of the tree is s_0; (ii) the set of nodes at date t is denoted by Σ_t (where we set $\Sigma_1 := \{s_0\} \times S$ and $\Sigma_t := \Sigma_{t-1} \times S$ for $t \geq 2$); and (iii) $\Sigma := \bigcup_{t\geq 1} \Sigma_t$ and $\Gamma := \{s_0\} \cup \Sigma$.[10] In each period, we assume that the state is realized at the beginning of the period. We denote the set of all probability measures on S as Δ_S. There is a single perishable commodity, called the consumption good in each period. No storage technology or production technology is available.

In each period, one new agent enters the economy after the state is realized and lives for two periods. In the rest of this chapter, we concentrate on the stationary situation. Therefore, agents are distinguished by the state in which they are born, and not the time or the past history of the realized states. An agent born in state s_t and period t is endowed with $\omega^y_{s_t}$ units of the consumption good in the first period of their life, and $\omega^o_{s_{t+1}}$ in state s_{t+1} in the second period. We assume that $(\omega^y_s, (\omega^o_{s'})_{s' \in S}) \in \mathbb{R}_{++} \times \mathbb{R}^S_{++}$ for all $s \in S$. Note that the second-period endowment is assumed to be independent of the shock in the first period. Therefore, the economy is represented by a point $(\omega^y_s, \omega^o_{s'})_{s,s' \in S}$ in the positive orthant of the finite-dimensional Euclidean space, $\mathbb{R}^{S\times S}_{++}$, given the agent's preferences described below.

6.3.2 *Preferences*

We denote the contingent consumption stream of an agent born in state s_t at date t as $c_{s_t} = (c^y_{s_t}, (c^o_{s_t s'})_{s' \in S}) \in \mathbb{R}_+ \times \mathbb{R}^S_+$. Each agent born in state s_t at date t is assumed to rank the consumption streams c_{s_t} according to their lifetime utility function

[9]Except for the preferences, the ingredients of our model are similar to those in Labadie's work (2004). However, her objective was to examine the financial arrangements that could result in the optimal allocations, rather than to examine the in/determinacy of stationary monetary equilibrium.

[10]This definition of the date-event tree is standard, and can be seen in, for example, Chattopadhyay (2001).

$U^{s_t}: \mathbb{R}_+ \times \mathbb{R}_+^S \to \mathbb{R}$. Furthermore, each agent born in state s is assumed to form a belief about an occurrence of the next period's state that is represented by a *set* of priors that are totally subjective, given the state realized in the period when they were born.[11] Throughout this chapter, we assume that an agent born in state s has an MEU preference.[12] That is, there exists a strictly monotonic increasing and strictly concave real-valued function u on $\mathbb{R}_+ \times \mathbb{R}_+$, which is continuously differentiable on the interior of its domain, and a compact and convex subset $\mathcal{P}_s$ of $\Delta_S \cap \mathbb{R}_{++}^S$ such that

$$(\forall c_s \in \mathbb{R}_+ \times \mathbb{R}_+^S) \quad U^s(c_s) = \min_{\pi_s \in \mathcal{P}_s} \sum_{s' \in S} u(c_s^y, c_{ss'}^o)\pi_{ss'}. \tag{6.1}$$

Note that we assume that u is common to all agents. When $\mathcal{P}_s$ is a singleton for each $s \in S$, the preference degenerates into the standard subjective expected utility. In such a case, $\mathcal{P}_s = \{\pi_s\}$ for some $\pi_s \in \Delta_S$ for each s and we may write $U^s(c_s)$ as $U(\pi_s)(c_s)$ because U^s does not depend on s directly by the commonality of u. Then, because $U(\pi_s)(c_s)$ is clearly continuous in π_s for each c_s and because $\mathcal{P}_s$ is compact by the assumption, the minimum in (6.1) can be actually achieved. Hence, U^s is well defined. We often write $U^s(c_s)$ as $U_{\mathcal{P}_s}(c_s)$ again because U^s depends on $\mathcal{P}_s$, and not directly on s. We define the nonempty set of priors that achieve the minimum in (6.1) by $\mathcal{M}$ as follows: $(\forall s \in S)(\forall c_s \in \mathbb{R}_+ \times \mathbb{R}_+^S)\ \mathcal{M}_s(c_s) := \arg\min_{\pi_s \in \mathcal{P}_s} U(\pi_s)(c_s)$. One can easily verify that this lifetime utility function is strictly concave because of the strict concavity of u. We will use this fact when we characterize the equilibria and when we show their conditional Pareto optimality.

Remark 6.3.1 The present model is very close to those of Magill and Quinzii (2003), and Labadie (2004).[13] However, the interpretations on the agents' beliefs in this chapter and in previous works are different. For example, Magill and Quinzii (2003) require that the (unique) subjective probability measure should coincide with the true probability measure that follows from a Markov process. On the other hand, in the present model, subjective beliefs do not necessarily coincide with the true or objective probability measures even when such measures exist. In other words, the formation of the agent's belief that is represented by a set of priors, whether it is a singleton or not, is totally subjective and it could be totally irrelevant to the true or objective probability measures. This interpretation on the agents' beliefs might be considered as a kind of bounded rationality and is different from those of Magill and Quinzii (2003), and Labadie (2004).

---

[11]That is, the formation of the belief is independent of the past history of realized states. Furthermore, the set of priors may not be common to all agents who are distinguished by the states at which they are born.

[12]Gilboa and Schmeidler (1989) axiomatized the MEU preferences over lottery acts and Casadesus-Masanell et al. (2000) axiomatized the MEU preferences over Savage acts. Their axiomatization does not depend on whether the state space is finite or infinite, and hence, it may be applied to our situation with a finite state space.

[13]Labadie (2004) considered a time-separable utility index function.

We sometimes write $\mathcal{P} = (\mathcal{P}_s)_{s\in S}$ and call it the *transition probability correspondence*. Here, we give an example of the transition probability correspondence.

Example 6.3.1 Suppose that there exist some $\hat{\pi} : S \to \Delta_S$ and $\varepsilon : S \to [0, 1]$ such that, for each $s \in S$, $\mathcal{P}_s = \{(1-\varepsilon_s)\hat{\pi}_s + \varepsilon_s\mu_s : \mu_s \in \Delta_S\}$, which is often called the *ε-contamination* of $\hat{\pi}_s$.[14] Obviously, this is an example of transition probability correspondence. Then, the associated lifetime utility function (6.1) takes the form: $U^s(c_s) = \min_{\pi_s\in\mathcal{P}_s} \sum_{s'\in S} u(c_s^y, c_{ss'}^o)\pi_{ss'} = (1-\varepsilon_s)\sum_{s'\in S} u(c_s^y, c_{ss'}^o)\hat{\pi}_{ss'} + \varepsilon_s \min_{s'\in S} u(c_s^y, c_{ss'}^o)$. Note that an increase in ε_s increases Knightian uncertainty in the sense that $\mathcal{P}_s$ dilates. The effect of this type of increase in Knightian uncertainty is considered in Sect. 6.7. ■

6.3.3 Stationary Monetary Equilibrium

We next turn to the definition of a stationary *monetary* equilibrium, which is a stationary equilibrium wherein money circulates. To describe the intergenerational trade via money, we introduce an infinitely lived outside asset that yields no dividends and is in constant supply. We denote the stock of fiat money as $M > 0$, which is constant over the date-events. We also let p_s be the real price of the money and q_s be the real money balance at state $s \in S$. By definition, $p_s M = q_s$ and therefore p_s and q_s have a one-to-one correspondence. A *stationary monetary equilibrium* is then defined by a pair (q^*, c^*) of a contingent real money balance $q^* \in \mathbb{R}^S_{++}$ and a contingent consumption stream $c^* = (c_s^{*y}, (c_{ss'}^{*o})_{s'\in S})_{s\in S}$, such that there exists an $m^* \in \mathbb{R}^S$ satisfying that, for all $s \in S$, (i) (c_s^*, m_s^*) belongs to the set

$$\underset{(c_s^y,(c_{ss'}^o)_{s'\in S},m_s)\in\mathbb{R}_{++}\times\mathbb{R}^S_{++}\times\mathbb{R}}{\arg\max} \left\{ U^s(c_s) \;\middle|\; \begin{array}{l} c_s^y = \omega_s^y - p_s^* m_s, \\ (\forall s' \in S)\;\; c_{ss'}^o = \omega_{s'}^o + p_{s'}^* m_s \end{array} \right\}$$

given $p_\tau^* := q_\tau^*/M$ for each $\tau \in S$ and (ii) $m_s^* = M$.

Condition (i) requires that the pair of the consumption stream $(c_s^{*y}, (c_{ss'}^{*o})_{s'\in S})$ and money holding m_s^* must be the solution of the (lifetime) utility-maximizing problem of the agent born in state s. Condition (ii) is the market-clearing condition of fiat money.[15] We can easily verify that, in any stationary monetary equilibrium, the market-clearing conditions for the contingent commodities hold (Walras' law). That is, for each $s, s' \in S$, $c_s^{*y} + c_{s's}^{*o} = \omega_s^y + \omega_s^o$. This also implies that the second-period consumptions at a stationary monetary equilibrium are independent of the state realized in the first period of an agent's life; that is, $c_{s's}^{*o} = c_{s''s}^{*o}$ for each $s, s', s'' \in S$.

[14]For the ε-contamination, see Sect. 2.3.3 and Chap. 12.

[15]In (i), we assume that the budget constraints hold with equalities. We can do this for the first budget constraint without loss of generality by the strict increase of u. For the other budget constraints, we simply assume it. Also note that we exclude corner solutions by assuming that $(c^y, (c_{s'}^o)_{s'\in S}) \in \mathbb{R}_{++} \times \mathbb{R}^S_{++}$ and (ii).

A stationary monetary equilibrium is called *fully insured* (with respect to the second-period consumptions) if, for each $s, s', s'' \in S$, $c_{ss'}^{*o} = c_{ss''}^{*o}$. This type of stationary monetary equilibrium plays an important role in the following analyses.

Finally, note that, after an equilibrium real money balance q^* has been chosen (and the money market has cleared), the equilibrium consumption stream c^* is automatically and uniquely determined from the budget constraints. Therefore, we can identify a stationary monetary equilibrium (q^*, c^*) with an equilibrium positive real money balance q^*. By using this convenient property, the agents' optimization problems can be simplified to the ones of choosing an optimal money holding. For later references, we define the utility function V_s of the money holding m_s for each agent born at state s facing the real money balance $q^* \in \mathbb{R}_{++}^S$. Formally, for each $s \in S$, let

$$(\forall q^*)(\forall m_s) \quad V_s^{q^*}(m_s) := U_{\mathcal{P}_s}(c_s^{m_s}(q^*)), \tag{6.2}$$

where $c_{ss'}^{m_s}(q^*) := (\omega_s^y - (q_s^*/M)m_s, \omega_{s'}^o + (q_{s'}^*/M)m_s)$ and $c_s^{m_s}(q^*) := (\omega_s^y - (q_s^*/M)m_s, (\omega_{s'}^o + (q_{s'}^*/M)m_s)_{s' \in S})$. Note that V_s is concave because of the strict concavity of u. We often suppress the superscript $^{q^*}$ when it is obvious from the context.

6.4 Two-State Illustrative Examples

Before conducting formal analyses, this section offers two examples that provide intuitions on the mechanism that generates indeterminacy of equilibria.

The next example assumes only two states and constructs economies that exhibit indeterminacy of equilibria. In particular, it shows that the indeterminacy is caused by the non-differentiability of the MEU preferences at consumption streams that are fully insured with respect to the second-period consumptions.

Example 6.4.1 Suppose that $S = \{\alpha, \beta\}$. In addition, we specify the model by assuming that $(\omega_\alpha^y, \omega_\beta^y, \omega_\alpha^o, \omega_\beta^o) = (6, 3, 1, 2)$, $u(c_s^y, c_{ss'}^o) = \ln c_s^y + \ln c_{ss'}^o$, and $\mathcal{P}_s = \left\{(\pi_{s\alpha}, \pi_{s\beta}) \in \Delta_S \,\middle|\, \varepsilon \le \pi_{s\alpha} \le \delta\right\}$ for each $s \in S$, where $0 < \varepsilon \le \delta < 1$.[16] Because we consider a two-state model, the optimization problem in Condition (i) of the definition of stationary monetary equilibrium can be rewritten as

$$\mathop{\arg\max}_{(c_s, m_s) \in (\mathbb{R}_+ \times \mathbb{R}_+^S) \times \mathbb{R}} \left\{ U^s(c_s^y, c_{s\alpha}^o, c_{s\beta}^o) \,\middle|\, \begin{array}{c} c_s^y = \bar{\omega}_s - c_{ss}^o, m_s = (c_{ss}^o - \omega_s^o)M/q_s^* \\ c_{s\beta}^o = \dfrac{q_\beta^*}{q_\alpha^*} c_{s\alpha}^o - \dfrac{q_\beta^*}{q_\alpha^*}\omega_\alpha^o + \omega_\beta^o \end{array} \right\},$$

[16]The MEU preferences in the Cobb-Douglas form as in this example have been axiomatized by Faro (2013).

where $\bar{\omega}_s := \omega_s^y + \omega_s^o$. In this condition, c_s^y and m_s completely depend on the selection of $(c_{s\alpha}^o, c_{s\beta}^o)$, especially c_{ss}^o, for each $s \in S$. Furthermore, the first constraint, $c_s^y = \bar{\omega}_s - c_{ss}^o$, implies that $(c_{s\alpha}^o, c_{s\beta}^o) \in X_s := \{(x_\alpha^o, x_\beta^o) \in \mathbb{R}_+^2 | x_s^o \leq \bar{\omega}_s\}$ because $c_s^y, c_{ss}^o \geq 0$. Therefore, we can consider that each agent born at state $s \in S$ chooses $(x_\alpha^o, x_\beta^o) \in X_s$ so as to maximize $\hat{U}^s(x_\alpha^o, x_\beta^o) := U^s(\bar{\omega}_s - x_s^o, x_\alpha^o, x_\beta^o)$ subject to the "budget line," $x_\beta^o = (q_\beta^*/q_\alpha^*)x_\alpha^o - (q_\beta^*/q_\alpha^*)\omega_\alpha^o + \omega_\beta^o$, between two commodities contingent upon state α and β. This means that we can consider solutions of the MEU-maximizing problem and stationary monetary equilibrium using a "box diagram" with indifference curves derived from $\hat{U}^s$ and the budget line. In Fig. 6.1, the boxes depict the space $X_\alpha \cap X_\beta$ and indifference curves, derived from $\hat{U}^s$, through $(x_\alpha, x_\beta) = (1, 1)$ and $(x_\alpha, x_\beta) = (2, 2)$. The U-shaped and $\subset$-shaped curves are related to indifference curves for agents born at states α and β, respectively. Note that $\hat{U}^s(1, 1) < \hat{U}^s(2, 2)$. It is assumed that $\varepsilon = \delta = 0.5$ in Fig. 6.1a and $(\varepsilon, \delta) = (0.25, 0.75)$ in Fig. 6.1b. Therefore, Fig. 6.1a, b are related to cases without and with Knightian uncertainty, respectively. Notably, the agent's indifference curves in Fig. 6.1b exhibit kinks on the 45-degree line. This is because the lifetime MEU function is not differentiable on this line.[17] Figure 6.2 introduces the budget lines to the box diagram and depicts the stationary monetary equilibria. In this figure, the point $(x_\alpha^o, x_\beta^o) = (1, 2)$ corresponds to the initial endowment, and straight lines through it represent the "budget lines." A second-period consumption (x_α^o, x_β^o) at a stationary monetary equilibrium then corresponds to a point on a "budget line" when it is tangential to the indifference curves of both agents (α and β). When $\varepsilon = \delta$ (no Knightian uncertainty), we can find a unique stationary monetary equilibrium, as in Fig. 6.2a. Here, the dashed line depicts the set of points at which the indifference curves of agents α and β are tangential to each other.[18]

When $\varepsilon < \delta$ (Knightian uncertainty exists), there exists a continuum of stationary monetary equilibria, as in Fig. 6.2b. Here, a second-period consumption $x^o = x_\alpha^o =$

---

[17] To be more precise, the marginal rates of substitution for indifferent curves derived from $\hat{U}^s$, denoted by $\widehat{MRS}_s(x^o)$, is calculated using

$$\widehat{MRS}_\alpha(x^o) = -\frac{\hat{U}_1^\alpha(x^o)}{\hat{U}_2^\alpha(x^o)} = \begin{cases} \dfrac{[(1+\varepsilon)x_\alpha^o - \varepsilon\bar{\omega}_\alpha]x_\beta^o}{(1-\varepsilon)(\bar{\omega}_\alpha - x_\alpha^o)x_\alpha^o} & \text{if } x_\alpha^o > x_\beta^o, \\ \dfrac{[(1+\delta)x_\alpha^o - \delta\bar{\omega}_\alpha]x_\beta^o}{(1-\delta)(\bar{\omega}_\alpha - x_\alpha^o)x_\alpha^o} & \text{if } x_\alpha^o < x_\beta^o, \end{cases}$$

and

$$\widehat{MRS}_\beta(x^o) = -\frac{\hat{U}_1^\beta(x^o)}{\hat{U}_2^\beta(x^o)} = \begin{cases} \dfrac{\varepsilon(\bar{\omega}_\beta - x_\beta^o)x_\beta^o}{[(2-\varepsilon)x_\alpha^o - (1-\varepsilon)\bar{\omega}_\beta]x_\alpha^o} & \text{if } x_\alpha^o > x_\beta^o, \\ \dfrac{\delta(\bar{\omega}_\beta - x_\beta^o)x_\beta^o}{[(2-\delta)x_\alpha^o - (1-\delta)\bar{\omega}_\beta]x_\alpha^o} & \text{if } x_\alpha^o < x_\beta^o \end{cases}$$

if $x_\alpha^o \neq x_\beta^o$. However, it cannot be calculated at x^o with $x_\alpha^o = x_\beta^o$, if $\varepsilon < \delta$.

[18] To be more precise, the uniqueness of stationary monetary equilibrium follows from, for example, Proposition 1 of Magill and Quinzii (2003) or Theorem 1 of Ohtaki (2015).

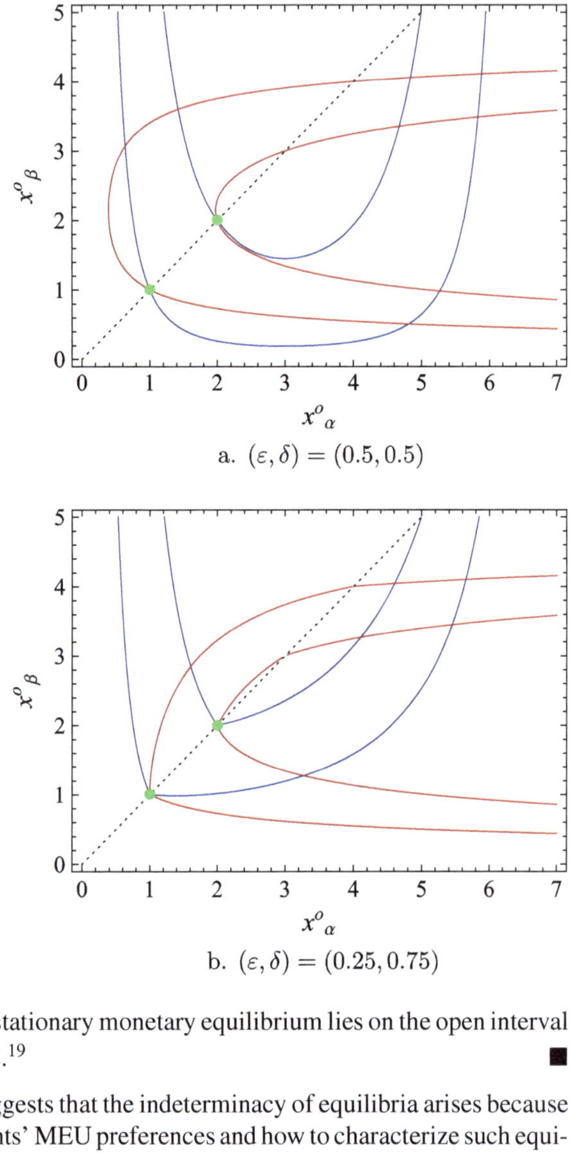

a. $(\varepsilon, \delta) = (0.5, 0.5)$

b. $(\varepsilon, \delta) = (0.25, 0.75)$

Fig. 6.1 "Edgeworth box": **a** there is no Knightian uncertainty, **b** there is Knightian uncertainty

x^o_β that corresponds to some stationary monetary equilibrium lies on the open interval of approximately 2.83–3.12.[19] ■

The previous example suggests that the indeterminacy of equilibria arises because of nonsmoothness of the agents' MEU preferences and how to characterize such equilibria is not yet clear. The next example also assumes only two states and gives an intuition for the characterization of the stationary monetary equilibria under Knightian uncertainty.

Example 6.4.2 Suppose that $S = \{\alpha, \beta\}$ and $\omega^o_\alpha < \omega^o_\beta$. Because $\mathcal{P}_s$ is compact and convex for each $s \in S$, we can write it as $\mathcal{P}_s = \{\pi_s \in \Delta_S | \, \mu_{s\alpha} \leq \pi_{s\alpha} \leq \nu_{s\alpha}\}$ for some

[19]The detail of the box diagram presented here is provided in Ohtaki (2014) for a case of no Knightian uncertainty.

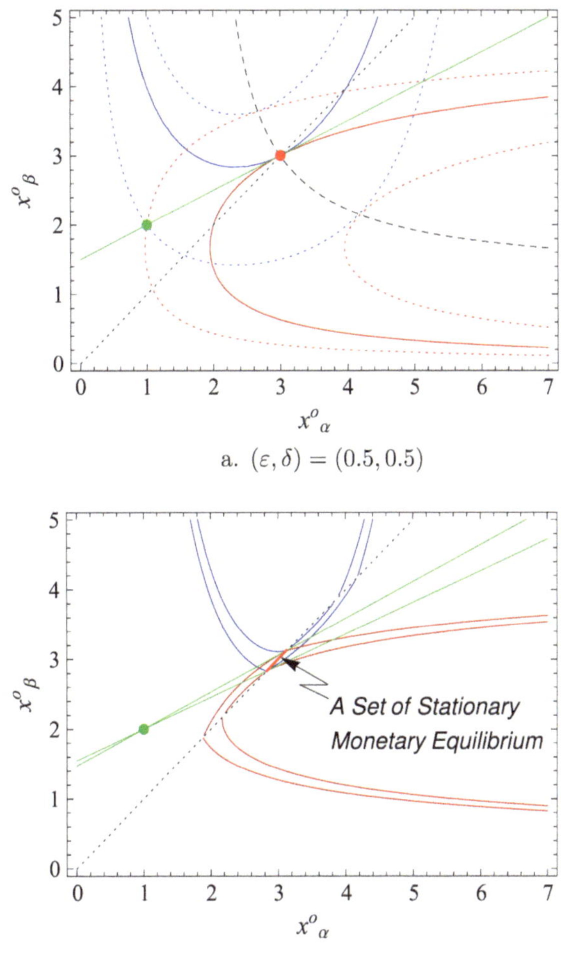

Fig. 6.2 Stationary monetary equilibria: **a** there is no Knightian uncertainty; **b** there is Knightian uncertainty

$\mu_s, \nu_s \in \Delta_S$ such that $0 < \mu_{s\alpha} < \nu_{s\alpha} < 1$. In addition, suppose that $u(c^y_s, c^o_{ss'}) = v_y(c^y_s) + v_o(c^o_{ss'})$ for some strictly monotonically increasing and strictly concave real-valued functions v_y and v_o on $\mathbb{R}_+$, which are continuously differentiable on the interior of its domain. Assume that there exists a stationary monetary equilibrium (q^*, c^*), wherein $\omega^o_\alpha + q^*_\alpha = \omega^o_\beta + q^*_\beta := \bar{c}^{*o}$ for each $s, s' \in S$. We have observed in Example 6.4.1 that there exists at least one economy generating such an equilibrium. Note that $q^*_\alpha > q^*_\beta$ because $\omega^o_\alpha < \omega^o_\beta$, and $\sum_{s' \in S} q^*_{s'} \mu_{ss'} < \sum_{s' \in S} q^*_{s'} \nu_{ss'}$ for each $s \in S$. Then, we can show that V_s is not differentiable at M, which must be chosen at any stationary monetary equilibrium. This is easy to verify. First, we can obtain $V_s(M) = v_y(\omega^y_s - q^*_s) + v_o(\bar{c}^{*o})$ and, for any real number h that is sufficiently close to but not equal to 0,

$$
\begin{aligned}
&V_s(M+h) \\
&= v_y(\omega_s^y - q_s^* - (q_s^*/M)h) + \min_{\pi_s \in \mathcal{P}_s} \sum_{s' \in S} v_o(\bar{c}^{*o} + (q_{s'}^*/M)h)\pi_{ss'} \\
&= v_y(\omega_s^y - q_s^* - (q_s^*/M)h) + \begin{cases} \sum_{s' \in S} v_o(\bar{c}^{*o} + (q_{s'}^*/M)h)\mu_{ss'} & \text{if } h > 0, \\ \sum_{s' \in S} v_o(\bar{c}^{*o} + (q_{s'}^*/M)h)\nu_{ss'} & \text{if } h < 0 \end{cases}
\end{aligned}
$$

because $q_\alpha^* > q_\beta^*$. Then, it follows that $R_s := \lim_{h \downarrow 0}(V_s(M+h) - V_s(M))/h = -(q_s^*/M)v_y'(\omega_s^y - q_s^*) + (1/M)v_o'(\bar{c}^{*o}) \sum_{s' \in S} q_{s'}^* \mu_{ss'}$ and $L_s := \lim_{h \uparrow 0}(V_s(M+h) - V_s(M))/h = -(q_s^*/M)v_y'(\omega_s^y - q_s^*) + (1/M)v_o'(\bar{c}^{*o}) \sum_{s' \in S} q_{s'}^* \nu_{ss'}$. Therefore, V_s is not differentiable at M because $R_s < L_s$. However, we should remark that M maximizes V_s if and only if $R_s \le 0 \le L_s$; that is, given $s \in S$

$$
\sum_{s' \in S} \frac{q_{s'}^*}{q_s^*} \mu_{ss'} \le \frac{v_y'(c_s^{*y})}{v_o'(\bar{c}^{*o})} \le \sum_{s' \in S} \frac{q_{s'}^*}{q_s^*} \nu_{ss'}, \tag{6.3}
$$

which gives us a partial characterization of the stationary monetary equilibrium. ■

6.5 Robust Indeterminacy

This section presents the first two out of four achievements we mentioned in the Introduction and Summary and it constitutes the main body of this chapter. Section 6.5.1 characterizes the stationary monetary equilibria by the solutions to the system of difference *inclusions*. Section 6.5.2 shows that there exists a continuum of equilibria and that it is *robust* in the sense that there exists an open set of economies, all elements of which generate such indeterminacy of equilibria.

6.5.1 Characterization of Stationary Monetary Equilibria

The inequalities in (6.3) in Example 6.4.2 can be interpreted as a requirement that, in a stationary monetary equilibrium, the marginal rate of substitution between the first-period and second-period consumptions lies in the range of expected rates of the return of the money. We may thus say that (6.3) represents a trade-off existing between intertemporal consumption smoothing and aversion to Knightian uncertainty and that agents can avoid uncertainty in the second-period consumption by sacrificing smoothing between the first-period and second-period consumptions. Furthermore, the range of the marginal rates of substitution that are admitted at a solution of the agents' optimization problems is *non*degenerate by the presence of Knightian uncertainty. All of these suggest that, under the MEU preference, a stationary monetary equilibrium may be characterized by the solution to the system of difference *inclusions*, not of difference equations.

The conjecture made in the previous paragraph is in fact correct as we show below. It is well known that if a stationary monetary equilibrium exists, it can be characterized by the solution to the system of difference *equations* that are derived from the first-order conditions of the agents' optimization problems *provided* the agents' preferences are represented by standard smooth utility functions.[20] In contrast, the stationary monetary equilibria in our model with the MEU preference, if they exist, can be characterized by the solutions to the system of difference *inclusions* by invoking Aubin's theorem (Theorem 4.2.1):

Theorem 6.5.1 *A positive vector $q^* \in \mathbb{R}^S_{++}$ is a stationary monetary equilibrium if and only if* $(\forall s \in S)$

$$0 \in \left\{ -\sum_{s' \in S} q_s^* u_1(c_{ss'}^M(q^*))\pi_{s'} + \sum_{s' \in S} q_{s'}^* u_2(c_{ss'}^M(q^*))\pi_{s'} \,\middle|\, \pi \in \mathcal{M}_s(c_s^M(q^*)) \right\} \tag{6.4}$$

where u_i is the derivative of u with respect to the i-th argument.

This is a natural extension of the characterization of a stationary monetary equilibrium in a stochastic OLG model with a single prior. In fact, if $\mathcal{P}_s$ is a singleton for all $s \in S$, this system of inclusions degenerates into a system of equations. Then this result turns out to be the same as the one of a stochastic OLG model with a single prior, as shown in, for example, Definition 2 of Magill and Quinzii (2003).

To close this subsection, we provide the characterization of *fully insured* stationary monetary equilibria, which is an immediate consequence of Theorem 6.5.1.

Corollary 6.5.1 *A positive vector $q^* \in \mathbb{R}^S_{++}$ such that $\omega_s^o + q_s^* = \omega_{s'}^o + q_{s'}^* =: \bar{c}^{*o}$ for each $s, s' \in S$, is a fully insured stationary monetary equilibrium if and only if*

$$(\forall s \in S) \quad \min_{\pi_s \in \mathcal{P}_s} \sum_{s' \in S} \frac{q_{s'}^*}{q_s^*} \pi_{ss'} \leq \frac{u_1(c_s^{*y}, \bar{c}^{*o})}{u_2(c_s^{*y}, \bar{c}^{*o})} \leq \max_{\pi_s \in \mathcal{P}_s} \sum_{s' \in S} \frac{q_{s'}^*}{q_s^*} \pi_{ss'}, \tag{6.5}$$

where $c_s^{*y} = \omega_s^y - q_s^*$.

The inequalities in (6.5) are obviously natural extensions of the inequalities in (6.3). Therefore, this result can also be interpreted as a trade-off between intertemporal consumption smoothing and aversion to Knightian uncertainty. We will exploit this corollary to find economies that certainly generate a continuum of stationary monetary equilibria.

---

[20] See, for example, Magill and Quinzii (2003); Ohtaki (2011).

6.5.2 Existence and Robust Indeterminacy of Equilibria

This subsection shows the robust indeterminacy of stationary monetary equilibria under the presence of Knightian uncertainty. We demonstrate that there exists a nonempty open set of economies, each element of which generates a continuum of stationary monetary equilibria. To this end, we need to do two things. First, we need to show the existence of a *continuum* of stationary monetary equilibria. However, even when there exists no Knightian uncertainty, the stochastic OLG model with money may generate a continuum of *nonstationary* monetary equilibria (Proposition 2, Magill and Quinzii, 2003).[21] On the other hand, a *stationary* monetary equilibrium can be unique when, for example, the preferences are time-separable and the degree of relative risk aversion of the second-period utility function is less than or equal to one (Proposition 1, Magill and Quinzii, 2003).[22] More generally, we can deduce from Theorem 1 of Gottardi (1996) that the *stationary* monetary equilibrium is locally isolated and hence cannot be a continuum when the preferences are smooth.[23] To present a stark contrast between stochastic OLG models with and without Knightian uncertainty, we demonstrate the indeterminacy of the *stationary* monetary equilibrium.

Second, we need to show that the indeterminacy is robust. We do this by showing the existence of a nonempty open set of economies in which the indeterminacy arises. This forces us to show that the indeterminacy may arise even when there exists the aggregate uncertainty. In fact, each element of the set of economies whose existence is to be proved exhibits the aggregate uncertainty (see Remark 6.5.1 below).

In the previous subsection, we observed that the stationary monetary equilibria can be characterized by the solutions to the system of difference inclusions. However, we have not yet shown the existence of such solutions. Consider an equilibrium real money balance $q^* \in \mathbb{R}^S_{++}$, such that for any $s', s'' \in S$, $\omega^o_{s'} + q^*_{s'} \neq \omega^o_{s''} + q^*_{s''}$ whenever $s' \neq s''$. In this case, there exists a neighborhood of q^* in which $\mathcal{M}_s(c^M_s(q))$ is "constant and a singleton" for each s.[24] We refer to this unique measure (which

---

[21] To be more precise, Proposition 2 of Magill and Quinzii (2003) show the indeterminacy of the candidates for "expectation functions," each of which constructs a nonstationary rational expectations equilibrium with circulating money.

[22] See also Theorem of Ohtaki (2015).

[23] As shown by Gottardi (1996), a "zero-th order" stationary monetary equilibrium (where money prices only depend on the current states) is locally isolated. In contrast, Spear et al. (1990) showed that the "first-order" and "second-order" stationary monetary equilibria (where money prices may depend on the past states) are indeterminate. In this chapter, the stationarity always refers to the "zero-th order."

[24] The basic idea is as follows: let $s_1 := \arg\min_{s' \in S} \omega^o_{s'} + q^*_{s'}$ and let $\mathcal{M}_1$ be the set of probability measures in $\mathcal{P}_s$ that assign the largest probability to s_1. Then, let $s_2 := \arg\min_{s' \in S\setminus\{s_1\}} \omega^o_{s'} + q^*_{s'}$ and let $\mathcal{M}_2$ be the set of probability measures in $\mathcal{M}_1$ that assign the largest probability to s_2. Continuing this process can lead to a single probability measure in $\mathcal{P}_s$ that is the unique element of $\mathcal{M}_s(c^M_s(q))$. In general, however, the success of this procedure hinges upon the nature of $\mathcal{P}_s$. In this sense, the argument of this footnote stands only heuristically. For example, if $\mathcal{P}_s$ is characterized by the ε-contamination (Example 6.3.1), the above procedure will determine a single probability measure.

depends on s because $\mathcal{P}_s$ depends on s) as μ_s. The system of inclusions, (6.4), is then a system of simultaneous equations: $(\forall s \in S)\ 0 = -\sum_{s' \in S} q_s^* u_1(\omega_s^y - q_s^*, \omega_{s'}^o + q_{s'}^*)\mu_{ss'} + \sum_{s' \in S} q_{s'}^* u_2(\omega_s^y - q_s^*, \omega_{s'}^o + q_{s'}^*)\mu_{ss'}$. Any solution to this system is an equilibrium of the economy. Its local nature (including the existence of a continuum of solutions) is the same as the standard stochastic OLG model and is well known. There is nothing new here and so we have not pursued this line any further.[25]

Next, we consider a *partially insured* equilibrium in the following sense. Let S' be a subset of S with $|S'| \geq 2$. Consider an equilibrium real money balance $q^* \in \mathbb{R}_{++}^S$ such that, for any $s', s'' \in S'$, $\omega_{s'}^o + q_{s'}^* = \omega_{s''}^o + q_{s''}^*$. Then, $\mathcal{M}_s(c_s^M(q^*))$ includes all the probability measures in $\mathcal{P}_s$ that assign the same probability to S'. However, because q^* need *not* be constant over S' (although $\omega^o + q^*$ must be), the set in (6.4) is not necessarily a singleton. Therefore, a continuum of solutions to the system of inclusions (6.4) may arise. To spell out the configuration of endowments that allow such indeterminacy could be very difficult. However, we may choose a continuum of q^* values appropriately so as to keep $\omega^o + q^*$ constant over some set but to make its (constant) value vary as q^* varies. This "endogenized flatness" can be further exploited to show the indeterminacy of *fully insured* equilibria.

Recall that a pair of first-period and second-period endowments, $(\omega^y, \omega^o) \in \mathbb{R}_{++}^S \times \mathbb{R}_{++}^S$, is called an *economy*. We say that an economy *exhibits equilibrium indeterminacy* if the stationary monetary equilibrium for it exists and is indeterminate. Furthermore, we define the function $f : \mathbb{R}_{++}^2 \to \mathbb{R}_{++}$ by $f(c^y, c^o) := u_1(c^y, c^o)/u_2(c^y, c^o)$ for each $(c^y, c^o) \in \mathbb{R}_{++}^2$, which is the marginal rate of substitution between the first-period and second-period consumptions. Note that f is continuous because u is continuously differentiable. We can now demonstrate the robust indeterminacy of stationary monetary equilibria.

Theorem 6.5.2 *There exists a nonempty open set $\Omega \subseteq \mathbb{R}_{++}^S \times \mathbb{R}_{++}^S$ of economies that generate a continuum of fully insured stationary monetary equilibria, if there are two distinct probability measures on S that belong to $\mathcal{P}_s$ for each $s \in S$, and $f(\cdot, c^o)$ is surjective for each $c^o > 0$.*

Therefore, we can find an open set of economies that exhibit equilibrium indeterminacy. More precisely, in the proof of this theorem (see the Appendix), we show that the fully insured second-period consumption satisfying (6.5), $(\bar{c}^{*o})$, becomes indeterminate. This implies that the corresponding equilibrium real money balance q^* (calculated using $q_s^* = \bar{c}^{*o} - \omega_s^o$ for each $s \in S$) is also indeterminate. Hence, we can obtain *nominal* and *real* indeterminacy; that is, indeterminacy of both the equilibrium nominal commodity prices and the equilibrium allocations.

Remark 6.5.1 Gottardi (1996) showed that in a more general stochastic OLG model with many agents that have convex preferences and with many securities, a stationary monetary equilibrium generically exists (Gottardi, 1996, Theorem 1.i). We can

[25] As stated in the previous footnote, the system of equations can possibly be a system of inclusions. Because we are concerned with a *sufficient* condition for multiple equilibria, we can neglect such a situation for our purpose.

deduce from this result that a stationary monetary equilibrium generically exists in our model with a convex MEU preference. In addition, Gottardi showed that the equilibrium is locally isolated when the agents' preferences are *smooth* (Gottardi, 1996, Theorem 1.ii). To be more precise, he showed that *any* open set of economies has its open subset of full Lebesgue measure such that each element of it generates a locally isolated stationary monetary equilibrium under convex and smooth preferences.[26] His observations still hold in our model provided that the agent's belief about the uncertain situation is summarized by a single probability measure. In contrast with his result, however, Theorem 6.5.2 shows the existence of *some* open set of economies that exhibit equilibrium indeterminacy under the MEU preference, which is convex but not smooth. Therefore, Theorem 6.5.2 is in stark contrast to previous results under smooth preferences.

We can provide an important property about economies that generate fully insured stationary monetary equilibria. As argued in the following remark, such economies exhibit aggregate uncertainty.

Remark 6.5.2 Let $\omega := (\omega^y, \omega^o) \in \mathbb{R}^S_{++} \times \mathbb{R}^S_{++}$ be an arbitrary economy generating indeterminacy of fully insured stationary monetary equilibria. Let $\bar{c}^{*o}$ be a second-period consumption corresponding to some fully insured stationary monetary equilibrium given the economy. We can observe that this economy exhibits aggregate uncertainty. To be more precise, it holds that $\omega^y_s + \omega^o_s \neq \omega^y_{s'} + \omega^o_{s'}$ for some $s, s' \in S$. First, suppose that $\omega^y_s = \omega^y_{s'} =: \bar{\omega}^y$ and $\omega^o_s = \omega^o_{s'} =: \bar{\omega}^o$ for each $s, s' \in S$. Then, $q^*_s = \bar{c}^{*o} - \bar{\omega}^o = q^*_{s'} =: \bar{q}^*$ for each $s, s' \in S$ and (6.5) degenerates into $u_1(\bar{\omega}^y - \bar{q}^*, \bar{\omega}^o + \bar{q}^*)/u_2(\bar{\omega}^y - \bar{q}^*, \bar{\omega}^o + \bar{q}^*) = 1$. This characterizes a stationary monetary equilibrium of a deterministic OLG model with the initial endowment $(\bar{\omega}^y, \bar{\omega}^o)$. However, we can deduce from Kehoe and Levine (1984, Proposition 3.5) that solutions of this equation must be locally isolated, which contradicts the hypothesis that ω exhibits indeterminacy. Therefore, there exist some $\tau, \kappa \in S$ such that $\omega^y_\tau \neq \omega^y_\kappa$ or $\omega^o_\tau \neq \omega^o_\kappa$. Now, suppose that $\omega^y_s + \omega^o_s = \omega^y_{s'} + \omega^o_{s'} =: \bar{\omega}$ for each $s, s' \in S$. Using the previous argument, it holds that $\omega^o_\tau \neq \omega^o_\kappa$. Then, (6.5) can be rewritten as $\min_{\pi \in \mathcal{P}_s} \sum_{s' \in S} (\bar{c}^{o*} - \omega^o_{s'})\pi_{s'}/(\bar{c}^{*o} - \omega^o_s) \leq u_1(\bar{\omega} - \bar{c}^{*o}, \bar{c}^{*o})/u_2(\bar{\omega} - \bar{c}^{*o}, \bar{c}^{*o}) \leq \max_{\pi \in \mathcal{P}_s} \sum_{s' \in S} (\bar{c}^{o*} - \omega^o_{s'})\pi_{s'}/(\bar{c}^{*o} - \omega^o_s)$ for each $s \in S$. However, we find that there is no constant $u_1(\bar{\omega} - \bar{c}^{*o}, \bar{c}^{*o})/u_2(\bar{\omega} - \bar{c}^{*o}, \bar{c}^{*o})$ that satisfies the last inequality for each s.[27] Therefore, each economy found in Theorem 6.5.2 exhibits aggregate uncertainty.

The last condition in Theorem 6.5.2 can be replaced with a simpler condition when the utility function u is additively time-separable. In the rest of this section, we concentrate our attention on the case where u is additively time-separable.

---

[26] Interested readers may refer to Cass et al. (1992), which also provided the existence and regularity results for the stationary monetary equilibrium in a more complicated stochastic OLG model.

[27] Consider $\bar{s}$ and $\underline{s}$ such that $\omega_{\bar{s}} = \max_{s \in S} \omega^o_s$ and $\omega_{\underline{s}} = \min_{s \in S} \omega^o_s$. Because $\pi \gg 0$ for each $\pi \in \mathcal{P}_s$, $\bar{c}^{*o}$ should satisfy that $1 < \min_{\pi \in \mathcal{P}_{\underline{s}}} \sum_{s' \in S} (\bar{c}^{o*} - \omega^o_{s'})\pi_{s'}/(\bar{c}^{*o} - \omega^o_{\underline{s}}) \leq u_1(\bar{\omega} - \bar{c}^{*o}, \bar{c}^{*o})/u_2(\bar{\omega} - \bar{c}^{*o}, \bar{c}^{*o}) \leq \max_{\pi \in \mathcal{P}_{\bar{s}}} \sum_{s' \in S} (\bar{c}^{o*} - \omega^o_{s'})\pi_{s'}/(\bar{c}^{*o} - \omega^o_{\bar{s}}) < 1$. However, this is a contradiction.

Corollary 6.5.2 *Suppose that u is time-separable; that is, there exist some strictly monotone increasing and strictly concave real-valued functions v_y and v_o on $\mathbb{R}_+$, which are continuously differentiable on the interior of its domain, such that $u(c^y, c^o) = v_y(c^y) + v_o(c^o)$ for each $(c^y, c^o) \in \mathbb{R}_+ \times \mathbb{R}_+$. Then, there exists a non-empty open set of economies that exhibit equilibrium indeterminacy if $\mathcal{P}_s$ has two distinct probability measures for each $s \in S$ and v_y satisfies the Inada condition; that is,* $\lim_{c^y \downarrow 0} v_y'(c^y) = +\infty$ *and* $\lim_{c^y \uparrow +\infty} v_y'(c^y) = 0$.

Remark 6.5.3 By restricting the preferences to those that are convex and smooth, we can find economies that generate a unique stationary monetary equilibrium. Under the assumption of additive separability of u, Proposition 1 of Magill and Quinzii (2003) provides a sufficient condition for the uniqueness of stationary monetary equilibrium. Following their result, if there is a stationary monetary equilibrium under a unique prior, it can be unique when the degree of relative risk aversion of the utility function for the second-period consumption is less than or equal to one.[28] However, it follows from Corollary 6.5.2 that there exists a continuum of stationary monetary equilibria under the MEU preference even when the degree of relative risk aversion of the second-period utility function is less than or equal to one. Therefore, Corollary 6.5.2 is a stark contrast to previous results under the smooth and additively time-separable preferences.[29]

In this subsection, we have found the robust indeterminacy of stationary monetary equilibria. This indeterminacy is proved via the "endogenized flatness"; that is, the fact that we can choose equilibrium real money balances so that the second-period consumptions can be constant over all states.

In the following two sections, we provide further results on the fully insured stationary monetary equilibria.

6.6 Comparative Statics

This section shows that an increase in Knightian uncertainty implies both an increase in the "degree" of indeterminacy and the dilation of the set of economies that exhibit a continuum of fully insured stationary monetary equilibria. Given an economy $\omega = (\omega^y, \omega^o)$ and a transition probability correspondence $\mathcal{P}$, we define the set of second-period consumptions at fully insured stationary monetary equilibria by $\hat{C}^o_{\mathcal{P}}(\omega)$. That is, we let $\hat{C}^o_{\mathcal{P}}(\omega) := \{\bar{c}^o \in \mathbb{R}_{++} \mid \bar{c}^o$ satisfies (6.5) under $\mathcal{P}$

[28] This result can be extended to slightly more general preferences. See Ohtaki (2015).

[29] In the framework of additively time-separable preferences, Manuelli (1990) also provides uniqueness results under an additional assumption that the states' evolution follows an *i.i.d.* process. He considers a stochastic OLG model with a general state space, and hence, it includes a finite state space case as in our model as a special case. Note that even when the set of priors, $\mathcal{P}_s$, is independent of s, Corollary 6.5.2 still demonstrates the existence of a continuum of stationary monetary equilibria.

and ω}. Note that $\hat{C}^o_{\mathcal{P}}(\omega)$ may be empty for some ω. In addition, we define $\hat{\Omega}_{\mathcal{P}}$ by $\hat{\Omega}_{\mathcal{P}} := \{\omega \in \mathbb{R}^S_{++} \times \mathbb{R}^S_{++} \mid \hat{C}^o_{\mathcal{P}}(\omega) \neq \phi\}$. Note that $\hat{\Omega}_{\mathcal{P}}$ is the set of economies in which a fully insured stationary monetary equilibrium exists. Finally, we write $\mathcal{P} \subseteq \mathcal{Q}$ when $\mathcal{P}_s \subseteq \mathcal{Q}_s$ for each $s \in S$. In accordance with the notion of Ghirardato and Marinacci (2002), we may say that $\mathcal{Q}$ represents more Knightian uncertainty (and more Knightian uncertainty aversion given the MEU preference) than $\mathcal{P}$, when $\mathcal{P} \subseteq \mathcal{Q}$. We can then prove the following theorem.

Theorem 6.6.1 *Let $\mathcal{P}$ and $\mathcal{Q}$ be two transition probability correspondences such that $\mathcal{P} \subseteq \mathcal{Q}$. Also assume that u and $\mathcal{P}$ satisfy all the assumptions of Theorem 6.5.2 (and hence, $\hat{\Omega}_{\mathcal{P}}$ is nonempty by Theorem 6.5.2). Then, (a) $\hat{C}^o_{\mathcal{P}}(\omega) \subseteq \hat{C}^o_{\mathcal{Q}}(\omega)$ for any $\omega \in \hat{\Omega}_{\mathcal{P}}$; and (b) $\hat{\Omega}_{\mathcal{P}} \subseteq \hat{\Omega}_{\mathcal{Q}}$.*

Recall that $\hat{\Omega}_{\mathcal{P}}$ and $\hat{C}^o_{\mathcal{P}}(\omega)$ are the set of economies that exhibit indeterminacy (of the fully insured equilibrium) and the set of second-period consumptions for some fully insured equilibrium. As mentioned above, the theorem indicates that an increase in uncertainty increases the degree of indeterminacy of the fully insured stationary monetary equilibrium and, at the same time, expands the set of economies that exhibit a continuum of fully insured equilibria.

Remark 6.6.1 The above observation is made by the comparative statics with respect to Knightian uncertainty. Following Ghirardato and Marinacci (2002), we define "greater Knightian uncertainty" as dilation of the set of priors. As argued in Klibanoff et al. (2005), such a definition of greater Knightian uncertainty cannot disentangle an attitude toward Knightian uncertainty from Knightian uncertainty itself.[30] In other words, our definition of greater Knightian uncertainty involves the effects of both increasing Knightian uncertainty and increasing Knightian uncertainty aversion. Theorem 6.6.1 then states that such a greater Knightian uncertainty increases the sizes of both the set of stationary monetary equilibria and the set of economies that exhibit equilibrium indeterminacy. To the best of our knowledge, Ohtaki and Ozaki (2015), on which this chapter is based, is the first work that conducts comparative statics with respect to Knightian uncertainty in a stochastic OLG model with money.

6.7 Optimality

We have shown the existence of a continuum of stationary monetary equilibria. A question that naturally arises is whether the allocations corresponding to these stationary monetary equilibria are optimal. The answer is that they are, in some sense. We begin with some definitions.

---

[30] Klibanoff et al. (2005) attempt to separate these two essentially distinct aspects of the preference. See footnote 35 of Chap. 1. Snow (2010) proposes a definition of "an increase in ambiguity" in the framework of Klibanoff et al. (2005). Gajdos et al. (2008) also separate them by using "objective" uncertainty.

Let $S_0 := \{s_0\} \cup S$. A *stationary feasible allocation* is a pair of $c^y \in \mathbb{R}^S_{++}$ and $c^o \in \mathbb{R}^{S_0 \times S}_{++}$ that satisfy $(\forall (s', s) \in S_0 \times S)\ c^y_s + c^o_{s's} = \omega^y_s + \omega^o_s$, where $c^o_{s_0 s}$ is the consumption of the *initial old*, who lives for one period in period 1 and in state s. From this equation and the assumption that the endowment depends only on the current state (see the discussion right after the definition of stationary monetary equilibrium in Sect. 6.3.3), it follows that $c^o_{s's}$ is independent of s'. Thus, we define a stationary feasible allocation as $c = (c^y_s, c^o_s)_{s \in S}$. A stationary feasible allocation $b = (b^y_s, b^o_s)_{s \in S}$ is *conditionally Pareto superior to* a stationary feasible allocation $c = (c^y_s, c^o_s)_{s \in S}$ if $(\forall s \in S)\ U_s(b^y_s, (b^o_{s'})_{s' \in S}) \geq U_s(c^y_s, (c^o_{s'})_{s' \in S})$ and $b^o_s \geq c^o_s$ with at least one strict inequality. The latter set of inequalities means that the initial old will not be worse off when moving from c to b, where we implicitly assume that the initial old will never be satiated. A stationary feasible allocation c is *conditionally Pareto optimal* if there is no other stationary feasible allocation that is conditionally Pareto superior to c.

We are now ready to state the main result of this section.

Theorem 6.7.1 *Every stationary monetary equilibrium achieves conditional Pareto optimality.*

Theorem 6.7.1 claims that even when there exists a continuum of stationary monetary equilibrium allocations because of the MEU preferences, each element of the continuum is conditionally Pareto optimal.[31] In other words, all equilibria found in Theorem 6.5.2 are incompatible with each other in the sense of the Pareto superiority.

Remark 6.7.1 When the agents' preferences are smooth, the conditionally Pareto optimal allocations are characterized by the dominant root of the matrix of marginal rates of substitution being less than or equal to one (see, among others, Aiyagari and Peled 1991; Chattopadhyay and Gottardi 1999; Chattopadhyay 2001; Ohtaki 2013). However, as we have already observed, the MEU preferences are nonsmooth. Therefore, we cannot directly apply the characterization results developed by the studies mentioned above to the current model. Instead of applying the established characterization results, we can more directly demonstrate the optimality of the stationary monetary equilibria by tailoring Sakai's (1988) proof to our model. Sakai demonstrates the conditional Pareto optimality of the stationary monetary equilibrium allocations in a stochastic OLG model with the standard expected utility preferences while his proof does not hinge upon this specific form of preferences.

References

Aiyagari, S.R., and D. Peled. 1991. Dominant root characterization of Pareto optimality and the existence of optimal equilibria in stochastic overlapping generations models. *Journal of Economic Theory* 54: 69–83.

[31] Note that the proof of Theorem 6.7.1 does not require continuous differentiability of u.

Billot, A., A. Chateauneuf, I. Gilboa, and J.-M. Tallon. 2000. Sharing beliefs: Between agreeing and disagreeing. *Econometrica* 68: 685–694.

Casadesus-Masanell, R., P. Klibanoff, and E. Ozdenoren. 2000. Maxmin expected utility over savage acts with a set of priors. *Journal of Economic Theory* 92: 35–65.

Cass, D., R.C. Green, and S.E. Spear. 1992. Stationary equilibria with incomplete markets and overlapping generations. *International Economic Review* 33: 495–512.

Chateauneuf, A., R.-A. Dana, and J.-M. Tallon. 2000. Risk sharing rules and equilibria with non-additive expected utilities. *Journal of Mathematical Economics* 61: 953–957.

Chattopadhyay, S. 2001. The unit root property and optimality: A simple proof. *Journal of Mathematical Economics* 36: 151–159.

Chattopadhyay, S., and P. Gottardi. 1999. Stochastic OLG models, market structure, and optimality. *Journal of Economic Theory* 89: 21–67.

Dana, R.-A. 2004. Ambiguity, uncertainty aversion and equilibrium welfare. *Economic Theory* 23: 569–587.

Demange, G., and G. Laroque. 1999. Social security and demographic shocks. *Econometrica* 67: 527–542.

Diamond, P.A. 1965. National debt in a neoclassical growth model. *American Economic Review* 55: 1126–1150.

Dow, J., and S.R.C. Werlang. 1992. Uncertainty aversion, risk aversion, and the optimal choice of portfolio. *Econometrica* 60: 197–204.

Epstein, L.G., and T. Wang. 1994. Intertemporal asset pricing under Knightian uncertainty. *Econometrica* 62: 283–322.

Epstein, L.G., and T. Wang. 1995. Uncertainty, risk-neutral measures and security price booms and crashes. *Journal of Economic Theory* 67: 40–82.

Faro, J.H. 2013. Cobb-Douglas preferences under uncertainty. *Economic Theory* 54: 273–285.

Fukuda, S.-I. 2008. Knightian uncertainty and poverty trap in a model of economic growth. *Review of Economic Dynamics* 11: 652–663.

Gajdos, T., T. Hayashi, J.-M. Tallon, and J.-C. Vergnaud. 2008. Attitude toward imprecise information. *Journal of Economic Theory* 140: 27–65.

Ghirardato, P., and M. Marinacci. 2002. Ambiguity made precise. *Journal of Economic Theory* 102: 251–289.

Gilboa, I., and D. Schmeidler. 1989. Maxmin expected utility with non-unique prior. *Journal of Mathematical Economics* 18: 141–153.

Gottardi, P. 1996. Stationary monetary equilibria in overlapping generations models with incomplete markets. *Journal of Economic Theory* 71: 75–89.

Guidolin, M., and F. Rinaldi. 2013. Ambiguity in asset pricing and portfolio choice: A review of the literature. *Theory and Decision* 74: 183–217.

Kehoe, T.J., and D.K. Levine. 1984. Regularity in overlapping generations exchange economies. *Journal of Mathematical Economics* 13: 69–93.

Klibanoff, P., M. Marinacci, and S. Mukerji. 2005. A smooth model of decision making under ambiguity. *Econometrica* 73: 1849–1892.

Labadie, P. 2004. Aggregate risk sharing and equivalent financial mechanisms in an endowment economy of incomplete participation. *Economic Theory* 27: 789–809.

Lucas Jr., R.E. 1978. Asset prices in an exchange economy. *Econometrica* 46: 1429–1445.

Maccheroni, F., M. Marinacci, and A. Rustihici. 2006. Ambiguity aversion, robustness, and the variational representation of preferences. *Econometrica* 74: 1447–1498.

Magill, M., and M. Quinzii. 1997. Which improves welfare more: A nominal or an indexed bond? *Economic Theory* 10: 1–37.

Magill, M., and M. Quinzii. 2003. Indeterminacy of equilibrium in stochastic OLG models. *Economic Theory* 21: 435–454.

Mandler, M. 2013. Endogenous indeterminacy and volatility of asset prices under ambiguity. *Theoretical Economics* 8: 729–750.

Manuelli, R. 1990. Existence and optimality of currency equilibrium in stochastic overlapping generations models: The pure endowment case. *Journal of Economic Theory* 51: 268–294.

Mukerji, S., and J.-M. Tallon. 2001. Ambiguity aversion and incompleteness of financial markets. *Review of Economic Studies* 68: 883–904.

Mukerji, S., and J.-M. Tallon. 2004a. An overview of economic applications of David Schmeidler's models of decision making under uncertainty. In *Uncertainty in Economic Theory*, ed. I. Gilboa. New York: Routledge.

Mukerji, S., and J.-M. Tallon. 2004b. Ambiguity aversion and the absence of indexed debt. *Economic Theory* 3: 665–685.

Ohtaki, E. 2011. A note on the existence of monetary equilibrium in a stochastic OLG model with a finite state space. *Economics Bulletin* 31: 485–492.

Ohtaki, E. 2013. Golden rule optimality in stochastic OLG economies. *Mathematical Social Sciences* 65: 60–66.

Ohtaki, E. 2014. Tractable graphical device for analyzing stationary stocastic OLG Economies. *Journal of Macroeconomics* 40: 16–26.

Ohtaki, E. 2015. A note on the existence and uniqueness of stationary monetary equilibrium in a stochastic OLG model. *Macroeconomic Dynamics* 19: 701–707.

Ohtaki, E., and H. Ozaki. 2013: Optimality in a stochastic OLG model with ambiguity. Tokyo Center for Economic Research Paper No. E-69. Available at SSRN: http://ssrn.com/abstract=2377585.

Ohtaki, E., and H. Ozaki. 2015. Monetary equilibria and Knightian uncertainty. *Economic Theory* 59: 435–459.

Ozsoylev, H., and J. Werner. 2011. Liquidity and asset prices in rational expectations equilibrium with ambiguous information. *Economic Theory* 48: 469–491.

Rigotti, L., and C. Shannon. 2012. Sharing risk and ambiguity. *Journal of Economic Theory* 147: 2028–2039.

Rinaldi, F. 2009. Endogenous incompleteness of financial markets: The role of ambiguity and ambiguity aversion. *Journal of Mathematical Economics* 45: 880–901.

Sakai, Y. 1988. Conditional Pareto optimality of stationary equilibrium in a stochastic overlapping generations model. *Journal of Economic Theory* 44: 209–213.

Snow, A. 2010. Ambiguity and the value of information. *Journal of Risk and Uncertainty* 40: 133–145.

Spear, S.E., S. Srivastava, and M. Woodford. 1990. Indeterminacy of stationary equilibrium in stochastic overlapping generations models. *Journal of Economic Theory* 50: 265–284.

Tallon, J.-M. 1998. Do sunspots matter when agents are Choquet-expected-utility maxmizers? *Journal of Economic Dynamics and Control* 22: 357–368.

Chapter 7
Dynamic Programming

7.1 Introduction and Summary

Ozaki and Streufert (1996) and Ozaki (2002) developed a theory of stochastic dynamic programming by generalizing the expectation operator E to a more abstract operator M, which maps a measurable function to another measurable function. They call M a *stochastic aggregator*.

This chapter specifies the stochastic aggregator M by

$$(\forall s \in S)(\forall u \in B(S, \mathcal{A})) \quad M_s u := \int_S u(s')\, \theta_s(ds')$$

where θ is a capacitary kernel from S to S and the integral is the *Choquet integral*. The *capacitary kernel* is defined in Sect. 2.5 and it plays a central role in the following chapters. We then adapt Ozaki and Streufert (1996) and Ozaki (2002) to this specific stochastic aggregator M to formally develop dynamic programming techniques that are applicable to economic models with Knightian uncertainty.

After developing a general theory according to Ozaki and Streufert (1996), we present two special dynamic programming theories: one is *non-negative* dynamic programming à la Blackwell's (1965) discounted dynamic programming, and the other is *non-positive* dynamic programming à la Strauch's (1966) negative dynamic programming. In particular, we argue that while the former needs *patience exceeding growth*, *ergodicity*, and *integrability*, the latter requires only quite weak assumptions.

Ozaki and Streufert (1996) can be adapted to the current model with Knightian uncertainty because the Choquet integral satisfies all of the important assumptions they impose on the stochastic aggregator M with respect to its mathematical nature. One such assumption is met by the Choquet integral thanks to Theorem 2.4.3 proved by Nishimura and Ozaki (2004). According to that theorem, we can reproduce the squeezing argument made by Ozaki and Streufert (1996) in the context of Knightian uncertainty modeled by the Choquet integral. Since the reproduction is quite simple

K.G. Nishimura and H. Ozaki, *Economics of Pessimism and Optimism*,
DOI 10.1007/978-4-431-55903-0_7

given Theorem 2.4.3, we do not provide the proofs of the results in this chapter. For them, the readers are referred to Ozaki and Streufert (1996).

The mathematical tools of dynamic programming developed in this chapter are essential to analyze the dynamic models that appear in later chapters.

7.2 Recursive Utility Function

7.2.1 *Stochastic Environment*

Throughout this chapter, the state space S is a nonempty Borel-measurable subset of a *Polish* space (that is, a Borel-measurable subset of a topological space that is a homeomorph of a *complete separable metric* space). Let $\mathcal{A}$ be the Borel σ-algebra on S. In this chapter, we set $\mathcal{A} = \mathcal{B}_S$.[1]

For each $t = 1, 2, \ldots$, let $(S^t, \mathcal{B}_{S^t})$ be the t-fold self-product measurable space constructed from $(S, \mathcal{B}_S)$; that is, $S^t = S \times \cdots \times S$ and $\mathcal{B}_{S^t} = \mathcal{B}_S \otimes \cdots \otimes \mathcal{B}_S$, where the products are $(t-1)$-times.[2] A generic element of S^t, which we call a *history*, is denoted by ${}_1\boldsymbol{s}_t = (s_1, s_2, \ldots, s_t)$.

7.2.2 *Consumption Plan*

For each $t = 0, 1, 2, \ldots$, let $L(S^t, \mathbb{R}_+)$ be the set of all functions from S^t into $\mathbb{R}_+$ that are $\mathcal{B}_{S^t}$-measurable, where we set $L(S^0, \mathbb{R}_+) := \mathbb{R}_+$. A *consumption plan* is any element of $\prod_{t \geq 0} L(S^t, \mathbb{R}_+)$ and we denote it by ${}_0\boldsymbol{c} = (c_0, c_1, c_2, \ldots)$. That is, ${}_0\boldsymbol{c}$ is a nonnegative real-valued stochastic process that is $\langle \mathcal{B}_{S^t} \rangle_{t \geq 0}$*-adapted*. Given a history ${}_1\boldsymbol{s}_t$ and a consumption plan ${}_0\boldsymbol{c}$, we define ${}_t\boldsymbol{c}$ by ${}_t\boldsymbol{c} := (c_t({}_1\boldsymbol{s}_t), c_{t+1}({}_1\boldsymbol{s}_t, \cdot), c_{t+2}({}_1\boldsymbol{s}_t, \cdot, \cdot), \ldots)$. Then, it holds that ${}_t\boldsymbol{c} \in \prod_{t \geq 0} L(S^t, \mathbb{R}_+)$ and we call it a *continuation of* ${}_0\boldsymbol{c}$ *after a realization of* ${}_1\boldsymbol{s}_t$.

7.2.3 *Return Function and Feasibility Correspondence*

Let A be a nonempty finite set of *assets* and let $F : S \times \mathbb{R}^A_+ \to \mathbb{R}_+$ be a *return function* that satisfies

F1. F is upper semi-continuous.

---

[1]See Sect. 2.5 for the definition of $\mathcal{B}_S$.

[2]Because S is assumed to be Polish, there is no notational ambiguity between $(\mathcal{B}_S)^t$ and $\mathcal{B}_{(S^t)}$ in defining it.

Use F to define the *feasibility correspondence* $\Gamma : \mathbb{R}_+ \twoheadrightarrow \mathbb{R}_+ \times \mathbb{R}_+^A$ by $(\forall y \in \mathbb{R}_+)\ \Gamma(y) := \{(c, x) \in \mathbb{R}_+ \times \mathbb{R}_+^A | c + \sum_{a \in A} x^a \leq y\}$. A consumption plan ${}_0\boldsymbol{c}$ is *feasible from* y if there exists an *investment plan* ${}_0\boldsymbol{x} \in \prod_{t \geq 0} L(S^t, \mathbb{R}_+^A)$ such that $(c_0, x_0) \in \Gamma(y)$ and $(\forall t \geq 1)\ (c_t, x_t) \in \Gamma(F(x_{t-1}))$, where we set $L(S^0, \mathbb{R}_+^A) := \mathbb{R}_+^A$.

7.2.4 Utility Function and Upper-Convergence

We define the *overly optimistic* return function $\bar{F} : S \times \mathbb{R}_+ \to \mathbb{R}_+$ by $(\forall s \in S)(\forall y \in \mathbb{R}_+)\ \bar{F}_s(y) := \max\{F_s(x) | \sum_{a \in A} x^a \leq y\}$. Given $y \in \mathbb{R}_+$, we define ${}_0\bar{\boldsymbol{F}}(y)$ by ${}_0\bar{\boldsymbol{F}}(y) := (y, \bar{F}(y), \bar{F}^2(y), \ldots)$. Here, $\bar{F}^t$ denotes the t-fold self-composition of $\bar{F}$; that is, $\bar{F}^0(y) := y$ and $(\forall t \geq 1)\ \bar{F}^t(y) = \bar{F}_{s_t} \circ \cdots \circ \bar{F}_{s_1}(y)$, where the products are $(t-1)$-times. Conveniently, it holds that $(\forall y)\ {}_0\bar{\boldsymbol{F}}(y) \in \prod_{t \geq 0} L(S^t, \mathbb{R}_+)$; that is, the "overly optimistic consumption plan," ${}_0\bar{\boldsymbol{F}}(y)$, is $\langle \mathcal{B}_{S^t} \rangle_{t \geq 0}$-adapted.[3] Given that, for any $y \in \mathbb{R}_+$ and for any consumption plan ${}_0\boldsymbol{c}$, which is feasible from y, it is obviously true that ${}_0\boldsymbol{c} \leq {}_0\bar{\boldsymbol{F}}(y)$. It is therefore sufficient to consider, as the *domain* of a utility function (defined below immediately), the set $\boldsymbol{C}$, which is defined by $\boldsymbol{C} := \{{}_0\boldsymbol{c} \in \prod_{t \geq 0} L(S^t, \mathbb{R}_+) \mid (\exists y \in \mathbb{R}_+)\ {}_0\boldsymbol{c} \leq {}_0\bar{\boldsymbol{F}}(y)\}$.

Let U be any extended real-valued (that is, $\bar{\mathbb{R}}$-valued) function defined on $S \times \boldsymbol{C}$. We call U a *utility function*. Note that we allow a utility function to be dependent on a state s, which we interpret as the initial state. A utility function U is *monotonic* if

U1. $(\forall s)(\forall {}_0\boldsymbol{c}, {}_0\boldsymbol{c}' \in \boldsymbol{C}) \quad {}_0\boldsymbol{c} \geq {}_0\boldsymbol{c}' \Rightarrow U_s({}_0\boldsymbol{c}) \geq U_s({}_0\boldsymbol{c}')$,

and it is *upper-convergent* if

U2. $(\forall s)(\forall y)(\forall {}_0\boldsymbol{c} \leq {}_0\bar{\boldsymbol{F}}(y)) \quad \lim_{t \to +\infty} U_s({}_0\boldsymbol{c}_{t-1}, {}_t\bar{\boldsymbol{F}}(y)) = U_s({}_0\boldsymbol{c})$,

in the latter of which the limit exists if U is monotonic because the sequence of consumption plans defining the upper-convergence is nonincreasing. (Here, the "limit" is defined in terms of the Euclidean topology on $\bar{\mathbb{R}}$).

While the monotonicity is not uncommon, the upper-convergence needs some explanation. The upper-convergence first appeared in Streufert (1990) in a deterministic environment, and then it was extended to a stochastic environment by Ozaki and Streufert (1996). It requires that the consumer should be indifferent to the far future in the sense that she would not care if her consumption would be replaced by the "best" one among those that are feasible in the extremely far future. It embodies some sort of discounting of the future, but importantly, it is a joint assumption on *both* the utility function *and* the return function.

[3] We say "overly optimistic" because ${}_0\bar{\boldsymbol{F}}(y)$ is not actually attainable under the feasibility requirement.

7.2.5 Recursivity and Koopmans' Equation

Let θ be a *convex* and *continuous* capacitary kernel on $S \times S$. Assume that a set $T \subseteq \bar{\mathbb{R}}$ satisfies

$$(\forall u \in L(S,T))(\forall s \in S) \quad \int_S u(s')\,\theta_s(ds') \in T\,, \tag{7.1}$$

where $L(S,T)$ is the set of all T-valued $\mathcal{B}_S$-measurable functions on S. We call T a *utility space*. The definition of a utility space requires that the Choquet integral should be well defined; that is, it is not "$\infty - \infty$." Later, we set $T = \bar{\mathbb{R}}_+$, or $T = \bar{\mathbb{R}}_-$. However, T can be any set as far as it satisfies (7.1).

A function $W : \mathbb{R}_+ \times T \to T$ is a *dynamic aggregator* if it satisfies

W1. W is nondecreasing in its second argument and is (jointly) upper semi-continuous.

A utility function U is *recursive* if there exists a dynamic aggregator W together with which U satisfies

U3. $(\forall s)(\forall\,{}_0\boldsymbol{c}) \quad U_s({}_0\boldsymbol{c}) = W\left(c_0, \int_S U_{s_1}({}_1\boldsymbol{c})\,\theta_s(ds_1)\right)$.

The equation in U3 is called *Koopmans' equation* (Koopmans 1960). The agent whose preference is represented by a recursive utility function is *time-consistent* in that she has no aggressive incentive to change later her consumption plan in the initial period and as uncertainty is gradually resolved because the dynamic aggregator is nondecreasing in its second argument by definition.

We define the *overly optimistic value function* $J^+ : S \times \mathbb{R}_+ \to T$ by $J_s^+(y) := U_s({}_0\bar{\boldsymbol{F}}(y))$.[4] We then consider

U4. $(\forall y)$ θ is upper quasi-continuous (u.q.c.) beneath $J^+ \circ \bar{F}(y)$,

where the upper quasi-continuity is defined in Sect. 2.5 and the function $J^+ \circ \bar{F}(y)$ is defined by a composite map $s \mapsto J_s^+ \circ \bar{F}_s(y)$ for each $y \in \mathbb{R}_+$. Note that U4 is an assumption that is jointly imposed on *both U and* the return function F, like the upper-convergence.

7.3 Dynamic Programming: A General Theory

We define the *true value function* $J^* : S \times \mathbb{R}_+ \to T$ by $J_s^*(y) := \max\{\, U_s({}_0\boldsymbol{c}) \mid {}_0\boldsymbol{c}$ is feasible from $y\,\}$. Note that the true value function is defined as the maximum and its existence remains to be proven.(See Theorem 7.3.1 below.) A consumption plan ${}_0\boldsymbol{c}$ is

[4]We say "overly optimistic" because $U_s({}_0\bar{\boldsymbol{F}}(y))$ is not actually attained as a utility number under the feasibility requirement.

optimal from $(s, y) \in S \times \mathbb{R}_+$ if it is feasible from y and it satisfies $U_s({}_0\boldsymbol{c}) = J_s^*(y)$. If the true value function exists, we define the *policy correspondence* $K^* : S \times \mathbb{R}_+ \twoheadrightarrow \mathbb{R}_+^2$ by

$$K_s^*(y) := \arg\max\left\{ W\left(c, \int_S J_{s'}^* \circ F_{s'}(x)\, \theta_s(ds')\right) \middle| (c, x) \in \Gamma(y) \right\}.$$

Note that the existence of the policy correspondence remains to be proven even when the true value function exists.[5] (See Theorem 7.3.1 below.)A consumption plan ${}_0\boldsymbol{c}$ is *recursively optimal* from $(s, y) \in S \times \mathbb{R}_+$ if there exists an investment plan ${}_0\boldsymbol{x}$ such that $(c_0, x_0) \in K_s^*(y)$ and $(\forall t \geq 1)\ (c_t, x_t) \in K^* \circ F(x_{t-1})$, where $K^* \circ F$ is the correspondence defined as a composite of K^* and F by $s \mapsto\!\!\!\!\to K_s^* \circ F_s(x)$ for each $x \in \mathbb{R}_+^A$. Note that the existence of recursive optima requires the existence of a measurable selection.

A function $J : S \times \mathbb{R}_+ \to T$ is an *admissible value function* if it is upper semi-continuous, nondecreasing in its second argument, and satisfies $J \leq J^+$. (Conveniently, it can be shown that J^+ is admissible under the assumptions of F1, U1, and U2.) We define the *Bellman operator* B from the set of admissible value functions into itself by

$$(\forall s, y)\ \ BJ_s(y) = \max\left\{ W\left(c, \int_S J_{s'} \circ F_{s'}(x)\, \theta_s(ds')\right) \middle| (c, x) \in \Gamma(y) \right\}.$$

Note that B needs to be well defined; that is, it must be proved that BJ exists and is admissible whenever J is admissible. An admissible value function J *solves Bellman's equation* if $J = BJ$.

One of the main results of this chapter is the next theorem.

Theorem 7.3.1 *Assume F1, W1, and U1–U4. Then J^* exists, and it is the largest admissible solution to Bellman's equation and it equals* $\lim_{n\to+\infty} B^n J^+$. *Furthermore, recursive optimality implies optimality.*

In the theorem, "largest" refers to the pointwise comparison between functions. Also, B^n denotes the n-fold self-composite of B; that is, $B \circ \cdots \circ B$ where the products are $(n-1)$-times, and the limit is pointwise.

The proof of Theorem 7.3.1 is a straightforward extension of Ozaki and Streufert (1996) and thus only a sketch of the proof is provided here. First, we adopt the proof of Ozaki and Streufert to a specific operator defined by the Choquet integral with respect to the capacitary kernel θ; that is, the one defined in the Introduction and Summary. Then we show that all the requirements that the stochastic aggregator M must satisfy *are* in fact satisfied by the Choquet integral by means of the results about it developed in Chap. 2.

---

[5]In addition to the existence of arg max, the measurability of the integrand is still unknown.

7.4 Non-negative Dynamic Programming

This section sets $T = \bar{\mathbb{R}}_+ := \mathbb{R}_+ \cup \{+\infty\}$ and constructs the utility function U from a capacitary kernel and a dynamic aggregator. To this end, let θ be a convex continuous capacitary kernel and let $W : \mathbb{R}_+ \times T \to T$ be a dynamic aggregator that may or may not satisfy the next assumption, which is somewhat strengthening W1.

A1. W is nondecreasing, upper semi-continuous, and continuous in its second argument.

We then *define* the utility function $U : S \times \prod_{t \geq 0} L(S^t, \mathbb{R}_+) \to T$ by

$$U_s({}_0\boldsymbol{c}) :=$$

$$\lim_{t \to +\infty} W\left(c_0, \int_S W\left(c_1, \int_S \cdots W(c_t, 0) \cdots \theta_{s_1}(ds_2)\right) \theta_s(ds_1)\right) \tag{7.2}$$

Because each component of the sequence is well defined by the Fubini property (Theorem 2.5.1) and because the sequence is nondecreasing by Proposition 2.4.2, the limit always exists. The utility function U is thus well defined. Furthermore, A1 and the monotone convergence theorem (Theorem 2.4.6) imply that U satisfies Koopmans' equation (U3).

We derive the parameters from the model's primitives; that is, the return function F and the dynamic aggregator W.

First, we use the return function F to find two functions $\zeta, \gamma \in L(S, \mathbb{R}_+)$ that jointly satisfy $(\forall s)(\forall y)\ \bar{F}_s(y) \leq \zeta_s + \gamma_s y$. When such ζ and γ exist, we henceforth fix them.

Second, we use W to define two parameters, $\delta, \bar{\delta} \in \mathbb{R}_+$ by $\delta := \overline{\lim}_{m \to +\infty} \sup_c \sup_{m' > m}(W(c, m') - W(c, m))/(m' - m)$ and $\bar{\delta} := \sup_{m \to +\infty} \sup_c \sup_{m' > m}(W(c, m') - W(c, m))/(m' - m)$. In general, W discounts the future nonlinearly, and impatience (reciprocal of discount factor) is variable depending on the "mean" future utility, m. Here, δ is the *asymptotic* impatience and $\bar{\delta}$ is the *uniform* impatience.

Third and finally, we use W again to find a parameter $\varepsilon \in (0, 1]$ that satisfies $(\exists \kappa_1, \kappa_2 \in \mathbb{R}_+)(\forall c)\ W(c, 0) \leq \kappa_1 + \kappa_2 c^\varepsilon$. When such an ε exists, we henceforth fix it, like ζ and γ.

We then consider the following assumptions on the capacitary kernel θ and the parameters derived above.

A2. $\bar{\delta} < 1$.

A3. $(\forall s)(\forall t \geq 1)\ g_s^t := \int_S \cdots \int_S \prod_{q=1}^t \gamma_{s_q}^\varepsilon\, \theta'_{s_{t-1}}(ds_t) \cdots \theta'_s(ds_1)$ is finite.

A4. $\lambda_g := \sup_s \overline{\lim_{t \to +\infty}} \left(g_s^t\right)^{1/t} < \delta^{-1}$.

A5. $(\forall s)(\forall t \geq 1)\ z_s^t := \int_S \cdots \int_S \sum_{r=1}^{t} \left(\prod_{q=r+1}^{t} \gamma_{s_q}^{\varepsilon} \right) \zeta_{s_r}^{\varepsilon}\, \theta'_{s_{t-1}}(ds_t) \cdots \theta'_s(ds_1)$ is finite.

A6. $\lambda_z := \sup_s \varlimsup_{t \to +\infty} \left(z_s^t \right)^{1/t} < \delta^{-1}$.

A7. $(\forall k_1, k_2 \in \mathbb{R}_+)(\forall d < (\lambda_g \vee \lambda_z)^{-1})(\forall y)$ θ is upper quasi-continuous beneath $\bar{\bar{u}} \in L(S, \bar{\mathbb{R}}_+)$, which is defined by

$$(\forall s)\ \ \bar{\bar{u}}_s := k_1 + k_2 \sum_{t=0}^{+\infty} d^t \left(z_s^t + g_s^t \left(\zeta_s^{\varepsilon} + \gamma_s^{\varepsilon} y^{\varepsilon} \right) \right).$$

In these assumptions, the vacuous products are set equal to 1, $g_s^0 := 1$, and $z_s^0 := 0$.

The functions g_s^t and z_s^t denote the growth component of the model up to time t, and hence, λ_g and λ_z may be thought of as the "average" growth. Given this, A4 and A6 require that *impatience exceeds growth*. Note that if the order of "sup" and "lim sup" in A4 and A6 were interchanged, we could never expect A4 and A6 to hold unless the "support of the distribution" is compact.[6] Therefore, A4 and A6 require that the model should possess some sort of *ergodic* structure. Finally, A7 is a *uniform integrability* requirement for the Choquet integral with respect to a capacitary kernel.

We then have the following theorem.

Theorem 7.4.1 *Assume F1 and A1. Further assume that $\zeta, \gamma, \delta, \bar{\delta}$, and ε exist and satisfy A2–A7. Then all the assumptions of Theorem 7.3.1 are satisfied.*

The proof is a straightforward extension of that in Ozaki and Streufert (1996). We only emphasize that Theorem 2.4.3 plays a crucial role in proving this theorem.

7.4.1 A Special Case: Bounded Returns

When the return function F is *bounded* on S, the story will become much simpler.

Proposition 7.4.1 *Assume F1, A1 and that θ is upper quasi-continuous beneath any constant real-valued function. Further assume that $\bar{\delta}$, δ, and ε exist and that $z, g \in \mathbb{R}_+$ satisfy $(\forall s, y)\ \bar{F}_s(y) \leq z + gy$. Finally, assume $\bar{\delta} < 1$ and $\delta g^{\varepsilon} < 1$. Then all the assumptions of Theorem 7.4.1 are met.*

Note that when the return is bounded, the integrability is almost trivial, impatience exceeding growth is quite easy to see, and the ergodicity is irrelevant. The proposition

[6]This means that our dynamic programming technique will be applicable even if the common severe assumption of compact-supportness of the distribution were violated.

shows that the result that is still much stronger than the well-known one can be derived as a corollary of Theorem 7.4.1.

For a proof, we refer the readers to Ozaki and Streufert (1996) again. (Also, see Sect. 7.1).

7.4.2 *An Example: CRRA Utility and AK Production*

Let ρ and β be real numbers such that $\rho \in [0, 1)$ and $\beta \in (0, 1)$, respectively. We define $W : \mathbb{R}_+ \times T \to T$ by $(\forall c, m)\ W(c, m) := c^{1-\rho} / (1 - \rho) + \beta m$. Furthermore, let A be a singleton and let γ be any function such that $\gamma \in L(S, \mathbb{R}_+)$. Finally, we define a return function F by $(\forall s, x)\ \ F_s(x) := \gamma_s x$.

Then, under these settings, all the assumptions of Theorem 7.4.1 are satisfied if

$$\lambda_g := \sup_s \overline{\lim_{t \to +\infty}} \left(\int_S \cdots \int_S \prod_{q=1}^{t} \gamma_{s_q}^{1-\rho}\, \theta'_{s_{t-1}}(ds_t) \cdots \theta'_s(ds_1) \right)^{1/t} < \beta^{-1}$$

and if $(\forall k_1, k_2 \in \mathbb{R}_+)(\forall d < \lambda_g^{-1})(\forall y)\ \ \theta$ is upper quasi-continuous beneath

$$k_1 + k_2 \sum_{t=0}^{+\infty} d^t \left(\int_S \cdots \int_S \prod_{q=0}^{t} \gamma_{s_q}^{1-\rho}\, \theta'_{s_{t-1}}(ds_t) \cdots \theta'_s(ds_1) \right) y^{1-\rho},$$

where $s_0 := s$.

Here, it is highlighted that we need *impatience dominating growth*, *ergodicity*, and *uniform integrability*.

Ozaki and Streufert (1996) provide concrete examples of economic growth models where these requirements are all met, the distribution is defined by a capacitary kernel that is a distortion of a stochastic kernel which is not compactly supported, and sustained growth is possible.

7.5 Non-positive Dynamic Programming

This section sets $T = \bar{\mathbb{R}}_- := \mathbb{R}_- \cup \{-\infty\}$ and constructs the utility function U from a capacitary kernel and a dynamic aggregator. To this end, let θ be a convex continuous capacitary kernel and let $W : \mathbb{R}_+ \times T \to T$ be a dynamic aggregator that may or may not satisfy the next assumption, which is somewhat strengthening W1 but still weakening A1.

B1. W is nondecreasing and upper semi-continuous.

We then *define* the utility function $U : S \times \prod_{t \geq 0} L(S^t, \mathbb{R}_+) \to T$ by (7.2). Because each component of the sequence is well defined by the Fubini property (Theorem 2.5.1) and because the sequence is nonincreasing by Proposition 2.4.2, the limit always exists. The utility function U is thus well defined. Furthermore, B1 and the monotonic convergence theorem (Theorem 2.4.6) imply that U satisfies Koopmans' equation (U3).

We consider the following assumption on the capacitary kernel θ.

U5. For any Polish space X, θ is upper *semi*-continuous on $S \times X$ beneath 0,

where the upper semi-continuity is defined in Sect. 2.5. We then have the following theorem.

Theorem 7.5.1 *Assume F1, B1, and U5. Then, all the conclusions of Theorem 7.3.1 are correct.*

For a proof, we refer the reader to Ozaki (2002), which substantially weakens the assumptions employed by Ozaki and Streufert (1996) for a non-positive utility function. (Replace the stochastic aggregator M in Ozaki (2002) by the Choquet integral defined by the capacitary kernel θ.)

Note that this theorem shows that dynamic programming techniques are available with quite weak assumptions when the preference is non-positive in the sense that the utility function representing it is bounded from above. In particular, U5 is always satisfied if θ is a stochastic kernel (that is, if it is additive), as pointed out by Ozaki (2002).

Also, note that B1 and U5 in Theorem 7.5.1 are met if the dynamic aggregator W is the one defined in Sect. 7.4.2 for any $\beta > 0$, as far as $\rho > 1$.

References

Blackwell, D. 1965. Discounted dynamic programming. *Annals of Mathematical Statistics*, *36*, 226–235.

Koopmans, T.C. 1960. Stationary ordinal utility and impatience. *Econometrica* 28: 287–309.

Nishimura, K. G., and Ozaki, H. 2004. Search and Knightian uncertainty, Journal of. *Economic Theory*, *119*, 299–333.

Ozaki, H. 2002. Dynamic programming with upper semi-continuous stochastic aggregator. *Advances in Mathematical Economics* 4: 25–39.

Ozaki, H., and Streufert, P.A. 1996. Dynamic programming for non-additive stochastic objectives. *Journal of Mathematical Economics* 25: 391–442.

Strauch, R. E. 1966. Negative dynamic programming. *Annals of mathematical statistics*, *37*, 871–890.

Streufert, P.A. 1990. Stationary recursive utility and dynamic programming under the assumption of biconvergence. *Review of Economic Studies* 57: 79–97.

Chapter 8
Dynamic Asset Pricing

8.1 Introduction and Summary

One of the main objectives of this chapter is to show that the indeterminacy of equilibria may show up in a truly dynamic framework. In this sense, this chapter is very closely related to Chaps. 4–6.

To this end, we take up a famous model by Epstein and Wang (1994), which essentially only changes a risk-averse and uncertainty-*neutral* representative agent into a risk-averse and uncertainty-*averse* representative agent in the pure-exchange dynamic asset-pricing model of Lucas (1978). We use as the objective function of the representative agent the *iterated Choquet expected utility* whose axiomatic foundation was discussed in Sect. 3.13. The dynamic programming technique developed in Chap. 7 is invoked in this treatment.

Our framework allows a much more general stochastic environment than that of Epstein and Wang because we can handle a distribution of the return whose support is not necessarily bounded. The framework of Epstein and Wang (1994) only deals with distributions with compact supports. This flexibility is possible because we invoke the dynamic programming techniques of Chap. 7, which can be applied to a fairly general stochastic environment. This technical aspect should be regarded as a particular contribution of this chapter.

We show that (1) the mechanics generating the indeterminacy is essentially the same as that of Dow and Werlang (1992) analyzed in Chap. 4, and that Epstein–Wang is a natural extension of Dow–Werlang to a dynamic framework; (2) indeterminacy can arise in the Epstein–Wang model even in the presence of aggregate shock, while the Dow–Werlang model assumes no aggregate shock; and (3) Epstein–Wang still needs *partial* absence of aggregate shock in the indeterminacy result. This indeterminacy result is not "robust" because it disappears when the economy is perturbed when the state space is finite, which is the same feature of indeterminacy in Dana's (2004) model analyzed in Chap. 5. We also show that (4) the indeterminacy in Epstein–Wang

K.G. Nishimura and H. Ozaki, *Economics of Pessimism and Optimism*,
DOI 10.1007/978-4-431-55903-0_8

only concerns price indeterminacy and not the real indeterminacy of goods allocation. To generate robust and real indeterminacy, a new mechanism is necessary and one such mechanism was presented in Chap. 6.

8.2 Lucas–Epstein–Wang Economy

This section describes a dynamic asset-pricing model based on that of Epstein and Wang (1994). However, it is important to note that they assume that the state space is a topological space and the consumption plans are *continuous* with respect to this topology, rather than simply being measurable. This is because the measurability is an assumption that is too weak mathematically to keep its track in a dynamic framework. It is, however, an assumption that is too strong to interpret economically. To avoid this difficulty, Epstein and Wang (1995) assume that the consumption plans are only *analytic*, rather than being measurable. See Remarks 2.3.1 and 2.5.1 for the analyticity. While the analyticity is weak enough to keep its track in a dynamic framework, the analysis is difficult because of its mathematical subtlety. We assume that the consumption plans are measurable, which is a natural assumption to impose both mathematically and economically. This becomes possible by assuming that the capacitary kernel is continuous in the sense defined in Sect. 2.5.

We continue to assume that the state space S is a nonempty Borel-measurable subset of a Polish space. Let u be a *felicity function* or an *instantaneous utility function* defined on $\mathbb{R}_+$ that is monotonically nondecreasing, differentiable, and strictly concave. We assume that the range of u is contained by $\mathbb{R}_+$ (Case (i)) or that it is contained by $\mathbb{R}_-$ (Case (ii)). Let $\beta \in (0, 1)$ be the discount factor and let θ be a convex continuous capacitary kernel. We assume that the agent's preference is represented by a utility function $U : S \times \prod_{t \geq 0} L(S^t, \mathbb{R}_+) \to \bar{\mathbb{R}}$ that is defined by

$$U_{s_0}({}_0\boldsymbol{c}) := \lim_{T \to +\infty} u(c_0) + \beta \int_S \cdots \\ \beta \int_S \left(u(c_{T-1}) + \beta \int_S u(c_T)\, \theta_{s_{T-1}}(ds_T) \right) \theta_{s_{T-2}}(ds_{T-1}) \cdots \theta_{s_0}(ds_1)\,.$$

Note that U is well defined for Case (i) and Case (ii) from the discussion in Sects. 7.4 and 7.5, respectively, because the dynamic aggregator W is now defined by $W(c, u) = u(c) + \beta u$.

Assume that there exists a "tree" in the economy. The "tree" bears "fruit" in each period, and the fruit will be divided among stockholders according to the share ownership of the tree. A *dividend process* is any element of $\prod_{t \geq 0} L(S^t, \mathbb{R}_{++})$ and is denoted by ${}_0\boldsymbol{d} = (d_0, d_1, d_2, \ldots)$. That is, ${}_0\boldsymbol{d}$ is a positive real-valued, $\langle \mathcal{B}_{S^t} \rangle_{t \geq 0}$-adapted stochastic process. (Recall that we set $L(S^0, \mathbb{R}_{++}) := \mathbb{R}_{++}$.) Here, we understand that $d_t \in L(S^t, \mathbb{R}_{++})$ is the amount of "fruit" at time t given to the agent when she owns the whole tree at that time.

A *price process* is any element of $\prod_{t\geq 0} L(S^t, \mathbb{R}_+)$ and is denoted by ${}_0\boldsymbol{q} = (q_0, q_1, q_2, \ldots)$. That is, ${}_0\boldsymbol{q}$ is a non-negative real-valued, $\langle \mathcal{B}_{S^t} \rangle_{t\geq 0}$-adapted stochastic process. Here, we understand that $q_t \in L(S^t, \mathbb{R}_+)$ is the price of the tree prevailing in the market at time t.

An *investment plan* is any element of $\prod_{t\geq 0} L(S^t, \mathbb{R}_+)$ and is denoted by ${}_1\boldsymbol{z} = (z_1, z_2, \ldots)$. That is, ${}_1\boldsymbol{z}$ is a non-negative real-valued, $\langle \mathcal{B}_{S^t} \rangle_{t\geq 0}$-adapted stochastic process. Here, we understand that $z_{t+1} \in L(S^t, \mathbb{R}_+)$ is the portion of the tree held by the agent at the beginning of period $t+1$ (and hence, it must be bought at time t).

Given a dividend process ${}_0\boldsymbol{d}$ and a price process ${}_0\boldsymbol{q}$, a pair of a consumption plan and an investment plan (henceforth, simply, a *plan*), $({}_0\boldsymbol{c},\ {}_1\boldsymbol{z})$, is *feasible from* an income $y > 0$ if $c_0 = y - q_0 z_1$ and $(\forall t \geq 1)\ c_t = (d_t + q_t)z_t - q_t z_{t+1}$. A plan $({}_0\boldsymbol{c},\ {}_1\boldsymbol{z})$ is *optimal* given $({}_0\boldsymbol{d},\ {}_0\boldsymbol{q})$, s and y if $({}_0\boldsymbol{c},\ {}_1\boldsymbol{z}) \in \arg\max\{ U_s({}_0\boldsymbol{c}) |\, ({}_0\boldsymbol{c},\ {}_1\boldsymbol{z})$ is feasible from y given $({}_0\boldsymbol{d},\ {}_0\boldsymbol{q})\}$.

Given an initial state s and a dividend process ${}_0\boldsymbol{d}$, a triplet, $({}_0\boldsymbol{c},\ {}_1\boldsymbol{z},\ {}_0\boldsymbol{q})$, is an *equilibrium* if $({}_0\boldsymbol{c},\ {}_1\boldsymbol{z})$ is optimal given $({}_0\boldsymbol{d},\ {}_0\boldsymbol{q})$, s and $y := d_0 + q_0$, and if $(\forall t \geq 1)\ z_t = 1$. In the first condition, setting y to be equal to $d_0 + q_0$ means that the agent holds the whole tree at the beginning.The second condition is the assumption of the *representative agent*, and it requires that the claim to the tree should equal its supply (that is, unity). As a result, all fruit in the economy is consumed by the single representative agent. A price process ${}_0\boldsymbol{q}$ is an *equilibrium price* if there exists a plan $({}_0\boldsymbol{c},\ {}_1\boldsymbol{z})$ with which $({}_0\boldsymbol{c},\ {}_1\boldsymbol{z},\ {}_0\boldsymbol{q})$ is an equilibrium.

A stochastic process ${}_0\boldsymbol{f} \in \prod_{t\geq 0} L(S^t, \mathbb{R}_+)$ is *Markovian* if $(\forall t \geq 1)(\exists f_t \in L(S, \mathbb{R}_+))(\forall\, {}_1s_t)\ f_t({}_1s_t) = f_t(s_t)$. A Markovian stochastic process ${}_0\boldsymbol{f} \in \prod_{t\geq 0} L(S^t, \mathbb{R}_+)$ is *stationary* if $(\exists f \in L(S, \mathbb{R}))(\forall t \geq 1)(\forall s_t)\ f_t(s_t) = f(s_t)$. We are, in particular, interested in the equilibrium price that is stationary.

8.3 Principle of Optimality

In this section, we invoke the dynamic programming techniques developed in Chap. 7.

To this end, we assume that the dividend process ${}_0\boldsymbol{d}$ is stationary and that $0 < \inf_s d_s \leq \sup_s d_s < +\infty$. Then, we characterize the optimal plan given such a dividend process and some stationary price process ${}_0\boldsymbol{q}$ as follows.

We first define the *value function* $J^* : S \times \mathbb{R}_+ \to \mathbb{R}_+$ by $J_s^*(y) := \max\{ U_s({}_0\boldsymbol{c}) |$ $({}_0\boldsymbol{c},\ {}_1\boldsymbol{z})$ is feasible from $y\}$. Note that the existence of the value function remains to be proven. If the value function exists, we define the *policy correspondence* $K^* : S \times \mathbb{R}_+ \twoheadrightarrow \mathbb{R}_+$ by

$$K_s^*(y) := \arg\max \left\{ u(y - q_s z') + \beta \int J_{s_+}^*((d_{s_+} + q_{s_+})z')\theta_s(ds_+) \,\middle|\, z' \geq 0 \text{ and } y - q_s z' \geq 0 \right\}.$$

Again, note that the existence of the policy correspondence remains to be proven even if the value function exists. A function $J : S \times \mathbb{R}_+ \to \bar{\mathbb{R}}_+$ *solves Bellman's equation* if $(\forall s)(\forall y)$

$$J_s(y) = \max \left\{ u(y - q_s z') + \beta \int J_{s_+}((d_{s_+} + q_{s_+})z')\theta_s(ds_+) \,\middle|\, z' \geq 0 \text{ and } y - q_s z' \geq 0 \right\}.$$

First, consider Case (i) and assume that there exists a real number $\varepsilon \in (0, 1]$ that satisfies $(\exists \kappa_1, \kappa_2 \in \mathbb{R}_+)(\forall c)\; u(c) \leq \kappa_1 + \kappa_2 c^{\varepsilon}$. Also, assume that the given price process ${}_0\boldsymbol{q}$ is such that both $\beta\lambda_g < 1$ and $(\forall k_1, k_2 \in \mathbb{R}_+)(\forall d < \lambda_g^{-1})(\forall y)\; \theta$ is upper quasi-continuous beneath

$$k_1 + k_2 \sum_{t=0}^{+\infty} d^t \left(\int_S \cdots \int_S \prod_{q=0}^{t} \left(d_{s_q} + q_{s_q}\right)^{\varepsilon} \theta'_{s_{t-1}}(ds_t) \cdots \theta'_s(ds_1) \right) y^{\varepsilon},$$

where

$$\lambda_g := \sup_s \overline{\lim_{t \to +\infty}} \left(\int_S \cdots \int_S \prod_{q=1}^{t} \left(d_{s_q} + q_{s_q}\right)^{\varepsilon} \theta'_{s_{t-1}}(ds_t) \cdots \theta'_s(ds_1) \right)^{1/t}.$$

Second, consider Case (ii) and assume that for any Polish space X, θ is upper semi-continuous on $S \times X$ beneath 0.

Then, for Case (i) and Case (ii), Theorems 7.4.1 and 7.5.1 show that J^* exists, that it is the unique solution to Bellman's equation, that K^* exists, and that recursive optimality implies optimality in the sense that $\arg\max\{U_s({}_0\boldsymbol{c}) \mid ({}_0\boldsymbol{c},\ {}_1\boldsymbol{z}) \text{ is feasible from } y\} \supseteq \{({}_0\boldsymbol{c},\ {}_1\boldsymbol{z}) \mid z_1 \in K_s^*(y),\ c_0 = y - q_0 z_1, (\forall t \geq 1)\ z_{t+1} \in K_{s_t}^*((d_{s_t} + q_{s_t})z_t) \text{ and } c_t = (d_{s_t} + q_{s_t})z_t - q_{s_t} z_{t+1}\}$. A "full-support condition" like the one in Epstein and Wang (1994) might allow "$\supseteq$" to be replaced by "=" (recursive optimality is implied by optimality). In general, however, this is not always the case even then because there might be an adapted optimal plan that may not be generated by measurable selections. See Stokey and Lucas (1989, p. 253).

8.4 The Euler Inequalities

In the first half of this section, we intuitively derive the Euler inequalities that the stationary equilibrium price should satisfy. The second half formally presents some theorems that characterize the stationary equilibrium price.

By the convexity of θ and hence by the sub-additivity of the Choquet integral (Proposition 2.4.4), the fact that J^* solves Bellman's equation implies that J^* is concave with respect to y. Therefore, the objective function defining the policy correspondence is *strictly concave* in z' under the current assumption that u is strictly concave. It then follows that the policy correspondence will be the policy *function* and the optimal investment (which we denote by z'^*) is uniquely determined. The first-order condition for z'^* to satisfy turns out to be: $(\forall s)(\forall y)$

$$\frac{d}{dz'_+}\left[u(y - q_s z'^*) + \beta \int J^*_{s_+}((d_{s_+} + q_{s_+})z'^*)\theta_s(ds_+)\right]$$
$$\leq 0 \leq \frac{d}{dz'_-}\left[u(y - q_s z'^*) + \beta \int J^*_{s_+}((d_{s_+} + q_{s_+})z'^*)\theta_s(ds_+)\right]$$

(see the proof of Theorem 4.3.1), and thus, we have: $(\forall s)(\forall y)$

$$\beta\frac{d}{dz'_+}\int J^*_{s_+}((d_{s_+} + q_{s_+})z'^*)\theta_s(ds_+)$$
$$\leq q_s u'(y - q_s z'^*) \leq \beta\frac{d}{dz'_-}\int J^*_{s_+}((d_{s_+} + q_{s_+})z'^*)\theta_s(ds_+)\,.$$

By the envelope theorem,[1] we know that J^* is differentiable with respect to y and that its derivative is given by $J^{*\prime}_s(y) = u'(y - q_s z'^*) = u'(c^*)$, where c^* is the optimal consumption level in the current period and the second equality is definitional. Because this relation must also hold true in the next period, it follows that $J^{*\prime}_{s_+}((d_{s_+} + q_{s_+})z'^*) = u'((d_{s_+} + q_{s_+})z'^* - q_{s_+}z''^*) = u'(c'^*)$, where z''^* is the investment level for the next period optimally chosen in the current period depending on both s_+ and $(d_{s_+} + q_{s_+})z'^*$, and c'^* is the optimal consumption level for the next period. Again, the second equality is definitional.

Now, we define the set $\mathcal{P}_s(z'^*)$ by

$$\mathcal{P}_s(z'^*) := \mathcal{P}(\theta_s, J^*_{s_+}((d_{s_+} + q_{s_+})z'^*))\,, \tag{8.1}$$

where $\mathcal{P}$ in the right-hand side is defined by (2.16) in Sect. 2.4. Then, by Theorem 4.2.2, it holds that $(\forall s)$

$$\frac{d}{dz'_+}\int J^*_{s_+}((d_{s_+} + q_{s_+})z'^*)\theta_s(ds_+)$$
$$= \min\left\{\int \frac{d}{dz'}J^*_{s_+}((d_{s_+} + q_{s_+})z'^*)P(ds_+)\,\middle|\, P \in \mathcal{P}_s(z'^*)\right\}$$
$$= \min\left\{\int J^{*\prime}_{s_+}((d_{s_+} + q_{s_+})z'^*)(d_{s_+} + q_{s_+})P(ds_+)\,\middle|\, P \in \mathcal{P}_s(z'^*)\right\}$$

---

[1] See, for example, Stokey and Lucas (1989, pp. 84-85). Note that the theorems there can be applied to the current situation under Knightian uncertainty.

$$= \min \left\{ \int u'(c'^*)(d_{s_+} + q_{s_+})P(ds_+) \,\middle|\, P \in \mathcal{P}_s(z'^*) \right\} .$$

Symmetrically, it holds that $(\forall s)$

$$\frac{d}{dz'_-} \int J^*_{s_+}((d_{s_+} + q_{s_+})z'^*)\theta_s(ds_+)$$
$$= \max \left\{ \int u'(c'^*)(d_{s_+} + q_{s_+})P(ds_+) \,\middle|\, P \in \mathcal{P}_s(z'^*) \right\} .$$

We have thus reached the *Euler inequalities* for the representative agent's utility-maximization problem: $(\forall s)$

$$\beta \min \left\{ \int u'(c'^*)(d_{s_+} + q_{s_+})P(ds_+) \,\middle|\, P \in \mathcal{P}_s(z'^*) \right\}$$
$$\leq q_s u'(c^*) \leq \beta \max \left\{ \int u'(c'^*)(d_{s_+} + q_{s_+})P(ds_+) \,\middle|\, P \in \mathcal{P}_s(z'^*) \right\} .$$

We now move to characterize the stationary equilibrium prices. First, we define the stochastic process $U^d \in \prod_{t \geq 0} L(S^t, \bar{\mathbb{R}})$, by $(\forall t)(\forall_0 s_t)\ U^d({}_0s_t) = U({}_t\boldsymbol{d}({}_1s_t))$, where ${}_t\boldsymbol{d}$ is the continuation of ${}_0\boldsymbol{d}$ after a realization of ${}_1s_t$. Then, it turns out that it is well defined (that is, it is $\langle \mathcal{B}_{S^t} \rangle_{t \geq 0}$-adapted) by the way of defining the utility function, mainly owing to the Fubini property (Theorem 2.5.1). Furthermore, U^d *is* stationary because the dividend process ${}_0\boldsymbol{d}$ is assumed to be stationary.

Note that at any equilibrium of the economy, it must be true that $(\forall t \geq 0)\ z_t = 1$ because the total supply of the "tree" is unity and only the representative agent demands the "tree,"and hence it must be true that $(\forall t \geq 0)\ c^*_t = d_t$. This means that at any equilibrium, it must be optimal for the representative consumer to consume all of her dividend in each period, and hence, it holds true that $(\forall t \geq 1)(\forall s_t)\ J^*_{s_t}(d_{s_t} + q_{s_t}) = U_{s_t}({}_t\boldsymbol{d}) = U^d_{s_t}$. Therefore, in turn, at any equilibrium, it must be true that $\mathcal{P}_s(z'^*) = \mathcal{P}_s(1) = \mathcal{P}(\theta_s, J^*_{s_+}(d_{s_+} + q_{s_+})) = \mathcal{P}(\theta_s, U^d)$, where $\mathcal{P}_s$ is defined above by (8.1).

Given all these, we have finally arrived at the *Euler inequalities*: $(\forall s)$

$$\beta \min \left\{ \int u'(d_{s_+})(d_{s_+} + q_{s_+})P(ds_+) \,\middle|\, P \in \mathcal{P}(\theta_s, U^d) \right\} \leq q_s u'(d_s)$$
$$\leq \beta \max \left\{ \int u'(d_{s_+})(d_{s_+} + q_{s_+})\, P(ds_+) \,\middle|\, P \in \mathcal{P}(\theta_s, U^d) \right\} . \qquad (8.2)$$

A formal characterization of the stationary equilibrium prices is provided by the following theorem.

Theorem 8.4.1 *Case (i): Suppose that a stationary price process q satisfies the conditions described in the previous subsection for Case (i). Then, q is an equilibrium stationary price if and only if it satisfies the Euler inequalities (8.2). Case (ii): The set of stationary equilibrium prices coincides with the set of q that satisfies the Euler inequalities (8.2).*

Epstein and Wang (1994) proved that there exists a stationary equilibrium price that is bounded over the state space. Because we (and they) assume that the dividend d is bounded above and bounded away from zero, any stationary price that satisfies the Euler inequalities (8.2) and that is bounded *is* an equilibrium price because the conditions described in the previous subsection for Case (i) are satisfied. Note, however, that there could be a stationary price that satisfies (8.2), but at the same time *fails* to be an equilibrium price. This is because there might be a price that satisfies (8.2), under which the representative consumer fails to solve the maximization problem because the conditions in the previous subsection for Case (i) are not satisfied.

The proof of Theorem 8.4.1 can be accomplished by combining Theorems 7.4.1 and 7.5.1with the proof by Epstein and Wang (1994) that employ a squeezing argument. Note, however, that Theorem 8.4.1 is more general than the original theorem of Epstein and Wang (1994) because they assume that all relevant distributions have compact supports, while we do not. We omit the full detail of the proof.

When θ is a stochastic kernel (θ_s is additive and a probability measure for each s assuming that θ is continuous), $\mathcal{P}_s$ is a singleton and the Euler inequalities are reduced to the *Euler equation* (see Lucas 1978):

$$q_s u'(d_s) = \beta \int u'(d_{s_+})(d_{s_+} + q_{s_+})\, \theta_s(ds_+) .$$

Note that the bounded stationary equilibrium price in this case is unique under the boundedness assumption on d.

Theorem 8.4.1 and the intermediate-value theorem immediately imply the next corollary.[2]

Corollary 8.4.1 *Case (i): Suppose that a stationary price process q satisfies the conditions described in the previous subsection for Case (i). Then, q is an equilibrium stationary price if and only if for any $s \in S$, there exists $Q \in \mathcal{P}_s$ such that*

$$q_s u'(d_s) = \beta \int u'(d_{s_+})(d_{s_+} + q_{s_+})\, Q_s(ds_+) . \tag{8.3}$$

Case (ii): A stationary price is an equilibrium price if and only if for any $s \in S$, there exists $Q \in \mathcal{P}_s$ such that (8.3) holds.

[2] By the same reason used above, our corollary is more general than the counterpart of Epstein and Wang (1994).

8.5 In/determinacy of Equilibrium Prices

8.5.1 *Uniqueness of Equilibrium Prices*

We show in this subsection that equilibrium prices are determinate and unique for some situations.

Suppose that $u'(d)(d+q)$ is U^d*-measurable* (Sect. 2.4.3). Then, Theorem 2.4.2 implies that the Euler inequality is reduced to the Euler equality. Because the bounded solution to the Euler equation is unique (see Lucas 1978), the bounded equilibrium price in Epstein and Wang's model is also unique.

Next, suppose that (a) $u'(d)d$ is U^d*-ordered* (Sect. 2.4.3) and that (b) if v is U^d-ordered, then the mapping defined by

$$s \mapsto \int_S v(s')\,\theta_s(ds')$$

is also U^d-ordered. Then, $u'(d)(d+q)$ is U^d-ordered as far as q is bounded and $\beta \in (0,1)$ because $(\forall s)$

$$\begin{aligned}
u'(d_s)(d_s+q_s) \;&=\; u'(d_s)d_s + \beta \int u'(d_{s_1})(d_{s_1}+q_{s_1})\, Q_s^1(ds_1) \\
&= u'(d_s)d_s + \beta \int u'(d_{s_1})d_{s_1}\, Q_s^1(ds_1) + \beta \int u'(d_{s_1})q_{s_1}\, Q_s^1(ds_1) \\
&= u'(d_s)d_s + \beta \int u'(d_{s_1})d_{s_1}\, \theta_s(ds_1) \\
&\quad + \beta \int \beta \int u'(d_{s_2})(d_{s_2}+q_{s_2})\, Q_{s_1}^2(ds_2)\, Q_s^1(ds_1) \\
&= u'(d_s)d_s + \beta \int u'(d_{s_1})d_{s_1}\, \theta_s(ds_1) \\
&\quad + \beta^2 \int\int u'(d_{s_2})d_{s_2}\, Q_{s_1}^2(ds_2)\, Q_s^1(ds_1) \\
&\quad + \beta^2 \int\int u'(d_{s_2})q_{s_2}\, Q_{s_1}^2(ds_2)\, Q_s^1(ds_1) \\
&= u'(d_s)d_s + \beta \int u'(d_{s_1})d_{s_1}\, \theta_s(ds_1) \\
&\quad + \beta^2 \int\int u'(d_{s_2})d_{s_2}\, \theta_{s_1}(ds_2)\, \theta_s(ds_1) \\
&\quad + \beta^2 \int\int u'(d_{s_2})q_{s_2}\, Q_{s_1}^2(ds_2)\, Q_s^1(ds_1) \\
&= \cdots \\
&= u'(d_s)d_s + \beta \int u'(d_{s_1})d_{s_1}\, \theta_s(ds_1)
\end{aligned}$$

$$+\beta^2 \int \int u'(d_{s_2}) d_{s_2}\, \theta_{s_1}(ds_2)\, \theta_s(ds_1) + \cdots .$$

Here, Q^1 is a probability measure in $\mathcal{P}_s$ whose existence is guaranteed by Corollary 8.4.1, and the first equality holds by the same corollary. In the third equality, the replacement of the second term is justified by assumptions (a) and (b) and by the latter half of Theorem 2.4.2. For the replacement of the third term, we invoke Corollary 8.4.1 again. In the fifth equality, the replacement of the third term is justified by the iterated use of the assumptions (a) and (b) and the latter half of Theorem 2.4.2. Repeating these procedures leads to the last equality because we are assuming that d and q are bounded and that $\beta \in (0, 1)$. The far right-hand side is U^d-ordered because each term appearing there is U^d-ordered, which verifies the claim. Therefore, under assumptions (a) and (b), the bounded stationary equilibrium price is unique from the discussion in the previous paragraph.

Note that when the state space S is an ordered set (say, an interval in $\mathbb{R}$), assumption (b) is a *stochastic nondecrease* (Sect. 2.5). This is a convenient assumption and we use it in Chap. 11 to find a closed-form solution for some dynamic economic model with Knightian uncertainty.

Another situation where indeterminacy does not arise is where the capacitary kernel does not depend on the current state (when it is actually not a kernel). If this is the case, by Koopmans' equation (U3 of Sect. 7.2.5), it holds that

$$(\forall s) \quad U_s^d = u(d_s) + \beta \int U_{s_+}^d\, \theta(ds_+) ,$$

and hence, d is U^d-ordered because u is nondecreasing by the assumption. Furthermore, if $u'(d)d$ is nondecreasing in d, then it is d-ordered, and hence, it is U^d-ordered. In summary, if θ is independent of s and if $u'(d)d$ is nondecreasing in d, assumptions (a) and (b) in the third paragraph of this subsection are satisfied. (Note that (b) is automatic because any constant can be ordered by any function.) For instance, if θ is independent of s and u is given by $u(c) = c^{1-\rho}/(1-\rho)$ with $\rho \in (0, 1)$, then the bounded stationary equilibrium price is unique in Epstein and Wang's (1994) model.

8.5.2 *Finite State Space*

This subsection discusses indeterminacy of equilibrium prices in Epstein and Wang's (1994) model with a finite state space. First, assume that $S = \{1, 2\}$. Without loss of generality, let $U_1^d > U_2^d$. Then, it is obvious that any function, including $u'(d)(d+q)$, is U^d-measurable, implying no indeterminacy arises by the observation made in the previous subsection. Therefore, for indeterminacy to arise, it is necessary that $U_1^d = U_2^d$. In such a case, however, Koopmans' equation in the previous subsection implies that $d_1 = d_2$ regardless of whether θ depends on s. Thus, the stationary equilibrium price is determinate by $\beta d/(1-\beta)$ as far as $\beta \in (0, 1)$ and no indeterminacy can arise.

Next, assume that the cardinality of the state space is more than two. Then, we can construct a Lucas–Epstein–Wang economy where indeterminacy arises as the following example shows.

Example 8.5.1 Let $S := \{1, 2, 3\}$ and let $d := \left(\frac{13-2\sqrt{22}}{8}, \frac{11-\sqrt{57}}{6}, \frac{29-\sqrt{165}}{6}\right)$. Here, $d_1 < d_2 < d_3$. Let $(\forall c)\ u(c) := c + c^{1/2}$ and let $\beta := 1/2$. To define a capacitary kernel θ, let P be a Markov chain defined by

$$P := \begin{bmatrix} \frac{1}{4} & \frac{1}{4} & \frac{1}{2} \\ \frac{1}{3} & \frac{1}{3} & \frac{1}{3} \\ \frac{1}{3} & \frac{1}{3} & \frac{1}{3} \end{bmatrix}.$$

Then, we define θ by $(\forall s)(\forall A \subseteq S)\ \theta_s(A) := P_s^2(A) = (P_s(A))^2$. For example, $\theta_1(\{2, 3\}) = (1/4 + 1/2)^2 = 9/16$.

Note that $(u(d_1), u(d_2), u(d_3)) = (9/8, 4/3, 13/3)$. The vector U^d is determined as the solution to the Koopmans' equation:

$$(\forall s) \quad U_s^d = u(d_s) + \frac{1}{2}\int U_{s_+}^d\, P_s^2(ds_+)\,.$$

To solve this system of linear equations, we estimate that $U_1^d = U_2^d < U_3^d$. Then the above system turns out to be

$$\begin{cases} U_1^d = \frac{9}{8} + \frac{1}{2}\left(\frac{3}{4}U_1^d + \frac{1}{4}U_3^d\right) \\ U_1^d = \frac{4}{3} + \frac{1}{2}\left(\frac{8}{9}U_1^d + \frac{1}{9}U_3^d\right) \\ U_3^d = \frac{13}{3} + \frac{1}{2}\left(\frac{8}{9}U_1^d + \frac{1}{9}U_3^d\right). \end{cases}$$

By solving this system, we obtain $\left(U_1^d, U_2^d, U_3^d\right) = (3, 3, 6)$. This verifies the estimate and hence it is certainly the U^d in this model.

Note that the dividend d is *not* U^d-ordered and there exist uncountably many stationary equilibrium prices in this model. Two examples of such prices are $(q_1, q_2, q_3) = (0.812907, 0.747157, 0.950250)$ and $(q_1, q_2, q_3) = (0.817222, 0.751834, 0.956197)$, each of which corresponds to each of following selections of $\mathcal{P}(\theta_s, U^d)$:

$$\begin{bmatrix} \frac{1}{16} & \frac{11}{16} & \frac{1}{4} \\ \frac{1}{9} & \frac{7}{9} & \frac{1}{9} \\ \frac{1}{9} & \frac{7}{9} & \frac{1}{9} \end{bmatrix}, \begin{bmatrix} \frac{11}{16} & \frac{1}{16} & \frac{1}{4} \\ \frac{7}{9} & \frac{1}{9} & \frac{1}{9} \\ \frac{7}{9} & \frac{1}{9} & \frac{1}{9} \end{bmatrix}.$$

■

On one hand, Example 8.5.1 shows that indeterminacy may arise if the cardinality of the state space is more than two. On the other hand, however, it is easy to see that the indeterminacy in Example 8.5.1 is not "robust" in the sense that if we perturb the dividend scheme just slightly, the indeterminacy immediately disappears. In fact, this is a remarkable feature of Epstein and Wang's model with a finite state space, to which we will return at the end of the next section.

8.6 Economy with Endowments

If we introduce an endowment process into the model, the indeterminacy of equilibrium prices shows up more easily. This subsection takes a look at such a mechanism.

8.6.1 Endowment Process

An *endowment process* is an element of $\prod_{t\geq 0} L(S^t, \mathbb{R}_+)$ and is denoted by ${}_0\boldsymbol{\omega} = (\omega_0, \omega_1, \ldots)$. That is, ${}_0\boldsymbol{\omega}$ is a non-negative real-valued $\langle \mathcal{B}_{S^t} \rangle_{t\geq 0}$-adapted stochastic process. Here, $\omega_t \in L(S^t, \mathbb{R}_+)$ is understood to be consumption goods available at time t to the representative agent (that falls from the sky apart from the "fruit.") Henceforth, we assume that the endowment process is stationary as in the dividend process d and that $\sup_s \omega_s < +\infty$.

8.6.2 Feasible Plans and Optimal Plans

Except for the addition of an endowment process, the model in this subsection is the same as that of Sect. 8.2. Given a dividend process ${}_0\boldsymbol{d}$, an endowment process ${}_0\boldsymbol{\omega}$, and a price process ${}_0\boldsymbol{q}$, a pair of adapted stochastic processes, $({}_0\boldsymbol{c},\ {}_1\boldsymbol{z})$, is a *feasible plan from* an income $y > 0$ if $c_0 = y - q_0 z_1$ and $(\forall t \geq 1)\ c_t = (d_t + q_t)z_t + \omega_t - q_t z_{t+1}$.[3] A plan $({}_0\boldsymbol{c},\ {}_1\boldsymbol{z})$ is *optimal* given $({}_0\boldsymbol{d},\ {}_0\boldsymbol{\omega},\ {}_0\boldsymbol{q})$, s and y if $({}_0\boldsymbol{c},\ {}_1\boldsymbol{z}) \in \arg\max\{U_s({}_0\boldsymbol{c}) | ({}_0\boldsymbol{c},\ {}_1\boldsymbol{z})$ is feasible from y given $({}_0\boldsymbol{d},\ {}_0\boldsymbol{\omega},\ {}_0\boldsymbol{q})\}$. Given an initial state s, a stationary dividend process ${}_0\boldsymbol{d}$ and a stationary endowment process ${}_0\boldsymbol{\omega}$, $({}_0\boldsymbol{c},\ {}_1\boldsymbol{z},\ {}_0\boldsymbol{q})$ is an *equilibrium* if $({}_0\boldsymbol{c},\ {}_1\boldsymbol{z})$ is optimal given $({}_0\boldsymbol{d},\ {}_0\boldsymbol{\omega},\ {}_0\boldsymbol{q})$, s and $y =$

[3]Consider the following normalization. Let $\hat{z}_t$ denote the volume of a net trade from a position in which the agent holds the whole "tree." That is, let $\hat{z}_t := z_t - 1$. Then, the feasibility constraint in the main text will be $c_t = (d_t + q_t)\hat{z}_t + d_t + \omega_t - q_t\hat{z}_{t+1} = (d_t + q_t)\hat{z}_t + \hat{\omega}_t - q_t\hat{z}_{t+1}$, where $\hat{\omega}_t := d_t + \omega_t$. This constraint turns out to be equivalent to that of Epstein and Wang (1994, p.297). Furthermore, the feasibility constraint in Sect. 9.2 à la Lucas is a special case of that of Epstein and Wang (1994) where $\hat{\omega}_t = d_t$, i.e., $\omega_t = 0$. If we rewrite the feasibility constraint according to Epstein and Wang (1994), it holds that $\hat{z}_t = 0$ at any equilibrium, which corresponds to an emergence of "inertia" of trades in Dow and Werlang's (1992) model. This strongly suggests that the model in this chapter is a dynamic extension of that of Dow and Werlang (1992). Also, while we assume that $z_t \geq 0$ in this chapter, this assumption can be weakened to the assumption on the lower bound of short sales à la Epstein and Wang (1994).

$d_0 + \omega_0 + q_0$, and if $(\forall t \geq 1)\ z_t = 1$. At any equilibrium, it holds by definition that $(\forall t \geq 0)\ (c_t, z_{t+1}) = (d_t + \omega_t, 1)$. This means that the representative agent owns the whole "tree" and consumes all "fruit" and endowments falling from the sky.

8.6.3 *The Euler Inequalities and Partial Aggregate Shocks*

By almost the same procedure as in Sect. 8.4, we obtain the Euler inequalities that characterize the stationary equilibrium prices as follows: $(\forall s)$

$$\beta \min \left\{ \int u'(d_{s_+} + \omega_{s_+})(d_{s_+} + q_{s_+}) P(ds_+) \,\middle|\, P \in \mathcal{P}(\theta_s, U^{d+\omega}) \right\}$$
$$\leq q_s u'(d_s + \omega_s)$$
$$\leq \beta \max \left\{ \int u'(d_{s_+} + \omega_{s_+})(d_{s_+} + q_{s_+}) P(ds_+) \,\middle|\, P \in \mathcal{P}(\theta_s, U^{d+\omega}) \right\},$$

where $(\forall s)\ U_s^{d+\omega} := U_s({}_1\boldsymbol{d}(s) + {}_1\boldsymbol{\omega}(s))$.

To see that the indeterminacy of equilibria shows up more easily than when there exists no endowment process, we first consider the extreme case in which no aggregate shocks exist. That is, we assume that $(\forall s, t \in S)\ d_s + \omega_s = d_t + \omega_t$. In this case, the total amount of consumption goods available to the representative consumer does not vary at all across states of the world.

Then, we observe that

$$\begin{aligned}
&\min \left\{ \int u'(d_{s_+} + \omega_{s_+})(d_{s_+} + q_{s_+}) P(ds_+) \,\middle|\, P \in \mathcal{P}(\theta_s, U^{d+\omega}) \right\} \\
&= \min \left\{ \int u'(d_{s_+} + \omega_{s_+})(d_{s_+} + q_{s_+}) P(ds_+) \,\middle|\, P \in \mathrm{core}(\theta_s) \right\} \\
&= \int u'(d_{s_+} + \omega_{s_+})(d_{s_+} + q_{s_+})\, \theta_s(ds_+) \\
&= u'(d + \omega) \int (d_{s_+} + q_{s_+})\, \theta_s(ds_+),
\end{aligned}$$

where the first equality holds because $U^{d+\omega}$ is constant by the assumption of no aggregate shock; the second equality holds by the fundamental theorem of the Choquet integral; and the third equality also holds by the assumption of no aggregate shock.

Symmetrically, we observe that

$$\max \left\{ \int u'(d_{s_+} + \omega_{s_+})(d_{s_+} + q_{s_+}) P(ds_+) \,\middle|\, P \in \mathcal{P}(\theta_s, U^{d+\omega}) \right\}$$

$$= \max \left\{ \int u'(d_{s_+} + \omega_{s_+})(d_{s_+} + q_{s_+}) P(ds_+) \,\middle|\, P \in \mathrm{core}(\theta_s) \right\}$$

$$= \int u'(d_{s_+} + \omega_{s_+})(d_{s_+} + q_{s_+})\, \theta'_s(ds_+)$$

$$- u'(d + \omega) \int (d_{s_+} + q_{s_+})\, \theta'_s(ds_+) \,.$$

As a result, the Euler inequalities in this case will become the next simple inequalities:

$$(\forall s) \quad \beta \int (d_{s_+} + q_{s_+})\, \theta_s(ds_+) \leq q_s \leq \beta \int (d_{s_+} + q_{s_+})\, \theta'_s(ds_+) \,,$$

from which we easily find that any arbitrary constant $q \in \mathbb{R}_+$ *is* a stationary equilibrium price if it satisfies

$$(\forall s) \quad \frac{\beta}{1-\beta} \int d_{s_+} \theta_s(ds_+) \leq q \leq \frac{\beta}{1-\beta} \int d_{s_+} \theta'_s(ds_+) \,. \tag{8.4}$$

Here, the left integral is typically strictly smaller that the right integral because θ is convex and the right integral is defined by its conjugate (recall Corollary 2.4.1, for instance).

By these analyses, we may conclude at least four important facts. First, the Euler inequalities (8.4) are essentially the *same* as the bid-ask spread by Dow and Werlang (1992). This shows that any price is an equilibrium if it is between the "worst" expected discounted present value of the dividend stream obtained by holding an asset and the "best" expected discounted present value of that dividend stream. As Footnote 3 suggests, the equilibrium price is the very price at which no net trade would take place. This is nothing other than the inertia of Dow and Werlang (1992). We thus conclude that Epstein and Wang's (1994) model and Dow and Werlang's (1992) model are basically the same except for whether it is static or dynamic *as far as* there exists no aggregate shock. (Recall that in Dow and Werlang, the agent does not face any uncertainty at the current position.)

Second, consider a *partial* aggregate shock. That is, assume that there exists a proper subset S' of S such that $(\forall s, t \in S')\ d_s + \omega_s = d_t + \omega_t$. The calculation of this subsection shows that there will still be indeterminacy of equilibrium prices in this case. This is a noticeable difference between the two models. Unless the aggregate amount of consumption goods available to the representative agent changes across the states, indeterminacy may arise. Epstein and Wang (1994) showed this fact in a truly dynamic model. It is important, however, to note that in their model the structure of aggregate shock in the economy does not vary over time.

Third, assume that the state space is *finite*. Then, the economy can be embedded into the finite-dimensional Euclidean space. (An economy can be represented as a point in such a space by its dividend and endowment profile.) Then, the set of economies such that the total amount of consumption goods are the same between at least two distinct states has at most zero Lebesgue measure. That is, if such an economy was slightly perturbed, indeterminacy would vanish. In other words, indeterminacy in Epstein and Wang's model with a finite state space is not *robust*. To generate a robust indeterminacy in an economy with a finite state space, we need a mechanism like that used in Chap. 6.

Fourth and finally, indeterminacy shown in Epstein and Wang's model is only about equilibrium prices. They show that there could be many prices that support the unique allocation as the equilibrium allocation, where the representative agent consumes everything. To generate *real* indeterminacy, a similar treatment to that used in Chap. 6 would be required.

References

Dana, R.-A. 2004. Ambiguity, uncertainty aversion and equilibrium welfare. *Economic Theory* 23: 569–587.

Dow, J., and S.R.C. Werlang. 1992. Uncertainty aversion, risk aversion, and the optimal choice of portfolio. *Econometrica* 60: 197–204.

Epstein, L.G., and T. Wang. 1994. Intertemporal asset pricing under Knightian uncertainty. *Econometrica* 62: 283–322.

Epstein, L.G., and T. Wang. 1995. Uncertainty, risk-neutral measures and security price booms and crashes. *Journal of Economic Theory* 67: 40–82.

Lucas Jr., R.E. 1978. Asset prices in an exchange economy. *Econometrica* 46: 1429–1445.

Stokey, N. L., & Lucas, R. E. Jr. (1989). Recursive methods in economic dynamics. Cambridge: Harvard University Press.

Chapter 9
Search and Knightian Uncertainty

9.1 Introduction and Summary

Consider an unemployed worker who is searching for a job. Suppose that "uncertainty" about labor market conditions has increased. Does this change induce her to search longer and more intensively, or shorter and less intensively? The answer to this question has utmost importance both in macroeconomics concerning the aggregate unemployment rate and microeconomics explaining worker behavior. The purpose of this chapter is to show that the answer is drastically different depending on the kind of "uncertainty" involved. If an increase in "uncertainty" is an increase in the variance of the wage offer distribution that the worker thinks she faces, the worker searches for a longer time. If an increase in "uncertainty" is a decrease in her confidence about the wage distribution, the worker searches for a shorter time.

This chapter applies the idea of Knightian uncertainty to the job search model, and compares the effect of its increase on the worker's search behavior with that of an increase in risk. To this end, we extend the stylized model of job search without recall (see, for example, Sargent 1987, p. 66) by assuming that the unemployed worker's preference is modeled by the intersection of the CEU and the MEU models. In effect, this is a model that is represented by the CEU with a convex probability capacity. Because we focus on the role of Knightian uncertainty, we assume the time-consistent intertemporal structure in the worker's preference over time. A time-consistent extension of the atemporal MEU model to a dynamic setting was axiomatized by Epstein and Schneider (2003),[1] and thus the preference we consider is based upon a sound behavioral foundation. Under these settings, we show that the

[1]See Klibanoff (1995) and Wang (2003) for alternative axiomatizations. Also see Sect. 3.13 of this book.

K.G. Nishimura and H. Ozaki, *Economics of Pessimism and Optimism*,
DOI 10.1007/978-4-431-55903-0_9

optimal stopping rule exists, that this optimal stopping rule has a reservation property, and that the reservation wage is characterized by a functional equation, namely, *Bellman's equation*.[2]

Then, we exploit the functional equation determining the reservation wage to examine the effect of an increase in Knightian uncertainty. In the traditional framework where uncertainty is specified by a single probability distribution, an increase in uncertainty (an increase in *risk*) is modeled by a mean-preserving spread of the given distribution. Then, it turns out that the mean-preserving spread, that is, an increase in risk, causes an increase in the reservation wage (see Rothschild and Stiglitz 1970, 1971); Kohn and Shavell 1974; or Sect. 9.2.1 of this chapter). Thus, the unemployed worker is inclined to keep searching for a job when risk has increased. In contrast, we formulate Knightian uncertainty in such a way that the worker does not have confidence that a given wage distribution is the true one, and that instead she assumes a set of probability distributions and maximizes the minimum of expected utilities based on each probability distribution. We then show that the reservation wage is *decreased* when Knightian uncertainty increases, and hence, the worker tends to accept the job offer more quickly. This result confirms our intuition that, when people lose confidence in their forecast about what happens in the future, they generally prefer certainty to uncertainty. An immediate acceptance of the wage offer implies that the uncertainty is turned into certainty.

This chapter is based on Nishimura and Ozaki (2004). For development of optimal stopping theories with Knightian uncertainty after this paper was published in similar discrete-time settings, see Riedel (2009) and Miao and Wang (2011).

The organization of the chapter is as follows. Section 9.2 explains the main result of this chapter by using a simple example based on the uniform distribution of the wage offer. Technical discussions are kept to a minimum in this section. Section 9.3 bridges nontechnical Sect. 9.2 and technical Sect. 9.4 in explaining the maxmin expected utility, Choquet expected utility, and some continuity problems that must be solved. Section 9.4 presents the main result in a general framework. This section also explains how the result of Sect. 9.2 is derived from the general framework.

9.2 An Example: Risk Versus Knightian Uncertainty

Let us first consider a simple job search model (for example, see a stylized example in Sargent 1987, p. 66). In each period, an unemployed worker draws a wage offer from a wage distribution F_0.[3] *The worker is assumed to know the true distribution*

[2]Klibanoff (1995) uses a similar objective function to show that in an optimal search model with learning, an uncertainty-averse agent's optimal stopping rule has a reservation property. He considers a specific learning procedure of the agent, a finite horizon, and a finite support of a wage distribution, and does not provide any comparative static result. In contrast, we are concerned with an infinite horizon, general distribution functions, and comparative statics examining the effect of uncertainty on the reservation wage.

[3]$F_0(x)$ denotes the probability that the wage offer is no greater than x.

F_0. If the unemployed worker accepts the offer, he earns that wage from this period onward. If he declines the offer, he gets unemployment compensation, $c > 0$, in this period[4] and will make a draw again in the next period. Let T denote the period that the worker accepts the wage offer. The unemployed worker's objective is, by choosing a suitable stopping rule, to maximize his expected lifetime income

$$E_0 \sum_{t=0}^{\infty} \beta^t y_t$$

where

$$y_t = \begin{cases} c & \text{for } t < T \\ w_T & \text{for } t \geq T \end{cases}$$

Under general conditions on F_0, (1) there exists the optimal stopping rule and (2) the stopping rule has a reservation property. That is, the optimal stopping rule is to accept the wage offer if it is no smaller than the reservation wage R and to wait for another offer if otherwise, where the reservation wage R is determined by a choice between accepting this period's offer or waiting for next period's offer[5]:

$$R = c + \frac{\beta}{1-\beta} \int_R^{\infty} (1 - F_0(x))\, dx\,. \tag{9.1}$$

To make our analysis as simple as possible, we further specify the wage distribution to be a uniform distribution over $[a, b]$ where $0 < a < b$. However, it should be noted that the result obtained in this section does not depend on this particular distributional assumption but it holds true for general distributions. The uniform-distribution assumption greatly reduces complexity and allows us to obtain an explicit solution of the reservation wage. We further assume that $b > c$ because otherwise continuing the search forever would be trivially optimal, and we assume that the parameters of the model satisfy the following conditions:

$$b - a > \beta(2c - a - b) \tag{9.2}$$

$$\text{and} \quad 2(c - a) > \beta(2c - a - b) \tag{9.3}$$

to assure that $R \in (a, b)$ holds. Then by (9.1), we have

$$R = c + \frac{\beta}{1-\beta} \int_R^b \frac{b-x}{b-a}\, dx = c + \frac{\beta(b-R)^2}{2(1-\beta)(b-a)}\,. \tag{9.4}$$

[4]The basic structure of the model is unchanged if instead we assume that the unemployed worker pays a search cost, rather than receiving unemployment compensation. In the case of the search cost, we have $c < 0$.

[5]Equation (9.1) is easily derived from Corollary 9.4.2 as a special case.

By solving this quadratic equation, we get[6]

$$R = \frac{1}{\beta}\left(b - (1-\beta)a - D^{1/2}\right) \tag{9.5}$$

where $D := (1-\beta)(b-a)\,(b-a-\beta(2c-a-b))$.

9.2.1 Increased Risk: Mean-Preserving Spread

Suppose that "uncertainty"over wage offers is slightly increased for the worker. In the above example, the wage distribution may be slightly more dispersed by γ, over $[a-\gamma, b+\gamma]$.

See Fig. 9.1, where F_0 (the dotted line) is the probability distribution function of the uniform distribution over $[a, b]$ and the solid line is a new uniform distribution over $[a-\gamma, b+\gamma]$. This is a mean-preserving spread, characterizing *increased risk* (see Rothschild and Stiglitz 1970). If this is the case, (9.4) is modified to

$$R = c + \frac{\beta(b+\gamma-R)^2}{2(1-\beta)(b-a+2\gamma)}. \tag{9.6}$$

We denote the solution R to this equation by $R(\gamma)$ as a function of γ. Then, the implicit function theorem shows that

$$\left.\frac{dR(\gamma)}{d\gamma}\right|_{\gamma=0} = \frac{\beta(b-R)(R-a)}{(b-a)[(1-\beta)(b-a)+\beta(b-R)]},$$

where R in the right-hand side is given by (9.5). Because $a < R < b$ by (9.2) and (9.3), $dR(\gamma)/d\gamma|_{\gamma=0} > 0$. This result shows that increased "uncertainty" in the form of increasing risk (a mean-preserving spread) increases the reservation wage.[7]

---

[6]Let us conjecture that $R \in (a, b)$ to derive (9.4) from (9.1). We then verify that the reservation wage R thus derived in (9.5) certainly satisfies this condition under (9.2) and (9.3). First, note that $D > 0$ by $b > a$ and by (9.2). Second, note that the conjugate solution to the quadratic equation (9.4), $\bar{R} := (1/\beta)\left(b-(1-\beta)a + D^{1/2}\right)$, violates the condition because $\bar{R} > b$ by $D > 0$ and by the fact that $(1/\beta)(b-(1-\beta)a) > b$, which is equivalent to $(1-\beta)(b-a) > 0$. Third, note that we have $R < b$ because we get $R < b$ if and only if $b > c$, which holds under our assumption. Finally, note that $R > a$ because $R > a$ if and only if $2(c-a) > \beta(2c-a-b)$, which holds because we have (9.3). The conjecture is thus verified.

[7]This remains true even when the assumption of the uniform distribution is relaxed. Let $\langle F_r \rangle_{r\in X}$ ($X \subseteq \mathbb{R}$) be an indexed family of distributions whose supports are contained by a single compact set and let $R(r)$ be the reservation wage characterized by (9.1) with F_0 replaced by F_r. In the example in the text, we set $r = \gamma$ and assume that F_γ is the uniform distribution with the support $[a-\gamma, b+\gamma]$. Here, F_r need not be a uniform distribution. Then, in this more general setting, it holds that, if $F_{r'}$ is obtained by applying a mean-preserving spread to F_r, $R(r')$ is no less than $R(r)$ (Kohn and Shavell 1974, p. 115, Corollary 20; Sargent 1987, pp. 63–70). The claim

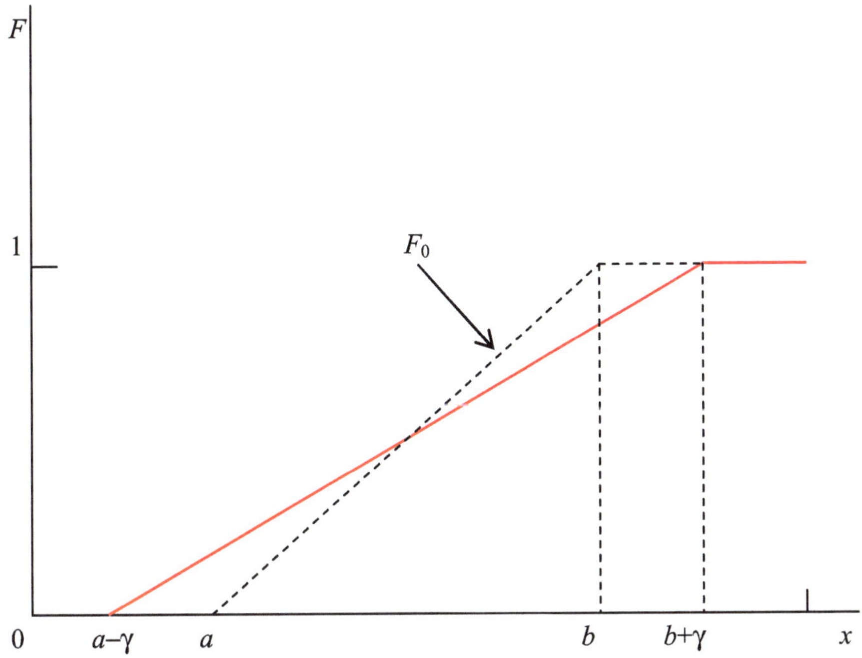

Fig. 9.1 The mean-preserving spread

9.2.2 Increased Knightian Uncertainty: ε-Contamination

In the case of the mean-preserving spread, the worker is still certain of the shape of the wage distribution. It is a uniform distribution $[a - \gamma, b + \gamma]$, spreading the original distribution by exactly γ. The worker has firm confidence about the new wage distribution.

In reality, however, the worker may not have such firm confidence in the wage distribution when economic conditions are changed. The worker may become uncertain about the shape of the wage distribution itself. The wage distribution may be different from the uniform distribution over $[a, b]$ with a positive (though small) probability. Moreover, the worker may have no idea about the shape of the wage distribution if in fact it is different. It may still be uniform and spreading out by γ ($[a - \gamma, b + \gamma]$), but the worker does not have any confidence about the value of γ. It may be wildly different from a uniform distribution. This "uncertainty" that the worker faces clearly cannot be reduced to a change in parameters of known distribution. Thus, the "uncertainty" here is Knightian uncertainty.

(Footnote 7 continued)
made in the text is thus a special case of this more general result. Also, Bikhchandani and Sharma (1996) show that basically the same result holds in an optimal search model with learning where the searcher updates her prior according to Bayes' rule based upon observations.

The problem that the worker faces is similar to that of a Bayesian statistician who confronts "uncertainty" in a prior distribution of the Bayesian learning process. One procedure that the Bayesian statistician often follows is to introduce a set of priors obtained by "contaminating" a single hypothetical prior and then investigating the robustness of the learning process. This procedure is often called *ε-contamination*.[8] We follow this Bayesian tradition in formulating Knightian uncertainty by "contaminating" the original wage distribution.

We formulate the worker's problem in three steps. First, following the ε-contamination literature, we specify the uncertainty that the worker faces by a *set* of distributions, rather than by a single distribution in the traditional framework. Second, we postulate an appropriate optimal search problem of the worker facing this multi-distribution uncertainty, using the framework of Gilboa and Schmeidler (1989). Third, we examine whether the optimal strategy has the reservation wage property and if it has, whether increased uncertainty increases the reservation wage.

To follow the ε-contamination literature, we need to be a bit formalistic. Let W be a Borel subset of $\mathbb{R}_+$ and $\mathcal{B}_W$ be the Borel σ-algebra on W. Let P_0 be the probability charge on W corresponding to F_0. In our example, W is $[a, b]$ and P_0 is the uniform distribution over $[a, b]$. Let $\mathcal{M}$ be the set of all probability charges on $\mathcal{B}_W$ and let $\varepsilon > 0$. In our example, $\mathcal{M}$ is the set of all probability charges corresponding to distributions over $[a, b]$. Then, the *ε-contamination* of the original distribution is the set of probability charges on W defined by

$$\mathcal{P}_0 := \{\, (1-\varepsilon)P_0 + \varepsilon\mu \mid \mu \in \mathcal{M}\,\}. \tag{9.7}$$

In fact, if $\varepsilon = 0$, then $\mathcal{P}_0 = \{P_0\}$, and the problem is reduced to the traditional search one. An increase in ε implies that the worker becomes less certain that P_0 is in fact the true distribution. Thus, an increase in ε can be interpreted as an increase in Knightian uncertainty.[9]

To concentrate our attention on Knightian uncertainty itself, we assume that the unemployed worker faces the same uncertainty characterized by $\mathcal{P}_0$ in each period. That is, we do not consider explicitly the worker's learning about the uncertainty. In contrast to search models with learning where the uncertainty is specified by a single distribution of some distribution family with an unknown parameter, the worker here does not know even the type of the true distribution, let alone its parameters. The uncertainty that the worker faces is much broader and deeper, and thus, our assumption of no learning taking place is a reasonable one for Knightian uncertainty.[10]

---

[8]See Sect. 2.3.3. Early works that consider the ε-contamination include, for example, Berger (1985) and Wasserman and Kadane (1990). For the use of ε-contamination in economics, see Epstein and Wang (1994, 1995).

[9]The formal definition of more Knightian uncertainty is given in Sect. 9.4.5.

[10]For search models with learning where the uncertainty is specified by a single distribution, see DeGroot (1970) and Rothschild (1974). Even for Knightian uncertainty, we could incorporate explicitly some updating rule. Nishimura and Ozaki (2008), on which Chap. 14 of this book is based, use the Dempster-Shafer rule, which is given some axiomatic foundation by

Because Knightian uncertainty is now defined by a set $\mathcal{P}_0$ of distributions rather than a single distribution, we must redefine the objective function accordingly. We postulate that the unemployed worker's objective is to maximize the minimum of his expected discounted future income

$$\min\left\{ \int_W I(w)\, dP(w) \,\middle|\, P \in \mathcal{P}_0 \right\}, \tag{9.8}$$

where $I(w)$ is the discounted future income, which is a bounded measurable function of the observed offer w.[11] The exact formula of $I(w)$ is complicated (see (9.18) below). As we argue below, this decision rule can be shown to have an axiomatic foundation along the lines of Gilboa and Schmeidler (1989) and Epstein and Schneider (2003).

Under these settings, we can show (see Sect. 9.4.4) that (1) there exists the optimal stopping rule and (2) the optimal stopping rule has a reservation property.[12] Furthermore, it turns out that R is characterized as the solution to the following equation for sufficiently small $\varepsilon > 0$:

$$\begin{aligned} R &= c + \frac{\beta}{1-\beta} \int_R^{\infty} (1-\varepsilon) P_0(\{\, w \mid w \geq x \,\})\, dx \\ &= c + \frac{\beta}{1-\beta}(1-\varepsilon) \int_R^{\infty} P_0(\{\, w \mid w \geq x \,\})\, dx \\ &= c + \frac{\beta(1-\varepsilon)(b-R)^2}{2(1-\beta)(b-a)} \end{aligned} \tag{9.9}$$

(see right after Corollary 9.4.2). By solving this equation, we can write R as $R(\varepsilon)$ as a function of ε. The implicit function theorem shows that

$$\left. \frac{dR(\varepsilon)}{d\varepsilon} \right|_{\varepsilon=0} = -\frac{\beta(b-R)^2}{2(1-\beta)(b-a) + 2\beta(b-R)},$$

where R on the right-hand side is given by (9.5). Because $R < b$ by (9.2) and (9.3), $dR(\varepsilon)/d\varepsilon|_{\varepsilon=0} < 0$, which shows that an increase in Knightian uncertainty, specified by an increase in ε, *decreases* the reservation wage. This is exactly the opposite to an increase in risk, specified by an increase in γ. As we already mentioned in the Introduction and Summary, this makes sense economically. When people become

(Footnote 10 continued)
Gilboa and Schmeidler (1993), to show that in many cases the adoption of the Dempster-Shafer rule does not resolve the uncertainty characterized by $\mathcal{P}_0$. A similar result is also obtained for other rules (see Chap. 14).

[11] The minimum is attained because I is assumed to be bounded and measurable, and $\mathcal{P}_0$ is weak * compact by the Alaoglu theorem.

[12] For an application of the formal analysis of Sect. 9.4, the objective function (9.8) needs to be slightly modified so that it may comply with some technical requirement, which we discuss carefully in Sect. 9.3.2. With (9.8) thus modified, the statements in the text are correct up to full technicality.

less confident in what happens in the future, they may prefer "certainty" much more to "uncertainty." The uncertainty is resolved immediately when the worker accepts the wage offer. Hence, an increase in Knightian uncertainty is likely to persuade the worker to cancel any further search.

Section 9.4.5 extends this example to a more general setting and shows that a similar result holds globally (not only locally) and for a more general set of preferences. See right after Theorem 9.4.2.

9.2.3 Risk Aversion

This section briefly discusses the effect caused by an increase in uncertainty on the *risk-averse* unemployed worker, whose expected lifetime *utility* is given by

$$E_0 \sum_{t=0}^{\infty} \beta^t u(y_t)$$

where $u : \mathbb{R}_+ \to \mathbb{R}$ is an increasing, differentiable and concave utility function.[13] Equation (9.1), which characterizes the reservation wage, is now turned into

$$u(R) = u(c) + \frac{\beta}{1-\beta} \int_R^{\infty} (1 - F_0(x))\, u'(x)\, dx \,. \tag{9.10}$$

We first consider the case where uncertainty increases in the sense of mean-preserving spread. To this end, we specify F_0 by the uniform distribution over $[a, b]$ as we did in Sect. 9.2.1. Also, we specify the utility function u by $(\forall y)\ u(y) = -y^{-\rho}/\rho$ where $\rho \geq -1$ and $\rho \neq 0$. When $\rho = -1$, the worker is risk-neutral. The larger the value of ρ, the more risk-averse the worker becomes.

Then, Eq. (9.10) is further simplified to

$$\frac{\beta\rho}{1-\rho} R^{1-\rho} + (b - a + a\beta) R^{-\rho} = (1-\beta)(b-a)c^{-\rho} + \frac{\beta}{1-\rho} b^{1-\rho} \,. \tag{9.11}$$

When $\rho = -1$, (9.11) is reduced to (9.4) and we know that $R \in (a, b)$. To see the value of R when ρ is large, assume that $b > c > 1$, $b - a > \beta(c - a)$, and $\beta > 1$.[14] Then, it turns out that when ρ goes to $+\infty$, R which solves Eq. (9.11) converges

[13] Here we do not provide formal justification for the results that follow, although we conjecture that the analysis similar to the one provided in Sect. 9.4 should be sufficient.

[14] The discount (upcount) factor, which is greater than unity, is admissible when the utility number is negative. In particular, the dynamic optimization problem is well defined in that case. See, for example, Ozaki and Streufert (1996) and Sect. 7.5 of this book.

from the right to $(b - a + a\beta)/\beta$.[15] Because $(b - a + a\beta)/\beta \in (a, b)$ under the stated assumptions, we may conclude that $R \in (a, b)$ when ρ is large.

Now suppose that F_0 is turned into the new uniform distribution over $[a - \gamma, b + \gamma]$. If we denote the reservation wage R by $R(\gamma)$ as a function of γ, the implicit function theorem shows that

$$\left.\frac{dR(\gamma)}{d\gamma}\right|_{\gamma=0} = \frac{\beta - 2 + 2(1-\beta)(R/c)^{\rho} + \beta(R/b)^{\rho}}{\rho R^{-1}(\beta R - b + a - a\beta)}. \tag{9.12}$$

We know that this is positive when $\rho = -1$ from the analysis of Sect. 9.2.1. Therefore, it is still positive when ρ is greater than but close to -1; that is, when the degree of worker's risk aversion is mild. On the other hand, when ρ is sufficiently large,(9.12) turns out to be negative,[16] showing that the mean-preserving spread decreases, rather than increases, the reservation wage. Thus, the effect on the reservation wage caused by an increase in uncertainty in the sense of the mean-preserving spread is "ambiguous" when we assume that the worker is risk-averse and it may depend on the degree of the worker's risk aversion.

We next turn to the case where Knightian uncertainty increases. To this end, we specify Knightian uncertainty by the ε-contamination as in Sect. 9.2.2. The Eq. (9.1), which characterizes the reservation wage, is now turned into

$$u(R) = u(c) + \frac{\beta}{1-\beta}\int_R^{\infty} (1-\varepsilon) P_0\left(\{\, w \mid w \geq x \,\}\right) u'(x)\, dx\,.$$

An increase in ε decreases the value of the integrand for each x as far as $u' > 0$. The only change in the value of R that is consistent with this increase in ε is its decrease. Therefore, an increase in ε *unambiguously* decreases the reservation wage R.

The discussion so far provides another sharp distinction between an increase in risk and that in Knightian uncertainty. The former has an ambiguous effect on the reservation wage while the latter unambiguously decreases it. Therefore, including risk aversion in the model will not have the same effect as including Knightian-uncertainty aversion, and the latter delivers an intuitive prediction described in Sect. 9.2.2.

---

[15] When ρ is larger than 1, the right-hand side of Eq. (9.11) is negative by the assumption that $\beta > 1$. Furthermore, when ρ becomes larger, the equation itself becomes closer to $-\beta R + b - a + a\beta = 0$ by the assumption that $b > c > 1$. The claim in the text then follows.

[16] Suppose that ρ is sufficiently large. Then, (a) $R > c$ because R is close to $(b - a + a\beta)/\beta$ and because $b - a > \beta(c - a)$ by the assumption; (b) $R < b$ as we already noted; and (c) $\beta R - b + a - a\beta > 0$ because R converges to $(b - a + a\beta)/\beta$ from the right. The assumption that $\beta > 1$, (a), and (b) show that the numerator of the right-hand side of (9.12) goes to $-\infty$ as ρ goes to $+\infty$ and (c) shows that its denominator is positive. Hence, (9.12) is negative when ρ is sufficiently large.

9.3 Some Technical Issues

Before proceeding with a formal analysis of Sect. 9.4, we deal in this section with two technical issues concerning dynamical analysis. In Sect. 9.4, we assume the objective function is intertemporally well defined. Preferences need to be "continuous" for this property to hold. The maxmin preferences illustrated by the Example in the previous section are not well suited for the characterization of this continuity requirement. Thus, in Sect. 9.3.1, we reformulate preferences as those represented by a Choquet integral with respect to a convex probability capacity. In Sect. 9.3.2, we explain problems that may arise if the capacity is not continuous in the Choquet-integral-cum-probability-capacity formulation. We thus impose the continuity assumption directly on the probability capacity.

9.3.1 Representation by Convex CEU

Let P_0 be a probability charge on W and let $\varepsilon > 0$. Then, we define $\theta_0 : \mathcal{B}_W \to [0, 1]$ by

$$(\forall A) \quad \theta_0(A) := \begin{cases} (1-\varepsilon)P_0(A) & \text{if } A \neq W \\ 1 & \text{if } A = W\,. \end{cases} \tag{9.13}$$

This is the ε-contamination introduced in Example 2.3.2 and we know that θ_0 is a convex probability capacity. Furthermore, as Example 2.3.5 shows, the core of θ_0 satisfies $\text{core}(\theta_0) = \mathcal{P}_0$ Therefore, it follows that

$$\begin{aligned} (\forall I) \quad \int_W I(w)\, d\theta_0(w) &= \min\left\{ \int_W I(w)\, dP(w) \,\middle|\, P \in \text{core}(\theta_0) \right\} \\ &= \min\left\{ \int_W I(w)\, dP(w) \,\middle|\, P \in \mathcal{P}_0 \right\} \end{aligned}$$

where the far left integral of the above relations is the Choquet integral and the first equality holds by the fundamental theorem of the Choquet integral (Theorem 2.4.1). This shows that the maxmin preferences given by (9.8) are identical to the preferences that are represented by the Choquet integral with respect to the convex capacity (9.13).

The axiomatic foundations of the Choquet expected utility model, with and without convex capacities, are discussed in Schmeidler (1982, 1989) (see also Gilboa 1987).

For mathematical tractability (see Sect. 9.3.2), we formulate a general search model under Knightian uncertainty in the next section with preferences represented by a Choquet integral with respect to a convex probability capacity. It should, however, be kept in mind that we lose some mathematical generality by this procedure, although not much in economics. In particular, although the maxmin representation and the Choquet representation of the preference coincide exactly for the case of the ε-contamination, they are not always so. In fact, while the preferences represented by a Choquet integral with respect to a convex capacity are a proper subset of the maxmin preferences, the converse is not necessarily true (e.g., see Huber and Strassen 1973, and Examples 3.11.1 and 3.11.2 of this book).

9.3.2 δ-Approximation of ε-Contamination

A convex capacity that is *not* continuous poses technical difficulty in a dynamic context. (For the definition of the continuity of a probability capacity, see Sect. 2.3.1.) To see this point, let us consider the capacity θ_0 corresponding to the original ε-contamination. It can be shown that θ_0 is not continuous.[17] Let $I(w_-, w)$ denote the discounted future income when the wage offer w_- has been observed today and the wage offer w will be observed tomorrow. Then, it turns out that

$$\int_W I(w_-, w) d\theta_0(w) = (1-\varepsilon) \int_W I(w_-, w) dP_0(w) + \varepsilon \inf_{w \in W} I(w_-, w) . \tag{9.14}$$

For the unemployed worker's objective function to be well defined over time, (9.14) must be measurable in w_- today because *yesterday* the worker had computed the expectation of (9.14) over w_-. However, it is well known that $\inf_{w \in W} I(w_-, w)$ is not necessarily measurable in w_- even if I is measurable jointly in (w_-, w). See Example 2.5.1. More generally, the Choquet integral

$$\int_W I(w_-, w)\, d\theta(w) \tag{9.15}$$

is not necessarily measurable in w_- unless θ is continuous.

To avoid this mathematical problem, we introduce the δ-approximation of the ε-contamination (Example 2.3.4) as follows: let δ be a (small) positive number, and let $\mathcal{M}(P_0, \delta)$ be defined by $\mathcal{M}(P_0, \delta) := \{ \mu \in \mathcal{M} \mid (\forall A)\ \delta\mu(A) \leq P_0(A) \}$. Note that $\mathcal{M}(P_0, 1) = \{P_0\}$, $\mathcal{M}(P_0, 0) = \mathcal{M}$ and $\mathcal{M}(P_0, \delta) \subseteq \mathcal{M}(P_0, \delta')$ whenever $\delta' < \delta$. The *δ-approximation of the ε-contamination*, $\mathcal{P}_\delta$, is defined by

$$\mathcal{P}_\delta := \{ (1-\varepsilon)P_0 + \varepsilon\mu \mid \mu \in \mathcal{M}(P_0, \delta) \} . \tag{9.16}$$

---

[17] This is so because θ_0 is not continuous from below. To see this, consider the increasing sequence of sets, $\langle W_n \rangle_n$, each of which is not equal to W and such that $\cup_n W_n = W$. Such a sequence exists, for example, when W is an open interval.

Note that $\mathcal{P}_\delta$ equals $\mathcal{P}_0$ when $\delta = 0$, it equals $\{P_0\}$ when $\delta = 1$, and $\mathcal{P}_\delta \subseteq \mathcal{P}_{\delta'}$ whenever $\delta' < \delta$. As an argument right after Corollary 9.4.2 shows, we may use $\mathcal{P}_\delta$ as an approximation of $\mathcal{P}_0$ when δ is sufficiently small.[18]

Define $\theta_\delta : \mathcal{B}_W \to [0, 1]$ by $(\forall A)$

$$\theta_\delta(A) := \begin{cases} (1-\varepsilon)P_0(A) & \text{if } P_0(A) \leq 1-\delta \\ (1-\varepsilon)P_0(A) + \varepsilon\left(\frac{P_0(A)-1)}{\delta} + 1\right) & \text{if } P_0(A) > 1-\delta\,. \end{cases} \tag{9.17}$$

This capacity was introduced in Example 2.3.4. As we claimed there, θ_δ is a convex probability capacity. Furthermore, it turns out that the core of θ_δ satisfies core $(\theta_\delta) = \mathcal{P}_\delta$. Therefore, it follows from the fundamental theorem of the Choquet integral (Theorem 2.4.1) that

$$\begin{aligned} (\forall I) \quad \int_W I(w)\, d\theta_\delta(w) &= \min\left\{ \int_W I(w)\, dP(w) \,\middle|\, P \in \text{core}(\theta_\delta) \right\} \\ &= \min\left\{ \int_W I(w)\, dP(w) \,\middle|\, P \in \mathcal{P}_\delta \right\}. \end{aligned}$$

The last expression is a slight variant of the maxmin preferences given by (9.8).

Although θ_0 is not continuous in general (see the remark given in Example 2.3.2), θ_δ defined by (9.17) *is* continuous as far as P_0 is a measure (that is, countably additive) because θ_δ is a continuous transformation of P_0 (see the remark given in Example 2.3.4). Recall that (9.15) is always measurable in w_- when the capacity is continuous by the Fubini property (Theorem 2.5.1). Thus, the worker's objective is well defined in this case. If the ε-contamination is replaced by its δ-approximation in Sect. 9.2.2, formal analysis of Sect. 9.4 may be invoked to show that the results there are certainly correct. See right after Corollary 9.4.2 and right after Theorem 9.4.2.

The ε-contamination and its δ-approximation are best explained in our uniform-distribution example by Figs. 9.2 and 9.3, which we draw in terms of distribution functions, rather than probability measures. In our example, $W = [a, b]$ and P_0 is the uniform distribution. We denote by F_0 the distribution function corresponding to P_0, consistent with the notation in Sect. 9.2. In Fig. 9.2, the ε -contamination of P_0, $\mathcal{P}_0$, is given by the set of all distribution functions that are above $(1-\varepsilon)F_0$ and below $(1-\varepsilon)F_0 + \varepsilon$ for all $x \in (a, b)$ and whose slope is no less than that of $(1-\varepsilon)F_0$.[19] An example of such an admissible distribution function is depicted as a

[18] In particular, observe that for $A \neq W$, $\lim_{\delta\to 0} \inf\{\, P(A) \mid P \in \mathcal{P}_\delta \,\} = (1-\varepsilon)P_0(A) = \inf\{\, P(A) \mid P \in \mathcal{P}_0 \,\}$ whenever $P_0(A) \neq 1$.

[19] From (9.7), we get the following alternative expression for $\mathcal{P}_0$: $\mathcal{P}_0 = \{\, P \in \mathcal{M} \mid (\forall A)\ P(A) \geq (1-\varepsilon)P_0(A) \,\}$. From this expression, we immediately know that there is the lower bound $(1-\varepsilon)F_0$ for admissible distribution functions as described in Fig. 9.2. Moreover, the inequality in the expression must hold for the complement of A. This implies that there is also the upper bound $(1-\varepsilon)F_0 + \varepsilon$ for admissible distribution functions, as described in the figure. The requirement about the slope of admissible distribution functions follows because for any c and d such that $a < c < d < b$, $(F(d) - F(c))/(d-c) = P([c, d])/(d-c) \geq (1-\varepsilon)P_0([c, d])/(d-c) = (1-\varepsilon)(F_0(d) - F_0(c))/(d-c)$.

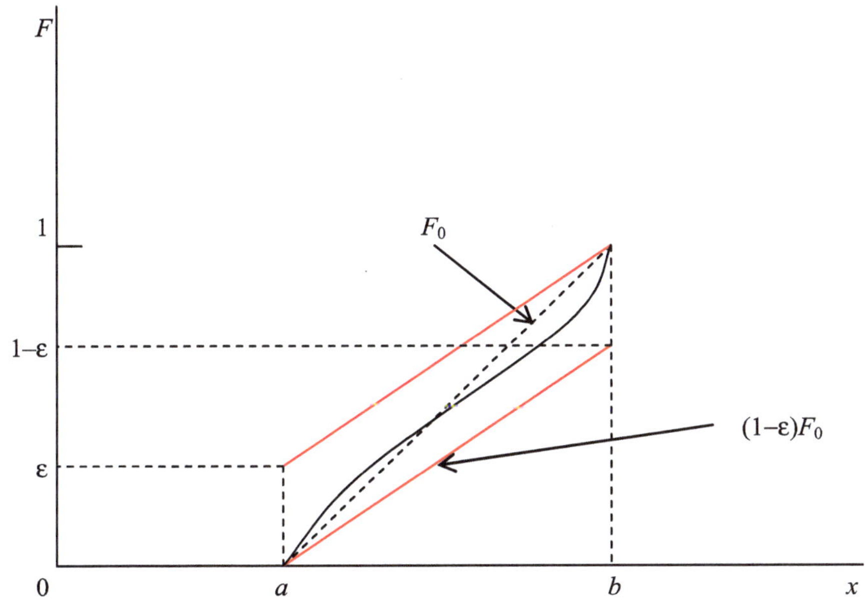

Fig. 9.2 The ε-contamination

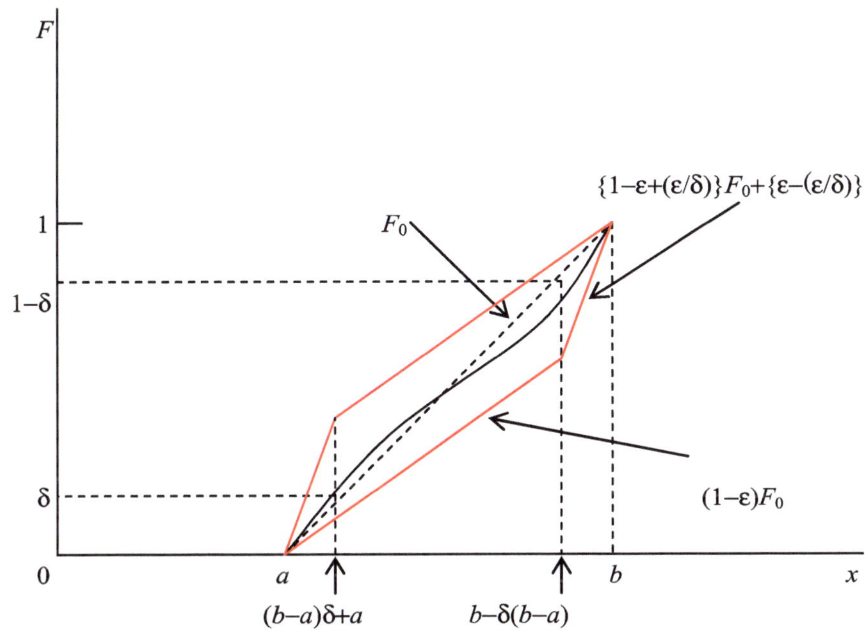

Fig. 9.3 The δ-approximation of the ε-contamination

curve in the figure. It is evident from this figure that $\inf\{P([a,x])|P \in \mathcal{P}_0\}$ is equal to $(1-\varepsilon)F_0(x)$ for all $x \in [a,b)$, and that we have $\inf\{P([a,x])|P \in \mathcal{P}_0\} = 1$ at $x = b$. Thus, $\inf\{P([a,x])|P \in \mathcal{P}_0\}$ becomes discontinuous at $x = b$, which reflects the fact that θ_0 is a *discontinuous* capacity.

In Fig. 9.3, the δ-approximation of the ε-contamination of P_0, $\mathcal{P}_\delta$, is given by the set of all distribution functions that are (i) above $(1-\varepsilon)F_0$ for $x \in [a,y]$ and above $(1-\varepsilon)F_0 + \varepsilon((F_0-1)/\delta+1)$ for $x \in [y,b]$, where $F_0(y) = 1-\delta$; (ii) below $(1-\varepsilon)F_0 + \varepsilon F_0/\delta$ for $x \in [a,z]$ and below $(1-\varepsilon)F_0 + \varepsilon$ for $x \in [z,b]$, where $F_0(z) = \delta$; and (iii) corresponding to measures in (9.16).[20] An example of such an admissible distribution function is depicted as a curve in the figure. It is evident by construction that $\inf\{\, P([a,x]) \mid P \in \mathcal{P}_\delta\}$ is continuous for all $x \in [a,b]$, which reflects the fact that θ_δ is a continuous capacity when $\delta > 0$. The figures also show that the δ-approximation of the ε-contamination, $\mathcal{P}_\delta$, expands toward the ε-contamination, $\mathcal{P}_0$, as δ decreases, and that we can "approximate" the latter by the former as close as possible by appropriately choosing a small δ.

One mathematical advantage of formulating preferences with a Choquet integral with respect to a convex capacity, rather than maxmin preferences, is that we can impose the continuity assumption directly on the primitive of the model by assuming that the capacity is continuous. This procedure greatly simplifies formal dynamic analysis without losing any economic insights.

9.4 The Formal Model

9.4.1 Stochastic Environment

Let $(W, \mathcal{B}_W)$ be a measurable space, where W is a Borel subset of $\mathbb{R}_+$ and $\mathcal{B}_W$ is the Borel σ-algebra on W. We regard each element $w \in W$ as an offer of wage in each single period. For any $t \geq 0$, we construct the t-dimensional product measurable space $(W^t, \mathcal{B}_{W^t})$ (we let $\mathcal{B}_{W^0} := \{\phi, W^\infty\}$) and embed it in the infinite-dimensional product measurable space $(W^\infty, \mathcal{B}_{W^\infty})$ as follows.

First, let $W^\infty = W \times W \times \cdots$ be the countably infinite Cartesian product of W with itself, and let $W^t = W \times \cdots \times W$ be the $(t-1)$-time Cartesian product of W with itself. That is, W^∞ is the set of infinite sequences $(w_1, w_2, \ldots)$, and W^t is the set of finite sequences $(w_1, \ldots, w_t)$, where $(\forall i)\ w_i \in W$. Second, let $\mathcal{B}_{W^\infty}$ be the σ-algebra on W^∞ generated by the family of sets of the form $E_1 \times E_2 \times \cdots$,

---

[20] From (9.16), we get the following alternative expressions for $\mathcal{P}_\delta$: $\mathcal{P}_\delta = \{\, P \in \mathcal{M} \mid (\forall A)\ P(A) \geq (1-\varepsilon)P_0(A)$ if $P_0(A) \leq 1-\delta$; and $P(A) \geq (1-\varepsilon)P_0(A) + \varepsilon((P_0(A)-1)/\delta+1)$ if $P_0(A) > 1-\delta\,\}$. We obtain the lower bound for admissible distribution functions in Fig. 9.3 immediately from this expression. The upper bound for them is obtained by substituting for A its complement in the above formula. As an implication of (iii), note that an admissible distribution function cannot jump whenever $\delta > 0$. This is because any probability measure in $\mathcal{P}_\delta$ assigns the zero-probability to a single point by the definition of $\mathcal{M}(P_0, \delta)$ under the assumption that P_0 is the uniform distribution.

and let $\mathcal{B}_{(W^t)}$ be the σ-algebra on W^t generated by the family of sets of the form $E_1 \times \cdots \times E_t$, where for each i, $E_i \in \mathcal{B}_W$; that is, E_i is a Borel set. Because W is a separable metric space, $\mathcal{B}_{(W^t)}$ is identical to $(\mathcal{B}_W)^t := \mathcal{B}_W \otimes \cdots \otimes \mathcal{B}_W$, the $(t-1)$-time product measurable space of $\mathcal{B}_W$. Third and finally, we define the σ-algebra $\hat{\mathcal{B}}_{W^t}$ on W^∞ (*not* on W^t) as the σ-algebra generated by the family of cylinder sets $E_1 \times \cdots \times E_t \times W \times W \times \cdots$, where $(\forall i)$ E_i is a Borel set. In particular, $\hat{\mathcal{B}}_{W^0} := \{\phi, W^\infty\}$ represents *no* information. Then, any function defined on W^∞ that is $\hat{\mathcal{B}}_{W^t}$-measurable takes on the same value given the realization of $(w_1, \ldots, w_t)$ regardless of the realization of $(w_{t+1}, w_{t+2}, \ldots)$; hence, it can be identified with the function defined on $\mathcal{B}_{(W^t)}$. In this manner, we can embed $\mathcal{B}_{(W^t)}$ in $\hat{\mathcal{B}}_{W^t}$. Therefore, we do not distinguish these two objects and use the notation $\mathcal{B}_{W^t}$ to represent both. This convention is convenient when we consider stopping rules that are defined on W^∞. We write a history of realized offers as ${}_1\boldsymbol{w}_t := (w_1, w_2, \ldots, w_t) \in W^t$, ${}_1\boldsymbol{w} := (w_1, w_2, \ldots) \in W^\infty$, and so on.

Let θ be a *capacitary kernel*; that is, let $\theta : W \times \mathcal{B}_W \to [0, 1]$ be a function such that $(\forall w \in W)$ θ_w is a probability capacity on $(W, \mathcal{B}_W)$ and $(\forall B \in \mathcal{B}_W)$ $\theta_{\cdot}(B)$ is $\mathcal{B}_W$-measurable. A capacitary kernel θ is *convex* (resp. *continuous*) if $(\forall w)$ θ_w is convex (resp. continuous). *Throughout the chapter, we assume that θ is convex and continuous.* We specify the uncertainty about the offer of the next period when the current wage offer is w by the core of θ_w. That is, we assume that the offer in each period is "distributed" in a Markovian manner according to core(θ_w). Note that while we now allow that the uncertainty is Markovian, we still assume as in Sect. 9.2.2, that no learning process takes place by restricting θ to be time-homogeneous.

9.4.2 Objective Function

An *income process* ${}_0\boldsymbol{y} = (y_0, y_1, y_2, \ldots)$ is an $\mathbb{R}_+$-valued stochastic process that is $\langle \mathcal{B}_{W^t} \rangle$-adapted; that is, it satisfies $(\forall t \geq 0)$ y_t is $\mathcal{B}_{W^t}$-measurable. Given an income process ${}_0\boldsymbol{y}$, we denote the *continuation* of ${}_0\boldsymbol{y}$ after the realization of a history ${}_1\boldsymbol{w}_t$ by ${}_t\boldsymbol{y}|_{{}_1\boldsymbol{w}_t} := (y_t({}_1\boldsymbol{w}_t), y_{t+1}({}_1\boldsymbol{w}_t, \cdot), y_{t+2}({}_1\boldsymbol{w}_t, \cdot, \cdot), \ldots)$. Obviously, the continuation ${}_t\boldsymbol{y}|_{{}_1\boldsymbol{w}_t}$ is $\langle \mathcal{B}_{W^t} \rangle$-adapted given ${}_1\boldsymbol{w}_t$.

Given any adapted income process ${}_0\boldsymbol{y}$ and an initial wage offer $w_0 \in W$, we define the *lifetime expected income* $I_{w_0}({}_0\boldsymbol{y})$ by[21]

$$I_{w_0}({}_0\boldsymbol{y}) = \lim_{t \to \infty} y_0 + \beta \int_W \Bigg(y_1 + \beta \int_W \Bigg(y_2 + \cdots \beta \int_W y_t \, \theta(dw_t) \cdots \Bigg) \theta(dw_2) \Bigg) \theta_{w_0}(dw_1) \quad (9.18)$$

[21]In (9.18), we suppressed the arguments of the integrand: it should be kept in mind that for every t, $y_t = y_t({}_1\boldsymbol{w}_t)$.

where $\beta \in (0, 1)$ is the discount factor and $\int_W \cdot \, d\theta$ is the *Choquet integral* with respect to a capacitary kernel θ. Note that each element of the sequence defining I is well defined by the continuity of θ and by the Fubini property (Theorem 2.5.1), and that the limit exists (allowing $+\infty$) because the sequence is nondecreasing by the non-negativity of y_t values and by Proposition 2.4.2.

The objective functions that resemble (9.18) and possess a dynamically consistent intertemporal structure have been axiomatized by Epstein and Schneider (2003), Nishimura and Ozaki (2003, reprinted in Sect. 3.13 of this book), and Wang (2003). These studies on axiomatic characterization provide a sound behavioral foundation of an objective function given by (9.18).

This paragraph presents an axiomatic foundation of the objective function (9.18) provided by Epstein and Schneider (2003). To this end, consider a probability measure on $(W^\infty, \mathcal{B}_{W^\infty})$ of the form: $p = p_0 \times p_1 \times p_2 \times \cdots$, where p_0 is a probability measure in $\text{core}(\theta_{w_0})$, p_t is a measurable selection of $w \mapsto\!\!\!\!\rightarrow \text{core}(\theta_w)$ (that is, p_t is a stochastic kernel) for each $t \geq 1$, and the product measure is constructed in a manner described, for example, in Stokey and Lucas (Stokey and Lucas 1989, Sect. 8.2). Denote the set of all such measures by $\mathcal{P}_{w_0}$. Note that in the construction of the product, any combination of stochastic kernels is permitted. The set of measures on $(W^\infty, \mathcal{B}_{W^\infty})$ thus constructed satisfies the *rectangularity* property of Epstein and Schneider (2003). By the rectangularity, (9.18) can be rewritten as

$$\min_{p \in \mathcal{P}_{w_0}} E^p \left[\sum_{t=0}^{\infty} \beta^t y_t \right], \tag{9.19}$$

where E^p denotes the expectation taken with respect to p. Epstein and Schneider (2003, Appendix B) provide a set of axioms in Anscombe and Aumann (1963) framework, which characterizes a preference that is represented by (9.19) for some discount factor β, some utility index (which is given by a linear function in (9.19)), and some rectangular set $\mathcal{P}_{w_0}$. The counterparts of Gilboa and Schmeidler (1989) axioms in a dynamic setting and the dynamic consistency are their two key axioms, the latter of which is essential for the rectangularity and the recursive structure in (9.18). Note that they do *not* assume that a set of stochastic kernels is either time-stationary or represented as a core of a convex capacity. We do assume both, and, in particular, the time-stationarity precludes us from incorporating the decision-maker's learning behavior into the model. See, however, a discussion in Sect. 9.2.2 as well as footnote 10.[22]

---

[22]Klibanoff (1995) and Wang (2003) provide alternative axiomatizations of a preference that is similar to (9.19). (Klibanoff considers only a finite horizon.) They employ preference domains that possess a complicated hierarchical structure, and, as a result, their axioms are more complicated than those of Epstein and Schneider.

The assumed continuity of θ and the monotone theorem (Theorem 2.4.6) imply that

$$(\forall\, {}_0\boldsymbol{y})(\forall w_0) \quad I_{w_0}({}_0\boldsymbol{y}) = y_0 + \beta \int_W I_{w_1}({}_1\boldsymbol{y}|_{w_1})\theta_{w_0}(dw_1)\,,$$

which is called *Koopmans' equation.*

When it happens to be the case that θ is a stochastic kernel, the objective function (9.18) is reduced to

$$\begin{aligned} I_{w_0}({}_0\boldsymbol{y}) &= \lim_{t\to\infty} y_0 + \beta \int_W \left(y_1 + \beta \int_W \left(y_2 + \cdots \beta \int_W y_t\, d\theta \cdots \right) d\theta \right) d\theta_{w_0} \\ &= \lim_{t\to\infty} y_0 + \beta \int_W y_1\, d\theta_{w_0} + \beta^2 \int_W \int_W y_2\, d\theta d\theta_{w_0} \\ &\quad + \cdots + \beta^t \int_W \int_W \cdots \int_W y_t\, d\theta \cdots d\theta d\theta_{w_0} \\ &= E_{w_0} \sum_{t=0}^{\infty} \beta^t y_t\,, \end{aligned}$$

where the expectation operator E in the last line is taken with respect to the infinite-dimensional product probability measure constructed from θ. When θ is not a stochastic kernel, the second equality may not hold because y_t and $\int_W y_{t+1}\theta(dw_{t+1})$ may not be co-monotonic (see Propositions 2.4.4 and 2.4.5), and the third equality may not hold because the "product capacity" is not uniquely well defined.[23]

9.4.3 Stopping Rule and Optimization Problem

In each period, the prospective worker is given an offer w. Upon observing the value of w, she has two alternatives; to accept it or to reject it. If she accepts the offer, she will obtain w for each period from that period on; if she rejects the offer, she will get unemployment compensation $c > 0$ for that period and will be given a random offer again in the next period.

A $\{0, 1, 2, \ldots\} \cup \{+\infty\}$-valued random variable d on $(W^\infty, \mathcal{B}_{W^\infty})$ is called a *stopping rule* if it satisfies $(\forall t = 0, 1, 2, \ldots)\ \{d = t\} \in \mathcal{B}_{W^t}$, where $\{d = t\}$ abbreviates $\{\, {}_1\boldsymbol{w} \mid d({}_1\boldsymbol{w}) = t\,\}$. We allow d to be $+\infty$ for some history. We denote the

[23] Let $(X, \mathcal{X})$ and $(Y, \mathcal{Y})$ be two measurable spaces, let $(Z, \mathcal{Z}) = (X \times Y, \mathcal{X} \otimes \mathcal{Y})$ be the product measurable space, and let μ and ν be a capacity on $\mathcal{X}$ and $\mathcal{Y}$, respectively. Consider a capacity σ on $\mathcal{Z}$ that satisfies $(\forall S \in \mathcal{X})(\forall T \in \mathcal{Y})\ \sigma(S \times T) = \mu(S)\nu(T)$. If both μ and ν are probability charges, such a product capacity σ is uniquely determined. However, if at least one of them (μ and ν) is not additive, there could be many capacities (σ) that satisfy the above relation. This implies that the "product capacity" cannot be determined uniquely from the "marginal capacity." For more details, see Ghirardato (1997).

set of all stopping rules by Δ. Given any stopping rule $d \in \Delta$, we define a process ${}_0\boldsymbol{y}^d = (y_0^d, y_1^d, y_2^d, \ldots)$ by

$$(\forall t \geq 0) \quad y_t^d = \begin{cases} c & \text{if } d > t \\ w_T & \text{if } d = T \quad (T = 0, 1, \ldots, t) \end{cases}$$

Lemma A.4.1 in the Appendix shows that ${}_0\boldsymbol{y}^d$ is $\langle \mathcal{B}_{W^t} \rangle$-adapted, and hence it is actually an income process. Given an initial wage offer $w_0 \in W$, we denote the lifetime expected income under a stopping rule $d \in \Delta$ by the symbol I for notational simplicity (there should be no confusion about this): $I_{w_0}(d) := I_{w_0}({}_0\boldsymbol{y}^d)$. Similarly, given any $t \geq 1$ and any history ${}_1\boldsymbol{w}_t \in W^t$, we denote the income under $d \in \Delta$ after the realization of ${}_1\boldsymbol{w}_t$ by $I_{w_t}(d|_{{}_1\boldsymbol{w}_t})$; that is, $I_{w_t}(d|_{{}_1\boldsymbol{w}_t}) := I_{w_t}({}_t\boldsymbol{y}^d|_{{}_1\boldsymbol{w}_t})$, where ${}_t\boldsymbol{y}^d|_{{}_1\boldsymbol{w}_t}$ is the continuation of ${}_0\boldsymbol{y}^d$ after the realization of ${}_1\boldsymbol{w}_t$ as is defined in Sect. 9.4.2. Lemma A.4.2 in the Appendix proves that

$$I_{w_0}(d) = \frac{w_0}{1-\beta} \chi_{\{d=0\}} + \left(c + \beta \int I_{w_1}(d|_{w_1}) d\theta_{w_0} \right) \chi_{\{d>0\}} \,. \tag{9.20}$$

Here, χ denotes the indicator function on W^∞.[24] Equation (9.20) is Koopmans' equation for a stopping rule d.

A stopping rule $d \in \Delta$ is *optimal* from w_0 if $d \in \arg\max\{ I_{w_0}(d) \mid d \in \Delta \}$. A stopping rule d is *admissible* if it dictates more searching as long as the observed offer is strictly less than c. Any stopping rule that is not admissible is suboptimal because it is dominated by the stopping rule which never stops, and hence, it can be safely ignored. When an optimal stopping rule exists, we define the *value function* $V^* : W \to \bar{\mathbb{R}}_+$ by $(\forall w \in W)\ V^*(w) := I_w(d_w^*)$, where we denote an optimal stopping rule from w by d_w^*.

9.4.4 *Existence and Characterization of Optimal Stopping Rule*

Given random variables w, w_0, ..., w_t, let $c \vee w$ and $\vee_{i=0}^t w_i$ denote the random variables defined by $\max\{c, w\}$ and $\max\{w_1, \ldots, w_t\}$. Throughout the rest of this chapter, we assume that the primitives of the model satisfy the following two conditions: $(\forall w_0)$

---

[24] For example,

$$\chi_{\{d=t\}} = \begin{cases} 1 & \text{if } \omega \in \{d = t\},\ \textit{i.e.},\ d(\omega) = t \\ 0 & \text{if } \omega \notin \{d = t\},\ \textit{i.e.},\ d(\omega) \neq t \,. \end{cases}$$

Because d is a stopping rule, $\chi_{\{d=t\}}$ and $\chi_{\{d>t\}}$ are $\mathcal{B}_{W^t}$-measurable.

E1. $(\forall t > 0)\ \bar{W}^t(w_0) := \int \cdots \int \left(c \vee \vee_{i=0}^t w_i\right) \theta'(dw_t) \cdots \theta'_{w_0}(dw_1) < +\infty$

E2. $\overline{\lim}_{t\to\infty} \left(\bar{W}^t(w_0)\right)^{1/t} < \beta^{-1}$

where θ' is the conjugate of θ (see Sect. 2.3.1). The integrand in E1, $c \vee \vee_{i=0}^t w_i$, is the overly optimistic income the worker expects in time t. It is *overly* optimistic because it is the highest offer up to time t (our model is on search *without* recall). The integral in E1 is its overly optimistic "expectation" evaluated at time 0. This is *overly* optimistic because it is evaluated by the *conjugate* of θ rather than θ itself.[25] E1 assumes that this is finite for any t. This optimistic "expected" income, $\bar{W}^t$, grows as t increases because it takes the maximum offer up to time t. The left-hand side of E2 defines the time-average of the rate of growth in $\bar{W}^t$. Hence, E2 as a whole assumes that this time-average is lower than the worker's impatience. When E2 holds, the effect caused by the high income in the far future can be safely ignored because the worker's impatience dominates the income growth along any optimistic path. This is an analogue to the condition for the dynamic programming technique introduced in Ozaki and Streufert (1996) and the Condition A4 in Sect. 7.4 of this book. If θ is simply a probability measure, the left-hand side of E2 is 1 as long as the expectation of w is finite (Chung 1974, p. 49), and hence, E2 is automatically satisfied.

Define a (constant) function $V^- : W \to \mathbb{R}_+$ by $(\forall w)\ V^-(w) := c/(1-\beta)$ and a function $V^+ : W \to \bar{\mathbb{R}}_+$ by $(\forall w_0)$

$$V^+(w_0) := \lim_{T\to\infty} (c \vee w_0) + \beta \int \Bigg((c \vee \vee_{i=0}^1 w_i) + \cdots \\ \beta \int (c \vee \vee_{i=0}^T w_i)\theta(dw_T) \cdots \Bigg) \theta_{w_0}(dw_1)\,,$$

which is a well-defined $\mathcal{B}_W$-measurable function (let $y_T := c \vee \vee_{i=0}^T w_i$ in (9.18)). Clearly, $V^- \le V^+$, and Lemma A.4.3 in the Appendix shows that $(\forall w_0)\ V^+(w_0) < +\infty$.

A $\mathcal{B}_W$-measurable function $V : W \to \mathbb{R}_+$ is *admissible* if it satisfies $V^- \le V \le V^+$. Note that for any admissible stopping rule d, $I.(d)$ is admissible. Let $\mathcal{V}$ be the space of all admissible functions from W into $\mathbb{R}_+$, and let B be the operator from $\mathcal{V}$ into itself defined by $(\forall V \in \mathcal{V})(\forall w \in W)$

$$BV(w) := \max\left\{ \frac{w}{1-\beta}\,,\ c + \beta \int_W V(w')\theta_w(dw') \right\}. \tag{9.21}$$

Lemma A.4.4 in the Appendix shows that BV is admissible for any admissible function V, and hence, that B is well defined.

---

[25] When we prove that the solution to Bellman's equation (specified later) is the value function, we apply the method of "squeezing" (see Lemma A.4.6 in the Appendix). To "squeeze," we need to bound the increment by the Choquet integral with respect to the conjugate (Theorem 2.4.3). This is why we need to define the "expected" income via the conjugate capacity in E1.

A function $V \in \mathcal{V}$ *solves Bellman's equation* if $BV = V$. We then have the main result of this chapter, summarized in the following theorem.

Theorem 9.4.1 *The value function V^* exists and is the unique admissible solution to Bellman's equation. Furthermore, V^* is attained by the stopping rule d^* such that for all $t \geq 0$, $d^* = t$ as soon as*

$$\frac{w_t}{1-\beta} \geq c + \beta \int_W V^*(w_{t+1})\theta_{w_t}(dw_{t+1})$$

holds; and $d^* > t$ otherwise.

Let $R : W \to \mathbb{R}_+$ be a $\mathcal{B}_W$ -measurable function defined by

$$(\forall w) \quad R(w) := (1-\beta)\left(c + \beta \int_W V^*(w')\theta_w(dw')\right) .$$

We call $R(w)$ the *reservation wage* at state w. We say that the capacitary kernel θ is *monotonic* if for any nondecreasing function $y : W \to \mathbb{R}_+$ and for any $x \geq 0$, $w' \geq w \Rightarrow \theta_{w'}(\{\, y \geq x \,\}) \geq \theta_w(\{\, y \geq x \,\})$. Note that if W is an interval and θ is stochastically nondecreasing (Sect. 2.5), θ is monotonic because we may set $h := \chi_{\{y \geq x\}}$ in (2.19) and h is nondecreasing. The next result is an extension of Lippman and McCall (1976, Theorem 1).

Corollary 9.4.1 *If θ is monotonic, then R is nondecreasing in w.*

The next result further characterizes the reservation wage when the capacitary kernel θ is *i.i.d.*; that is, when θ is independent of the current wage offer w.

Corollary 9.4.2 *If the capacitary kernel θ is independent of the current wage offer, then the reservation wage $R(w)$ will be constant and is given by the solution R to the next equation:*

$$\begin{aligned} R &= c + \frac{\beta}{1-\beta} \int_R^\infty \theta(\{\, w \mid w \geq x \,\})\, dx \\ &= c + \frac{\beta}{1-\beta} \int_R^\infty (1 - F_{\theta'}(x))\, dx\,, \end{aligned}$$

where $F_{\theta'}$ is the "distribution" of θ' defined by $F_{\theta'}(x) := \theta'(\{\, w \mid w \leq x \,\})$.

As an application of Corollary 9.4.2, we show that (9.9) characterizes the reservation wage for sufficiently small ε and δ in the Example of the δ -approximation of the ε-contamination provided in Sects. 9.2.2 and 9.3.2. First, let $\varepsilon > 0$ be small enough to be such that $R(\varepsilon) > a$ where $R(\varepsilon)$ is the solution to (9.9). This is possible because $R(\cdot)$ is continuous and $R(0) > a$ by (9.2) and (9.3). Second, let $\delta > 0$ be small enough to be such that $a + (b-a)\delta < R(\varepsilon)$. This is possible because $R(\varepsilon) > a$. Third, note that for any $R > a + (b-a)\delta$, it holds that

$$c + \frac{\beta}{1-\beta} \int_R^\infty \theta_\delta\left(\{w \,|w \geq x\}\right) dx = c + \frac{\beta}{1-\beta} \int_R^\infty (1-\varepsilon) P_0\left(\{w \,|w \geq x\}\right) dx$$

by the definition of θ_δ. Finally, note that

$$R(\varepsilon) = c + \frac{\beta}{1-\beta} \int_{R(\varepsilon)}^\infty \theta_\delta\left(\{\, w \mid w \geq x \,\}\right) dx\,. \tag{9.22}$$

This holds because $R(\varepsilon)$ solves (9.9) and because $R(\varepsilon) > a + (b-a)\delta$. Therefore, the continuity of θ_δ, Corollary 9.4.2, and (9.22) imply that $R(\varepsilon)$ is certainly the reservation wage.

9.4.5 An Increase in Uncertainty

Let θ^1 and θ^2 be two capacitary kernels that are convex and continuous. We say that θ^2 *represents more Knightian uncertainty than* θ^1 if

$$(\forall w)(\forall B) \quad \theta_w^1(B) \geq \theta_w^2(B)\,. \tag{9.23}$$

Under the assumption that θ^1 and θ^2 are convex, it turns out that (9.23) is equivalent to

$$(\forall w) \quad \mathrm{core}(\theta_w^2) \supseteq \mathrm{core}(\theta_w^1)\,, \tag{9.24}$$

which substantiates our definition of more Knightian uncertainty. Ghirardato and Marinacci (2002) developed a notion of comparative ambiguity aversion and related it to (9.23), which also provides some behavioral foundation of our notion of more Knightian uncertainty.[26]

Let R^1 and R^2 be a reservation wage of an unemployed worker with θ^1 and θ^2, respectively. The next result shows that the reservation wage decreases if Knightian uncertainty increases.

Theorem 9.4.2 *If θ^2 represents more Knightian uncertainty than θ^1, then $(\forall w)$ $R^2(w) \leq R^1(w)$.*

---

[26]To be more precise, let θ^1 and θ^2 be two (not necessarily convex nor continuous) capacities, and let the preference relation $\succeq_i$ $(i = 1, 2)$ be represented by

$$(\forall I) \quad \int_W I(w)\, d\theta^i(w) \quad (i = 1, 2) \tag{9.25}$$

where I denotes the random income. Then, $(\forall B)\ \theta^1(B) \geq \theta^2(B)$ if and only if for any *non*random money amount x and any random income I, $x \succeq_1 (\succ_1) I \Rightarrow x \succeq_2 (\succ_2) I$, where $(\forall i)$ $\succ_i$ is the asymmetric component of $\succeq_i$ (Ghirardato and Marinacci 2002, Theorem 17(i)). Note that they use the term "ambiguity" in a similar sense as "Knightian uncertainty" here.

As an application of Theorem 9.4.2, we show that an increase in ε decreases the reservation wage for any $\delta > 0$ in the Example of the δ-approximation of the ε-contamination provided in Sects. 9.2.2 and 9.3.2. (Recall that we made only a local analysis in Sect. 9.2.2.) Let $\delta > 0$ and let $\varepsilon_2 > \varepsilon_1 > 0$. We write $\mathcal{P}_\delta$ explicitly as $\mathcal{P}_\delta^\varepsilon$ to denote its dependence on ε. Also, suppose that θ_δ^i is the probability capacity corresponding to $\mathcal{P}_\delta^{\varepsilon_i}$. Then, it turns out that $(\forall A)$

$$\theta_\delta^2(A) = \begin{cases} \dfrac{1-\varepsilon_2}{1-\varepsilon_1}\theta_\delta^1(A) & \text{if } \theta_\delta^1(A) \leq (1-\varepsilon_1)(1-\delta) \\ \dfrac{\delta - \varepsilon_2\delta + \varepsilon_2}{\delta - \varepsilon_1\delta + \varepsilon_1}\theta_\delta^1(A) - \dfrac{(\varepsilon_2 - \varepsilon_1)(1-\delta)}{\delta - \varepsilon_1\delta + \varepsilon_1} & \text{if } \theta_\delta^1(A) > (1-\varepsilon_1)(1-\delta)\,. \end{cases}$$

This shows that

$$(\forall A) \quad \theta_\delta^2(A) = g(\theta_\delta^1(A)) \tag{9.26}$$

for some convex, strictly increasing, and surjective function $g : [0,1] \to [0,1]$,[27] which in turn implies (9.23). Therefore, Theorem 9.4.2 shows that an increase in ε decreases the reservation wage.

References

Anscombe, F.J., and R.J. Aumann. 1963. A definition of subjective probability. *Annals of Mathematical Statistics* 34: 199–205.

Berger, J.O. 1985. *Statistical decision theory and Bayesian analysis* (2nd edn.). Berlin: Springer.

Bikhchandani, S., and S. Sharma. 1996. Optimal search with learning. *Journal of Economic Dynamics and Control* 20: 333–359.

Chung, K.L. 1974. *A course in probability theory*, 2nd ed. Cambridge: Academic Press.

DeGroot, M.H. 1970. *Optimal statistical decisions*. New York: McGraw-Hill.

Epstein, L.G., and M. Schneider. 2003. Recursive multiple-priors. *Journal of Economic Theory* 113: 1–31.

Epstein, L.G., and T. Wang. 1994. Intertemporal asset pricing under Knightian uncertainty. *Econometrica* 62: 283–322.

Epstein, L.G., and T. Wang. 1995. Uncertainty, risk-neutral measures and security price booms and crashes. *Journal of Economic Theory* 67: 40–82.

Epstein, L.G., and J. Zhang. 1999. Least convex capacities. *Economic Theory* 13: 263–286.

Ghirardato, P. 1997. On independence for non-additive measures, with a Fubini theorem. *Journal of Economic Theory* 73: 261–291.

Ghirardato, P., and M. Marinacci. 2002. Ambiguity made precise. *Journal of Economic Theory* 102: 251–289.

Gilboa, I. 1987. Expected utility theory with purely subjective non-additive probabilities. *Journal of Mathematical Economics* 16: 141–153.

[27] Epstein and Zhang (1999) adopt this notion as a definition of more Knightian uncertainty aversion when the capacities are *convex*. Suppose that the preference relation $\succeq_i$ is represented by (26) with θ^1 and θ^2 both convex. Then, they say that $\succeq_2$ exhibits more Knightian uncertainty aversion than $\succeq_1$ if (9.26) (with $_\delta$ ignored) holds. For further discussion, see Epstein and Zhang (1999, Theorem 3.1).

Gilboa, I., and D. Schmeidler. 1989. Maxmin expected utility with non-unique prior. *Journal of Mathematical Economics* 18: 141–153.
Gilboa, I., and D. Schmeidler. 1993. Updating ambiguous beliefs. *Journal of Economic Theory* 59: 33–49.
Huber, P.J., and V. Strassen. 1973. Minimax tests and the Neyman-Pearson lemma for capacities. *The Annals of Statistics* 1: 251–263.
Klibanoff, P. 1995. Dynamic choice with uncertainty aversion. mimeo, Northwestern University.
Kohn, M.G., and S. Shavell. 1974. The theory of search. *Journal of Economic Theory* 9: 93–123.
Lippman, S.A., and J.J. McCall. 1976. Job search in a dynamic economy. *Journal of Economic Theory* 12: 365–390.
Miao, J., and N. Wang. 2011. Risk, uncertainty, and option exercise. *Journal of Economic Dynamics and Control* 35: 442–461.
Nishimura K.G., and H. Ozaki. 2003. A simple axiomatization of iterated Choquet objectives, unpublished manuscript.
Nishimura, K.G., and H. Ozaki. 2004. Search and Knightian uncertainty. *Journal of Economic Theory* 119: 299–333.
Nishimura, K.G., and H. Ozaki 2008. Learning may increase perceived uncertainty: A model of confidence erosion under Knightian uncertainty, mimeo, Keio University. (Revised version of Nishimura and Ozaki, 2002)
Ozaki, H., and P.A. Streufert. 1996. Dynamic programming for non-additive stochastic objectives. *Journal of Mathematical Economics* 25: 391–442.
Riedel, F. 2009. Optimal stopping with multiple priors. *Econometrica* 77: 857–908.
Rothschild, M. 1974. Searching for the lowest price when the distribution of prices is unknown. *Journal of Political Economy* 82: 689–711.
Rothschild, M., and J. Stiglitz. 1970. Increasing risk I: A definition. *Journal of Economic Theory* 2: 225–243.
Rothschild, M., and J. Stiglitz. 1971. Increasing risk II: Its economic consequences. *Journal of Economic Theory* 3: 66–84.
Sargent, T.J. 1987. *Dynamic macroeconomic theory*. Cambridge: Harvard University Press.
Schmeidler, D. 1982. Subjective probability without additivity, (Temporary Title), Working Paper, The Foerder Institute for Economic Research, Tel Aviv University.
Schmeidler, D. 1989. Subjective probability and expected utility without additivity. *Econometrica* 57: 571–587. (Its working paper is first published in 1982)
Stokey, N.L. and R.E. Lucas, Jr. 1989. *Recursive methods in economic dynamics*. Cambridge: Harvard University Press.
Wang, T. 2003. Conditional preferences and updating. *Journal of Economic Theory* 108: 286–321.
Wasserman, L.A., and J.B. Kadane. 1990. Bayes' theorem for Choquet capacities. *The Annals of Statistics* 18: 1328–1339.

Chapter 10
Irreversible Investment and Knightian Uncertainty

10.1 Introduction and Summary

The investment decisions of any firm typically involve three features. First, future market conditions are uncertain. Second, the cost of investment cannot be retrieved and thus investment is irreversible. Third, the opportunity to invest does not vanish at once such that choosing a time to invest becomes a critical decision. This irreversibility of investment under uncertainty coupled with the optimal investment timing problem has attracted considerable attention in recent years, especially after McDonald and Siegel (1986) successfully applied financial option pricing techniques to this problem and Dixit and Pindyck (1994) related option-theoretic results to neoclassical investment theory. Most irreversible investment studies, however, assume more than that future market conditions are uncertain. In these studies, future uncertainty is characterized by a certain probability charge over states of nature. This amounts to assuming that the firm is *perfectly certain* that future market conditions are governed by this particular probability charge. However, this assumption may be far-fetched: the firm may not be so sure about future uncertainty. It may think other probability charges are also likely and it might have no idea of the relative "plausibility" of these charges. Uncertainty that is *not* reducible to a single probability charge and thus characterized by a *set* of probability charges is often called *Knightian uncertainty*, or *ambiguity* in some cases (see Chap. 1). In contrast, uncertainty that *is* reducible to a single probability charge with known parameters is referred to as *risk*. That is, a firm may face Knightian uncertainty in contemplating investment, facing not a single probability charge but a set of probability charges.

The purpose of this chapter is to show that the effect of uncertainty on the value of irreversible investment opportunity differs drastically between risk and Knightian uncertainty. Specifically, the standard result that an increase in uncertainty increases the value of irreversible investment opportunities is reversed if uncertainty is not risk but Knightian uncertainty. That is, an increase in Knightian uncertainty (properly defined) reduces the value of an irreversible investment opportunity, while the opposite is true for an increase in risk in the form of an increase in variance. In contrast,

K.G. Nishimura and H. Ozaki, *Economics of Pessimism and Optimism*,
DOI 10.1007/978-4-431-55903-0_10

both of them have the same effect on the value of waiting: they increase the value of waiting and make it more likely.

In this chapter, we take a patent as an example of irreversible investment. To highlight the effect of Knightian uncertainty, the firm is assumed to be risk-neutral but *uncertainty-averse* in the sense that it computes the expected profit by using the "worst" element in the set of probability charges characterizing Knightian uncertainty and chooses its strategy to maximize it (maxmin criterion).[1]

Following the standard procedure of irreversible investment studies, we assume that (1) to utilize a patent, the firm has to build a factory and construction costs are sunk after its completion, and (2) the profit flow after construction is characterized by a geometric Brownian motion with a drift. Then, the firm first calculates the value of the utilized patent, and then contemplates when to build a factory by taking into account the value of the utilized patent and the cost of investment. The firm's problem is thus formulated as an optimal stopping problem in continuous time.[2]

Unlike the standard case, however, we assume that the firm is not perfectly certain that the profit flow is generated by a particular geometric Brownian motion with say, variance σ^2 and drift μ, or equivalently, by a probability charge underlying this geometric Brownian motion, say P. The firm may think that the profit flow is generated by other probability charges slightly different from P. The firm has no idea about which of these probability charges is "true." Thus, the firm faces Knightian uncertainty with respect to probability charges characterizing the profit flow.

We assume that the firm thinks these probability charges are not far from P. First, we assume that these probability charges agree with P with respect to zero probability events. (That is, if a particular event's probability is zero with P, then it is also zero with these probability charges.) Then, these probability charges can be shown as a perturbation of P by a particular "density generator." Second, the deviation of these probabilities from P is not large in the sense that the corresponding density generator's move is confined in a range, $[-\kappa, \kappa]$, where κ can be described as a degree of this Knightian uncertainty. This specification of Knightian uncertainty in continuous time is called κ-ignorance by Chen and Epstein (2002) in a different context.

These two assumptions, although they seem quite general, have strong implications. Under the first assumption, for each of the probability charges constituting the firm's Knightian uncertainty, the profit flow is characterized by a "geometric Brownian motion" of the same variance σ^2 with respect to this probability charge. Thus, "geometric Brownian motions" corresponding to these probability charges

[1]For axiomatization of such behavior, see Gilboa and Schmeidler (1989). Such behavior is also closely related to the one represented by Choquet-expected-utility maximization. See Schmeidler (1982, 1989), Gilboa (1987), and Chap. 3 of this book.

[2]The standard procedure is to apply financial option pricing techniques to this problem, exploiting the fact that an *un*utilized patent can be considered a call option whose primal asset is a *utilized* patent that generates a stochastic flow of profits, and whose exercise price is a fixed cost of building a factory to produce patented products. (For example, see Dixit and Pindyck 1994.) This approach and the optimal stopping approach are two ways of formulating the same problem and produce the same result.

differ only in the drift term. (In fact, this is a direct consequence of the well-known Girzanov theorem in the literature of mathematical finance. See for example, Karatzas and Shreve 1991.) Under the second assumption, the minimum drift term among them becomes $\mu - \kappa\sigma$. Note that the uncertainty-averse firm evaluates the present value of the patent according to the "worst" scenario. Loosely speaking, this amounts to calculating the patent's value using the probability charge corresponding to a geometric Brownian motion with variance σ^2 and minimum drift $\mu - \kappa\sigma$. Thus, an increase in κ, the degree of Knightian uncertainty, leads to a lower value of the utilized patent at the time of investment, because it is evaluated by a less favorable Brownian motion process governing the profit flow from the utilized patent. Consequently, the value of the unutilized patent is also reduced.

This is in sharp contrast with the positive effect of an increase in risk (that is, an increase in σ) on the value of the unutilized patent when there is no Knightian uncertainty. An increase in σ under no Knightian uncertainty implies that when the firm waits, it will undertake investment only when market conditions are more favorable (because it does not have to undertake investment when market conditions are less favorable). Consequently, an increase in σ increases the value of the unutilized patent.

Despite such differences, both an increase in risk and in Knightian uncertainty similarly raise the value of waiting and thus make the firm more likely to postpone investment. However, the reason for waiting is critically different. An increase in risk (σ) under no Knightian uncertainty leaves the value of a utilized patent unchanged, but increases the value of an unutilized patent, and thus makes waiting more profitable. An increase in Knightian uncertainty (κ) reduces both the value of the utilized patent and that of the unutilized patent, but it lowers the former more than the latter. This is because the value of the unutilized patent depends not only on the proceeds from undertaking investment (the utilized patent), but also on the proceeds from not undertaking investment, which is independent of the value of the utilized patent. Because the value of the utilized patent is reduced more than that of the unutilized patent, the firm finds waiting more profitable.

While in this chapter an increase in Knightian uncertainty raises the value of waiting, the opposite holds true in the previous chapter's search model, which is set up in a discrete-time infinite-horizon framework. It showed that an increase in Knightian uncertainty lowers the reservation wage and hence shortens waiting. The value of waiting is thus reduced.

Although both the job search model in Chap. 9 and the irreversible investment models in this chapter are formulated as optimal stopping problems, there is a fundamental difference between the two in the nature of uncertainty. In Chap. 9, the decision-maker determines when she stops the search and resolves uncertainty. Thus, an increase in Knightian uncertainty makes the uncertainty-averse decision-maker more likely to stop the search and to resolve uncertainty. In contrast, in this chapter, the decision-maker contemplates when to begin investment and face uncertainty. Thus, an increase in Knightian uncertainty makes the uncertainty-averse decision-maker more likely to postpone investment to avoid facing uncertainty.

Optimal stopping theories with Knightian uncertainty and their applications to real options developed in similar continuous-time settings after Nishimura and Ozaki (2007), on which this chapter is based, was published include Asano (2010), Trojanowska and Kort (2010), Asano and Shibata (2011), Schröder (2011), Thijssen (2011), and Cheng and Riedel (2013).

This chapter is organized as follows. In Sect. 10.2, we present a simple two-period, two-state example and explain intuitions behind the result of this chapter. In Sect. 10.3, we present some mathematics that are necessary to formally define Knightian uncertainty in continuous time. In Sects. 10.4–10.6, we formulate the firm's irreversible investment problem in continuous time, derive an explicit formula for a utilized patent, and investigate the optimal investment timing problem. In Sect. 10.7, we conduct a sensitivity analysis and present the main result of this chapter: differing effects of uncertainty between an increase in risk and Knightian uncertainty. All proofs are relegated to the Appendix.

10.2 A Two-Period, Two-State Example

This section offers an illustrative example of the differing effects of risk and Knightian uncertainty. The example is a simple patent-pricing scenario and is essentially the same as the widget-factory example of Dixit and Pindyck (1994, Chap. 2). We compare the effect of an increase in risk on the value of a patent with that of an increase in Knightian uncertainty. We show that an increase in Knightian uncertainty reduces the value of the patent, while an increase in risk increases its value. In contrast, both have the same effect on the value of waiting: they make waiting more likely.

Consider a risk-neutral firm contemplating whether to buy a patent (or a venture firm, vacant lot, etc.).[3] After purchasing the patent, the firm has to spend a large amount of money to utilize it. The firm may have to build a new factory to produce patented products. The factory is product-specific and cannot be used for other purposes. Thus, the investment is irreversible and becomes sunk afterward.

Suppose that there are two periods: period 0 and period 1. There is no uncertainty in period 0 and the operating profit from producing and selling the products is π_0. There is uncertainty in period 1, where the state is either *boom* (b) or *slump* (s). Let π_1 be the operating profit in period 1, which equals π_b in boom and π_s in slump.

To utilize this patent, the firm has to build a factory to produce the product. Let I be the cost of building the factory. We assume that $\pi_s < I < \pi_b$. The firm has a choice between building the factory in period 0 or in period 1. Let p_b be the probability of boom in period 1 and let r be the rate of interest. Then, if the firm builds a factory in period 0, the expected discounted cash flow from this patent is

[3] Nishimura and Ozaki (2004) and Chap. 9 of this book discuss the effect of an increase in both risk and Knightian uncertainty in a discrete-time search model where the decision-maker is both risk-averse and uncertainty-averse.

$$(\pi_0 - I) + \frac{1}{1+r}\left(p_b \pi_b + (1-p_b)\,\pi_s\right) , \tag{10.1}$$

while if it postpones investment until period 1, the expected discounted cash flow of this patent is

$$\frac{p_b}{1+r}\left(\pi_b - I\right) , \tag{10.2}$$

because the period 1 cash flow is $\pi_b - I$ in boom and 0 in slump (that is, the firm does not want to build the factory in slump because $\pi_s < I$).

If the firm is perfectly certain that the boom probability is p_b, the model is exactly the same as the Dixit-Pindyck example. The firm compares (10.1) and (10.2) and determines the optimal timing for investment. Then, the value of the unutilized patent is determined accordingly. Thus, if

$$\pi_0 - \left(1 - \frac{p_b}{1+r}\right) I + \frac{1}{1+r}\left(1-p_b\right)\pi_s < 0 \tag{10.3}$$

holds, then postponement is the optimal strategy. If otherwise, investment in period 0 is optimal. Consequently, if (10.3) holds true (that is, postponement is optimal), then (10.2) is the value of the patent at period 0. If not, (10.1) is the value of the patent at period 0.

In the real world, however, it is highly unlikely that the firm is absolutely certain about boom probability. The firm may think that p_b is likely to be boom probability, but at the same time may consider that another probability, say p'_b, is also plausible. Moreover, the firm may not be at all certain whether a particular boom probability is "more plausible" than others. In summary, the firm may have a set of boom probabilities, instead of having one boom probability as in the Dixit-Pindyck example. Moreover, the firm may not be certain about the "relative plausibility" of these boom probabilities. Such a multiplicity of probability distributions is called *Knightian uncertainty*.

Let $\mathcal{P}$ be a compact set of boom probabilities that the firm thinks plausible. It is known (see Gilboa and Schmeidler 1989) that in multiple-probability-charge cases of this kind, if the firm acts in accordance with certain sensible axioms, then its behavior can be characterized as being *uncertainty-averse*: when the firm evaluates its position, it will use a probability corresponding to the "worst" scenario. This means (10.1) is replaced by

$$\begin{aligned}&(\pi_0 - I) + \frac{1}{1+r}\min_{p_b \in \mathcal{P}}\left(p_b \pi_b + (1-p_b)\,\pi_s\right)\\ &= (\pi_0 - I) + \frac{1}{1+r}\left[\pi_s + \left(\min_{p_b \in \mathcal{P}} p_b\right)(\pi_b - \pi_s)\right]\end{aligned} \tag{10.4}$$

because $\pi_b > \pi_s$, and (10.2) is now

$$\frac{1}{1+r}\min_{p_b\in\mathcal{P}} p_b(\pi_b - I) = \frac{1}{1+r}\left(\min_{p_b\in\mathcal{P}} p_b\right)(\pi_b - I) \tag{10.5}$$

because $\pi_b > I$. Consequently, the postponement criterion is now

$$(\pi_0 - I) + \frac{\pi_s}{1+r} + \frac{1}{1+r}\left(\min_{p_b\in\mathcal{P}} p_b\right)(I - \pi_s) < 0\,. \tag{10.6}$$

Let us now consider in turn an increase in risk and uncertainty. To simplify exposition, let us further assume $p_b = 1/2$ and $\mathcal{P} = [(1/2) - \varepsilon, (1/2) + \varepsilon]$. Here, $\varepsilon \in (0, 1/2)$ is a real number that can be described as the degree of "contamination" of confidence in $p_b = 1/2$. We hereafter call this specification the *ε-contamination*.[4] An increase in ε can be considered as an increase in Knightian uncertainty.[5]

An increase in risk is characterized by a mean-preserving spread of the second-period operating profit π_1. Suppose that there is no Knightian uncertainty and risk is increased so that (π_s, π_b) now spread out to $(\pi_s - \gamma, \pi_b + \gamma)$. It is evident from (10.2) that the mean-preserving spread always increases the value of an *un*utilized patent, or the value of a patent when the firm postpones investment. Intuitively, this is because an increase in risk implies that, when the firm waits, it can undertake investment only when market conditions are more favorable than before. At the same time, it leaves the value of the utilized patent unchanged (see (10.1)). Consequently, the value of investment opportunity increases with an increase in risk.

Furthermore, (10.1) and (10.2) show that the firm is more likely to find it profitable to postpone investment than before when the mean-preserving spread takes place. This is also clear from (10.3). Its left-hand side is decreased by the mean-preserving spread and hence the criterion for postponement is more easily satisfied.

Next, suppose that there is Knightian uncertainty, and thus the value of the utilized patent is (10.4) and that of the unutilized patent is (10.5). Suppose further that Knightian uncertainty is increased in the sense that the degree of confidence contamination, ε, is increased.[6] It is plain to see from (10.4) and (10.5) that an increase in ε always decreases the value of both the utilized and unutilized patent. Therefore,

---

[4]The concept of ε-contamination can be applied to multiple-state cases. Let $\mathcal{M}$ be the set of all probability charges over states, and let $P_0 \in \mathcal{M}$. Then, the *ε-contamination* of P_0, $\{P_0\}^{\varepsilon}$, is defined by $\{P_0\}^{\varepsilon} := \{(1-\varepsilon)P_0 + \varepsilon Q \mid Q \in \mathcal{M}\}$, where $\varepsilon \in [0, 1)$. Some behavioral foundation for ε-contamination is provided by Nishimura and Ozaki (2006) and Chap. 12 of this book. Also, Nishimura and Ozaki (2004) and Chap. 9 of this book apply ε-contamination to a discrete-time search model and Nishimura and Ozaki (2002, 2008) and Chap. 14 of this book explore learning behavior under ε-contamination.

[5]More generally, an expansion of $\mathcal{P}$ (in terms of set inclusion) can be interpreted as an increase in Knightian uncertainty. Ghirardato and Marinacci (2002) develop the notion of comparative Knightian-uncertainty aversion, or in their terms, "comparative ambiguity aversion," and relate it to this set expansion, which provides some behavioral foundation of our notion of an increase in Knightian uncertainty. See Sect. 9.4.5.

[6]The following observations still hold with some minor modification (such as a replacement of "increases" by "nondecreases") even if an increase in Knightian uncertainty is modeled more generally by an expansion of $\mathcal{P}$. See the previous footnote.

the value of investment opportunity *de*creases rather than increases with increases in Knightian uncertainty. Intuitively, an increase in Knightian uncertainty leads to a lower value of the utilized patent at the time of investment because it is evaluated by a less favorable profit from the utilized patent, and hence, the value of the unutilized patent is also reduced.

It is also evident from (10.4) and (10.5) that reduction in value is larger in the utilized patent than in the unutilized patent, implying that the firm is again more likely to postpone investment than before. This is also clear from (10.6). Its left-hand side is decreased by an increase in ε and hence the criterion for postponement is more easily satisfied.

We therefore observe that an increase in Knightian uncertainty and an increase in risk have opposite effects on the value of an unutilized patent (the investment opportunity) although they have the same effect on the timing of investment.

In the following sections, the simple two-period, two-state example of building a factory for patented products in this section is generalized to a continuous-time model, and we argue that basically the same observations hold true.

10.3 Knightian Uncertainty in Continuous Time

In this section, Knightian uncertainty is introduced into the continuous-time model, and three ways to characterize it are discussed; strong rectangularity, *i.i.d.* uncertainty, and κ-ignorance. κ-Ignorance is a special case of *i.i.d.* uncertainty, and *i.i.d.* uncertainty is in turn a special case of strong rectangularity.

As in the simple example of Sect. 10.2, it is not likely that the firm has perfect confidence in the probability P. There may be other candidate probabilities that the firm considers probable. Thus, the firm faces Knightian uncertainty, in which the firm confronts a set of probabilities instead of a single probability P. However, these candidate probabilities are not likely to be wildly different from P, but it is rather a small deviation from P, like ε-contamination in the example of the previous section.

To model this type of Knightian uncertainty in the continuous-time framework, we follow Chen and Epstein (2002) who characterized Knightian uncertainty in continuous time in a different context. First, we assume that the firm considers only a set of probabilities that have perfect agreement with P with respect to zero probability events. This amounts to assuming that probability measures we consider are absolutely continuous with respect to P and one another. Two probabilities are called equivalent if they are absolutely continuous with each other. Thus, we are concerned with probabilities equivalent to P.[7] (See Sect. 10.3.1.)

It is known (Girsanov's theorem) in the mathematical finance literature that an equivalent probability is generated by a "density generator" from an original probability, and that a Brownian motion (with respect to the original probability) perturbed

[7] This is a weaker concept of Knightian uncertainty than that in the discrete-time model (see, for example, the previous chapter).

by this density generator is still a Brownian motion (with respect to the generated equivalent probability). Moreover, all equivalent probabilities to P can be generated in this way. This property in turn implies that "geometric Brownian motions" corresponding to probabilities equivalent to P, which describe the movement of profit π_t under these probabilities, are different only in their drift term, not in the volatility term. (See Sect. 10.3.2.)

We impose a restriction on the form of Knightian uncertainty thus defined, which Chen and Epstein call *rectangularity*. Actually, we adopt its stronger version, which we call "strong" rectangularity to simplify the argument. (See Sect. 10.3.3.)

After the value of a utilized patent is derived for the case of strong rectangularity in Sect. 10.4 and the optimal investment decision for this case is formulated and characterized in Sect. 10.5, we assume that the firm considers only small perturbations from P; that is, the density generator is confined to a small range. In particular, we are mostly concerned with a continuous-time counterpart to the ε-contamination in Sect. 10.2, which Chen and Epstein call *κ-ignorance*. Specifically, κ-ignorance assumes that the density generator moves only in the range $[-\kappa, \kappa]$ and thus κ can be considered as the degree of Knightian uncertainty or ignorance. (See Sect. 10.3.4.)

Later, in Sect. 10.6, an analytic formula determining the value of an unutilized patent is derived for the case of κ-ignorance and infinite horizon. This formula will be utilized in the sensitivity analysis of Sect. 10.7, which examines the effect of risk and Knightian uncertainty.

10.3.1 Density Generators

We proceed with a mathematically more rigorous manner. Let T be the expiration date of the patent, which is assumed to be finite for the time being. For simplicity, we assume the patent produces no profit after its expiration date T.[8] Later, we consider a case in which T is infinite.

Let $(\Omega, \mathcal{F}_T, P)$ be a probability space. In the remainder of this chapter, we assume that P is a probability measure (countably additive), not only a probability charge (finitely additive). Let $(B_t)_{0\leq t\leq T}$ be a standard Brownian motion with respect to P. As a filtration $(\mathcal{F}_t)_{0\leq t\leq T}$, we take the *standard filtration* for $(B_t)_{0\leq t\leq T}$.[9]

Let us now define the "density generators" that are utilized in formulating Knightian uncertainty in this chapter. Let $\mathcal{L}$ be the set of real-valued, measurable,[10] and $(\mathcal{F}_t)$-adapted stochastic processes on $(\Omega, \mathcal{F}_T, P)$ with an index set $[0, T]$, and let $\mathcal{L}^2$ be a subset of $\mathcal{L}$, which is defined by

---

[8]To incorporate the possibility of after-expiration profit flow is straightforward but makes analysis cumbersome.

[9]A filtration $(\mathcal{F}_t)_{0\leq t\leq T}$ is the *standard filtration* for $(B_t)_{0\leq t\leq T}$ if for each $t \geq 0$, $\mathcal{F}_t$ is the smallest σ-algebra that contains all P-null sets and with respect to which $(B_k)_{0\leq k\leq t}$ are all measurable.

[10]A real-valued stochastic process $(X_t)_{0\leq t\leq T}$ on $(\Omega, \mathcal{F}_T, P)$ is *measurable* if a function $(t, \omega) \mapsto X_t(\omega)$ is $(\mathcal{B}([0, T]) \otimes \mathcal{F}_T)$-measurable, where $\mathcal{B}([0, T])$ is the Borel σ-algebra on $[0, T]$.

$$\mathcal{L}^2 := \left\{ (\theta_t)_{0 \le t \le T} \in \mathcal{L} \;\middle|\; \int_0^T \theta_t^2 \, dt < +\infty \; P\text{-a.s.} \right\}.$$

Given $\theta := (\theta_t)_{0 \le t \le T} \in \mathcal{L}^2$, we define a stochastic process $\left(z_t^\theta\right)_{0 \le t \le T}$ by

$$(\forall t) \quad z_t^\theta := \exp\left(-\frac{1}{2}\int_0^t \theta_s^2 \, ds - \int_0^t \theta_s dB_s\right), \tag{10.7}$$

where the stochastic integral, $\int_0^t \theta_s dB_s$, is well defined for each t because $\theta \in \mathcal{L}^2$.[11] A stochastic process $\theta \in \mathcal{L}^2$ is a *density generator* if $z^\theta := \left(z_t^\theta\right)_{0 \le t \le T}$ thus defined is an $(\mathcal{F}_t)$-martingale.[12]

As the name suggests, a density generator generates another probability measure from a given probability measure, and the resulting measure is equivalent to the original measure. To see this, let θ be a density generator and define the probability measure Q^θ by

$$(\forall A \in \mathcal{F}_T) \quad Q^\theta(A) := \int_A z_T^\theta(\omega) dP(\omega). \tag{10.9}$$

Because z^θ is a martingale, $Q^\theta(\Omega) = E^P[z_T^\theta] = z_0^\theta = 1$, and hence, Q^θ is certainly a probability measure that is absolutely continuous with respect to P. Furthermore, because z_T^θ is strictly positive, P is absolutely continuous with respect to Q^θ. Therefore, Q^θ is equivalent to P. Conversely, any probability measure that is equivalent to P can be generated via (10.9) by some density generator (see Duffie 1996, p. 289).

We assume that the firm's set of probability measures describing its Knightian uncertainty consists of probability measures equivalent to P. The standard results described in the previous paragraph then imply that the firm's Knightian uncertainty is characterized as an "expansion" of the set of probability measures from a singleton set $\{P\}$ through density generators.

Let Θ be a set of density generators. We then define the set of probability measures generated by Θ, $\mathcal{P}^\Theta$, on $(\Omega, \mathcal{F}_T)$ by

$$\mathcal{P}^\Theta := \{ Q^\theta \mid \theta \in \Theta \}, \tag{10.10}$$

where Q^θ is derived from P according to (10.9). Thus, the firm's Knightian uncertainty is characterized by $\mathcal{P}^\Theta$ for some Θ.

---

[11]Equivalently, $\left(z_t^\theta\right)_{0 \le t \le T}$ is defined as a unique solution to the stochastic differential equation: $dz_t^\theta = -z_t^\theta \theta_t dB_t$ with $z_0^\theta = 1$.

[12]A sufficient condition for z^θ to be an $(\mathcal{F}_t)$-martingale and thus for θ to be a density generator is *Novikov's condition*:

$$E^P\left[\exp\left(\frac{1}{2}\int_0^T \theta_s^2 \, ds\right)\right] < +\infty \tag{10.8}$$

(see Karatzas and Shreve 1991, p. 199, Corollary 5.13).

10.3.2 The Set of Stochastic Differential Equations

Let μ and σ be real numbers. We assume that $\sigma \geq 0$ without loss of generality[13] and $\sigma \neq 0$ to exclude a deterministic case. Then, suppose that the operating profit from the utilized patent is a real-valued stochastic process $(\pi_t)_{0 \leq t \leq T}$ that is generated by a geometric Brownian motion such that $d\pi_t = \mu \pi_t dt + \sigma \pi_t dB_t$, where $\pi_0 > 0$ and (B_t) is a Brownian motion with respect to the probability measure P. Because $dB_t^\theta = dB_t + \theta_t dt$ by Girsanov's theorem,[14] we have for any $\theta \in \Theta$,

$$d\pi_t = (\mu - \sigma\theta_t)\pi_t dt + \sigma \pi_t dB_t^\theta \,. \tag{10.12}$$

Thus, (π_t) is also the solution of the stochastic differential equation (10.12) if Q^θ is the underlying probability measure because in this case, $\left(B_t^\theta\right)$ is a Brownian motion with respect to Q^θ by Girsanov's theorem. Under uncertainty characterized by Θ, the decision-maker considers all stochastic differential equations, (10.12), with $\theta \in \Theta$ varying. It should be noted that θ affects only the drift term, and not the volatility term, in (10.12).

Let $\theta \in \Theta$. Then, by (10.12) and an application of Ito's lemma to the logarithm of π_t by regarding Q^θ as the true probability measure, we obtain

$$(\forall t \geq 0) \quad \pi_t = \pi_0 \exp\left(\left(\mu - \frac{1}{2}\sigma^2\right)t - \sigma \int_0^t \theta_s \, ds + \sigma B_t^\theta\right) . \tag{10.13}$$

10.3.3 Strong Rectangularity

We assume that the firm considers a "small deviation" from the original P. This means that the range that density generators can move is restricted to some "neighborhood" set of P. In particular, we consider a counterpart to the ε-contamination of Sect. 10.2, which is called κ-ignorance (Chen and Epstein 2002).

It is now necessary to formally define κ-ignorance. However, because some of our results in this chapter hold true under weaker conditions than κ-ignorance, it is worthwhile to also define these conditions, called rectangularity and *i.i.d.* uncertainty by Chen and Epstein.

A set of density generators, Θ, is called *strongly rectangular* if there exist a nonempty compact subset $\mathcal{K}$ of $\mathbb{R}$ and a compact-valued, measurable correspondence

[13]If necessary, take $(-B_t)$ instead of (B_t) in the following.

[14]Girsanov's theorem states that if we define, for each $\theta \in \Theta$, a stochastic process $\left(B_t^\theta\right)_{0 \leq t \leq T}$ by

$$(\forall t) \quad B_t^\theta := B_t + \int_0^t \theta_s \, ds \,, \tag{10.11}$$

then $\left(B_t^\theta\right)_{0 \leq t \leq T}$ turns out to be a standard Brownian motion with respect to $(\mathcal{F}_t)$ on $(\Omega, \mathcal{F}_T, Q^\theta)$ (Karatzas and Shreve 1991, p. 191, Theorem 5.1).

$K : [0, T] \twoheadrightarrow \mathcal{K}$ such that[15]

$$\Theta = \left\{ \theta \in \mathcal{L}^2 \,\middle|\, \theta_t(\omega) \in K_t \quad (m \otimes P)\text{-a.s.} \right\}, \tag{10.14}$$

where m denotes the Lebesgue measure restricted on $\mathcal{B}([0, T])$.[16] Any element of a set Θ defined by (10.14) satisfies Novikov's condition (10.8) because $(\forall t)\ K_t \subseteq \mathcal{K}$ and $\mathcal{K}$ is compact, and hence, it is certainly a density generator. We denote by Θ^K the set defined by (10.14).

The next theorem is an important implication of strong rectangularity.

Theorem 10.3.1 *Let $0 \leq s \leq t \leq T$, let x be an $\mathcal{F}_T$-measurable function, and let Θ be a strongly rectangular set of density generators. Then, it holds that*

$$\begin{aligned}\min_{\theta\in\Theta} E^{Q^\theta}[x \mid \mathcal{F}_s] &= \min_{\theta\in\Theta} E^{Q^\theta}\left[E^{Q^\theta}[x \mid \mathcal{F}_t] \,\middle|\, \mathcal{F}_s \right] \\ &= \min_{\theta\in\Theta} E^{Q^\theta}\left[\min_{\theta'\in\Theta} E^{Q^{\theta'}}[x \mid \mathcal{F}_t] \,\middle|\, \mathcal{F}_s \right] \end{aligned} \tag{10.15}$$

as long as the minima exist.

Note that while the first equality in Theorem 10.3.1 always holds by the law of iterated integrals, the second equality may not hold if Θ is not strongly rectangular.[17] The "recursive" structure (10.15) under strong rectangularity is exploited when we solve an optimal stopping problem for the firm.

10.3.4 I.I.D. Uncertainty and κ-Ignorance

The *i.i.d.* uncertainty is a special case of strong rectangularity in which K_t is independent of time t. To be precise, the uncertainty characterized by Θ is an *i.i.d. uncertainty* if there exists a compact subset K of $\mathbb{R}$ such that $0 \in K$ and $\Theta = \left\{ \theta \in \mathcal{L}^2 \,\middle|\, \theta_t(\omega) \in K \quad (m \otimes P) - a.s. \right\}$.

κ-Ignorance is a special case of *i.i.d.* uncertainty, where the set K is further specified as $K = [-\kappa, \kappa]$ for some $\kappa \geq 0$. It is evident that if $\kappa = 0$, Knightian uncertainty

[15] A compact-valued correspondence $K : [0, T] \twoheadrightarrow \mathcal{K}$ is *measurable* if $\{ t \in [0, T] \mid K_t \cap U \neq \phi \} \in \mathcal{B}([0, T])$ holds for any open set U.

[16] Chen and Epstein (2002) adopt a weaker definition of rectangularity than ours. That is, a set of density generators, Θ, is *rectangular* if there exists a set-valued stochastic process $(K_t)_{0\leq t\leq T}$ such that $\Theta = \left\{ \theta \in \mathcal{L}^2 \,\middle|\, \theta_t(\omega) \in K_t(\omega) \quad (m \otimes P)\text{-a.s.} \right\}$ and, for each t, $K_t : \Omega \twoheadrightarrow \mathbb{R}$ is compact-valued and satisfies some additional regularity conditions. Our definition of strong rectangularity further restricts K_t to be degenerate (that is, nonstochastic). This restriction makes the following analysis much easier.

[17] Note that the second equality in (10.15) also holds under the weaker requirement of rectangularity of Chen and Epstein (2002) (see the previous footnote). Strong rectangularity is needed to show Proposition 10.4.1 below, where the rectangularity is not sufficient.

vanishes. If κ increases, it means that the firm is less certain than before that candidate probability measures are close to P. Thus, κ-ignorance can be considered as a continuous-time counterpart of ε-contamination in Sect. 10.2.

10.4 The Value of a Utilized Patent

Let us now consider the value of a utilized patent under Knightian uncertainty described in the previous section. We first derive its exact formula. Here, it turns out that strong rectangularity, of which *i.i.d.* uncertainty (and thus κ-ignorance) is a special case, is sufficient to obtain a simple formula.

Suppose that $\mathcal{P}^{\Theta}$ is Knightian uncertainty that the firm faces, where $\mathcal{P}^{\Theta}$ is the set of measures defined by (10.10) with some strongly rectangular set of density generators, $\Theta = \Theta^K$. Then, the corresponding profit process (π_t) follows (10.12). As in Sect. 10.2, we assume that the firm is uncertainty-averse. Then, the value at time t of the utilized patent with expiration time T, which has the current profit flow π_t, is defined by

$$W(\pi_t, t) := \inf_{Q \in \mathcal{P}^{\Theta}} E^Q \left[\int_t^T e^{-\rho(s-t)} \pi_s \, ds \,\middle|\, \mathcal{F}_t \right], \tag{10.16}$$

where $\rho > 0$ is the firm's discount rate and $E^Q[\cdot|\mathcal{F}_t]$ denotes the expectation with respect to Q conditional on $\mathcal{F}_t$. We assume $\rho > \mu$. The infimum operator reflects the firm's uncertainty aversion.

Before presenting Proposition 10.4.1 that gives an exact formula, we need to define an "upper-rim" density generator, which plays a pivotal role in our analysis. Given $(K_t)_{0 \le t \le T}$, we define an *upper-rim density generator*, θ^*, by

$$(\forall t) \quad \theta_t^* := \arg\max\{ \sigma x \,|\, x \in K_t \} = \max K_t\,, \tag{10.17}$$

where equality holds by $\sigma > 0$ and the compact-valuedness of K. Note that we write $\max K_t$ instead of $\{\max K_t\}$. Then, θ^* turns out to be a degenerate (that is, nonstochastic) measurable process,[18] and hence, $\theta^* \in \mathcal{L}$. Therefore, it follows that $\theta^* \in \Theta^K$ by (10.17). Obviously, if Knightian uncertainty is κ-ignorance so that $(\forall t)\ K_t = [-\kappa, \kappa]$, then $\theta^* = \kappa$.

We are now ready to present the exact formula.

Proposition 10.4.1 *Suppose that the firm faces Knightian uncertainty characterized by Θ^K, where Θ^K is a strongly rectangular set of density generators defined by (10.14) for some K. Then the value of the utilized patent in (10.16) is given by*

[18] Let $a \in \mathbb{R}$. Then, $\{ t \mid \max K_t > a \} = \{ t \mid K_t \cap (a, +\infty) \neq \phi \} \in \mathcal{B}([0, T])$ by measurability of K, which shows that $\max K_t$ is $\mathcal{B}([0, T])$-measurable (see Footnote 15).

$$W(\pi_t, t) = \int_t^T \pi_t \exp\left(-(\rho - \mu)(s-t) - \int_t^s \sigma\theta_r^* \, dr\right) ds\,, \tag{10.18}$$

where θ^* is defined by (10.17).

We notice that even though the firm is assumed to be risk-neutral, the risk factor σ sneaks in and an increase in risk also influences the value of the unutilized patent under Knightian uncertainty, whereas the risk factor does not influence the value when there is no Knightian uncertainty (when $\theta^* = 0$). Thus, Knightian uncertainty in the continuous-time framework makes the value of the utilized patent depend not only on Knightian uncertainty itself, but also on risk.

10.5 The Optimal Investment Decision

In this section, we formulate the investment problem of the firm as an optimal stopping problem under Knightian uncertainty, and relate the investment problem to the value of the utilized patent described in the previous section.

Consider the investment of building a factory to produce patented products, which costs I and in return generates a profit flow $(\pi_s)_{s\geq t}$ when made at time t. The firm faces the same Knightian uncertainty as in the previous section: $(\pi_s)_{s\geq t}$ follows (10.12) with strongly rectangular $\Theta = \Theta^K$. The firm possessing the patent has an investment opportunity and contemplates optimal timing of this investment.

Then, at time t, the firm faces the optimal stopping problem of maximizing:

$$\min_{Q\in\mathcal{P}^\Theta} E^Q\left[\int_{t'}^T e^{-\rho(s-t)}\pi_s \, ds - e^{-\rho(t'-t)} I \,\middle|\, \mathcal{F}_t\right]$$

by choosing an $(\mathcal{F}_t)$-stopping time,[19] t' ($t' \in [t, T]$), when the investment is to be made.[20] The maximum of this problem is denoted by V_t:

$$V_t := \max_{t'\geq t} \min_{Q\in\mathcal{P}^\Theta} E^Q\left[\int_{t'}^T e^{-\rho(s-t)}\pi_s \, ds - e^{-\rho(t'-t)} I \,\middle|\, \mathcal{F}_t\right]. \tag{10.19}$$

[19]That is, t' is such that $(\forall t \geq 0)\ \{t' \leq t\} \in \mathcal{F}_t$.

[20]An alternative approach to modeling the firm's behavior under uncertainty is to apply *robust control theory*. Then, the firm's objective would be to maximize:

$$\min_{Q\in\mathcal{P}^\Theta}\left(E^Q\left[\int_{t'}^T e^{-\rho(s-t)}\pi_s \, ds - e^{-\rho(t'-t)} I \,\middle|\, \mathcal{F}_t\right] + \eta R_t(Q)\right),$$

where η is a constant and $R_t(\cdot)$ measures the degree of deviation of the "true" probability measure Q from the "approximating" probability measure P, or the cost of model-misspecification when Q is the true probability measure. The preference behind this control problem is *not* based on the maxmin expected utility à la Gilboa and Schmeidler (1989) which underlies the specification of Knightian uncertainty in the current chapter. However, both preferences generate the same optimal path for some class of optimization problems. See Hansen et al. (2001).

Then, V_t is the value of the investment opportunity.

Now consider the two options available to the firm: invest now (at time t) or wait for a short time interval, dt, and reconsider whether to invest after that (at time $t + dt$). Then, as A.5.3 in the Appendix shows, V_t solves a version of the *Hamilton-Jacobi-Bellman equation*:

$$V_t = \max \left\{ W_t - I,\ \min_{Q \in \mathcal{P}^\Theta} E^Q[\, dV_t \mid \mathcal{F}_t\,] + V_t - \rho V_t\, dt \right\} . \tag{10.20}$$

Here, the first term on the right-hand side is the value of "stopping right now" and the second term is the value of "waiting," each of which corresponds to one of the two options mentioned above.

10.6 The Value of an Unutilized Patent

In general, it is difficult to derive an analytical solution of the functional equation (10.20) and get a simple formula for the value of the unutilized patent. However, analysis is greatly simplified if (a) underlying Knightian uncertainty is further restricted to κ-ignorance,[21] (b) the planning horizon is infinite, and (c) the patent never expires. (In the terminology of option theory, we are now considering irreversible investment as an American option.) In this section, we explicitly solve the optimal stopping problem in such a case and get a simple pricing formula of the unutilized patent.

10.6.1 κ-Ignorance and Infinite Horizon

Under κ-ignorance, the upper-rim density generator θ^* defined by (10.17) is independent of t and is given by

$$\theta^* = \arg\max\{\, \sigma x \mid x \in [-\kappa, \kappa]\} = \kappa . \tag{10.21}$$

Therefore, (10.18) is simplified to

$$W(\pi_t, t) = \int_t^T \pi_t e^{(-\rho+\mu-\kappa\sigma)(s-t)}\, ds = \frac{\pi_t}{\lambda}\left(1 - e^{-\lambda(T-t)}\right) , \tag{10.22}$$

where $\lambda \in \mathbb{R}$ is defined by

$$\lambda := \rho - (\mu - \kappa\sigma) . \tag{10.23}$$

[21] This section can easily be extended to the case of *i.i.d.* uncertainty.

In what follows, we let T go to infinity, and assume that relations between variables in the limit hold true in the infinite horizon case. We have assumed that $\rho > \mu$, and then, λ defined by (10.23) turns out to be positive because $\kappa \geq 0$. Consequently, under κ-ignorance, as T approaches infinity, (10.22) approaches

$$W(\pi_t) = \frac{\pi_t}{\lambda}, \tag{10.24}$$

which is independent of time. We hereafter assume that (10.24) holds in the infinite horizon case.[22]

Then, applying Ito's lemma by regarding P as the true probability measure, we have that (W_t) solves

$$dW_t = \mu W_t dt + \sigma W_t dB_t \tag{10.25}$$

with $W_0 := \pi_0/\lambda$. Hence, (10.11) implies that for any $\theta \in \Theta$, (W_t) solves

$$dW_t = (\mu - \sigma\theta_t)W_t dt + \sigma W_t dB_t^\theta . \tag{10.26}$$

This shows that when Q^θ is the true probability measure, (W_t) solves the stochastic differential equation defined by (10.26).

10.6.2 The Hamilton-Jacobi-Bellman Equation

Let us return to the optimal stopping problem of the previous section. If the planning horizon is infinite and (W_t) follows (10.25) (and (10.26)), then V_t defined by (10.19) depends only on W_t, and not on physical time t. Therefore, we are allowed to write it as $V_t = V(W_t)$ with some $V : \mathbb{R}_+ \to \mathbb{R}$. In this case, the Hamilton-Jacobi-Bellman equation turns out to be

$$\begin{aligned} V(W_t) = & \\ & \max \left\{ W_t - I,\ \min\nolimits_{Q\in\mathcal{P}^\Theta} E^Q\left[\, dV_t \mid \mathcal{F}_t \,\right] + V(W_t) - \rho V(W_t)\, dt \right\} . \end{aligned} \tag{10.27}$$

Let us now solve the above Hamilton-Jacobi-Bellman equation. We conjecture that there exists W^* such that the optimal strategy of the firm takes the form of "stop right now if $W_t \geq W^*$ and wait if $W_t < W^*$." This conjecture shall be verified to be true later.

---

[22] When the planning horizon and the patent expiration date are infinite in κ-ignorance, W becomes independent of t. However, conditions guaranteeing that (10.24) holds in the infinite horizon case are not yet known. We do not attempt to derive such conditions here, and instead we simply assume they are satisfied in our model. This is because we need more mathematical apparatus than we have in this chapter. For example, Girsanov's theorem is usually stated in a finite-horizon framework and thus some sophistication is required to extend it to an infinite horizon (see Karatzas and Shreve 1991, p. 192, Corollary 5.2).

In the continuation region, that is, when $W_t < W^*$, it holds from (10.27) that

$$\min_{Q \in \mathcal{P}^\Theta} E^Q [\, dV_t \mid \mathcal{F}_t \,] = \rho V(W_t)\, dt \,. \tag{10.28}$$

Here, the left-hand side is the minimum capital gain of holding the investment opportunity during $[t, t + dt]$, and the right-hand side is its opportunity cost measured in terms of the firm's discount rate. Equation (10.28) shows that both must be equal in the continuation region.

We now derive from Eq. (10.28) a nonstochastic ordinary differential equation for V. We conjecture that V is twice differentiable in the continuation region. Then, by Ito's lemma and (10.26), we have for each θ,

$$dV_t = V'(W_t)\left((\mu - \sigma\theta_t) W_t dt + \sigma W_t dB_t^\theta\right) + \frac{1}{2}\sigma^2 W_t^2 V''(W_t)\, dt \,. \tag{10.29}$$

At this stage, we conjecture that V' is positive. Then, the left-hand side of (10.28) is rewritten as

$$\min_{Q \in \mathcal{P}^\Theta} E^Q [\, dV_t \mid \mathcal{F}_t \,] = V'(W_t)(\mu - \kappa\sigma) W_t dt + \frac{1}{2}\sigma^2 W_t^2 V''(W_t)\, dt \tag{10.30}$$

(see A.5.4 in the Appendix). From (10.28) to (10.30), we obtain a (nonstochastic) second-order ordinary differential equation for V such that

$$\frac{1}{2}\sigma^2 W_t^2 V''(W_t) + (\mu - \kappa\sigma) W_t V'(W_t) - \rho V(W_t) = 0 \,, \tag{10.31}$$

which must hold in the continuation region.

To solve (10.31) for V, we need two boundary conditions. One boundary condition is given by the condition that if the utilized patent has no value, the investment opportunity also has no value[23]:

$$V(0) = 0 \,. \tag{10.32}$$

The other boundary condition comes from the Hamilton-Jacobi-Bellman equation (10.27) as

$$V(W^*) = W^* - I \,, \tag{10.33}$$

where W^* is the "reservation value" whose existence is now assumed.

Because W^* must be optimally chosen by the firm, (10.33) serves as a free-boundary condition. To determine the value of W^*, we need an additional condition for V, which is obtained from the optimization with respect to W^*. To find this, consider the gain the firm would obtain if it made an investment upon observing W_t.

---

[23]From (10.26), it follows that $W_T = 0$ for any $T \geq t$ if $W_t = 0$. Hence, it is optimal for the firm never to invest, leading to (10.32) by (10.19).

It would be the value of the project minus the value of the investment opportunity (the value of not making investment now) and it is given by $W_t - V(W_t)$. Because W^* should be chosen so as to maximize this, it must hold that

$$V'(W^*) = 1 \tag{10.34}$$

from the first-order condition for maximization.[24]

10.6.3 The Optimal Strategy

The ordinary differential equation (10.31) with boundary conditions (10.32), (10.33), and (10.34) can be explicitly solved to obtain

$$V(W_t) = \left(\frac{I}{\alpha - 1}\right)^{1-\alpha} \alpha^{-\alpha} W_t^{\alpha} =: A W_t^{\alpha} \tag{10.35}$$

as far as $W_t < W^*$ (see A.5.5 in the Appendix), where the reservation value W^* is given by

$$W^* = \frac{\alpha I}{\alpha - 1} \tag{10.36}$$

and α is a constant defined by

$$\alpha := \frac{-\left\{(\mu - \kappa\sigma) - \frac{1}{2}\sigma^2\right\} + \sqrt{\left\{(\mu - \kappa\sigma) - \frac{1}{2}\sigma^2\right\}^2 + 2\rho\sigma^2}}{\sigma^2}. \tag{10.37}$$

Under the maintained assumption that $\rho > \mu$ and $\kappa \geq 0$, it holds that $\alpha > 1$ (see A.5.6 in the Appendix). Hence, W^* and V are well defined.

Therefore, the value of the investment opportunity or the patent, V, is given by

$$V(W_t) = \begin{cases} \left(\frac{I}{\alpha - 1}\right)^{1-\alpha} \alpha^{-\alpha} W_t^{\alpha} & \text{if } W_t < W^* \\ W_t - I & \text{if } W_t \geq W^* \end{cases} \tag{10.38}$$

(see Fig. 10.1). Recall that we have made three conjectures: (a) there exists a unique reservation value W^*; (b) V is twice differentiable in the continuation region; and (c) V' is positive. These conjectures are easily verified to hold true from (10.38) ((b) and (c) are immediate and see Fig. 10.1 for (a)).

[24] We will find later that V is convex, and hence, the second-order condition turns out to be satisfied.

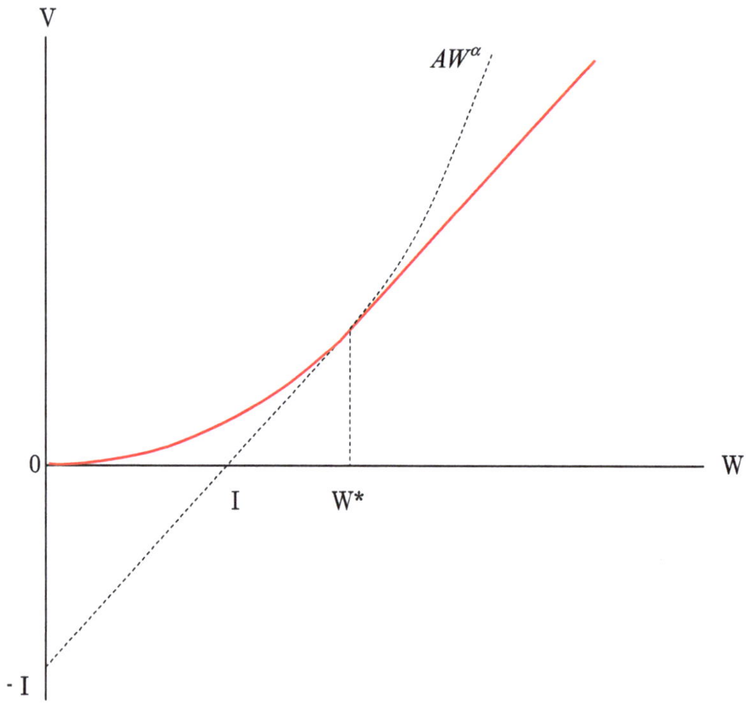

Fig. 10.1 The value function

To summarize, we have proved

Proposition 10.6.1 *Assume that Knightian uncertainty the firm faces is κ-ignorance, and further assume that relations among variables in the finite-horizon case converge, as the horizon goes to infinity, to those in the infinite-horizon case. Then, in the case of the infinite horizon, the value of the unutilized patent, that is, $V(W_t)$ in the continuation region ($W_t < W^*$), is given by (10.35) with W^* and α defined by (10.36) and (10.37), respectively.*

10.7 Sensitivity Analysis

This section compares the effect of an increase in Knightian uncertainty and that of an increase in risk on the value of a patent and on optimal timing of investment. We show that the same result holds in the continuous-time case as in the simple two-period, two-state example of Sect. 10.2.

10.7.1 An Increase in Risk

Let us consider the effect of an increase in risk when there is no Knightian uncertainty, or when we assume that $\kappa = 0$. It is evident from (10.23) and (10.24) that σ^2 does not influence the value of the utilized patent. In contrast, σ^2 changes the value of the unutilized patent. With some calculation, we have

$$\frac{\partial \alpha}{\partial \sigma^2} < 0 . \tag{10.39}$$

We also obtain $\partial V(W_t)/\partial \alpha < 0$ for the unutilized patent (that is, when $W_t < W^*$).[25] Combining these, we have $\partial V(W_t)/\partial \sigma^2 > 0$ for the value of the unutilized patent. Thus, an increase in σ^2 increases the value of the unutilized patent. Finally, because $\partial W^*/\partial \alpha < 0$ (see (10.36)), we obtain $\partial W^*/\partial \sigma^2 > 0$ by (10.39). Therefore, we obtain

Proposition 10.7.1 *In the case of no Knightian uncertainty, an increase in σ^2, that is, an increase in risk, induces (a) an increase in the value of the unutilized patent and no change in the value of the utilized patent, and (b) an increase in the reservation value W^* (see Fig. 10.2).*

10.7.2 An Increase in Knightian Uncertainty

Let us now consider a case where the Knightian uncertainty that the firm faces is characterized as κ-ignorance, which is a continuous-time counterpart of the ε-contamination seen in the two-period, two-state example of Sect. 10.2.

Consider first the value of the utilized patent. We have from (10.23) and (10.24), $W_t = W(\pi_t) = \pi_t / (\rho - (\mu - \kappa\sigma))$. Consequently, an increase in κ reduces the value of the utilized patent. This contrasts with the case of no Knightian uncertainty where an increase in σ^2 has no effect on the value of the utilized patent.

Let us now turn to the value of the unutilized patent. It is evident from (10.35) that an increase in κ reduces the value of the unutilized patent by lowering W. Moreover, an increase in κ further reduces the value of the unutilized patent through α. It follows from (10.37) with some calculation that

$$\frac{\partial \alpha}{\partial \kappa} > 0 . \tag{10.40}$$

Thus, the effect of an increase in κ on α is opposite to that of an increase in σ^2 under no Knightian uncertainty. Combining this effect and $\partial V(W_t)/\partial \alpha < 0$ when

[25] The claim holds because $\partial \ln V(W_t)/\partial \alpha = -\ln I + \ln(\alpha - 1) - \ln \alpha + \ln W_t < -\ln I + \ln(\alpha - 1) - \ln \alpha + \ln W^* = -\ln I + \ln(\alpha - 1) - \ln \alpha + \ln(\alpha I/(\alpha - 1)) = 0$.

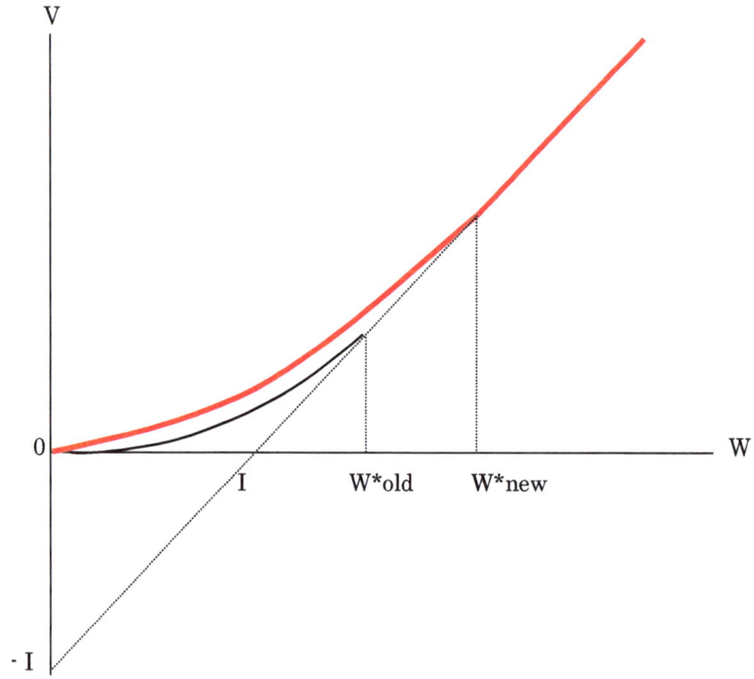

Fig. 10.2 An increase in risk

$W_t < W^*$ from Footnote 25, we have $(\partial V(W_t)/\partial\alpha)\,(\partial\alpha/\partial\kappa) < 0$ when $W_t < W^*$. Consequently, an increase in κ reduces the value of the unutilized patent (that is, $V(W_t)$ when $W_t < W^*$) by raising α. The direct effect of lowering W and the indirect effect of raising α both reduce the value of the unutilized patent.

Finally, because $\partial W^*/\partial\alpha < 0$, we obtain $\partial W^*/\partial\kappa < 0$ by (10.40). Thus, we conclude that the next proposition holds.

Proposition 10.7.2 *Assume the same assumptions as Proposition 10.6.1. Then an increase in κ, that is, an increase in Knightian uncertainty, induces (a) a* decrease *in the value of utilized and unutilized patents, and (b) a* decrease *in the reservation value W^* (see Fig. 10.3).*

This proposition provides a sharp contrast to an increase in the "risk" in the previous subsection. While an increase in risk increases the value of the unutilized patent (and leaves the value of the utilized patent unchanged), an increase in Knightian uncertainty (an increase in κ) decreases the value of the unutilized patent (as well as the value of the utilized patent).

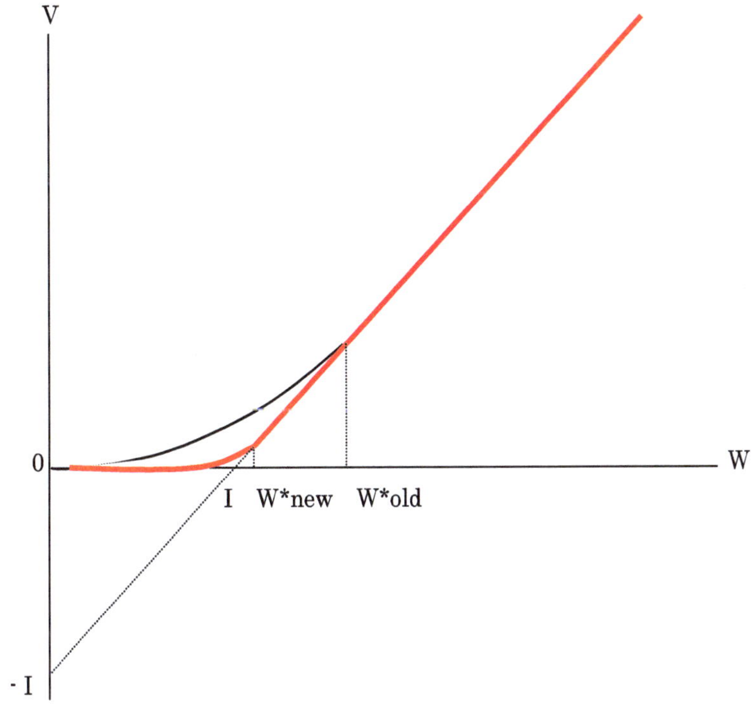

Fig. 10.3 An increase in Knightian uncertainty

10.7.3 *Value of Waiting*

To analyze the value of waiting, it is worthwhile reinterpreting the reservation value W^* in Propositions 10.7.1 and 10.7.2 in terms of the reservation profit flow π^* defined as

$$\pi^* := \begin{cases} (\rho - \mu)W^* & \text{under no Knightian uncertainty} \\ (\rho - (\mu - \kappa\sigma))\ W^* & \text{under Knightian uncertainty } (\kappa\text{-ignorance}). \end{cases}$$

Note that $W_t = \pi_t/(\rho - \mu)$ under no Knightian uncertainty and $W_t = \pi_t/\,(\rho - (\mu - \kappa\sigma))$ under κ-ignorance. When the current profit flow, π_t, is less than π^*, the value of the utilized patent, W_t, is less than W^* because $\rho - \mu > 0$ under no Knightian uncertainty and $\rho - (\mu - \kappa\sigma) > 0$ under κ-ignorance. Hence, waiting is the optimal strategy. On the other hand, when the current profit flow is greater than π^*, the value of the utilized patent is greater than W^* and hence "stopping right now" is the optimal strategy. Therefore, π^* thus defined serves as the reservation profit flow.

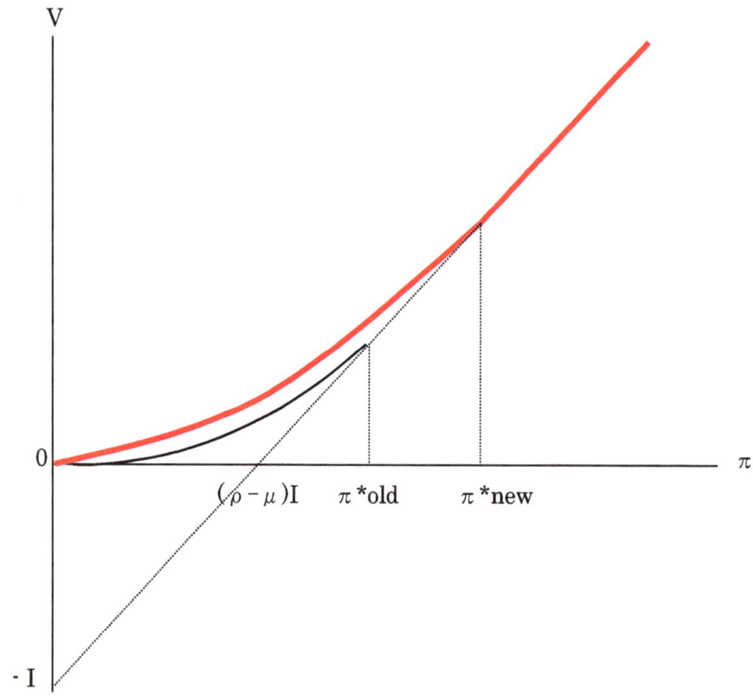

Fig. 10.4 An increase in risk (The x-axis is measured in terms of profit flow)

It follows that $\partial\pi^*/\partial\sigma^2 > 0$ under no Knightian uncertainty because $\partial W^*/\partial\sigma^2 > 0$ (see Sect. 10.7.1), and calculation shows that $\partial\pi^*/\partial\kappa > 0$ under κ-ignorance.[26] Thus, both an increase in risk under no Knightian uncertainty and an increase in κ-ignorance under Knightian uncertainty *in*crease the reservation profit flow, and thus the value of waiting is increased (see Figs. 10.4 and 10.5). This result conforms to that of Sect. 10.2, where increases in both risk and Knightian uncertainty make it more profitable for the firm to postpone irreversible investment.

This waiting-enhancing effect of an increase in Knightian uncertainty is in stark contrast to its waiting-reducing effect in the job search model investigated by Nishimura and Ozaki (2004, Chap. 9 of this book). They show that in a discrete-time infinite-horizon job search model, an increase in Knightian uncertainty unambiguously reduces the reservation wage and thus shortens waiting.

Although both the job search and irreversible investment models are formulated as optimal stopping problems, there is a fundamental difference between the two as to the nature of uncertainty. In the job search model, the decision-maker determines when to stop the search and thus resolve uncertainty. Thus, an increase in Knightian uncertainty makes the uncertainty-averse decision-maker more likely to stop the search and resolve uncertainty. In contrast, in the irreversible investment model, the

[26] In fact, it can be shown that $\partial\pi^*/\partial\kappa > 0$ if $\alpha > 1$.

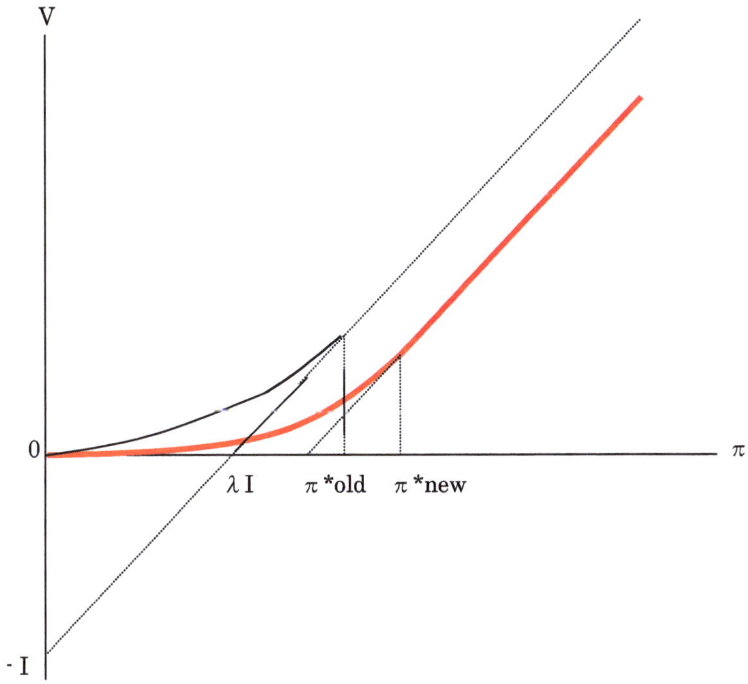

Fig. 10.5 An increase in Knightian uncertainty (The x-axis is measured in terms of profit flow)

decision-maker contemplates when to begin investment and face uncertainty. Thus, an increase in Knightian uncertainty makes the uncertainty-averse decision-maker more likely to postpone investment to avoid facing uncertainty.

References

Asano, T. 2010. Precautionary principle and the optimal timing of environmental policy under ambiguity. *Environmental and Resource Economics* 47: 173–196.

Asano, T., and A. Shibata. 2011. Optimal pricing and quality choice of a monopolist under Knightian uncertainty. *International Journal of Industrial Organization* 29: 746–754.

Chen, Z., and L. Epstein. 2002. Ambiguity, risk and asset returns in continuous time. *Econometrica* 70: 1403–1443.

Cheng, X., and F. Riedel. 2013. Optimal stopping under ambiguity in continuous time. *Mathematics and Financial Economics* 7: 29–68.

Dixit, A., and R. Pindyck. 1994. *Investment under uncertainty*. Princeton: Princeton University Press.

Duffie, D. 1996. *Dynamic asset pricing theory*, 2nd ed. Princeton: Princeton University Press.

Ghirardato, P., and M. Marinacci. 2002. Ambiguity made precise. *Journal of Economic Theory* 102: 251–289.

Gilboa, I. 1987. Expected utility theory with purely subjective non-additive probabilities. *Journal of Mathematical Economics* 16: 141–153.

Gilboa, I., and D. Schmeidler. 1989. Maxmin expected utility with non-unique prior. *Journal of Mathematical Economics* 18: 141–153.

Hansen, L.P., T.J. Sargent, G.A. Turmuhambetova and N. Williams. 2001. Robustness and uncertainty aversion, University of Chicago, mimeo.

Karatzas, I. and S.E. Shreve. 1991. *Brownian motion and stochastic calculus* (2nd edn.). Berlin: Springer.

McDonald, R., and D. Siegel. 1986. The value of waiting to invest. *Quarterly Journal of Economics* 101: 707–728.

Nishimura, K.G. and H. Ozaki. 2002. Economics of self-feeding fear, Discussion Paper 2002-CF-175, University of Tokyo.

Nishimura, K.G., and H. Ozaki. 2004. Search and Knightian uncertainty. *Journal of Economic Theory* 119: 299–333.

Nishimura, K.G., and H. Ozaki. 2006. An axiomatic approach to ε-contamination. *Economic Theory* 27: 333–340.

Nishimura, K.G., and H. Ozaki. 2007. Irreversible investment and Knightian uncertainty. *Journal of Economic Theory* 136(1): 668–694.

Nishimura, K.G. and H. Ozaki. 2008. Learning may increase perceived uncertainty: A model of confidence erosion under Knightian uncertainty, mimeo, Keio University. (Revised version of Nishimura and Ozaki, 2002)

Schmeidler, D. 1982. Subjective probability without additivity (Temporary Title), Working Paper, The Foerder Institute for Economic Research, Tel Aviv University.

Schmeidler, D. 1989. Subjective probability and expected utility without additivity. *Econometrica* 57: 571–587. (Its working paper is first published in 1982)

Schröder, D. 2011. Investment under ambiguity with the best and worst in mind. *Mathematics and Financial Economics* 4: 107–133.

Thijssen, J.J. 2011. Incomplete markets, ambiguity, and irreversible investment. *Journal of Economics Dynamics and Control* 35: 909–921.

Trojanowska, M., and P.M. Kort. 2010. The worst case of real options. *Journal of Optimization Theory and Applications* 146: 709–734.

Chapter 11
Liquidity Preference and Knightian Uncertainty

11.1 Introduction and Summary

11.1.1 Money Offering Flexibility

Without doubt, money is the most liquid asset. The conversion of money to other assets is immediate and costless, whereas the conversion of nonmoney assets to other assets including money involves time and substantial transaction costs. Thus, money enables prompt movement among various forms of investment, both financial and real. In a sense, money offers liquidity services. It is natural to assume that these liquidity services are one of the most important determinants of money demand. In fact, this is the heart of speculative demand for money, as opposed to transaction and precautionary demand for money. Unfortunately, however, there are relatively few examinations of the liquidity or speculative motive of holding money, as compared with the transaction and precautionary motives.

The model we consider in this chapter is based on the classical model of the cash-in-advance economy in Stokey and Lucas (1989, Chap. 13).[1] While their model assumes that money is required to buy commodities, we assume that money is required to make investment. Thus, while money is an enabler of consumption transactions in the Stokey–Lucas model, money is an enabler of investment transactions in our model. In this sense, we consider money as liquid assets and other assets as illiquid assets (illiquid for one period). Otherwise, our basic set-up is the same as that of Stokey and Lucas, and their model can be regarded as a special case of ours.

In the linear-utility model of Stokey and Lucas (1989, p. 401), the representative agent's current-period utility is the current consumption times the marginal utility parameter, which is identically and independently distributed. In our model, we

---

[1]Their model is quite similar to Taub's (1988) model, which itself specifies Lucas' (1980) model by assuming that a decision-maker is risk-neutral.

K.G. Nishimura and H. Ozaki, *Economics of Pessimism and Optimism*,
DOI 10.1007/978-4-431-55903-0_11

assume the portfolio manager's current period "utility" is the current investment times gross rates of return under a Markovian stochastic environment. Moreover, we consider Knightian uncertainty about these gross rates of return in the form of the Choquet integral framework. Thus, when our Choquet integral framework is reduced to the usual (Lebesgue) integral framework *and* when our Markovian stochastic environment is reduced to the *i.i.d.* stochastic environment, then our model turns out to be the same as the cash-in-advance pure-currency economy model of Stokey and Lucas.

Among existing literature of the liquidity motive of holding money, Jones and Ostroy's (1984) formulation has attracted much attention. They argue that money, as an asset of the least transaction cost, offers flexibility to its holder, which other assets cannot provide. Under the presence of liquidation (transaction) costs on other assets, money is held to enable the option of waiting for tomorrow to resolve uncertainty rather than investing today under uncertainty. Thus, their formulation of liquidity services of money can be considered as an enabler of options.

In this chapter, by extending the Stokey–Lucas cash-in-advance model to investment opportunities under Knightian uncertainty, we re-examine the idea of Jones and Ostroy in two ways. First, we put their idea into a truly dynamic framework of the infinite horizon. Second, we consider not only the case in which a decision-maker is reasonably confident about the nature of uncertainty she faces and her view about her probabilistic environment is summarized by a particular probability, but also the case in which her confidence about her probabilistic environment is much lower and she is not certain about even relative plausibility of possible probabilities. Specifically, we consider a behavior of a risk-neutral fund manager who contemplates in each period whether to make an illiquid investment which, if made, generates some returns. Furthermore, we assume that the fund manager faces true uncertainty, rather than mere risk, about the realization of these returns.

We set up a fund manager's problem so that she should maximize the sum of discounted future gross returns from an investment by tactically choosing its amount in each period, where the uncertainty about the returns is evaluated according to the CEU preference with a convex capacity in a manner that time consistency holds. This time consistency is crucial because we apply dynamic programming techniques to solve the problem. The contribution of this chapter includes proving the existence of the optimal investment strategy and presenting that strategy in a closed form under the assumption of stochastic nondecrease of a convex capacitary kernel. Here, a *convex capacitary kernel* is a convex extension of a transition probability and the *stochastic nondecrease* means that the state space is ordered in an appropriate manner.[2] It then turns out that the optimal investment strategy takes a form of reservation strategy: there exists the reservation function, a function of a current return, such that if a current return exceeds the value of this function, the fund manager should invest all the money subject to a cash-in-advance constraint; if it does not, she should

[2]The formal definitions of the capacitary kernel and the stochastic nondecrease appear in Sect. 2.5.

not conduct any investment. Furthermore, we present a condition on the convex capacitary kernel under which the reservation function becomes a constant.

The existence of cash reserve provides the fund manager with an option not to invest in the current period but to wait until next period. The results mentioned in the previous paragraph show that the fund manager has a call option when she has cash in hand and exercises this option when the return exceeds some reservation level. This facilitates the interpretation of cash as an "enabler" of call options and substantiates the meaning of flexibility according to Jones and Ostroy (1984).

The organization of this chapter is as follows. In the remainder of this section, we will first explain in nontechnical terms the differing effects on the speculative demand for money between increase in risk and increase in (Knightian) uncertainty. We also summarize new mathematical results. Section 11.2 formulates the stochastic environment underlying the model and formally presents the fund manager's problem. Section 11.3 gives the exact solution of the fund manager's problem and shows that the solution has the form of reservation strategy, while Sect. 11.4 conducts sensitivity analyses for when risk increases and when uncertainty increases. Lemmas and proofs are relegated to the Appendix.

11.1.2 Increase in Risk Versus Increase in Uncertainty

Given that the optimal investment strategy is characterized by the reservation function, we are next interested in the behavior of this function when the stochastic environment changes. As was claimed in the previous subsection, we distinguish a risky situation from an uncertain situation and hence we need to analyze these two cases separately.

First, suppose that uncertainty is summarized by a single probability; that is, the uncertainty is reduced to risk. Suppose further that the situation becomes riskier in the sense of mean-preserving spread according to Rothschild and Stiglitz (1970). We then prove that the reservation function is raised in response to this increase in risk. Intuitively, an increase in risk tends to raise the reservation function for the fund manager to exploit potentially more favorable future opportunities. An increase in risk or volatility thus increases the value of a waiting option. Because money as liquidity is an enabler of this option, the value of money as liquidity increases when the risk increases.

Second, we analyze the effects of an increase in uncertainty on the reservation function. We say that uncertainty increases if the capacity that describes the uncertain situation becomes more convex. To understand this rather mathematical definition in a more intuitive way, it should be noted that this "increased convexity" leads to the expansion of the core of the capacity. Because the CEU with a convex capacity equals the minimum among the expected utilities, each of which is calculated by an element of the core of the capacity, the expansion of the core implies more uncertainty *and* more uncertainty aversion at the same time (due to the characteristics of "min" operator). We then prove that an increase in uncertainty in this sense *lowers* the reservation function. This seems to be quite intuitive. When the uncertainty increases, the fund manager that hates uncertainty prefers to make the gross return determinate rather than to keep it indeterminate as a random variable depending on the future states' realization. Therefore, she accelerates investment by lowering the reservation function. That is, the fund manager prefers to resolve uncertainty by making an unambiguous investment now. (Note that given the return of the current period, the gross return on that investment is also determined.)

These results present a stark contrast between the risk and uncertainty with respect to the effects on decision-making. In a job search context, Nishimura and Ozaki (2004, Chap. 9 of this book) showed that an unemployed worker, who seeks to maximize her lifetime income, uses the reservation strategy: there exists the reservation wage such that she accepts the wage offer if it exceeds the reservation wage and she does not otherwise. Then, they showed that this reservation wage increases if risk increases and it decreases if uncertainty increases. There, both the increase of risk and that of uncertainty are defined in the same manner as this chapter. One can see clear resemblance between their paper and this chapter; however, there are important differences between them. First, the action space is discrete in Nishimura and Ozaki (2004). It consists of the two alternatives: to accept the job offer, or to reject it. In this chapter, the action space is a continuum. The action is the amount of investment and it takes on any non-negative real number as long as it satisfies the cash-in-advance constraint. Second, the decision is once and for all in Nishimura and Ozaki (2004). Once the unemployed worker accepts the offer, she is supposed to keep working at that wage level from that time on. On the other hand, in this chapter, the decision is made in each period. Even if the investment is made once, the fund manager needs to contemplate whether to invest in the next period. The fact that we obtain similar results in spite of these differences suggests a robust and contrasting difference between risk and uncertainty.[3]

As a closing comment of this subsection, we point out one implication of our analyses on the money demand. An increase in risk raises the reservation function and increases the average cash holdings. Hence, the demand for money increases. On the contrary, an increase in uncertainty lowers the reservation function and decreases the demand for money.

Given that the model in this chapter can be interpreted as a cash-in-advance model of consumption with stochastic preference, it also gives us interesting implications on consumption. The results of this chapter imply that if a consumer feels that the future is fundamentally more uncertain (her future preferences are more uncertain in the sense of Frank Knight), she wants to increase current consumption rather than to save for the future. In contrast, if she thinks that the future is risky in the form of mean-preserving spread, she wants to save more for the future than to consume

[3]To be fair, the risk neutrality of the fund manager is crucial for us to obtain that the optimal strategy takes the form of the reservation strategy. Without it, this property of the optimal strategy vanishes. In the discrete action space model of Nishimura and Ozaki (2004) the reservation strategy continues to be optimal even when the fund manager is risk-averse. This may be thought of as another difference between the two models.

today. In other words, if the future is uncertain, it is better to enjoy now. If the future is risky, it is better to save today to prepare for tomorrow.

11.1.3 Some Technical Aspects

To obtain the results stated in the preceding two subsections, we develop some mathematical tools in this chapter. In particular, we prove that Bellman's principle of optimality holds for our model by developing some dynamic programming techniques that are very similar to those developed in Chap. 7. That is, we prove that any solution to Bellman's equation is the value function and that recursive optimality implies optimality. As stated earlier in this chapter, when our Choquet integral framework is reduced to the usual (Lebesgue) integral framework *and* when our Markovian stochastic environment is reduced to the *i.i.d.* stochastic environment, then our model is the same as Stokey and Lucas' (1989, p. 401) model of pure-currency economy. We prove that Bellman's principle of optimality holds if we extend Stokey and Lucas' framework of an *i.i.d.* probability measure to that of a convex capacitary kernel, which is a convex "transformation" of a transition function or a stochastic kernel in the terminology of Stokey and Lucas (1989).

To this end, we develop an assumption of upper semi-continuity (u.s.c.) of a capacitary kernel. The u.s.c. is concerned with some continuity property of a capacitary kernel when both a set and a current state change simultaneously and it is mainly used when we prove that the Bellman operator is well defined.[4]

Given Bellman's principle of optimality, we need to solve Bellman's equation to find the exact solution of the fund manager's problem. We do this by assuming that a capacitary kernel is stochastically nondecreasing. The stochastic nondecrease appears in Topkis (1998) for a stochastic kernel and appears in Ozaki and Streufert (2001) for a capacitary kernel with a finite state space. This assumption amounts to saying that the Choquet integral of a nondecreasing function is nondecreasing as a function of a current state. Because of the stochastic nondecrease, all relevant functions become nondecreasing and hence mutually "co-monotonic." By the fact that the Choquet integral of the sum of mutually co-monotonic functions is equal to the sum of their Choquet integrals (Theorem 2.4.5), we can interchange the sum and the integral freely, which enables us to solve Bellman's equation. Similarly to the case of u.s.c., Sect. 2.5 provides a sufficient condition for a capacitary kernel to be stochastically nondecreasing and present a family of capacitary kernels that satisfy this condition.

---

[4]The formal definitions of u.s.c., a closely related concept of upper quasi-continuity (u.q.c.) and some results on them appear in Sect. 2.5. There, we provide a sufficient condition for a capacitary kernel to be u.s.c. and present a family of capacitary kernels that satisfy this condition.

11.2 The Model

This section defines the stochastic environment of our model and introduces the fund manager's problem.

11.2.1 Stochastic Environment

Let $Z := [\underline{z}, \bar{z}]$ be a closed interval in $\mathbb{R}_+$ such that $0 \leq \underline{z} < \bar{z} < +\infty$ and let $\mathcal{B}_Z$ be the Borel σ-algebra on Z. An element z_t of Z represents the gross rate of return on investment made in period t. In our model, z_t also serves as a state variable. We construct the t-fold self-product measurable space from $(Z, \mathcal{B}_Z)$ and denote it by $(Z^t, \mathcal{B}_{Z^t})$; that is, $(Z^t, \mathcal{B}_{Z^t}) := (Z \times \cdots \times Z, \mathcal{B}_Z \otimes \cdots \otimes \mathcal{B}_Z)$, where the products are t-fold. A generic element of $(Z^t, \mathcal{B}_{Z^t})$, which is denoted by $(z_1, \ldots, z_t)$ or ${}_1z_t$, is a history of states realized up to period t.

We assume that z_t is "distributed" according to a convex and continuous capacitary kernel $\theta : Z \times \mathcal{B}_Z \to [0, 1]$. Recall that a capacitary kernel θ is *stochastically nondecreasing* if for each nondecreasing function $h : Z \to \mathbb{R}$, the mapping defined by

$$z \mapsto \int_Z h(z')\,\theta_z(dz') \tag{11.1}$$

is nondecreasing. The stochastic nondecrease is very closely related to the concept of stochastically ordered columns of a finite Markov chain and their monotonic transformation developed by Ozaki and Streufert (2001), and plays a crucial role for us to obtain the exact solution to the fund manager's problem.

Throughout this chapter, we assume that θ is stochastically nondecreasing and that it is upper semi-continuous (u.s.c.) on $Z \times \mathbb{R}_+$ beneath any constant function. We need the latter assumption for us to invoke some dynamic programming techniques, for which the readers are referred to Chap. 7. We note that there certainly exists a class of convex and continuous capacitary kernels that are both stochastically nondecreasing and u.s.c. See right after Example 2.5.2.

11.2.2 The Fund Manager's Problem

In this subsection, we consider the problem facing a risk-neutral fund manager who contemplates in each period whether to make an irreversible investment, which, if made, generates some return.

An *investment strategy* is any $\mathbb{R}_+$-valued, $\langle \mathcal{B}_{Z^t} \rangle$-adapted stochastic process and is denoted by ${}_0\boldsymbol{x}$ or $\langle x_t \rangle_{t=0}^{\infty}$. Here, the $\langle \mathcal{B}_{Z^t} \rangle$-adaptedness requires that $x_0 \in \mathbb{R}_+$ and $(\forall t \geq 1)\ x_t : Z^t \to \mathbb{R}_+$ should be $\mathcal{B}_{Z^t}$-measurable. A *money-holding strategy*, denoted ${}_1\boldsymbol{m}$ or $\langle m_t \rangle_{t=1}^{\infty}$, is any $\mathbb{R}_+$-valued, $\langle \mathcal{B}_{Z^{t-1}} \rangle$-adapted stochastic process. That is, $m_1 \in \mathbb{R}_+$ and $(\forall t \geq 2)$ m_t is $\mathcal{B}_{Z^{t-1}}$-measurable.

Let $y > 0$ be an income that is given in each period. Given $m_0 \geq 0$, an investment strategy ${}_0\boldsymbol{x}$ is *feasible from* m_0 if there exists a money-holding strategy ${}_1\boldsymbol{m}$ such that the *budget constraint*:

$$(\forall t \geq 0) \quad x_t + m_{t+1} \leq y + m_t\,, \tag{11.2}$$

and the *liquidity constraint on investment* (or, the *cash-in-advance constraint on investment, CIA*):

$$(\forall t \geq 0) \quad x_t \leq m_t \tag{11.3}$$

are both met. The CIA requires the fund manager should hold in advance money amount much enough to cover the cost of investment.

Let $\beta := 1/(1+r)$, where $r > 0$ is the net rate of interest. The expected present value of all the future gross returns on investment is given by

$$I_{z_0}({}_0\boldsymbol{x}) := \lim_{T \to +\infty} x_0 z_0 + \beta \int_Z \cdots \beta \int_Z x_T z_T \, \theta_{z_{T-1}}(dz_T) \cdots \theta_{z_0}(dz_1)\,, \tag{11.4}$$

when the initial state is z_0 and the investment strategy ${}_0\boldsymbol{x}$ is chosen. Because each component of the sequence is well defined by the Fubini property (Theorem 2.5.1) and the sequence is nondecreasing, the limit exists (allowing $+\infty$). The monotone convergence theorem (Theorem 2.4.6) shows that this objective function satisfies *Koopmans' equation*:

$$(\forall z_0)(\forall {}_0\boldsymbol{x}) \quad I_{z_0}({}_0\boldsymbol{x}) = x_0 z_0 + \beta \int_Z I_{z_1}({}_1\boldsymbol{x})\, \theta_{z_0}(dz_1)\,,$$

where ${}_1\boldsymbol{x}$ is a continuation of ${}_0\boldsymbol{x}$ after the realization of z_1. This recursive structure of the objective function enables us to apply dynamic programming techniques.

The fund manager maximizes the objective (11.4) given z_0 by choosing an investment strategy ${}_0\boldsymbol{x}$ and a money-holding strategy ${}_1\boldsymbol{m}$ under the budget constraint (11.2) and the CIA (11.3). More formally, let a function $v^* : \mathbb{R}_+ \times Z \to \mathbb{R}$ be called the *value function* for the fund manager's problem if it satisfies $(\forall m, z)$ $v^*(m, z) = \max \{\, I_z({}_0\boldsymbol{x}) \mid {}_0\boldsymbol{x}$ is feasible from $m \,\}$, where ${}_0\boldsymbol{x}$ is *feasible from* m if there exists a money-holding strategy with which ${}_0\boldsymbol{x}$ satisfies both (11.2) and (11.3) with $m_0 := m$. Note that the existence of the value function (existence of the maximum) needs to be proven. An investment strategy ${}_0\boldsymbol{x}$ is *optimal from* $(m, z) \in \mathbb{R}_+ \times Z$ if it is feasible from m and satisfies $I_z({}_0\boldsymbol{x}) = v^*(m, z)$ when the value function exists. In the next section, we prove that the value function certainly exists, and then we characterize the optimal investment strategy for the fund manager.

11.3 The Exact Solution

This section gives the solution to the fund manager's problem presented in Sect. 11.2. We show in the first subsection some dynamic programming results that justify the exactness of our solution to the problem. We then present the exact solution to the problem in the next subsection. In the final subsection of this section, we show that the solution may be further simplified with an additional assumption of stochastic convexity.

11.3.1 Dynamic Programming

The value function for the fund manager's problem is (possibly) unbounded. Hence, the commonly used contraction-mapping theorem cannot be invoked to prove the existence of the value function. In this section, we invoke the dynamic programming techniques developed in Chap. 7 for this specific problem and show the existence of the value function.

We start with a series of definitions. We define the *feasibility correspondence* $\Gamma : \mathbb{R}_+ \twoheadrightarrow \mathbb{R}_+^2$ by $(\forall m)\ \Gamma(m) := \left\{ (x, m') \in \mathbb{R}_+^2 \,\middle|\, x + m' \leq y + m \text{ and } x \leq m \right\}$. When v^* exists, we define the *policy correspondence* $g : \mathbb{R}_+ \times Z \twoheadrightarrow \mathbb{R}_+^2$ by

$$(\forall m, z) \quad g(m, z) := \arg\max \left\{ xz + \beta \int_Z v^*(m', z')\, \theta_z(dz') \,\middle|\, (x, m') \in \Gamma(m) \right\}. \tag{11.5}$$

For the policy correspondence to be well defined, v^* must be such that $(\forall m')\ v^*(m', \cdot)$ is $\mathcal{B}_Z$-measurable and the right-hand side of (11.5) is nonempty. We show the existence of the policy correspondence soon. An investment strategy ${}_0\boldsymbol{x}$ is *recursively optimal* from $(m, z) \in \mathbb{R}_+ \times Z$ if there exists a money-holding strategy ${}_1\boldsymbol{m}$ such that $(x_0, m_1) \in g(m, z)$ and $(\forall t \geq 1)\ (x_t, m_{t+1}) \in g(m_t, z_t)$. Among the requirements of recursive optimality is the existence of a measurable selection of g.

We define the function $v^+ : \mathbb{R}_+ \to \mathbb{R}_+$ by $(\forall m)$

$$\begin{aligned} v^+(m) &:= \lim_{T \to +\infty} m\bar{z} + \cdots + \beta^{T-1}\left((T-1)y + m\right)\bar{z} + \beta^T (Ty + m)\bar{z} \\ &= \sum_{t=0}^{\infty} \beta^t m\bar{z} + \sum_{t=0}^{\infty} t\beta^t y\bar{z} = \frac{m\bar{z}}{1-\beta} + \frac{\beta y\bar{z}}{(1-\beta)^2} \quad =: \; B^+ m + A^+ . \end{aligned}$$

The function v^+ may be called the *overly optimistic value function* because for any investment strategy ${}_0\boldsymbol{x}$ that is feasible from m, it holds that $(\forall z)\ I_z({}_0\boldsymbol{x}) \leq v^+(m)$. A function $v : \mathbb{R}_+ \times Z \to \mathbb{R}$ is *admissible* if it is upper semi-continuous (u.s.c.), nondecreasing in its first argument, and satisfies $(\forall m, z)\ 0 \leq v(m, z) \leq v^+(m)$. Obviously, v^+ is admissible.

We define the *Bellman operator*, which maps an admissible function v to another function Bv, by $(\forall v)(\forall m, z)$

$$Bv(m,z) := \max\left\{ xz + \beta \int_Z v(m',z')\,\theta_z(dz') \;\middle|\; (x,m') \in \Gamma(m) \right\}. \qquad (11.6)$$

The next lemma shows that when v is admissible, the right-hand side of (11.6) is well defined.

Lemma 11.3.1 *The Bellman operator is well defined. That is, for any admissible function v and any m', $v(m',\cdot)$ is $\mathcal{B}_Z$-measurable and the maximum in (11.6) exists.*

By this lemma, we know that when v^* exists and is admissible (which is among the conclusions of Theorem 11.3.1 below), the policy correspondence exists.

Lemma 11.3.2 *$Bv^+ \leq v^+$, and for any admissible function v, Bv is admissible.*

This lemma shows that the Bellman operator maps the space of admissible functions into itself.

Finally, an admissible function v *solves Bellman's equation* if $v = Bv$. Our main result of this section is the following.

Theorem 11.3.1 *The value function exists, it is the unique admissible solution to Bellman's equation, and recursive optimality implies optimality.*

We rely on this theorem to characterize the optimal investment strategy, which will be conducted in the next subsection.

11.3.2 Finding the Exact Solution

This subsection gives the solution to the fund manager's problem that was presented in Sect. 11.2. Suppose that $R : Z \to \mathbb{R}$ is a nondecreasing (and hence $\mathcal{B}_Z$-measurable) function. We define the operator T that maps such a function R to another nondecreasing function TR by

$$(\forall R)(\forall z) \quad TR(z) := \beta \int_Z \max\left\{z', R(z')\right\} \theta_z(dz'). \qquad (11.7)$$

To see that TR is certainly nondecreasing, note that $\max\left\{z', R(z')\right\}$ is nondecreasing in z' and that θ is assumed to be stochastically nondecreasing.

Lemma 11.3.3 *There exists a unique fixed point R^* that satisfies $(\forall z)\ 0 \leq R^*(z) \leq \bar{z}$ to the operator T defined by (11.7). Furthermore, R^* is u.s.c., nondecreasing, and given by $R^* = \lim_{n\to\infty} T^n\bar{z} = \lim_{n\to\infty} T^n 0$, where T^n denotes the n-fold self-composition of T, $T \circ \cdots \circ T$.*

Given $t \geq 1$, $z \in Z$ and a nondecreasing function $h : Z \to \mathbb{R}$, we denote by $E_z^t[h]$ the t-fold iterated expectation of h with respect to θ:

$$E_z^t[h] := \int_Z \cdots \int_Z \int_Z h(z_t)\,\theta_{z_{t-1}}(dz_t)\,\theta_{z_{t-2}}(dz_{t-1}) \cdots \theta_z(dz_1)\,.$$

We define E^0 by $(\forall h, z)$ $E_z^0[h] := h(z)$ and we often write E^1 as E. Clearly, $E_z^t[h]$ is well defined and nondecreasing in z because θ is stochastically nondecreasing. We then define a function $A : Z \to \mathbb{R}_+$ by

$$(\forall z) \quad A(z) := y \sum_{s=0}^{\infty} \beta^s E_z^s[R^*]\,. \tag{11.8}$$

Note that A is well defined and finite valued because R^* is a $\mathcal{B}_Z$-measurable bounded function and $\beta \in (0, 1)$. Furthermore, A is nondecreasing because the sum of nondecreasing functions is nondecreasing and because A is the limit of a sequence of such nondecreasing functions.

We find the value function by solving Bellman's equation and then find the policy correspondence. Such a procedure is justified by Theorem 11.3.1. As a result, we have the next theorem, whose proof can be found in the Appendix.

Theorem 11.3.2 *The value function v^* exists and is given by:* $(\forall m, z)$

$$v^*(m, z) = \begin{cases} R^*(z)m + A(z) & \text{if } z \le R^*(z) \\ zm + A(z) & \text{if } z > R^*(z) \end{cases} \tag{11.9}$$

and the policy correspondence g exists and is given by: $(\forall m, z)$

$$g(m, z) = \begin{cases} \{(0, m + y)\} & \text{if } z < R^*(z) \\ \{(x, m') \in \Gamma(m) | x + m' = y + m\} & \text{if } z = R^*(z) \\ \{(m, y)\} & \text{if } z > R^*(z)\,. \end{cases} \tag{11.10}$$

Furthermore, recursive optimality implies optimality.

We construct an investment strategy ${}_0\boldsymbol{x}^*$ (and its associated money-holding strategy ${}_1\boldsymbol{m}$) that is recursively optimal from (m, z) as follows:

$$(\forall t \ge 0) \quad (x_t^*, m_{t+1}) = \begin{cases} (0, m_t + y) & \text{if } z_t \le R^*(z_t) \\ (m_t, y) & \text{if } z_t > R^*(z_t) \end{cases} \tag{11.11}$$

where $m_0 := m$ and $z_0 := z$. The stochastic process ${}_0\boldsymbol{x}^*$ thus defined is $\langle \mathcal{B}_{Z^t} \rangle$-adapted because R^* is $\mathcal{B}_Z$-measurable. Therefore, it is certainly an investment strategy and recursively optimal from (m, z) by (11.10) and the definition of recursive optimality. By the last statement of Theorem 11.3.2, we know that ${}_0\boldsymbol{x}^*$ is an optimal investment strategy from (m, z).

The existence of cash reserve provides the fund manager with an option not to invest in the current period and to wait until next period. This shows that the fund manager has a call option when she has cash in hand. Here, cash is an "enabler" of this call option, or flexibility in terms of Jones and Ostroy (1984). Cash is endowed with this function by the liquidity services it provides, and ultimately by transaction costs implicit in the irreversibility of investment.

11.3.3 Reservation Property

Recall that a capacitary kernel θ is *stochastically convex* if for each nondecreasing function $h : Z \to \mathbb{R}$, the mapping defined by (11.1) is convex. This subsection assumes that θ is stochastically convex. An example of a stochastically convex capacitary kernel is provided right after Example 2.5.2.

Under the assumption of stochastic convexity, it can be shown that the trigger function R^* is constant. More formally, the optimal investment strategy ${}_0\boldsymbol{x}^*$ *has a reservation property* if there exists a *constant* $z^* \geq 0$, called *reservation value*, such that

$$(\forall t \geq 0) \quad (x_t^*, m_{t+1}) = \begin{cases} (0, m_t + y) & \text{if } z_t \leq z^* \\ (m_t, y) & \text{if } z_t > z^* . \end{cases}$$

We can prove the following result.

Theorem 11.3.3 *Suppose that the capacitary kernel θ is stochastically convex. Then, the optimal investment strategy has a reservation property. Furthermore, if $\beta E_{\underline{z}}[z'] \geq \underline{z}$, then there exists a unique $z^* \in Z$ such that $z^* = R^*(z^*)$ and the reservation value equals z^*.*

11.4 Sensitivity Analyses

This section conducts two sensitivity analyses. First, we consider a case where uncertainty does not exist and we assume that the risk increases in the sense of a mean-preserving spread. We then show that such an increase in risk raises the reservation function. Second, we assume that uncertainty exists and that uncertainty increases in the sense that the core of a capacity expands. We then show that an increase in uncertainty lowers the reservation function in contrast to an increase in risk. These results show that an increase either in risk or in uncertainty affects the money demand in the opposite directions.

11.4.1 An Increase in Risk

In this subsection, we assume that there is no uncertainty. Given a probability measure P on $(Z, \mathcal{B}_Z)$, we denote by F the (cumulative) distribution function derived from P; that is, $(\forall z)\ F(z) := P([\underline{z}, z])$. Let P^0 and P^1 be two probability measures on $(Z, \mathcal{B}_Z)$. We denote by F^0 and F^1 the distribution functions associated with P^0 and P^1, respectively. We say that P^1 *is obtained from* P^0 *by a mean-preserving spread* if it holds that

$$\int_Z z\,dF^0(z) = \int_Z z\,dF^1(z) \text{ and } (\forall x \in \mathbb{R})\ \int_{-\infty}^{x} F^0(z)\,dz \le \int_{-\infty}^{x} F^1(z)\,dz\,.$$

A capacitary kernel $\theta : \mathcal{B}_Z \times Z \to [0, 1]$ is called a *stochastic kernel* (Stokey and Lucas 1989, p. 226) if $(\forall z)\ \theta_z(\cdot)$ is countably additive (that is, a probability measure). Clearly, a stochastic kernel is a convex and continuous capacitary kernel. We say that a stochastic kernel P^1 *is obtained from* P^0 *by a mean-preserving spread* if $(\forall z \in Z)\ P^1_z(\cdot)$ is obtained from $P^0_z(\cdot)$ by the mean-preserving spread.

Theorem 11.4.1 *Let P^0 be a stochastic kernel that is stochastically nondecreasing, u.s.c., and stochastically convex and let P^1 be a stochastic kernel that is u.s.c. Furthermore, assume that P^1 is obtained from P^0 by the mean-preserving spread. Then, $(\forall z \in Z)\ R^{*1}(z) \ge R^{*0}(z)$, where R^{*i} is the fixed point of T^i corresponding to P^i for each $i = 0, 1$.*

Corollary 11.4.1 *Let P^0 and P^1 be as in Theorem 11.4.1. Also, suppose that $z_t \le z^{*0}$, where z^{*0} is the reservation value corresponding to P^0 whose existence is guaranteed by Theorem 11.3.3. Then, it holds that $z_t \le R^{*1}(z_t)$.*

In this corollary, note that the existence of the reservation *value*, not reservation *function*, corresponding to P^1 is not known. The corollary shows that if making investment is not an optimal strategy before the risk increases, it cannot be so after the risk has increased. Therefore, an increase in risk tends to increase cash balances to be carried over to the next period to exploit potentially more favorable future opportunities. Money cash balances work as a provider of this option, which is more favorable under more risk.

11.4.2 An Increase in Uncertainty

Let θ^0 and θ^1 be two capacitary kernels. We say that θ^1 *represents more (Knightian) uncertainty than* θ^0 if

$$(\forall A)(\forall z) \quad \theta^0_z(A) \ge \theta^1_z(A)\,. \tag{11.12}$$

Under the assumption that θ^0 and θ^1 are convex, it turns out that (11.12) is equivalent to

$$(\forall z) \quad \mathrm{core}(\theta_z^0) \subseteq \mathrm{core}(\theta_z^1)\,, \tag{11.13}$$

which substantiates our definition of more uncertainty, and the definition of more uncertainty aversion given the fundamental theorem of the Choquet integral (Theorem 2.4.1). Ghirardato and Marinacci (2002) develop a notion of comparative ambiguity aversion and relate it to (11.12). They also provide some behavioral foundation of our notion of more uncertainty. See Sect. 9.4.5.

In the theorem below, we assume that θ^0 and θ^1 are convex and continuous capacitary kernels that are stochastically nondecreasing and u.s.c., and we let R^0 and R^1 be the reservation function associated with θ^0 and θ^1, respectively.

When a capacitary kernel θ^1 is defined by

$$(\forall A)(\forall z) \quad \theta_z^1(A) := g \circ \theta_z^0(A) \tag{11.14}$$

with some θ^0 and some continuous and convex function $g : [0, 1] \to [0, 1]$, then θ^1 satisfies all the requirements if so does θ^0 (Theorem 2.5.6). Furthermore, if θ^1 is defined by (11.14), it satisfies (11.12) and hence represents more uncertainty than θ^0.[5]

The next result shows that the reservation function is lowered if uncertainty increases in the sense of (11.12).

Theorem 11.4.2 *Suppose that θ^0 and θ^1 are convex and continuous capacitary kernels that are stochastically nondecreasing and u.s.c. Also, suppose that θ^1 represents more uncertainty than θ^0. Then, $(\forall z)\ R^{*1}(z) \le R^{*0}(z)$, where R^{*i} is the fixed point of T^i corresponding to θ^i for each $i = 0, 1$.*

References

Epstein, L.G., and J. Zhang. 1999. Least convex capacities. *Economic Theory* 13: 263–286.

Ghirardato, P., and M. Marinacci. 2002. Ambiguity made precise. *Journal of Economic Theory* 102: 251–289.

Jones, R.A., and J.M. Ostroy. 1984. Flexibility and uncertainty. *Review of Economic Studies* 51: 13–32.

Lucas Jr., R.E. 1980. Equilibrium in a pure currency economy. *Economic Inquiry* 18: 203–220.

Nishimura, K.G., and H. Ozaki. 2004. Search and Knightian uncertainty. *Journal of Economic Theory* 119: 299–333.

Ozaki, H., and P.A. Streufert. 2001. Solutions for some dynamic problems with uncertainty aversion. *The Japanese Economic Review* 52: 251–283.

Rothschild, M., and J. Stiglitz. 1970. Increasing risk I: a definition. *Journal of Economic Theory* 2: 225–243.

[5]Epstein and Zhang (1999) adopt the notion (11.14) as a definition of more uncertainty (and more uncertainty aversion) when the capacities are convex.

Stokey, N.L., and R.E. Lucas Jr. 1989. *Recursive methods in economic dynamics*. Cambridge: Harvard University Press.
Taub, B. 1988. Efficiency in a pure currency economy with inflation. *Economic Inquiry* 26: 567–583.
Topkis, D.M. 1998. *Supermodularity and complementarity*. Princeton: Princeton University Press.

Chapter 12
A Simple Characterization of Pessimism and Optimism: ε-Contamination Versus ε-Exuberance

12.1 Introduction and Summary

On Wall Street, there are bulls and bears among professional investors. On Main Street, ordinary people are sometimes overly optimistic about their future and at other times excessively pessimistic. Bulls and bears on Wall Street often have starkly different views about the markets even though the available information is not so different among them. People on Main Street often switch from optimism to pessimism and *vice versa* quite easily even though there may not be noticeable change in their conditions.

The purpose of this chapter is to present a simple characterization of optimism and pessimism of this kind. We show that seemingly irrational, overly optimistic or excessively pessimistic behavior described in the previous paragraph can be in fact "rational" in the sense that it is consistent with axioms that are "reasonable," under fundamental uncertainty (that is, Knightian uncertainty) about the future.

The organization of this chapter is as follows. The remainder of this section explains the main results and their implications in a nontechnical manner. Section 12.2 presents mathematical preliminaries. Section 12.3 deals with pessimism and presents axioms. Section 12.4 contains the main result whose proof is relegated to the Appendix. Section 12.5 extends our analysis to the case of optimism, and presents axioms and main results. Section 12.6 relates our results to the Anscombe–Aumann theory and shows that our approach is a natural extension of their theory. Section 12.7 presents implications of our theory in the distribution-function framework. In particular, these implications are intuitive and easily applicable to economic problems.

12.1.1 Pessimism: The ε-Contamination

Consider firstly pessimistic behavior. Suppose that (1) an economic agent is $(1-\varepsilon) \times 100\%$ certain that the uncertainty she faces is characterized by a particular

K.G. Nishimura and H. Ozaki, *Economics of Pessimism and Optimism*,
DOI 10.1007/978-4-431-55903-0_12

probability, but that (2) she has a fear that, with $\varepsilon \times 100\%$ chance, her opinion is completely wrong and she is left perfectly ignorant about the true probability in the future. In particular, there is always the possibility of the worst case. This situation is often called "ε-contamination." That is, her confidence is partially contaminated by the fear of ignorance.

The ε-contamination is a special case of Knightian uncertainty or ambiguity in which the decision-maker faces not a single probability but a set of probabilities. Because it is analytically tractable, several authors have examined the ε-contamination or its variants in search behavior (Nishimura and Ozaki 2004, and Chap. 9 of this book), portfolio choice (Chen and Epstein 2002), learning (Nishimura and Ozaki 2002, 2008, and Chap. 14 of this book), and voting (Chu and Liu 2002). The ε-contamination also comes up in the statistics literature on robustness. See, for example, Berger (1985).

The first purpose of this chapter is to provide a simple set of behavioral axioms under which the decision-maker's preference is represented by the Choquet expected utility with the ε-contamination. These axioms are formal representations of concepts (1) and (2) described earlier.

12.1.2 Optimism: The ε-Exuberance

We next consider optimistic behavior. Suppose that (3) an economic agent is $(1-\varepsilon) \times 100\%$ certain that uncertainty she faces is characterized by a particular probability, but that (4) she is a little optimistic that, with $\varepsilon \times 100\%$ chance, her opinion is wrong and she comes across the best possible opportunity that she can imagine in the future, although she is ignorant about the true probability. This situation can be called "ε-exuberance," following the famous quote of "irrational exuberance" by Alan Greenspan.[1] This economic agent has a conviction that, however small, there is always a chance of a very successful outcome, although she is ignorant of the true probability of the future.

The second purpose of this chapter is to provide a simple set of behavioral axioms under which the decision-maker's preference is represented by the maximax criterion and equivalently the Choquet expected utility with the ε-exuberance. These axioms are formal representations of concepts (3) and (4) described earlier.

In the ε-contamination, we hypothesize that a decision-maker is not perfectly certain about the most likely probability and she thinks there is always the possibility that the worst case may occur. In the ε-exuberance, we assume the opposite: there is always the possibility that the best-case scenario occurs.

The ε-exuberance is an intuitive representation of optimistic behavior under Knightian uncertainty or ambiguity in which the decision-maker faces not a single probability but a set of probabilities. Optimistic behavior has recently been analyzed

[1]See Remarks by Chairman Alan Greenspan at the Annual Dinner and Francis Boyer Lecture of the American Enterprise Institute for Public Research, Washington, D.C., December 5, 1996.

in insurance markets by Bracha and Brown (2013), who also explored its axiomatic foundation based on the framework of variational preferences developed by Maccheroni et al. (2006). In contrast, we employ the lottery framework of Anscombe and Aumann (1963), which enables an intuitive interpretation of ε-exuberance.

12.1.3 Pessimism and Optimism: A Symmetry

In our framework, pessimism and optimism are symmetric. Investors on Wall Street almost agree on the most likely probability, with $(1-\varepsilon)\times 100\%$ certainty, which is based on the information available to them. If there is no insider (private) information, their most likely probability is not so different. However, as mortal beings, investors have different attitudes toward Knightian uncertainty in the future. Some are pessimistic thinking of the worst case and others are optimistic hoping for the best outcome. However, there is no *a priori* rationale for choosing one against the other: both are equally plausible and acceptable.

A similar argument may hold for workers and consumers in Main Street. Facing Knightian uncertainty in the future, and having no convincing guidance, they may change from ε-contamination to ε-exuberance and *vice versa*. In retrospect, we observe such a flip-flop change in behavior in everyday life.

12.2 Preliminaries

Let $(S, \mathcal{A})$ be a measurable space, where $\mathcal{A}$ is an algebra on S. We fix it throughout this chapter. To describe the decision-maker's preference, we employ Anscombe–Aumann's framework of lottery acts. See Sect. 3.8 for definitions of lottery acts and others used in their framework. In what is different from the orthodox Anscombe–Aumann representation result, the following discussion shows the "worst-limit" constant act and the "best-limit" constant act play a crucial role. Given a simple lottery act $f \in L_0$, let $Y_{\min f}$ be the subset of Y representing the f worst-limit constant acts, defined by $Y_{\min f} := \{\, y \in Y \mid (\forall s)\ y \preceq f(s) \text{ and } (\exists s)\ y = f(s)\,\}$. Because f is a simple lottery act, $Y_{\min f}$ is nonempty when $\succeq$ is a weak order. We henceforth denote by $y_{\min f}$ an arbitrary element of $Y_{\min f}$. Also, $Y_{\max f}$ and $y_{\max f}$ are defined symmetrically.

Let $f, g \in L_0$ and $\lambda \in [0, 1]$. In this chapter, we denote also by $f_\lambda g$ the compound lottery act $\lambda f + (1-\lambda)g$.[2] A special case of the compound lottery act will become important. We often consider $\lambda y_{\min f} + (1-\lambda)y_{\max f}$; that is, a compound lottery act of the worst-limit constant act with probability λ and the best-limit constant act with probability $1-\lambda$. We call this act λ-*weighted worst-best combination*, which itself is a *constant* lottery act.

[2]See Sect. 3.8.1 for the definition of the compound lottery act.

12.3 Pessimistic Behavior: Axioms

In addition to Schmeidler's (1982; 1989) well-known axioms[3]: (i) weak order; (ii) comonotonic independence; (iv) continuity; (v) monotonicity; and (vii) nondegeneracy, we consider the following axioms that may be imposed on a binary relation $\succeq$ defined on L_0. In the axioms, f and g denote arbitrary elements in L_0 and λ denotes an arbitrary real number such that $\lambda \in (0, 1]$.

The first axiom requires that any simple lottery act f should be dominated by some compound lottery act of its worst-limit and best-limit constant acts. In the axiom, ε is a real number such that $\varepsilon \in [0, 1)$. The axiom requires that the given relation should hold with respect to this specific ε. Therefore, whether the axiom is satisfied depends on ε, and hence, it is labeled (viii-ε), rather than (viii).

(viii-ε) (ε-Dominance of ε-Weighted Worst-Best Combination over Any Lottery)

$$(1-\varepsilon)y_{\max f} + \varepsilon y_{\min f} \succeq f. \tag{12.1}$$

Under (i), (ii), (iv), (v), (vii), and (viii-ε), it can be shown (see Lemma A.7.1 in the Appendix) that all $f \in L_0$ has the following *ε-contamination equivalence*:

$$(\forall f \in L_0)(\exists y_f \in L_c)\;\; f \sim (1-\varepsilon)y_f + \varepsilon y_{\min f}\,, \tag{12.2}$$

where ε is the one with which (viii-ε) holds. This property shows that all simple lottery acts have their own equivalent compound constant act consisting of its worst-limit constant act with probability ε and some constant act y_f with probability $1-\varepsilon$. Clearly, y_f defined in (12.2) is one way of representing f. We hereafter call it *f's equivalent constant act in ε-contamination equivalence*.

The next axiom concerns ordering among these equivalent constant acts in ε-contamination equivalence. In the axiom, ε is a real number such that $\varepsilon \in [0, 1)$. By the same reason given for (viii-ε), we label it (ix-ε), rather than (ix).

(ix-ε) (Worst-Limit Irrelevance) Both of the following hold:

(ix-ε-1) (Affine Irrelevance) If there exist y_f, y_g, $y_{f\lambda g} \in L_c$ such that $f \sim (1-\varepsilon)y_f + \varepsilon y_{\min f}$, $g \sim (1-\varepsilon)y_g + \varepsilon y_{\min g}$, and $f\lambda g \sim (1-\varepsilon)y_{f\lambda g} + \varepsilon y_{\min f\lambda g}$, then $y_{f\lambda g} \sim \lambda y_f + (1-\lambda)y_g$; and

[3]Each of the following axioms corresponds to each of Axioms S1–S5 in Sect. 3.9.1. For explicit statements of these axioms, the readers are referred there. However, note that we state the axioms in terms of a weak order here, instead of a preference order as used earlier. This does not cause any essential difference in the following exposition. For this, see Sect. 3.2.

(ix-ε-2) (Monotone Irrelevance) If $(\forall s)\ f(s) \succsim g(s)$ and there exist $y_f,\ y_g \in L_c$ such that $f \sim (1-\varepsilon)y_f + \varepsilon y_{\min f}$ and $g \sim (1-\varepsilon)y_g + \varepsilon y_{\min g}$, then $y_f \succsim y_g$.

Axiom (ix-ε-1) means that if y_f, y_g, and $y_{f\lambda g}$ are the equivalent acts of f, g, and $f\lambda g$ in ε-contamination equivalence, respectively, then $y_{f\lambda g} \sim \lambda y_f + (1-\lambda)y_g$, regardless of characteristics of the worst limits $y_{\min f}$, $y_{\min g}$, and $y_{\min f\lambda g}$. Similarly, Axiom (ix-ε-2) implies that if $f(s) \succsim g(s)$ for all s, then $y_f \succsim y_g$, regardless of characteristics of the worst limits $y_{\min f}$ and $y_{\min g}$. These two axioms imply that the worst limits are irrelevant in ordering among equivalent constant acts in ε-contamination equivalence.

Basically, both (ix-ε-1) and (ix-ε-2) require that the worst case should be irrelevant to the agents of the type we are now thinking of because these agents always take the worst case into consideration. That is, it is irrelevant in the choice between two lotteries *because it is always relevant*.

Axioms (viii-ε) and (ix-ε) are closely related to the axioms of Anscombe and Aumann (1963), especially their independence axiom.[4] In fact, our model can be considered as a natural extension of the Anscombe–Aumann model to the case in which the decision-maker has a fear of the worst outcome with the possibility of ε all the time. We will turn to this issue later.

12.4 Pessimistic Behavior: Main Results

The main results of this chapter are the next theorem and the following two corollaries.

Theorem 12.4.1 *Given any $\varepsilon \in [0, 1)$, a binary relation $\succsim$ defined on L_0 satisfies (i), (ii), (iv), (v), (vii), (viii-ε), and (ix-ε) if and only if there exist a unique probability charge μ on $(S, \mathcal{A})$, an affine function $u : Y \to \mathbb{R}$, which is unique up to a positive affine transformation, such that*

$$f \succsim g \Leftrightarrow (1-\varepsilon)\int_S u(f(s))\,d\mu(s) + \varepsilon \min_{s\in S} u(f(s)) \geq (1-\varepsilon)\int_S u(g(s))\,d\mu(s) + \varepsilon \min_{s\in S} u(g(s))\,.$$

Recall from Example 2.3.5 that the *ε-contamination of* a probability charge μ on $(S, \mathcal{A})$ is defined as the set $\{\ (1-\varepsilon)\mu + \varepsilon q \mid q \in \mathcal{M}(S, \mathcal{A})\ \}$ and that this set is denoted by $\{\mu\}^{\varepsilon}$. It is easy to see that $(\forall f \in L_0)$

[4] Axiom AA2 in Sect. 3.8.2. Note that Schmeidler (1982, 1989) names it *Axiom (iii)*.

$$\int_S u(f(s))\, d\{\mu\}^{\varepsilon}(s) := \min\left\{ \int_S u(f(s))\, dp(s) \,\middle|\, p \in \{\mu\}^{\varepsilon} \right\}$$
$$= (1-\varepsilon)\int_S u(f(s))\, d\mu(s) + \varepsilon \min_{s\in S} u(f(s)),$$

where the first equality is definitional. Therefore, the following corollary is immediate.

Corollary 12.4.1 *Given any $\varepsilon \in [0, 1)$, a binary relation $\succeq$ defined on L_0 satisfies (i), (ii), (iv), (v), (vii), (viii-ε), and (ix-ε) if and only if there exist a unique probability charge μ on $(S, \mathcal{A})$, an affine function $u : Y \to \mathbb{R}$, which is unique up to a positive affine transformation, such that*

$$f \succeq g \Leftrightarrow \int_S u(f(s))\, d\{\mu\}^{\varepsilon}(s) \geq \int_S u(g(s))\, d\{\mu\}^{\varepsilon}(s).$$

Corollary 12.4.1 clearly shows that our representation result is a very special case of Gilboa and Schmeidler's (1989) *maxmin expected utility* (MEU) discussed in Sect. 3.10. Here, the set of multiple priors is further characterized by the ε-contamination of some probability charge. This fact immediately proves that the set of axioms we impose here as a whole is stronger that that of Gilboa and Schmeidler (Axioms GS1–GS6 in Sect. 3.10.1).

Another corollary follows from the fundamental theorem of the Choquet integral (Theorem 2.4.1) and the fact that the ε-contamination of a probability charge μ is exactly equal to the core of the probability capacity defined by

$$(\forall A \in \mathcal{A}) \quad \theta(A) = \begin{cases} (1-\varepsilon)\mu(A) & \text{if } A \neq S \\ 1 & \text{if } A = S \end{cases} \tag{12.3}$$

(see Examples 2.3.2 and 2.3.5). That is, we have the next corollary.

Corollary 12.4.2 *Given any $\varepsilon \in [0, 1)$, a binary relation $\succeq$ defined on L_0 satisfies (i), (ii), (iv), (v), (vii), (viii-ε), and (ix-ε) if and only if there exist a unique probability charge μ on $(S, \mathcal{A})$, an affine function $u : Y \to \mathbb{R}$, which is unique up to a positive affine transformation, such that*

$$f \succeq g \Leftrightarrow \int_S u(f(s))\, d\theta(s) \geq \int_S u(g(s))\, d\theta(s),$$

where the probability capacity θ is defined from μ by (12.3) and the integral is the Choquet integral.

This corollary clearly shows that our representation result is a very special case of Schmeidler's (1982; 1989) *Choquet expected utility* (CEU) with a *convex* probability capacity as discussed in Sect. 3.9. Here, the convex probability capacity is further characterized by the ε-contamination of some probability charge. This fact immediately proves that the set of axioms we impose here as a whole is stronger that that of Schmeidler plus uncertainty aversion (Axioms S1–S5 plus uncertainty aversion in

Sects. 3.9.1 and 3.9.3). To put it differently, we assume all the axioms of Schmeidler's theorem (Theorem 3.9.1), where the derived capacity is *not* necessarily convex. This implies that, in the presence of these axioms, our axioms of the ε-dominance and the worst-limit irrelevance are stronger than the uncertainty aversion of Schmeidler and they are strong enough for the decision-maker's preference to be forced to be represented by the form of ε-contamination.

12.5 Optimistic Behavior: Axioms and Main Results

We introduce two sets of axioms, each of which corresponds to the counterpart in the representation by ε-contamination. In the axioms, f and g denote arbitrary elements in L_0 and λ denotes an arbitrary real number such that $\lambda \in (0, 1]$.

The first axiom requires that any simple lottery act f dominates some compound lottery act of its worst-limit and best-limit constant acts. In the axiom, ε is a real number such that $\varepsilon \in [0, 1)$. The axiom requires that the given relation should hold with respect to this ε. Therefore, whether the axiom is satisfied depends on ε, and hence, it is labeled (viii$'$-ε), rather than (viii$'$).

(viii$'$-ε) (ε-Dominance of any Lottery over $(1-\varepsilon)$-Weighted Worst-Best Combination) $(\forall f \in L_0)\ \ f \succeq (1-\varepsilon)y_{\min f} + \varepsilon y_{\max f}$.

Under (i), (ii), (iv), (v), (vii), and (viii$'$-ε), it can be shown very similarly to the proof of Lemma A.7.1 in the Appendix, that all $f \in L_0$ has the following *ε-exuberance equivalence*:

$$(\forall f \in L_0)(\exists y_f \in L_c)\ \ f \sim (1-\varepsilon)y_f + \varepsilon y_{\max f}, \tag{12.4}$$

where ε is the one with which (viii$'$-ε) holds. This property shows that all simple lottery acts have their own equivalent compound constant act consisting of its best-limit constant act with probability ε and some constant act y_f with probability $1-\varepsilon$. Clearly, y_f defined in (12.4) is one way of representing f. We hereafter call it *f's equivalent constant act in ε-exuberance equivalence*.

The next axiom concerns ordering among these equivalent constant acts in ε-exuberance equivalence. In the axiom, ε is a real number such that $\varepsilon \in [0, 1)$. By the same reason given for (viii$'$-ε), we label it (ix$'$-ε), rather than (ix$'$).

(ix$'$-ε) (Best-Limit Irrelevance) Both of the following hold:

(ix$'$-ε-1) (Affine Irrelevance) If there exist $y_f,\ y_g,\ y_{f_\lambda g} \in L_c$ such that $f \sim (1-\varepsilon)y_f + \varepsilon y_{\max f}$, $g \sim (1-\varepsilon)y_g + \varepsilon y_{\max g}$, and $f_\lambda g \sim (1-\varepsilon)y_{f_\lambda g} + \varepsilon y_{\max f_\lambda g}$, then $y_{f_\lambda g} \sim \lambda y_f + (1-\lambda)y_g$; and

(ix$'$-ε-2) (Monotone Irrelevance) If $(\forall s)\ f(s) \succeq g(s)$ and there exist $y_f,\ y_g \in L_c$ such that $f \sim (1-\varepsilon)y_f + \varepsilon y_{\max f}$ and $g \sim (1-\varepsilon)y_g + \varepsilon y_{\max g}$, then $y_f \succeq y_g$.

Axiom (ix$'$-ε-1) means that if y_f, y_g, and $y_{f_\lambda g}$ are the equivalent acts of f, g, and $f_\lambda g$ in ε-exuberance equivalence, respectively, then $y_{f_\lambda g} \sim \lambda y_f + (1-\lambda)y_g$, regardless of characteristics of the best limits $y_{\max f}$, $y_{\max g}$, and $y_{\max f\lambda g}$. Similarly, Axiom (ix-ε-2) implies that if $f(s) \succeq g(s)$ for all s, then $y_f \succeq y_g$, regardless of the characteristics of the best limits $y_{\max f}$ and $y_{\max g}$. These two axioms imply that the best limits are irrelevant in ordering among equivalent constant acts in ε-exuberance equivalence.

Basically, both (ix$'$-ε-1) and (ix$'$-ε-2) require that the *best* case should be irrelevant to the agents of the type we are now thinking of because these agents always take the *best* case into consideration. That is, it is irrelevant in the choice between two lotteries *because it is always relevant*.

The main results of this chapter are the next theorem and the following two corollaries. The proof of the theorem can be conducted in an exactly symmetrical manner to that of Theorem 12.4.1, and hence, it is omitted.

Theorem 12.5.1 *Given any $\varepsilon \in [0, 1)$, a binary relation $\succeq$ defined on L_0 satisfies (i), (ii), (iv), (v), (vii), (viii$'$-ε), and (ix$'$-ε) if and only if there exist a unique probability charge μ on $(S, \mathcal{A})$, an affine function $u : Y \to \mathbb{R}$, which is unique up to a positive affine transformation, such that*

$$f \succeq g \Leftrightarrow (1-\varepsilon)\int_S u(f(s))d\mu(s) + \varepsilon \max_{s\in S} u(f(s)) \geq$$

$$(1-\varepsilon)\int_S u(g(s))\,d\mu(s) + \varepsilon \max_{s\in S} u(g(s))$$

Because it holds true that $(\forall f \in L_0)$

$$\max\left\{\int_S u(f(s))\,dp(s)\,\middle|\, p \in \{\mu\}^{\varepsilon}\right\} = (1-\varepsilon)\int_S u(f(s))\,d\mu(s) + \varepsilon \max_{s\in S} u(f(s)),$$

the following corollary is immediate.

Corollary 12.5.1 *Given any $\varepsilon \in [0, 1)$, a binary relation $\succeq$ defined on L_0 satisfies (i), (ii), (iv), (v), (vii), (viii$'$-ε), and (ix$'$-ε) if and only if there exist a unique probability charge μ on $(S, \mathcal{A})$, an affine function $u : Y \to \mathbb{R}$, which is unique up to a positive affine transformation, such that*

$$f \succeq g \Leftrightarrow$$

$$\max\left\{\int_S u(f(s))\,dp(s)\,\middle|\, p \in \{\mu\}^{\varepsilon}\right\} \geq \max\left\{\int_S u(g(s))\,dp(s)\,\middle|\, p \in \{\mu\}^{\varepsilon}\right\}.$$

Another corollary follows immediately from Corollaries 12.5.1 and 2.4.1 That is, we have the next corollary.

Corollary 12.5.2 *Given any $\varepsilon \in [0, 1)$, a binary relation $\succeq$ defined on L_0 satisfies (i), (ii), (iv), (v), (vii), (viii$'$-ε), and (ix$'$-ε) if and only if there exist a unique probability charge μ on $(S, \mathcal{A})$, an affine function $u : Y \to \mathbb{R}$, which is unique up to a positive affine transformation, such that*

$$f \succeq g \Leftrightarrow \int_S u(f(s))\, d\theta'(s) \geq \int_S u(g(s))\, d\theta'(s)\,,$$

where the probability capacity θ is defined from μ by (12.3), θ' is the conjugate of θ, and the integral is the Choquet integral.

12.6 Anscombe–Aumann's Theory: Revisited

Recall from Sect. 3.8.2, that Anscombe and Aumann (1963) assume the independence axiom (Axiom (iii)) instead of co-monotonic independence axiom (Axiom (ii)), of which the former is much stronger, and that they prove the representation theorem by subjective expected utility. Our set of axioms can be considered as an extension of the Anscombe–Aumann axioms to the case where the decision-maker considers the possibility of the worst outcome with the possibility of ε *all the time* (ε-contamination), or considers the possibility of the best outcome with the possibility of ε *all the time* (ε-exuberance).

The next proposition substantiates this view by showing that axioms (i), (ii), (iv), (v), (vii), and (viii-0) and (ix-0) (resp. (viii′-0) and (ix′-0)) are necessary and sufficient for the Anscombe–Aumann axioms (i), (iii), (iv), (v), and (vii), where (viii-0) and (ix-0) (resp. (viii′-0) and (ix′-0)) are special cases of (viii-ε) and (ix-ε) (resp. (viii′-ε) and (ix′-ε)) by setting $\varepsilon := 0$.

Proposition 12.6.1 *(i), (ii), (iv), (v), (vii), (viii-0), and (ix-0) $\Leftrightarrow$ (i), (iii), (iv), (v), and (vii). Similarly, (i), (ii), (iv), (v), (vii), (viii′-0), and (ix′-0) $\Leftrightarrow$ (i), (iii), (iv), (v), and (vii).*

12.7 The Distribution-Function Framework

This section assumes that the outcome is *monetary* and that people's conviction is given by a unique or multiple *distribution functions*. This makes our theory more intuitive and applicable to economic problems.

12.7.1 Distribution Functions with Compact Supports

Let $\varepsilon \in (0, 1)$ and let $[a, b]$ be a *compact* interval in $\mathbb{R}$. For simplicity, we assume that an economic agent's utility index is linear.[5] Let F_0 be any distribution function with its support completely contained by $[a, b]$; that is, F_0 is nondecreasing on $\mathbb{R}$ and such that $F_0(a) = 0$ and $F_0(b) = 1$. Here, we understand that a distribution is for

[5]This assumption is not essential in what follows and can be dispensed with easily.

uncertain monetary outcomes, and hence, for an uncertain utility distribution under the linearity assumption.

Suppose that an economic agent is $(1-\varepsilon) \times 100\%$ certain that the uncertainty she faces is characterized by F_0 and that she thinks otherwise that *any (possibly, quite bad) distribution whose support is contained by* $[a, b]$ *is possible*. Then, she evaluates an uncertain monetary outcome x by using the distribution function F defined by $(\forall x \in [a, b])\ F(x) := (1-\varepsilon)F_0(x) + \varepsilon$ because she puts a point-mass at $\{a\}$ with $\varepsilon \times 100\%$ *fear*.

Symmetrically, suppose that an economic agent is $(1-\varepsilon) \times 100\%$ certain that the uncertainty she faces is characterized by F_0 and that she thinks otherwise that *any (possibly, quite good) distribution whose support is contained by* $[a, b]$ *is possible*. Then, she evaluates an uncertain monetary outcome x by using the distribution function F defined by $(\forall x \in [a, b))\ F(x) := (1-\varepsilon)F_0(x)$ and $F(b) := 1$ because she puts a point-mass at $\{b\}$ with $\varepsilon \times 100\%$ *hope*.

Example 12.7.1 (*Uniform Distribution*) Let $\varepsilon \in (0, 1)$ and let $-\infty < a < b < +\infty$. Suppose that an economic agent is $(1-\varepsilon) \times 100\%$ certain that the uncertainty she faces is characterized by the uniform distribution over $[a, b]$, F_0, given by $F_0(x) := (x-a)/(b-a)$ for $x \in [a, b]$. Now assume that her belief is represented by the *ε-contamination* of F_0. Then, the distribution function F is given by $(\forall x \in [a, b])\ F(x) = (1-\varepsilon)(x-a)/(b-a) + \varepsilon$. Next assume that her belief is represented by the *ε-exuberance* of F_0. Then, the distribution function F is given by $(\forall x \in [a, b))\ F(x) = (1-\varepsilon)(x-a)/(b-a)$ and $F(b) = 1$. See Fig. 9.2. ■

12.7.2 Density Functions

Let $a \in \mathbb{R}$ and let δ_a be something like a real-valued function on $\mathbb{R}$ that satisfies

$$\int_{-\infty}^{\infty} f(x)\delta_a(x)\,\mu(dx) = f(a) \tag{12.5}$$

for any continuous function $f : \mathbb{R} \to \mathbb{R}$, where μ is the Lebesgue measure on $(\mathbb{R}, \mathcal{B}_{\mathbb{R}})$. Note that δ_a *cannot* be a function. For instance, let f be a constant function that always takes on some positive real number and let $a \in \mathbb{R}$. Then, we can always find a sequence of *continuous* functions $\langle f_n \rangle_{n=1}^{\infty}$ such that $(\forall n)\ f_n(a) = f(a)$ and $f_n(x) = 0$ whenever $|x-a| > 1/n$. Whichever function we take as δ_a, the left-hand side of (12.5) goes to zero for such a sequence while its right-hand side remains as $f(a) > 0$. In fact, as this example suggests, it turns out that δ_a satisfying (12.5) can be defined only as a limit of some sequence of functions. This object, which is *not* a function in the usual sense, is known as the *delta distribution* or *Dirac's delta*, and it is often denoted by δ_a as we do.

The specification that uses Dirac's delta is applicable whenever the distribution function F_0 has a density and it makes it easy to apply the concepts of ε-contamination and ε-exuberance to economic problems.

Example 12.7.2 (Uniform Distribution) Let $\varepsilon \in (0, 1)$ and let $-\infty < a < b < +\infty$. Suppose that an economic agent is $(1 - \varepsilon) \times 100\%$ certain that the uncertainty she faces is characterized by the uniform distribution over $[a, b]$, F_0, given by $F_0(x) := (x - a)/(b - a)$ for $x \in [a, b]$. Then, the "density function" of the ε-contamination of F is given by $(\forall x \in [a, b])\ f(x) = (1 - \varepsilon)\chi_{(a,b]}(x)/(b - a) + \varepsilon\delta_a(x)$, and the "density function" of the ε-exuberance of F is given by $(\forall x \in [a, b])\ f(x) = (1 - \varepsilon)\chi_{[a,b)}(x)/(b - a) + \varepsilon\delta_b(x)$, where χ denotes the indicator function as usual. ■

12.7.3 Distribution Functions with Unbounded Supports

This subsection shows that the distribution-function approach works as far as the range of an economic agent's utility index is bounded even when the support of distributions of monetary outcomes is *un*bounded. Let $\varepsilon \in (0, 1)$ and let F_0 be *any* distribution function. Let $u : \mathbb{R} \to \mathbb{R}$ be the *utility function of money* and assume that $\min_{x\in\mathbb{R}} u(x)$ exists.[6]

Suppose that an economic agent is $(1 - \varepsilon) \times 100\%$ certain that the uncertainty she faces is characterized by F_0 and that she thinks otherwise that *any (possibly, quite bad) distribution is possible*. Then, she evaluates an uncertain prospect of money *measured by her utility index*, $u(x)$, by using the "distribution" function F defined by $(\forall x)\ F(x) = (1 - \varepsilon)F_0(x) + \varepsilon$ because she assigns a probability of unity to the set defined by $\arg\min_{x\in\mathbb{R}} u(x)$ with $\varepsilon \times 100\%$ fear. We say that F is a "distribution" because it may not be a distribution in a truly mathematical sense because it may not be the case that $\lim_{x\downarrow-\infty} F(x) = 0$, which is the property a distribution must satisfy when we characterize it axiomatically.

Symmetrically, suppose that an economic agent is $(1 - \varepsilon) \times 100\%$ certain that the uncertainty she faces is characterized by F_0 and that she thinks otherwise that *any (possibly, quite good) distribution is possible*. Assume that $\max_{x\in\mathbb{R}} u(x)$ exists.[7] Then, she evaluates an uncertain prospect of money *measured by her utility index*, $u(x)$, by using the distribution function F defined by

$$F(x) = \begin{cases} (1 - \varepsilon)F_0(x) & \text{if } x \notin \arg\max_{x\in\mathbb{R}} u(x) \\ 1 & \text{if } x \in \arg\max_{x\in\mathbb{R}} u(x) \end{cases}$$

because she assigns a probability of unity to the set defined by $\arg\max_{x\in\mathbb{R}} u(x)$ with $\varepsilon \times 100\%$ fear.

---

[6] By assuming this, we avoid a subtle argument that would be necessary when the infimum is not achieved. Our idea can be conveyed neatly under this simplifying assumption.

[7] See the previous footnote.

References

Anscombe, F.J., and R.J. Aumann. 1963. A definition of subjective probability. *Annals of Mathematical Statistics* 34: 199–205.

Berger, J.O. 1985. *Statistical decision theory and bayesian analysis*, 2nd ed. Berlin: Springer.

Bracha, A., and D. Brown. 2013. (Ir)rational exuberance: optimism, ambiguity, and risk, Cowles Foundation Discussion Paper No. 1898.

Chen, Z., and L. Epstein. 2002. Ambiguity, risk and asset returns in continuous time. *Econometrica* 70: 1403–1443.

Chu, C.Y.C., and W.-F. Liu. 2002. Knightian uncertainty and the voting paradox, mimeo, University of Washington.

Gilboa, I., and D. Schmeidler. 1989. Maxmin expected utility with non-unique prior. *Journal of Mathematical Economics* 18: 141–153.

Maccheroni, F., M. Marinacci, and A. Rustihici. 2006. Ambiguity aversion, robustness, and the variational representation of preferences. *Econometrica* 74: 1447–1498.

Nishimura, K.G., and H. Ozaki. 2002. Economics of self-feeding fear, Discussion Paper 2002-CF-175, University of Tokyo.

Nishimura, K.G., and H. Ozaki. 2004. Search and Knightian uncertainty. *Journal of Economic Theory* 119: 299–333.

Nishimura, K.G., and H. Ozaki. 2008. Learning may increase perceived uncertainty: A model of confidence erosion under Knightian uncertainty, mimeo, Keio University. (Revised version of Nishimura and Ozaki, 2002).

Schmeidler, D. 1982. Subjective probability without additivity (Temporary Title), Working Paper, The Foerder Institute for Economic Research, Tel Aviv University.

Schmeidler, D. 1989. Subjective probability and expected utility without additivity. *Econometrica* 57: 571–587. Its working paper is first published in 1982.

Chapter 13
Persistent Pessimism and Optimism in Forecasts: Implicit Means and Law of Iterated Integrals

13.1 Introduction and Summary

Economic activities have become increasingly complicated in recent years. For example, financial innovation, past and present, has increased the complexity of financial information. Securitization is one manifestation of this trend, and it generates an extraordinary degree of complexity. Information and communication technology in general has vastly expanded the scope and amount of information that firms have to know when they decide on their prices, production, and investment.

Complexity leads to the dependency of investors on external as well as internal expert information: professional forecasts (valuation) of rating agencies, forecast firms, and market analysts as well as in-house professionals. In particular, the forecasts of international organizations such as the IMF and the OECD have become very influential, not only for investors but also for national policy makers. Experts' forecasts determine market sentiment and thus move the market and ultimately the economy.

The conventional, neoclassical wisdom is that, firstly, an economic agent's forecast of an economic variable should be unbiased so long as she is "rational". In particular, her forecast is assumed to be the mathematical expectation of the economic random variable. Second, any biases found in one point of time should not be persistent, because a rational economic agent learns from the past history to rectify her bias. Mathematically, the law of iterated integrals or expectations holds: the unconditional expectation of the conditional expectation of variable x on variable y is equal to the unconditional expectation of variable x. However, we have often observed biased forecasts and their persistence even among the forecasts of experts we mentioned above. For example, IMF forecasts have been persistently overly optimistic for years. In particular, the IMF has failed to predict the collapse of the bubble in Japan in the 1990s, the subprime crisis of the United States in the 2000s, and the European sovereign debt crisis in the 2010s. Market analysts of securities houses are often regarded as persistently optimistic about the performance of firms with which these securities houses are involved with.

K.G. Nishimura and H. Ozaki, *Economics of Pessimism and Optimism*,
DOI 10.1007/978-4-431-55903-0_13

The purpose of this chapter is to show that a small deviation from this neoclassical paradigm, that is, an economic agent's forecast of an economic variable is the mathematical expectation of this variable, leads to a more realistic view of economic forecasts than the neoclassical one. In particular, the observed persistence of bias in these forecasts can be explained in the framework of rationality, that is, decision theory.

It should be noted that the mathematical expectation (or more simply, "mean") is chosen as the "optimal forecast" when the symmetric mean squared errors are chosen as the loss function of forecast errors. However, forecasters may have an asymmetric loss function: they may regret positive forecast errors more than negative forecast errors. For instance, securities houses' market analysts may be more concerned with clients' lost opportunities to invest in particular stocks, rather than lost opportunity of disinvest from them. We show that the "optimal forecast" based on this upwardly skewed loss function of forecast errors is biased upward with respect to the mean. Moreover, we also show that the unconditional optimal forecast of the conditional optimal forecast of variable x (e.g., the earnings of a particular firm) on variable y (e.g., new information) is higher than or equal to the unconditional optimal forecast of variable x (see the case of "bearishness" in Sect. 13.4.4). New information does not decrease the bias of this economic agent's forecast with respect to the mean. It rather increases (or at least leaves unchanged) the bias on average. Thus, the bias persists as new information comes in. Thus, optimism and pessimism in the economic agent's forecast persists in terms of bias in her forecast with respect to the mathematical expectation. In other words, the law of iterated optimal forecasts that holds for mathematical expectation or mean does not hold in this asymmetric loss function of forecast errors. This chapter examines other loss functions of forecast errors as well (we hereafter call them *error functions*).

To achieve the stated goal, this chapter adopts a new framework that generalizes the concept of "conditional expectation" to mean values that are implicitly defined as unique solutions to some functional equation according to the theory developed by Ozaki (2009). We call such a mean value an *implicit mean*. The implicit mean was axiomatized by Fishburn (1986) and has been extensively applied to economics (for example, Epstein 1986) and decision theory (for example, Chew 1983, 1989; Dekel 1986; Grant et al. 2000). A very special example of an implicit mean is the *quasi-linear mean*, which was axiomatized by Nagumo (1930) and Kolmogorov (1930) and has also been applied to economics (for example, Epstein and Zin 1989; Farmer 1990; Weil 1990) and decision theory (for example, Kreps and Porteus 1978).

Specifically, this chapter provides a procedure to define *the* conditional implicit mean and analyzes its properties. To this end, we first show that the implicit mean can be alternatively characterized as the unique solution to the problem of "best" approximating a random variable by the constant where the approximation error is measured by some function, which we call an *error function*. When the error function is specified by the squared loss, the solution to the problem is given by the ordinary expectation and hence the implicit mean turns out to be equal to the expectation. Given any implicit mean, we find (actually, we can always find, as is shown in this chapter) the "unique" error function (see below) with respect to which the given implicit mean solves the approximation problem. Then, *that* error function is employed to define another approximation problem where a random variable is approximated by a function, rather than a constant, which is measurable with respect to the sub-σ-algebra on which the implicit mean is to be conditioned. We prove that the "best" approximation always exists uniquely and define it as a *conditional* implicit mean. Again, when the error function happens to be the squared loss, the conditional implicit mean turns out to equal the ordinary conditional expectation.

A question that naturally arises for such a procedure is whether it can be defined unambiguously. It turns out immediately that there are many error functions for which the given implicit mean gives the "best" approximation. Therefore, for the procedure to be unambiguous, it must hold that each of these error functions should generate the same solution to the problem of approximating within the class of measurable functions. We show that this certainly holds, and hence, that the procedure defines *the* conditional implicit mean unambiguously.

The scheme of conditional and unconditional implicit mean thus defined has a feature that is quite different from that of the ordinary expectation. The implicit mean is in general "biased" in the sense that the unconditional implicit mean of the conditional implicit mean is not necessarily equal to the unconditional implicit mean. In other words, an analogue of the law of iterated expectations, which holds true for the ordinary expectation, does not hold in general for the implicit mean. It is interesting to know under what additional conditions imposed on the implicit mean the law holds. We show that it holds if and only if the implicit mean happens to be the quasi-linear mean. The quasi-linear mean is still more general than the ordinary expectation and this result provides a characterization of the former in terms of conditioning.

We emphasize here that the term of "information" that appears in this chapter is exclusively used in the sense of Sect. 1.1.2.

The organization of the chapter is as follows. The next section defines the implicit mean as the solution to some functional equation and then characterizes it alternatively as the solution of some approximation problem. Section 13.3 defines the conditional implicit mean along the line described above and then characterizes the quasi-linear mean as the unique implicit mean that satisfies the law of iterated expectations.

Section 13.4 provides examples of implicit means. It discusses quasi-linear means, the implicit mean based on an L^q-error function, and in particular, the implicit mean based on an asymmetric error function. They are defined in terms of error functions that extend the mean squared loss. Here we explicitly show that quasi-linear means satisfy the law of iterated expectations while the latter two violate the law and hence they are persistently "biased." In particular, we present an example of asymmetric mean squared errors in which "positive-surprise" aversion implies persistent upward bias in the forecast, while "negative-surprise" aversion leads to persistent downward bias.

Section 13.5 offers other applications to economics. The first application is to show that people may exhibit "information aversion". We construct the decision-maker's optimization problem in which a size of information, along with an act, is a choice variable. Because more information allows available acts to increase, it may seem that more information is always more preferred. However, we show that the decision-maker could prefer remaining uninformed even if the information is free. The second application is the resolution of Ellsberg's paradox. We show that if the decision-maker is "negative-surprise" averse in a sense that is described by using asymmetric loss function (Sect. 13.4.3), her choice is the one observed in Ellsberg's paradox. All proofs for propositions and a corollary are relegated to the Appendix.

13.2 The Implicit Mean

13.2.1 Preliminaries

We take as primitive a probability space, $(\Omega, \mathcal{F}, \mu)$. Here, $\mathcal{F}$ is a σ-algebra consisting of subsets (or, *events*) of Ω and μ is a (σ-additive) probability measure on $\mathcal{F}$. We denote by $L^\infty(\mathcal{F})$ the space of real-valued, essentially bounded, and $\mathcal{F}$-measurable functions on Ω, which we denote also by F for notational simplicity; that is, $F := L^\infty(\mathcal{F}) := \{\, f : \Omega \to \mathbb{R} \mid f \text{ is } \mathcal{F}\text{-measurable and } \|f\|_\infty < +\infty \,\}$, where $\|\cdot\|_\infty$ denotes the *essential supremum* and is defined for each real-valued $\mathcal{F}$-measurable function f, by $\|f\|_\infty := \inf\{a \geq 0 \mid \mu(\{\omega \in \Omega \mid |f(\omega)| > a\}) = 0\}$ (we set $\inf \phi := +\infty$). We follow the usual convention that the two functions f and f' define a single element of F whenever $f = f'$ μ-almost everywhere (μ-a.e.),[1] and regard F as the set of μ-equivalence classes of functions. Hence, a (not necessarily $\mathcal{F}$-measurable) function f is an element of F if and only if there exists an essentially bounded $\mathcal{F}$-measurable function f' such that $f = f'$ μ-a.e.

From Sect. 2.2.2, recall the definition of the convex-rangedness and the nonatomicity. Also, recall that the two concepts coincide under this section's setting that $\mathcal{F}$ is the σ-algebra and μ is σ-additive (Proposition 2.2.1). For example, the finite-dimensional Euclidean space endowed with the Lebesgue (or Borel) measurable sets and the Lebesgue measure is convex-ranged (or equivalently, nonatomic). Intuitively, the probability space has a "rich" structure under the assumption of convex-rangedness. *Throughout the chapter, we assume that* $(\Omega, \mathcal{F}, \mu)$ *is convex-ranged.*

Given $z \in \mathbb{R}$, we denote by z^Ω, or more simply by z (no confusion is expected), the element f of F such that $(\forall \omega)\ f(\omega) = z$. Also, given $E \in \mathcal{F}$, we denote by χ_E the indicator function of E.[2]

A real-valued function defined on F is called a *functional*, and a functional $N : F \to \mathbb{R}$ is called a *generalized mean* if it satisfies $(\forall z \in \mathbb{R})\ N(z^\Omega) = z$. A familiar example of the generalized mean is the integral with respect to μ or the *expectation*, which we denote by E^μ or E. That is,

---

[1]We say that $f = f'$ μ-a.e. by definition if there exists a set $N \in \mathcal{F}$ such that $\{\, \omega \in \Omega \mid f(\omega) \neq f'(\omega) \,\} \subseteq N$ and $\mu(N) = 0$.

[2]The *indicator function* is defined in Sect. 2.2.3.

$$(\forall f \in F) \quad E^{\mu}[f] := E[f] := \int_{\Omega} f(\omega)\, d\mu(\omega)\,.$$

This chapter is concerned with the *implicit mean*, which is some class of generalized means that includes the expectation as a very special case.

13.2.2 The Betweenness Function and Its Uniqueness

To define the implicit mean, we first introduce a betweenness function. A function $\varphi : \mathbb{R}^2 \to \mathbb{R}$ is a *betweenness function* if it satisfies

B1. $(\forall x)\ \ \varphi(x, x) = 0$;
B2. $(\forall x)\ \ \varphi(x, \cdot)$ is strictly increasing or
$(\forall x)\ \ \varphi(x, \cdot)$ is strictly decreasing; and
B3. φ is continuous.

Note that when φ is a betweenness function, so is $-\varphi$; that is, $-\varphi$ satisfies B1–B3. Let $f \in F$, let φ be a betweenness function, and consider the following equation in $m \in \mathbb{R}$:

$$\int_{\Omega} \varphi(f(\omega), m)\, d\mu(\omega) = 0\,.$$

Then, by B1–B3 and the intermediate-value theorem, the solution m to this equation is uniquely determined. Furthermore, when $f = z$ for some $z \in \mathbb{R}$, it follows from B1 that $m = z$.

We now define a class of generalized means called an implicit mean. A functional $M : F \to \mathbb{R}$ is an *implicit mean* if there exists a betweenness function φ such that

$$(\forall f \in F) \quad \int_{\Omega} \varphi(f(\omega), M(f))\, d\mu(\omega) = 0\,. \tag{13.1}$$

An implicit mean with a betweenness function satisfying an additional assumption of skew-symmetry was axiomatized by Fishburn (1986).[3]

The remarks in the first paragraph of this subsection imply that any betweenness function φ uniquely determines a functional M, which we denote also by M^{φ}, as a solution to Eq. (13.1) and that such a functional is a generalized mean.

A question that naturally arises is that of uniqueness of the betweenness function that generates a given implicit mean. Suppose that two betweenness functions φ and φ' generate the same implicit mean M; that is, assume that $M = M^{\varphi} = M^{\varphi'}$. Then,

---

[3] An assumption of skew-symmetry is introduced later. For Fishburn's axiomatization, see the next footnote. In related works, Chew (1983, 1989) and Dekel (1986) axiomatized preferences that are represented as the unique solutions to functional equations similar to (13.1) in the framework of risk. Grant et al. (2000) extended it to the framework of uncertainty.

what relation should hold between φ and φ' ? The following proposition gives an answer.

Proposition 13.2.1 *Let φ and φ' be two betweenness functions. Then, $M^{\varphi} = M^{\varphi'}$ if and only if there exists a continuous positive function $a : \mathbb{R} \to \mathbb{R}_{++}$ or a continuous negative function $a : \mathbb{R} \to \mathbb{R}_{--}$ such that $(\forall x, z)\ \ \varphi'(x, z) = a(z)\varphi(x, z)$.*

For later use, we further restrict a class of implicit means. A betweenness function φ is *skew-symmetric* if it satisfies $(\forall x, z \in \mathbb{R})\ \varphi(z, x) = -\varphi(x, z)$. An implicit mean M is *skew-symmetric* if there exists a skew-symmetric betweenness function that generates M via Eq. (13.1).[4] As an immediate corollary, it follows that if φ and φ' are skew-symmetric betweenness functions that both generate the same implicit mean, then there exists a nonzero *constant a* such that $(\forall x, z)\ \varphi'(x, z) = a\varphi(x, z)$.[5]

A betweenness function is *separable* if there exists a continuous and strictly monotonic function $\hat{\varphi} : \mathbb{R} \to \mathbb{R}$ such that $(\forall x, z \in \mathbb{R})\ \varphi(x, z) = \hat{\varphi}(x) - \hat{\varphi}(z)$. An implicit mean M is *quasi-linear* if there exists a separable betweenness function that generates M via Eq. (13.1). The quasi-linear implicit mean, or more simply, the *quasi-linear mean*, is extensively studied in the literature (see, for example, Hardy et al. 1952, Chap. 3 and the literature cited in Introduction and Summary). The quasi-linear mean M is clearly skew-symmetric because a separable betweenness function is skew-symmetric, and it can be explicitly written as $(\forall f \in F)\ M(f) = \hat{\varphi}^{-1} \circ E[\,\hat{\varphi} \circ f\,]$, where $\hat{\varphi}^{-1}$ is the inverse of $\hat{\varphi}$ whose existence is guaranteed by the continuity and strict monotonicity of φ. When $\hat{\varphi}$ is a linear function, the quasi-linear mean is reduced to the expectation.

13.2.3 Alternative Characterization of Implicit Mean

This subsection provides an alternative characterization of the implicit mean. To this end, we introduce an error function. A function $\phi : \mathbb{R}^2 \to \mathbb{R}$ is an *error function* if it satisfies

---

[4] Fishburn (1986) axiomatizes the skew-symmetric implicit mean. To be more precise, he considers seven axioms that may be imposed on a real-valued function defined on a convex set of probability measures on a real interval, and then shows that such a function is the skew-symmetric implicit mean if and only if it satisfies all the seven axioms, one of which is his *cancellation axiom* that is responsible for skew-symmetry. Note that the definition of the skew-symmetric implicit mean requires only an existence of *some* skew-symmetric betweenness function. It is clear in light of Proposition 13.2.1 that there *does* exist (many) non-skew-symmetric betweenness functions that generate the same skew-symmetric implicit mean.

[5] Let φ and φ' be such betweenness functions. Then, by Proposition 13.2.1 and the skew-symmetry, there exists a function $a : \mathbb{R} \to \mathbb{R}$ that satisfies $(\forall x, z)\ a(z)\varphi(x, z) = \varphi'(x, z) = -\varphi'(z, x) = -a(x)\varphi(z, x) = a(x)\varphi(x, z)$. This shows that $(\forall x, z)\ a(z) = a(x)$; that is, the function a is constant.

E1. $(\forall x, z)\ \ \phi(x, z) \geq 0$;
E2. $\phi(x, z) = 0 \ \Leftrightarrow\ z = x$;
E3. $(\forall x)\ \ \phi(x, \cdot)$ is strictly convex ;
E4. ϕ is continuous ; and
E5. ϕ_2 exists and is continuous.

In E5, ϕ_2 denotes the partial derivative of ϕ with respect to its second argument. Given an error function ϕ, we define a correspondence $M^\phi : F \twoheadrightarrow \mathbb{R}$ by

$$(\forall f \in F) \quad M^\phi(f) := \arg\min\left\{ \int_\Omega \phi(f(\omega), z)\, d\mu(\omega) \,\middle|\, z \in \mathbb{R} \right\}. \tag{13.2}$$

Intuitively, $M^\phi(f)$ gives the best approximation to f within the real numbers, where the approximation is the "best" in the sense that the approximation error measured by an error function ϕ is minimized. If we define ϕ^2 by $(\forall x, z)\ \phi^2(x, z) := |x - z|^2$, then ϕ^2 is clearly an error function. Furthermore, as we will see later (in particular, see (13.4)), it holds that $M^{\phi^2} = E$. Therefore, M^ϕ generalizes E.

The well-defined nature (the nonempty-valuedness) of M^ϕ is included in the next proposition.

Proposition 13.2.2 *Let ϕ be an error function. Then, for each $f \in F$, $M^\phi(f)$ is nonempty and a singleton. Furthermore, for each $f \in F$, $M^\phi(f)$ is characterized as a unique solution z to*

$$\int_\Omega \phi_2(f(\omega), z)\, d\mu(\omega) = 0\,.$$

As a convention, we write as $M^\phi(f) = z$, rather than as $M^\phi(f) = \{z\}$, with $z \in \mathbb{R}$. By the first conclusion of Proposition 13.2.2 and this convention, we may regard M^ϕ as a functional. By E1 and E2, M^ϕ is a generalized mean. Furthermore, ϕ_2 is a betweenness function by E1–E5 (in particular, it is strictly increasing in its second argument by E3) and hence M^ϕ is an implicit mean by the second conclusion of Proposition 13.2.2. Therefore, any error function generates an implicit mean.

The next proposition establishes its converse. That is, any implicit mean can be generated as the best approximation with some error function.

Proposition 13.2.3 *Let M be an implicit mean. Then, there exists an error function ϕ such that $M = M^\phi$.*

Note that an error function ϕ that generates M in the sense that $M = M^\phi$ is not unique. In fact, Propositions 13.2.1 and 13.2.2 show that for any two error functions ϕ and ϕ', $M^\phi = M^{\phi'}$ if and only if there exists a continuous positive function $a : \mathbb{R} \to \mathbb{R}_{++}$ or a continuous negative function $a : \mathbb{R} \to \mathbb{R}_{--}$ such that $(\forall x, z)\ \phi'_2(x, z) = a(z)\phi_2(x, z)$.

13.3 The Conditional Implicit Mean

13.3.1 Information Structure

We denote by $\mathcal{F}^*$ the space of all sub-σ-algebras of $\mathcal{F}$, and denote by $\mathcal{F}^\circ$ the space of all sub-σ-algebras of $\mathcal{F}$ that contain all μ-null sets.[6] Given $\mathcal{G} \in \mathcal{F}^*$, we define two functional spaces, $F(\mathcal{G})$ and $L^\infty(\mathcal{G})$, as follows: $f \in F(\mathcal{G})$ if and only if there is a bounded $\mathcal{G}$-measurable function f' such that $f' = f$ μ-a.e.[7] and $f \in L^\infty(\mathcal{G})$ if and only if there is a bounded $\mathcal{G}$-measurable function f' such that there exists a set $N \in \mathcal{G}$ (*not* "$\in \mathcal{F}$") such that $\{\, \omega \in \Omega \mid f'(\omega) \neq f(\omega) \,\} \subseteq N$ and $\mu(N) = 0$. For elements in $F(\mathcal{G})$, we identify f with f' if $f = f'$ μ-a.e., while for elements in $L^\infty(\mathcal{G})$, we do so if $f = f'$ "almost everywhere" in the sense defined above. Note that $F(\mathcal{G}) \subseteq F$ and that "our" $L^\infty(\mathcal{G})$ coincides with the "usual" $L^\infty(\mathcal{G})$ defined on the probability space $(\Omega, \mathcal{G}, \mu)$. Also note that while $F(\mathcal{G})$ and $L^\infty(\mathcal{G})$ coincide when $\mathcal{G}$ happens to equal $\mathcal{F}$, they are distinct in general.[8] However, it turns out that for any $\mathcal{G} \in \mathcal{F}^\circ$, $F(\mathcal{G})$ and $L^\infty(\mathcal{G})$ coincide. In what follows, we always consider $\mathcal{F}^\circ$, rather than $\mathcal{F}$, and denote both spaces commonly by $F(\mathcal{G})$.

Given a sub-σ-algebra $\mathcal{G} \in \mathcal{F}^\circ$, we frequently interpret $\mathcal{G}$ as representing information we possess. For each event $E \in \mathcal{G}$, we know whether E has occurred. For each event $E \in \mathcal{F} \backslash \mathcal{G}$, we know that E is an event; that is, we know that there are two possibilities that either E has happened or not, but we do not know whether it has actually occurred. For example, the event E may be "Martians live." Under this interpretation, we assume that we are able to assign a probability to each event regardless of whether we know its occurrence. For this interpretation, see Sect. 1.1.2.

13.3.2 Defining Conditional Implicit Mean

This subsection proposes a new concept of the conditional implicit mean, which can be naturally interpreted and extends the concept of conditioning beyond that for the expectation.

We proceed with an analogy to the conditional expectation to motivate our concept. Let $\mathcal{G} \in \mathcal{F}^\circ$. Then, the *conditional expectation* given $\mathcal{G}$, $E[\cdot|\mathcal{G}]$, is *defined* by[9]

---

[6]A subset E of Ω is a *μ-null set* by definition if $E \in \mathcal{F}$ and $\mu(E) = 0$.

[7]See Footnote 1.

[8]To see that $F(\mathcal{G}) \neq L^\infty(\mathcal{G})$ in general, consider a simple example: $\Omega := \{\omega_1, \omega_2, \omega_3\}$; $\mathcal{F} := 2^\Omega$; $\mathcal{G} := \{\phi, \{\omega_1\}, \{\omega_2, \omega_3\}, \Omega\}$; $\mu(\{\omega_1\}) = \mu(\{\omega_2\}) := 1/2$ and $\mu(\{\omega_3\}) := 0$; $f \in F$ is such that $f(\omega_1) = f(\omega_2) := 1$ and $f(\omega_3) := 2$. Then, $f \in F(\mathcal{G})$, but $f \notin L^\infty(\mathcal{G})$. Note that $\mathcal{G} \notin \mathcal{F}^\circ$.

[9]Equation (13.4) is typically applied to L^2 spaces, as a definition of conditional expectation, in which case the minimum is always uniquely attained by the orthogonal projection because $L^2(\mathcal{G})$ is a closed subspace of $L^2(\mathcal{F})$. Because $L^\infty \subseteq L^2$, this definition can be directly applied to the current context. Furthermore, if it is extended to the L^1 space by the standard approximation argument, it coincides with a more common definition of the conditional expectation:

$$(\forall f \in F) \quad E[f|\mathcal{G}] := \arg\min \{ \| f - g \|_2 \mid g \in F(\mathcal{G}) \} , \tag{13.4}$$

where $\| \cdot \|_2$ denotes the L^2-norm and is defined by

$$(\forall f \in F) \quad \| f \|_2 := \left(\int_\Omega |f(\omega)|^2 \, d\mu(\omega) \right)^{1/2} .$$

That is, the conditional expectation of f given $\mathcal{G}$ is the best approximation to f within the class of $\mathcal{G}$-measurable functions, where the approximation is the "best" in the sense that the approximation error measured by the L^2-metric, $\|f - g\|_2$, is minimized.

As an *implication* of the definition (13.4) of conditional expectation, it holds that

$$(\forall f \in F) \quad E[\, f \,|\{\phi, \Omega\}] = E[\, f \,], \tag{13.5}$$

where $\{\phi, \Omega\}$ denotes the σ-algebra generated by all μ-null subsets of Ω.[10] That is, the conditional expectation given "no information," or the "best" approximation within the real numbers with an approximation error measured by L^2-metric, is the *un*conditional expectation.

We "reverse" the procedure to define the conditional implicit mean. Given an implicit mean M, we find an error function that generates M via (13.2). The existence of such an error function is guaranteed by Proposition 13.2.2. We then use *that* error function, say ϕ, to define the conditional implicit mean as the best approximation within the class of measurable functions, where the approximation is the "best" in the sense that the approximation error measured by ϕ is minimized. When M happens to equal the expectation, such an error function ϕ will be given by the L^2-metric and the conditional implicit mean generated by ϕ is exactly the conditional expectation defined by (13.4). Note that the L^2-metric satisfies E1–E5 and is certainly an error function. Therefore, our definition naturally extends that of conditional expectation.

The rest of this subsection shows that this procedure works nicely. First, we prove that for any error function, the best approximation always exists uniquely. Given an error function ϕ and a sub-σ-algebra $\mathcal{G} \in \mathcal{F}^\circ$, we define a correspondence $M^\phi(\cdot|\mathcal{G}) : F \to F(\mathcal{G})$ by: $(\forall f \in F)$

(Footnote 9 continued)
$E[f|\mathcal{G}]$ is defined as a $\mathcal{G}$-measurable integrable function that satisfies

$$(\forall h \in L^\infty(\mathcal{G})) \quad \int_\Omega (f(\omega) - E[f|\mathcal{G}](\omega))\, h(\omega)\, d\mu(\omega) = 0 . \tag{13.3}$$

For the definitions of L^1 and L^2 spaces and other details, see Billingsley (1986, in particular, p. 477, 34.15).

[10]Equation (13.5) holds true even if we understand as usual that $\{\phi, \Omega\}$ represents the σ-algebra generated by ϕ and Ω. The text definition of $\{\phi, \Omega\}$ is to ensure that $\{\phi, \Omega\} \in \mathcal{F}^\circ$.

$$M^{\phi}(f|\mathcal{G}) := \arg\min \left\{ \int_{\Omega} \phi(f(\omega), g(\omega))\, d\mu(\omega) \,\middle|\, g \in F(\mathcal{G}) \right\}. \tag{13.6}$$

The well-defined nature (the nonempty-valuedness) of $M^{\phi}(\cdot|\mathcal{G})$ is included in the next proposition.

Proposition 13.3.1 *Let ϕ be an error function. Then, for each $f \in F$ and each $\mathcal{G} \in \mathcal{F}^{\circ}$, $M^{\phi}(f|\mathcal{G})$ is nonempty and a singleton.*

Note that $M^{\phi}(f|\mathcal{G})$ is a singleton as a set of μ-equivalence classes. As a convention, we write as $M^{\phi}(f|\mathcal{G}) = g$, rather than as $M^{\phi}(f|\mathcal{G}) = \{g\}$, with $g \in F(\mathcal{G})$. Also, note that $(\forall f \in F)\ M^{\phi}(f) = M^{\phi}(f|\{\phi, \Omega\})$, where the left-hand side is defined by (13.2) and the right-hand side is defined by (13.6) with $\mathcal{G} = \{\phi, \Omega\}$ denoting the σ-algebra generated by all μ-null subsets of Ω. Hence, Proposition 13.3.1 generalizes the first half of Proposition 13.2.2. The next proposition generalizes its second half.

Proposition 13.3.2 *Let $f \in F$ and let $\mathcal{G} \in \mathcal{F}^{\circ}$. Then, $g = M^{\phi}(f|\mathcal{G})$ if and only if g satisfies $g \in F(\mathcal{G})$ and*

$$(\forall h \in F(\mathcal{G})) \qquad \int_{\Omega} \phi_2(f(\omega), g(\omega)) h(\omega)\, d\mu(\omega) = 0\,. \tag{13.7}$$

We turn to the next step in defining the conditional implicit mean. Let M be an implicit mean. Then, by Proposition 13.2.3, there exists an error function ϕ such that $M = M^{\phi}$, where M^{ϕ} is defined by (13.2). We may use *this* ϕ to define the conditional implicit mean $M(\cdot|\cdot)$ by $M(\cdot|\cdot) := M^{\phi}(\cdot|\cdot)$, where $M^{\phi}(\cdot|\cdot)$ is defined by (13.6). However, an error function ϕ such that $M = M^{\phi}$ is not unique (see the remark right after Proposition 13.2.3). Therefore, for the definition of the conditional implicit mean to be unambiguous, each of such error functions needs to generate the same $M^{\phi}(\cdot|\cdot)$. The next proposition shows that is certainly the case.

Proposition 13.3.3 *Let M be an implicit mean and let ϕ and ϕ' be two error functions such that $M = M^{\phi} = M^{\phi'}$. Then, $(\forall f \in F)(\forall \mathcal{G} \in \mathcal{F}^{\circ})\ M^{\phi}(f|\mathcal{G}) = M^{\phi'}(f|\mathcal{G})$, where the equality holds μ-a.e.*

We are now ready to state the definition of *the* conditional implicit mean. Given an implicit mean M, we define its *conditional mean*, denoted $M(\cdot|\cdot)$, by

$$(\forall f \in F)(\forall \mathcal{G} \in \mathcal{F}^{\circ}) \quad M(f|\mathcal{G}) := M^{\phi}(f|\mathcal{G}) \tag{13.8}$$

where ϕ is an error function such that $M = M^{\phi}$ whose existence is guaranteed by Proposition 13.2.3 and the right-hand side is defined by (13.6). By Proposition 13.3.3, the conditional implicit mean is well defined; that is, the definition does not depend on a choice of an error function.

We may apply this definition also when we begin with an error function. To be more precise, suppose that an error function ϕ' is given as a primitive, and define the implicit mean M by $M := M^{\phi'}$ via (13.2) and the conditional implicit mean

$M(\cdot|\cdot)$ by $M(\cdot|\cdot) := M^{\phi'}(\cdot|\cdot)$ via (13.6). Then, $M(\cdot|\cdot)$ thus defined coincides with the one derived from M by (13.8). Therefore, whether we begin with a betweenness function or an error function, we will obtain a consistent system of conditional and unconditional implicit means.

Finally, we relate the conditional implicit mean to the betweenness function.

Corollary 13.3.1 *Let M be an implicit mean defined by a betweenness function φ via (13.1) (which we denoted by M^{φ} in the previous section). Also, let $f \in F$ and let $\mathcal{G} \in \mathcal{F}^{\circ}$. Then, $g = M(f|\mathcal{G})$ if and only if g satisfies $g \in F(\mathcal{G})$ and*

$$(\forall h \in F(\mathcal{G})) \quad \int_{\Omega} \varphi(f(\omega), g(\omega))h(\omega)\, d\mu(\omega) = 0\,. \tag{13.9}$$

If φ were defined by $(\forall x, z)\ \varphi(x, z) := x - z$, M would be equal to E (see the end of Sect. 13.2.2), (13.9) would be the same as (13.3) (see Footnote 9) and the scheme of conditional implicit means would be precisely reduced to the one of conditional expectations.

13.3.3 The Law of Iterated Integrals and Characterization of Quasi-linear Mean

Among implications of the conditional expectation, which is defined by (13.3) or (13.4), is

$$(\forall f \in F)(\forall \mathcal{G} \in \mathcal{F}^{\circ}) \quad E[f] = E[E[f|\mathcal{G}]]\,, \tag{13.10}$$

which is known as the *law of iterated expectations*. Now, consider a similar statement for the implicit mean, M:

$$(\forall f \in F)(\forall \mathcal{G} \in \mathcal{F}^{\circ}) \quad M(f) = M(M(f|\mathcal{G}))\,, \tag{13.11}$$

where $M(\cdot)$ terms on the left-hand side and the outer of the right-hand side are the given implicit mean and $M(\cdot|\cdot)$ inside of the right-hand side is the conditional implicit mean derived from $M(\cdot)$ via (13.8). When M satisfies (13.11), we say that it satisfies the *law of iterated integrals*. In general, the implicit mean M does not necessarily satisfy the law of iterated integrals unless it is generated by the L^2-metric, ϕ^2, via (13.2). This "biasedness", rather than "unbiasedness", of the implicit mean will be further illustrated by the examples in the next section.

The next proposition shows that the quasi-linear mean is the only skew-symmetric implicit mean that satisfies the law of iterated integrals. Hence, the proposition characterizes the quasi-linear mean in terms of a scheme of conditioning.

Proposition 13.3.4 *Let M be a skew-symmetric implicit mean. Then, M is quasi-linear if and only if it satisfies (13.11).*

13.4 Examples of the Implicit Mean

This section offers three examples of implicit means, and we derive the conditional mean for each. The first example is the quasi-linear mean and we directly verify that it satisfies the law of iterated integrals, which conforms to Proposition 13.3.4. The second and third examples are defined with respect to the error functions that extend the squared loss. We show that they violate the law of iterated integrals and we discuss the direction of their "biasedness."

13.4.1 Quasi-linear Mean

We have already introduced the quasi-linear mean and shown that it is the only skew-symmetric implicit mean that satisfies the law of iterated integrals (Proposition 13.3.4). In this subsection, we will find its conditional mean explicitly and then verify that it satisfies the law of iterated integrals directly.

Let M be a quasi-linear mean defined via (13.1) with a betweenness function φ such that $(\forall x, z)\ \varphi(x, z) = \hat{\varphi}(x) - \hat{\varphi}(z)$ for some continuous and strictly monotonic function $\hat{\varphi} : \mathbb{R} \to \mathbb{R}$. First, we claim that

$$(\forall f \in F)(\forall \mathcal{G} \in \mathcal{F}^{\circ}) \quad M(f|\mathcal{G}) = \hat{\varphi}^{-1} \circ E[\hat{\varphi} \circ f|\mathcal{G}] \tag{13.12}$$

where $E[\cdot|\cdot]$ is the conditional expectation and $\hat{\varphi}^{-1}$ is the inverse of $\hat{\varphi}$ whose existence is guaranteed by the continuity and strict monotonicity of $\hat{\varphi}$. To prove the claim, let $g := \hat{\varphi}^{-1} \circ E[\hat{\varphi} \circ f|\mathcal{G}]$ and let $h \in F(\mathcal{G})$. Then, it holds that

$$0 = \int_{\Omega} \big(\hat{\varphi} \circ f(\omega) - \hat{\varphi} \circ g(\omega)\big)\, h(\omega)\, d\mu(\omega) = \int_{\Omega} \varphi(f(\omega), g(\omega)) h(\omega)\, d\mu(\omega)\,,$$

where the first equality holds by (13.3) (see Footnote 9) because $\hat{\varphi} \circ g = E[\hat{\varphi} \circ f|\mathcal{G}]$ and the second equality holds by the definition of φ. Because h is arbitrary, Corollary 13.3.1 proves the claim.

Second, we verify that M satisfies the law of iterated integrals. Note that $(\forall f)\ M(f) = \hat{\varphi}^{-1} \circ E[\hat{\varphi} \circ f]$ by (13.1). Therefore, $(\forall f \in F)(\forall \mathcal{G} \in \mathcal{F}^{\circ})$

$$\begin{aligned} M(M(f|\mathcal{G})) &= \hat{\varphi}^{-1} \circ E[\hat{\varphi} \circ M(f|\mathcal{G})] \\ &= \hat{\varphi}^{-1} \circ E\left[\hat{\varphi} \circ \hat{\varphi}^{-1} \circ E[\hat{\varphi} \circ f|\mathcal{G}]\right] \\ &= \hat{\varphi}^{-1} \circ E\left[E[\hat{\varphi} \circ f|\mathcal{G}]\right] = \hat{\varphi}^{-1} \circ E[\hat{\varphi} \circ f] = M(f) \end{aligned}$$

where the second equality holds by (13.12) and the fourth equality holds by (13.10).

13.4.2 L^q-Error Function

Let $q \in (1, +\infty)$ and let $\phi^q : \mathbb{R}^2 \to \mathbb{R}$ be defined by $(\forall x, z \in \mathbb{R})$ $\phi^q(x, z) := |x - z|^q$. Then, it is easily verified that ϕ^q satisfies E1-E5 and hence ϕ^q is an error function, which we call the *L^q-error function*. We denote by M^q and $M^q(\cdot|\cdot)$ the unconditional and conditional implicit means generated from ϕ^q via (13.2) and (13.6), respectively. In these notations, we have $M^2 = E$ and $M^2(\cdot|\cdot) = E[\cdot|\cdot]$.

The implicit mean M^q becomes more sensitive to the underlying probability when q becomes closer to 1 and it becomes more sensitive to the values the random variable assumes when q becomes larger. This point will be highlighted if we consider an extreme case. Let $\langle E_1, E_2 \rangle$ be a partition of Ω such that $(\forall i)$ $p_i := \mu(E_i) > 0$, let $x_1, x_2 \in \mathbb{R}$, and define $\hat{f} \in F$ by $\hat{f} := x_1\chi_{E_1} + x_2\chi_{E_2}$. When $q = 1$, $M^q(\hat{f}) = x_i$, where $i = \arg\max_{j=1,2} p_j$, and the underlying probability is decisive in determining the value of M^q.[11] On the other hand, when $q = +\infty$, $M^q(\hat{f}) = (x_1 + x_2)/2$ regardless of p_i values, and the values the random variable assumes are decisive in it.[12]

The betweenness function φ that defines M^q via (13.1) turns out to be $(\forall x, z)$ $\varphi(x, z) = -q|x - z|^{q-1}\mathrm{sgn}(x - z)$ by Proposition 13.2.2. This betweenness function is skew-symmetric while it is not separable unless $q = 2$.[13] Therefore, Proposition 13.3.4 shows that M^q does not satisfy the law of iterated integrals unless $q = 2$.

To see the "biasedness" of M^q more closely, consider the following example. Let $\langle E_1, E_2, E_3 \rangle$ be a partition of Ω such that $0 < p_1 := \mu(E_1) = \mu(E_3) =: p_3 < \frac{1}{2}$ and $p_2 := \mu(E_2) > 0$, let $\mathcal{G}$ be the σ-algebra generated by $E_2 \cup E_3$ and all μ-null subsets of Ω, and let $\mathcal{G}'$ be the σ-algebra generated by $E_1 \cup E_2$ and all μ-null subsets of Ω. The information given by $\mathcal{G}$ cannot distinguish the event E_3 from the event E_2, while the information given by $\mathcal{G}'$ cannot distinguish the event E_1 from the event E_2. Furthermore, the events E_1 and E_3 are assumed to be equally likely to occur. Also, let $x \in \mathbb{R}$, let $\varepsilon > 0$, and define $\hat{f} \in F$ by $\hat{f} := (x - \varepsilon)\chi_{E_1} + x\chi_{E_2} + (x + \varepsilon)\chi_{E_3}$. Finally, let $r := 1/(q - 1)$ for notational ease. Then, several lines of calculation lead to $M^q(\hat{f}) = x$,

[11] When $p_1 = p_2$, any real number between x_1 and x_2 can be a solution of the minimization problem defining (13.2), and hence, M^q is not well defined. This is why we excluded the case where $q = 1$ at the outset. Thus, the argument in the text stands only heuristically.

[12] When $q = +\infty$, we think of the minimization problem defining (13.2) as

$$\min_{z \in \mathbb{R}} \lim_{q \to +\infty} \left(\int_{\Omega} |f(\omega) - z|^q \, d\mu(\omega) \right)^{1/q}.$$

Again, the argument remains only heuristic.

[13] In fact, any betweenness function φ' that is "equivalent" to φ in the sense that $(\exists a)(\forall x, z)$ $\varphi'(x, z) = a(z)\varphi(x, z)$ is not separable. See Proposition 13.2.1.

$$M^q(M^q(\hat{f}|\mathcal{G})) = p_1^r \frac{(p_2+p_3)^r - (p_2^r + p_3^r)}{(p_2^r + p_3^r)(p_1^r + (p_2+p_3)^r)}\varepsilon + x \text{ , and}$$
$$M^q(M^q(\hat{f}|\mathcal{G}')) = p_1^r \frac{(p_1^r + p_2^r) - (p_1+p_2)^r}{(p_1^r + p_2^r)((p_1+p_2)^r + p_3^r)}\varepsilon + x$$

which in turn shows that

$$q < 2 \Leftrightarrow M^q(M^q(\hat{f}|\mathcal{G}')) < M^q(\hat{f}) < M^q(M^q(\hat{f}|\mathcal{G})); \tag{13.13}$$
$$q > 2 \Leftrightarrow M^q(M^q(\hat{f}|\mathcal{G}')) > M^q(\hat{f}) > M^q(M^q(\hat{f}|\mathcal{G})). \tag{13.14}$$

The relations (13.13) and (13.14) clearly show that M^q does not satisfy the law of iterated integrals unless $q = 2$. Because M^2 satisfies the law, we may conclude that M^q satisfies the law if and only if $q = 2$.

To see the intuition behind (13.13), suppose that $q < 2$. In this case, making an intermediate aggregation among relatively "good" states (that is, calculating $M^q(\hat{f}|\mathcal{G})$ first) "helps", while doing so among relatively "bad" states (calculating $M^q(\hat{f}|\mathcal{G}')$ first) does not. To see why, recall from the second paragraph of this subsection that the implicit mean M^q tends to be more sensitive to the underlying probability, rather than to the values the random variable assumes, when $q < 2$. An intermediate aggregation raises the probabilities of both the good event (E_3) and the bad event (E_1), and hence, it makes the good event better and the bad event worse under M^q, leading to (13.13).

To see the intuition behind (13.14), suppose that $q > 2$. In this case, making an intermediate aggregation among relatively "good" states "dampens", while doing so among relatively "bad" states does not. To see why, recall from the second paragraph of this subsection that the implicit mean M^q is relatively *in*sensitive to the underlying probability and it tends to simply take the expectation by putting an equal weight to each value the random variable assumes when $q > 2$. An intermediate aggregation averages the good events (E_2 and E_3) downward and it averages the bad events (E_2 and E_1) upward, and hence, it makes the good events *less* good and the bad events *less* bad under M^q, leading to (13.14).

13.4.3 Asymmetric Error Function

Let $q \in (1, +\infty)$, let $\gamma > 0$, and let $\phi^{q,\gamma} : \mathbb{R}^2 \to \mathbb{R}$ be defined by

$$(\forall x, z \in \mathbb{R}) \quad \phi^{q,\gamma}(x,z) := \begin{cases} \gamma|x-z|^q & \text{if } x \geq z \\ |x-z|^q & \text{if } x < z. \end{cases}$$

Then, it is easily verified that $\phi^{q,\gamma}$ satisfies E1-E5 and hence $\phi^{q,\gamma}$ is an error function, which we call the *asymmetric error function*. We denote by $M^{q,\gamma}$ and $M^{q,\gamma}(\cdot|\cdot)$ the unconditional and conditional implicit means generated from $\phi^{q,\gamma}$ via (13.2) and (13.6), respectively. In these notations, we have $M^{2,1} = E$ and $M^{2,1}(\cdot|\cdot) = E[\cdot|\cdot]$.

When $\gamma = 1$, $\phi^{q,\gamma}$ is reduced to ϕ^q in the previous subsection. Otherwise, $\phi^{q,\gamma}$ treats an underestimate ($z < x$) and an overestimate ($z > x$) *asymmetrically*. When $\gamma < 1$, an overestimate is more "penalized" than an underestimate because the error caused by the latter is tolerated by γ while that caused by the former is not. On the other hand, when $\gamma > 1$, the underestimate is more "penalized" than the overestimate because the error caused by the former is exaggerated by γ while that caused by the latter is not.

The betweenness function φ that defines $M^{q,\gamma}$ via (13.1) turns out to be

$$(\forall x, z) \quad \varphi(x, z) = \begin{cases} -\gamma q(x-z)^{q-1} & \text{if } x \geq z \\ q(z-x)^{q-1} & \text{if } x < z \end{cases} \tag{13.15}$$

by Proposition 13.2.2. The betweenness function given by (13.15) is *not* skew-symmetric, and hence, we can*not* invoke Proposition 13.3.4 to see whether $M^{q,\gamma}$ satisfies the law of iterated integrals.

To study the "biasedness" of $M^{q,\gamma}$ further, let $q = 2$ in what follows. Then, the following example shows that $M^{2,\gamma}$ does not satisfy the law of iterated integrals unless $\gamma = 1$. Let $\langle E_1, E_2, E_3 \rangle$ be a partition of Ω such that $(\forall i)\ p_i := \mu(E_i) > 0$ and let $\mathcal{G}$ be the σ-algebra generated by $E_1 \cup E_2$ and all μ-null subsets of Ω. Also, let $x_1, x_2 \in \mathbb{R}$ be such that $x_1 < x_2$ and define $\hat{f} \in F$ by $\hat{f} := x_1\chi_{E_1} + x_2\chi_{E_2 \cup E_3}$. Then, lengthy but straightforward calculation leads to $\gamma < 1 \Leftrightarrow M^{2,\gamma}(\hat{f}) > M^{2,\gamma}(M^{2,\gamma}(\hat{f}|\mathcal{G}))$ and $\gamma > 1 \Leftrightarrow M^{2,\gamma}(\hat{f}) < M^{2,\gamma}(M^{2,\gamma}(\hat{f}|\mathcal{G}))$. This clearly shows that $M^{2,\gamma}$ does not satisfy the law of iterated integrals unless $\gamma = 1$. Because $M^{2,1}$ satisfies the law, we may conclude that $M^{2,\gamma}$ satisfies the law if and only if $\gamma = 1$.

This example can be generalized to the next proposition.

Proposition 13.4.1 *Let $M^{2,\gamma}$ be the implicit mean generated by the asymmetric error function $\phi^{2,\gamma}$. Then,*

$$\gamma < 1 \Leftrightarrow (\forall f \in F)(\forall \mathcal{G} \in \mathcal{F}^\circ) \ \ M^{2,\gamma}(f) > M^{2,\gamma}(M^{2,\gamma}(f|\mathcal{G}))\,; \tag{13.16}$$

$$\gamma > 1 \Leftrightarrow (\forall f \in F)(\forall \mathcal{G} \in \mathcal{F}^\circ) \ \ M^{2,\gamma}(f) < M^{2,\gamma}(M^{2,\gamma}(f|\mathcal{G}))\,. \tag{13.17}$$

When $\gamma < 1$, each application of $M^{2,\gamma}$ tends to underestimate because the cost of an underestimation is tolerated, and hence, its iterated applications lower the mean value. To the contrary, when $\gamma > 1$, each application of $M^{2,\gamma}$ tends to overestimate because the cost of an underestimation is exaggerated, and hence, its iterated applications raise the mean value.

13.4.4 Persistent Bearishness and Bullishness

In this subsection, we consider agents that are endowed with the asymmetric error function in the previous subsection and interpret such agents as exhibiting *surprise aversion/affinity*. First, assume that $\gamma < 1$. Then, an agent with $\phi^{2,\gamma}$ punishes an overestimate more than an underestimate. Given that an overestimate can be understood to be a "negative-surprise" in the sense that a realized value of a random variable is *lower* than she thought, we may say that she exhibits *negative-surprise aversion*. By way of definition, it is immediate that $(\forall f)\ M^{2,\gamma}(f) \leq M^{2,1}(f) = E[f]$. That is, the agent who exhibits negative-surprise aversion always reports a lower value than the expected value and can be characteristically called "bearish."

We can see that a "bearish" agent's behavior is *persistent* in the following sense. Keep assuming that $\gamma < 1$. Then, Proposition 13.4.1 shows $(\forall f)(\forall \mathcal{G}) M^{2,\gamma}(M^{2,\gamma}(f|\mathcal{G})) < M^{2,\gamma}(f) \leq E[f]$. That is, even if the agent foresees further information becoming available in the future, her outlook does not improve and she remains "bearish." Importantly, additional information is not available now but it will become available in the future. The agent foresees this future availability now, but this fact does not change her attitude (that is, an aversion) toward negative surprise.

Symmetrically, assume that $\gamma > 1$. Then, an agent with $\phi^{2,\gamma}$ punishes an underestimate more than an overestimate. Because an underestimate can be understood to be a "*positive* surprise" in the sense that a realized value of a random variable is *higher* than she thought, we may say that she exhibits *positive-surprise affinity*. Furthermore, given that for such an agent, Proposition 13.4.1 shows $(\forall f)(\forall \mathcal{G})\ M^{2,\gamma}(M^{2,\gamma}(f|\mathcal{G})) > M^{2,\gamma}(f) \geq E[f]$. she can be characteristically called "bullish" and her bullishness is *persistent* in the sense described in the previous paragraph.

13.5 Applications: Information Aversion and Ellsberg's Paradox Revisited

This section provides two economic applications of the theory developed in this chapter. We first offer a model where the agent endowed with an asymmetric error function exhibits an aversion to more information. It is well known that in a game situation, an agent may benefit from the fact that he knows less *if* other players know that he knows less. On the contrary, the model we present below is that with purely a single agent. She shows an aversion to more information (and hence, an affinity to less information) when her error function is asymmetric with $\gamma < 1$ because she is then negative-surprise averse in the sense of Sect. 13.4.4.

As another application, we take up Ellsberg's paradox given in Sect. 3.7. We show that the preference pattern that showed up in Ellsberg's paradox *can* be explained by an agent's *single* prior, rather than her multiple priors, if we assume that she is negative-surprise averse. This clearly shows that the multiplicity of probability charges the decision-maker possesses is not necessary for explaining the paradox.

13.5.1 Information Aversion

This subsection constructs the decision-maker's optimization problem in which the size of information, along with the act, is a choice variable and the agent might exhibit information aversion.

We construct the model in four steps. First, consider the simple information structure as follows: $\Omega = E_1 \cup E_2 \cup E_3, (\forall i)\ E_i \in \mathcal{F}, (\forall i \neq j)\ E_i \cap E_j = \phi, (\forall i)\ p_i := \mu(E_i) > 0$; $\mathcal{G}$ is the σ-algebra generated by $E_2 \cup E_3$ and all μ-null subsets of Ω; and $\mathcal{G}'$ is the σ-algebra generated by all μ-null subsets of Ω. Here, $\mathcal{G}$ represents information that cannot distinguish the third event from the second event and $\mathcal{G}'$ represents no information.

Second, let $X := \mathbb{R}$ be an outcome space and let $\Gamma : \Omega \twoheadrightarrow X$ be a *feasibility correspondence* defined by

$$(\forall \omega) \quad \Gamma(\omega) := \begin{cases} [0, \bar{a}] & \text{if} \quad \omega \in E_1 \\ [0, \bar{a} + \varepsilon] & \text{if} \quad \omega \in E_2 \cup E_3 \end{cases} \tag{13.18}$$

where $\bar{a}$ and ε are positive constants. A *feasible act* is a function $a_0 : \Omega \to \mathbb{R}$ such that $(\forall \omega)\ a_0(\omega) \in \Gamma(\omega)$. The feasibility of an act requires that the agent must choose an act whose outcome will be feasible should any state be realized. We assume that the choice of an act is made before the true state is revealed, so the feasibility requirement must be met for each of the states.

Third, let $\hat{u} \in F$ be a stochastic "future" utility defined by

$$(\forall \omega) \quad \hat{u}(\omega) = \begin{cases} 0 & \text{if} \quad \omega \in E_1 \cup E_2 \\ b & \text{if} \quad \omega \in E_3 \end{cases}$$

where $b > 0$ is a given constant. The third event is a special one: the agent gets "bonus" utility, b, only when this event occurs. Note that $\hat{u}$ need be only $\mathcal{F}$-measurable, rather that $\mathcal{G}$- or $\mathcal{G}'$-measurable. Also note that we assume that an act does not affect $\hat{u}$.[14]

Finally, we assume that the agent chooses a feasible act a_0 and information $\mathcal{H}$ so as to maximize

$$M^q(a_0 + M^q(\hat{u}|\mathcal{H})) \tag{13.19}$$

subject to the following constraints: $\mathcal{H} \in \{\mathcal{G}, \mathcal{G}'\}$ and

$$a_0 \in F(\mathcal{H})\,. \tag{13.20}$$

Here, $q > 1$ and M^q in (13.19) is the implicit mean defined in Sect. 13.4.2.

[14]The function $\hat{u}$ may be regarded as a summary statistic of all relevant factors that could affect the agent's overall utility.

We assume that the utility index on $X(=\mathbb{R})$ is linear. Hence, the total current utility before the state ω is realized is given by $a_0 + M^q(\hat{u}|\mathcal{H})$. Because this is still stochastic, the decision-maker needs to compute its mean by using M^q, which leads to (13.19). We also assume that obtaining the information does not incur any cost.[15]

Once the model has been constructed, we activate it to show that the agent shows an aversion to information. In the above optimization problem, the amount of information $\mathcal{H}$ has two roles. First, if $\mathcal{H}$ becomes finer (that is, if the amount of information increases), more feasible acts will become available (see (13.20)). Second, $\mathcal{H}$ filters the $\mathcal{F}$-measurable function $\hat{u}$ to the $\mathcal{H}$-measurable function by using M^q.

When $q = 2$, we have (13.19) $= M^2(a_0 + M^2(\hat{u}|\mathcal{H})) = E[a_0 + E[\hat{u}|\mathcal{H}]] = E[a_0] + E[E[\hat{u}|\mathcal{H}]] = E[a_0] + E[\hat{u}]$ where the last equation holds by the law of iterated expectations. Therefore, more information is preferred to (or at least as preferred as) less information because more feasible acts will be available under more information because the measurability requirement will become weaker.

However, when $q \neq 2$, the story is not that straightforward. To see this, observe that the decision-maker who chooses $\mathcal{G}$ will choose the act a such that

$$a(\omega) = \begin{cases} \bar{a} & \text{if} \quad \omega \in E_1 \\ \bar{a} + \varepsilon & \text{if} \quad \omega \in E_2 \cup E_3 \end{cases}$$

while the one who chooses $\mathcal{G}'$ will choose the act a' such that $(\forall \omega)\ a'(\omega) = \bar{a}$ by (13.18) and (13.20). Then, we have

$$M^q(a + M^q(\hat{u}|\mathcal{G})) = \bar{a} + \frac{(p_2 + p_3)^r}{p_1^r + (p_2 + p_3)^r}\varepsilon + \frac{p_3^r(p_2 + p_3)^r}{(p_2^r + p_3^r)(p_1^r + (p_2 + p_3)^r)}b$$

$$\text{and} \quad M^q(a' + M^q(\hat{u}|\mathcal{G}')) = \bar{a} + \frac{p_3^r}{(p_1 + p_2)^r + p_3^r}b,$$

where $r := 1/(q-1)$. Furthermore, it turns out that

$$\frac{p_3^r(p_2 + p_3)^r}{(p_2^r + p_3^r)(p_1^r + (p_2 + p_3)^r)} < \frac{p_3^r}{(p_1 + p_2)^r + p_3^r} \Leftrightarrow q > 2,$$

which shows that $M^q(a + M^q(\hat{u}|\mathcal{G})) > M^q(a' + M^q(\hat{u}|\mathcal{G}'))$ if $q \le 2$ because $\varepsilon > 0$. This means that the information is always preferred in this model if $q \le 2$. However, if $q > 2$ *and* either ε is small enough or b is large enough, it could be the case that $M^q(a' + M^q(\hat{u}|\mathcal{G}')) > M^q(a + M^q(\hat{u}|\mathcal{G}))$. For instance, if $q > 2$ (and hence, if $r < 1$) and if $p_1 = p_2 = p_3$, it follows that $M^q(a' + M^q(\hat{u}|\mathcal{G}')) > M^q(a + M^q(\hat{u}|\mathcal{G}))$ if and only if $b > [2^r/(1 - 2^{r-1})]\varepsilon$. From the discussion of Sect. 13.4.2, the case $q > 2$ is considered to model the behaviour of the agent who is relatively insensitive

---

[15]This is simply because we like to show an aversion to the information. Introducing the cost merely facilitates our job.

to the underlying probability. This example shows that such a person could prefer remaining uninformed even if the information is free.

13.5.2 Ellsberg's Paradox Revisited

Consider Ellsberg's (1961) paradox given in Sect. 3.7. Let $S := \{R, B, W\}$ and $\mathcal{F} := 2^S$. Contrary to CEU theory (Sect. 3.9) or MEU theory (Sect. 3.10), we assume that the decision-maker is endowed with a *single probability charge* p such that $p(\{R\}) = p(\{B\}) = p(\{W\}) = 1/3$. We also assume that the decision-maker evaluates each outcome by the utility index that is unique up to a positive affine transformation, as in CEU or MEU theory. Without loss of generality, we set $u(\$0):= 0$ and $u(\$1{,}000):= 1$.

Here, assume that the decision-maker's overall preference over acts is now characterized by an asymmetric error function with $\gamma > 0$ as described in Sect. 13.4.3. Let f_1, f_2, f_3, and f_4 be the acts appearing in Ellsberg's paradox. Finally, let $\mathcal{G} := \{\phi, \{R\}, \{B, W\}, S\}$ be a sub-σ-algebra of $\mathcal{F}$, which is one specification of partial information the decision-maker may possess. Then, a calculation reveals the next proposition.

Proposition 13.5.1 *The following relation holds true:*

$$\gamma < 1 \quad \Leftrightarrow \quad M^{2,\gamma}(M^{2,\gamma}(u \circ f_1|\mathcal{G})) > M^{2,\gamma}(M^{2,\gamma}(u \circ f_2|\mathcal{G})) \text{ as well as}$$
$$M^{2,\gamma}(M^{2,\gamma}(u \circ f_4|\mathcal{G})) > M^{2,\gamma}(M^{2,\gamma}(u \circ f_3|\mathcal{G}))\,.$$

Recall that the rankings $f_1 \succ f_2$ and $f_4 \succ f_3$ are exactly those in Ellsberg's paradox. Therefore, assuming that the decision-maker is *negative-surprise averse*, Proposition 13.5.1 explains Ellsberg's paradox.[16] Essentially, if the decision-maker exhibits negative-surprise aversion and if she foresees that she would know later if the color of ball she has drawn is R or not, then her ranking is in accordance with the one in the paradox. The important point here is not that she will actually know if the color is R or not, but that she foresees she would know it. For example, the experimenter may say so actually, or rather, she may simply believe that he would do that.

Ozaki (2013) provides an axiomatic foundation for the class of preferences under uncertainty where the agent employs an error function that may be different from the mean squared error. He weakens Savage's axioms, in particular, by replacing his sure-thing principle with a weaker axiom of *weak decomposability* by Grant et al. (2000). If the sure-thing principle is restored, then the error function will coincide with the mean squared error function.

However, Ozaki fixes the information structure and the preference thus characterized turns out to be probabilistically sophisticated. Therefore, the preference with a general error function can*not* explain Ellsberg's paradox as it is (see Sect. 3.7).

[16]For the negative-surprise aversion, see Sect. 13.4.4.

Some additional framework concerning the information structure like those in this subsection appears necessary to resolve the paradox by the agent's error-minimizing behaviors with a single probability charge.

References

Billingsley, P. 1986. *Probability and Measure* (2nd ed.), Wiley-Interscience.

Chew, S.H. 1983. A generalization of the quasilinear mean with applications to the measurement of income inequality and decision theory resolving the Allais paradox. *Econometrica* 51: 1065–1092.

Chew, S.H. 1989. Axiomatic utility theories with the betweenness property. *Annals of Operations Research* 19: 273–298.

Dekel, E. 1986. An axiomatic characterization of preferences under uncertainty. *Journal of Economic Theory* 40: 304–318.

Ellsberg, D. 1961. Risk, ambiguity, and the Savage axioms. *Quarterly Journal of Economics* 75: 643–669.

Epstein, L.G. 1986. Implicitly additive utility and the nature of optimal economic growth. *Journal of Mathematical Economics* 15: 111–128.

Epstein, L.G., and S.E. Zin. 1989. Substitution, risk aversion, and the temporal behavior of consumption and asset returns: A theoretical framework. *Econometrica* 57: 937–970.

Farmer, R.E.A. 1990. RINCE preferences. *Quarterly Journal of Economics*, February, 43–60.

Fishburn, P.C. 1986. Implicit mean value and certainty equivalence. *Econometrica* 54: 1197–1205.

Grant, S., A. Kajii, and B. Polak. 2000. Decomposable choice under uncertainty. *Journal of Economic Theory* 92: 169–197.

Hardy, G., Littlewood, J.E and Pólya, G. 1952: *Inequalities* (2nd ed.), Cambridge University Press.

Kolmogorov, A. 1930. Sur la notion de la moyenne. *Rendiconti Accademia dei Lincei* 6 (12): 388–391.

Kreps, D.M., and E.L. Porteus. 1978. Temporal resolution of uncertainty and dynamic choice theory. *Econometrica* 46: 185–200.

Nagumo, M. 1930. Uber eine Klasse der Mittelwerte. *Japan Journal of Mathematics* 7: 71–79.

Ozaki, H. 2009. Conditional implicit mean and the law of iterated integrals. *Journal of Mathematical Economics* 45: 1–15.

Ozaki, H. 2013. Subjective error measure, Keio University, mimeo. Presented at Risk, Uncertainty and Decision 2013 (Paris).

Weil, P. 1990. Nonexpected utility in macroeconomics. *Quarterly Journal of Economics*, February, 29–42.

Chapter 14
Learning Under Knightian Uncertainty

14.1 Introduction and Summary

Economic agents including policy makers face various uncertainties when they make decisions. Here we must distinguish between two different kinds of uncertainty. The first one, which is often called *risk*, is formulated as a known probability distribution with possibly unknown parameters that can be learned from past experience of, say, stock prices and the GDP growth rate in the near future. The second kind of uncertainty deserves the name of true fundamental uncertainty. This uncertainty cannot be reduced to a known distribution, and is often called *Knightian uncertainty* in recognition of the works of Frank Knight. Not only are economic agents uncertain about the future value of stock prices and GDP growth in a known probability distribution, but also they do not have clear knowledge of their probability distribution. In other words, they do not have clear confidence in the "stochastic model" that they often use to describe economic activities in the real world.

One way to cope with the uncertain world is to gather information about unknown economic conditions, and to learn about underlying parameters from it. Thus, learning, which is often formulated as Bayesian learning, is considered to reduce the magnitude of uncertainty. In fact, if the uncertainty that agents face is risk, Bayesian learning is shown to reduce the magnitude of uncertainty.

The purpose of this chapter is to show that this is not always the case when facing Knightian uncertainty.[1] In contrast to risk, Knightian uncertainty is characterized as a

[1]In the statistics literature, Seidenfeld and Wasserman (1993) presented necessary and sufficient conditions that dilation of uncertainty (which corresponds to erosion of confidence discussed later) take place in the case of the "no-narrowing" Bayes rule if uncertainty is formulated as a set of distributions (that is, Knightian uncertainty). However, these conditions are hard to explain and thus they are difficult to apply in economic problems of our interest. The contribution of this chapter is, first, to show that confidence erosion can occur under relatively simple, not-so-implausible conditions in the case of ε-contamination; and second, to present sufficient conditions under which dilation still occurs in the "range-narrowing" maximum-likelihood rule.

K.G. Nishimura and H. Ozaki, *Economics of Pessimism and Optimism*,
DOI 10.1007/978-4-431-55903-0_14

set of distributions, instead of a single distribution. Hence, learning is characterized by an update process of the set of distributions after each random sampling. In this chapter, ε-contamination of confidence is taken as an example of Knightian uncertainty. Suppose that an economic agent is $(1 - \varepsilon) \times 100\%$ certain that the uncertainty she faces is characterized by a particular dynamic stochastic model, but that she has fear that, with $\varepsilon \times 100\%$ chance, her conviction is wrong and she is left ignorant about the "true" model. We call this situation ε-contamination of confidence and $1 - \varepsilon$ can be taken as a charge of confidence. It is a convenient characterization of the fundamental uncertainty that economic agents face,[2] and it has axiomatic foundation.[3]

Suppose further that the economic agent follows a Bayesian procedure or its variant, which is considered rational in the theory of economics.[4] Then, we show that her confidence erodes (the degree of confidence $1 - \varepsilon$ decreases) after having a new observation if the initial degree of confidence in the stochastic model is not strong compared with the new observation's "informational value."[5] The reason for confidence erosion is that new information brings in a new dynamic possibility that was not previously considered seriously.

This chapter is organized as follows. In Sect. 14.2, we present a simple example of confidence erosion in the learning model developed by Rothschild (1974). A general model of confidence erosion is presented in Sects. 14.3–14.5. In Sect. 14.3, we formulate a stochastic environment and the decision-maker's objective function, and define "dilation of uncertainty;" that is, a phenomenon that "new observation reduces confidence." Section 14.4 defines and examines two "sensible" updating rules: the maximum-likelihood rule and the multi-prior Bayesian rule.[6] Section 14.5 contains the main results: In the case of ε-contamination, if the initial degree of confidence is not strong compared with a new observation's "informational value," dilation of uncertainty occurs regardless of whether the maximum-likelihood rule or

[2]The concept of ε-contamination defined in this chapter is used in Nishimura and Ozaki (2004) who examine search behavior under Knightian uncertainty. (See Chap. 9 of this book).

[3]Nishimura and Ozaki (2006) show that if economic agents' behaviors are in accordance with several axioms, then their perceived uncertainty can be characterized as ε-contamination of confidence. (See Chap. 12 of this book.) Their axioms are not at all singular. Thus, their results suggest that ε -contamination of confidence may commonly be observed.

[4]We consider the maximum-likelihood rule and a multi-prior Bayesian rule because they are intuitive and sensible. After a new observation, the maximum-likelihood rule chooses, among all distributions in the set characterizing Knightian uncertainty, those that put the highest probability on the occurrence of an actual observation, and updates the chosen distributions by using the Bayes rule. The multi-prior Bayesian rule updates all distributions in the set by using the Bayes rule. Both rules are based on Bayesian ideas.

[5]See Theorem 14.5.2 below. The exact meaning of "informational value" will be clarified later in this chapter. The result is surprising particularly in the case of the maximum-likelihood "update" rule, in which substantial "narrowing" of the range of probability charges seems to occur after obtaining a new observation through the maximum-likelihood principle.

[6]In fact, to our knowledge, there is no other update rule that has been discussed as widely and intensively as these rules in the literature.

the Bayesian rule is utilized. All proofs of Lemma and Theorems are relegated to the Appendix.

14.2 An Example: Rothschild's Learning Model

Let us consider a case examined by Rothschild (1974), which has been one of the most well-known examples in the economics of learning. An unemployed worker is searching for a job. Different firms offer different wages. The subject participates in a series of job interviews and receives a wage quotation at each interview. To simplify our analysis, we consider a two-period model.[7]

In Rothschild's model, the unemployed worker is risk-neutral, and contemplates her optimal policy in terms of expected income. She does not know the wage distribution, and learns about the distribution by observation. In particular, the unemployed worker assumes that the wage-offer distribution is a multinomial distribution with a support of $W := \{w_1, \ldots, w_k\}$, where $(\forall i)\ w_i \geq 0$. However, she does not know the probability p_i of a particular w_i.

It is then assumed that the unemployed worker thinks that the p_i values are distributed according to a Dirichlet distribution over a set $\mathcal{P}$, where

$$\mathcal{P} := \left\{ \boldsymbol{p} = (p_1, \ldots, p_k) \in \mathbb{R}^k \;\middle|\; (\forall i)\ p_i > 0 \text{ and } \sum_{i=1}^{k} p_i = 1 \right\},$$

whose density function f is

$$f(\boldsymbol{p}|\boldsymbol{\alpha}) = \frac{\Gamma(\alpha_1 + \cdots + \alpha_k)}{\Gamma(\alpha_1) \cdots \Gamma(\alpha_k)} p_1^{\alpha_1 - 1} \ldots p_{k-1}^{\alpha_{k-1}-1} (1 - \textstyle\sum_{i=1}^{k-1} p_i)^{\alpha_k - 1},$$

where $\boldsymbol{\alpha} \in \mathbb{R}^k_{++}$ is a parameter vector and $\Gamma(\cdot)$ is the gamma function. The mean of each marginal, p_i $(i = 1, \ldots, k)$, is given by

$$E[p_i] = \frac{\alpha_i}{\sum_{\ell=1}^{k} \alpha_\ell}. \tag{14.1}$$

Suppose that the decision-maker observed a wage offer w_i in the first period. Then, by DeGroot (1970, p. 174, Theorem 1), the posterior wage-offer distribution, updated by Bayes' rule upon observing w_i, turns out to be the Dirichlet distribution with the parameter vector

$$\boldsymbol{\alpha}'_i := (\alpha_1, \ldots, \alpha_{i-1}, \alpha_i + 1, \alpha_{i+1}, \ldots, \alpha_k). \tag{14.2}$$

[7]Rothschild (1974) considers an infinite horizon. We deviate from his work in this respect to make our argument simple and transparent.

The learning process of the unemployed worker has the following interpretation. Suppose that the agent has a "prior" wage distribution that is multinomial with parameters $\boldsymbol{p}^0 := (p_1^0, \ldots, p_k^0)$ over the wage offer in the second period, where for each j, p_j^0 is a probability of w_j's occurrence and it is defined by $p_j^0 := E[p_j]$. Then, from (14.1), her "prior" second-period expected wage income will be

$$\sum_{j=1}^{k} w_j p_j^0 = \sum_{j=1}^{k} w_j E[p_j] = \frac{\sum_{j=1}^{k} w_j \alpha_j}{\sum_{\ell=1}^{k} \alpha_\ell}. \tag{14.3}$$

Then, the worker receives the wage offer w_i for some i in the first period. Upon observing w_i, she revises her prior distribution, $\boldsymbol{p}^0$, to the posterior one, $\boldsymbol{p}_i' := (p_1'(w_i), \ldots, p_k'(w_i))$, where $p_j'(w_i) := E[p_j|w_i]$. Then, with some calculation,[8] her "prior" second-period expected income (14.3) is revised to the "posterior" second-period expected income *given* the observation of the first period: $\sum_{j=1}^{k} w_j p_j'(w_i) = \sum_{j=1}^{k} w_j E[p_j|w_i] = \sum_{j\neq i} w_j\alpha_j / \left(\sum_{\ell=1}^{k} \alpha_\ell + 1\right) + w_i\, (\alpha_i + 1) / \left(\sum_{\ell=1}^{k} \alpha_\ell + 1\right) = \left(\sum_{j=1}^{k} w_j\alpha_j + w_i\right) / \left(\sum_{\ell=1}^{k} \alpha_\ell + 1\right)$. The unemployed worker then uses this posterior second-period expected wage income in contemplating her optimal strategy: whether to stop searching now or to go on to the next period.

The above example of Rothschild assumes that the unemployed worker is *perfectly* certain that the wage distribution is a multinomial one and the distribution of the wage-occurrence probability is a Dirichlet distribution. However, there is no *a priori* rationale that the worker assumes this particular combination.

Let us now deviate from Rothschild's specification, and consider a case in which the unemployed worker is *almost* certain that the true distribution is the multinomial distribution with the known parameter $\boldsymbol{p}^0 = (p_1^0, \ldots, p_k^0)$, but that she is not completely certain about that. Thus, she fears that, with $\varepsilon \times 100\%$ probability, the true distribution is different from this multinomial distribution, and moreover, she may not have any information about the true parameter values if $\boldsymbol{p}^0$ is not the true one. In other words, the unemployed worker is almost $((1-\varepsilon) \times 100\%)$ certain about the wage distribution but has an $\varepsilon \times 100\%$ fear that she is wrong and is ignorant about the true distribution.[9] In this setting, it is natural to see ε as a measure to gauge ignorance, or equivalently, $1-\varepsilon$ as the degree of confidence.[10]

---

[8]Letting $E[\cdot|w_i]$ be the posterior mean, (14.1) and the paragraph containing (14.2) imply that $(\forall j \neq i)\ E[p_j|w_i] = \alpha_j/(\sum_{\ell=1}^{k} \alpha_\ell + 1)$ and $E\,[p_i|w_i] = (\alpha_i + 1)/(\sum_{\ell=1}^{k} \alpha_\ell + 1)$.

[9]Nishimura and Ozaki (2006, and Chap. 12 of this book) show that, if the decision-maker's behavior is consistent with certain plausible axioms, her decision-making is characterized as maximizing the minimum of her expected utility over multiple priors that are characterized by ε-contamination of confidence explained in the text. The set of axioms they presented are an extension of Schmeidler's (1982, 1989) axioms.

[10]The ε-contamination has been widely used in statistics literature to specify a set of charges (see, for example, Berger 1985). There, the sensitivity of an estimator to the assumed prior distribution $((\boldsymbol{p}^0, \boldsymbol{p}^0)$ in the text) is the main concern in the context of Bayesian estimation problems. While we also specify a set of charges or Knightian uncertainty by ε-contamination, our main concern is

Given that the unemployed worker is risk-neutral and thus maximizes expected income, her situation is the same as that of a decision-maker facing (a restricted form of) *ε-contamination* of the distribution.[11] Formally, let $\varepsilon \in (0, 1)$ and let $\mathcal{P} \times \mathcal{P}$ be a set of pairs of $\boldsymbol{p}$ in the first period and $\boldsymbol{p}'$ in the second period[12]: $\mathcal{P} \times \mathcal{P} = \left\{ (\boldsymbol{p}, \boldsymbol{p}') \mid \boldsymbol{p}, \boldsymbol{p}' \in \mathcal{P} \right\}$. Then, the ε-contamination of $(\boldsymbol{p}, \boldsymbol{p}') = (\boldsymbol{p}^0, \boldsymbol{p}^0)$ considered in this section, $\left\{(\boldsymbol{p}^0, \boldsymbol{p}^0)\right\}^{\varepsilon}$, is $\left\{(\boldsymbol{p}^0, \boldsymbol{p}^0)\right\}^{\varepsilon} := \left\{ (1-\varepsilon)(\boldsymbol{p}^0, \boldsymbol{p}^0) + \varepsilon(\boldsymbol{q}, \boldsymbol{q}') \mid (\boldsymbol{q}, \boldsymbol{q}') \in \mathcal{P} \times \mathcal{P} \right\}$. (For this notation, see Example 2.3.5 and Sect. 12.4)

We now examine what happens to the degree of confidence after the new observation. However, to proceed with our analysis, we should specify the decision-maker's objective function and the procedure of updating priors in the case of Knightian uncertainty or multiple probability distributions.

First, it is known (see Schmeidler 1982, 1989; Gilboa and Schmeidler 1989; and Chap. 3 of this book) that in multiple-probability cases of this kind, if the decision-maker's behavior is in accordance with certain sensible axioms, then her behavior is characterized as being *uncertainty-averse*: when the decision-maker evaluates her position, she uses probability corresponding to the "worst" scenario. Following this line of argument, we assume that the unemployed worker is uncertainty-averse. Second, we assume that the decision-maker uses a Bayesian procedure to multiple priors by applying it to all probabilities in $\left\{(\boldsymbol{p}^0, \boldsymbol{p}^0)\right\}^{\varepsilon}$.[13]

Let us now consider this Bayesian process. Let (w_i, w_j') denote an event that the first-period wage observation is w_i and that in the second period is w_j. Then, the probability of this event evaluated by one element, $(1-\varepsilon)(\boldsymbol{p}^0, \boldsymbol{p}^0) + \varepsilon(\boldsymbol{q}, \boldsymbol{q}')$, of $\left\{(\boldsymbol{p}^0, \boldsymbol{p}^0)\right\}^{\varepsilon}$ is $\Pr(w_i, w_j') := (1-\varepsilon)\, p_i^0 p_j^0 + \varepsilon q_i q_j'$ and a corresponding second-period marginal probability is $\Pr(w_j') := (1-\varepsilon)\, p_j^0 + \varepsilon q_j'$. Hence, the set of the prior second-period probabilities is given by

$$\left\{ (1-\varepsilon)\, \boldsymbol{p}^0 + \varepsilon \boldsymbol{q}' \;\middle|\; \boldsymbol{q}' \in \mathcal{P} \right\}. \tag{14.4}$$

Suppose as before that w_i is observed for some i. The unemployed worker updates each element in the set of the prior second-period probabilities to their posterior, so that we have

$$\Pr\left(w_j' \middle| w_i\right) = \frac{\Pr(w_i, w_j')}{\Pr(w_i)} = \left(1-\varepsilon'\right) p_j^0 + \varepsilon' q_j' \tag{14.5}$$

---

not robustness of a specfic estimator but the set itself, which reflects the decision-maker's lack of confidence.

[11]In this section, we restrict contamination, $(\boldsymbol{q}, \boldsymbol{q}')$, to be a product probability charge to make a proof simple and intuitive. However, in general, contamination is not restricted to a product probability charge, but it is allowed to be any probability charge defined over the product space. We consider these general cases in the formal analysis of Sects. 14.3, 14.4 and 14.5. See in particular Eq. (14.14) in Sect. 14.5.

[12]In other words, $\mathcal{P} \times \mathcal{P}$ is the set of all product charges of the form: $\boldsymbol{p} \otimes \boldsymbol{p}'$ when we regard $\boldsymbol{p}$ and $\boldsymbol{p}'$ as probability charges on W. In the text, we denote $\boldsymbol{p} \otimes \boldsymbol{p}'$ by $(\boldsymbol{p}, \boldsymbol{p}')$.

[13]The case of the maximum-likelihood rule is discussed in Sects. 14.3 and 14.4. Here we analyze the Bayesian rule because it is more tractable than the maximum-likelihood rule.

where

$$\varepsilon' := \frac{\varepsilon q_i}{(1-\varepsilon)\,p_i^0 + \varepsilon q_i}. \tag{14.6}$$

The set of corresponding posteriors is the set of all these probabilities obtained by varying both $\boldsymbol{q}$ and $\boldsymbol{q}'$.

Let $\bar{\varepsilon}' := \varepsilon/((1-\varepsilon)p_i^0 + \varepsilon)$. Then, we have $(1-\varepsilon')p_j^0 + \varepsilon' q_j' = (1-\bar{\varepsilon}')p_j^0 + \bar{\varepsilon}'((1-\varepsilon'/\bar{\varepsilon}')p_j^0 + (\varepsilon'/\bar{\varepsilon}')q_j')$. Because $\bar{\varepsilon}' \geq \varepsilon'$ and that $\mathcal{P}$ is the set of all conceivable $\boldsymbol{q}'$, we know $(1-\varepsilon'/\bar{\varepsilon}')\boldsymbol{p}^0 + (\varepsilon'/\bar{\varepsilon}')\boldsymbol{q}' \in \mathcal{P}$. Consequently, the set of corresponding posteriors is a subset of

$$\left\{ \left(1-\bar{\varepsilon}'\right) \boldsymbol{p}^0 + \bar{\varepsilon}' \boldsymbol{q}' \,\middle|\, \boldsymbol{q}' \in \mathcal{P} \right\}. \tag{14.7}$$

Conversely, take one element of (14.7), $\left(1-\bar{\varepsilon}'\right) \boldsymbol{p}^0 + \bar{\varepsilon}'\bar{\boldsymbol{q}}'$. Then, it is always possible to find $\varepsilon' \in [0, \bar{\varepsilon}']$ (and ultimately $\boldsymbol{q} \in \mathcal{P}$) and $\boldsymbol{q}' \in \mathcal{P}$ satisfying that $\left(1-\varepsilon'\right) \boldsymbol{p}^0 + \varepsilon'\boldsymbol{q}' = \left(1-\bar{\varepsilon}'\right) \boldsymbol{p}^0 + \bar{\varepsilon}'\bar{\boldsymbol{q}}'$ and then $q_i \in [0, 1]$ satisfying (14.6). Because the set of posterior distributions corresponding to (14.4) is characterized by (14.5) and (14.6) with $\boldsymbol{q}$ and $\boldsymbol{q}'$ varying (see the paragraph containing (14.5) and (14.6)), (14.7) is a subset of that set. Thus, all things considered, we conclude that the set of posteriors after w_i is observed is equal to (14.7).

Let us now compare the set of priors (14.4) and that of posteriors (14.7). The latter shows that the unemployed worker is now $(1-\bar{\varepsilon}') \times 100\%$ certain about $\boldsymbol{p}^0$: her fear that her conviction is wrong is increased from ε to $\bar{\varepsilon}'$ (note that $\bar{\varepsilon}' > \varepsilon$ as far as $p_i^0 < 1$). *The decision-maker's degree of confidence is decreased after the observation of* w_i. Note that there is no "surprise" justifying a decrease in confidence.

It is clear that the dynamic nature of Knightian uncertainty plays a crucial role in eroding this confidence. Here, Knightian uncertainty is dynamic in the sense that the decision-maker thinks that the true distribution may change over time.[14] Loosely speaking, the above argument reveals that a new observation makes the decision-maker "find" a combination of probabilities over two periods leading to a posterior probability that was not considered by her before (probability outside her prior beliefs).

In this section, we have presented an example that new information reduces confidence of the decision-maker about the uncertain world. However, the argument we have employed is based on a specific example of a multinomial distribution à la Rothschild. Thus, one may question the generality of the results. In the rest of this chapter, we extend our model to a general setting and show that the same result holds in general cases.

In the next section, we reformulate the basic problem of this section in a general framework of behavior under dynamic Knightian uncertainty. We consider two

[14]If the wage distribution of the first period is perfectly correlated with that of the second period, then we cannot have confidence erosion. A perfect correlation means that if the decision-maker gets wage w_i in the first period then she gets w_i in the second period. In this case, uncertainty is completely resolved in the first period. However, so long as the correlation is not perfect, there is a possibility of confidence erosion.

updating rules commonly utilized in the literature for this kind of problem: the maximum-likelihood rule and the (generalized) Bayesian rule. The formal exposition of these updating rules is given in Sect. 14.4. In Sect. 14.5, we show that, under general conditions, the same results as observed in this section hold true for general probability charges and for both updating rules in general ε-contamination cases: new information reduces the decision-maker's confidence.[15]

14.3 The Two-Period Model of Knightian Uncertainty

To make a formal analysis, we have to set up a dynamic model in which the decision-maker has multiple probability charges about her economic environment. In the following, we first specify a stochastic environment and consider an update rule. We then incorporate the update rule into the decision-maker's objective function to represent evolution of her view of the world in the form of multiple probability charges over the stochastic environment. We exclusively consider a two-period model. An extension to multi-period cases is straightforward but notationally cumbersome.

In the following, notations are somewhat involved because of the complexity introduced by dynamic Knightian uncertainty: the decision-maker does not have perfect confidence not only about a "true" probability charge for each period but also how it changes over periods. Consequently, the model, including the objective function and updating rules, is specified in an entire dynamic structure of the decision-maker's stochastic environment.

14.3.1 *Information Structure*

Let W be a state space for each single period and let $\Omega := W \times W$ be the whole state space. A generic element of Ω is denoted by (w_1, w_2).

The information structure, which represents the basis of the decision-maker's view of the world, is exogenously given by a filtration $\mathcal{F} := \langle \mathcal{F}_t \rangle_{t=0,1,2}$. Let $m, n \geq 2$ and let $\langle E_i \rangle_{i=1}^m$ and $\langle F_j \rangle_{j=1}^n$ be two finite partitions of W. We assume that $\mathcal{F}_0 = \{\phi, \Omega\}$, that $\mathcal{F}_1$ is represented by a finite partition of Ω of the form: $\langle E_i \times W \rangle_i$, and that $\mathcal{F}_2$ is represented by a finite partition of Ω of the form: $\langle E_i \times F_j \rangle_{i,j}$. Clearly, it holds that $\mathcal{F}_0 \subseteq \mathcal{F}_1 \subseteq \mathcal{F}_2$, and this represents an increase of information as time goes by in a sense described in Sect. 1.1.2.

Given $p \in \mathcal{M}(\Omega, \mathcal{F}_2)$, we denote by $p|_1$ its restriction on $(\Omega, \mathcal{F}_1)$. Although $p|_1$ is formally a charge on Ω, it can be naturally regarded as the one on $(W, \langle E_i \rangle_i)$ and in that case, $p|_1(\cdot) = p(\cdot \times W)$. Thus viewed, $p|_1$ can be considered as the *first-period marginal probability charge* of p. Similarly, we define the *second-period marginal*

[15] These updating rules of multiple probability charges correspond to those of some convex probability capacities. See Sect. 2.3.5.

probability charge, $p|_2$, of p. That is, let $p|_2 \in \mathcal{M}(W, \langle F_j \rangle_j)$ be defined by $p|_2(\cdot) := p(W \times \cdot)$. Here, we abuse a notation to denote by $(W, \langle E_i \rangle_i)$ the measurable space on which the algebra is generated by the partition $\langle E_i \rangle_i$ and we denote the set of all probability charges on it by $\mathcal{M}(W, \langle E_i \rangle_i)$. Similar notations apply to other cases in obvious manners.

The decision-maker's view of the world is represented by not a single probability charge but a set of probability charges (Knightian uncertainty). Formally, we assume that the decision-maker's *Knightian uncertainty* is represented by $\mathcal{P} \subseteq \mathcal{M}(\Omega, \mathcal{F}_2)$.

Finally, let us now define "priors." Given $\mathcal{P} \subseteq \mathcal{M}(\Omega, \mathcal{F}_2)$, we define the *(prior) second-period marginal Knightian uncertainty*, $\mathcal{P}|_2$, as a set of second-period marginal probability charges such that $\mathcal{P}|_2 := \{\ p|_2 \mid p \in \mathcal{P}\,\}$. Here, the adjective *prior* emphasizes the fact that this is a set of the second-period marginal probability charges before the decision-maker obtains an observation in the first period.

14.3.2 Income Process

An income in each period, denoted by y_1 and y_2, is a function from $\Omega = W \times W$ into $\mathbb{R}_+$. We call (y_1, y_2) an *income process* if it is $\mathcal{F}$-adapted; that is, $(\forall t)$ y_t is $\mathcal{F}_t$-measurable. Given an income process (y_1, y_2), we write the value of y_2 as $y_2|_{w_1 \in E,\, w_2 \in F}$ if $(w_1, w_2) \in E \times F$ for some $E \times F \in \mathcal{F}_2$. The $\mathcal{F}$-adaptedness allows us to write the value of y_1 as $y_1|_{w_1 \in E}$ if $w_1 \in E$ for some E such that $E \times W \in \mathcal{F}_1$. We denote the set of $\mathcal{F}$ -adapted income processes by $Y(\mathcal{F})$.

14.3.3 Updating Rules

Let p be a probability charge on $(\Omega, \mathcal{F}_2)$; that is, let $p \in \mathcal{M}(\Omega, \mathcal{F}_2)$. After observing E_i in the first period, the decision-maker updates her probability charges.

Let us now first consider the ordinary Bayesian updating procedure. Given E_i such that $p(E_i \times W) > 0$, we denote by $p|_2(\cdot|E_i)$ the (posterior) probability charge on $(\Omega, \mathcal{F}_2)$ conditional on the occurrence of $E_i \times W$. Here, the adjective *posterior* signifies the fact that this is a probability charge after the decision-maker obtains an observation E_i. That is, $(\forall i, j)$ $p|_2(E_i \times F_j|E_i) := p(E_i \times F_j)/p(E_i \times W)$. By writing $p|_2(\cdot|E_i) := p|_2(E_i \times \cdot|E_i)$, $p|_2(\cdot|E_i)$ may be regarded as a probability charge on $(W, \langle F_j \rangle_j)$. (It should be noted here that $p|_2(\cdot) = p|_2(\cdot|W)$, where $p|_2(\cdot)$ is defined in Sect. 14.3.1.). The *Bayesian procedure* is defined as a function: $(p, E_i) \mapsto p|_2(\cdot|E_i)$, which maps a pair of charges p on $(\Omega, \mathcal{F}_2)$ and an event E_i in the first period, to the charge on $(W, \langle F_j \rangle_j)$ according to the manner defined in this paragraph.

An updating rule we consider in this chapter generalizes the function $p|_2$ in the ordinary Bayesian procedure to the case of multiple charges; that is, where there exists Knightian uncertainty. Formally, an *updating rule* is a function that maps a pair $(\mathcal{P}, E)$, where $\mathcal{P}$ is the decision-maker's Knightian uncertainty (a nonempty compact subset of $\mathcal{M}(\Omega, \mathcal{F}_2)$) and E is an event such that $E \times W \in \mathcal{F}_1$ and $(\forall p \in \mathcal{P})\ p(E \times W) > 0$, to a set of (posterior) probability charges, which is a nonempty compact subset of $\mathcal{M}(W, \langle F_j \rangle_j)$. We denote an updating rule by ϕ and its specific value by $\phi(\mathcal{P}, E)$. (This seemingly cumbersome notation is necessary for taking account of dynamic Knightian uncertainty, as we will see later in this and following sections.)

There is one natural restriction on sensible updating rules. When $\mathcal{P}$ happens to be a singleton, they should coincide with ordinary Bayes' rule:

$$\phi(\{p\}, E) = \{\, p|_2(\cdot|E) \,\}\,. \tag{14.8}$$

In what follows, we consider only updating rules that satisfy (14.8).

14.3.4 Objective Function

Let us now turn to the issue of formulating the objective function of the decision-maker. As in the previous section, we assume that the minimum of the "expected" lifetime income, V, is her objective function to be maximized, which is given by:

$$V(y_1, y_2) = \min_{p \in \mathcal{P}} \sum_{i=1}^{m} \Big[\big(y_1|_{w_1 \in E_i}\big) + \beta \min_{q \in \phi(\mathcal{P}, E_i)} \sum_{j=1}^{n} \big(y_2|_{w_1 \in E_i,\, w_2 \in F_j}\big)\, q(F_j) \Big] p(E_i \times W)\,, \tag{14.9}$$

where $(y_1, y_2) \in Y(\mathcal{F})$, ϕ is an updating rule, $\beta\ (> 0)$ is a discount or upcount factor, and $\mathcal{P}$ is the decision-maker's Knightian uncertainty, which is a subset of $\mathcal{M}(\Omega, \mathcal{F}_2)$. For this definition to be meaningful, $\mathcal{P}$ must be a nonempty compact subset of $\mathcal{M}(\Omega, \mathcal{F}_2)$ satisfying $(\forall p \in \mathcal{P})(\forall i)\ p(E_i \times W) > 0$.

Preferences represented by special cases of the Eq. (14.9), where the updating rules are further specified, are axiomatized by Epstein and Schneider (2003) and Wang (2003). (See the next section.)

14.3.5 Dilation of Knightian Uncertainty

We now define "dilation" of Knightian uncertainty. Let $\mathcal{P} \in \mathcal{M}(\Omega, \mathcal{F}_2)$ be Knightian uncertainty that the decision-maker faces and let ϕ be her updating rule. The *dilation of Knightian uncertainty* takes place upon the occurrence of $E \in \langle E_i \rangle_i$ if the set of *posterior* probability charges generated by the update rule is strictly "greater" than the set of *prior* probability charges, or equivalently if it holds that $\phi(\mathcal{P}, E) \supsetneq \mathcal{P}|_2$, where the set-inclusion is strict. In this case, the set of prior probability charges does not shrink, but dilates: the decision-maker faces larger uncertainty than before the observation.[16]

In contrast, if the opposite strict set inclusion holds for some $E \in \langle E_i \rangle_i$, we describe it as a *contraction of Knightian uncertainty* upon the occurrence of E. In this case, the decision-maker faces a smaller uncertainty than before the observation.

14.4 The (Generalized) Bayesian and Maximum-Likelihood Rules

We consider two updating rules that have been extensively studied in the literature.[17] The (generalized) *Bayesian rule* (henceforth, the *GB rule*)[18] is denoted by ϕ_{GB} and is defined by: $(\forall \mathcal{P} \subseteq \mathcal{M}(\Omega, \mathcal{F}_2))(\forall E \in \langle E_i \rangle_i)$

$$\phi_{GB}(\mathcal{P}, E) := \{ p|_2(\cdot|E) \mid p \in \mathcal{P} \}. \tag{14.11}$$

[16] In the statistics literature, the dilation is defined with respect to lower- and upper-probabilities. To be more precise, let $\mathcal{P} \subseteq \mathcal{M}(\Omega, \mathcal{F}_2)$ and let $B \in \mathcal{F}_2$ be such that $(\forall p \in \mathcal{P})\ p(B) > 0$. Then, we define the *lower-probability*, denoted $\underline{\mathcal{P}}$, by $(\forall A \in \mathcal{F}_2)\ \underline{\mathcal{P}}(A) := \inf_{p \in \mathcal{P}} p(A)$ and define the *conditional lower-probability*, denoted $\underline{\mathcal{P}}(\cdot|B)$, by $(\forall A \in \mathcal{F}_2)\ \underline{\mathcal{P}}(A|B) := \inf_{p \in \mathcal{P}} p(A \cap B)/p(B)$. The upper-probability $\overline{\mathcal{P}}$ and the conditional upper-probability $\overline{\mathcal{P}}(\cdot|B)$ are defined symmetrically. Each of these "probabilities" turns out to be a nonadditive probability charge, or probability capacity. It is said that B *dilates* A if the following holds:

$$\underline{\mathcal{P}}(A|B) < \underline{\mathcal{P}}(A) \leq \overline{\mathcal{P}}(A) < \overline{\mathcal{P}}(A|B). \tag{14.10}$$

For this concept of dilation and a study of its properties, see Seidenfeld and Wasserman (1993). Herron et al. (1997) contains some additional analysis. Walley (1991) extensively studies the lower- and upper-probabilities.

In particular, Seidenfeld and Wasserman (1993) derives a necessary and sufficient condition for the dilation to take place in the sense of (14.10), for cases including the ε-contamination. Their condition, however, is based on a particular event A (not on a set of charges) so that its application to economic models is rather difficult if not impossible.

In Sect. 14.5, we derive a sufficient condition for the dilation to take place for the ε-contamination in the sense defined in the text. Our definition is more general than (14.10) because it is applied directly to a set of charges and not to a particular event A. We consider the maximum-likelihood updating rule as well as the generalized Bayesian updating rule (see the next section) while (14.10) is related only to the generalized Bayesian rule. Furthermore, we consider the dynamic nature of Knightian uncertainty explicitly to derive the economic intuition behind the dilation.

[17] See Dempster (1967, 1968); Shafer (1976); Fagin and Halpern (1990); Gilboa and Schmeidler (1993); and Denneberg (1994).

[18] The generalized Bayesian rule was originally proposed as an update rule for a capacity. More precisely, the rule was developed for $\mathcal{P}$, which is characterized as the *core* of a convex capacity (Fagin and Halpern 1990; Denneberg 1994). The text use of the rule is its natural extension to the case of a more general $\mathcal{P}$. See Sect. 2.3.5.

This means that the decision-maker updates all probability charges according to the ordinary Bayesian procedure. In particular, she does not discard any of these charges after the observation. It is evident that the procedure we employed in Sect. 14.2 corresponds to this rule. When ϕ is specified by ϕ_{GB}, the decision-maker's objective function becomes

$$V(y_1, y_2) = \min_{p \in \mathcal{P}} \sum_{i=1}^{m} \Big[\left(y_1|_{w_1 \in E_i}\right) + \beta \min_{p \in \mathcal{P}} \sum_{j=1}^{n} \left(y_2|_{w_1 \in E_i,\, w_2 \in F_j}\right) p|_2(F_j|E_i) \Big] p(E_i \times W) . \tag{14.12}$$

A preference-theoretic foundation of this updating rule is given by Epstein and Schneider (2003). They axiomatize the preference relation represented by (14.12) with $\mathcal{P}$ being "rectangular" and ϕ being the GB rule. (See Epstein and Schneider (2003) for details including the concept of rectangularity. Also, see Sect. 10.3.3.)

To define the *maximum-likelihood rule* (henceforth, the *ML rule*),[19] let $\mathcal{P}^*$ be defined by $(\forall E \in \langle E_i \rangle_i)\ \mathcal{P}^*(E) := \arg\max \{\, p|_1(E) \mid p \in \mathcal{P}\}$. Then, the ML rule is defined by: $(\forall \mathcal{P} \subseteq \mathcal{M}(\Omega, \mathcal{F}_2))(\forall E \in \langle E_i \rangle_i)$

$$\phi_{ML}(\mathcal{P}, E) := \{\, p|_2(\cdot|E) \mid p \in \mathcal{P}^*(E)\,\} . \tag{14.13}$$

A preference-theoretic foundation of this updating rule is given by Wang (2003). He axiomatizes the preference relation represented by (14.12) with $\mathcal{P}$ being the core of some convex probability capacity and ϕ being the GB rule and the ML rule (see Wang (2003), for details).[20]

Both the GB and ML rules satisfy the requirement we impose on updating rules, (14.8).

Lemma 14.4.1 *Assume that* $\mathcal{P} = \{p\}$ *for some* $p \in \mathcal{M}(\Omega, \mathcal{F}_2)$ *such that* $(\forall i)$ $p(E_i \times W) > 0$. *Then,* $(\forall i)\ \phi_{GB}(\mathcal{P}, E_i) = \phi_{ML}(\mathcal{P}, E_i) = \{p|_2(\cdot|E_i)\}$.

This lemma shows that both rules extend Bayes' rule to the case where the prior is not unique. Finally, it immediately follows from the definition that $(\forall \mathcal{P})(\forall i)\ \phi_{ML}(\mathcal{P}, E_i) \subseteq \phi_{GB}(\mathcal{P}, E_i)$. That is, the "degree of (Knightian) uncertainty" in the posteriors implied by the ML rule is no more than that implied by the GB rule.

[19]The maximum-likelihood rule was originally proposed as an updating rule for a capacity (Dempster 1967, 1968; Shafer 1976). Later, Gilboa and Schmeidler (1993) showed that this rule is identical to the maximum-likelihood updating rule, which we extend to the case of a more general $\mathcal{P}$ in the text. See Sect. 2.3.5.

[20]For a related work that provides some axiomatic foundation to the ML rule, see Gilboa and Schmeidler (1993).

14.5 The ε-Contamination and Dilation of Knightian Uncertainty

In this section, we consider a case where the decision-maker's Knightian uncertainty, $\mathcal{P}$, is specified by a general ε-contamination. Here, ε-contamination is "general," because we do not restrict it to be of a product probability charge. We give a simple and easily verifiable condition under which dilation takes place. Using this condition, we then show that if the ε-contamination under consideration is a restricted one, that is, one of a product of probability charges (as in the case of Sect. 14.2), the decision-maker *always* experiences dilation of uncertainty *regardless of whether the updating rule is GB or ML.*

Formally, let p^0 be a probability charge on $(\Omega, \mathcal{F}_2)$ such that $(\forall i)\ p^0(E_i \times W) > 0$, and let $\varepsilon \in (0, 1)$. We assume that the decision-maker's $\mathcal{P}$ $(\subseteq \mathcal{M}(\Omega, \mathcal{F}_2))$ is characterized by the *ε-contamination* of p^0, such that

$$\mathcal{P} = \left\{p^0\right\}^{\varepsilon} := \left\{ (1-\varepsilon)p^0 + \varepsilon q \;\middle|\; q \in \mathcal{M}(\Omega, \mathcal{F}_2) \right\}. \tag{14.14}$$

In the following analysis, the one-period counterpart of the two-period ε-contamination (14.14) turns out to be important. Applying the same idea to the one-period case, we define for each $\varepsilon \in (0, 1)$ and each $E \in \langle E_i \rangle_i$, the ε-contamination of $p^0|_2(\cdot|E)$ $(\in \mathcal{M}(W, \langle F_j \rangle_j))$ by $\{p^0|_2(\cdot|E)\}^{\varepsilon} := \{(1-\varepsilon)p^0|_2(\cdot|E) + \varepsilon q_2 | q_2 \in \mathcal{M}(W, \langle F_j \rangle_j)\}$.

The following lemma shows that the second-period "restriction" of the ε-contamination of p^0 is the same as the ε-contamination of the second-period "restriction" of p^0. In a sense, the "operator" of taking ε-contamination and the "operator" of taking the second-period "restriction" or marginal are interchangeable with respect to p^0, which is a probability charge on $(\Omega, \mathcal{F}_2)$ such that $(\forall i)\ p^0(E_i \times W) > 0$.

Formally, $\left\{p^0\right\}^{\varepsilon}\big|_2$, the (prior) second-period marginal Knightian uncertainty of the ε-contamination of p^0, is equal to $\left\{p^0|_2\right\}^{\varepsilon}$, the ε-contamination of the (prior) second-period marginal probability charge $p^0|_2 = p^0|_2(\cdot|W)$:

Lemma 14.5.1 *Taking the marginal, $\cdot|_2$, and taking ε-contamination, $\{\cdot\}^{\varepsilon}$, are interchangeable with respect to p^0: that is, $(\forall \varepsilon \in (0, 1))$ $\left\{p^0\right\}^{\varepsilon}\big|_2 = \left\{p^0|_2\right\}^{\varepsilon}$.*

We now present a result characterizing posterior second-period (marginal) Knightian uncertainty derived by the two updating rules in the case of ε-contamination.

Theorem 14.5.1 *Let $\varepsilon \in (0, 1)$ and let $E \in \langle E_i \rangle_i$. Then, $\phi_{GB}\left(\left\{p^0\right\}^{\varepsilon}, E\right) = \phi_{ML}$ $\left(\left\{p^0\right\}^{\varepsilon}, E\right) = \left\{p^0|_2(\cdot|E)\right\}^{\varepsilon'}$ where $\varepsilon' := \varepsilon'(\varepsilon, E) := \varepsilon/((1-\varepsilon)p^0|_1(E) + \varepsilon) > \varepsilon$.*

Let us now define a measure of the "informational value" of the observation E with respect to p^0, the "pre-contaminated" probability charge. Let $E \in \langle E_i \rangle_i$ and let $\delta(E) \in [0, 1]$ be defined by $\delta(E) := \max_{j=1,\ldots,n} |p^0|_2(F_j|E) - p^0|_2(F_j)|$. The real number $\delta(E)$ is the maximum of the "probability change" caused by the observation E with respect to the pre-contaminated probability charge p^0, which can be considered as a charge of the informational value of the observation E for p^0.

The next theorem shows that, if ε, the degree of contamination of p^0, is sufficiently large with respect to $\delta(E)$, the informational value of observation E with respect to p^0, then the dilation takes place.

Theorem 14.5.2 *Let $\mathcal{P}$ be given by $\{p^0\}^\varepsilon$ and let $E \in \langle E_i \rangle_i$. Suppose that the degree of contamination of p^0 is sufficiently large compared with the informational value of the observation E with respect to p^0; that is, suppose that the following inequality holds:*

$$\varepsilon > \frac{p^0|_1(E)}{\left(1 - p^0|_1(E)\right) \min_j p^0|_2(F_j)} \delta(E) . \tag{14.15}$$

Then, the dilation occurs in the sense that it holds that $\left[\phi_{GB}\left(\{p^0\}^\varepsilon, E\right) = \phi_{ML}\left(\{p^0\}^\varepsilon, E\right) = \right] \{p^0|_2(\cdot|E)\}^{\varepsilon'} \supsetneqq \{p^0|_2\}^\varepsilon \left[= \{p^0\}^\varepsilon|_2\right]$, where the inclusion is strict and ε' is as defined in Theorem 14.5.1.

This theorem shows that the dilation occurs when the degree of confidence in p^0 is small (that is, ε is large) compared with the informational value of the observation with respect to p^0 (that is, $\delta(E)$).

An important special case is where $p^0 = p_1^0 \otimes p_2^0$ for some $p_1^0 \in \mathcal{M}(W, \langle E_i \rangle_i)$ and $p_2^0 \in \mathcal{M}(W, \langle F_j \rangle_j)$; that is, p^0 is a product of two probability charges. An example of this case is analyzed in Sect. 14.2. In this example, there is no informational value in observation E with respect to p^0. To see this, note that $p^0|_2(F_j|E) = p^0|_2(F_j) = p_2^0(F_j)$ for all F_j. It is clear that $\delta(E) = 0$ for all events E. Theorem 14.5.2 implies the following corollary in this case.

Corollary 14.5.1 *Suppose that $p^0 = p_1^0 \otimes p_2^0$ for some $p_1^0 \in \mathcal{M}(W, \langle E_i \rangle_i)$ and $p_2^0 \in \mathcal{M}(W, \langle F_j \rangle_j)$. Also, suppose that $\mathcal{P}$ is given by $\{p^0\}^\varepsilon$. Then, for any $E \in \langle E_i \rangle_i$, it holds that $\phi_{GB}(\{p^0\}^\varepsilon, E_i) = \phi_{ML}(\{p^0\}^\varepsilon, E_i) \supsetneqq \mathcal{P}|_2$, where the inclusion is strict.*

This corollary shows a striking result. In the case of ε-contamination of a product of probability charges, the GB rule and even the ML rule, which are considered to have some behavioral foundation and thus to be sensible in the multiple-prior framework, actually *increase*, rather than decrease, the degree of Knightian uncertainty. In a sense, new information worsens the decision-maker's confused state of confidence, rather than improves it.

References

Berger, J.O. 1985. *Statistical decision theory and bayesian analysis*, Second ed. Berlin: Springer.

DeGroot, M.H. 1970. *Optimal statistical decisions*: McGraw-Hill.

Dempster, A.P. 1967. Upper and lower probabilities induced by a multivalued map. *Annals of Mathematical Statistics* 38: 325–339.

Dempster, A.P. 1968. A generalization of Bayesian inference. *Journal of Royal Statistics Society, Series B* 30: 205–247.

Denneberg, D. 1994. Conditioning (updating) non-additive measures. *Annals of Operations Research* 52: 21–42.

Epstein, L.G., and M. Schneider. 2003. Recursive multiple-priors. *Journal of Economic Theory* 113: 1–31.

Fagin, R., and J.Y. Halpern. 1990. A new approach to updating beliefs. In *Proceedings of the 6th conference on uncertainty in AI.*

Gilboa, I., and D. Schmeidler. 1989. Maxmin expected utility with non-unique prior. *Journal of Mathematical Economics* 18: 141–153.

Gilboa, I., and D. Schmeidler. 1993. Updating ambiguous beliefs. *Journal of Economic Theory* 59: 33–49.

Herron, T., T. Seidenfeld, and L. Wasserman. 1997. Divisive conditioning: Further results on dilation. *Philosophy of Science* 64: 411–444.

Nishimura, K.G., and H. Ozaki. 2004. Search and Knightian uncertainty. *Journal of Economic Theory* 119: 299–333.

Nishimura, K.G., and H. Ozaki. 2006. An axiomatic approach to ε-contamination. *Economic Theory* 27: 333–340.

Rothschild, M. 1974. Searching for the lowest price when the distribution of prices is unknown. *Journal of Political Economy* 82: 689–711.

Schmeidler, D. 1982. Subjective probability without additivity (Temporary Title), Working Paper, The Foerder Institute for Economic Research, Tel Aviv University.

Schmeidler, D. 1989. Subjective probability and expected utility without additivity. *Econometrica* 57, 571–587. (Its working paper is first published in 1982).

Seidenfeld, T., and L. Wasserman. 1993. Dilation for convex sets of probabilities. *Annals of Statistics* 21: 1139–1159.

Shafer, G. 1976. *A mathematical theory of evidence*. Princeton: Princeton University Press.

Walley, P. 1991. *Statistical reasoning with imprecise probabilities*. London: Chapman and Hall.

Wang, T. 2003. Conditional preferences and updating. *Journal of Economic Theory* 108: 286–321.

Chapter 15
Areas of Further Research

This chapter briefly reviews further and ongoing research along the lines developed in this book.

15.1 Error-Functional Approach and Multiple Updating Schemes

In the dynamic analyses in the latter half of this book, we treated the capacitary kernel θ as exogenously given. (Note, however, that we deviate from this convention in Sects. 2.3.5, 3.13 and Chap. 14.) This means that the decision-maker's *updated* view about future prospects after observing a realization of the current state is also exogenously determined by θ_s when the current state has been known to be s.

In this section, we employ the error-functional approach developed in Chap. 13 to "endogenize" the way the decision-maker updates her view (preferences) when new information arrives. Here, her view is represented by an atemporal probability capacity, rather than an exogenously given capacitary kernel.

In particular, we show that if the decision-maker's initial view about the world is described by Knightian uncertainty (the decision-maker is unsure about which probability charge to apply to evaluate an uncertain prospect), then the way of updating her belief after making an observation becomes multiple or "indeterminate." In fact, this "indeterminacy" is not about the resulting updated beliefs, but about how to update the initial view in the form of multiple priors. It is shown that this "indeterminacy" is an exact counterpart of the indeterminacy of equilibria discussed in Chaps. 4, 5, 6, and 8.

Further development of the theory proposed in this section will be of interest and importance in understanding the role played by fundamental uncertainty in the process of decision-making.[1]

[1] This section is partially based on Ozaki (2000).

K.G. Nishimura and H. Ozaki, *Economics of Pessimism and Optimism*,
DOI 10.1007/978-4-431-55903-0_15

15.1.1 Error Functionals that Generate the Choquet Integral

Let $(S, \mathcal{A})$ be a measurable space. For the sake of simplicity, we assume that S is a finite set. Suppose that the decision-maker is a Choquet-expected-utility maximizer who is characterized by a convex probability capacity θ on $(S, \mathcal{A})$, as in Sect. 3.9. We assume that the decision-maker exhibits uncertainty aversion, while the uncertainty-affinity case would be handled similarly with a suitable modification of the following argument.

Given $x \in B(S, \mathcal{A})$, we interpret x as a random variable representing random utility numbers, instead of writing $u \circ f$ by introducing an outcome space, a utility index as well as the concept of act, again for the sake of simplicity. Then, the decision-maker's overall utility given x is defined by

$$\int_S x(s)\, \theta(ds) \tag{15.1}$$

where the integral is the Choquet integral defined by (2.13).

Recall that $\mathcal{P}(\theta, x)$ is the set of probability charges that are "equivalent" to θ. (Its formal definition is given by (2.16).) We regard the mapping defined by $x \mapsto\!\!\!\to \mathcal{P}(\theta, x)$, where θ is fixed, as a correspondence. Because $\mathcal{P}(\theta, x)$ is nonempty by the remark right after (2.16) because θ is now assumed to be convex, this is certainly a correspondence. Furthermore, by the same remark, it is *not* in general a function (that is, not singleton-valued). Let ν be any *selection* of this correspondence; that is, assume that a function ν satisfies $(\forall x)\ \nu(x) \in \mathcal{P}(\theta, x)$. We write the value of ν at x as ν_x rather than $\nu(x)$.

Given any such selection ν, we define a functional $\Phi_\nu : B(S, \mathcal{A}) \times B(S, \mathcal{A}) \to \mathbb{R}$, which we call an *error functional*, by: $(\forall x, z \in B(S, \mathcal{A}))$

$$\Phi_\nu(x, z) := \int_S (x(s) - z(s))^2\, \nu_x(ds)\,, \tag{15.2}$$

where the right-hand side is the Dunford–Schwartz integral with respect to a probability charge ν_x.[2]

An error functional can be considered as a variant of the *error function* in Chap. 13. We call it a function*al*, rather than a function, because it is defined on a more abstract vector space, rather than on a more concrete space like $\mathbb{R}^2$. The interpretation of them, however, is very similar. That is, an error functional Φ_ν measures the "distance" between two random utility numbers x and z, or an "error" when we are estimating x by using z.

Given $x \in B(S, \mathcal{A})$ and a sub-σ-algebra $\mathcal{G}$ of $\mathcal{A}$, we define a $\mathcal{G}$-measurable function on S, $M_\nu(x|\mathcal{G})$, by

---

[2]For the Dunford–Schwartz integral with respect to a charge, see Sect. 2.3.3. Note, however, that the right-hand side of (15.2) is simply a "summation" under the current assumption of a finite state space.

$$M_\nu(x|\mathcal{G}) := \arg\min\{\, \Phi_\nu(x, z) \mid z \in B(S, \mathcal{G}) \,\}\,. \tag{15.3}$$

Under the assumption that S is finite, it is easy to see that $M_\nu(x|\mathcal{G})$ is well defined and that $M_\nu(x|\mathcal{G})(s)$ is a singleton set as far as $\theta(s) > 0$. The $\mathcal{G}$-measurable function $M_\nu(x|\mathcal{G})$ thus defined is the "best" approximate of x within the $\mathcal{G}$-measurable functions, where the approximation error is measured by the error functional defined by (15.2). This is, at least in spirit, exactly the same thing as $M(\cdot|\mathcal{G})$ that appeared in Chap. 13.

The decision-maker uses (15.3) to make a "better" re-evaluation of a random utility number x when she obtained a new piece of information represented by $\mathcal{G}$. (For this interpretation of a sub-σ-algebra as partial information, see Sect. 1.1.2.) One rationale of this procedure is the following. When $\mathcal{G} = \{\phi, S\}$, that is, when the decision-maker has no information at all, we simply write $M_\nu(x|\mathcal{G})$ as $M_\nu(x)$ instead of $M_\nu(x|\{\phi, S\})$. Note that $M_\nu(x)$ is a constant. Then, we have

$$(\forall x \in B(S, \mathcal{A})) \quad M_\nu(x) = \int_S x(s)\, \nu_x(ds) = \int_S x(s)\, \theta(ds)\,.$$

Here, the first equality follows from the first-order condition for the minimization problem in (15.3), where the first-order condition is such that the derivative of the right-hand side of (15.2) with respect to (constant) z should be zero,[3] and the second equality holds because $(\forall x)\ \nu_x \in \mathcal{P}(\theta, x)$ by definition.

The preceding paragraph shows that the decision-maker evaluates an uncertain prospect by the Choquet integral when she has no information, which is exactly what we supposed at the very beginning of this section. We thus conclude that the decision-maker's conditioning scheme that uses the error functional defined by (15.2) when only partial information $\mathcal{G}$ is given is quite natural and totally consistent with her behavior when she has no information at all.

15.1.2 Multiplicity of Updating Schemes

The error functional that generates the Choquet integral when the sub-σ-algebra is specified by $\mathcal{G} := \{\phi, S\}$ is *not* unique. This is because the selection ν corresponding to θ is not unique, which is in turn because $\mathcal{P}(\theta, x)$ may not be a singleton for some x unless θ happens to be a probability charge. Therefore, the "conditional Choquet expectation" is not unique in general. The next example illustrates this fact.

Example 15.1.1 Let $S := \{1, 2, 3\}$, let $\mathcal{A} := 2^S$, let p, q_1, q_2 be probability charges defined by $p := (1/3, 1/3, 1/3)$, $q_1 := (1/9, 5/9, 1/3)$, and $q_2 := (5/9, 1/9, 1/3)$, respectively, and let θ be a probability capacity defined by $(\forall A \in \mathcal{A})\ \theta(A) := (p(A))^2$. Also, let ν_1 and ν_2 be selections of $x \mapsto\!\!\!\to \mathcal{P}(\theta, x)$ such that $\nu_1(x) := q_1$

[3]The differentiability is guaranteed by the dominated convergence theorem for the Dunford–Schwartz integral. See Dunford and Schwartz (1988, p.124, Theorem III.3.7).

if $x(1) = x(2)$ and $\nu_1(x) := p$ if otherwise, and $\nu_2(x) := q_2$ if $x(1) = x(2)$ and $\nu_2(x) := p$ if otherwise, respectively. It can be easily verified that ν_1 and ν_2 are, in fact, selections. Finally, let $\mathcal{G} := \{\phi, \{1\}, \{2, 3\}, S\}$. Then, it is not difficult to see that $M_{\nu_1}(x|\mathcal{G})(2) \neq M_{\nu_2}(x|\mathcal{G})(2)$ for any x such that $x(1) = x(2)$. ■

Note that the multiplicity of the "conditional Choquet expectation" is caused by the multiplicity in the updating scheme itself and that this multiplicity in the updating scheme is in turn caused by the multiplicity of probability charges (or the nonadditivity of probability capacity) representing the decision-maker's preference.

Note that the multiplicity or indeterminacy here is deep because it is not simply the decision-maker's updated beliefs, but rather that of the updating rules themselves. In this respect, the multiplicity of this section is in stark contrast with that in Chap. 14. There, the updated beliefs are multiple because each of the multiple beliefs is updated according to a *single* rule, but the rule itself is unique whether it is the generalized Bayesian rule or maximum-likelihood rule.

It is interesting to see that the mechanism that generates the multiplicity or indeterminacy of the updating rules is essentially the same as the one generating the multiplicity of the supporting prices in Chap. 4 and the multiplicity of equilibrium prices in Chaps. 5 and 8. All come from the multiplicity of probability charges that are "equivalent" to the given probability capacity with respect to the operation of taking the integral.

As the discussions in Chap. 5 suggest, indeterminacy of this kind may disappear if we "shake" the model even slightly. In fact, Example 15.1.1 shows that the indeterminacy may be "rare" in the sense that the "conditional Choquet expectation" is common for all the functions that take different values at each of the distinct states. However, its indeterminacy is *robust* in the sense that such functions are "abundant," rather than "rare." For example, think of an indicator function of any nonempty subset of S.

The next two subsections discuss this issue in more detail.

15.1.3 Updating Probability Capacity Revisited

Given $A \in \mathcal{A}$, let χ_A be the *indicator function* of A. When P is a probability charge on $(S, \mathcal{A})$ and when A and B are $\mathcal{A}$-measurable subsets of S (that is, when they are two events), the *conditional probability charge of A given B* is denoted by $P_B(A)$ and defined by $P_B(A) := P(A \cap B)/P(B)$ as far as $P(B) > 0$.[4] It is well known that

$$P_B(A) = E[\chi_A|\{\phi, B, B^c, S\}](s), \tag{15.4}$$

where the conditional expectation is in the usual sense with respect to P and s is any element of B. Recall from Chap. 13 that the conditional expectation is the best

[4]The conditional probability can be any real number between 0 and 1 inclusively when $P(B) = 0$. However, we do not consider this case in what follows.

approximation of χ_A within the family of $\{\phi, B, B^c, S\}$-measurable functions, and hence, it takes on the identical value on B. The right-hand side of (15.4) represents this common value. Also, recall that it is the "best" in the sense that the approximation error between χ_A and (15.4) is minimized when that error is measured by the L^2-metric with respect to P.

The Eq. (15.4) strongly suggests a way of defining the "conditional probability capacity," once that we have defined the "conditional Choquet expectation." Let θ be a convex probability capacity on $(S, \mathcal{A})$ and let ν be any selection of the correspondence defined by $x \mapsto\mapsto \mathcal{P}(\theta, x)$ as we did in the previous subsection. Then, we propose to define "the" conditional probability capacity of an event A given another event B *via* ν, to be denoted $\theta_B^\nu(A)$, by

$$\theta_B^\nu(A) := M_\nu(\chi_A | \{\phi, B, B^c, S\})(s) \tag{15.5}$$

where s is any element of B. As we see in the previous subsection, $\theta_B^\nu(A)$ is well defined uniquely as far as $\theta(B) > 0$. Furthermore, it is easy to see that θ_B^ν thus defined satisfies (2.1) and (2.3) as well as $\theta_B^\nu(S) = 1$. Therefore, θ_B^ν is in fact a probability capacity.

If θ happens to be a probability charge, this definition leads to the conditional probability charge given by $P(A \cap B)/P(B)$, which is uniquely determined. If otherwise, however, each of multiple selections ν defines a distinct updating rule for a probability capacity. While this multiplicity is troublesome, each of these updating rules can be regarded as reasonable because of its rationale mentioned in Sect. 15.1.1.

Given a selection ν, from (15.3) we can identify $\theta_B^\nu(A)$, for any $B \in \mathcal{A}$ such that $\theta(B) > 0$ and any $A \in \mathcal{A}$, as the unique solution to the minimization problem defined by $\min_{x \in [0,1]} (1 - x)^2 \nu_{\chi_A}(A \cap B) + x^2 \nu_{\chi_A}(A^c \cap B)$, where $\nu_{\chi_A} \in \mathcal{P}(\theta, \chi_A)$ is the value of ν evaluated at χ_A. By solving this, we have an explicit formula for θ_B^ν as follows: $(\forall A \in \mathcal{A})$

$$\theta_B^\nu(A) = \frac{\nu_{\chi_A}(A \cap B)}{\nu_{\chi_A}(B)} = \frac{\nu_{\chi_A}(A \cap B)}{\nu_{\chi_A}(A \cap B) + \nu_{\chi_A}(A^c \cap B)}, \tag{15.6}$$

which is well defined as far as $\theta(B) > 0$ because $\nu_{\chi_A}(B) \geq \theta(B) > 0$. This formula also shows the multiplicity of updating rules under the current scheme because of the multiplicity of selections, ν.

15.1.4 General Updating Rule à la Denneberg

In Sect. 2.3.5, we introduced three updating rules for a probability capacity that have been studied in the literature: the *generalized Bayesian* updating rule, Denneberg's (1994) *general* updating rule, and the *maximum-likelihood* updating rule. We also note that Denneberg's general updating rule, θ^G, is more "cautious" or "pessimistic" than the Dempster-Shafer updating rule, θ^{DS}, in the sense that $(\forall A, B)\ \theta_B^G(A) \leq \theta_B^{DS}(A)$ as far as $\theta(B) > 0$. (See Sect. 2.3.5.)

Furthermore, the Eq. (2.11) strongly suggests that Denneberg's general updating rule is fairly "pessimistic" in its nature. This idea of "pessimism" can be made precise. That is, we can characterize Denneberg's general updating rule as the most "pessimistic" updating rule among the rules under the current scheme that employs the error functional given by (15.2).

Proposition 15.1.1 *Let θ be a convex probability capacity on $(S, \mathcal{A})$ and let $B \in \mathcal{A}$ be such that $\theta(B) > 0$. Then, for any $A \in \mathcal{A}$,*

$$\min_{\nu} \theta_B^{\nu}(A) = \theta_B^G(A) \ \textit{and} \tag{15.7}$$

$$\max_{\nu} \theta_B^{\nu}(A) = \frac{\theta(A) - \theta(A \cap B^c)}{\theta(A \cup B) - \theta(A \cap B^c)}, \tag{15.8}$$

where the minimum and the maximum are when ν moves among all the selections of the correspondence defined by $x \mapsto\!\!\!\rightarrow \mathcal{P}(\theta, x)$.

The updating rule defined by the right-hand side of (15.8) is not studied in the literature to the best of our knowledge.

Denneberg's general updating rule is a plausible updating scheme for a decision-maker that shows "pessimism" when her preference is represented by a convex probability capacity θ. This is because Denneberg's general updating rule is the "most" pessimistic in the sense given by Proposition 15.1.1 among the rules that have some consistency with the original probability capacity as described in Sect. 15.1.2.

15.2 Two Distinct Types of Learning

This section differentiates two types of learning and suggests further research for these areas.

15.2.1 Learning to Elaborate One's Belief

The first type of learning is made by the decision-maker with an intention of improving or elaborating her belief about the occurrence of uncertain events. One of the most important remarks here is that the evolution of information represented by a filtration in terms of mathematics (a sequence of sub-σ-algebras that become finer over time) is *exogenous* and completely *fixed*. This is a convention adopted by most research so far in the literature.

Chapter 14 of this book is an example of research concerning this type of learning. It places an exogenous information filtration on a two-period dynamic model at the outset and examines a learning behavior of the decision-maker who attempts to elaborate her belief given by multiple priors. This occurs when the decision-maker faces Knightian uncertainty, and makes an observation in the form of random sampling. The chapter then shows that an update of multiple priors according to both the generalized Bayesian rule and the maximum-likelihood rule may increase the degree of Knightian uncertainty in that the set of priors characterizing uncertainty may dilate. Note that the information filtration is fixed throughout the analyses and learning takes place only with respect to the precision of the decision-maker's belief.

Behind this story, we assumed that the decision-maker's preference is given by a recursion of MEU-type atemporal preference. See (14.9).[5] Through the "min" operator, the decision-maker's pessimistic view about the world is incorporated into her preference.

An interesting extension of the model of Chap. 14 would be to include a decision-maker's eagerness to learn as another explicit choice variable. Here, the decision-maker's "eagerness" of learning may be measured by her intended intensity of making observations. Because learning, or equivalently in this context, making more observations, may lead to an expansion of the set of priors representing the decision-maker's belief and because her preference is characterized by an MEU-type, it may be quite possible that she would prefer making no observation at all. If making an observation incurs some cost, this inclination may be easily strengthened.

Regardless of whether we can apply a sound axiomatic foundation, *any* atemporal preference can be composed into a recursive, and hence time-consistent, utility function defined over an infinite horizon. See (7.2), where we assume a dynamic aggregator W to be quite general. If we set $W(c, m) = u(c) + \beta m$ for some felicity function u and a discount factor β, then the preference axiomatized by Wang (2003) and Epstein and Schneider (2003) would appear as special cases of (7.2). Because a preference that is time-*in*consistent is difficult to justify[6] and because the models with time-consistent preferences are quite operational given that dynamic programming techniques can be invoked for them,[7] research like that proposed in the previous paragraph may be promising.

[5] An infinite-horizon version of the preference similar to (14.9) was axiomatized by Wang (2003). The preference he axiomatized is recursive (time-consistent) and is a recursion of a CEU-type atemporal preference, rather than that of an MEU-type. The preference axiomatized by Wang can exhibit non-indifference between distinct information filtration, and hence, between differing timing of uncertainty resolution. Note, however, that the information filtration is exogenously given at the outset and that the decision-maker's motivation for obtaining finer or coarser information algebra over time (that is, the second type of learning behavior we will discuss in the next subsection) cannot be handled in Wang's framework. A simplification of Wang's axioms, for example, an extension of the preference axiomatized in Sect. 3.13 of this book to an infinite-horizon model, would be interesting research because his axiomatization is fairly complicated and hard to verify. An axiomatization of a recursion of an MEU-type atemporal preference is made by Epstein and Schneider (2003).

[6] However, see the discussion made in Sect. 1.4.4.

[7] See Chap. 7. This is exactly what we show in Chaps. 8, 9, 10, and 11 of this book.

15.2.2 Learning to "Chop" the State Space

Another type of learning made by the decision-maker is described as a procedure of obtaining more precise "information"[8] about the occurrence of the true state, not that of obtaining more confidence in her belief of it. This learning process is represented by a sequence of sub-σ-algebras that become finer over time because the finer the σ-algebra is, the better the decision-maker knows the true state. Here, the information itself is the object of learning, while learning in the previous subsection involved the decision-maker updating a set of priors or a single prior that is nonadditive under the information filtration that is exogenously given and fixed.

The mathematical model provided in Chap. 13 is an example of a framework that can explain that situation, where the extent of information is a choice variable the decision-maker should choose tactically. This is because anticipating the acquisition of further information in the future *does* affect the decision-maker's current utility level, while it cannot happen in the traditional models that employ mathematical expectation. Although Chap. 13 assumes that the decision-maker possesses a unique subjective probability charge, that chapter can show that there is a case in which she prefers to remain ignorant, rather than being well informed, in a single-agent framework.

The study of axiomatization of preferences defined jointly on both acts f and the extent of information $\mathcal{G}$ that can be represented in a form of $M(M(u \circ f|\mathcal{G}))$, like the one in Chap. 13, has never been done before to the best of our knowledge.[9] The axiomatic derivation of the prior(s), regardless of whether it is unique or they are multiple, in such a framework has never been considered anywhere. These will be fruitful areas of research in decision theory.

Furthermore, extension of this work to a truly dynamic framework of an infinite horizon with time consistency still preserved should be of great interest in terms of theory and applications. As we remarked at the end of the previous subsection, a recursive extension of the atemporal preference is always possible theoretically.[10] In such a model, the decision-maker chooses the optimal extent of information in each period, and hence, the timing of uncertainty resolution would be determined endogenously as a result of the decision-maker's optimizing behavior. In such a case, it is possible that the decision-maker may prefer "uncertainty" to never be resolved.

15.3 Other Ongoing Research

We close this book by briefly mentioning some ongoing research themes of the authors that are closely related to the contents of the book.

---

[8]For the meaning of "information" here, see Sect. 1.1.2.

[9]However, see Ozaki (2013) and the remark at the end of Sect. 13.5.2.

[10]We refer the readers to Ozaki and Streufert (1996).

Ohtaki and Ozaki (2013) advance the model presented in Chap. 6 further. It has been known that, in the overlapping generations (OLG) model with the complete market, the optimality of an equilibrium allocation can be judged by examining the associated equilibrium price. (See Peled (1984), for example.) They re-examine this observation in a stochastic OLG model with the generations equipped with MEU preferences. It is then shown that, under such preferences, optimality of an equilibrium allocation depends on the set of possible supporting prices, and not necessarily on the associated equilibrium price itself. Therefore, observations of an equilibrium price do not necessarily tell us the optimality of the equilibrium allocation. What is worse, the possible supporting price may not be unique in this kind of economy as we see in Chap. 6. Therefore, we need to know all the supporting prices, most of which are not realized, in order to judge the optimality of the equilibrium price in the presence of Knightian uncertainty.

Kishishita and Ozaki (2015) introduce Knightian uncertainty into a game-theoretic model of a public good, focusing on the case where the sum of the contributions must exceed some threshold for the public good to be provided. There exist many social issues that can be approximated by such a public goods game with threshold. For example, environmental problems such as international cooperation for preventing climate change are typical applications of this game. In this game, players may be reluctant to contribute the provision of public goods when the value of the threshold is uncertain. We explore the case where players face ambiguity (Knightian uncertainty) about the threshold. Then, it is shown that in the case of "full" ambiguity, no contribution constitutes a unique Nash equilibrium and in the case of "partial" ambiguity, the maximal amount of contribution in equilibria decreases with the degree of ambiguity. This is completely different from what McBride (2006) shows in the case where the uncertainty about the threshold is described by a probability distribution that is known. Also, this result is consistent with a result of an experimental study made by Dannenberg's et al. (2015).[11]

Finally, Nishimura and Ozaki (2014) extend the concept of the rational-expectations equilibrium, from a traditional single-belief framework to a multi-belief one. In the traditional framework of single belief, agents are supposed to know the equilibrium price "correctly." We relax this requirement in the framework of multiple beliefs. While agents do not have to know the equilibrium price exactly, they must be correct in that it must be always contained in the support of each probability distribution they think possible. We call this equilibrium concept a *multi-belief rational-expectations equilibrium*. We then show that such an equilibrium exists, that indeterminacy and complexity of equilibria can occur even when the degree of risk aversion is moderate, and, in particular, that a decreasing price sequence can be an equilibrium. The last property is highlighted in a linear-utility example where any decreasing price sequence is a multi-belief rational-expectations equilibrium while only possible single-belief rational-expectations equilibrium price

[11]Note the close resemblance between Kishishita and Ozaki (2015) and Chap. 9 of this book. It would be interesting to see that given the other players' strategies, each player faces the problem that is similar to a job search model.

sequences are those that are constant over time. The concept of the multi-belief rational-expectations equilibrium proposed in this paper is interesting as a suitable concept of the equilibrium when people are "pessimistic" as discussed repeatedly in this book. Above all, the theory thus developed is convincing because it can explain the "sustained deflation" that Japan has experienced over the past two decades.

References

Dannenberg, A., A. Löschel, G. Paolacci, C. Reif, and A. Tavoni. 2015. On the provision of public goods with probabilistic and ambiguous thresholds. *Environmental and Resource Economics* 61: 365–383.

Denneberg, D. 1994. Conditioning (updating) non-additive measures. *Annals of Operations Research* 52: 21–42.

Dunford, N. and J. T. Schwartz 1988. *Linear Operator Part I: General Theory*, Wiley Classics Library.

Epstein, L.G., and M. Schneider. 2003. Recursive multiple-priors. *Journal of Economic Theory* 113: 1–31.

Kishishita, D. and H. Ozaki 2015. Public goods game with ambiguous threshold. The University of Tokyo, mimeo.

McBride, M. 2006. Discrete public goods under threshold uncertainty. *Journal of Public Economics* 90: 1181–1199.

Nishimura K.G. and Ozaki, H. 2014. Multi-belief rational-expectations equilibria: Indeterminacy, complexity and sustained deflation, Discussion Paper Series CARF-F-354, The University of Tokyo. http://www.carf.e.u-tokyo.ac.jp/english/workingpaper/F354.html

Ohtaki, E. and H. Ozaki 2013. Optimality in a stochastic OLG model with ambiguity, Tokyo Center for Economic Research Paper No. E-69. Available at SSRN: http://ssrn.com/abstract=2377585.

Ozaki, H. 2000. Conditional expectation with Choquet capacities. Tohoku University, mimeo.

Ozaki, H. 2013. Subjective error measure. Keio University, mimeo. Presented at Risk, Uncertainty and Decision 2013 (Paris).

Ozaki, H., and P.A. Streufert. 1996. Dynamic programming for non-additive stochastic objectives. *Journal of Mathematical Economics* 25: 391–442.

Peled, D. 1984. Stationary Pareto optimality of stochastic asset equilibria with overlapping generations. *Journal of Economic Theory* 34: 396–403.

Wang, T. 2003. Conditional preferences and updating. *Journal of Economic Theory* 108: 286–321.

Appendix
Proofs of Lemmas and Theorems

A.1 Proofs for Chap. 2

A.1.1 Proof of Corollary 2.2.1

First, we prove that if a functional I is additive, it is homogeneous with respect to rational numbers. That is, we prove that $(\forall a \in B(K))(\forall r \in \mathbb{Q})\ I(ra) = rI(a)$. Let $a \in B(K)$ and let $r \in \mathbb{Q}_+$ be a positive rational number such that $r = m/n$, where $m, n \in \mathbb{N}$. The additivity of I implies that $nI((m/n)a) = I(n(m/n)a) = I(ma) = mI(a)$, and hence, $I(ra) = rI(a)$. Then, let r be a negative rational number. Note that $I(a) = -I(-a)$ holds because $0 = I(a-a) = I(a) + I(-a)$ by the additivity. Therefore, $I(ra) = I(-|r|a) = |r|I(-a) = -|r|I(a) = rI(a)$, which proves the claim.

Second, we prove that if a functional $I : B(K) \to \mathbb{R}$ is additive, monotonic, and satisfies $I(\chi_S) = 1$, then I is norm-continuous. To this end, let $\varepsilon > 0$ and let $\langle a_n \rangle_{n=1}^{\infty}$ be convergent to a in the norm topology. Also, let δ be a positive rational number such that $0 < \delta < \varepsilon$ and let $N \in \mathbb{N}$ be such that $(\forall n \geq N)\ \ \|a - a_n\| < \delta$. Then, for any $n \geq N$, it holds that $I(a) - I(a_n) = I(a) + I(-a_n) = I(a - a_n) \leq I(\|a - a_n\|\chi_S) \leq I(\delta\chi_S) = \delta I(\chi_S) = \delta < \varepsilon$, where the first equality holds because $0 = I(a_n - a_n) = I(a_n) + I(-a_n)$ by the additivity; the second equality holds by the additivity; the first inequality holds by the monotonicity and the definition of the norm; the second inequality holds by the monotonicity and the definition of δ; the third equality holds by the fact proven in the first paragraph; and the strict inequality holds by the definition of δ. Similarly, we can show that $I(a_n) - I(a) < \varepsilon$. The claim thus follows.

Third, we prove that if a functional $I : B(K) \to \mathbb{R}$ is additive, monotonic, and satisfies $I(\chi_S) = 1$, then I is homogeneous. To this end, let $\lambda \in \mathbb{R}$ and let $\langle r_n \rangle_n$ be any sequence of rational numbers that converges to λ. Then, for any $a \in B(K)$, $r_n a$ converges to λa in the norm topology. Therefore, it holds that $I(\lambda a) = I(\lim_{n\to\infty} r_n a) = \lim_{n\to\infty} I(r_n a) = \lim_{n\to\infty} r_n I(a) = \lambda I(a)$, where the second equality holds by the norm-continuity proven in the second paragraph, and the third

K.G. Nishimura and H. Ozaki, *Economics of Pessimism and Optimism*,
DOI 10.1007/978-4-431-55903-0

equality holds by the homogeneity with respect to rational numbers proven in the first paragraph.

Therefore, by the additivity, the monotonicity, and the assumption that $I(\chi_S) = 1$, we conclude that I is norm-continuous from the second paragraph and that it is homogeneous from the previous paragraph.

Given all this, we extend the domain of I from $B(K)$ to B as follows and name the resultant functional $\hat{I}$: $(\forall a \in B)\ \hat{I}(a) := \bar{a}I(a/\bar{a})$, where $\bar{a} := \sup_s |a(s)|$. Then, $a/\bar{a} \in B([-1, 1]) \subseteq B(K)$ given that $[-1, 1] \subseteq K$ by assumption. Thus, $\hat{I} \in B$. Because $\hat{I}$ thus defined is linear and norm-continuous given that I is additive, homogeneous, and norm-continuous, and because it holds that $\hat{I}(\chi_S) = 1 \cdot I(\chi_S/1) = I(\chi_S) = 1$, $\hat{I}$ satisfies all the assumptions of the Riesz Representation Theorem (Theorem 2.2.1). Finally, I and $\hat{I}$ coincide on $B(K)$ by the homogeneity of I and the definition of $\hat{I}$, the proposition follows from Theorem 2.2.1. ■

A.1.2 Proof of Claim Made in First Paragraph of Sect. 2.3.2

We show that when both g and θ are convex, $g \circ \theta$ is convex. The other claims follow immediately or from similar reasoning. Let g and θ be convex and let $A, B \in \mathcal{A}$. Without loss of generality, assume that $\theta(A) \geq \theta(B)$. Note that the convexity of θ implies that $\theta(A \cup B) - \theta(A) \geq \theta(B) - \theta(A \cap B)$. First, suppose that $\theta(A \cup B) = \theta(A)$. Then, it holds that $\theta(A \cap B) = \theta(B)$, from which it follows that $g \circ \theta(A \cup B) + g \circ \theta(A \cap B) = g \circ \theta(A) + g \circ \theta(B)$. Second, suppose that $\theta(B) = \theta(A \cap B)$. Then, it holds that $g \circ \theta(A \cup B) + g \circ \theta(A \cap B) \geq g \circ \theta(A) + g \circ \theta(B)$ by the nondecrease of g. Third and finally, suppose that $\theta(A \cup B) - \theta(A) \geq \theta(B) - \theta(A \cap B) > 0$. Then, this assumption, the convexity of f, and $\theta(A \cup B) \geq \theta(A) \lesseqgtr \theta(B) \geq \theta(A \cap B)$ imply that $(g \circ \theta(A \cup B) - g \circ \theta(A))/(\theta(B) - \theta(A \cap B)) \geq (g \circ \theta(A \cup B) - g \circ \theta(A))/(\theta(A \cup B) - \theta(A)) \geq (g \circ \theta(B) - g \circ \theta(A \cap B))/(\theta(B) - \theta(A \cap B))$. Because all possibilities are exhausted, the proof is complete. ■

A.1.3 Proof of Theorem 2.3.1 (Scott's Theorem)

We follow Gilboa (1985). The necessity of weak additivity follows immediately because $g \circ p((A \backslash E) \cup F) > g \circ p((B \backslash E) \cup F) \Rightarrow g(p(A) - p(E) + p(F)) > g(p(B) - p(E) + p(F)) \Rightarrow p(A) > p(B)$ (by the nondecrease of g) $\Rightarrow g \circ p(A) > g \circ p(B)$ (by the strict increase of g).

To prove sufficiency, assume that θ is a convex-ranged probability capacity that is weakly additive and we define a binary relation $\succ_\ell$ on 2^S by $(\forall A, B)\ A \succ_\ell B \Leftrightarrow \theta(A) > \theta(B)$. Then, it turns out that $\succ_\ell$ is a *qualitative probability*. See Sect. 3.5.1 for the definition of qualitative probability. In fact, QP1, QP2, and QP3 follow immediately. QP4 follows because $E \cup G \succ_\ell F \cup G \Rightarrow \theta(E \cup G) > \theta(F \cup G) \Rightarrow \theta(E) > \theta(F)$ (by the weak additivity of θ) $\Rightarrow E \succ_\ell F$, and because $E \succ_\ell F \Rightarrow (E \cup G)\backslash G \succ_\ell (F \cup G)\backslash G \Rightarrow \theta((E \cup G)\backslash G) > \theta((E \cup G)\backslash G) \Rightarrow \theta(E \cup G) > \theta(F \cup G)$ (by the weak additivity of θ) $\Rightarrow \theta(E) > \theta(F)$ (by the weak additivity of θ again) $\Rightarrow E \succ_\ell F$. It can be also proved that $\succ_\ell$ satisfies QP5. (See Gilboa 1985.)

Therefore, Savage's Subjective Probability Theorem (Theorem 3.5.1) implies that there exists a unique convex-ranged probability charge p on $(S, 2^S)$ such that

$$(\forall A, B) \quad p(A) > p(B) \Leftrightarrow A \succ_\ell B \Leftrightarrow \theta(A) > \theta(B), \tag{A.1}$$

where the second equivalence holds by the definition of $\succ_\ell$. The convex-rangedness of p implies that for any $r \in [0, 1]$, there exists a set A such that $p(A) = r$. We choose such a set A arbitrarily and denote it by $p^{-1}(r)$. Then, we define a function $g : [0, 1] \to [0, 1]$ by $g(r) := \theta(p^{-1}(r))$. Because it holds that $\theta(A) = \theta(B)$ whenever $p(A) = p(B)$ by (A.1), the choice of a specific set does not affect the value g, and thus, g is well defined. It also follows that $g(0) = 0$ and $g(1) = 1$ because $\theta(\phi) = 0$ and $\theta(S) = 1$. Furthermore, g is strictly increasing because $(\forall r, r' \in [0, 1])\ r > r' \Rightarrow p(p^{-1}(r)) > p(p^{-1}(r')) \Rightarrow \theta(p^{-1}(r)) > \theta(p^{-1}(r'))$ (by (A.1)) $\Rightarrow g(r) > g(r')$.

We complete the proof by showing that $\theta = g \circ p$. However, this is immediate because for any set A with $p(A) = r$, $\theta(A) = \theta(p^{-1}(r)) = g(r) = g \circ p(A)$. ■

A.1.4 Proof of Theorem 2.4.3

Let $u, v \in B$ and let θ be convex. Then, the theorem follows because

$$\begin{aligned}
&\int u\, d\theta - \int v\, d\theta = \int u\, d\theta - \int (v - u + u) d\theta \\
&\le \int u\, d\theta - \left[\int (v - u) d\theta + \int u\, d\theta\right] = - \int (v - u) d\theta \\
&= \int (u - v) d\theta' \le \int |u - v|\, d\theta'
\end{aligned}$$

where the first inequality holds by the sub-additivity of the Choquet integral with respect to a convex capacity (Proposition 2.4.4); the third equality holds by Proposition 2.4.1; and the last inequality holds by the monotonicity of the Choquet integral (Proposition 2.4.2). ■

A.1.5 Proof of Theorem 2.4.6 (Monotone Convergence Theorem)

Note that (b) follows from (a) if we let $\langle u_n \rangle$ and θ be $\langle -u_n \rangle$ and θ' in (a). We thus prove only (a). We first note that it holds that $\theta(\{u \geq x\}) = \theta(\{u > x\})$ for almost all x. Obviously, $\theta(\{u \geq x\}) \geq \theta(\{u > x\})$ holds for all x. On the other hand, $x \mapsto \theta(\{u > x\})$ is weakly decreasing in x, and hence, it is continuous at $x \notin X$, where X is some set that is at most countably infinite. Let x be a point at which $x \mapsto \theta(\{u > x\})$ is continuous. Then, $\theta(\{u > x\}) = \lim_{n\to\infty} \theta(\{u > x - 1/n\}) \geq \theta(\{u \geq x\})$. Therefore, (a) holds because

$$
\begin{aligned}
&\lim_{n\to\infty} \int u_n d\theta \\
&= \lim_{n\to\infty} \left[\int_{-\infty}^{0} (\theta(\{u_n \geq x\}) - 1)dx + \int_{0}^{\infty} \theta(\{u_n \geq x\})dx \right] \\
&= \lim_{n\to\infty} \left[\int_{-\infty}^{0} (\theta(\{u_n > x\}) - 1)dx + \int_{0}^{\infty} \theta(\{u_n > x\})dx \right] \\
&= \int_{-\infty}^{0} \lim_{n\to\infty} (\theta(\{u_n > x\}) - 1)dx + \int_{0}^{\infty} \lim_{n\to\infty} \theta(\{u_n > x\})dx \\
&= \int_{-\infty}^{0} (\theta(\cup_n\{u_n > x\}) - 1)dx + \int_{0}^{\infty} \theta(\cup_n\{u_n > x\})dx \\
&= \int_{-\infty}^{0} (\theta(\{\lim_{n\to\infty} u_n > x\}) - 1)dx + \int_{0}^{\infty} \theta(\{\lim_{n\to\infty} u_n > x\})dx \\
&= \int_{-\infty}^{0} (\theta(\{\lim_{n\to\infty} u_n \geq x\}) - 1)dx + \int_{0}^{\infty} \theta(\{\lim_{n\to\infty} u_n \geq x\})dx \\
&= \int \lim_{n\to\infty} u_n d\theta
\end{aligned}
$$

where the first and last equalities hold by the definition of the Choquet integral; the second and sixth equalities hold by the remark we have just made; the third equality holds by the Lebesgue monotone convergence theorem; the fourth equality holds by the continuity of θ from below; and the fifth equality holds by the strict inequality defining the set. ∎

A.1.6 Proof of Theorem 2.4.7 (Fatou's Lemma)

Let $\langle u_n \rangle$ be given as such. Then,

$$
\begin{aligned}
\limsup_{n\to\infty} \int u_n(s)\,\theta(ds) &= \limsup_{n\to\infty} \int_0^\infty \theta\left(\{s\,|u_n(s) \geq t\}\right) dt \\
&\leq \int_0^\infty \limsup_{n\to\infty} \theta\left(\{s\,|u_n(s) \geq t\}\right) dt \\
&\leq \int_0^\infty \limsup_{n\to\infty} \theta\left(\bigcup_{k=n}^{\infty} \{s\,|u_k(s) \geq t\}\right) dt \\
&\leq \int_0^\infty \theta\left(\bigcap_{n=1}^{\infty}\bigcup_{k=n}^{\infty} \{s\,|u_n(s) \geq t\}\right) dt \\
&\leq \int_0^\infty \theta\left(\left\{s \,\middle|\, \limsup_{n\to\infty} u_n(s) \geq t\right\}\right) dt \\
&= \int \limsup_{n\to\infty} u_n(s)\,\theta(ds)\,,
\end{aligned}
$$

where the first inequality holds by the "usual" Fatou's lemma because $\langle u_n \rangle$ is uniformly bounded from above; the second inequality is trivial; the third inequality holds by the assumption on θ; and the fourth inequality follows from the definition of the lim sup of a sequence of both sets and real numbers. ■

A.1.7 Proof of Theorem 2.5.1 (Fubini Property)

Given $E \in \mathcal{A} \otimes \mathcal{A}$ and $s \in S$, we denote by $E(s)$ the s-section of E: $E(s) = \{s' \in S \mid (s, s') \in E\}$. We first prove that the mapping $s \mapsto \theta_s(E(s))$ is $\mathcal{A}$-measurable for any $E \in \mathcal{A}\otimes\mathcal{A}$. We define $\mathcal{E}$ by $\mathcal{E} := \{E \in \mathcal{A}\otimes\mathcal{A} | s \mapsto \theta_s(E(s)) \text{ is } \mathcal{A}\text{-measurable}\}$. Then the collection of finite disjoint unions of rectangles is a subfamily of $\mathcal{E}$ because if $E = \cup_{i=1}^n (A_i \times B_i)$ where $A_i, B_i \in \mathcal{A}$ and $(A_i \times B_i) \cap (A_j \times B_j) = \phi$ for $i \neq j$, then $\theta_s(E(s)) = \max_{N' \subset \{1,2,\ldots,n\}} \theta_s(\cup_{i\in N'} B_i) I_{\cap_{i\in N'} A_i}(s)$ (see Dellacherie and Meyer 1988, p. 184) and the right-hand side is $\mathcal{A}$-measurable. It remains to show that $\mathcal{E}$ is a monotone class. To this end, let $\langle E_n \rangle_{n=1}^\infty \subseteq \mathcal{E}$ and $E_n \uparrow E$. Then $E_n(s) \uparrow E(s)$ for any $s \in S$ and $\lim_{n\to\infty} \theta_s(E_n(s)) = \theta_s(E(s))$ by the continuity of $\theta_s(\cdot)$, which implies $E \in \mathcal{E}$. A similar argument applies to decreasing sequences.

We now prove the theorem for the simple functions, which is sufficient thanks to the monotone convergence theorem (Theorem 2.4.6). Let u be a simple function on $S \times S$. Then, we can write $u(s, s_+) = \sum_{i=1}^n a_i \chi_{E_i}(s, s_+)$, where $0 < a_1 < \cdots < a_n$, χ is the indicator function, and $\langle E_i \rangle$ is a partition of $S \times S$. It follows that $(\forall s \in S)$

$$\begin{aligned}
\int u(s, s_+)\, \theta_s(ds_+) &= \int \sum_{i=1}^{n} a_i \chi_{E_i}(s, s_+)\, \theta_s(ds_+) \\
&= \int \sum_{i=1}^{n} a_i \chi_{E_i(s)}(s_+)\, \theta_s(ds_+) \\
&= \sum_{i=1}^{n} (a_i - a_{i-1}) \theta_s(\, \cup_{k=i}^{n} (E_k(s))\,) \\
&= \sum_{i=1}^{n} (a_i - a_{i-1}) \theta_s(\, (\cup_{k=i}^{n} E_k)(s)\,),
\end{aligned}$$

where $a_0 := 0$ and the third equality holds by the definition of the Choquet integral. Then the claim follows because the last expression is $\mathcal{A}$-measurable by the first paragraph. ■

A.1.8 Proof of Theorem 2.5.3 (Upper Semi-continuity)

This paragraph proves that under the stated assumptions, for any decreasing sequence of $\mathcal{B}_S$-measurable subsets of S, $\langle A_n \rangle_{n=1}^{\infty}$, and for any sequence $\langle s^n \rangle_{n=1}^{\infty} \subseteq S$ such that $s^n \to s^0$,

$$\overline{\lim_{n\to\infty}}\, \theta_{s^n}(A_n) \leq \theta_{s^0}\left(\lim_{n\to\infty} A_n \right). \tag{A.2}$$

To prove the claim, let $\langle A_n \rangle_{n=1}^{\infty} \subseteq \mathcal{B}_S$ be such that $A_n \supseteq A_{n+1} \supseteq \cdots$, let $\langle s^n \rangle_{n=1}^{\infty} \subseteq S$ be such that $s^n \to s^0$ and let $\varepsilon > 0$ be arbitrarily chosen. Then, there exists $N_1 \in \mathbb{N}$ such that $n > N_1$ implies $|\theta_{s^n}(A_n) - \theta_{s^0}(A_n)| < \varepsilon/2$ because θ is strongly continuous by the assumption. Furthermore, there exists $N_2 \in \mathbb{N}$ such that $n > N_2$ implies $|\theta_{s^0}(A_n) - \theta_{s^0}(\lim_{n\to\infty} A_n)| < \varepsilon/2$ because $\theta_{s^0}(\cdot)$ is continuous from above by the assumption and because $A_n \downarrow \lim_{n\to+\infty} A_n$ as $n \to +\infty$. Let $N := \max\{N_1, N_2\}$. Then for any $n > N$, it holds that $|\theta_{s^n}(A_n) - \theta_{s^0}(\lim_{n\to\infty} A_n)| \leq |\theta_{s^n}(A_n) - \theta_{s^0}(A_n)| + |\theta_{s^0}(A_n) - \theta_{s^0}(\lim_{n\to\infty} A_n)| < \varepsilon$, which in turn implies that for any $n > N$, $\theta_{s^n}(A_n) < \theta_{s^0}(\lim_{n\to\infty} A_n) + \varepsilon$. Because $\varepsilon > 0$ is arbitrary, the proof of (A.2) is complete.

This paragraph completes the proof. To this end, let $u : S \times X \to \mathbb{R}$ be upper semi-continuous. Note that proving the claim is equivalent to proving that the mapping defined by $(x, s) \mapsto \int_S u(s', x)\, \theta_s(ds')$ is u.s.c. To show this, let $\langle (x^n, s^n) \rangle_{n=1}^{\infty}$ be a sequence in $X \times S$ that converges to (x^0, s^0). Then, it holds that, for each $t \geq 0$,

$$\begin{aligned}
\overline{\lim_{n\to\infty}} \left\{ s' \,\middle|\, u(s', x^n) \geq t \right\} &= \bigcap_{n=1}^{\infty} \bigcup_{k=n}^{\infty} \left\{ s' \,\middle|\, u(s', x^k) \geq t \right\} \\
&\subseteq \left\{ s' \,\middle|\, \overline{\lim_{n\to\infty}}\, u(s', x^n) \geq t \right\} \\
&\subseteq \left\{ s' \,\middle|\, u(s', x^0) \geq t \right\},
\end{aligned} \tag{A.3}$$

where the equality is definitional; the first inclusion follows from the definition of $\overline{\lim}$ of a sequence of both sets and real numbers; and the second inclusion follows from the u.s.c. of u. Hence, it holds that, for each $t \geq 0$

$$\begin{aligned}\overline{\lim_{n\to\infty}}\, \theta_{s^n}\left(\left\{s' \left| u(s', x^n) \geq t\right.\right\}\right) &\leq \overline{\lim_{n\to\infty}}\, \theta_{s^n}\left(\bigcup_{k=n}^{\infty}\left\{s' \left| u(s', x^k) \geq t\right.\right\}\right) \\ &\leq \theta_{s^0}\left(\bigcap_{n=1}^{\infty}\bigcup_{k=n}^{\infty}\left\{s' \left| u(s', x^k) \geq t\right.\right\}\right) \\ &= \theta_{s^0}\left(\overline{\lim_{n\to\infty}}\left\{s' \left| u(s', x^n) \geq t\right.\right\}\right) \\ &\leq \theta_{s^0}\left(\left\{s' \,\middle|\, u(s', x^0) \geq t\right\}\right),\end{aligned}$$

where the first inequality holds by the monotonicity of θ; the second inequality holds by (A.2) because the sequence of sets in the parentheses is decreasing; the next equality is definitional; and the last inequality holds by (A.3). Finally, we arrive at

$$\begin{aligned}\overline{\lim_{n\to\infty}} \int_S u(s', x^n)\, \theta_{s^n}(ds') &= \overline{\lim_{n\to\infty}} \int_0^{\infty} \theta_{s^n}\left(\left\{s' \left| u(s', x^n) \geq t\right.\right\}\right) dt \\ &\leq \int_0^{\infty} \overline{\lim_{n\to\infty}}\, \theta_{s^n}\left(\left\{s' \left| u(s', x^n) \geq t\right.\right\}\right) dt \\ &\leq \int_0^{\infty} \theta_{s^0}\left(\left\{s' \,\middle|\, u(s', x^0) \geq t\right\}\right) dt \\ &= \int_S u(s', x^0)\, \theta_{s^0}(ds'),\end{aligned}$$

where both equalities follow from the definition of the Choquet integral; the first inequality follows from Fatou's lemma (Theorem 2.4.7) assuming that for any s' and any $n \geq 1$, $u(s', x^n) \leq \bar{u}$ for some constant $\bar{u}$ as presupposed for the upper semi-continuity. The proof is thus complete. ■

A.1.9 Proof of Theorem 2.5.4 (Stochastic Nondecrease)

($\Rightarrow$) Suppose that θ is stochastically nondecreasing and let $t \geq 0$. Also let $\chi_{\{w \in Z | w \geq t\}}$ be the indicator function of the set $\{w \in Z | w \geq t\}$. Because $\chi_{\{w \in Z | w \geq t\}}(z')$ is nondecreasing in z' on Z, the stochastic nondecrease of θ implies that

$$\int_Z \chi_{\{w \in Z | w \geq t\}}(z') \theta_z(dz') = \theta_z(\{z' \in Z | z' \geq t\})$$

is nondecreasing in z, which proves the claim.

($\Leftarrow$) Suppose that $\theta_z(\{z' \in Z | z' \geq t\})$ is nondecreasing in z for each $t \geq 0$. Let $h : Z \to \mathbb{R}_+$ be a nondecreasing function. For $k \geq 1$, let $i(k) := k2^k + 1$. For $i \in \{1, \dots, i(k) - 1\}$ and $k \geq 1$, let $S(i,k) := \{z | (i-1)/2^k \leq h(z) < i/2^k\}$ and $a_{i,k} := (i-1)/2^k$. Let $S(i(k),k) := \{z | (i(k)-1)/2^k \leq h(z)\}$ and let $a_{i(k),k} := (i(k)-1)/2^k$. Finally, we define h_k by $h_k(z) := \sum_{i=1}^{i(k)} a_{i,k}\chi_{S(i,k)}(z)$ for each $z \in Z$ and $k \geq 1$. Note that the sequence of functions $\langle h_k \rangle_{k=1}^{\infty}$ converges upwards to h pointwise. Then, by definition of h_k and the Choquet integral,

$$\begin{aligned}
&\int_Z h_k(z')\theta_z(dz') \\
&= \frac{1}{2^k}\theta_z\left(\bigcup_{i=2}^{i(k)} S(i,k)\right) + \frac{1}{2^k}\theta_z\left(\bigcup_{i=3}^{i(k)} S(i,k)\right) + \cdots + \frac{1}{2^k}\theta_z\left(S(i(k),k)\right) \\
&= \frac{1}{2^k}\Big[\theta_z(\{z' | h_k(z') \geq 1/2^k\}) + \theta_z(\{z' | h_k(z') \geq 2/2^k\}) + \\
&\quad \cdots + \theta_z(\{z' | h_k(z') \geq k2^k/2^k\})\Big].
\end{aligned}$$

Note that $\theta_z(\{z' | h_k(z') \geq i/2^k\})$ is nondecreasing in z for each $i \in \{1, \dots, k2^k\}$ by the supposition of the theorem given that h_k is nondecreasing. Because $\int_Z h_k(z')\theta_z(dz')$ is a sum of nondecreasing functions, it is nondecreasing in z. Finally, $\int_Z h(z')\theta_z(dz')$ is nondecreasing in z because it is the limit of the sequence of nondecreasing functions by the monotone convergence theorem (Theorem 2.4.6). ■

A.1.10 Proof of Theorem 2.5.5 (Stochastic Convexity)

The proof is the same as that for Theorem 2.5.4 except that we use the fact that a sum of convex functions is convex and the fact that the limit of a sequence of convex functions is convex. ■

A.1.11 Proof of Theorem 2.5.6

That $f \circ \theta$ is a convex and continuous capacitary kernel follows from Sect. A.1.2. The stochastic nondecrease of $f \circ \theta$ follows by Theorem 2.5.4 and by the fact that f is nondecreasing. Its stochastic convexity follows by Theorem 2.5.5 and by the convexity of f. Finally, its u.s.c. follows by the definition of u.s.c. and by the nondecrease and the continuity of f. ■

A.1.12 Proof of Example 2.5.2

(a) Stochastic nondecrease. Note that

$$(\forall z, t) \quad P_z(\{z' \in Z | z' \geq t\}) = 1 - F_z(t) = \max\{0, 1 - (2 - z)t\}\ , \qquad (A.4)$$

where the first equality holds because the Lebesgue measure is atomless. Because $1 - F_z(t)$ is nondecreasing in z for each t, the stochastic nondecrease follows from Theorem 2.5.4. (b) Strong continuity. Scheffé's theorem (Billingsley 1986, p. 218, Theorem 16.11) shows that $\| P_{z_n}(\cdot) - P_{z_0}(\cdot) \| \to 0$ as $n \to +\infty$ because the density function of $P_{z_n}(\cdot)$ exists and converges to that of $P_{z_n}(\cdot)$ except at $1/(2-z_0)$, where $\|\cdot\|$ is the total variation norm, which implies the strong continuity of P. (c) Stochastic convexity. From (A.4), we see that $1 - F_z(t)$ is convex in z for each t. Hence, the stochastic convexity follows from Theorem 2.5.5. ■

A.2 Proofs for Chap. 3

A.2.1 Proof of Theorem 3.3.1 (von Neumann–Morgenstern's Theorem)

The necessity of the axioms are easily seen, and hence, we show only the sufficiency of the axioms below. Also, we only give a sketch of a proof, closely following Kreps (1988).

We first prove the next lemma.

Lemma A.2.1 *If a binary relation $\succ$ on $\mathcal{P}$ satisfies Axioms A1, A2, and A3, then the following holds:*
(a) If $p \succ q$ and $0 \leq a < b \leq 1$, then $bp + (1-b)q \succ ap + (1-a)q$.
(b) If $p \succeq q \succeq r$ and $p \succ r$, then there exists a unique $a^* \in [0, 1]$ such that $q \sim a^* p + (1 - a^*)r$.
(c) If $p \sim q$ and $a \in [0, 1]$, then for any $r \in \mathcal{P}$, it holds that $ap + (1-a)r \sim aq + (1-a)r$.

Proof of (a). If $a = 0$, then the claim follows immediately from A2. Hence, assume that $a > 0$. We define r by $r := bp + (1-b)q$. Then, A2 implies $r \succ q$, and hence, it follows that $r = (1 - (a/b))r + (a/b)r \succ (1 - (a/b))q + (a/b)r = (1-(a/b))q + (a/b)(bp + (1-b)q) = ap + (1-a)q$, which completes the proof.
Proof of (b). If a^* exists, it must be unique by (a). Therefore, it suffices to show the existence of a^*. Assume that $p \succ q \succ r$. (Otherwise, the existence of a^* is trivial.) We define a real number a^* by $a^* := \sup\{a \in [0, 1] \,|\, q \succeq ap + (1-a)r\}$. First, assume that $a^* p + (1-a^*)r \succ q \succ r$. Then, A3 implies that there exists $b \in (0, 1)$ such that $b(a^* p + (1-a^*)r) + (1-b)r = ba^* p + (1 - ba^*)r \succ q$.

Furthermore, $ba^* < a^*$ holds because $a^* \neq 0$. This and the definition of a^* implies the existence of a' such that $ba^* < a' < a^*$ and $q \succeq a'p + (1 - a')r$. Then, (a) implies $q \succ ba^*p + (1 - ba^*)r$, which is a contradiction. Similarly, assuming $p \succ q \succ a^*p + (1 - a^*)r$ leads to a contradiction. Therefore, (b) holds. We omit a proof for (c). See Kreps (1988). Note, however, that iterated applications of (c) show that $p \sim q$ and $r \sim w \Rightarrow \lambda p + (1 - \lambda)r \sim \lambda q + (1 - \lambda)w$.

When all probability measures are indifferent to each other, we may take any constant function as u. Hence, we assume that there exist a pair of probability measures p and q such that $p \succ q$ and fix them. For any r such that $p \succeq r \succeq q$, we define $u(r)$ by a real number which satisfies $u(r) \in [0, 1]$ and $u(r)p + (1 - u(r))q \sim r$. By (b) of Lemma A.2.1, such a $u(r)$ is uniquely determined. Then, for any r and r' such that $p \succeq r \succeq q$ and $p \succeq r' \succeq q$, it holds that $r \succ r' \Leftrightarrow u(r)p + (1 - u(r))q \succ u(r')p + (1 - u(r'))q \Leftrightarrow u(r) > u(r')$ where the second equivalence follows from (a) of Lemma A.2.1. Furthermore, for any such r and r' and for any $\lambda \in [0, 1]$, it holds that $\lambda r + (1 - \lambda)r' \sim \lambda(u(r)p + (1 - u(r))q) + (1 - \lambda)(u(r')p + (1 - u(r'))q) = (\lambda u(r) + (1 - \lambda)u(r'))p + (\lambda(1 - u(r)) + (1 - \lambda)(1 - u(r')))q = (\lambda u(r) + (1 - \lambda)u(r'))p + (1 - \lambda u(r) - (1 - \lambda)u(r'))q$. Here, the equivalence follows from (c) of Lemma A.2.1 and the remark at the end of the previous paragraph. This and the definition of u imply $u(\lambda r + (1 - \lambda)r') = \lambda u(r) + (1 - \lambda)u(r')$.

The function u thus defined preserves its properties (representation and affinity) through a positive affine transformation. Therefore, we may assume without loss of generality that $u(p) = 1$ and $u(q) = 0$. Furthermore, for any r such that $r \succ p$, we find an $a \in (0, 1)$ that satisfies $ar + (1 - a)q \sim p$ (such an a can be found uniquely) and we define $u(r) := 1/a$. Also, for any r such that $q \succ r$, we find an $a \in (0, 1)$ that satisfies $ap + (1 - a)r \sim q$ (such an a can be found uniquely) and we define $u(r) := -a/(1 - a)$. The function u thus defined can be easily verified to be an affine function that represents $\succ$ on $\mathcal{P}$ and the proof is complete. ∎

A.2.2 *Proof of Theorem 3.5.2 (Savage's Theorem)*

The necessity of the axioms is easily seen, and hence, we show only the sufficiency of the axioms below. Also, we only give a sketch for a proof along the lines developed by Kreps (1988), which in turn is based upon Fishburn (1970).

For any pair of events A and B, we specify that $A \succ_\ell B$ whenever it holds that for some pair of outcomes x, x' with $x \succ x'$,

$$\begin{bmatrix} x \text{ on } A \\ x' \text{ on } A^c \end{bmatrix} \succ \begin{bmatrix} x \text{ on } B \\ x' \text{ on } B^c \end{bmatrix}.$$

Axiom P4 guarantees that $\succ_\ell$ is well defined; that is, $\succ_\ell$ does not depend on a specific choice of x and x'. Also, it follows from P1, P2, P3, P4, and P5 that $\succ_\ell$ turns out to be a qualitative probability on S. Furthermore, it can be verified that $\succ_\ell$ satisfies QP5 by P6. By the Subjective Probability Theorem (Theorem 3.5.1), there exists the unique convex-ranged probability charge μ, which represents $\succ_\ell$.

Given any simple act $f \in F_0$, the probability charge μ derived in the previous paragraph defines the simple probability charge p_f on X by $(\forall x \in X) \quad p_f(x) = \mu(f^{-1}(\{x\}))$. Note that for any $p \in P_0(X)$, we can always find some $f \in F_0$ such that $p = p_f$. Also, it can be shown that $(\forall f, g \in F_0)$

$$p_f = p_g \Rightarrow f \sim g. \tag{A.5}$$

The property (A.5) is known as *probabilistic sophistication*. (See Sect. 3.6.) Therefore, we may unambiguously define a binary relation $\succ_P$ on $P_0(X)$ by $(\forall p, q \in P_0(X)) \quad p \succ_P q \Leftrightarrow p = p_f,\ q = p_g$ and $f \succ g$.

It turns out that the binary relation $\succ_P$ defined at the end of the previous paragraph satisfies Axioms A1, A2, and A3 of Theorem 3.3.1. We can thus invoke Theorem 3.3.1 to conclude that there exists a von Neumann–Morgenstern index u on X, which is unique up to a positive affine transformation, such that

$$\begin{aligned} f \succ g \Leftrightarrow p_f \succ_P p_g \Leftrightarrow \int_X u(x)\, dp_f(x) &> \int_X u(x)\, dp_g(x) \\ \Leftrightarrow \int_S u(f(s))\, d\mu(s) &> \int_S u(g(s))\, d\mu(s), \end{aligned}$$

which completes the proof. ■

A.2.3 Proof of Theorem 3.6.1

The necessity of the axioms is easily seen, and hence, we show only the sufficiency of the axioms below.

Axiom P5 implies that there exist two outcomes x, x' such that $x \succ x'$. Then, let $X^* := \{x, x'\}$. Also, let F_0^* be the subset of F_0 consisting of all X^*-valued acts and denote the restriction of $\succ$ on F_0^* by $\succ^*$. Then, it can be easily verified that Axioms P1, P3, P4, P5, and P6 are met when restricting us to $(S, \mathcal{E}, X^*, F_0^*, \succ^*)$. Furthermore, P4* and P2 are equivalent under this restriction, and hence, the proof of Savage's Theorem (Theorem 3.5.2) shows that there exists the unique convex-ranged probability charge μ on S such that for any act $f, g \in F_0^*$, $f \succ g \Leftrightarrow \mu(f^{-1}(\{x\})) > \mu(g^{-1}(\{x\}))$ because μ represents $\succ_\ell$ and because $x \succ x'$. (See the second paragraph of the proof of Theorem 3.5.2.)

On the other hand, it follows that

$$\begin{aligned} A \succ_\ell B &\Leftrightarrow A\backslash B \succ_\ell B\backslash A \\ &\Leftrightarrow \begin{bmatrix} x \text{ on } A\backslash B \\ x' \text{ on } B\backslash A \\ x' \text{ on } (A\triangle B)^c \end{bmatrix} \succ \begin{bmatrix} x' \text{ on } A\backslash B \\ x \text{ on } B\backslash A \\ x' \text{ on } (A\triangle B)^c \end{bmatrix} \\ &\Leftrightarrow \mu(A\backslash B) > \mu(B\backslash A) \Leftrightarrow \mu(A) > \mu(B), \end{aligned}$$

where the first and second equivalence are definitional; the third equivalence holds from the conclusion of the previous paragraph; and the last equivalence holds by the additivity of μ. Thus, we have shown that μ represents $\succ_\ell$.

Next, suppose that $\mu(A) = \mu(B)$ holds for some mutually disjoint events, A and B. Given any pair of outcomes y, y' and any act h, we use these events to define the two acts f and g by

$$f := \begin{bmatrix} y \text{ on } A \\ y' \text{ on } B \\ h \text{ on } (A\cup B)^c \end{bmatrix} \quad \text{and} \quad g := \begin{bmatrix} y' \text{ on } A \\ y \text{ on } B \\ h \text{ on } (A\cup B)^c \end{bmatrix}.$$

By the fact that μ represents $\succ_\ell$, both $A \succeq_\ell B$ and $B \succeq_\ell A$ hold. Therefore, we may conclude that $f \sim g$. To see this, first assume that $y \succ y'$. Then, $f \sim g$ follows directly from (3.2). Second, we assume that $y \sim y'$. Then, $f \sim g$ follows by the successive applications of Axiom P3. The observation made in this paragraph shows that two acts, one of which is made up by exchanging outcomes the other assumes over mutually disjoint events having the same probability, are indifferent to each other. This fact in turn shows that two acts f and g are indifferent if $p_f = p_g$ (that is, $\succ$ is probabilistically sophisticated) because, if so, one act can be made up from the other by a finite iteration of these exchanging procedures. Finally, we conclude that we may define unambiguously a preference order $\succ_P$ on $P_0(X)$ by $p_f \succ_P p_g \Leftrightarrow f \succ g$. (See the third paragraph of the proof of Theorem 3.5.2.)

We can prove that the preference order $\succ_P$ defined in the previous paragraph satisfies both the monotonicity and the mixture-continuity. Let $x^*, x_* \in X$ be such that $x^* \succ x_*$, whose existence is guaranteed by Axiom P5, and use them to define the subset $\mathcal{P}$ of $P_0(X)$ by $\mathcal{P} := \{\, p \in P_0(X) \mid \delta_{x^*} \succeq_P p \succeq_P \delta_{x_*} \,\}$. Then, for any $p \in \mathcal{P}$, there exists λ_p that satisfies $p \sim_P \lambda_p \delta_{x^*} + (1-\lambda_p)\delta_{x_*}$ by the mixture-continuity and Lemma A.2.1(b). (Recall that the mixture-continuity is a stronger assumption on a preference order than the continuity (A3) and that Lemma A.2.1(b) requires only A1 and A3.) Furthermore, by the monotonicity of $\succ_P$, λ_p is uniquely determined. Let us define $V(p) := \lambda_p$. Then, for any $p, q \in \mathcal{P}$ such that $p \succeq_P (\succ_P)\, q$, it holds that $V(p)\delta_{x^*} + (1-V(p))\delta_{x_*} \sim_P p \succeq_P (\succ_P)\, q \sim_P V(q)\delta_{x^*} + (1-V(q))\delta_{x_*}$, implying that $V(p) \geq (>)\, V(q)$ again by monotonicity. We thus conclude that V represents $\succ_P$ on $\mathcal{P}$. Finally, V can be extended to $P_0(X)$ so that it should still represent $\succ_P$, which completes the proof. ■

A.2.4 Proof of Theorem 3.8.1

We show that Axioms AA1–AA5 imply the representation. Other claims are easy to verify and their proofs are omitted. Because L_0 is a mixture space and because $\succ$ satisfies Axioms B1, B2, and B3 (because it satisfies AA1, AA2, and AA3), Theorem 3.4.1 immediately implies that there exists an affine function on L_0 that represents $\succ$. We name this function J. We use J to define an affine function u on Y by $(\forall y \in Y)\ u(y) := J(y)$, where y on the right-hand side is understood to be the constant lottery act that always takes on y. AA4 and AA5 imply the existence of a pair of simple lotteries, $y^*, y_* \in Y$, such that $y^* \succ y_*$. To see this, suppose on the contrary that $(\forall y, y' \in Y)\ y \sim y'$. Then, for any pair of simple lottery acts f and g, it holds that $(\forall s)\ f(s) \sim g(s)$, and then, that $f \sim g$ by AA4, which contradicts AA5. Therefore, we have $u(y^*) > u(y_*)$. By applying an appropriate affine transformation to J, we can normalize u so that $u(y^*) = 1$ and $u(y_*) = -1$ without any loss of generality.

Let $K := u(Y) \subseteq \mathbb{R}$. Then, K is convex by the affinity of u and because Y is a mixture space. We thus conclude that $[-1, 1] \subseteq K$ by the normalization made at the end of the previous paragraph. We define a function $U : L_0 \to B_0(K)$ by $(\forall f)(\forall s)\ U(f)(s) := u(f(s))$. The function U thus defined turns out to be surjective. To see this, let $a \in B_0(K)$. Then, we can always find such an act $f \in L_0$ that $(\forall s)\ u(f(s)) = a(s) \in K$ because $K = u(Y)$. Also, note that $f \sim g$ whenever $(\forall s)\ U(f)(s) = U(g)(s)$ because the latter implies that $(\forall s)\ u(f(s)) = u(g(s))$ by the definition of U and because this implies $f \sim g$ by both AA4 and the fact that u is a representation on Y. As a final remark about U, note that $(\forall \alpha \in [0, 1])(\forall f, g)(\forall s)\ U(\alpha f + (1-\alpha)g)(s) = u(\alpha f(s) + (1-\alpha)g(s)) = \alpha u(f(s)) + (1-\alpha)u(g(s)) = \alpha U(f)(s) + (1-\alpha)U(g)(s)$ by the affinity of u.

We now define a functional I on $B_0(K)$ by $(\forall a \in B_0(K))\ I(a) := J(U^{-1}(a))$, where $U^{-1}(a)$ denotes any representative of such an act f that $(\forall s)\ U(f)(s) = a(s)$. By one of the remarks made in the previous paragraph and by the fact that J is a representation of $\succ$ on L_0, the functional I is well defined. The rest of this paragraph shows that $I(0) = 0$ where 0 on the left-hand side denotes the element of $B_0(K)$ that always takes on 0 as its value. To see this, let $f^* := (1/2)y^* + (1/2)y_*$ be the constant lottery act. Then, $(\forall s)\ U(f^*)(s) = u((1/2)y^* + (1/2)y_*) = (1/2)u(y^*) + (1/2)u(y_*) = 0$ by the affinity of u and by the normalization made in the first paragraph, which proves the claim because $I(0) = J(f^*) = u(f^*) = 0$ by the definition of I.

This paragraph shows that the following equation holds:

$$(\forall a, b)(\forall \alpha \in [0, 1]) \quad I(\alpha a + (1-\alpha)b) = \alpha I(a) + (1-\alpha)I(b)\,. \tag{A.6}$$

Let $a, b \in B_0(K)$ and let $\alpha \in [0, 1]$. Note that $\alpha a + (1-\alpha)b \in B_0(K)$. The surjectivity of U, which is proved in the second-last paragraph, allows us to let $f, g \in L_0$ be such that $(\forall s)\ U(f)(s) = a(s),\ U(g)(s) = b(s)$. Note that $(\forall s)\ U(\alpha f + (1-\alpha)g)(s) = u(\alpha f(s) + (1-\alpha)g(s)) = \alpha u(f(s)) + (1-\alpha)u(g(s)) = \alpha U(f)(s) + (1-\alpha)U(g)(s) = \alpha a(s) + (1-\alpha)b(s)$. This shows that $I(\alpha a + (1-\alpha)b) =$

$J(U^{-1}(\alpha a+(1-\alpha)b))$ by the definition of I. Therefore, this and one of the claims made in the second-last paragraph prove the claim because $I(\alpha a+(1-\alpha)b) = J(U^{-1}(\alpha a+(1-\alpha)b)) = J(U^{-1}(\alpha U(f)+(1-\alpha)U(g))) = J(U^{-1}(U(\alpha f + (1-\alpha)g))) = J(\alpha f+(1-\alpha)g) = \alpha J(f)+(1-\alpha)J(g) = \alpha I(a)+(1-\alpha)I(b)$. Note that, in particular, we used the full affinity of J on L_0 here.

This paragraph proves that the functional I satisfies all the assumptions of Corollary 2.2.1. (i) *The fact that* $I(\chi_S) = 1$. This is easy. Note that $(\forall s)\ U(y^*)(s) = u(y^*) = 1 = \chi_S(s)$. Thus, $I(\chi_S) = J(y^*) = u(y^*) = 1$. (ii) *Additivity*. Letting $b := 0$ in (A.6) shows $(\forall a)(\forall \alpha \in [0,1])\ I(\alpha a) = \alpha I(a)$ because $I(0) = 0$ as proven at the end of the second-last paragraph. The additivity thus holds by this and (A.6) where α is set equal to $1/2$. (iii) *Monotonicity*. Let $a, b \in B_0(K)$ and let $f, g \in L_0$ be such that $(\forall s)\ U(f)(s) = a(s),\ U(g)(s) = b(s)$. This is possible again by the surjectivity of U. Then, it follows that $(\forall s)\ a(s) \geq b(s) \Rightarrow (\forall s)\ U(f)(s) \geq U(g)(s) \Rightarrow (\forall s)\ u(f(s)) \geq u(g(s)) \Rightarrow (\forall s)\ f(s) \succeq g(s) \Rightarrow f \succeq g \Rightarrow J(f) \geq J(g) \Rightarrow I(a) \geq I(b)$, where we used AA4, proving the monotonicity.

Given that all the assumptions for Corollary 2.2.1 are satisfied, it can be invoked to conclude that, defining the probability charge p on $(S, \mathcal{A})$ by $(\forall A)\ p(A) := I(\chi_A)$, we have

$$(\forall a \in B_0(K)) \quad I(a) = \int_S a(s)\, dp(s)\,.$$

Then, for any $f, g \in L_0$, it follows that

$$\begin{aligned} f \succ g \;\Leftrightarrow\; J(f) > J(g) \;\Leftrightarrow\; I(U(f)) > I(U(g)) \\ \Leftrightarrow \int_S U(f)(s)\, dp(s) > \int_S U(g)(s)\, dp(s) \\ \Leftrightarrow \int_S u(f(s))\, dp(s) > \int_S u(g(s))\, dp(s)\,, \end{aligned}$$

which completes the proof. ∎

A.2.5 *Proof of Theorem 3.9.1*

We show that Axioms S1–S5 imply the representation. Other claims are easy to verify and their proofs are omitted. The rest of this paragraph proves the existence of a function J on L_0 that represents $\succ$ and *whose restriction on L_c is an affine function*, where the latter statement makes sense because L_c is a mixture space. Note that any pair of acts in L_c are co-monotonic, and hence, that $\succ$, when restricted on L_c, satisfies Axioms B1, B2, and B3 because $\succ$ satisfies Axioms S1, S2, and S3. Therefore, Theorem 3.4.1 immediately implies that there exists an affine function on L_c that represents the restriction of $\succ$ on L_c. We name this function u. The affinity of u and Axioms S4 and S5 allow us to use exactly the same reasoning as the one in the first paragraph of Sect. A.2.4 to conclude that we may assume the existence of y^*, $y_* \in Y$ such that $y^* \succ y_*$, $u(y^*) = 1$, and $u(y_*) = 0$. Furthermore, note that given an even *not necessarily constant* act $f \in L_0$, any two out of three acts, f, y^*, and y_*, are mutually co-monotonic. Therefore, both Lemma A.2.1 and exactly the same reasoning as the rest of Sect. A.2.1 do apply. Thus, we may define $J(f)$ via u by $J(f) := a^*$ or $1/a^*$ or $-a^*/(1-a^*)$, depending upon the three cases described, where a^* is as defined in Lemma A.2.1. The affinity of u completes the proof of the claim.

Let $K := u(Y)$ and define a function $U : L_0 \to B_0(K)$ by $(\forall f)(\forall s)\ U(f)(s) := u(f(s))$. Then, exactly the same argument as the second paragraph of Sect. A.2.4 shows that U is surjective and "affine." Then, we define a functional I on $B_0(K)$ by $(\forall a \in B_0(K))\ I(a) := J(U^{-1}(\{a\}))$, where U^{-1} is as defined in the third paragraph of Sect. A.2.4 and the argument there shows that I is well defined.

This paragraph proves that I defined in the previous paragraph satisfies all the assumptions of a corollary of Schmeidler's Representation Theorem (Theorem 2.4.5). (i) Let $\lambda \in K$ and let $y \in Y$ be such that $u(y) = \lambda$. Then, it follows that $I(\lambda\chi_S) = J(y) = u(y) = \lambda$ because $(\forall s)\ U(y)(s) = u(y) = u(y)\chi_S(s) = \lambda\chi_S(s)$. (ii) Let $a, b, c \in B_0(K)$ be such that any two of them are co-monotonic and let $f, g, h \in L_0$ be such that $U(f) = a$, $U(g) = b$, and $U(h) = c$. Then, by the previous paragraph, it holds that, for any $\alpha \in (0, 1)$, $I(a) > I(b) \Rightarrow J(f) > J(g) \Rightarrow f \succ g \Rightarrow \alpha f + (1-\alpha)h \succ \alpha g + (1-\alpha)h \Rightarrow J(\alpha f + (1-\alpha)h) > J(\alpha g + (1-\alpha)h) \Rightarrow I(U(\alpha f + (1-\alpha)h)) > I(U(\alpha g + (1-\alpha)h)) \Rightarrow I(\alpha U(f) + (1-\alpha)U(h)) > I(\alpha U(g) + (1-\alpha)U(h)) \Rightarrow I(\alpha a + (1-\alpha)c) > I(\alpha b + (1-\alpha)c)$, where the second and fourth implications hold by the fact that J represents $\succ$ on L_0 (proven in the first paragraph); the third implication holds because $\succ$ is co-monotonic independent (Axiom S2); the fifth implication holds by the definition of I; the sixth implication holds by the "affinity" of U; and the last implication holds by the definitions of the acts. Note that we did not use the affinity of J, which is not the case for the current J, and that this is a significant difference from the proof for Theorem 3.8.1. Finally, (iii) can be proved in exactly the same way as (iii) in Sect. A.2.4.

We now invoke Theorem 2.4.5. We define a probability capacity θ by $(\forall A)$ $\theta(A) := I(\chi_A)$. Then, the theorem implies that

$$(\forall a) \quad I(a) = \int_S a(s)\, d\theta(s)\,.$$

From this, it follows that

$$\begin{aligned} & f \succ g \ \Leftrightarrow\ J(f) > J(g) \ \Leftrightarrow\ I(U(f)) > I(U(g)) \\ \Leftrightarrow\ & \int_S U(f)(s)\, d\theta(s) > \int_S U(g)(s)\, d\theta(s) \\ \Leftrightarrow\ & \int_S u(f(s))\, d\theta(s) > \int_S u(g(s))\, d\theta(s)\,, \end{aligned}$$

which completes the proof. ∎

A.2.6 Proof of Theorem 3.9.2

This paragraph proves that the uncertainty aversion and the next condition are equivalent:

$$(\forall a, b)(\forall \alpha \in [0, 1]) \quad I(\alpha a + (1-\alpha)b) \geq \min\{I(a), I(b)\}\,. \tag{A.7}$$

Assume the uncertainty aversion and that $I(a) \geq I(b)$ without loss of generality. Let f and g be such that $U(f) = a$ and $U(g) = b$. Then, $f \succeq g$ given that $J(f) = I(a) \geq I(b) = J(g)$, and this and the uncertainty aversion imply that for any $\alpha \in [0, 1]$, it holds that $\alpha f + (1-\alpha)g \succeq g$. This in turn implies that $I(\alpha a + (1-\alpha)b) = I(\alpha U(f) + (1-\alpha)U(g)) = I(U(\alpha f + (1-\alpha)g)) = J(\alpha f + (1-\alpha)g) \geq J(g) = I(b)$ and then (A.7) follows. Conversely, assume that (A.7) holds and let $f, g \in L_0$ be such that $f \succeq g$. Then, because $I(U(f)) = J(f) \geq J(g) = I(U(g))$, it holds that $J(\alpha f+(1-\alpha)g) = I(U(\alpha f+(1-\alpha)g)) = I(\alpha U(f) + (1-\alpha)U(g)) \geq \min\{I(U(f)), I(U(g))\} \geq I(U(g)) = J(g)$, and hence, the uncertainty aversion follows.

This paragraph proves the necessity of the convexity. To do this, assume that uncertainty aversion holds. It then follows from (A.7) that $(\forall a, b)(\forall \alpha \in [0, 1])\ I(\alpha a + (1-\alpha)b) \geq I(a)$ whenever $I(a) = I(b)$. This and the positive homogeneity of the Choquet integral (Proposition 2.4.3) imply that

$$(\forall a, b) \quad I(a+b) = 2I\,(a/2+b/2) \geq 2I(a) = I(a) + I(b) \tag{A.8}$$

whenever $I(a) = I(b)$. Let $E, F \in \mathcal{A}$ be such that $\theta(E) \geq \theta(F)$, and let $\gamma \geq 1$ be such that $\theta(E) = \gamma\theta(F)$. Then, because $I(\chi_E) = \theta(E) = \gamma\theta(F) = \gamma I(\chi_F) = I(\gamma\chi_F)$, (A.8) implies that

$$I(\chi_E + \gamma\chi_F) \geq \theta(E) + \gamma\theta(F)\,. \tag{A.9}$$

On the other hand, because $\chi_E+\gamma\chi_F = \chi_{E\cap F}+(\gamma-1)\chi_F+\chi_{E\cup F}$, the co-monotonic additivity of the Choquet integral (Proposition 2.4.5) implies that $I(\chi_E + \gamma\chi_F) = I(\chi_{E\cap F} + (\gamma-1)\chi_F + \chi_{E\cup F}) = I(\chi_{E\cap F}) + I((\gamma-1)\chi_F) + I(\chi_{E\cup F}) = \theta(E \cap F) + (1-\gamma)\theta(F) + \theta(E \cup F)$. Combining this and (A.9) leads to the definition of the convexity of θ.

This paragraph proves the sufficiency of the convexity. When θ is convex, the subadditivity of the Choquet integral (Proposition 2.4.4) and its positive homogeneity (Proposition 2.4.3) immediately imply that $(\forall a, b)(\forall \alpha \in [0, 1])\ I(\alpha a+(1-\alpha)b) \geq \alpha I(a) + (1-\alpha)I(b)$. This implies (A.7), and then uncertainty aversion by the first paragraph of this proof. ■

A.2.7 *Proof of Theorem 3.10.1*

We give only a sketch of a proof for the sufficiency of the axioms. For the details, see Gilboa and Schmeidler (1989). Similarly to Sect. A.2.5, it can be shown that there exists a representation of $\succ$ on L_0 whose restriction on L_c is an affine function. Furthermore, if we define a function $U : L_0 \to B_0(K)$ by $(\forall f)(\forall s)\ U(f)(s) := u(f(s))$ and if we define a functional I on a functional space $B_0(K)$ by $(\forall a \in B_0(K))\ I(a) := J(U^{-1}(\{a\}))$, it can be shown similarly that I is well defined and that $I(\chi_S) = 1$ by an appropriate normalization of u.

It can be proved that the functional I thus defined satisfies for any $a, b \in B_0$, for any $\alpha \geq 0$ and for any $\gamma \in \mathbb{R}$,

Monotonicity	$a \geq b \Rightarrow I(a) \geq I(b)$
Positive Homogeneity	$I(\alpha a) = \alpha I(a)$
Super Additivity	$I(a+b) \geq I(a) + I(b)$
C-Additivity	$I(a + \gamma\chi_S) = I(a) + I(\gamma\chi_S)$

and that I can be extended to B so that it should satisfy these conditions.

Any functional I that satisfies Monotonicity, Positive Homogeneity, Super Additivity, C-Additivity, and $I(\chi_S) = 1$ can be shown to be represented by

$$(\forall a \in B) \quad I(a) = \min\left\{ \int_S a(s)\,dp(s) \,\middle|\, p \in C \right\}$$

for some closed convex set C of probability charges, from which the sufficiency of the axioms follows. ■

A.2.8 *Proof of Theorem 3.13.1*

Showing that the axioms in the theorem are necessary for the representation is straightforward in view of the co-monotonic additivity of the Choquet integral (Proposition 2.4.5), and hence, it is omitted. We prove the sufficiency of the axioms in several steps.

Step 1. We show that there exists a representation of $\succ_0$ whose restriction on constant acts is affine. However, this can be conducted in exactly the same way as Sect. A.2.5 because of Axioms A1, A2(0), A3, A4, and A5. We name it J.

Step 2. Let L'_0 be the space of simple lottery acts whose domain is T. Given any $f \in L_0$ and any $s \in S$, it obviously holds that $f(s, \cdot) \in L'_0$. For each $i \in \{1, \ldots, m\}$, we define a binary relation $\succ'_i$ on L'_0 by: $(\forall f', g' \in L'_0)$

$$f' \succ'_i g' \Leftrightarrow$$
$$(\forall f, g \in L_0)\ \left[f(s_i, \cdot) = f' \text{ and } g(s_i, \cdot) = g' \Rightarrow f \succ_i g \right]. \quad \text{(A.10)}$$

Two acts, f' and g', are *co-monotonic with respect to* $\succ_i'$ if $(\forall t, t' \in T)$ $f'(t) \succ_i' f'(t') \Rightarrow g'(t) \not\prec_i' g'(t')$, where $f'(t)$, say, should be understood to be a constant act on T. The rest of this step shows that the following holds: $(\forall f', g' \in L_0')$

$$f' \succ_i' g' \;\Leftrightarrow\; (\exists f, g \in L_0)\; f(s_i, \cdot) = f',\; g(s_i, \cdot) = g' \text{ and } f \succ_i g\,. \tag{A.11}$$

To show $(\Rightarrow)$, suppose that $f' \succ_i' g'$. Then, the right-hand side of (A.11) clearly holds true by (A.10) because we can always find f and g such that $f(s_i, \cdot) = f'$ and $g(s_i, \cdot) = g'$ for any f' and g'. To show $(\Leftarrow)$, suppose that the right-hand side of (A.11) holds; that is, assume that there exist $\hat{f}$ and $\hat{g}$ such that $\hat{f}(s_i, \cdot) = f'$, $\hat{g}(s_i, \cdot) = g'$, and $\hat{f} \succ_i \hat{g}$. Let f, g be any pair of acts such that $f(s_i, \cdot) = f'$ and $g(s_i, \cdot) = g'$. Then, Axiom A6 implies that $\hat{f} \sim_i f$ and $\hat{g} \sim_i g$, and hence, it follows that $f \succ_i g$ by Axiom A1. Therefore, $f' \succ_i' g'$ holds by (A.10).

Step 3. Let $i \in \{1, 2, \ldots, n\}$ be arbitrary. This step proves that $\succ_i'$ defined in Step 2 satisfies all the axioms of Theorem 3.9.1.

(Ordering) We need to show that $\succ_i'$ is asymmetric and negatively transitive. The asymmetry is immediate from (A.10) and the asymmetry of $\succ_i$ (Axiom A1). To show negative transitivity, let $f', g', h' \in L_0'$ be such that $f' \not\succ_i' g'$ and $g' \not\succ_i' h'$. Then, by (A.10), there exist $f, g \in L_0$ such that $f(s_i, \cdot) = f'$, $g(s_i, \cdot) = g'$, and $f \not\succ_i g$ and there exist $\hat{g}, h \in L_0$ such that $\hat{g}(s_i, \cdot) = g'$, $h(s_i, \cdot) = h'$, and $\hat{g} \not\succ_i h$. Given that Axiom A6 implies that $g \sim_i \hat{g}$ and because $\succ_i$ is a preference order (Axiom A1), it follows that $f \not\succ_i h$. Therefore, we have $f' \not\succ_i' h'$ by (A.10), which completes the proof of the negative transitivity. We derive $\succeq_i'$ and $\sim_i'$ from $\succ_i'$ as usual.

(Co-monotonic Independence) Let $f', g', h' \in L_0'$ be pairwise co-monotonic with respect to $\succ_i'$ and such that $f' \succ_i' g'$. We need to show that for any $\lambda \in (0, 1)$,

$$\lambda f' + (1 - \lambda)h' \succ_i' \lambda g' + (1 - \lambda)h'\,. \tag{A.12}$$

Let $\lambda \in (0, 1)$ and let $f, g, h \in L_0$ be such that $(\forall s)$ $f(s, \cdot) = f'$, $g(s, \cdot) = g'$, and $h(s, \cdot) = h'$. This paragraph proves that f, g, h thus defined are pairwise co-monotonic with respect to $\succ_i$. To see this, let $s, s' \in S$ and $t, t' \in T$ be such that $f(s, t) \succ_i f(s', t')$. Because $f(s, t) = f'(t)$ and $f(s', t') = f'(t')$, it follows that $f'(t) \succ_i' f'(t')$ by (A.11) and that $g'(t) \not\prec_i' g'(t')$ by the co-monotonicity of f' and g' with respect to $\succ_i'$. Because $g(s, t) = g'(t)$ and $g(s', t') = g'(t')$, (A.11) also implies that $g(s, t) \not\prec_i g'(s', t')$. The same argument applies to the other pairs of acts.

This paragraph completes the proof. Note that $f \succ_i g$ by (A.10) and the assumption that $f' \succ_i' g'$. Therefore, Axiom A2(1) and the pairwise co-monotonicity of f, g, h proven in the previous paragraph imply that $\lambda f + (1-\lambda)h \succ_i \lambda g + (1-\lambda)h$. Finally, (A.12) follows from (A.11) because $(\lambda f + (1-\lambda)h)(s_i, \cdot) = \lambda f(s_i, \cdot) + (1-\lambda)h(s_i, \cdot) = \lambda f' + (1-\lambda)h'$ and $(\lambda g + (1-\lambda)h)(s_i, \cdot) = \lambda g(s_i, \cdot) + (1-\lambda)h(s_i, \cdot) = \lambda g' + (1-\lambda)h'$.

(Continuity) Let $f', g', h' \in L_0'$ be such that $f' \succ_i' g'$ and $g' \succ_i' h'$. We need to show the existence of $\alpha, \beta \in (0, 1)$ such that $\alpha f' + (1 - \alpha)h' \succ_i' g'$ and $g' \succ_i' \beta f' + (1 - \beta)h'$. To do this, let $f, g, h \in L_0$ be such that $f(s_i, \cdot) = f'$, $g(s_i, \cdot) = g'$

and $h(s_i, \cdot) = h'$. Then, (A.10) shows that $f \succ_i g$ and $g \succ_i h$. Therefore, Axiom A3 implies that there exists $\alpha \in (0, 1)$ such that $\alpha f + (1 - \alpha)h \succ_i g$. Finally, (A.11) shows that $\alpha f' + (1 - \alpha)h' \succ_i' g'$ because $(\alpha f + (1 - \alpha)h)(s_i, \cdot) = \alpha f(s_i, \cdot) + (1 - \alpha)h(s_i, \cdot) = \alpha f' + (1 - \alpha)h'$. The existence of β can be proven similarly.

(Monotonicity) We first show that for any $y, y' \in Y$, $y \succ_i' y'$ if and only if $y \succ_i y'$. To do this, suppose that $y \succ_i' y'$ and let $f, g \in L_0$ be constant acts such that $(\forall \omega \in \Omega)$ $f(\omega) = y$ and $g(\omega) = y'$. Then, (A.10) immediately implies that $f \succ_i g$, and hence, that $y \succ_i y'$. Next, suppose that $y \succ_i y'$. Then, it follows that $y \succ_i' y'$ from (A.11) by letting f and g there be the constant acts defined above.

This paragraph completes the proof of the monotonicity. Let $f', g' \in L_0'$ be such that $(\forall t \in T)$ $f'(t) \succeq_i' g'(t)$. We need to show that $f' \succeq_i' g'$. To do this, let $f, g \in L_0$ be such that $(\forall s \in S)$ $f(s, \cdot) = f'$ and $g(s, \cdot) = g'$. Then, from the assumption that $(\forall t)$ $f'(t) \succeq_i' g'(t)$, it follows that $(\forall \omega \in \Omega)$ $f(\omega) \succeq_i' g(\omega)$, and hence, that $(\forall \omega \in \Omega)$ $f(\omega) \succeq_i g(\omega)$ by the claim proven in the previous paragraph. Therefore, Axiom A4 implies that $f \succeq_i g$, which in turn implies that $f' \succeq_i' g'$ by (A.10).

(Nondegeneracy) We need to show that there exist $f', g' \in L_0'$ such that $f' \succ_i' g'$. To do this, note that there exist $y^*, y_* \in Y$ such that $y^* \succ_0 y_*$ by Axioms A4 and A5. Then, Axiom A7 implies that $y^* \succ_i y_*$, and hence, the claim proven in the first paragraph of the proof of monotonicity shows that $y^* \succ_i' y_*$, which completes this step.

Step 4. By Step 3, we may apply Theorem 3.9.1 to $\succ_i$ for each $i \in \{1, \ldots, m\}$, and conclude that there exist a unique probability capacity θ_{s_i} on T and an affine function $u_i : Y \to \mathbb{R}$, which is unique up to a positive affine transformation, such that $(\forall f, g \in L_0')$

$$f' \succ_i' g' \;\Leftrightarrow\; \int_T u_i(f'(t))\,\theta_{s_i}(dt) > \int_T u_i(g'(t))\,\theta_{s_i}(dt)\,. \tag{A.13}$$

In the remainder of this step, we prove (3.5) in the theorem. Arbitrarily, let $i \in \{1, \ldots, m\}$. First, we show that $(\forall f, g \in L_0)$

$$f \succ_i g \;\Leftrightarrow\; \int_T u_i(f(s_i, t))\,\theta_{s_i}(dt) > \int_T u_i(g(s_i, t))\,\theta_{s_i}(dt)\,. \tag{A.14}$$

To show $(\Leftarrow)$, let $f, g \in L_0$ be such that the right-hand side of (A.14) holds. Then, by (A.13), it holds that $f(s_i, \cdot) \succ_i' g(s_i, \cdot)$ by regarding f' and g' as $f(s_i, \cdot)$ and $g(s_i, \cdot)$. Then, by (A.10), it follows that $f \succ_i g$. To show $(\Rightarrow)$, let $f, g \in L_0$ be such that $f \succ_i g$ and such that the right-hand side of (A.14) does *not* hold. Then, by (A.13), it holds that $f(s_i, \cdot) \not\succ_i' g(s_i, \cdot)$. On the other hand, the assumption that $f \succ_i g$ implies that $f(s_i, \cdot) \succ_i' g(s_i, \cdot)$ by (A.11), which contradicts the asymmetry of $\succ_i'$ as established in (Ordering) of Step 3.

Second, note that there exist $y^*, y_* \in Y$ such that $y^* \succ_0 y_*$. (See Nondegeneracy in Step 4.) Therefore, Axiom A7 implies that $y^* \succ_i y_*$. On the other hand, let u be the restriction of J on Y (see Step 1). Then, u is an affine function such that $u(y^*) > u(y_*)$ because J is a representation of $\succ_0$ (see Step 1 again). Therefore, by making a suitable positive affine transformation on u_i, we may assume without loss of generality that $u_i(y^*) = u(y^*)$ and $u_i(y_*) = u(y_*)$. Because two affine functions that intersect at two distinct points coincide perfectly, it follows that $(\forall y \in Y)\ u_i(y) = u(y)$. Finally, we conclude that there exist a unique class of probability capacities, $\langle \theta_{s_i} \rangle_{i=1}^m$, on T and an affine function $u : Y \to \mathbb{R}$ such that $(\forall f, g \in L_0)$

$$f \succ_i g \Leftrightarrow \int_T u(f(s_i, t))\, \theta_{s_i}(dt) > \int_T u(g(s_i, t))\, \theta_{s_i}(dt)\,, \tag{A.15}$$

proving (3.5).

Step 5. Let $K := u(Y) \subseteq \mathbb{R}$. Note that K is convex by the affinity of u. We denote by $\hat{B}_0(K)$ the space of K-valued simple functions *on* S. Two elements, $a, b \in \hat{B}_0(K)$, are naturally called *co-monotonic* if $(\forall s, s' \in S)\ (a(s) - a(s'))(b(s) - b(s')) \geq 0$. This step defines a functional I on $\hat{B}_0(K)$. Given any $f \in L_0$, a mapping defined by

$$s \mapsto \int_T u(f(s, t))\, \theta_s(dt)$$

is an element of $\hat{B}_0(K)$. Furthermore, for any $a \in \hat{B}_0(K)$, we can find a first-period-measurable act $f \in L_0$ such that

$$(\forall s \in S) \quad a(s) = \int_T u(f(s, t))\, \theta_s(dt) = u(f(s)) \tag{A.16}$$

because $K = u(Y)$. (Recall that we may denote the outcome of a first-period-measurable act by $f(s)$, instead of $f(s, t)$.) We then define a functional $I : \hat{B}_0(K) \to \mathbb{R}$ by $(\forall a \in B_0(K))\ I(a) = J(f)$, where $f \in L_0$ is an act that satisfies

$$(\forall s \in S) \quad a(s) = \int_T u(f(s, t))\, \theta_s(dt)\,.$$

We know that such an act certainly exists even within first-period-measurable acts by (A.16). To show the well-defined nature of I, let $a \in B_0(K)$ and let $f, g \in L_0$ be any pair of acts such that

$$(\forall i) \quad a(s_i) = \int_T u(f(s_i, t))\, \theta_{s_i}(dt) = \int_T u(g(s_i, t))\, \theta_{s_i}(dt)\,.$$

Then, (A.15) implies that $(\forall i)\ f \sim_i g$, which in turn implies that $f \sim_0 g$ by Axiom A8 (Dynamic Consistency). We thus conclude the well-defined nature of I by $J(f) = J(g)$ because J is a representation of $\succ_0$. As an immediate consequence of the definition of I, note that

$$(\forall f \in L_0) \quad J(f) = I\left(\int_T u(f(\cdot, t))\, \theta_{\cdot}(dt)\right)\,. \tag{A.17}$$

In particular, when f is first-period-measurable, we have

$$J(f) = I\left(u(f(\cdot))\right). \tag{A.18}$$

Step 6. In this step, we show that the functional I defined in Step 5 satisfies all the assumptions of Theorem 2.4.5, which proves that I can be represented by

$$(\forall a \in \hat{B}_0(K)) \quad I(a) = \int_S a(s)\,\theta_0(ds)$$

with some probability capacity θ_0 on S. This and (A.17) prove (3.4) because J is a representation of $\succ_0$.

(i) Let $\lambda \in K$. We need to show that $I(\lambda\chi_S) = \lambda$. To do this, let $y \in Y$ be an outcome such that $u(y) = \lambda$ and let $f \in L_0$ be a first-period-measurable act such that $(\forall s)\ f(s) = y$. Then, $I(\lambda\chi_S) = I\left(u(f(\cdot))\right) = U(f) = u(y) = \lambda$, where the second equality holds by (A.18) and the third equality holds because f is a constant act and u is a restriction of J on Y (see Step 4).

(ii) Let $a, b, c \in \hat{B}_0(K)$ be pairwise co-monotonic. We need to show that for any $\alpha \in (0, 1)$,

$$I(a) > I(b) \Rightarrow I(\alpha a + (1-\alpha)c) > I(\alpha b + (1-\alpha)c). \tag{A.19}$$

To do this, let f, g, h be first-period-measurable acts such that $(\forall s)\ u(f(s)) = a(s)$, $u(g(s)) = b(s)$ and $u(h(s)) = c(s)$. Such f, g, and h certainly exist by (A.16). Then, f and g are co-monotonic because for any $s, s' \in S$, $f(s) \succ_0 f(s') \Leftrightarrow f(s) \succ_i f(s') \Leftrightarrow u(f(s)) > u(f(s')) \Leftrightarrow a(s) > a(s') \Rightarrow b(s) \not< b(s') \Leftrightarrow u(g(s)) \not< u(g(s')) \Leftrightarrow g(s) \not\prec_i g(s') \Leftrightarrow g(s) \not\prec_0 g(s')$, where the first and last equivalences hold by Axiom A7; the second and fifth equivalences hold by (A.15) and first-period-measurability of f and g; and the one-way implication holds by the co-monotonicity between a and b. By similar reasoning, any other pair among f, g, and h turns out to be mutually co-monotonic. Thus, (A.19) holds because $I(a) > I(b) \Rightarrow I\left(u(f(\cdot))\right) > I\left(u(g(\cdot))\right) \Rightarrow J(f) > J(g) \Rightarrow J(\alpha f + (1-\alpha)h) > J(\alpha g + (1-\alpha)h) \Rightarrow I\left(u(\alpha f(\cdot) + (1-\alpha)h(\cdot))\right) > I\left(u(\alpha g(\cdot) + (1-\alpha)h(\cdot))\right) \Rightarrow I\left(\alpha u(f(\cdot)) + (1-\alpha)u(h(\cdot))\right) > I\left(\alpha u(g(\cdot)) + (1-\alpha)u(h(\cdot))\right) \Rightarrow I(\alpha a + (1-\alpha)c) > I(\alpha a + (1-\alpha)c)$, where the second and fourth implications hold by (A.18); the third implication holds by the assumption that f, g, h are first-period-measurable, the fact that they are pairwise co-monotonic (proven just above), A2(0) and the fact that J represents $\succ$; and the fifth implication holds by the affinity of u on Y.

(iii) Let $a, b \in B_0(K)$ be such that $a \geq b$. We need to prove that $I(a) \geq I(b)$. To do this, let f and g be first-period-measurable acts such that $(\forall s)\ u(f(s)) = a(s)$ and $u(g(s)) = b(s)$. Such f and g certainly exist by (A.16). Then, $I(a) \geq I(b)$ holds because $(\forall s)\ a(s) \geq b(s) \Leftrightarrow (\forall s)\ u(f(s)) \geq u(g(s)) \Leftrightarrow (\forall s)\ f(s) \succeq_0 g(s) \Rightarrow f \succeq_0 g \Leftrightarrow J(f) \geq J(g) \Leftrightarrow I(u(f(\cdot))) \geq I(u(g(\cdot))) \Leftrightarrow I(a) \geq I(b)$, where the second equivalence holds because u is a representation of $\succ_0$ on Y; the one-way implication holds by Axiom A4; the third equivalence holds because J represents $\succ_0$; and the fourth equivalence holds by (A.18). ■

A.3 Proofs for Chap. 6

A.3.1 Proof of Theorem 6.5.1

Because $U_{\mathcal{P}_s}(\cdot)$ is strictly concave, a real number $m \in \mathbb{R}$ is a solution of the degenerate optimization problem in (6.2) if and only if $(\forall s \in S)\ dV_s(m)/dm_+ \leq 0 \leq dV_s(m)/dm_-$, where $dV_s(m)/dm_+$ and $dV_s(m)/dm_-$ are the left- and right-derivatives of $V_s(m)$ taken with respect to m. Therefore, we can characterize a stationary equilibrium by a system of inequalities: $(\forall s \in S)\ dV_s(M)/dm_+ \leq 0 \leq dV_s(M)/dm_-$. Because Theorem 4.2.2 implies

$$\frac{dV_s(m)}{dm_+} = \min_{\pi \in \mathcal{M}_s(c_s^m(q^*))} \left(-\sum_{s' \in S} q_s^* u_1(c_{ss'}^m(q^*))\pi_{s'} + \sum_{s' \in S} q_{s'}^* u_2(c_{ss'}^m(q^*))\pi_{s'} \right),$$
$$\frac{dV_s(m)}{dm_-} = \max_{\pi \in \mathcal{M}_s(c_s^m(q^*))} \left(-\sum_{s' \in S} q_s^* u_1(c_{ss'}^m(q^*))\pi_{s'} + \sum_{s' \in S} q_{s'}^* u_2(c_{ss'}^m(q^*))\pi_{s'} \right)$$

for all $m \in \mathbb{R}$, we obtain (6.4). ■

A.3.2 Lemma A.3.1

We need the following lemma to prove Theorem 6.5.2.

Lemma A.3.1 *Suppose that there are two distinct probability measures $\mu, \nu \in \Delta_S$, such that $\mu, \nu \in \mathcal{P}_s$ for each $s \in S$. Then, there exists $\hat{\omega}^o \in \mathbb{R}^S_{++}$ such that $\min\left\{\sum_{s' \in S} \hat{\omega}^o_{s'}\pi_{s'} \,\middle|\, \pi \in \mathcal{P}_{\hat{s}}\right\} < \max\left\{\sum_{s' \in S} \hat{\omega}^o_{s'}\pi_{s'} \,\middle|\, \pi \in \mathcal{P}_{\tilde{s}}\right\}$ for each $\hat{s}, \tilde{s} \in S$, or equivalently,*

$$\max_{s \in S} \min_{\pi \in \mathcal{P}_s} \sum_{s' \in S} \hat{\omega}^o_{s'}\pi_{s'} < \min_{s \in S} \max_{\pi \in \mathcal{P}_s} \sum_{s' \in S} \hat{\omega}^o_{s'}\pi_{s'}. \tag{A.20}$$

Proof Because μ and ν are distinct probability measures on S, there exists at least one $t \in S$ such that $0 \leq \nu_t < \mu_t$. We define $\bar{\alpha} > 0$ by $\bar{\alpha} := \sum_{s' \neq t}(\nu_{s'} - \mu_{s'})/(1 - \nu_t/\mu_t)$. Because $\sum_{s' \neq t}(\nu_{s'} - \mu_{s'}) > 0$ and $1 - \nu_t/\mu_t > 0$, it follows that $\bar{\alpha} > 0$. Therefore, we can arbitrarily choose $\alpha \in (0, \bar{\alpha})$. Now, we define $\hat{\omega}^2 \in \mathbb{R}^S_{++}$ by

$$(\forall s' \in S) \quad \hat{\omega}^o_{s'} := \begin{cases} \alpha/\mu_t & \text{if } s' = t, \\ 1 & \text{otherwise.} \end{cases}$$

It follows from $\alpha < \bar{\alpha}$ that $\alpha(1 - (\nu_t/\mu_t)) + \sum_{s' \neq t}(\mu_{s'} - \nu_{s'}) < 0$, so we can obtain $\sum_{s' \in S} \hat{\omega}^o_{s'} \mu_{s'} - \sum_{s' \in S} \hat{\omega}^o_{s'} \nu_{s'} = (\alpha + \sum_{s' \neq t} \mu_{s'}) - (\alpha \nu_t/\mu_t + \sum_{s' \neq t} \nu_{s'}) = \alpha(1 - \nu_t/\mu_t) + \sum_{s' \neq t}(\mu_{s'} - \nu_{s'}) < 0$, that is, $\sum_{s' \in S} \hat{\omega}^o_{s'} \mu_{s'} < \sum_{s' \in S} \hat{\omega}^o_{s'} \nu_{s'}$. Finally, because $\mu, \nu \in \mathcal{P}_s$ for each $s \in S$, it holds that $\min\{\sum_{s' \in S} \hat{\omega}^o_{s'} \pi_{s'} | \pi \in \mathcal{P}_{\hat{s}}\} \leq \sum_{s' \in S} \hat{\omega}^o \mu_{s'} < \sum_{s' \in S} \hat{\omega}^o \nu_{s'} \leq \max\{\sum_{s' \in S} \hat{\omega}^o_{s'} \pi_{s'} | \pi \in \mathcal{P}_{\tilde{s}}\}$ for each $\hat{s}, \tilde{s} \in S$. This completes the proof. ■

A.3.3 Proof of Theorem 6.5.2

Let $\hat{\omega}^o$ be an element of $\mathbb{R}^S_{++}$ whose existence is proved by Lemma A.3.1. Then there exist $m, M \in \mathbb{R}_{++}$ such that $(\forall s \in S)$ $\min_{\pi \in \mathcal{P}_s} \sum_{s' \in S} \hat{\omega}^o_{s'} \pi_{s'} < m < M < \max_{\pi \in \mathcal{P}_s} \sum_{s' \in S} \hat{\omega}^o_{s'} \pi_{s'}$ by (A.20). Because $\max_{\pi \in \mathcal{P}_s} \sum_{s' \in S} \omega^o_{s'} \pi_{s'}$ and $\min_{\pi \in \mathcal{P}_s} \sum_{s' \in S} \omega^o_{s'} \pi_{s'}$ are continuous in ω^o for each $s \in S$ according to the maximum theorem (Berge 1963), there exists an open neighborhood, Ω^o_s, of $\hat{\omega}^o$ for each $s \in S$ such that any element of Ω^o_s satisfies $\min_{\pi \in \mathcal{P}_s} \sum_{s' \in S} \omega^o_{s'} \pi_{s'} < m < M < \max_{\pi \in \mathcal{P}_s} \sum_{s' \in S} \omega^o_{s'} \pi_{s'}$. We define Ω^o by $\Omega^o := \bigcap_{s \in S} \omega^o_s$. Obviously, Ω^o is open and nonempty because $\hat{\omega}^o \in \Omega^o$. There then exist $\underline{\omega}^o_1, \bar{\omega}^o_1, \ldots, \underline{\omega}^o_{|S|}, \bar{\omega}^o_{|S|}$ such that $\hat{\omega}^o \in (\underline{\omega}^o_1, \bar{\omega}^o_1) \times \cdots \times (\underline{\omega}^o_{|S|}, \bar{\omega}^o_{|S|}) \subset \Omega^o$, where we write $S = \{1, 2, \ldots, |S|\}$. Let $\hat{c}^o$ be any real number such that $\hat{c}^o > \max_{s \in S} \bar{\omega}^o_s$. Then, from the above inequalities, it holds that, for any $\omega^o \in (\underline{\omega}^o_1, \bar{\omega}^o_1) \times \cdots \times (\underline{\omega}^o_{|S|}, \bar{\omega}^o_{|S|})$ and for any $s \in S$, $\hat{c}^o - \max_{\pi \in \mathcal{P}_s} \sum_{s' \in S} \omega^o_{s'} \pi_{s'} < \hat{c}^o - M < \hat{c}^o - m < \hat{c}^o - \min_{\pi \in \mathcal{P}_s} \sum_{s' \in S} \omega^o_{s'} \pi_{s'}$.

Let $s \in S$. We define a function $g : \mathbb{R}^2_{++} \to \mathbb{R}$ by $(\forall(\omega^y_s, \omega^o_s))$ $g(\omega^y_s, \omega^o_s) := (\hat{c}^o - \omega^o_s) u_1(\omega^y_s + \omega^o_s - \hat{c}^o, \hat{c}^o)/u_2(\omega^y_s + \omega^o_s - \hat{c}^o, \hat{c}^o)$. By the assumption that f is surjective with respect to its first argument, there exists $\hat{\omega}^y_s \in \mathbb{R}_{++}$ such that $g(\hat{\omega}^y_s, \hat{\omega}^o_s) \in (\hat{c}^o - M, \hat{c}^o - m)$, where $\hat{\omega}^o_s$ is found in the first paragraph of this proof. Because g is continuous according to the continuity of f, $g^{-1}((\hat{c}^o - M, \hat{c}^o - m))$ is open. Therefore, there exist open sets Ω^y_s and $\hat{\Omega}^o_s$ such that $\hat{\omega}^y_s \in \Omega^y_s$, $\hat{\omega}^o_s \in \hat{\Omega}^o_s$, and $\Omega^y_s \times \hat{\Omega}^o_s \subset g^{-1}((\hat{c}^o - M, \hat{c}^o - m))$. Let $\tilde{\Omega}^o_s := (\underline{\omega}^o_s, \bar{\omega}^o_s) \cap \hat{\Omega}^o_s$. Then, $\tilde{\Omega}^o_s$ is open and nonempty because $\hat{\omega}^o_s$ is included in both sets. Finally, we define Ω by $\Omega := \Omega^y_1 \times \cdots \times \Omega^y_{|S|} \times \tilde{\Omega}^o_1 \times \cdots \times \tilde{\Omega}^o_{|S|}$.

Let $(\omega^y, \omega^o) \in \Omega$. Then, $\hat{c}^o$ (found in the first paragraph of this proof) satisfies (6.5) with strict inequalities for each $s \in S$. Because f is continuous, there exists an open neighborhood, $\hat{C}^o_s$, of $\hat{c}^o$ such that for any $c^o \in \hat{C}^o_s$, c^o satisfies (6.5) with strict inequalities. We define C^o by $C^o := \bigcap_{s \in S} \hat{C}^o_s$. This is the desired set and the proof is complete. ■

A.3.4 Proof of Corollary 6.5.2

Under the stated assumptions, the function f will become $f(x, y) = v_y'(x)/v_o'(y)$ for each x and y. According to the Inada condition on v_y, $f(\cdot, y)$ is clearly surjective for each y, which completes the proof. ■

A.3.5 Proof of Theorem 6.6.1

(a) Let $\omega \in \hat{\Omega}_{\mathcal{P}}$ and $\bar{c}^o \in \hat{C}^o_{\mathcal{P}}(\omega)$. These definitions are valid because $\hat{\Omega}_{\mathcal{P}}$ is nonempty owing to our assumption and Theorem 6.5.2, and because $\hat{C}^o_{\mathcal{P}}(\omega)$ is nonempty according to the definition of $\hat{\Omega}_{\mathcal{P}}$. Then, for each $s \in S$, $\bar{c}^o - \max_{\pi \in \mathcal{Q}_s} \sum_{s' \in S} \omega^o_{s'} \pi_{s'} \leq \bar{c}^o - \max_{\pi \in \mathcal{P}_s} \sum_{s' \in S} \omega^o_{s'} \pi_{s'} \leq (\bar{c}^o - \omega^o_s) f(\omega^y_s + \omega^o_s - d, d) \leq \bar{c}^o - \min_{\pi \in \mathcal{P}_s} \sum_{s' \in S} \omega^o_{s'} \pi_{s'} \leq \bar{c}^o - \min_{\pi \in \mathcal{Q}_s} \sum_{s' \in S} \omega^o_{s'} \pi_{s'}$. Here, the first and the last inequalities hold because $\mathcal{P}_s \subset \mathcal{Q}_s$, and the second and third inequalities hold because of the assumption that $d \in \hat{C}^o_{\mathcal{P}}(\omega)$. Therefore, $d \in \hat{C}^o_{\mathcal{Q}}(\omega)$, and hence, $\hat{C}^o_{\mathcal{P}}(\omega) \subseteq \hat{C}^o_{\mathcal{P}}(\omega)$.

(b) Let $\omega \in \hat{\Omega}_{\mathcal{P}}$. Then, $\hat{C}^o_{\mathcal{P}}(\omega)$ is nonempty, and $\hat{C}^o_{\mathcal{Q}}(\omega)$ is also nonempty because $\hat{C}^o_{\mathcal{P}}(\omega) \subseteq \hat{C}^o_{\mathcal{Q}}(\omega)$ according to (a). Therefore, $\omega \in \hat{\Omega}_{\mathcal{Q}}$, which completes the proof. ■

A.3.6 Proof of Theorem 6.7.1

Sakai (1988) proves that if $U^s : \mathbb{R}_{++} \times \mathbb{R}^S_{++} \to \mathbb{R}$ is increasing and strictly quasi-concave for all $s \in S$, then for any stationary feasible allocation c corresponding to a stationary monetary equilibrium, there exists no other stationary feasible allocation b that is conditionally Pareto superior to c. (Sakai (1988) assumes that U^s is represented by an expected utility function with a utility index that satisfies some regularity conditions. However, his proof only requires that U^s should be increasing and strictly quasi-concave.) Clearly, U^s is increasing. Furthermore, because U^s is strictly concave, it is strictly quasi-concave.[1] Therefore, the proof is complete. ■

A.4 Proofs for Chap. 9

A.4.1 Lemmas

Lemma A.4.1 *${}_0y^d$ is $\langle \mathcal{B}_{W^t} \rangle$-adapted.*

[1]See, for example, Theorem 1.E.1(i) of Takayama (1974).

Proof This is immediate because for any $t \geq 0$, $y_t^d = \sum_{T=0}^{t} w_T \chi_{\{d=T\}} + c\chi_{\{d>t\}}$ and the components on the right-hand side are all $\mathcal{B}_{W^t}$-measurable. ■

Lemma A.4.2 *For any $d \in \Delta$, it holds that*

$$I_{w_0}(d) = \frac{w_0}{1-\beta}\chi_{\{d=0\}} + \left(c + \beta \int I_{w_1}(d|_{w_1}) d\theta_{w_0}\right)\chi_{\{d>0\}} .$$

Proof This holds because

$$\begin{aligned}
&I_{w_0}(d)\\
&= \lim_{T\to\infty} y_0^d + \beta \int \left(y_1^d + \cdots \beta \int y_T^d \, d\theta \cdots \right) d\theta_{w_0}\\
&= \lim_{T\to\infty} \left[\left(y_0^d + \beta \int \left(y_1^d + \cdots \beta \int y_T^d \, d\theta \cdots \right) d\theta_{w_0}\right)\chi_{\{d=0\}}\right.\\
&\quad \left. + \left(y_0^d + \beta \int \left(y_1^d + \cdots \beta \int y_T^d \, d\theta \cdots \right) d\theta_{w_0}\right)\chi_{\{d>0\}}\right]\\
&= \lim_{T\to\infty} \left[\left(w_0 + \beta \int \left(w_0 + \cdots \beta \int w_0 \, d\theta \cdots \right) d\theta_{w_0}\right)\chi_{\{d=0\}}\right.\\
&\quad \left. + \left(c + \beta \int \left(y_1^d + \cdots \beta \int y_T^d \, d\theta \cdots \right) d\theta_{w_0}\right)\chi_{\{d>0\}}\right]\\
&= \lim_{T\to\infty} \left[\left(\frac{1-\beta^{T+1}}{1-\beta} w_0\right)\chi_{\{d=0\}}\right.\\
&\quad \left. + \left(c + \beta \int \left(y_1^d + \cdots \beta \int y_T^d \, d\theta \cdots \right) d\theta_{w_0}\right)\chi_{\{d>0\}}\right]\\
&= \frac{w_0}{1-\beta}\chi_{\{d=0\}} + \left(c + \beta \lim_{T\to\infty} \int \left(y_1^d + \cdots \beta \int y_T^d \, d\theta \cdots \right) d\theta_{w_0}\right)\chi_{\{d>0\}}\\
&= \frac{w_0}{1-\beta}\chi_{\{d=0\}} + \left(c + \beta \int \lim_{T\to\infty} \left(y_1^d + \cdots \beta \int y_T^d \, d\theta \cdots \right) d\theta_{w_0}\right)\chi_{\{d>0\}}\\
&= \frac{w_0}{1-\beta}\chi_{\{d=0\}} + \left(c + \beta \int I_{w_1}(d|_{w_1}) d\theta_{w_0}\right)\chi_{\{d>0\}} ,
\end{aligned}$$

where the second-last equality holds by the monotone convergence theorem (Theorem 2.4.6). ■

Lemma A.4.3 $(\forall w_0 \in W)\ \ V^{+}(w_0) < +\infty$.

Proof Let $w_0 \in W$, and let $\hat{\beta}$ and $\hat{t}$ be such that $\hat{\beta} > \beta$ and $(\forall t \geq \hat{t})\ (\bar{W}^t(w_0))^{1/t} < \hat{\beta}^{-1}$. Such $\hat{\beta}$ and $\hat{t}$ exist by E2. Then,

$$
\begin{aligned}
V^+(w_0) &\le \lim_{T\to\infty} (c \vee w_0) + \beta \int (c \vee \vee_{i=0}^{1} w_i) d\theta'_{w_0} + \cdots \\
&\quad + \beta^T \int \cdots \int (c \vee \vee_{i=0}^{T} w_i) d\theta'_{w_{T-1}} \cdots d\theta'_{w_0} \\
&= \lim_{T\to\infty} \bar{W}^0(w_0) + \beta \bar{W}^1(w_0) + \cdots + \beta^T \bar{W}^T(w_0) \\
&\le \lim_{T\to\infty} \bar{W}^0(w_0) + \beta \bar{W}^1(w_0) + \cdots \\
&\quad + \beta^{\hat{t}-1} \bar{W}^{\hat{t}-1}(w_0) + \beta^{\hat{t}} \hat{\beta}^{-\hat{t}} + \cdots + \beta^T \hat{\beta}^{-T} \\
&= \bar{W}^0(w_0) + \beta \bar{W}^1(w_0) + \cdots + \beta^{\hat{t}-1} \bar{W}^{\hat{t}-1}(w_0) + \frac{(\beta/\hat{\beta})^{\hat{t}}}{1-\beta/\hat{\beta}},
\end{aligned}
$$

where the first inequality holds by the assumption that θ is convex, the fact that $\theta \le \theta'$, the concavity of θ', and the sub-additivity of the Choquet integral with respect to a concave capacity (Proposition 2.4.4). The last line of the whole inequality is finite by E1 and the fact that $\hat{\beta} > \beta$. ■

Lemma A.4.4 *$BV^- \ge V^-$, $BV^+ \le V^+$, and for any admissible function $V \in \mathcal{V}$, BV is admissible.*

Proof The first claim holds because $(\forall w_0)$

$$
\begin{aligned}
BV^-(w_0) &= \max\left\{\frac{w_0}{1-\beta},\ c + \beta \int V^-(w_1)\theta_{w_0}(dw_1)\right\} \\
&= \max\left\{\frac{w_0}{1-\beta},\ \frac{c}{1-\beta}\right\} \ \ge\ V^-(w_0)\,.
\end{aligned}
$$

The second claim holds because $(\forall w_0)$

$$
\begin{aligned}
& BV^+(w_0) \\
&= \max\left\{\frac{w_0}{1-\beta},\ c + \beta \int V^+(w_1)\theta_{w_0}(dw_1)\right\} \\
&= \max\left\{\frac{w_0}{1-\beta}, c + \beta \int \lim_{T\to\infty} \left((c \vee w_1) + \cdots \beta \int (c \vee \vee_{i=1}^{T} w_i) d\theta \cdots\right) d\theta_{w_0}\right\} \\
&= \max\left\{\frac{w_0}{1-\beta},\ \lim_{T\to\infty} c + \beta \int \left((c \vee w_1) + \cdots \beta \int (c \vee \vee_{i=1}^{T} w_i) d\theta \cdots\right) d\theta_{w_0}\right\} \\
&\le \max\left\{\frac{w_0}{1-\beta},\right. \\
&\quad \left. \lim_{T\to\infty} (c \vee w_0) + \beta \int \left((c \vee \vee_{i=0}^{1} w_i) + \cdots \beta \int (c \vee \vee_{i=0}^{T} w_i) d\theta \cdots\right) d\theta_{w_0}\right\} \\
&\le \max\left\{\frac{w_0}{1-\beta},\ V^+(w_0)\right\} \ = \ V^+(w_0)\,,
\end{aligned}
$$

where the third equality holds by the monotone convergence theorem (Theorem 2.4.6). The final claim follows from the first two claims and the fact that $BV \leq BV'$ whenever $V \leq V'$. ■

Lemma A.4.5 *For any* $w_0 \in W$,

$$\lim_{t\to\infty} \beta^t \int\int \cdots \int V^+(w_t)d\theta'_{w_{t-1}} \cdots d\theta'_{w_1} d\theta'_{w_0} = 0\,.$$

Proof Let $w_0 \in W$, and let $\hat{\beta}$ and $\hat{t}$ be such that $\hat{\beta} > \beta$ and $(\forall t \geq \hat{t})\ (\bar{W}^t(w_0))^{1/t} < \hat{\beta}^{-1}$. Such $\hat{\beta}$ and $\hat{t}$ exist by E2. Then, for any $t \geq \hat{t}$,

$$\begin{aligned}
&\beta^t \int \cdots \int V^+(w_t)d\theta'_{w_{t-1}} \cdots d\theta'_{w_0} \\
&\leq \beta^t \int \cdots \int \lim_{T\to\infty} \Big[(c \vee w_t) + \beta \int (c \vee \vee_{i=0}^{1} w_{t+i})d\theta'_{w_t} \\
&\quad + \cdots + \beta^T \int \cdots \int (c \vee \vee_{i=0}^{T} w_{t+i})d\theta'_{w_{t+T-1}} \cdots d\theta'_{w_t}\Big] d\theta'_{w_{t-1}} \cdots d\theta'_{w_0} \\
&= \lim_{T\to\infty} \beta^t \int \cdots \int \Big[(c \vee w_t) + \beta \int (c \vee \vee_{i=0}^{1} w_{t+i})d\theta'_{w_t} \\
&\quad + \cdots + \beta^T \int \cdots \int (c \vee \vee_{i=0}^{T} w_{t+i})d\theta'_{w_{t+T-1}} \cdots d\theta'_{w_t}\Big] d\theta'_{w_{t-1}} \cdots d\theta'_{w_0} \\
&\leq \lim_{T\to\infty} \beta^t \int \cdots \int \Big[(c \vee \vee_{i=0}^{t} w_i) + \beta \int (c \vee \vee_{i=0}^{t+1} w_i)d\theta'_{w_t} \\
&\quad + \cdots + \beta^T \int \cdots \int (c \vee \vee_{i=0}^{t+T} w_i)d\theta'_{w_{t+T-1}} \cdots d\theta'_{w_t}\Big] d\theta'_{w_{t-1}} \cdots d\theta'_{w_0} \\
&\leq \lim_{T\to\infty} \Big(\beta^t \int \cdots \int (c \vee \vee_{i=0}^{t} w_i)d\theta'_{w_{t-1}} \cdots d\theta'_{w_0} \\
&\quad + \beta^{t+1} \int \cdots \int (c \vee \vee_{i=0}^{t+1} w_i)d\theta'_{w_t} \cdots d\theta'_{w_0} \\
&\quad + \cdots + \beta^{t+T} \int \cdots \int (c \vee \vee_{i=0}^{t+T} w_i)d\theta'_{w_{t+T-1}} \cdots d\theta'_{w_0}\Big) \\
&= \lim_{T\to\infty} \beta^t \bar{W}^t(w_0) + \beta^{t+1}\bar{W}^{t+1}(w_0) + \cdots + \beta^{t+T}\bar{W}^{t+T}(w_0) \\
&\leq \lim_{T\to\infty} \beta^t\hat{\beta}^{-t} + \beta^{t+1}\hat{\beta}^{-(t+1)} + \cdots + \beta^{t+T}\hat{\beta}^{-(t+T)} = (\beta/\hat{\beta})^t/(1-\beta/\hat{\beta})\,,
\end{aligned}$$

where the first inequality holds by the concavity of θ' and the sub-additivity of the Choquet integral with respect to a concave capacity (Proposition 2.4.4); the first equality holds by the monotone convergence theorem (Theorem 2.4.6); and the third inequality holds by the concavity of θ' and the sub-additivity of the Choquet integral with respect to a concave capacity (Proposition 2.4.4). The last line of the whole inequality converges to 0 as $t \to \infty$ by the fact that $\hat{\beta} > \beta$. ■

Lemma A.4.6 *For any $d \in \Delta$ and for any admissible function V,*

$$\lim_{t\to\infty}\Bigg|I_{w_0}(d)-\Bigg[\frac{w_0}{1-\beta}\chi_{\{d=0\}}+\Bigg(c+\beta\int\Bigg(\frac{w_1}{1-\beta}\chi_{\{d=1\}}+\Bigg(c+ \cdots\beta\int\Bigg(\frac{w_{t-1}}{1-\beta}\chi_{\{d=t-1\}}+\Bigg(c+\beta\int V(w_t)d\theta_{w_{t-1}}\Bigg)\chi_{\{d>t-1\}}\Bigg)d\theta_{w_{t-2}} \cdots\Bigg)\chi_{\{d>1\}}\Bigg)d\theta_{w_0}\Bigg)\chi_{\{d>0\}}\Bigg]\Bigg|=0$$

Proof By the iterative applications of Eq. (9.20), we have for any $t > 0$,

$$\begin{aligned}
I_{w_0}(d) &= \frac{w_0}{1-\beta}\chi_{\{d=0\}}+\left(c+\beta\int I_{w_1}(d|_{w_1})d\theta_{w_0}\right)\chi_{\{d>0\}}\\
&= \frac{w_0}{1-\beta}\chi_{\{d=0\}}+\Bigg(c+\beta\int\Bigg(\frac{w_1}{1-\beta}\chi_{\{d=1\}}\\
&\quad+\left(c+\beta\int I_{w_2}(d|_{1}{}_{\mathbf{w}_2})d\theta_{w_1}\right)\chi_{\{d>1\}}\Bigg)d\theta_{w_0}\Bigg)\chi_{\{d>0\}}\\
&= \cdots\cdots\cdots\\
&= \frac{w_0}{1-\beta}\chi_{\{d=0\}}+\Bigg(c+\beta\int\Bigg(\frac{w_1}{1-\beta}\chi_{\{d=1\}}+\Bigg(c+\\
&\quad\cdots\beta\int\Bigg(\frac{w_{t-1}}{1-\beta}\chi_{\{d=t-1\}}+\left(c+\beta\int I_{w_t}(d|_{1}{}_{\mathbf{w}_t})d\theta_{w_{t-1}}\right)\chi_{\{d>t-1\}}\Bigg)d\theta_{w_{t-2}}\\
&\quad\cdots\Bigg)\chi_{\{d>1\}}\Bigg)d\theta_{w_0}\Bigg)\chi_{\{d>0\}}\,.
\end{aligned}$$

Therefore, for any $t > 0$,

$$\begin{aligned}
&\Bigg|I_{w_0}(d)-\Bigg[\frac{w_0}{1-\beta}\chi_{\{d=0\}}+\Bigg(c+\beta\int\Bigg(\frac{w_1}{1-\beta}\chi_{\{d=1\}}+\Bigg(c+\\
&\cdots\beta\int\Bigg(\frac{w_{t-1}}{1-\beta}\chi_{\{d=t-1\}}+\left(c+\beta\int V(w_t)d\theta_{w_{t-1}}\right)\chi_{\{d>t-1\}}\Bigg)d\theta_{w_{t-2}}\\
&\cdots\Bigg)\chi_{\{d>1\}}\Bigg)d\theta_{w_0}\Bigg)\chi_{\{d>0\}}\Bigg]\Bigg|\\
&=\beta\Bigg|\int\Bigg(\frac{w_1}{1-\beta}\chi_{\{d=1\}}+\Bigg(c+\cdots\beta\int\Bigg(\frac{w_{t-1}}{1-\beta}\chi_{\{d=t-1\}}\\
&\quad+\left(c+\beta\int I_{w_t}(d|_{1}{}_{\mathbf{w}_t})d\theta_{w_{t-1}}\right)\chi_{\{d>t-1\}}\Bigg)d\theta_{w_{t-2}}\cdots\Bigg)\chi_{\{d>1\}}\Bigg)d\theta_{w_0}\\
&\quad-\int\Bigg(\frac{w_1}{1-\beta}\chi_{\{d=1\}}+\Bigg(c+\cdots\beta\int\Bigg(\frac{w_{t-1}}{1-\beta}\chi_{\{d=t-1\}}
\end{aligned}$$

$$
+\left(c+\beta\int V(w_t)d\theta_{w_{t-1}}\right)\chi_{\{d>t-1\}}\Big)d\theta_{w_{t-2}}\cdots\Big)\chi_{\{d>1\}}\Big)d\theta_{w_0}\Bigg|\chi_{\{d>0\}}
$$

$$
\begin{aligned}
&\leq \beta\int\beta\Bigg|\int\left(\frac{w_2}{1-\beta}\chi_{\{d=2\}}+\cdots\beta\int\left(\frac{w_{t-1}}{1-\beta}\chi_{\{d=t-1\}}\right.\right.\\
&\quad+\left.\left.\left(c+\beta\int I_{w_t}\left(d|_{1}\mathbf{w}_t\right)d\theta_{w_{t-1}}\right)\chi_{\{d>t-1\}}\right)\cdots\right)d\theta_{w_1}\\
&\quad-\int\left(\frac{w_2}{1-\beta}\chi_{\{d=2\}}+\cdots\beta\int\left(\frac{w_{t-1}}{1-\beta}\chi_{\{d=t-1\}}\right.\right.\\
&\quad+\left.\left.\left(c+\beta\int V(w_t)d\theta_{w_{t-1}}\right)\chi_{\{d>t-1\}}\right)\cdots\right)d\theta_{w_1}\Bigg|\chi_{\{d>1\}}d\theta'_{w_0}\chi_{\{d>0\}}\\
&\leq\cdots\cdots\cdots\\
&\leq\beta\int\beta\int\cdots\\
&\quad\beta\int\left|I_{w_t}\left(d|_{1}\mathbf{w}_t\right)-V(w_t)\right|d\theta'_{w_{t-1}}\chi_{\{d>t-1\}}\cdots d\theta'_{w_1}\chi_{\{d>1\}}d\theta'_{w_0}\chi_{\{d>0\}}\\
&=\beta^t\int\int\cdots\int\left|I_{w_t}\left(d|_{1}\mathbf{w}_t\right)-V(w_t)\right|\chi_{\{d>t-1\}}d\theta'_{w_{t-1}}\cdots d\theta'_{w_1}d\theta'_{w_0}\\
&\leq\beta^t\int\int\cdots\int\max\{I_{w_t}\left(d|_{1}\mathbf{w}_t\right)\chi_{\{d>t-1\}},\ V(w_t)\}d\theta'_{w_{t-1}}\cdots d\theta'_{w_1}d\theta'_{w_0}\\
&\leq\beta^t\int\int\cdots\int V^+(w_t)\,d\theta'_{w_{t-1}}\cdots d\theta'_{w_1}d\theta'_{w_0},
\end{aligned}
$$

where a series of inequalities in the middle holds by successive applications of Theorem 2.4.3, and the last inequality holds by the admissibility of V. Finally, Lemma A.4.5 completes the proof. ∎

Lemma A.4.7 *Any admissible solution to Bellman's equation is the value function.*

Proof Let V be any admissible solution to Bellman's equation, and let $w_0 \in W$. This paragraph shows that $V(w_0) \geq I_{w_0}(d)$ for any $d \in \Delta$. Let $d \in \Delta$ be any stopping rule. Then, that V solves Bellman's equation implies that for any $t > 0$,

$$
\begin{aligned}
& V(w_0) \\
\geq\; & \frac{w_0}{1-\beta}\chi_{\{d=0\}} + \left(c + \beta \int V(w_1) d\theta_{w_0}\right) \chi_{\{d>0\}} \\
\geq\; & \frac{w_0}{1-\beta}\chi_{\{d=0\}} + \left(c + \beta \int \left(\frac{w_1}{1-\beta}\chi_{\{d=1\}} + \right.\right. \\
& \left.\left.\left(c + \beta \int V(w_2) d\theta_{w_1}\right)\chi_{\{d>1\}}\right) d\theta_{w_0}\right)\chi_{\{d>0\}} \\
\geq\; & \cdots\cdots\cdots \\
\geq\; & \frac{w_0}{1-\beta}\chi_{\{d=0\}} + \left(c + \beta \int \left(\frac{w_1}{1-\beta}\chi_{\{d=1\}} + \left(c + \right.\right.\right. \\
& \cdots \beta \int \left(\frac{w_{t-1}}{1-\beta}\chi_{\{d=t-1\}} + \left(c + \beta \int V(w_t) d\theta_{w_{t-1}}\right)\chi_{\{d>t-1\}}\right) d\theta_{w_{t-2}} \\
& \left.\left.\left.\cdots\right)\chi_{\{d>1\}}\right) d\theta_{w_0}\right)\chi_{\{d>0\}}.
\end{aligned}
$$

Hence, Lemma A.4.6 proves the claim by the admissibility of V.

This paragraph shows that there exists a stopping rule $d \in \Delta$ such that $V(w_0) = I_{w_0}(d)$. Let d be the stopping rule such that for all $t \geq 0$, $d = t$ as soon as

$$
\frac{w_t}{1-\beta} \geq c + \beta \int_W V(w_{t+1}) \theta_{w_t}(dw_{t+1})
$$

holds; and $d > t$ otherwise. Then, that V solves Bellman's equation implies that for any $t > 0$,

$$
\begin{aligned}
& V(w_0) \\
=\; & \frac{w_0}{1-\beta}\chi_{\{d=0\}} + \left(c + \beta \int V(w_1) d\theta_{w_0}\right) \chi_{\{d>0\}} \\
=\; & \frac{w_0}{1-\beta}\chi_{\{d=0\}} + \left(c + \beta \int \left(\frac{w_1}{1-\beta}\chi_{\{d=1\}} \right.\right. \\
& \left.\left. + \left(c + \beta \int V(w_2) d\theta_{w_1}\right)\chi_{\{d>1\}}\right) d\theta_{w_0}\right)\chi_{\{d>0\}} \\
=\; & \cdots\cdots\cdots \\
=\; & \frac{w_0}{1-\beta}\chi_{\{d=0\}} + \left(c + \beta \int \left(\frac{w_1}{1-\beta}\chi_{\{d=1\}} + \left(c + \right.\right.\right. \\
& \cdots \beta \int \left(\frac{w_{t-1}}{1-\beta}\chi_{\{d=t-1\}} + \left(c + \beta \int V(w_t) d\theta_{w_{t-1}}\right)\chi_{\{d>t-1\}}\right) d\theta_{w_{t-2}} \\
& \left.\left.\left.\cdots\right)\chi_{\{d>1\}}\right) d\theta_{w_0}\right)\chi_{\{d>0\}}.
\end{aligned}
$$

Again, Lemma A.4.6 proves the claim by the admissibility of V. ■

Lemma A.4.8 *Both* $\lim_{n\to\infty} B^n V^-$ *and* $\lim_{n\to\infty} B^n V^+$ *are admissible solutions to Bellman's equation.*

Proof $\langle B^n V^- \rangle$ is weakly increasing and $\langle B^n V^+ \rangle$ is weakly decreasing by Lemma A.4.4, and hence, the limits exist. Lemma A.4.4 also shows that these limits are admissible. Finally, the limits solve Bellman's equation by the monotone convergence theorem (Theorem 2.4.6). ■

A.4.2 Proof of Theorem 9.4.1

The first half of the claim follows immediately from Lemmas A.4.7 and A.4.8. The second half of the claim also follows immediately from the proof of Lemma A.4.7. ■

A.4.3 Proof of Corollary 9.4.1

It suffices to show that V^* is weakly increasing in w by the monotonicity of θ in the sense of (2.3) and the definition of R. This, however, follows immediately from the facts that BV is weakly increasing when V is weakly increasing by the monotonicity of θ, that V^- is weakly increasing (it is actually constant), and that $V^* = \lim_{n\to\infty} B^n V^-$. ■

A.4.4 Proof of Corollary 9.4.2

By the definition of the reservation wage, R is constant. Furthermore, R satisfies the first equation because

$$
\begin{aligned}
\frac{R}{1-\beta} &= c + \beta \int_W V^*(w)\theta(dw) \\
&= c + \beta \int_0^\infty \theta\left(\{\, w \mid V^*(w) \geq x \,\}\right) dx \\
&= c + \beta V^*(R) + \beta \int_{V^*(R)}^\infty \theta\left(\{\, w \mid V^*(w) \geq x \,\}\right) dx \\
&= c + \beta V^*(R) + \beta \int_{V^*(R)}^\infty \theta\left(\{\, w \mid w/(1-\beta) \geq x \,\}\right) dx
\end{aligned}
$$

$$= c + \frac{\beta}{1-\beta} R + \beta \int_{R/(1-\beta)}^{\infty} \theta(\{ w \mid w/(1-\beta) \geq x \})\, dx$$

$$= c + \frac{\beta}{1-\beta} R + \frac{\beta}{1-\beta} \int_{R}^{\infty} \theta(\{ w \mid w \geq x \})\, dx ,$$

where the first equality holds by the definition of R; the second equality holds by the definition of the Choquet integral; the third, fourth, and fifth equalities hold because V^* solves Bellman's equation (Theorem 9.4.1); and the final equality holds by the change of variable. For the second equality, note that for almost all x, it holds that $\theta(\{ w \mid w \geq x \}) = \theta(\{ w \mid w > x \})$ (see Sect. A.1.5). Then, it follows that

$$\begin{aligned}
\int_{R}^{\infty} \theta(\{ w \mid w \geq x \})\, dx &= \int_{R}^{\infty} \theta(\{ w \mid w > x \})\, dx \\
&= \int_{R}^{\infty} \theta\left(\{ w \mid w \leq x \}^c\right) dx \\
&= \int_{R}^{\infty} \left[1 - \left(1 - \theta\left(\{ w \mid w \leq x \}^c\right)\right)\right] dx \\
&= \int_{R}^{\infty} \left[1 - \theta'(\{ w \mid w \leq x \})\right] dx .
\end{aligned}$$

■

A.4.5 Proof of Theorem 9.4.2

For each $i = 1, 2$, let B^i and V^{i*} be the operator defined by (9.21) and the value function corresponding to θ^i. Then, $(\forall V)(\forall w)$

$$\begin{aligned}
B^2 V(w) &= \max \left\{ \frac{w}{1-\beta},\ c + \beta \int_W V(w') \theta_w^2(dw') \right\} \\
&\leq \max \left\{ \frac{w}{1-\beta},\ c + \beta \int_W V(w') \theta_w^1(dw') \right\} = B^1 V(w) ,
\end{aligned}$$

where the inequality holds by the fundamental theorem of the Choquet integral (Theorem 2.41) and (9.24). Therefore, it follows that $V^{2*} \leq V^{1*}$ by this, the fact that $B^i V' \geq B^i V$ whenever $V' \geq V$, and that $V^{i*} = \lim_{n\to\infty} (B^i)^n V^-$ by Lemma A.4.8. Finally, we conclude that $(\forall w)$

$$\begin{aligned}\frac{R^2(w)}{1-\beta} &= c + \beta \int_W V^{2*}(w')\theta^2_w(dw') \\ &\leq c + \beta \int_W V^{1*}(w')\theta^2_w(dw') \\ &\leq c + \beta \int_W V^{1*}(w')\theta^1_w(dw') \;=\; \frac{R^1(w)}{1-\beta},\end{aligned}$$

where the first inequality holds by the remark made above, and the second inequality holds by the fundamental theorem of the Choquet integral (Theorem 2.4.1) and (9.24). ■

A.5 Proofs for Chap. 10

A.5.1 *Proof of Theorem 10.3.1*

Let θ be a density generator, let $\left(z_t^\theta\right)$ be defined by (10.7), and define the measure Q_t^θ by: $(\forall t \in [0,T])(\forall A \in \mathcal{F}_T)$

$$Q_t^\theta(A) := \int_A z_t^\theta \, dP\,.$$

To show the theorem, we prepare a couple of lemmas.

The first lemma shows that Q_t^θ is a probability measure that coincides with Q^θ over $\mathcal{F}_t$. This is a direct implication of the martingale property of $\left(z_t^\theta\right)$.

Lemma A.5.1 *The measure Q_t^θ is a probability measure satisfying* $(\forall A \in \mathcal{F}_t)$ $Q_t^\theta(A) = Q^\theta(A)$, *where Q^θ is defined by* (10.9).

Proof Because $\left(z_t^\theta\right)$ is a martingale, it follows that $Q_t^\theta(\Omega) = E^P\left[z_t^\theta\right] = z_0^\theta = 1$, and hence, Q_t^θ is certainly a probability measure. To show the claimed equality, let $t \in [0,T]$ and $A \in \mathcal{F}_t$. Then,

$$Q_t^\theta(A) = \int_A z_t^\theta \, dP = \int_A E^P\left[z_T^\theta \middle| \mathcal{F}_t\right] dP = \int_A z_T^\theta \, dP = Q^\theta(A)\,,$$

where the second equality holds by the fact that $\left(z_t^\theta\right)$ is a martingale and the third equality holds by the definition of conditional expectation and the assumption that $A \in \mathcal{F}_t$. ■

The next lemma shows that, loosely speaking, the expectation with respect to Q^θ of an $\mathcal{F}_t$-measurable random variable conditional on $\mathcal{F}_s$ depends on the density generator θ only between s and t.

Lemma A.5.2 *Let* $0 \le s \le t \le T$ *and* x *be an* $\mathcal{F}_t$*-measurable random variable. Then,* $E^{Q^\theta}[x \mid \mathcal{F}_s]$ *depends only on* $(\theta_u)_{s \le u < t}$.

Proof First, note that

$$E^{Q^\theta}[x \mid \mathcal{F}_s] = \frac{1}{z_s^\theta} E^P\left[x z_t^\theta \mid \mathcal{F}_s\right]. \tag{A.21}$$

To see this, let $A \in \mathcal{F}_s$. Then,

$$\begin{aligned}
\int_A \frac{1}{z_s^\theta} E^P\left[x z_t^\theta \mid \mathcal{F}_s\right] dQ^\theta &= \int_A \frac{1}{z_s^\theta} E^P\left[x z_t^\theta \mid \mathcal{F}_s\right] dQ_s^\theta \\
&= \int_A \frac{1}{z_s^\theta} E^P\left[x z_t^\theta \mid \mathcal{F}_s\right] z_s^\theta \, dP \\
&= \int_A E^P\left[x z_t^\theta \mid \mathcal{F}_s\right] dP \\
&= \int_A x z_t^\theta \, dP = \int_A x \, dQ_t^\theta = \int_A x \, dQ^\theta,
\end{aligned}$$

where each equality holds by: Lemma A.5.1 and the fact that the integrand is $\mathcal{F}_s$-measurable (first); the definition of Q_s^θ (second); cancellation (third); the definition of conditional expectation and the fact that $A \in \mathcal{F}_s$ (fourth); the definition of Q_t^θ (fifth); and Lemma A.5.1 and the fact that the integrand is $\mathcal{F}_t$-measurable (sixth). Because the whole equality holds for any $A \in \mathcal{F}_s$, (A.21) follows by the definition of conditional expectation.

Second, the right-hand side of (A.21) is rewritten as

$$\frac{1}{z_s^\theta} E^P\left[x z_t^\theta \mid \mathcal{F}_s\right] = E^P\left[x \exp\left(-\frac{1}{2}\int_s^t \theta_u \, du - \int_s^t \theta_u \, dB_u\right) \Big| \, \mathcal{F}_s\right]$$

by the definition of $\left(z_t^\theta\right)$. This shows that $E^{Q^\theta}[x \mid \mathcal{F}_s]$ depends only on $(\theta_u)_{s \le u \le t}$. In fact, it depends only on $(\theta_u)_{s \le u < t}$ because stochastic processes $\left(\int_0^t \theta_u \, du\right)_t$ and $\left(\int_0^t \theta_u \, dB_u\right)_t$ have a continuous sample path for each $\omega \in \Omega$ (Karatzas and Shreve 1991, p. 140, Remark 2.11). This completes the proof. ∎

Proof of Theorem 10.3.1. To show that "$\ge$" holds, let θ^* be such that $E^{Q^{\theta^*}}[E^{Q^{\theta^*}}[x|\mathcal{F}_t]|\mathcal{F}_s] = \min_{\theta \in \Theta} E^{Q^\theta}[E^{Q^\theta}[x|\mathcal{F}_t]|\mathcal{F}_s]$. Then, $\min_{\theta \in \Theta} E^{Q^\theta}[E^{Q^\theta}[x|\mathcal{F}_t]|\mathcal{F}_s] = E^{Q^{\theta^*}}[E^{Q^{\theta^*}}[x|\mathcal{F}_t]|\mathcal{F}_s] \ge E^{Q^{\theta^*}}[\min_{\theta' \in \Theta} E^{Q^{\theta'}}[x|\mathcal{F}_t]|\mathcal{F}_s] \ge \min_{\theta \in \Theta} E^{Q^\theta}[\min_{\theta' \in \Theta} E^{Q^{\theta'}}[x|\mathcal{F}_t]|\mathcal{F}_s]$.

To show that "$\le$" holds, let θ^* and θ'^* be such that $E^{Q^{\theta^*}}[E^{Q^{\theta'^*}}[x|\mathcal{F}_t]|\mathcal{F}_s] = \min_{\theta \in \Theta} E^{Q^\theta}[\min_{\theta' \in \Theta} E^{Q^{\theta'}}[x|\mathcal{F}_t]|\mathcal{F}_s]$. Also, we define θ^{**} by: $\left(\theta_u^{**}\right)_{0 \le u < t} := \left(\theta_u^*\right)_{0 \le u < t}$ and $\left(\theta_u^{**}\right)_{t \le u \le T} := \left(\theta_u'^*\right)_{t \le u \le T}$. Then, strong rectangularity implies that $\theta^{**} \in \Theta$. Furthermore, $\min_{\theta \in \Theta} E^{Q^\theta}[\min_{\theta' \in \Theta} E^{Q^{\theta'}}[x|\mathcal{F}_t]|\mathcal{F}_s] = E^{Q^{\theta^*}}[E^{Q^{\theta'^*}}[x|\mathcal{F}_t]|$

$\mathcal{F}_s] = E^{Q^{\theta^{**}}}[E^{Q^{\theta^{**}}}[x|\mathcal{F}_t]|\mathcal{F}_s] \geq \min_{\theta\in\Theta} E^{Q^{\theta}}[E^{Q^{\theta}}[x|\mathcal{F}_t]|\mathcal{F}_s]$, where the second equality holds by Lemma A.5.2 and the inequality holds by the fact that $\theta^{**} \in \Theta$. ■

A.5.2 *Proof of Proposition 10.4.1*

We first show that for any $s \geq t$ and any $\theta \in \Theta^{(K_t)}$,

$$\begin{aligned} & E^{Q^{\theta}}\left[\exp\left(-\int_t^s \sigma\theta_r\,dr + \sigma\left(B_s^{\theta} - B_t^{\theta}\right)\right)\middle|\,\mathcal{F}_t\right] \\ & \geq E^{Q^{\theta^*}}\left[\exp\left(-\int_t^s \sigma\theta_r^*\,dr + \sigma\left(B_s^{\theta^*} - B_t^{\theta^*}\right)\right)\middle|\,\mathcal{F}_t\right]. \end{aligned} \tag{A.22}$$

To do this, let $s \geq t$ and $\theta \in \Theta^{(K_t)}$. Note that by the definition of (θ_t^*), it holds that $(\forall\omega)$

$$\exp\left(-\int_t^s \sigma\theta_r\,dr + \sigma\left(B_s^{\theta} - B_t^{\theta}\right)\right) \geq \exp\left(-\int_t^s \sigma\theta_r^*\,dr + \sigma\left(B_s^{\theta} - B_t^{\theta}\right)\right).$$

Thus, the monotonicity of conditional expectation (Billingsley 1986, p. 468, Theorem 34.2(iii)) implies that

$$\begin{aligned} & E^{Q^{\theta}}\left[\exp\left(-\int_t^s \sigma\theta_r\,dr + \sigma\left(B_s^{\theta} - B_t^{\theta}\right)\right)\middle|\,\mathcal{F}_t\right] \\ & \geq E^{Q^{\theta}}\left[\exp\left(-\int_t^s \sigma\theta_r^*\,dr + \sigma\left(B_s^{\theta} - B_t^{\theta}\right)\right)\middle|\,\mathcal{F}_t\right] \\ & = \exp\left(-\int_t^s \sigma\theta_r^*\,dr\right)\exp\left(\frac{1}{2}\sigma^2(s-t)\right) \\ & = E^{Q^{\theta^*}}\left[\exp\left(-\int_t^s \sigma\theta_r^*\,dr + \sigma\left(B_s^{\theta^*} - B_t^{\theta^*}\right)\right)\middle|\,\mathcal{F}_t\right], \end{aligned}$$

where we invoked the "degeneracy" of (θ_t^*) to show the equalities. Consequently, (A.22) holds.

We can now rewrite W as follows:

$$\begin{aligned} W(\pi_t, t) &= \inf_{\theta\in\Theta} E^{Q^{\theta}}\left[\int_t^T e^{-\rho(s-t)}\pi_s\,ds\,\middle|\,\mathcal{F}_t\right] \\ &= \inf_{\theta\in\Theta}\int_t^T E^{Q^{\theta}}\left[e^{-\rho(s-t)}\pi_s \,\middle|\, \mathcal{F}_t\right] ds \\ &= \inf_{\theta\in\Theta}\int_t^T \pi_t \exp\left(\left(\mu-\rho-\frac{1}{2}\sigma^2\right)(s-t)\right) \times \end{aligned}$$

$$
\begin{aligned}
& E^{Q^{\theta}}\left[\exp\left(-\int_t^s \sigma\theta_r\,dr+\sigma\left(B_s^{\theta}-B_t^{\theta}\right)\right)\,\middle|\,\mathcal{F}_t\right]ds \\
&= \int_t^T \pi_t \exp\left(\left(\mu-\rho-\frac{1}{2}\sigma^2\right)(s-t)\right)\times \\
&\quad E^{Q^{\theta^*}}\left[\exp\left(-\int_t^s \sigma\theta_r^*\,dr+\sigma\left(B_s^{\theta^*}-B_t^{\theta^*}\right)\right)\,\middle|\,\mathcal{F}_t\right]ds \\
&= \int_t^T \pi_t \exp\left(\left(\mu-\rho-\frac{1}{2}\sigma^2\right)(s-t)-\int_t^s \sigma\theta_r^*\,dr\right)\times \\
&\quad E^{Q^{\theta^*}}\left[\exp\sigma\left(B_s^{\theta^*}-B_t^{\theta^*}\right)\,\middle|\,\mathcal{F}_t\right]ds \\
&= \int_t^T \pi_t \exp\left(\left(\mu-\rho-\frac{1}{2}\sigma^2\right)(s-t)-\int_t^s \sigma\theta_r^*\,dr\right)\times \\
&\quad \exp\left(\frac{1}{2}\sigma^2(s-t)\right)ds \\
&= \int_t^T \pi_t \exp\left(-(\rho-\mu)(s-t)-\int_t^s \sigma\theta_r^*\,dr\right)ds\,,
\end{aligned}
$$

where the first equality holds by (10.10); the second equality holds by Fubini's theorem for conditional expectation (Ethier and Kurtz 1986, p. 74, Proposition 4.6)[2]; the third equality holds by (10.29); the fourth equality is derived from (10.21); the fifth equality holds by the fact that $\left(\theta_t^*\right)$ is a "degenerate" stochastic process; and the sixth equality holds by the fact that $\left(B_t^{\theta^*}\right)$ is the Brownian motion with respect to Q^{θ^*} and the formula for the expectation of a lognormal distribution (see, for example, Mood et al. 1974). Thus, the proof of Proposition 10.4.1 is complete. ■

[2] Given that Brownian motion is a measurable process (Billingsley 1986, p. 530, Theorem 37.2) and (θ_t) is a measurable process by assumption, (π_t) is also a measurable process by (10.13), and hence, a function $(s,\omega)\mapsto e^{-\rho(s-t)}\pi_s(\omega)$ is $(\mathcal{B}([t,T])\otimes\mathcal{F}_T)$-measurable. Furthermore, it also holds from (10.13) that

$$\int_t^T E^{Q^{\theta}}[\,|e^{-\rho(s-t)}\pi_s|\,]\,ds<+\infty\,.$$

Therefore, we may invoke Ethier and Kurtz (1986, p. 74, Proposition 4.6) to conclude that there exists a function $f:[t,T]\times\Omega\to\mathbb{R}$ such that f is $(\mathcal{B}([t,T])\otimes\mathcal{F}_t)$-measurable, $(\forall s,\omega)\ f(s,\omega)=E^{Q^{\theta}}[e^{-\rho(s-t)}\pi_s|\mathcal{F}_t](\omega)$, $\int_t^T|f(s,\omega)|\,ds<+\infty$ P-a.s., and

$$(\forall\omega)\quad \int_t^T f(s,\omega)\,ds=E^{Q^{\theta}}\left[\int_t^T e^{-\rho(s-t)}\pi_s\,ds\,\middle|\,\mathcal{F}_t\right](\omega)\,,$$

justifying the second equality.

A.5.3 Derivation of Hamilton–Jacobi–Bellman Equation (10.20)

We obtain

$$
\begin{aligned}
V_t &= \max_{t' \geq t} \min_{Q \in \mathcal{P}^{\Theta}} E^{Q}\left[\int_{t'}^{T} e^{-\rho(s-t)} \pi_s \, ds - e^{-\rho(t'-t)} I \,\middle|\, \mathcal{F}_t \right] \\
&= \max \left\{ \min_{Q \in \mathcal{P}^{\Theta}} E^{Q}\left[\int_{t}^{T} e^{-\rho(s-t)} \pi_s ds \,\middle|\, \mathcal{F}_t \right] - I, \right. \\
&\qquad \left. \max_{t' \geq t + dt} \min_{Q \in \mathcal{P}^{\Theta}} E^{Q}\left[\int_{t'}^{T} e^{-\rho(s-t)} \pi_s \, ds - e^{-\rho(t'-t)} I \,\middle|\, \mathcal{F}_t \right] \right\} \\
&= \max \left\{ W_t - I, \ \max_{t' \geq t+dt} \min_{Q \in \mathcal{P}^{\Theta}} E^{Q}\left[\int_{t'}^{T} e^{-\rho(s-t)} \pi_s \, ds - e^{-\rho(t'-t)} I \,\middle|\, \mathcal{F}_t \right] \right\} \\
&= \max \left\{ W_t - I, \ \max_{t' \geq t+dt} \min_{\theta \in \Theta} E^{Q^{\theta}}\left[\int_{t'}^{T} e^{-\rho(s-t)} \pi_s \, ds - e^{-\rho(t'-t)} I \,\middle|\, \mathcal{F}_t \right] \right\} \\
&= \max \left\{ W_t - I, \ e^{-\rho \, dt} \max_{t' \geq t+dt} \min_{\theta \in \Theta} E^{Q^{\theta}}\left[\right. \right. \\
&\qquad \left. \left. E^{Q^{\theta}}\left[\int_{t'}^{T} e^{-\rho(s-t-dt)} \pi_s ds - e^{-\rho(t'-t-dt)} I \,\middle|\, \mathcal{F}_{t+dt} \right] \middle|\, \mathcal{F}_t \right] \right\} \\
&= \max \left\{ W_t - I, e^{-\rho \, dt} \max_{t' \geq t+dt} \min_{\theta \in \Theta} E^{Q^{\theta}} \right. \\
&\qquad \left. \left[\min_{\theta' \in \Theta} E^{Q^{\theta'}}\left[\int_{t'}^{T} e^{-\rho(s-t-dt)} \pi_s ds - e^{-\rho(t'-t-dt)} I \,\middle|\, \mathcal{F}_{t+dt} \right] \middle|\, \mathcal{F}_t \right] \right\} \\
&= \max \left\{ W_t - I, e^{-\rho \, dt} \min_{\theta \in \Theta} E^{Q^{\theta}} \right. \\
&\qquad \left. \left[\max_{t' \geq t+dt} \min_{\theta' \in \Theta} E^{Q^{\theta'}}\left[\int_{t'}^{T} e^{-\rho(s-t-dt)} \pi_s ds - e^{-\rho(t'-t-dt)} I \,\middle|\, \mathcal{F}_{t+dt} \right] \middle|\, \mathcal{F}_t \right] \right\} \\
&= \max \left\{ W_t - I, \ e^{-\rho \, dt} \min_{\theta \in \Theta} E^{Q^{\theta}} \left[\ V_{t+dt} \mid \mathcal{F}_t \ \right] \right\} \\
&= \max \left\{ W_t - I, \ (1 - \rho \, dt) \left(\min_{\theta \in \Theta} E^{Q^{\theta}} \left[\, dV_t \mid \mathcal{F}_t \, \right] + V_t \right) \right\} \\
&= \max \left\{ W_t - I, \ \min_{\theta \in \Theta} E^{Q^{\theta}} \left[\, dV_t \mid \mathcal{F}_t \, \right] + V_t - \rho V_t dt \right\},
\end{aligned}
$$

where each equality holds by: the definition of V_t, (10.19) (first); splitting the decision between investing now (at time t) and waiting for a short time interval and reconsidering whether to invest afterward (at time $t + dt$) (second); the definition of W_t, (10.16) (third); the definition of $\mathcal{P}^{\Theta}$, (10.10) (fourth); the law of iterated integrals (fifth); the rectangularity, (10.15) (sixth); the fact that t' is restricted to be greater than or equal to $t + dt$ (seventh); the definition of V_t, (10.19), with t replaced by $t+dt$ (eighth); writing V_{t+dt} as $V_t + dV_t$ and approximating $e^{-\rho dt}$ by $(1-\rho dt)$ (such an approximation is justified because we let dt go to zero) (ninth); and eliminating the term that is of a higher order than dt (tenth). ∎

A.5.4 Derivation of Eq. (10.30)

We get

$$\begin{aligned}
&\min_{Q\in\mathcal{P}^{\Theta}} E^{Q}\left[\, dV_t \mid \mathcal{F}_t \,\right] = \min_{\theta\in\Theta} E^{Q^{\theta}}\left[\, dV_t \mid \mathcal{F}_t \,\right] \\
&= \min_{\theta\in\Theta} E^{Q^{\theta}}\Big[V'(W_t)\left((\mu - \sigma\theta_t)W_t dt + \sigma W_t dB_t^{\theta}\right) \\
&\quad + (1/2)\sigma^2 W_t^2 V''(W_t)\, dt \,\Big|\, \mathcal{F}_t \Big] \\
&= \min_{\theta\in\Theta} V'(W_t)(\mu - \sigma\theta_t)W_t dt + (1/2)\sigma^2 W_t^2 V''(W_t)\, dt \\
&= V'(W_t)(\mu - \kappa\sigma)W_t dt + (1/2)\sigma^2 W_t^2 V''(W_t)\, dt\,,
\end{aligned}$$

where the first equality holds by the definition of $\mathcal{P}^{\Theta}$; the second equality holds by the fact that (10.29) holds for each θ; the third equality holds by the fact that $\left(B_t^{\theta}\right)$ is the Brownian motion with respect to Q^{θ}; and the last equality holds by (10.21) and the conjecture that V' is positive. ∎

A.5.5 Solution of Eq. (10.31)

To solve (10.31) with boundary conditions (10.32)–(10.34), consider the following quadratic equation called the *characteristic equation* for (10.31): $\sigma^2 x(x-1)/2 + (\mu - \kappa\sigma)x - \rho = 0$, the solutions to which are given by α defined by (10.37) and its conjugate, β. It turns out that $\alpha > 1$ and $\beta < 0$ (see Sect. A.5.6 below). Furthermore, it can be easily verified that both W_t^{α} and W_t^{β} solve (10.31) and that the Wronskian of W_t^{α} and W_t^{β} is nonzero for any $W_t > 0$. (Here, the *Wronskian* of the two functions f_1 and f_2 is defined by $W(f_1, f_2) := f_1 f_2' - f_1' f_2$, and $W(W_t^{\alpha}, W_t^{\beta}) = (\beta-\alpha)W_t^{\alpha+\beta-1}$.) Hence, any solution to (10.31) can be expressed uniquely as a linear combination of W_t^{α} and W_t^{β}; that is,

$$V(W_t) = AW_t^{\alpha} + BW_t^{\beta}\,, \tag{A.23}$$

where A and B are some reals (Boyce 1986, p. 116, Theorem 3.4). Conversely, it is obvious that any function of the form (A.23) is a solution to (10.31). We conclude that (A.23) exhausts all the solutions to (10.31).

We now turn to the boundary conditions. The negativity of β and (10.32) immediately imply that $B = 0$, and hence, that $V(W_t) = AW_t^\alpha$, where A still remains undetermined. This, (10.33), and (10.34) imply the following two equations: $A(W^*)^\alpha = W^* - I$ and $\alpha A (W^*)^{\alpha-1} = 1$, which can be solved to give the solution in the text. ■

A.5.6 *Proof that* $\alpha > 1$ *and* $\beta < 0$

To see that $\alpha > 1$, note that

$$\alpha > \frac{-\left(\mu - \kappa\sigma - \frac{1}{2}\sigma^2\right) + \sqrt{\left(\mu - \kappa\sigma - \frac{1}{2}\sigma^2\right)^2 + 2(\mu - \kappa\sigma)\sigma^2}}{\sigma^2}$$

$$= \frac{-\left(\mu - \kappa\sigma - \frac{1}{2}\sigma^2\right) + \left|\mu - \kappa\sigma + \frac{1}{2}\sigma^2\right|}{\sigma^2},$$

where the strict inequality holds because $\rho > \mu - \kappa\sigma$ by the assumption that $\rho > \mu$ and $\kappa \geq 0$. Our claim follows because the last term is unity if $\mu - \kappa\sigma \geq -\frac{1}{2}\sigma^2$ and more than unity if $\mu - \kappa\sigma < -\frac{1}{2}\sigma^2$.

On the other hand, β, the conjugate of α, is negative because

$$\beta = \frac{-\left(\mu - \kappa\sigma - \frac{1}{2}\sigma^2\right) - \sqrt{\left(\mu - \kappa\sigma - \frac{1}{2}\sigma^2\right)^2 + 2\rho\sigma^2}}{\sigma^2}$$

$$< \frac{-\left(\mu - \kappa\sigma - \frac{1}{2}\sigma^2\right) - \left|\mu - \kappa\sigma - \frac{1}{2}\sigma^2\right|}{\sigma^2} \leq 0,$$

where the strict inequality holds because $\rho > 0$. ■

A.6 Proofs for Chap. 11

A.6.1 *Proof of Lemma 11.3.1*

First, we show that for any admissible function v, the mapping defined by

$$(m', z) \mapsto \int_Z v(m', z')\, \theta_z(dz')$$

is u.s.c. The admissibility of v implies that v is u.s.c. and that there exists $N \geq 1$ such that $(\forall n \geq N)(\forall z')\ v(m'_n, z') \leq v^+(m'_n) < v^+(m'_0) + 1$ because v^+ is u.s.c. (in fact, it is continuous). Therefore, we need to prove the upper semi-continuity of θ on $Z \times \mathbb{R}_+$ beneath any constant function. This is, however, the maintained assumption in this chapter, and hence, the proof of the claim is complete.

Second, we complete the proof by showing that for any admissible function v, Bv is well defined. However, this follows immediately because the maximand in (11.6) is u.s.c. in (x, m') by the fact proven in the previous paragraph and because Γ is compact-valued. ■

A.6.2 Proof of Lemma 11.3.2

The first half of the lemma follows because $(\forall m, z)$

$$\begin{aligned} Bv^+(m, z) &= \max\left\{ xz + \beta B^+ m' + \beta A^+ \;\middle|\; (x, m') \in \Gamma(m) \right\} \\ &\leq mz + \beta B^+(m + y) + \beta A^+ \\ &\leq m\bar{z} + \beta B^+(m + y) + \beta A^+ \\ &= m\bar{z}/(1 - \beta) + \beta y \bar{z}/(1 - \beta)^2 \;=\; v^+(m, z)\,. \end{aligned}$$

To show the latter half of the lemma, let v be an admissible function. Then, the admissibility of v, the fact that B is monotonically nondecreasing in v, and the inequality proven in the previous paragraph show that $0 \leq B0 \leq Bv \leq Bv^+ \leq v^+$. Furthermore, Bv is u.s.c. by the maximum theorem (Berge 1963) because the maximand in (11.6) is u.s.c. by Sect. A.6.1 and because Γ is continuous. Finally, the nondecrease is immediate. ■

A.6.3 Proof of Theorem 11.3.1

To prove the theorem, we need a series of lemmas.

Lemma A.6.1 *For any $m \geq 0$, any investment strategy ${}_0\mathbf{x}$ that is feasible from m and its associated money-holding strategy ${}_1\mathbf{m}$, and any admissible function v, it holds that* $(\forall z)$

$$I_z({}_0\mathbf{x}) = \lim_{T \to +\infty} x_0 z + \beta \int_Z \cdots$$

$$\beta \int_Z \left(x_{T-1} z_{T-1} + \beta \int_Z v(m_T, z_T)\, \theta_{z_{T-1}}(dz_T) \right) \theta_{z_{T-2}}(dz_{T-1}) \cdots \theta_z(dz_1)$$

Proof Let $(m, z) \in \mathbb{R}_+ \times Z$, let ${}_0\boldsymbol{x}$ be an investment strategy that is feasible from m and let v be an admissible function. The iterated applications of Koopmans' equation to ${}_0\boldsymbol{x}$ shows that $(\forall T \geq 1)$

$$I_z({}_0\boldsymbol{x}) = x_0 z + \beta \int_Z \cdots$$
$$\beta \int_Z \left(x_{T-1} z_{T-1} + \beta \int_Z I_{z_T}({}_T\boldsymbol{x})\, \theta_{z_{T-1}}(dz_T) \right) \theta_{z_{T-2}}(dz_{T-1}) \cdots \theta_z(dz_1),$$

where ${}_T\boldsymbol{x}$ is a continuation of ${}_0\boldsymbol{x}$ after the realization of ${}_1z_T$. Therefore, for any $T \geq 1$, it follows that

$$\Bigg| I_z({}_0\boldsymbol{x}) - \Bigg[x_0 z + \beta \int_Z \cdots \beta \int_Z \Bigg(x_{T-1} z_{T-1}$$
$$+ \beta \int_Z v(m_T, z_T) \theta_{z_{T-1}}(dz_T) \Bigg) \theta_{z_{T-2}}(dz_{T-1}) \cdots \theta_z(dz_1) \Bigg] \Bigg|$$
$$= \beta \Bigg| \int_Z \cdots \beta \int_Z \Bigg(x_{T-1} z_{T-1}$$
$$+ \beta \int_Z I_{z_T}({}_T\boldsymbol{x}) \theta_{z_{T-1}}(dz_T) \Bigg) \theta_{z_{T-2}}(dz_{T-1}) \cdots \theta_z(dz_1)$$
$$- \int_Z \cdots \beta \int_Z \Bigg(x_{T-1} z_{T-1}$$
$$+ \beta \int_Z v(m_T, z_T) \theta_{z_{T-1}}(dz_T) \Bigg) \theta_{z_{T-2}}(dz_{T-1}) \cdots \theta_z(dz_1) \Bigg|$$
$$\leq \beta \int_Z \Bigg| \Bigg(\cdots \beta \int_Z \Bigg(x_{T-1} z_{T-1}$$
$$+ \beta \int_Z I_{z_T}({}_T\boldsymbol{x}) \theta_{z_{T-1}}(dz_T) \Bigg) \theta_{z_{T-2}}(dz_{T-1}) \cdots \Bigg)$$
$$- \Bigg(\cdots \beta \int_Z \Bigg(x_{T-1} z_{T-1}$$
$$+ \beta \int_Z v(m_T, z_T)\, \theta_{z_{T-1}}(dz_T) \Bigg) \theta_{z_{T-2}}(dz_{T-1}) \cdots \Bigg) \Bigg| \theta'_z(dz_1)$$
$$\leq \cdots\cdots\cdots$$
$$\leq \beta^T \int_Z \cdots \int_Z \int_Z \left| I_{z_T}({}_T\boldsymbol{x}) - v(m_T, z_T) \right|$$
$$\theta'_{z_{T-1}}(dz_T) \theta'_{z_{T-2}}(dz_{T-1}) \cdots \theta'_z(dz_1)$$
$$\leq \beta^T \int_Z \cdots \int_Z \int_Z \max \left\{ I_{z_T}({}_T\boldsymbol{x}), v(m_T, z_T) \right\}$$
$$\theta'_{z_{T-1}}(dz_T) \theta'_{z_{T-2}}(dz_{T-1}) \cdots \theta'_z(dz_1)$$

$$\begin{aligned}&\leq \beta^T \int_Z \cdots \int_Z \int_Z v^+(Ty+m)\theta'_{z_{T-1}}(dz_T)\theta'_{z_{T-2}}(dz_{T-1})\cdots\theta'_z(dz_1)\\ &= \beta^T(B^+Ty + B^+m + A^+),\end{aligned}$$

where the first to third inequalities hold by Theorem 2.4.3 and the fifth inequality holds because $(\forall z_T)\ I_{z_T}({}_T\boldsymbol{x}) \leq v^+(Ty+m)$ by the fact that for any investment strategy ${}_0\boldsymbol{x}$ that is feasible from m, $x_T \leq Ty+m$. Because the last term of the above inequalities goes to 0 as $T \to +\infty$, we have

$$\lim_{T\to\infty}\Bigg| I_z({}_0\boldsymbol{x}) - \Bigg[x_0 z + \beta \int_Z \cdots \beta\int_Z \left(x_{T-1}z_{T-1} + \beta\int_Z v(m_T, z_T)\,\theta_{z_{T-1}}(dz_T)\right)\theta_{z_{T-2}}(dz_{T-1}) \cdots \theta_z(dz_1)\Bigg]\Bigg| = 0,$$

which completes the proof. ■

Lemma A.6.2 *Any admissible solution to Bellman's equation is the value function.*

Proof Let v be an admissible function that solves Bellman's equation and let $(m, z) \in \mathbb{R}_+ \times Z$. This paragraph shows that for any investment strategy ${}_0\boldsymbol{x}$ that is feasible from m, it holds that $v(m, z) \geq I_z({}_0\boldsymbol{x})$. Let ${}_0\boldsymbol{x}$ be such an investment strategy and let ${}_1\boldsymbol{m}$ be its associated money-holding strategy. Then,

$$\begin{aligned}v(m,z) &\geq x_0 z + \beta\int_Z v(m_1, z_1)\,\theta_z(dz_1)\\ &\geq x_0 z + \beta\int_Z \left(x_1 z_1 + \beta\int_Z v(m_2, z_2)\,\theta_{z_{T-1}}(dz_2)\right)\theta_z(dz_1)\\ &\geq \cdots\\ &\geq x_0 z + \beta\int_Z \left(x_1 z_1 + \cdots \beta\int_Z v(m_T, z_T)\,\theta_{z_{T-1}}(dz_T)\cdots\right)\theta_z(dz_1)\end{aligned}$$

where the first inequality holds because v solves Bellman's equation and $(x_0, m_1) \in \Gamma(m)$ by the feasibility, the second inequality holds because v solves Bellman's equation and $(x_1, m_2) \in \Gamma(m_1)$ by the feasibility, and so on. Given that the overall inequality holds for any $T \geq 1$, Lemma A.6.1 proves the claim.

This paragraph completes the proof by showing that there exists an investment strategy ${}_0\boldsymbol{x}$ that is feasible from m and satisfies $v(m, z) = I_z({}_0\boldsymbol{x})$. We define the investment strategy ${}_0\boldsymbol{x}$ and the money-holding strategy ${}_1\boldsymbol{m}$ recursively by

$$(x_0, m_1) \in \arg\max\left\{ xz + \beta\int_Z v(m', z')\,\theta_z(dz') \,\middle|\, (x, m') \in \Gamma(m)\right\}$$

and $(\forall t \geq 1)$

$$(x_t, m_{t+1}) \in \arg\max \left\{ x z_t + \beta \int_Z v(m', z')\, \theta_{z_t}(dz') \,\middle|\, (x, m') \in \Gamma(m_t) \right\}.$$

Such strategies are well defined by the measurable selection theorem (Wagner 1977, p. 880, Theorem 9.1(ii)). Then,

$$\begin{aligned} v(m, z) &= x_0 z + \beta \int_Z v(m_1, z_1)\, \theta_z(dz_1) \\ &= x_0 z + \beta \int_Z \left(x_1 z_1 + \beta \int_Z v(m_2, z_2)\, \theta_{z_1}(dz_2) \right) \theta_z(dz_1) \\ &= \cdots \\ &= x_0 z + \beta \int_Z \left(x_1 z_1 + \cdots \beta \int_Z v(m_T, z_T)\, \theta_{z_{T-1}}(dz_T) \cdots \right) \theta_z(dz_1) \end{aligned}$$

where the equalities hold by the definition of ${}_0\boldsymbol{x}$ and ${}_1\boldsymbol{m}$ and because v solves Bellman's equation. Because the overall inequality holds for any $T \geq 1$, Lemma A.6.1 proves the claim. ■

Lemma A.6.3 *A function v^∞ defined by $v^\infty := \lim_{n\to\infty} B^n v^+$ is an admissible solution to Bellman's equation, where B^n denotes the n-fold self-composition of B, $B \circ \cdots \circ B$.*

Proof By Lemma 11.3.2 and the fact that B is nondecreasing in v, $\langle B^n v^+ \rangle_{n=1}^\infty$ is a nonincreasing sequence of u.s.c. functions that are bounded from below by 0, and hence its limit exists and is u.s.c. Therefore, v^∞ is a well-defined admissible function. In the rest of this proof, we show that v^∞ solves Bellman's equation.

Note that $(\forall n \geq 1)$ $B^{n+1} v^+ = B \circ B^n v^+ \geq B \circ \lim_{n\to\infty} B^n v^+ = B v^\infty$. Therefore, we have $v^\infty = \lim_{n\to\infty} B^{n+1} v^+ \geq B v^\infty$.

To show the opposite inequality, let $(m, z) \in \mathbb{R}_+ \times Z$ and let $\langle (x_n, m'_n) \rangle_{n=1}^\infty$ be a sequence in $\mathbb{R}_+^2$ such that $(\forall n \geq 1)$

$$(x_n, m'_n) \in \arg\max \left\{ x z + \beta \int_Z B^n v^+(m', z')\, \theta_z(dz') \,\middle|\, (x, m') \in \Gamma(m) \right\}.$$

Such a sequence exists because the right-hand side is nonempty by Lemma 11.3.1 and the admissibility of $B^n v^+$. Given that $\Gamma(m)$ is compact, there exists a subsequence $\langle (x_{n(i)}, m'_{n(i)}) \rangle_{i=1}^\infty$ that converges to $(x_0, m'_0) \in \Gamma(m)$. Then,

$$\begin{aligned} B v^\infty(m, z) &= \max \left\{ x z + \beta \int_Z v^\infty(m', z')\, \theta_z(dz') \,\middle|\, (x, m') \in \Gamma(m) \right\} \\ &\geq x_0 z + \beta \int_Z v^\infty(m'_0, z')\, \theta_z(dz') \\ &= x_0 z + \beta \int_Z \lim_{n\to\infty} B^n v^+(m'_0, z')\, \theta_z(dz') \end{aligned}$$

$$
\begin{aligned}
&= x_0 z + \beta \int_Z \lim_{i\to\infty} B^{n(i)} v^+(m'_0, z')\, \theta_z(dz') \\
&\geq x_0 z + \beta \int_Z \lim_{i\to\infty} \limsup_{j\to\infty} B^{n(i)} v^+(m'_{n(j)}, z')\, \theta_z(dz') \\
&\geq x_0 z + \beta \int_Z \lim_{i\to\infty} \limsup_{j\to\infty} B^{n(j)} v^+(m'_{n(j)}, z')\, \theta_z(dz') \\
&= x_0 z + \beta \int_Z \limsup_{j\to\infty} B^{n(j)} v^+(m'_{n(j)}, z')\, \theta_z(dz') \\
&\geq x_0 z + \beta \limsup_{j\to\infty} \int_Z B^{n(j)} v^+(m'_{n(j)}, z')\, \theta_z(dz') \\
&= \limsup_{j\to\infty} \left(x_{n(j)} z + \beta \int_Z B^{n(j)} v^+(m'_{n(j)}, z')\, \theta_z(dz') \right) \\
&= \limsup_{j\to\infty} B^{n(j)+1} v^+(m, z) \\
&= \lim_{j\to\infty} B^{n(j)+1} v^+(m, z) \\
&= v^\infty(m, z) ,
\end{aligned}
$$

where the second inequality holds by the u.s.c. of $B^{n(i)} v^+$. To show the fourth inequality, let $J \geq 1$ be such that $(\forall j \geq J)\ m'_{n(j)} < m'_0 + 1$. Then, it follows that $(\forall j \geq J)(\forall z' \in Z)$

$$
B^{n(j)} v^+(m'_{n(j)}, z') \leq v^+(m'_{n(j)}, z') = B^+ m'_{n(j)} + A^+ < B^+(m'_0 + 1) + A^+ .
$$

Therefore, the desired inequality holds by Fatou's lemma (Theorem 2.4.7). ■

Proof of Theorem 11.3.1. Lemmas A.6.2 and A.6.3 show that v^∞ is a value function, and hence, the value function certainly exists. Suppose that v and v' are two admissible solutions to Bellman's equation. Then, it must be that $v = v'$ because both v and v' must be the value function by Lemma A.6.2 and because the value function is unique by its definition. Therefore, the admissible solution to Bellman's equation is unique and equals v^∞ because v^∞ is admissible by Lemma A.6.3. Finally, the second paragraph of the proof of Lemma A.6.2 shows that recursive optimality implies optimality. ■

A.6.4 *Proof of Lemma 11.3.3*

First, we define R^+ by $(\forall z)\ R^+(z) := \bar{z}$. Then, it follows that $(\forall z)$

$$
TR^+(z) = \beta \int_Z \max\left\{z', \bar{z}\right\} \theta_z(dz') = \beta \int_Z \bar{z}\, \theta_z(dz') = \beta\bar{z} \leq \bar{z} = R^+(z) .
$$

Because T is monotonic in the sense that $(\forall R, R')\ R \geq R' \Rightarrow TR \geq TR'$, $\langle T^n R^+ \rangle_{n=1}^{\infty}$ (where T^n denotes the t-fold self-composition of T) is a nonincreasing sequence of functions. Hence, its limit exists and is nondecreasing because each $T^n R^+$ is nondecreasing. We denote this by R^{∞}. We now see that R^{∞} is a fixed point of T because $(\forall z)$

$$\begin{aligned} TR^{\infty}(z) &= \beta \int_Z \max\left\{z', R^{\infty}(z')\right\} \theta_z(dz') \\ &= \beta \int_Z \max\left\{z', \lim_{n\to\infty} T^n R^+(z')\right\} \theta_z(dz') \\ &= \beta \int_Z \lim_{n\to\infty} \max\left\{z', T^n R^+(z')\right\} \theta_z(dz') \\ &= \lim_{n\to\infty} \beta \int_Z \max\left\{z', T^n R^+(z')\right\} \theta_z(dz') \\ &= \lim_{n\to\infty} T^{n+1} R^+(z) \;=\; R^{\infty}(z)\,, \end{aligned}$$

where the fourth inequality holds by the monotone convergence theorem (Theorem 2.4.6).

Second, we define R^- by $(\forall z)\ R^-(z) = 0$. Then, it follows that

$$(\forall z) \quad TR^-(z) = \beta \int_Z \max\left\{z', 0\right\} \theta_z(dz') \geq 0 = R^-(z)\,.$$

Because $(\forall R, R')\ R \geq R' \Rightarrow TR \geq TR'$, $\langle T^n R^- \rangle_{n=1}^{\infty}$ is a nondecreasing sequence of functions. Hence, its limit exists and is nondecreasing because each $T^n R^-$ is nondecreasing. We denote this by R_{∞}. We now see that R_{∞} is a fixed point of T because $(\forall z)$

$$\begin{aligned} TR_{\infty}(z) &= \beta \int_Z \max\left\{z', R_{\infty}(z')\right\} \theta_z(dz') \\ &= \beta \int_Z \max\left\{z', \lim_{n\to\infty} T^n R^-(z')\right\} \theta_z(dz') \\ &= \beta \int_Z \lim_{n\to\infty} \max\left\{z', T^n R^-(z')\right\} \theta_z(dz') \\ &= \lim_{n\to\infty} \beta \int_Z \max\left\{z', T^n R^-(z')\right\} \theta_z(dz') \\ &= \lim_{n\to\infty} T^{n+1} R^-(z) \;=\; R_{\infty}(z)\,, \end{aligned}$$

where the fourth inequality holds by the monotone convergence theorem (Theorem 2.4.6).

This paragraph shows that $R^{\infty} = R_{\infty}$. To this end, let $z \in Z$ and let $n \geq 1$. Then, we have

$$
\begin{aligned}
0 &\le \left|T^n R^+(z) - T^n R^-(z)\right| \\
&= \beta \left| \int_Z \max\left\{z', T^{n-1}R^+(z')\right\} \theta_z(dz') \right. \\
&\quad \left. - \int_Z \max\left\{z', T^{n-1}R^-(z')\right\} \theta_z(dz') \right| \\
&\le \beta \int_Z \left|\max\left\{z_1, T^{n-1}R^+(z_1)\right\} - \max\left\{z_1, T^{n-1}R^-(z_1)\right\}\right| \theta'_z(dz_1) \\
&\le \beta \int_Z \left|T^{n-1}R^+(z_1) - T^{n-1}R^-(z_1)\right| \theta'_z(dz_1) \\
&\le \beta^2 \int_Z \int_Z \left|T^{n-2}R^+(z_2) - T^{n-2}R^-(z_2)\right| \theta'_{z_1}(dz_2)\theta'_z(dz_1) \\
&\le \cdots \\
&\le \beta^n \int_Z \cdots \int_Z \int_Z \left|R^+(z_n) - R^-(z_n)\right| \theta'_{z_{n-1}}(dz_n)\theta'_{z_{n-2}}(dz_{n-1}) \cdots \theta'_z(dz_1) \\
&= \beta^n \int_Z \cdots \int_Z \int_Z \bar{z}\, \theta'_{z_{n-1}}(dz_n)\theta'_{z_{n-2}}(dz_{n-1}) \cdots \theta'_z(dz_1) \\
&= \beta^n \bar{z},
\end{aligned}
$$

where the second inequality holds by Theorem 2.4.3. Because the overall inequality holds for any n, taking the limit proves the claim.

Let R be any fixed point of T such that $R^- = 0 \le R \le \bar{z} = R^+$. Then, it holds that $TR^- \le TR = R \le TR^+$ by the monotonicity of T and the assumption that R is a fixed point of T. By iterating this procedure, we have $(\forall n)\ T^n R^- \le R \le T^n R^+$. Therefore, it follows that $R_\infty = \lim_{n\to\infty} T^n R^- \le R \le \lim_{n\to\infty} T^n R^+ = R^\infty$. This and the fact proven in the previous paragraph show that $R = R_\infty = R^\infty$, and hence, $R^* := R^\infty$ is the unique fixed point of T satisfying $0 \le R^* \le \bar{z}$.

That R^* is nondecreasing is immediate. Finally, we show that R^* is u.s.c. By the first paragraph of Sect. A.6.1, we know that $(\forall n)\ T^n R^+$ is u.s.c. in z under the assumption of u.s.c. of θ. Therefore, R^* is u.s.c. because it is the infimum of u.s.c. functions by $R^* = \lim_{n\to\infty} T^n R^+ = \inf_{n\ge 1}\langle T^n R^+\rangle$. ■

A.6.5 *Proof of Theorem 11.3.2*

Before proving Theorem 11.3.2, we prepare a lemma.

Lemma A.6.4 *The function A defined by (11.8) is u.s.c. and satisfies*

$$
(\forall z) \quad A(z) = R^*(z)y + \beta E_z[A]. \tag{A.24}
$$

Proof (U.s.c.) Because R^* is u.s.c. (by Lemma 11.3.3) and bounded from above (by $\bar{z}$), $(\forall s \ge 0)\ E^s_z[R^*]$ is u.s.c. in z by the first paragraph of Sect. A.6.1. Let $z_0 \in Z$ and let $\varepsilon > 0$. Given that $E_z^s[R^*]$ is uniformly bounded from above in s and z and because $\beta < 1$, there exists $S \geq 1$ such that $y \sum_{s=S+1}^{+\infty} \beta^s E_z^s[R^*] < \varepsilon/2$. Furthermore, because $\sum_{s=0}^{S} \beta^s E_z^s[R^*]$ is u.s.c. in z (because it is a *finite* sum of u.s.c. functions), there exists a neighborhood N of z_0 such that $(\forall z \in N)\ y \sum_{s=0}^{S} \beta^s E_z^s[R^*] < A(z_0) + \varepsilon/2$. Finally, we have $(\forall z \in N)\ A(z) < A(z_0) + \varepsilon$, which completes the proof.

(Equation (A.24)) The equation holds because

$$
\begin{aligned}
A(z) &= y \sum_{s=0}^{+\infty} \beta^s E_z^s[R^*] \\
&= R^*(z)y + \beta y \sum_{s=0}^{+\infty} \beta^s E_z^{s+1}[R^*] = R^*(z)y + \beta y \sum_{s=0}^{+\infty} \beta^s E_z\left[E_{z_1}^s[R^*]\right] \\
&= R^*(z)y + \beta y \lim_{T\to\infty} \sum_{s=0}^{T} \beta^s E_z\left[E_{z_1}^s[R^*]\right] \\
&= R^*(z)y + \beta y \lim_{T\to\infty} E_z\left[R^*(z_1)\right] + \beta E_z\left[E_{z_1}\left[R^*\right]\right] + \cdots + \beta^T E_z\left[E_{z_1}^T\left[R^*\right]\right] \\
&= R^*(z)y + \beta y \lim_{T\to\infty} E_z\left[R^*(z_1)\right] + E_z\left[\beta E_{z_1}\left[R^*\right]\right] + \cdots + E_z\left[\beta^T E_{z_1}^T\left[R^*\right]\right] \\
&= R^*(z)y + \beta y \lim_{T\to\infty} E_z\left[R^*(z_1) + \beta E_{z_1}\left[R^*\right] + \cdots + \beta^T E_{z_1}^T\left[R^*\right]\right] \\
&= R^*(z)y + \beta y \lim_{T\to\infty} \beta y E_z\left[\sum_{s=0}^{T} \beta^s E_{z_1}^s[R^*]\right] \\
&= R^*(z)y + \beta y E_z\left[\sum_{s=0}^{+\infty} \beta^s E_{z_1}^s[R^*]\right] \\
&= R^*(z)y + \beta E_z\left[y \sum_{s=0}^{+\infty} \beta^s E_{z_1}^s[R^*]\right] = R^*(z)y + \beta E_z[A],
\end{aligned}
$$

where the third equality holds by the definition of E^s; the seventh equality holds by the co-monotonic additivity of $E_z[\cdot]$ (Proposition 2.4.5) because each $E_{z_1}^t[R^*]$ $(0 \leq t \leq T)$ is nondecreasing in z_1 and hence mutually co-monotonic; and the ninth equality holds by the monotone convergence theorem (Theorem 2.4.6). ■

Proof of Theorem 11.3.2. First, we show that the function $\hat{v} : \mathbb{R}_+ \times Z \to \mathbb{R}$ defined by $(\forall m, z)\ \hat{v}(m, z) := \max\{z, R^*(z)\}m + A(z)$ is admissible; that is, $\hat{v}$ is u.s.c., nondecreasing in m, and satisfies $(\forall m, z)\ 0 \leq \hat{v}(m, z) \leq m\bar{z}/(1-\beta) + \beta y \bar{z}/(1-\beta)^2$. That $\hat{v}$ is u.s.c. follows because R^* is u.s.c. (by Lemma 11.3.3) and A is u.s.c. (by Lemma A.6.4). The nondecrease is obvious. To show the inequalities, note that $R^* \leq TR^+ = \beta\bar{z}$ by (11.7). Therefore, $0 \leq \hat{v}(m, z) = \max\{z, R^*(z)\}m + y \sum_{s=0}^{+\infty} \beta^s E_z^s[R^*] \leq \bar{z}m + y \sum_{s=0}^{+\infty} \beta^s \beta\bar{z} = \bar{z}m + y\beta\bar{z}/(1-\beta) \leq m\bar{z}/(1-\beta) + \beta y \bar{z}/(1-\beta)^2$.

Second, we show that $\hat{v}$ is the solution to Bellman's equation: $(\forall m, z)$

$$v(m,z) = \max\left\{ xz + \beta \int_Z v(m',z')\,\theta_z(dz') \,\middle|\, (x,m') \in \Gamma(m) \right\}.$$

We have

$$\begin{aligned}
&\max\left\{ xz + \beta \int_Z \hat{v}(m',z')\,\theta_z(dz') \,\middle|\, (x,m') \in \Gamma(m) \right\} \\
&= \max\left\{ xz + m'\beta \int_Z \max\left\{z', R^*(z')\right\}\theta_z(dz') \right. \\
&\quad \left. + \beta \int_Z A(z')\,\theta_z(dz') \,\middle|\, (x,m') \in \Gamma(m) \right\} \\
&= \max\left\{ xz + m'TR^*(z) + \beta E_z[A] \,\middle|\, (x,m') \in \Gamma(m) \right\} \\
&= \max\left\{ xz + m'R^*(z) + \beta E_z[A] \,\middle|\, (x,m') \in \Gamma(m) \right\} \\
&= \begin{cases} R^*(z)(m+y) + \beta E_z[A] & \text{if } z \le R^*(z) \\ mz + R^*(z)y + \beta E_z[A] & \text{if } z > R^*(z) \end{cases} \\
&= \begin{cases} R^*(z)m + R^*(z)y + \beta E_z[A] & \text{if } z \le R^*(z) \\ zm + R^*(z)y + \beta E_z[A] & \text{if } z > R^*(z) \end{cases} \\
&= \begin{cases} R^*(z)m + A(z) & \text{if } z \le R^*(z) \\ zm + A(z) & \text{if } z > R^*(z) \end{cases} \\
&= \hat{v}(m,z),
\end{aligned}$$

where the first equality holds by the co-monotonic additivity of the Choquet integral (Proposition 2.4.5) because both $\max\{z', R^*(z')\}$ and $A(z')$ are nondecreasing in z' and hence co-monotonic; the third equality holds by the fact that R^* is the fixed point of T; and the sixth equality holds by Eq. (A.24).

Finally, because $\hat{v}$ is an admissible solution to Bellman's equation as shown in the preceding paragraphs, we conclude that v^* defined by (11.9), which equals $\hat{v}$, is the value function by Theorem 11.3.1. Furthermore, the second paragraph of this proof shows that g defined by (11.10) is the policy correspondence. Finally, that recursive optimality implies optimality is among the conclusions of Theorem 11.3.1. ■

A.6.6 *Proof of Theorem 11.3.3*

We prepare a lemma.

Lemma A.6.5 *Suppose that the capacitary kernel θ is stochastically convex. Then, R^* is a convex function.*

Proof First, we show that for each $n \geq 1$, $T^n R^+$ is nondecreasing and convex in z. We prove this by induction. The statement holds true when $n = 0$ because $T^0 R^+ = R^+ = \bar{z}$ is constant and hence both nondecreasing and convex in z. Suppose that $T^{n-1} R^+$ is nondecreasing and convex in z. Then, $\max\{z', T^{n-1} R^+(z')\}$ is nondecreasing in z'. Therefore, $T^n R^+$ is nondecreasing and convex by the definition of T because θ is stochastically increasing and stochastically convex.

Given that R^* is a pointwise limit of a sequence of convex functions by Lemma 11.3.3 and by the fact proven in the previous paragraph, R^* is convex. ■

Proof of Theorem 11.3.3. By Lemma A.6.5, R^* is convex and hence continuous on $(\underline{z}, \bar{z})$. Because R^* is u.s.c. and nondecreasing by Lemma 11.3.3, it is continuous on $[\underline{z}, \bar{z})$ with only possible discontinuity occurring at $z = \bar{z}$. Furthermore, note that $R^*(\bar{z}) \leq T R^+(\bar{z}) = \beta \bar{z} < \bar{z}$. Therefore, the graph of R^* crosses the 45-degree line from above if and only if $R^*(\underline{z}) \geq \underline{z}$. First, suppose that $R^*(\underline{z}) < \underline{z}$. Then, any z^* such that $0 \leq z^* < \underline{z}$ serves as a reservation level and the optimal strategy clearly has a reservation property. Second, suppose that $R^*(\underline{z}) \geq \underline{z}$. Then, there exists a unique $z^* \in Z$ such that $z^* = R^*(z^*)$ and the optimal strategy has a reservation property because $\{ z \in Z \mid z \leq R^*(z) \} = \{ z \in Z \mid z \leq z^* \}$.

We complete the proof by showing that when $\beta E_{\underline{z}}[z'] \geq \underline{z}$, it holds that $R^*(\underline{z}) \geq \underline{z}$. To see this, suppose that it does not. Then, because R^* solves $R^* = T R^*$, it follows from (11.7) that $R^*(\underline{z}) = T R^*(\underline{z}) \geq \beta E_{\underline{z}}[z'] \geq \underline{z} > R^*(\underline{z})$, which is a contradiction. ■

A.6.7 *Proof of Theorem 11.4.1*

For each $i = 0, 1$, let T^i be the operator defined from P^i by (11.7). We show that for each $n \geq 1$, $(T^1)^n R^+ \geq (T^0)^n R^+$, which completes the proof because $(\forall i)\ R^{*i} = \lim_{n\to\infty} (T^i)^n R^+$. We prove the claim by induction. The statement clearly holds true when $n = 0$ because $(T^1)^0 R^+ = R^+ = (T^0)^0 R^+$. Suppose that $(T^1)^{n-1} R^+ \geq (T^0)^{n-1} R^+$. Then,

$$
\begin{aligned}
(T^1)^n R^+ &= T^1 \circ (T^1)^{n-1} R^+ \;\geq\; T^1 \circ (T^0)^{n-1} R^+ \\
&= \beta \int_Z \max\left\{z', (T^0)^{n-1} R^+(z')\right\} P^1_z(dz') \\
&\geq \beta \int_Z \max\left\{z', (T^0)^{n-1} R^+(z')\right\} P^0_z(dz') \\
&= T^0 \circ (T^0)^{n-1} R^+ \;=\; (T^0)^n R^+,
\end{aligned}
$$

where the first inequality holds by the induction hypothesis. To see that the second inequality holds, note that $\max\left\{z', (T^0)^{n-1} R^+(z')\right\}$ is convex in z' by the argument similar to the proof of Lemma A.6.5 and by the fact that the maximum of two convex functions is convex. Therefore, the inequality holds true by Rothschild and Stiglitz (1970, p. 237, Theorem 2) because P_z^1 is obtained from P_z^0 by the mean-preserving spread for each z. ■

A.6.8 *Proof of Corollary 11.4.1*

This follows because $z_t \leq R^{*0}(z_t) \leq R^{*1}(z_t)$ where the first inequality holds because $z_t \leq z^{*0}$ if and only if $z_t \leq R^{*0}(z_t)$ by Theorem 11.3.3 and the second inequality holds by Theorem 11.4.1. ■

A.6.9 *Proof of Theorem 11.4.2*

For each $i = 0, 1$, let T^i be the operator defined from θ^i by (11.7). We show that for each $n \geq 1$, $(T^1)^n R^+ \leq (T^0)^n R^+$, which completes the proof given that $(\forall i)\ R^{*i} = \lim_{n\to\infty}(T^i)^n R^+$. We prove the claim by induction. The statement clearly holds true when $n = 0$ because $(T^1)^0 R^+ = R^+ = (T^0)^0 R^+$. Suppose that $(T^1)^{n-1} R^+ \leq (T^0)^{n-1} R^+$. Then,

$$
\begin{aligned}
(T^1)^n R^+ &= T^1 \circ (T^1)^{n-1} R^+ \ \leq\ T^1 \circ (T^0)^{n-1} R^+ \\
&= \beta \int_Z \max\left\{z', (T^0)^{n-1} R^+(z')\right\} \theta_z^1(dz') \\
&= \beta \min\left\{ \int_Z \max\left\{z', (T^0)^{n-1} R^+(z')\right\} P(dz') \,\middle|\, P \in \mathrm{core}(\theta_z^1)\right\} \\
&\leq \beta \min\left\{ \int_Z \max\left\{z', (T^0)^{n-1} R^+(z')\right\} P(dz') \,\middle|\, P \in \mathrm{core}(\theta_z^0)\right\} \\
&= \beta \int_Z \max\left\{z', (T^0)^{n-1} R^+(z')\right\} \theta_z^0(dz') \\
&= T^0 \circ (T^0)^{n-1} R^+ \ =\ (T^0)^n R^+ ,
\end{aligned}
$$

where the first inequality holds by the induction hypothesis and the monotonicity of the Choquet integral (Proposition 2.4.2); the third equality holds by the fundamental theorem of the Choquet integral (Theorem 2.4.1); the second inequality holds because $\mathrm{core}(\theta_z^0) \subseteq \mathrm{core}(\theta_z^1)$ given that θ^1 represents more uncertainty than θ^0 by the assumption, and because (11.12) and (11.13) are equivalent; and the fourth equality holds also by the fundamental theorem of the Choquet integral (Theorem 2.4.1). ■

A.7 Proofs for Chap. 12

A.7.1 Proof of Theorem 12.4.1

We use the following lemma to prove the theorem.

Lemma A.7.1 *Let $\varepsilon \in [0, 1)$ and assume that (i), (ii), (iv), (v), (vii), and (viii-ε) hold. Then, $(\forall f \in L_0)(\exists y_f \in L_c)\ f \sim (1-\varepsilon)y_f + \varepsilon y_{\min f}$.*

Proof Let $f \in L_0$. Then, $y^* := (1-\varepsilon)y_{\max f} + \varepsilon y_{\min f} \succeq f \succeq y_{\min f} := y_*$, where the first and second orderings hold true by (viii-ε) and by (v), respectively. In the rest of proof, we assume that $y^* \succ f \succ y_*$ because the lemma would follow immediately otherwise. Then, because any pair out of three acts, y^*, f, and y_*, is co-monotonic, Lemma A.2.1(b) shows that $f \sim a^*y^* + (1-a^*)y_*$, where a^* is defined by $a^* := \sup\{a \in [0, 1] \mid f \succeq ay^* + (1-a)y_*\}$. On the other hand, $a^*y^*+(1-a^*)y_* = a^*((1-\varepsilon)y_{\max f}+\varepsilon y_{\min f})+(1-a^*)((1-\varepsilon)y_{\min f}+\varepsilon y_{\min f}) = (1-\varepsilon)(a^*y_{\max f} + (1-a^*)y_{\min f}) + \varepsilon y_{\min f}$. Therefore, defining $y_f := a^*y_{\max f} + (1-a^*)y_{\min f}$ completes the proof. ■

Proof of Theorem 12.4.1. This paragraph and those following define a binary relation $\succ^*$ on L_0, and then prove two lemmas. We use $\succ$ to define a binary relation $\succ^*$ on L_0 as follows: $f \succ^* g \Leftrightarrow [f \sim (1-\varepsilon)y_f+\varepsilon y_{\min f}$ and $g \sim (1-\varepsilon)y_g+\varepsilon y_{\min g} \Rightarrow y_f \succ y_g]$, where y_f and y_g are arbitrary elements of L_c. By definition, $f \succ^* g$ holds true whenever there does not exist such a y_f and/or y_g. Clearly, y_f $[y_g]$ is, when it exists, the equivalent constant act of f $[g]$ in ε-contamination equivalence. Thus, the binary relation $\succ^*$ is induced by the original preferences over these equivalent constant acts.

We define $\succeq^*$ and $\sim^*$ from $\succ^*$ as usual. A binary relation on Y is naturally induced from $\succeq^*$ as its restriction on L_c and it is denoted by the same symbol, $\succeq^*$. Then, the following two lemmas hold.

Lemma A.7.2 *Assume that (i) holds, let $f \in L_0$, and let $y_f \in L_c$. If $f \sim (1-\varepsilon)y_f + \varepsilon y_{\min f}$, then $f \sim^* y_f$.*

Proof Suppose that $f \sim (1-\varepsilon)y_f + \varepsilon y_{\min f}$. It always holds that $y_f \sim (1-\varepsilon)y_f + \varepsilon y_{\min y_f}$ because $y_{\min y_f} = y_f$. Furthermore, $y_f \not\succ y_f$ because $\succ$ is asymmetric by (i). Therefore, by the definition of $\succ^*$, it follows that $f \not\succ^* y_f$. Similarly, $y_f \not\succ^* f$. Therefore, $f \sim^* y_f$. ■

Lemma A.7.3 *Assume that (i) and (ii) hold. Then, $\succ$ and $\succ^*$ coincide on L_c.*

Proof Let $y, y' \in Y$. First, assume that $y \succ^* y'$. Note that $y \sim (1-\varepsilon)y+\varepsilon y_{\min y}$ and $y' \sim (1-\varepsilon)y' + \varepsilon y'_{\min y'}$ hold because $(\forall y \in Y)\ y_{\min y} = y$. Hence, it follows from the definition of $\succ^*$ that $y \succ y'$. Second, assume that $y \succ y'$. Let $\bar{y}$ and $\bar{y}'$ be arbitrary constant acts such that (a) $y \sim (1-\varepsilon)\bar{y} + \varepsilon y_{\min y}$ and (b) $y' \sim (1-\varepsilon)\bar{y}' + \varepsilon y'_{\min y'}$. From (a), it holds that $(1-\varepsilon)y + \varepsilon y_{\min y} = y \sim (1-\varepsilon)\bar{y} + \varepsilon y_{\min y}$. Therefore,

(i) and (ii) imply that $y \sim \bar{y}$ (recall that any pair of constant acts is co-monotonic). Similarly, it holds from (b) that $y' \sim \bar{y}'$. Finally, (i) and the assumption that $y \succ y'$ show that $\bar{y} \succ \bar{y}'$, which in turn shows that $y \succ^* y'$ by the definition of $\succ^*$. ■

This paragraph proves a lemma that shows that the binary relation $\succsim^*$ defined in the first paragraph of this proof satisfies Axioms AA1–AA5 postulated in Sect. 3.8.2. (Note that we rename them (i), (iii), (iv), (v), and (vii). Also, note that we state the axioms in terms of a weak order, instead of a preference order.) Let $\varepsilon \in [0, 1)$. We henceforth suppress "-ε" and simply write as (viii) and (ix). Throughout this and the following subsections, we always assume that $\succsim$ satisfies (i), (ii), (iv), (v), (vii), (viii), and (ix).

Lemma A.7.4 *The binary relation $\succsim^*$ satisfies (i), (iii), (iv), (v), and (vii).*

Proof **(i) Weak Order**. We prove this by showing that $\succ^*$ is asymmetric and negatively transitive (see footnote 3 of Chap. 12). (Asymmetry) Assume that $f \succ^* g$. Also suppose that $f \sim (1-\varepsilon)y_f + \varepsilon y_{\min f}$ and that $g \sim (1-\varepsilon)y_g + \varepsilon y_{\min g}$. The existence of constant acts, y_f and y_g, is guaranteed by Lemma A.7.1. Then, it follows from the definition of $\succ^*$ that $y_f \succ y_g$ and the asymmetry of $\succ$ implies that $y_g \not\succ y_f$. Hence, the definition of $\succ^*$ implies that $g \not\succ^* f$.

(Negative Transitivity) Assume that $f \not\succ^* g$ and $g \not\succ^* h$. Then, there exist constant acts y_f and y_g such that $f \sim (1-\varepsilon)y_f + \varepsilon y_{\min f}$, $g \sim (1-\varepsilon)y_g + \varepsilon y_{\min g}$, and $y_f \not\succ y_g$, and there exist constant acts y'_g and y_h such that $g \sim (1-\varepsilon)y'_g + \varepsilon y'_{\min g}$, $h \sim (1-\varepsilon)y_h + \varepsilon y_{\min h}$, and $y'_g \not\succ y_h$. It then holds that $(1-\varepsilon)y_g + \varepsilon y_{\min g} \sim g \sim (1-\varepsilon)y'_g + \varepsilon y'_{\min g} \sim (1-\varepsilon)y'_g + \varepsilon y_{\min g}$, where the last indifference relation holds by Lemma A.2.1(c) and the fact that $y_{\min g} \sim y'_{\min g}$ because $\succsim$ satisfies (i), (iii), and (iv) when restricted on L_c. Therefore, (i) and (ii) imply that $y_g \sim y'_g$ (recall that any pair of constant acts are co-monotonic). Hence, (i) implies that $y_f \not\succ y_h$, which shows that $f \not\succ^* h$.

(iii) Independence. Assume that $f \succ^* g$ and let $y_{f\lambda h}$ and $y_{g\lambda h}$ be any constant acts such that $\lambda f + (1-\lambda)h \sim (1-\varepsilon)y_{f\lambda h} + \varepsilon y_{\min f\lambda h}$ and $\lambda g + (1-\lambda)h \sim (1-\varepsilon)y_{g\lambda h} + \varepsilon y_{\min g\lambda h}$. We show that $y_{f\lambda h} \succ y_{g\lambda h}$, which completes the proof by the definition of $\succ^*$. By Lemma A.7.1 and the assumption that $f \succ^* g$, there exist constant acts y_f, y_g, and y_h such that $f \sim (1-\varepsilon)y_f + \varepsilon y_{\min f}$, $g \sim (1-\varepsilon)y_g + \varepsilon y_{\min g}$, $h \sim (1-\varepsilon)y_h + \varepsilon y_{\min h}$, and $y_f \succ y_g$. Because any pair of constant acts is co-monotonic, (ii) implies that $\lambda y_f + (1-\lambda)y_h \succ \lambda y_g + (1-\lambda)y_h$. On the other hand, (ix-1) implies that $\lambda y_f + (1-\lambda)y_h \sim y_{f\lambda h}$ and $\lambda y_g + (1-\lambda)y_h \sim y_{g\lambda h}$. Therefore, (i) shows that $y_{f\lambda h} \succ y_{g\lambda h}$.

(iv) Continuity. Assume that $f \succ^* g$ and $g \succ^* h$ and let y_f, y_g and y_h be any constant acts such that $f \sim (1-\varepsilon)y_f + \varepsilon y_{\min f}$, $g \sim (1-\varepsilon)y_g + \varepsilon y_{\min g}$, and $h \sim (1-\varepsilon)y_h + \varepsilon y_{\min h}$. Such y_f, y_g, and y_h exist by Lemma A.7.1. By the assumption that $f \succ^* g$ and $g \succ^* h$ and the definition of $\succ^*$, it follows that $y_f \succ y_g$ and $y_g \succ y_h$. Then, (iv) implies that there exists $\alpha \in (0, 1)$ such that $\alpha y_f + (1-\alpha)y_h \succ y_g$. Let $y_{f\alpha h}$ be any constant act such that $\alpha f + (1-\alpha)h \sim (1-\varepsilon)y_{f\alpha h} + \varepsilon y_{\min f\alpha h}$. Then, (ix-1) implies that $y_{f\alpha h} \sim \alpha y_f + (1-\alpha)y_h$. Therefore, (i) shows that $y_{f\alpha h} \succ y_g$, which in turn shows that $\alpha f + (1-\alpha)h \succ^* g$ by the definition of $\succ^*$. A similar proof applies for the existence of $\beta \in (0,1)$ such that $g \succ^* \beta f + (1-\beta)h$.

(v) Monotonicity. Suppose that $(\forall s \in S)\ f(s) \succeq^* g(s)$. Because $\succ^*$ and $\succ$ coincide on L_c (Lemma A.7.3), it follows that $(\forall s \in S)\ f(s) \succeq g(s)$. Let y_f and y_g be constant acts such that $f \sim (1-\varepsilon)y_f + \varepsilon y_{\min f}$ and $g \sim (1-\varepsilon)y_g + \varepsilon y_{\min g}$. Such y_f and y_g exist by Lemma A.7.1. Then, (ix-2) implies that $y_f \succeq y_g$, or equivalently, $y_g \not\succ y_f$. Therefore, it follows from the definition of $\succ^*$ that $g \not\succ^* f$, implying that $f \succeq^* g$.

(vii) Nondegeneracy. From (v) and (vii), it follows that $(\exists y, y' \in Y)\ y \succ y'$. Because $\succ^*$ and $\succ$ coincide on L_c (Lemma A.7.3), $y \succ^* y'$. ∎

This paragraph completes the proof. Lemma A.7.4 allows us to apply Theorem 3.8.1 to $\succ^*$, which shows that there exist a unique probability charge μ on $(S, \mathcal{A})$ and an affine function $u : Y \to \mathbb{R}$, which is unique up to a positive affine transformation, such that

$$f \succ^* g \Leftrightarrow \int_S u(f(s))\, d\mu(s) > \int_S u(g(s))\, d\mu(s)\,. \tag{A.25}$$

We define $J^* : L_0 \to \mathbb{R}$ by

$$(\forall f \in L_0) \quad J^*(f) := \int_S u(f(s))\, d\mu(s) \tag{A.26}$$

and then define $J : L_0 \to \mathbb{R}$ by $(\forall f \in L_0)\ J(f) := u((1-\varepsilon)y_f + \varepsilon y_{\min f})$, where $y_f \in L_c$ is the equivalent constant act of f in ε-contamination equivalence whose existence is guaranteed by Lemma A.7.1. Because u represents $\succ^*$ on L_c by (A.25) and $\succ^*$ and $\succ$ coincide on L_c by Lemma A.7.3, u represents $\succ$ on L_c. Therefore, J is well defined and represents $\succ$ on L_0. Finally, we have

$$\begin{aligned} J(f) &= u((1-\varepsilon)y_f + \varepsilon y_{\min f}) \;=\; (1-\varepsilon)u(y_f) + \varepsilon u(y_{\min f}) \\ &= (1-\varepsilon)J^*(y_f) + \varepsilon \min_S u(f(s)) \;=\; (1-\varepsilon)J^*(f) + \varepsilon \min_S u(f(s)) \\ &= (1-\varepsilon)\int_S u(f(s))\, d\mu(s) + \varepsilon \min_S u(f(s))\,, \end{aligned}$$

where the second equality holds by the affinity of u; the third equality holds by the definition of J^* and the fact that u represents $\succ$ on Y; the fourth equality holds by Lemma A.7.2 and the fact that J^* represents $\succ^*$; and the last equality holds by (A.26). Because J represents $\succ$ on L_0, the proof is complete. ∎

A.7.2 Proof of Proposition 12.6.1

This paragraph proves that (i), (iii), (iv), and (v) imply (viii-0) and (ix-0). It is immediate that (v) implies (viii-0) and that (i) and (v) imply (ix-0-2). To prove that (ix-0-1) holds, note that $(\forall f, g, h \in L_0)\ f \sim g \Rightarrow \lambda f + (1-\lambda)h \sim \lambda g + (1-\lambda)h$ by Lemma A.2.1(c) because $\succsim$ satisfies (i), (iii), and (iv) when restricted on L_c. This shows that if $f \sim y_f$, $g \sim y_g$ and $f_\lambda g \sim y_{f_\lambda g}$, then $\lambda y_f + (1-\lambda)y_g \sim \lambda y_f + (1-\lambda)g \sim \lambda f + (1-\lambda)g = f_\lambda g \sim y_{f_\lambda g}$, showing (ix-0-1).

This paragraph proves that (i), (ii), (iv), (v), (vii), (viii-0), and (ix-0) imply (iii). Lemma A.7.1 proves that $(\forall f \in L_0)(\exists y_f \in L_c)\ f \sim y_f$ (simply let $\varepsilon = 0$ there). Let $y_f, y_g, y_h, y_{f_\lambda h}, y_{g_\lambda h} \in L_c$ be such that $f \sim y_f$, $g \sim y_g$, $h \sim y_h$, $f_\lambda h \sim y_{f_\lambda h}$ and $g_\lambda h \sim y_{g_\lambda h}$, and let $f \succ g$. Then, (i) implies that $y_f \succ y_g$. Because any pair of constant acts is co-monotonic, (ii) implies that $\lambda y_f + (1-\lambda)y_h \succ \lambda y_g + (1-\lambda)y_h$. Finally, (i) and (viii-0-1) imply that $f_\lambda h \sim y_{f_\lambda h} \succ y_{g_\lambda h} \sim g_\lambda h$.

Combining the above two paragraphs completes the proof of the proposition. ■

A.8 Proofs for Chap. 13

A.8.1 Proof of Proposition 13.2.1

The 'if' part follows immediately. To prove the 'only if' part, let φ and φ' be betweenness functions such that $M^\varphi = M^{\varphi'}$. We first assume that both φ and φ' are strictly increasing in their second arguments. Let $x_*, z, x^* \in \mathbb{R}$ be such that $x_* < z < x^*$. Because $\varphi(x_*, z) > 0$ and $\varphi(x^*, z) < 0$ by B1 and the assumption that φ is strictly increasing in its second argument, there exists $p \in (0, 1)$ such that

$$\varphi(x_*, z)p + \varphi(x^*, z)(1-p) = 0 \tag{A.27}$$

by the intermediate-value theorem. Also, there exists an event $E \in \mathcal{F}$ such that $\mu(E) = p$ by the assumption that the probability space is nonatomic. Therefore, if we define $\hat{f} \in F$ by $\hat{f} = x_*\chi_E + x^*\chi_{\Omega\setminus E}$, then it holds that $M^\varphi(\hat{f}) = z$ by Eqs. (13.1) and (A.27). Because $M^{\varphi'}(\hat{f}) = z$ by the assumption that $M^\varphi = M^{\varphi'}$, Eq. (13.1) also implies that

$$\varphi'(x_*, z)p + \varphi'(x^*, z)(1-p) = 0\,. \tag{A.28}$$

Equations (A.27) and (A.28) together then imply that

$$\varphi'(x_*, z)/\varphi(x_*, z) = \varphi'(x^*, z)/\varphi(x^*, z)\,. \tag{A.29}$$

Because Eq. (A.29) holds for arbitrary x_*, z, and x^* such that $x_* < z < x^*$, we may define a function $a : \mathbb{R} \to \mathbb{R}$ by

$$(\forall z) \quad a(z) := \varphi'(x, z)/\varphi(x, z) \tag{A.30}$$

where x is any real number such that $x \neq z$. It follows that a is well defined and $(\forall z)\ a(z) > 0$ by the assumption that φ and φ' are strictly increasing in their second arguments. Therefore, it holds that $(\forall z)(\forall x \neq z)\ \varphi'(x, z) = a(z)\varphi(x, z)$, which also holds when $x = z$ by B1. The continuity of a follows from (A.30) and the continuity of φ and φ' in their second arguments (B3). Finally, when each or both of φ and φ' are strictly *de*creasing in their second arguments, we can apply the same argument as above to $-\varphi$ or $-\varphi'$ or both. ■

A.8.2 *Proof of Proposition 13.2.2*

For the first half of the claim, a proof similar to that for Proposition 13.3.1 applies (simply set $\mathcal{G} := \{\phi, \Omega\}$ there). Its second half follows from E3 and E5. ■

A.8.3 *Proof of Proposition 13.2.3*

Let M be an implicit mean and let φ be its associated betweenness function. Without loss of generality, we assume that φ is strictly decreasing in its second argument in the B2 statement. Then, we define $\phi : \mathbb{R}^2 \to \mathbb{R}$ by

$$(\forall x, z) \quad \phi(x, z) = -\int_x^z \varphi(x, t)dt\,.$$

Because φ is continuous by B3, ϕ is well defined. Also, B3 implies that ϕ_2 exists and that

$$(\forall x, z) \quad \phi_2(x, z) = -\varphi(x, z)\,. \tag{A.31}$$

We show that ϕ satisfies E1–E5 and hence that it is an error function: E1 and E2 follow from B1 and B2; E3 follows from (A.31) and B2; E4 follows from B3; and E5 follows from (A.31) and B3. Finally, (A.31) shows that

$$(\forall f \in F) \quad \int_\Omega \phi_2(f(\omega), M(f))\, d\mu = \int_\Omega \varphi(f(\omega), M(f))\, d\mu = 0\,,$$

which shows that $M = M^\phi$ by the latter half of Proposition 13.2.2. ■

A.8.4 Proof of Proposition 13.3.1

Let $f \in F$ and let $\mathcal{G} \in \mathcal{F}^\circ$. We first prove the existence of the best approximation. Note that $F(\mathcal{G}) = L^\infty(\mathcal{G})$ because $\mathcal{G} \in \mathcal{F}^\circ$ and we define $(L^\infty(\mathcal{G}))_1 := \{ g \in L^\infty(\mathcal{G}) \mid (\forall\omega)\ |g(\omega)| \le \|f\|_\infty \}$. By E1-E3, $\arg\min\{ \Phi(f, g) \mid g \in L^\infty(\mathcal{G}) \}$ must be in $(L^\infty(\mathcal{G}))_1$ if it exists, where we define Φ by

$$(\forall f, g \in F) \quad \Phi(f, g) := \int_\Omega \phi(f(\omega), g(\omega))\, d\mu(\omega)\,.$$

Let $\langle g_n \rangle_{n=1}^\infty$ be a sequence in $(L^\infty(\mathcal{G}))_1$ such that

$$\Phi(f, g_n) \to \inf_g \Phi(f, g) := \inf\{ \Phi(f, g) \mid g \in \left(L^\infty(\mathcal{G})\right)_1 \}\,. \tag{A.32}$$

Because $(L^\infty(\mathcal{G}))_1$ is weak * compact by Alaoglu's theorem (Dunford and Schwartz 1988, p. 424, Theorem 2), there exists a subsequence $\langle g_{n_i} \rangle_{i=1}^\infty$ and $g_0 \in (L^\infty(\mathcal{G}))_1$ such that g_{n_i} converges to g_0 in the weak * topology on $L^\infty(\mathcal{G})$. Consider the L^1-space on $(\Omega, \mathcal{G}, \mu)$, which we denote by $L^1(\mathcal{G})$. Then, it clearly holds that $\langle g_{n_i} \rangle_i \subseteq L^1(\mathcal{G})$ and $g_0 \in L^1(\mathcal{G})$. Furthermore, it holds that

$$\int_\Omega h(\omega) g_{n_i}(\omega)\, d\mu(\omega) \to \int_\Omega h(\omega) g_0(\omega)\, d\mu(\omega)$$

for any $h \in L^1(\mathcal{G})$ by the definition of the convergence in the weak * topology on $L^\infty(\mathcal{G})$, and hence, it holds for any $h \in L^\infty(\mathcal{G})$ because $L^\infty(\mathcal{G}) \subseteq L^1(\mathcal{G})$. Therefore, $\langle g_{n_i} \rangle_i$ converges to g_0 in the weak topology on $L^1(\mathcal{G})$.

This paragraph proves that $\Phi(f, g_0) = \inf_g \Phi(f, g)$ and completes the proof of the existence. Suppose to the contrary that $\Phi(f, g_0) > \inf_g \Phi(f, g)$ and let $\varepsilon > 0$ be such that

$$\Phi(f, g_0) > \inf_g \Phi(f, g) + \varepsilon\,. \tag{A.33}$$

It holds from (A.32), by discarding at most finite elements of the sequence if necessary, that

$$(\forall i) \quad \Phi(f, g_{n_i}) < \inf_g \Phi(f, g) + \varepsilon\,. \tag{A.34}$$

Furthermore, there exists a sequence $\langle \bar{g}_m \rangle_{m=1}^\infty \subseteq (L^\infty(\mathcal{G}))_1$ such that $\bar{g}_m \to g_0$ in the L^1-norm, where each $\bar{g}_m$ is some finite convex combination of elements in $\langle g_{n_i} \rangle_i$, by Mazur's lemma (Dunford and Schwartz 1988, p. 422, Corollary 14) and the claim established in the previous paragraph. Then, there exists a subsequence $\langle \bar{g}_{m_j} \rangle_j$ of $\langle \bar{g}_m \rangle_m$ such that $\bar{g}_{m_j} \to g_0$ μ-a.e. by Folland (1984, p. 62, Corollary 2.32), and hence, $\Phi(f, \bar{g}_{m_j}) \to \Phi(f, g_0)$ by E4 and the dominated convergence theorem (Folland 1984, p. 54). Therefore, (A.33) implies that $(\exists j)\ \Phi(f, \bar{g}_{m_j}) > \inf_g \Phi(f, g) + \varepsilon$. This, E3 and (A.34) imply that $(\exists N \in \mathbb{N})(\exists \langle c_k \rangle_{k=1}^N \text{ s.t. } \sum_{k=1}^N c_k = 1)\ \inf_g \Phi(f, g) + \varepsilon <$

$\Phi(f, \bar{g}_{m_j}) = \Phi(f, \sum_{k=1}^{N} c_k g_{n_{i_k}}) \le \sum_{k=1}^{N} c_k \Phi(f, g_{n_{i_k}}) < \inf_g \Phi(f, g) + \varepsilon$, which is a contradiction.

Finally, to prove that $\arg\min\{\, \Phi(f, g) \mid g \in F(\mathcal{G}) \,\}$ is a singleton, suppose that two functions g_1 and g_2 in $F(\mathcal{G})$ both attain the minimum. Suppose that $g_1 \neq g_2$; that is, $\mu(\{\, \omega \mid g_1(\omega) \neq g_2(\omega) \,\}) > 0$. Then, $\frac{1}{2}g_1 + \frac{1}{2}g_2 \in F(\mathcal{G})$ and $\Phi(f, \frac{1}{2}g_1 + \frac{1}{2}g_2) < \Phi(f, g_1) = \Phi(f, g_2)$ by E3, which contradicts the assumption that g_1 and g_2 attain the minimum. ∎

A.8.5 Proof of Proposition 13.3.2

To prove the 'only if' part, let $g = M^\phi(f \mid \mathcal{G})$ and let $h \in F(\mathcal{G})$ be arbitrarily chosen. Then, $g \in F(\mathcal{G})$ by the definition of $M^\phi(f \mid \mathcal{G})$. Furthermore, the map

$$\mathbb{R} \ni \varepsilon \mapsto \int_\Omega \phi(f, g + \varepsilon h)\, d\mu := \int_\Omega \phi(f(\omega), g(\omega) + \varepsilon h(\omega))\, d\mu(\omega)$$

has its minimum at $\varepsilon = 0$ by the definition of $M^\phi(f \mid \mathcal{G})$ because $(\forall \varepsilon)\ g + \varepsilon h \in F(\mathcal{G})$. Hence, the claim follows from E5.

To prove the 'if' part, suppose that $g \in F(\mathcal{G})$ satisfies (13.7) and suppose that there exists $g' \in F(\mathcal{G})$ such that

$$\int_\Omega \phi(f, g')\, d\mu < \int_\Omega \phi(f, g)\, d\mu\,.$$

Then, it holds that

$$0 > \int_\Omega \big(\phi(f, g') - \phi(f, g)\big)\, d\mu > \int_\Omega \phi_2(f, g)(g' - g)\, d\mu = 0\,,$$

where the second inequality holds by E3 and E5, and the equality holds by (13.7) because $g' - g \in F(\mathcal{G})$, leading to a contradiction. ∎

A.8.6 Proof of Proposition 13.3.3

Let M be an implicit mean and let ϕ and ϕ' be two error functions such that $M = M^\phi = M^{\phi'}$. Then, Propositions 13.2.1 and 13.2.2 imply that there exists a continuous positive function or a continuous negative function, a, such that $(\forall x, z)\ \phi'_2(x, z) = a(z)\phi_2(x, z)$. Let $f \in F$, $\mathcal{G} \in \mathcal{F}^\circ$, and $h \in F(\mathcal{G})$. Then, $h / a(M^{\phi'}(f \mid \mathcal{G}))$ is a well-defined function because a is nonzero and $h / a(M^{\phi'}(f \mid \mathcal{G})) \in F(\mathcal{G})$ because a is continuous. Therefore,

$$
\begin{aligned}
0 &= \int_\Omega \phi_2'(f, M^{\phi'}(f|\mathcal{G}))h/a(M^{\phi'}(f|\mathcal{G}))\, d\mu \\
&= \int_\Omega a(M^{\phi'}(f|\mathcal{G}))\phi_2(f, M^{\phi'}(f|\mathcal{G}))h/a(M^{\phi'}(f|\mathcal{G}))\, d\mu \\
&= \int_\Omega \phi_2(f, M^{\phi'}(f|\mathcal{G}))h\, d\mu\,,
\end{aligned}
$$

where the first equality holds by Proposition 13.3.2 and the fact that $h/a(M^{\phi'}(f|\mathcal{G})) \in F(\mathcal{G})$. Because the entire equality holds for an arbitrary h, Proposition 13.3.2 establishes that $M^{\phi'}(f|\mathcal{G}) = M^{\phi}(f|\mathcal{G})$. ■

A.8.7 *Proof of Corollary 13.3.1*

Let ϕ be any error function that generates M via (13.2), whose existence is guaranteed by Proposition 13.2.3. Then, it holds that $M(\cdot|\cdot) = M^{\phi}(\cdot|\cdot)$ by the definition of $M(\cdot|\cdot)$, (13.8). Furthermore, Propositions 13.2.1 and 13.2.2 imply that there exists a continuous positive function or a continuous negative function, a, such that $(\forall x, z)\ \phi_2(x, z) = a(z)\varphi(x, z)$ because both ϕ_2 and φ define M via (13.1).

To prove the ‘only if’ part, let $g = M(f|\mathcal{G})$ and let $h \in F(\mathcal{G})$. Then, $h/a(g)$ is a well-defined function in $F(\mathcal{G})$ because a is nonzero and continuous. Therefore, by Proposition 13.3.2 and the fact that $M(\cdot|\cdot) = M^{\phi}(\cdot|\cdot)$, it holds that

$$
0 = \int_\Omega \phi_2(f, g)h/a(g)\, d\mu = \int_\Omega a(g)\varphi(f, g)h/a(g)\, d\mu = \int_\Omega \varphi(f, g)h\, d\mu\,.
$$

Because the whole equality holds for an arbitrary h, the proof is complete.

To prove the ‘if’ part, assume that $g \in F(\mathcal{G})$ satisfies (13.9) and let $h \in F(\mathcal{G})$. Note that $a(g)h \in F(\mathcal{G})$ because a is continuous. Therefore, by (13.9), it holds that

$$
0 = \int_\Omega \varphi(f, g)a(g)h\, d\mu = \int_\Omega \phi_2(f, g)h\, d\mu\,.
$$

Because the whole equality holds for an arbitrary h, Proposition 13.3.2 shows that $g = M^{\phi}(f|\mathcal{G}) = M(f|\mathcal{G})$. ■

A.8.8 *Proof of Proposition 13.3.4*

To prove the ‘only if’ part, let φ be a betweenness function that defines M via (13.1) and let $\hat{\varphi}$ be a continuous and strictly monotonic function such that $(\forall x, z)\ \varphi(x, z) = \hat{\varphi}(x) - \hat{\varphi}(z)$. Also, let $f \in F$ and let $\mathcal{G} \in \mathcal{F}^{\circ}$. Then, (13.1) and Corollary 13.3.1 imply

$$\int_{\Omega} \varphi(f, M(f))\, d\mu = \int_{\Omega} \varphi(f, M(f|\mathcal{G}))\, d\mu = 0$$

(let h be χ_Ω in (13.9)). Hence, it holds that

$$\int_{\Omega} \hat{\varphi}(M(f))\, d\mu = \int_{\Omega} \hat{\varphi}(f) d\mu = \int_{\Omega} \hat{\varphi}(M(f|\mathcal{G}))\, d\mu\,,$$

which in turn implies that

$$\int_{\Omega} \varphi(M(f|\mathcal{G}), M(f))\, d\mu = \int_{\Omega} \big(\hat{\varphi}(M(f|\mathcal{G})) - \hat{\varphi}(M(f))\big)\, d\mu = 0\,.$$

Therefore, $M(f) = M(M(f|\mathcal{G}))$ by (13.1). Because this holds for arbitrary f and $\mathcal{G}$, the proof is complete.

To prove the 'if' part, let M be a skew-symmetric implicit mean and let φ be a skew-symmetric betweenness function that defines M via (13.1). Also, assume that (13.11) holds and let x_1, x_2, y, and x_3 be reals such that $x_1 < x_2 < y < x_3$. Then, by B1 and B2, there exists $a, b > 0$ such that $\varphi(x_1, x_2)a + \varphi(x_3, x_2) = 0$ and $\varphi(x_2, y)b + \varphi(x_3, y) = 0$. If we define $p_1 = a/(a+b+1)$, $p_2 = b/(a+b+1)$, and $p_3 = 1/(a+b+1)$, then it holds that $p_1 + p_2 + p_3 = 1$,

$$\varphi(x_1, x_2)p_1 + \varphi(x_3, x_2)p_3 = 0 \text{ and } \varphi(x_2, y)p_2 + \varphi(x_3, y)p_3 = 0\,. \tag{A.35}$$

Furthermore, by the maintained assumption of nonatomicity, there exist $E, F \in \mathcal{F}$ such that $F \subseteq E$, $\mu(E) = p_2 + p_3$ and $\mu(F) = p_3$. Let $\hat{f} \in F$ be defined by $\hat{f} = x_1\chi_{\Omega\setminus E} + x_2\chi_{E\setminus F} + x_3\chi_F$ and let $\mathcal{G}$ be the σ-algebra generated by E and all μ-null subsets of Ω. Then, (13.1) implies that $M(\hat{f}) = x_2$ because

$$\begin{aligned}\int_{\Omega} \varphi(\hat{f}, x_2)d\mu &= \int_{\Omega\setminus E} \varphi(x_1, x_2)d\mu + \int_{E\setminus F} \varphi(x_2, x_2)d\mu + \int_{F} \varphi(x_3, x_2)d\mu \\ &= \varphi(x_1, x_2)p_1 + \varphi(x_2, x_2)p_2 + \varphi(x_3, x_2)p_3 \\ &= \varphi(x_1, x_2)p_1 + \varphi(x_3, x_2)p_3 \;=\; 0\,,\end{aligned}$$

where the second equality holds by the definitions of E and F, the third equality holds by B1, and the last equality holds by (A.35). Also, Corollary 13.3.1 implies that $M(\hat{f}|\mathcal{G}) = x_1\chi_{\Omega\setminus E} + y\chi_E$ because any function in $F(\mathcal{G})$ can be represented by $h\chi_{\Omega\setminus E} + h'\chi_E$ with some reals, h and h', and because ($\forall h, h' \in \mathbb{R}$)

$$\begin{aligned}&\int_{\Omega} \varphi(\hat{f}, x_1\chi_{\Omega\setminus E} + y\chi_E)(h\chi_{\Omega\setminus E} + h'\chi_E)d\mu \\ &= \int_{\Omega\setminus E} \varphi(x_1, x_1)h\, d\mu + \int_{E\setminus F} \varphi(x_2, y)h'\, d\mu + \int_{F} \varphi(x_3, y)h'\, d\mu\end{aligned}$$

$$= \varphi(x_2, y)h' p_2 + \varphi(x_3, y)h' p_3$$
$$= h' (\varphi(x_2, y)p_2 + \varphi(x_3, y)p_3) \;=\; 0\,,$$

where the second equality holds by B1 and the definitions of E and F, and the last equality holds by (A.35). Therefore, it holds that

$$\begin{aligned}\varphi(x_1, x_2)p_1 + \varphi(y, x_2)(p_2 + p_3) &= \int_{\Omega\setminus E} \varphi(x_1, x_2)d\mu + \int_E \varphi(y, x_2)d\mu \\ &= \int_\Omega \varphi(M(\hat{f}|\mathcal{G}), M(\hat{f}))d\mu \\ &= 0\,, \end{aligned} \tag{A.36}$$

where the first equality holds by the definitions of E and F, the second equality holds by the expressions of $M(\hat{f})$ and $M(\hat{f}|\mathcal{G})$ derived above, and the last equality holds by (13.1) and (13.11). Finally, the skew-symmetry of φ, (A.35), and (A.36) imply

$$\varphi(x_2, y) + \varphi(y, x_3) + \varphi(x_3, x_2) = 0\,. \tag{A.37}$$

So far, we have established that (A.37) holds for any x_2, y, and x_3 such that $x_2 < y < x_3$.

Let $x_0 \in \mathbb{R}$ be arbitrarily fixed and define $\hat{\varphi} : \mathbb{R} \to \mathbb{R}$ by $(\forall x)\ \hat{\varphi}(x) = \varphi(x, x_0)$. Then, $\hat{\varphi}$ is continuous and strictly monotonic by B2, B3, and the skew-symmetry of φ. We show that $(\forall x, z)\ \varphi(x, z) = \hat{\varphi}(x) - \hat{\varphi}(z)$, which completes the proof. (a) Let $x, z \in \mathbb{R}$ be such that $x < z$. Then, there are five possible cases: $x < z < x_0, x < z = x_0, x < x_0 < z, x_0 = x < z$, and $x_0 < x < z$. First, suppose that $x < z < x_0$. Then, $\varphi(x, z) = -\varphi(z, x_0) - \varphi(x_0, x) = -\varphi(z, x_0) + \varphi(x, x_0) = -\hat{\varphi}(z) + \hat{\varphi}(x)$, where the first equality holds by (A.37), the second equality holds by the skew-symmetry, and the third equality holds by the definition of $\hat{\varphi}$. Second, suppose that $x < z = x_0$. Then, $\varphi(x, z) = \varphi(x, x_0) + \varphi(x_0, z) = \varphi(x, x_0) - \varphi(z, x_0) = \hat{\varphi}(x) - \hat{\varphi}(z)$, where the first equality holds by B1 and the assumption that $z = x_0$, the second equality holds by the skew-symmetry, and the third equality holds by the definition of $\hat{\varphi}$. A similar argument applies for each of the other three cases. (b) Let $x, z \in \mathbb{R}$ be such that $x > z$. Then, $\varphi(x, z) = -\varphi(z, x) = -\left(\hat{\varphi}(z) - \hat{\varphi}(x)\right) = \hat{\varphi}(x) - \hat{\varphi}(z)$, where the first equality holds by the skew-symmetry, and the second equality holds because the claim has already been proved for the case where the second argument is greater than the first. ■

A.8.9 *Proof of Proposition 13.4.1*

We prove only (13.16). A similar argument applies for (13.17). ($\Leftarrow$) follows from the example. To show ($\Rightarrow$), let $\gamma \leq 1$. Also, we define $\varphi : \mathbb{R}^2 \to \mathbb{R}$ by

$$(\forall x, z) \quad \varphi(x, z) := \begin{cases} \gamma(z - x) & \text{if} \quad x \geq z \\ z - x & \text{if} \quad x < z . \end{cases}$$

Then, φ turns out to be a betweenness function and $(\forall f \in F)$ $M^{2,\gamma}(f)$ is the unique solution z to

$$\int_\Omega \varphi(f(\omega), z)\, d\mu(\omega) = 0 \tag{A.38}$$

by (13.15). Let $f, h \in F$, and let $\mathcal{G} \in \mathcal{F}^\circ$. Then, by the convexity of φ in both arguments together, it holds that $(\forall \omega)$

$$\begin{aligned} &\varphi(f(\omega) + h(\omega), M^{2,\gamma}(f + h)) - \varphi(f(\omega), M^{2,\gamma}(f)) \\ &\geq \varphi_1^+(f(\omega), M^{2,\gamma}(f))h(\omega) + \varphi_2^-(f(\omega), M^{2,\gamma}(f))(M^{2,\gamma}(f + h) - M^{2,\gamma}(f)) \end{aligned}$$

where φ_1^+ is the partial derivative of φ with respect to its first argument from the right and φ_2^- is the partial derivative of φ with respect to its second argument from the left, both of which are well defined. Therefore, (A.38) implies that

$$\begin{aligned} &\int_\Omega \left[\varphi_1^+(f, M^{2,\gamma}(f))h + \varphi_2^-(f, M^{2,\gamma}(f))(M^{2,\gamma}(f + h) - M^{2,\gamma}(f))\right] d\mu \\ &\leq \int_\Omega \varphi(f + h, M^{2,\gamma}(f + h))d\mu - \int_\Omega \varphi(f, M^{2,\gamma}(f))d\mu \;=\; 0 . \end{aligned}$$

Because this holds for an arbitrary $h \in F$, we may set $h := M^{2,\gamma}(f|\mathcal{G}) - f$. Then, we have

$$M^{2,\gamma}(M^{2,\gamma}(f|\mathcal{G})) - M^{2,\gamma}(f) \leq -\frac{\int_\Omega \varphi_1^+(f, M^{2,\gamma}(f))(M^{2,\gamma}(f|\mathcal{G}) - f)d\mu}{\int_\Omega \varphi_2^-(f, M^{2,\gamma}(f))d\mu}$$

because the denominator on the right-hand side is strictly positive because $\int_\Omega \varphi_2^-(f, M^{2,\gamma}(f))d\mu \geq \gamma > 0$.

This paragraph completes the proof by showing that

$$\int_\Omega \varphi_1^+(f, M^{2,\gamma}(f))(M^{2,\gamma}(f|\mathcal{G}) - f)d\mu \geq 0 .$$

This inequality holds because

$$\begin{aligned} &\int_\Omega \varphi_1^+(f, M^{2,\gamma}(f))(M^{2,\gamma}(f|\mathcal{G}) - f)d\mu \\ &= \int_{\{f \geq M^{2,\gamma}(f)\}} -\gamma(M^{2,\gamma}(f|\mathcal{G}) - f)d\mu \\ &\quad + \int_{\{f < M^{2,\gamma}(f)\}} -(M^{2,\gamma}(f|\mathcal{G}) - f)d\mu \end{aligned}$$

$$
\begin{aligned}
&= (1-\gamma)\int_{\{f \geq M^{2,\gamma}(f)\}} (M^{2,\gamma}(f|\mathcal{G}) - f)d\mu - \int_{\Omega} (M^{2,\gamma}(f|\mathcal{G}) - f)d\mu \\
&\geq (1-\gamma)\int_{\{f \geq M^{2,\gamma}(f|\mathcal{G})\}} (M^{2,\gamma}(f|\mathcal{G}) - f)d\mu - \int_{\Omega} (M^{2,\gamma}(f|\mathcal{G}) - f)d\mu \\
&= -\int_{\{f \geq M^{2,\gamma}(f|\mathcal{G})\}} \gamma(M^{2,\gamma}(f|\mathcal{G}) - f)d\mu \\
&\quad -\int_{\{f < M^{2,\gamma}(f|\mathcal{G})\}} (M^{2,\gamma}(f|\mathcal{G}) - f)d\mu \\
&= -\int_{\Omega} \varphi(f, M^{2,\gamma}(f|\mathcal{G}))d\mu \;=\; 0,
\end{aligned}
$$

where the inequality holds by $\gamma \leq 1$ and the last equality holds by Corollary 13.3.1 (let h be χ_Ω in (13.9)). ■

A.9 Proofs for Chap. 14

A.9.1 Proof of Lemma 14.4.1

For the GB rule, the claim is immediate from (14.11). For the ML rule, the claim is also immediate from (14.13) and the fact that $(\forall i)\ \mathcal{P}^*(E_i) = \{p\}$. ■

A.9.2 Proof of Lemma 14.5.1

To show $\{p^0\}^\varepsilon|_2 \subseteq \{p^0|_2\}^\varepsilon$, let $p_2 \in \{p^0\}^\varepsilon|_2$. Then, there exists $p \in \{p^0\}^\varepsilon$ such that $p_2 = p(W \times \cdot)$. That $p \in \{p^0\}^\varepsilon$ in turn implies that there exists $q \in \mathcal{M}(\Omega, \mathcal{F}_2)$ such that $p = (1-\varepsilon)p^0 + \varepsilon q$. Hence, $p_2 = p(W \times \cdot) = (1-\varepsilon)p^0|_2(\cdot) + \varepsilon q|_2(\cdot)$. This shows that $p_2 \in \{p^0|_2\}^\varepsilon$ because $q|_2(\cdot) \in \mathcal{M}(W, \langle F_j\rangle_j)$.

To show $\{p^0\}^\varepsilon|_2 \supseteq \{p^0|_2\}^\varepsilon$, let $p_2 \in \{p^0|_2\}^\varepsilon$. Then, there exists $q_2 \in \mathcal{M}(W, \langle F_j\rangle_j)$ such that $p_2 = (1-\varepsilon)p^0|_2 + \varepsilon q_2$. Let $q_1 \in \mathcal{M}(W, \langle E_i\rangle_i)$ and let $p = (1-\varepsilon)p^0 + \varepsilon(q_1 \times q_2)$. Then, $p \in \{p^0\}^\varepsilon$ and $p|_2 = (1-\varepsilon)p^0|_2 + \varepsilon q_2 = p_2$, and hence, $p_2 \in \{p^0\}^\varepsilon|_2$. ■

A.9.3 Proof of Theorem 14.5.1

(a) ***The GB rule***. We define $\mathcal{R} \subseteq \mathcal{M}(W, \langle F_j\rangle_j)$ by

$$\mathcal{R} := \left\{ \frac{(1-\varepsilon)p^0|_1(E)}{(1-\varepsilon)p^0|_1(E)+\varepsilon q_1(E)}\, p^0|_2(\cdot|E) + \frac{\varepsilon q_1(E)}{(1-\varepsilon)p^0|_1(E)+\varepsilon q_1(E)}\, q_2 \;\middle|\; \begin{array}{l} q_1 \in \mathcal{M}(W, \langle E_i\rangle_i)\,, \\ q_2 \in \mathcal{M}(W, \langle F_j\rangle_j) \end{array} \right\}.$$

We first show that

$$\phi_{GB}\left(\{p^0\}^\varepsilon, E\right) = \mathcal{R}. \tag{A.39}$$

By the definition of ϕ_{GB}, it holds that

$$\begin{aligned} &\phi_{GB}\left(\{p^0\}^\varepsilon, E\right) \\ &= \left\{ p|_2(\cdot|E) \mid p \in \{p^0\}^\varepsilon \right\} = \left\{ \frac{p(E\times\cdot)}{p(E\times W)} \;\middle|\; p \in \{p^0\}^\varepsilon \right\} \\ &= \left\{ \frac{(1-\varepsilon)p^0|_1(E)}{(1-\varepsilon)p^0|_1(E)+\varepsilon q(E\times W)}\, p^0|_2(\cdot|E) \right. \\ &\quad \left. + \frac{\varepsilon}{(1-\varepsilon)p^0|_1(E)+\varepsilon q(E\times W)}\, q(E\times\cdot) \;\middle|\; q \in \mathcal{M}(\Omega, \mathcal{F}_2) \right\} \end{aligned} \tag{A.40}$$

where we invoked the fact that $p^0(E\times\cdot) = p^0|_1(E)\cdot p^0|_2(\cdot|E)$. Equation (A.40) shows that $\mathcal{R} \subseteq \phi_{GB}\left(\{p^0\}^\varepsilon, E\right)$ because $q_1 \times q_2 \in \mathcal{M}(\Omega, \mathcal{F}_2)$.

To show that the opposite inclusion also holds, let $p \in \phi_{GB}\left(\{p^0\}^\varepsilon, E\right)$. Then, there exists $q \in \mathcal{M}(\Omega, \mathcal{F}_2)$ such that

$$\begin{aligned} p = &\frac{(1-\varepsilon)p^0|_1(E)}{(1-\varepsilon)p^0|_1(E)+\varepsilon q(E\times W)}\, p^0|_2(\cdot|E) \\ &+ \frac{\varepsilon}{(1-\varepsilon)p^0|_1(E)+\varepsilon q(E\times W)}\, q(E\times\cdot) \end{aligned}$$

by (A.40). When $q(E\times W) = 0$, it follows that $p = p^0|_2(\cdot|E)$, and hence, $p \in \mathcal{R}$ (let q_1 be such that $q_1(E) = 0$ in the definition of $\mathcal{R}$). When $q(E\times W) \neq 0$, let $q_1 = q|_1$ and $q_2 = q|_2(\cdot|E)$, which is now well defined, in the definition of $\mathcal{R}$. Then, $q_1 \in \mathcal{M}(W, \langle E_i\rangle_i)$ and $q_2 \in \mathcal{M}(W, \langle F_j\rangle_j)$, and hence, $p \in \mathcal{R}$. Thus, we have proved that (A.39) holds true.

We next show that $\{p^0|_2(\cdot|E)\}^{\varepsilon'} = \mathcal{R}$, which completes the proof in the case of the GB rule. It immediately follows that $\{p^0|_2(\cdot|E)\}^{\varepsilon'} \subseteq \mathcal{R}$ (let q_1 be such that $q_1(E) = 1$). To show that the opposite inclusion also holds, let $p \in \mathcal{R}$. Then, there exist $q_1 \in \mathcal{M}(W, \langle E_i\rangle_i)$ and $q_2 \in \mathcal{M}(W, \langle F_j\rangle_j)$ such that

$$\begin{aligned} p &= \frac{(1-\varepsilon)p^0|_1(E)}{(1-\varepsilon)p^0|_1(E)+\varepsilon q_1(E)}\, p^0|_2(\cdot|E) + \frac{\varepsilon q_1(E)}{(1-\varepsilon)p^0|_1(E)+\varepsilon q_1(E)}\, q_2 \\ &= (1-\varepsilon')p^0|_2(\cdot|E) + \varepsilon'\left\{(1-\tilde{\varepsilon})p^0|_2(\cdot|E) + \tilde{\varepsilon} q_2\right\} \end{aligned}$$

where $\tilde{\varepsilon} := ((1-\varepsilon)p^0|_1(E)q_1(E) + \varepsilon q_1(E))/((1-\varepsilon)p^0|_1(E) + \varepsilon q_1(E))$. Because $(1-\tilde{\varepsilon})p^0|_2(\cdot|E) + \tilde{\varepsilon}q_2 \in \mathcal{M}(W, \langle F_j \rangle_j)$ by the fact that $\tilde{\varepsilon} \in [0, 1]$, it follows that $p \in \{p^0|_2(\cdot|E)\}^{\varepsilon'}$ as desired.

(b) ***The ML rule***. We only need to show that $\{p^0|_2(\cdot|E)\}^{\varepsilon'} \subseteq \phi_{ML}\left(\{p^0\}^{\varepsilon}, E\right)$ because the opposite inclusion holds by (a) and the fact that $\phi_{ML} \subseteq \phi_{GB}$ always holds. To prove this, first note that $(\forall E \in \langle E_i \rangle_i)$ we have $(\{p^0\}^{\varepsilon})^*(E) = \{(1-\varepsilon)p^0 + \varepsilon q | q \in \mathcal{M}(\Omega, \mathcal{F}_2)$ and $q(E \times W) = 1\}$ (see (14.13)), which in turn implies that

$$\begin{aligned}\phi_{ML}\left(\{p^0\}^{\varepsilon}, E\right) &= \left\{ p|_2(\cdot|E) \,\middle|\, p \in \left(\{p^0\}^{\varepsilon}\right)^*(E) \right\} \\ &= \left\{ \frac{(1-\varepsilon)p^0|_1(E)}{(1-\varepsilon)p^0|_1(E)+\varepsilon} p^0|_2(\cdot|E) + \frac{\varepsilon}{(1-\varepsilon)p^0|_1(E)+\varepsilon} q(E \times \cdot) \right. \\ &\qquad\qquad \left. \,\middle|\, q \in \mathcal{M}(\Omega, \mathcal{F}_2) \text{ and } q(E \times W) = 1 \right\}.\end{aligned}$$

Let $p_2 \in \{p^0|_2(\cdot|E)\}^{\varepsilon'}$. Then, there exists $q_2 \in \mathcal{M}(W, \langle F_j \rangle_j)$ such that $p_2 = (1-\varepsilon')p^0|_2(\cdot|E) + \varepsilon' q_2$. Let q_1 be the element of $\mathcal{M}(W, \langle E_i \rangle_i)$ such that $q_1(E) = 1$. Then, $q_1 \times q_2 \in \mathcal{M}(\Omega, \mathcal{F}_2)$, $(q_1 \times q_2)(E \times W) = 1$, and $p_2 = (1-\varepsilon')p^0|_2(\cdot|E) + \varepsilon' q_1(E)q_2(\cdot)$. Therefore, $p_2 \in \phi_{ML}\left(\{p^0\}^{\varepsilon}, E\right)$ as desired.

(c) ***To show*** $\varepsilon' > \varepsilon$. Because we have assumed that $(\forall i : i = 1, \ldots, m)$ $p^0(E_i \times W) > 0$ and $m \geq 2$ in Sect. 14.5, it follows that $(\forall i : i = 1, \ldots, m)$ $p^0(E_i \times W) = p^0|_1(E_i) < 1$. Therefore, it holds that $\varepsilon' > \varepsilon$. ■

A.9.4 *Proof of Theorem 14.5.2*

Note that the two equalities on the left-hand side were established by Theorem 14.5.1 and the equality on the right-hand side was established by Lemma 14.5.1; hence, the theorem claims that the strict inclusion holds.

We first prove $\{p^0|_2(\cdot|E)\}^{\varepsilon'} \supseteq \{p^0|_2\}^{\varepsilon}$, and then show that inclusion is strict.

(a) Proof of $\{p^0|_2(\cdot|E)\}^{\varepsilon'} \supseteq \{p^0|_2\}^{\varepsilon}$. Let $p_2 \in \{p^0|_2\}^{\varepsilon}$. Then, there exists $q_2 \in \mathcal{M}(W, \langle F_j \rangle_j)$ such that $p_2 = (1-\varepsilon)p^0|_2 + \varepsilon q_2$. Therefore, we have

$$\begin{aligned}p_2 &= (1-\varepsilon')p^0|_2(\cdot|E) + \varepsilon' \left(\frac{1-\varepsilon}{\varepsilon'} p^0|_2 - \frac{1-\varepsilon'}{\varepsilon'} p^0|_2(\cdot|E) + \frac{\varepsilon}{\varepsilon'} q_2 \right) \\ &= (1-\varepsilon')p^0|_2(\cdot|E) + \varepsilon' \mu, \qquad \text{(A.41)}\end{aligned}$$

where $\mu := ((1-\varepsilon)/\varepsilon')p^0|_2 - ((1-\varepsilon')/\varepsilon')p^0|_2(\cdot|E) + (\varepsilon/\varepsilon')q_2$. It immediately follows that μ is an (additive) signed charge such that $\mu(\phi) = 0$ and $\mu(W) = 1$. If $\mu \geq 0$, then $\mu \in \mathcal{M}(W, \langle F_j \rangle_j)$ and hence $p_2 \in \{p^0|_2(\cdot|E)\}^{\varepsilon'}$ implying $\{p^0|_2(\cdot|E)\}^{\varepsilon'} \supseteq \{p^0|_2\}^{\varepsilon}$. We now prove that $\mu \geq 0$. Note that if $(\forall F \in$

$\langle F_j \rangle_j$) $((1-\varepsilon)/\varepsilon')p^0|_2(F)-((1-\varepsilon')/\varepsilon')p^0|_2(F|E) \geq 0$, then $\mu \geq 0$ because $q_2 \geq 0$. Therefore, it is sufficient to show the above relation. If $\delta(E) = 0$, it is straightforward to show $((1-\varepsilon)/\varepsilon')p^0|_2(F) - ((1-\varepsilon')/\varepsilon')p^0|_2(F|E) = ((1-\varepsilon)/\varepsilon')(p^0|_2(F) - p^0|_2(F|E)) - ((\varepsilon - \varepsilon')/\varepsilon')p^0|_2(F|E) = ((\varepsilon' - \varepsilon)/\varepsilon')p^0|_2(F|E) \geq 0$, because $\delta(E) = \max_j \left| p^0|_2(F_j|E) - p^0|_2(F_j) \right| = 0$ and $\varepsilon' \geq \varepsilon$. If $\delta(E) > 0$, we have

$$\begin{aligned}
&\frac{1-\varepsilon}{\varepsilon'} p^0|_2(F) - \frac{1-\varepsilon'}{\varepsilon'} p^0|_2(F|E) \\
&= (1-\varepsilon)\left[\left(\frac{1-\varepsilon}{\varepsilon} p^0|_1(E) + 1\right) p^0|_2(F) - \frac{1}{\varepsilon} p^0|_1(E) p^0|_2(F|E)\right] \\
&\geq (1-\varepsilon)\left[\left(\frac{1-\varepsilon}{\varepsilon} p^0|_1(E) + 1\right) p^0|_2(F) - \frac{1}{\varepsilon} p^0|_1(E)\left(p^0|_2(F) + \delta(E)\right)\right] \\
&= (1-\varepsilon)\left[\left(1 - p^0|_1(E)\right) p^0|_2(F) - \frac{\delta(E)}{\varepsilon} p^0|_1(E)\right] \\
&\geq (1-\varepsilon)\left[\left(1 - p^0|_1(E)\right) \min_j p^0|_2(F_j) - \frac{\delta(E)}{\varepsilon} p^0|_1(E)\right] \\
&> (1-\varepsilon)\Bigg[\left(1 - p^0|_1(E)\right) \min_j p^0|_2(F_j) \\
&\quad - \delta(E)\, p^0|_1(E)\left(\frac{p^0|_1(E)}{\left(1 - p^0|_1(E)\right) \min_j p^0|_2(F_j)}\,\delta(E)\right)^{-1}\Bigg] \\
&= 0\,,
\end{aligned} \tag{A.42}$$

where the first equality holds by the definition of ε'; the first inequality holds by the definition of δ; the second inequality holds by the min operator; and the strict inequality holds by (14.15) and the assumptions that $\delta(E) > 0$ and $p^0|_1(E) > 0$. This completes the first half of the proof.

(b) Proof of strict inclusion. Let $F \in \langle F_j \rangle_j$ be such that $p^0|_2(F) > 0$, and let $\hat{p}_2 \in \left\{p^0|_2(\cdot|E)\right\}^{\varepsilon'}$ be such that $\hat{p}_2(F) = (1-\varepsilon')p^0|_2(F|E)$. We show $\hat{p}_2 \notin \left\{p^0|_2\right\}^{\varepsilon}$. If $\delta(E) = 0$, we have for any $p_2 \in \left\{p^0|_2\right\}^{\varepsilon}$, $p_2(F) \geq (1-\varepsilon)p^0|_2(F) = (1-\varepsilon')p^0|_2(F) + (\varepsilon' - \varepsilon)p^0|_2(F) > (1-\varepsilon')p^0|_2(F) = (1-\varepsilon')p^0|_2(F|E) = \hat{p}_2(F)$, where the strict inequality holds because $\varepsilon' > \varepsilon$ (Theorem 14.5.1) and $p^0|_2(F) > 0$ by the assumption of F, and its next equality holds because $p^0|_2(F) = p^0|_2(F|E)$ by the assumption that $\delta(E) = 0$. Therefore, we have $\hat{p}_2 \notin \left\{p^0|_2\right\}^{\varepsilon}$.

Finally, if $\delta(E) > 0$, we have for any $p_2 \in \left\{p^0|_2\right\}^{\varepsilon}$,

$$\begin{aligned}
p_2(F) &\geq (1-\varepsilon')p^0|_2(F|E) + \varepsilon'\left(\frac{1-\varepsilon}{\varepsilon'} p^0|_2(F) - \frac{1-\varepsilon'}{\varepsilon'} p^0|_2(F|E)\right) \\
&> (1-\varepsilon')p^0|_2(F|E) = \hat{p}_2(F)
\end{aligned}$$

where the first inequality follows from (A.41) and the second is implied by (A.42). Consequently, we have $\hat{p}_2 \notin \{p^0|_2\}^{\varepsilon}$. ■

A.9.5 *Proof of Corollary 14.5.1*

This follows immediately from Theorem 14.5.2 because $\delta(E) = 0$ when $p^0 = p_1^0 \otimes p_2^0$ for some p_1^0 and p_2^0. ■

A.10 Proofs for Chap. 15

A.10.1 *Proof of Proposition 15.1.1*

This proof employs a finite capacity that is not necessarily a probability capacity; that is, it may not gauge the state space by unity. More specifically, given a probability capacity θ on $(S, \mathcal{A})$ and a set $A \in \mathcal{A}$, we define the *capacity concentrated on* A, denoted θ_A, by

$$(\forall E \in \mathcal{A}) \quad \theta_A(E) = \theta(A \cap E)\,. \tag{A.43}$$

Then, it is easy to see that for any $A \in \mathcal{A}$, θ_A is convex (resp. concave, finitely additive) if θ is convex (resp. concave, finitely additive), where each of the convexity, the concavity, and the finite additivity of θ_A is defined by the natural manner except that it may not be the case that $\theta_A(S) = 1$. We define the *conjugate* of θ_A, denoted $(\theta_A)'$, by $(\forall E)$ $(\theta_A)'(E) = \theta_A(S) - \theta_A(E^c)$, and we define the *core* of θ_A, denoted core(θ_A), as the set of finite probability charges μ dominating θ_A setwise such that $\mu(S) = \theta_A(S) = \theta(A)$.

The next lemma is a key to the proof of Proposition 15.1.1.

Lemma A.10.1 *Let θ be a convex probability capacity, let μ be a probability charge, and let $A \in \mathcal{A}$. If $\mu \in core(\theta)$ and $\mu(A) = \theta(A)$, then*

$$\mu = \mu_A + \mu_{A^c}\,, \tag{A.44}$$

$$\mu_A \in core\,(\theta_A)\ \text{, and} \tag{A.45}$$

$$\mu_{A^c} \in core(((\theta')_{A^c})')\,, \tag{A.46}$$

where μ_A and μ_{A^c} are as defined in (A.43).

Conversely, if a probability charge μ can be written as $\mu = \mu_1 + \mu_2$ with some μ_1 and μ_2 such that $\mu_1 \in core\,(\theta_A)$ and $\mu_2 \in core(((\theta')_{A^c})')$, then $\mu \in core(\theta)$ and $\mu(A) = \theta(A)$.

Proof To prove the first half of the claim, let $B \in \mathcal{F}$ be arbitrary. Equation (A.44) always holds because $(\mu_A + \mu_{A^c})(B) = \mu_A(B) + \mu_{A^c}(B) = \mu(A \cap B) + \mu(A^c \cap B) =$

$\mu(B)$. Equation (A.45) follows because $\mu_A(S) = \mu(A) = \theta(A)$ and $\mu_A(B) = \mu(A \cap B) \geq \theta(A \cap B) = \theta_A(B)$, where we used the assumptions on μ. Finally, to prove (A.46), note that $\mu_{A^c}(S) = \mu(A^c) = \mu(S) - \mu(A) = \theta(S) - \theta(A) = \theta'(A^c) = (\theta')_{A^c}(S) - 0 = (\theta')_{A^c}(S) - (\theta')_{A^c}(\phi) = ((\theta')_{A^c})'(S)$, where again we used the assumption that $\mu(A) = \theta(A)$. Therefore, it suffices to show that $\mu_{A^c}(B) \geq ((\theta')_{A^c})'(B)$, which is equivalent to $\mu_{A^c}(S) - \mu_{A^c}(B^c) \geq (\theta')_{A^c}(S) - (\theta')_{A^c}(B^c)$. Because the first terms on both sides are identical as mentioned above and because B is arbitrary, we need to show that $\mu_{A^c}(B) \leq (\theta')_{A^c}(B)$. However, this holds because $\mu_{A^c}(B) = \mu(A^c \cap B) = \mu(S) - \mu(A \cup B^c) \leq \theta(S) - \theta(A \cup B^c) = \theta'(A^c \cap B) = (\theta')_{A^c}(B)$, where we use the assumptions on μ once again.

To prove the second half of the claim, let $B \in \mathcal{F}$ be arbitrary. Then, $\mu(B) = \mu_1(B) + \mu_2(B) \geq \theta_A(B) + ((\theta')_{A^c})'(B) = \theta(A \cap B) + ((\theta')_{A^c}(S) - (\theta')_{A^c}(B^c)) = \theta(A \cap B) + (\theta'(A^c) - \theta'(A^c \cap B^c)) = \theta(A \cap B) - \theta(A) + \theta(A \cup B) \geq \theta(B)$, where the first inequality holds by the assumptions on μ_1 and μ_2, and the second inequality holds by the convexity of θ. Therefore, we conclude that $\mu(S) \geq \theta(S)$ and $\mu(A) \geq \theta(A)$ given that B is arbitrary. Thus, to complete the proof, it suffices to show that $\mu(S) \leq \theta(S)$ and $\mu(A) \leq \theta(A)$, each of which holds because $\mu(S) = \mu_1(S) + \mu_2(S) \leq (\theta_A)'(S) + (\theta')_{A^c}(S) = \theta_A(S) - \theta_A(\phi) + \theta'(A^c) = \theta(A) - 0 + \theta(S) - \theta(A) = \theta(S)$ and $\mu(A) = \mu_1(A) + \mu_2(A) \leq (\theta_A)'(A) + (\theta')_{A^c}(A) = \theta_A(\Omega) - \theta_A(A^c) + \theta'(\phi) = \theta(A) - 0 + 0 = \theta(A)$, where both inequalities hold by the definition of the core, the convexity of θ, and the assumptions on μ_1 and μ_2. ■

Proof of Proposition 15.1.1. We prove only (15.7). A similar argument applies for (15.8). Let ν be any conditioning function for θ and let A, B be arbitrary. Then, because $\nu_{\chi_A} \in \text{core}(\theta)$ and $\nu_{\chi_A}(A) = \theta(A)$ by the definition of the conditioning function, the first half of Lemma A.10.1 shows that $\nu_{\chi_A}(A \cap B) = (\nu_{\chi_A})_A(B) \geq \theta_A(B) = \theta(A \cap B)$ and $\nu_{\chi_A}(A^c \cap B) = (\nu_{\chi_A})_{A^c}(B) \leq (\theta')_{A^c}(B) = \theta'(A^c \cap B)$. Hence, it follows from (15.6) and the definition of θ^G (Sect. 2.3.5) that $\theta^{\nu}_B(A) \geq \theta^G_B(A)$.

We complete the proof by showing that the lower bound is actually attained by some conditioning function, say $\bar{\nu}$. Let A, B be arbitrary and let μ_1 and μ_2 be such that $\mu_1 \in \text{core}\,(\theta_A)$ and $\mu_2 \in \text{core}\left(\left((\theta')_{A^c}\right)'\right)$. Such finite charges, μ_1 and μ_2, certainly exist because both θ_A and $\left((\theta')_{A^c}\right)'$ are convex because θ is convex. Furthermore, we can choose such μ_1 and μ_2 so that $\mu_1(A \cap B) = \theta_A(A \cap B) = \theta(A \cap B)$ and $\mu_2(A^c \cap B) = (\theta')_{A^c}(A^c \cap B) = \theta'(A^c \cap B)$ by the fundamental theorem of the Choquet integral and its corollary (Theorem 2.4.1 and Corollary 2.4.1). (Let a there be the indicator function.) We define μ by $\mu = \mu_1 + \mu_2$. We claim that μ thus defined is a probability charge. The finite additivity and $\mu(\phi) = 0$ are immediate. That $\mu(S) = 1$ also follows because $\mu(S) = \mu_1(S) + \mu_2(S) = \theta_A(S) + \left((\theta')_{A^c}\right)'(S) = \theta(A) + \left((\theta')_{A^c}\right)(S) - 0 = \theta(A) + \theta'(A^c) = \theta(A) + 1 - \theta(A) = 1$, where the second equality holds by the definition of the core for the concentrated capacity. Therefore, the second half of Lemma A.10.1 implies that $\mu \in \text{core}(\theta)$ and $\mu(A) = \theta(A)$. Thus, we may define the conditioning function $\hat{\nu}$ so that $\hat{\nu}_{\chi_A} = \mu$.

This paragraph completes the proof by showing that $\bar{\nu}$ defined in the previous paragraph attains the lower bound. First, note that from $\mu_2 \in \text{core}\left(\left((\theta')_{A^c}\right)'\right)$, $\mu_2(A \cap B) \leq (\theta')_{A^c}(A \cap B) = \theta'(\phi) = 0$, implying that $\mu_2(A \cap B) = 0$. Second, note that from $\mu_1 \in \text{core}(\theta_A)$, $\mu_1(A^c \cap B) \leq (\theta_A)'(A^c \cap B) = \theta_A(S) - \theta_A(A \cup B^c) = \theta(A) - \theta(A) = 0$, implying that $\mu_1(A^c \cap B) = 0$. Finally, by (15.6), we have

$$\begin{aligned}\theta_B^{\bar{\nu}}(A) &= \mu(A \cap B)/\mu(B) = \mu(A \cap B)/(\mu(A \cap B) + \mu(A^c \cap B)) \\ &= \mu_1(A \cap B)/(\mu_1(A \cap B) + \mu_2(A^c \cap B)) \\ &= \theta(A \cap B)/(\theta(A \cap B) + \theta(A^c \cap B)) \;=\; \theta_B^G(A)\end{aligned}$$

by the definition of θ^G. ■

References

Berge, C. 1963. *Topological spaces*. Edinburgh: Oliver and Boyd.

Billingsley, P. 1986. *Probability and measure*, 2nd ed. New York: Wiley-Interscience.

Boyce, W.E., and R.C. DiPrima. 1986. *Elementary differential equations and boundary value problems*, 4th ed. New York: Wiley.

Dellacherie, C., and P.A. Meyer. 1988. *Probabilities and potential C*. New York: North-Holland.

Dunford, N., and J.T. Schwartz. 1988. *Linear operator part i: general theory*. Wiley Classics Library.

Ethier, S.N., and T.G. Kurtz. 1986. *Markov processes*. New York: Wiley-Interscience.

Fishburn, P.C. 1970. *Utility thoery for decision making*. New York: Wiley.

Folland, G.B. 1984. *Real analysis*, 2nd ed. (1999). New York: Wiley Interscience.

Gilboa, I. 1985. Subjective distortions of probabilities and non-additive probabilities, Working Paper, The Foerder Institute for Economic Research, Tel Aviv University.

Gilboa, I., and D. Schmeidler. 1989. Maxmin expected utility with non-unique prior. *Journal of Mathematical Economics* 18: 141–153.

Karatzas, I., and S.E. Shreve. 1991. *Brownian motion and stochastic calculus*, 2nd ed. Berlin: Springer.

Kreps, D. 1988. *Notes on the theory of choice*. Boulder: Westview Press.

Mood, A.M., F.A. Graybill, and D.C. Boes. 1974. *Introduction to the theory of statistics*, 3rd ed. McGraw-Hill.

Rothschild, M., and J. Stiglitz. 1970. Increasing risk I: A definition. *Journal of Economic Theory* 2: 225–243.

Sakai, Y. 1988. Conditional Pareto optimality of stationary equilibrium in a stochastic overlapping generations Model. *Journal of Economic Theory* 44: 209–213.

Takayama, A. 1974. *Mathematical Economics*. Hinsdale: The Dryden Press.

Wagner, D.H. 1977. Survey of measurable selection theorems. *SIAM Journal of Control and Optimization* 15: 859–903.

Index

K.G. Nishimura and H. Ozaki, *Economics of Pessimism and Optimism*,
DOI 10.1007/978-4-431-55903-0

MIX
Papier aus verantwortungsvollen Quellen
Paper from responsible sources
FSC® C105338

FSC
www.fsc.org

If you have any concerns about our products,
you can contact us on
ProductSafety@springernature.com

In case Publisher is established outside the EU,
the EU authorized representative is:
Springer Nature Customer Service Center GmbH
Europaplatz 3, 69115 Heidelberg, Germany

Printed by Libri Plureos GmbH
in Hamburg, Germany